Progress in Psychological Science around the World

Volume 2: Social and Applied Issues

Progress in Psychological Science around the World Volumes 1 and 2 present the main contributions from the 28th International Congress of Psychology, held in Beijing in 2004. These expert contributions include the Nobel Laureate presentation, the Presidential address, and the Keynote and State-of-the-Art lectures. They are written by international leaders in psychology from 25 countries and regions around the world. The authors present a variety of approaches and perspectives that reflect cutting-edge advances in psychological science.

This second volume builds on the coverage of neural, cognitive, and developmental issues from the first volume, to address social and applied issues in modern psychology. The topics covered include: educational psychology and measurement; health psychology; and social and cultural psychology. Organizational, applied, and international psychology are also discussed.

Progress in Psychological Science around the World, with its broad coverage of psychological research and practice, and its highly select group of world-renowned authors, will be invaluable for researchers, professionals, teachers, and students in the field of psychology.

Qicheng Jing is Professor of Psychology at the Institute of Psychology, Chinese Academy of Sciences.

Mark R. Rosenzweig is Professor of Graduate Studies at the Department of Psychology, University of California, Berkeley.

Géry d'Ydewalle is Director of the Laboratory of Experimental Psychology, University of Leuven.

Houcan Zhang is Professor of Psychology at the School of Psychology, Beijing Normal University.

Hsuan-Chih Chen is Professor of Psychology at the Department of Psychology, Chinese University of Hong Kong.

Kan Zhang is Professor of Psychology at the Institute of Psychology, Chinese Academy of Sciences.

Progress in Psychological Science around the World

Volume 2: Social and Applied Issues

Congress Proceedings: XVIII International Congress of Psychology, Beijing, 2004

edited by
**Qicheng Jing, Mark R. Rosenzweig,
Géry d'Ydewalle, Houcan Zhang,
Hsuan-Chih Che, and Kan Zhang**

Ψ Psychology Press
Taylor & Francis Group
HOVE AND NEW YORK

First published 2006 by Psychology Press
27 Church Road, Hove, East Sussex, BN3 2FA

Simultaneously published in the USA and Canada
by Psychology Press
270 Madison Avenue, New York NY 10016

*Psychology Press is an imprint of the Taylor & Francis Group, an informa
business*

Copyright © 2006 International Union of Psychological Science

Typeset in Times by
RefineCatch Limited, Bungay, Suffolk
Printed and bound in Great Britain by
TJ International Ltd, Padstow, Cornwall
Cover design by Jim Wilkie

British Library Cataloguing in Publication Data
A catalogue record for this book is available from the British Library

Library of Congress Cataloging-in-Publication Data
A catalogue record has been requested

ISBN13: 978–1–84169–962–4 (hbk)

ISBN10: 1–84169–962–4 (hbk)

Contents

List of contributors   ix
List of committees   xiii
Preface   xv

SECTION I
Educational psychology and measurement   1

1 **Giving psychology away: From individual learning
   to learning organizations**   3
   LAUREN B. RESNICK, USA

2 **Which should be the contribution of psychology to education?**   23
   EMILIO RIBES-IÑESTA, MEXICO

3 **Activating historical and conceptual links in the realm of
   instruction in Latin America**   35
   ALFONSO ORANTES, VENEZUELA

4 **English classes without English teachers: The Pan Deng
   English learning program**   51
   QI DONG, SHA TAO, BEILEI LI, WENJING WANG, AND
   CHUANSHENG CHEN, CHINA

5 **Rules and tools of intelligence: How IQ became obsolete**   71
   J. P. DAS, CANADA

6 **A combined emic–etic approach to cross-cultural personality
   test development: The case of the CPAI**   91
   FANNY M. CHEUNG, HONG KONG (CHINA)

7   **Chinese personality: Structure and measurement**   105
DENGFENG WANG AND HONG CUI, CHINA

SECTION II
Health psychology   123

8   **Effects of stress, emotion, and Type-A behavior on**
     heart disease and psychological disorders   125
CHARLES D. SPIELBERGER, USA

9   **Temperament as a predictor of maladaptive**
     behavior under extreme stress: The Polish studies
     of natural disasters   139
JAN STRELAU, MAGDALENA KACZMAREK, AND
BOGDAN ZAWADZKI, POLAND

10 **The involvement of psychological processes**
     in immunocompetence   159
WENJUAN LIN, CHINA

11 **Self-regulatory processes in health behavior change**   167
RALF SCHWARZER, URTE SCHOLZ,
SONIA LIPPKE, FALKO F. SNIEHOTTA, AND
JOCHEN P. ZIEGELMANN, GERMANY

12 **Violence against women: A global health issue**   181
NANCY FELIPE RUSSO, USA

13 **Professional psychology around the world: A fifty-year**
     progress report   199
RAYMOND D. FOWLER, USA

SECTION III
Social and cultural psychology   207

14 **Cognition and perception: East and West**   209
RICHARD E. NISBETT, USA

15 **Cross-cultural psychology: An ecocultural approach**   229
JOHN B. BERRY, CANADA

16 Some metatheoretical issues in culture, parenting and
developmental science 245
MARC H. BORNSTEIN, USA

17 Dealing with norm and meta-norm violators: Cultural
differences in thoughts or motivated actions? 261
RAMADHAR SINGH, SINGAPORE

18 Culture and psychology: A SWOT analysis of
cross-cultural psychology 279
FONS J. R. VAN DE VIJVER, THE NETHERLANDS

19 Mind and body in Japanese culture 299
HAYAO KAWAI, JAPAN

20 The era of fluid culture: Conceptual implications for
cultural psychology 305
HIROSHI AZUMA, JAPAN

21 Self-esteem in cultural contexts: The case of the Japanese 319
SUSUMU YAMAGUCHI, CHUN-CHI LIN, AND SAYAKA AOKI, JAPAN

22 Understanding human potential, creativity and achievement:
Indigenous, cultural and psychological perspectives 331
UICHOL KIM AND YOUNG-SHIN PARK, KOREA

SECTION IV
Organizational, applied, and international psychology 349

23 Investigating five leadership themes: Roles, decisions,
character, relationships, and journeys 351
LEON MANN, AUSTRALIA

24 Leadership competency and implicit assessment modeling 371
ZHONG-MING WANG, CHINA

25 Control processes in the formation of task units 385
DANIEL GOPHER, ISRAEL

26 States of mind: Political systems as implicit theories
of psychology 405
DIANE F. HALPERN, USA

27 Russian psychology at the crossroads   417
VLADIMIR A. BARABANSCHIKOV, RUSSIA

28 Towards a history of applied psychology in the 20th century   433
HELIO CARPINTERO, SPAIN

Author index   443
Subject index   453

Contributors to Volume 2

Sayaka Aoki, Department of Social Psychology, Graduate School of Humanities and Sociology, University of Tokyo, Hongo 7–3–1, Bunkyo-ku, Tokyo 113–0033, Japan

Hiroshi Azuma, Seisen Jogakuin College, 2–120–8 Uwano, Nagano-shi 381–0085, Japan

Vladimir A. Barabanschikov, Institute of Psychology, Russian Academy of Sciences, 129366 Yaroslavskaya 13, Moscow, Russia

John B. Berry, Psychology Department, Queen's University at Kingston, Ontario K7L 3N6, Canada

Marc H. Bornstein, Child and Family Research, National Institute of Child Health and Human Development, Suite 8030, 6705 Rockledge Drive, Bethesda MD 20892–7971, USA

Helio Carpintero, SD, Psicologia Basica, Facultad de Filosofia (B-21), Universidad Complutense, Ciudad Universitaria, Madrid, 28040, Spain

Chuansheng Chen, Department of Psychology and Social Behavior, University of California, Irvine, CA 92697–7085, USA

Fanny M. Cheung, Department of Psychology, The Chinese University of Hong Kong, Shatin, NT, Hong Kong SAR

Hong Cui, Medical Psychology Division, General Hospital of People's Liberation Army, Beijing 100853, China

J. P. Das, Developmental Disabilities Centre, Education Building 6–123, University of Alberta, Edmonton T5G 2E5, Canada

Qi Dong, Institute of Cognitive Neuroscience and Learning, Beijing Normal University, Beijing 100875, China

Raymond D. Fowler, Department of Psychology, University of Alabama, Tuscaloosa, Al 35487, USA. Address for Correspondence: 8276 Caminito Maritimo, La Jolla, CA 92037, USA

Daniel Gopher, Faculty of Industrial Engineering and Management, Technion – Israel Institute of Technology, Haifa, 32000 Israel

Diane F. Halpern, Berger Institute for Work, Family, and Children, Claremont McKenna College, 850 Columbia Avenue, Claremont, CA 91711–6420, USA

Magdalena Kaczmarek, Warsaw School of Social Psychology, Chodakowska 19–31, 03–815 Warsaw, Poland

Hayao Kawai, Agency for Cultural Affairs, 527 Chaya-cho, Higashiyama-ku, Kyoto 605–0931, Japan

Uichol Kim, Department of Psychology, Inha University, Nam-gu Yonghyeon-dong, Inchon, 402–751, Korea

Beilei Li, Institute of Cognitive Neuroscience and Learning, Beijing Normal University, Beijing 100875, China

Chun-Chi Lin, Department of Social Psychology, Graduate School of Humanities and Sociology, University of Tokyo, Hongo 7–3–1, Bunkyo-ku, Tokyo 113–0033, Japan

Wenjuan Lin, Key Laboratory of Mental Health, Institute of Psychology, Chinese Academy of Sciences, Beijing, 100101, China

Sonia Lippke, Gesundheitspsychologie, Pf. 10, Freie Universität Berlin, Habelschwerdter Allee 45, D-14195 Berlin, Germany

Leon Mann, Centre for R&D Leadership, Faculty of Medicine, Dentistry and Health Sciences, The University of Melbourne, Victoria, 3010, Australia

Richard E. Nisbett, Department of Psychology, University of Michigan, Ann Arbor, MI 48109, USA

Alfonso Orantes, Central University of Venezuela, P.O. Box Apartado 47 120, Caracas 1041-A, Venezuela

Young-Shin Park, Department of Education, Inha University, Nam-gu Yonghyeon-dong, Inchon, 402–751, Korea

Lauren B. Resnick, Learning Research and Development Center, University of Pittsburgh, 3939 O'Hara Street, Room 824, Pittsburgh, PA 15260, USA

Emilio Ribes-Iñesta, Centro de Estudios e Investigaciones en Comportamiento, Apartado Postal 5–374, 45040 Zapopan, México

Nancy Felipe Russo, Department of Psychology, Box 1104, Arizona State University, Tempe, AZ 855028-4511, USA

Urte Scholz, Psychologisches Institut, Universität Zürich, Sozial- und Gesundheitspsychologie, Raemistrasse 66, CH-8001 Zürich, Switzerland

Ralf Schwarzer, Gesundheitspsychologie, Pf. 10, Freie Universität Berlin, Habelschwerdter Allee 45, D-14195 Berlin, Germany

Ramadhar Singh, Department of Social Work and Psychology, National University of Singapore, Blk AS6, 11 Law Link, Singapore 117570, Republic of Singapore

Falko F. Sniehotta, University of Aberdeen, School of Psychology, College of Life Sciences and Medicine, William Guild Building, Aberdeen AB24 2UB, UK

Charles D. Spielberger, Center for Research in Behavioral Medicine and Health Psychology, University of South Florida, Psychology Department, PCD 4118G, 4202 East Fowler Avenue, Tampa, FL 33620–7200, USA

Jan Strelau, Faculty of Psychology, University of Warsaw, Stawki 5/7, 00–183 Warsaw, Poland

Sha Tao, Institute of Cognitive Neuroscience and Learning, Beijing Normal University, Beijing 100875, China

Fons J. R. van de Vijver, Department of Psychology, Tilburg University, PO Box 90153, NL-5000 LE Tilburg, Netherlands

Dengfeng Wang, Department of Psychology and Research Center on Personality and Social Psychology, Peking University, Beijing 100871, China

Wenjing Wang, Institute of Cognitive Neuroscience and Learning, Beijing Normal University, Beijing 100875, China

Zhong-Ming Wang, School of Management, Zhejiang University, Zijin Campus, Hangzhou 310058, China

Susumu Yamaguchi, Department of Social Psychology, Graduate School of Humanities and Sociology, University of Tokyo, Hongo 7–3–1, Bunkyo-ku, Tokyo 113–0033, Japan

Bogdan Zawadzki, Faculty of Psychology, University of Warsaw, Warsaw, Poland

Jochen P. Ziegelmann, Gesundheitspsychologie, Pf. 10, Freie Universität Berlin, Habelschwerdter Allee 45, D-14195 Berlin, Germany

Editors

Hsuan-Chih Chen, Department of Psychology, Chinese University of Hong Kong, Shatin, NT, Hong Kong (China)

Géry d'Ydewalle, Department of Psychology, University of Leuven, B-3000 Leuven, Belgium

Qicheng Jing, Institute of Psychology, Chinese Academy of Sciences, 10A Datun Road, Beijing 100101, China

Mark R. Rosenzweig, Department of Psychology, 3210 Tolman Hall, University of California, Berkeley, CA 94720–1650, USA

Houcan Zhang, School of Psychology, Beijing Normal University, Beijing 100875, China

Kan Zhang, Institute of Psychology, Chinese Academy of Sciences, 10A Datun Road, Beijing 100101, China

NOTE

On the opening page of Chapters 4, 7, 9, 11, 21, and 22 only the first-named author is pictured.

Committees

Executive Committee

Qicheng Jing (President), Kan Zhang (Secretary-General), Houcan Zhang (IUPsyS Vice-President), Géry d'Ydewalle (IUPsyS Liaison), Hsuan-Chih Chen, Yongming Chen, Chongde Lin, Zhongxian Lin, Deli Shen, Su Wang, Yufang Yang, Yutai Zhang

Scientific Committee

Yufang Yang (Chair), Yanjie Su (Deputy Chair), Weimin Mou (Deputy Chair), Jing Chen, Jinhong Ding, Su Li, Ye Liu, Binwu Qiu, Jiannong Shi, Yuming Xuan, Jianxin Zhang

Organizing Committee

Kan Zhang (Chair), Xiaolan Fu (Deputy Chair), Hua Shu (Deputy Chair), Buxin Han (Deputy Secretary-General, EC), Xianghong Sun, Xiaomin Sun, Lili Wang, Shaoyuan Wu, Qingfang Zhang, Zhen Zhang, Liqi Zhu

International Advisory Committee

Kurt Pawlik (Chair), John Adair, Ruben Ardila, Hiroshi Azuma, A. V. Brushlinsky, Saths Cooper, Fergus Craik, Michel Denis, Raymond D. Fowler, Cigdem Kagitçibasi, Daniel Kahneman, Kevin McConkey, Jitendra Mohan, Elizabeth Nair, Lars-Göran Nilsson, Jose Prieto, Mark R. Rosenzweig, Herbert A. Simon, Harold W. Stevenson, Jan Strelau, Berhard Wilpert

IUPsyS Executive Committee (2000–2004)

Michel Denis (President), Géry d'Ydewalle (Past-President), Juan José Sanchez Sosa (Vice-President), Houcan Zhang (Vice-President), Michel Sabourin (Treasurer), Pierre Ritchie (Secretary-General), Merry Bullock (Deputy Secretary-General), John Adair, Ruben Ardila, Saths Cooper, Hiroshi Imada, Cigdem Kagitçibasi, Ingrid Lunt, Elizabeth Nair, Bruce Overmier, Ype Poortinga, Rainer Silbereisen

Preface

The two-volume *Progress in Psychological Science around the World, Proceedings of the 28th International Congress of Psychology* is a collection of invited papers presented at the Congress which was held in Beijing, 8–13 August 2004.

The first International Congress of Psychology was held in 1889 in Paris. Its closing banquet took place in the Eiffel Tower, which had been completed and inaugurated earlier that year. This was just 10 years after the founding of the first laboratory of psychology by Wilhelm Wundt. During the ensuing 115 years, International Congresses have taken place on four continents of the world. Eventually in 2004 the 28th International Congress of Psychology was held in Beijing, China, the first International Congress of Psychology held in an Asian developing country.

China is a country possessing both traditional cultural heritages and modern achievements. Beijing, which was the ancient capital of China through several dynasties, is now the capital of the People's Republic of China. It is a thriving center for political, scientific, and commercial endeavors, a place of global confluence and exchanges. Beijing is especially noted for its historical sites, such as the Great Wall, the Forbidden City, and the Temple of Heaven. The rich historical legacy of China reveals a long history of social changes and human interactions, providing a cultural environment especially suited to exchanges in the science of human behavior – psychology.

The Beijing Congress opened on the evening of 8 August 2004. At the opening ceremony, a welcome speech was made by the President of the Chinese Academy of Sciences, Vice-Chairman, National People's Congress of China, Professor Yongxiang Lu, followed by speeches by IUPsyS President Michel Denis and Congress President Qicheng Jing. It was highlighted by a Nobel Laureate address entitled "A perspective on cognitive illusions" by Dr Daniel Kahneman. Dr Kahneman was awarded the Nobel Prize in 2002. The opening addresses were followed by a Chinese acrobatic performance, a thrilling experience for all the participants. The Congress closed on the evening of 13 August. At the closing ceremony the organization of the next congress was handed to the German organizers, who will be hosting the 29th International Congress of Psychology in Berlin in 2008. It will be the fourth time that the International Congress has been held in Germany.

In addition to the Nobel Laureate presentation by Dr Daniel Kahneman and the Presidential address by Dr Michel Denis, the scientific program of the Congress consisted of 32 Keynote and 35 State-of-the-Art addresses, 237 invited symposia, 432 thematic oral sessions, and 15 poster sessions. The program provided a current overview of the multifaceted nature of the science of psychology; highly distinguished scientists presented updated accounts of the various fields of research across 25 major areas in psychology. Altogether 5598 papers were presented at the Congress. The high quality of the scientific program can be attested by the often full house attendance in the meeting rooms; this happened even at the final sessions just before the closing of the Congress. The Congress in cooperation with IUPsyS organized nine workshops, the Young Psychologists Program and Advanced Research and Training Seminars. Other international organizations of psychology sponsored meetings of various kinds. The Beijing Congress had a total attendance of 6261 delegates from 78 countries, including countries and regions from which psychologists rarely participate in international congresses, such as Iran, Vietnam and Macau. This Congress was the largest both in attendance and in scope in the history of International Congresses of Psychology. An impressive scene at the Congress was the 200 Chinese psychology students, in yellow shirts with the Congress logo, who contributed excellent service during the meetings.

The two Proceedings volumes include the Nobel Laureate presentation, the Presidential address, the Keynote and the State-of-the-Art addresses of the Congress. Considering that the selection of chapters represents the current status of the accumulated knowledge from psychological research around the world, we felt it appropriate to give the volumes a common title: *Progress in Psychological Science around the World*. Altogether 69 invited speakers presented papers at the Congress; however, 11 speakers, for various reasons, were unable to provide manuscripts. Thus the Proceedings include 58 presentations. Care has been taken to divide the contributions into approximately equal-sized volumes: Volume I, Neural, Cognitive and Developmental Issues, comprising four subsections with 30 chapters; Volume II, Social and Applied Issues, comprising four subsections with 28 chapters. We have also tried for the first time to publish photographs of the authors together with their papers in the Proceedings. We appreciate the authors' cooperation with this request.

In preparation of the Congress, Dr Raymond Fowler was invited to participate in a Scientific Committee meeting in Beijing in January 2003 to discuss the nomination of invited speakers and the planning of the scientific program of the Congress. His experience was important to the formulation of the final scientific program. The manuscripts submitted to be published in the Proceedings were reviewed by the editors and received positive support from the authors. However, due to the large number of papers and expertise required in so many fields of psychology, the following colleagues were also invited to participate in the reviewing process: Drs Winton Au, John Berry,

Him Cheung, Chi-Yue Chiu, Fuxi Fang, Kwok Leung, Patrick Leung, and Xuchu Weng. Their hard work, along with the close cooperation of the authors, brought the editorial work of the Proceedings to a conclusion. We greatly appreciate their support.

We would like to express our sincere thanks to the editorial staff, Drs Guomei Zhou, Yuhao Sun, and Ye Liu who provided help in the earlier phase of collection of the manuscripts. Particularly, we are indebted to Miss Hang Zhang; her skillful secretarial assistance and untiring dedication were indispensable to the publication of the two volumes. Finally, we would like to express our gratitude to the staff of Psychology Press who organized and oversaw the production of the Proceedings, particularly to Managing Editor Ms Imogen Burch, and Senior Production Editor Ms Kathryn Russel, and to Ms Jenny Millington and Dr Lewis Derrick for copy-editing the two volumes. Their experience has greatly facilitated the completion of the Proceedings.

Qicheng Jing, Mark R. Rosenzweig,
Géry d'Ydewalle, Houcan Zhang,
Hsuan-Chih Chen, and Kan Zhang
(*Editors*)

Section I

Educational psychology and measurement

1 Giving psychology away: From individual learning to learning organizations

Lauren B. Resnick

In 1969, George Miller gave a landmark Presidential Address to the American Psychological Association entitled, *Giving Psychology Away*. In it he argued that as a mature science, the discipline of psychology should focus substantial attention on how to make the fruits of scientific investigation useful in various important human endeavors. Ever since, many branches of psychology have indeed developed applications of their science and sought wide acceptance of the principles that their investigations have yielded. The task of making psychological science relevant has turned out to be as exciting as Miller envisaged, but perhaps more difficult than he was able to foresee 35 years ago. In this chapter I consider the complexities of "giving away" the knowledge of cognitive and learning processes that have been amassed over this period.

The first obvious question to pose is a broad one: How does one give away scientific and professional knowledge? There seem to be four broad possibilities:

1   We could *tell* people what we know about learning and instruction, and leave to "practitioners" (teachers and other education practitioners) the full task of making the knowledge useful, taking care to "translate" our technical and scientific language into terms accessible to people who are not trained in psychology.
2   Alternately we could *train* people as "practitioners" of learning and cognitive psychology. As part of this we would build study tools and processes that were explicitly designed to support specific kinds of professional learning.
3   We could create *protocols* of practice that, if used appropriately, would constitute good "applications" of our science.
4   Finally, we could also try to change the *organizations* in which people work and learn so that they become more optimal environments for professional learning and practice.

These four are not, of course, mutually exclusive. Each of the first three has been used by psychologists – perhaps most diligently those aiming to use psychology as a foundation for improvement of school-level education. But because each is expensive, individual research and development groups tend mostly to focus on one or the other, rather than on the mix of strategies likely to actually be most effective. What is more, as scholars in the discipline of psychology, we are much more familiar and comfortable with some of these strategies than with others. Our discipline is particularly undeveloped with respect to the fourth strategy – organizational change. In examining these four strategies, I will suggest that unless we can optimally combine them, psychology is likely to become increasingly marginalized as nations and societies around the world place education increasingly at the center of their social policies.

Telling what we know

This is the method of sharing our knowledge at which we as scholars are most adept. We write research articles and give presentations on a regular basis. For the most part, though, these publications and papers given at professional meetings are aimed at others like us: researchers and scholars. Only when we write textbooks or other books and articles aimed specifically for "practitioners" do we work to make our language and concepts accessible to audiences who are not specialists. In the fields of education and industrial training, future practitioners go through an educational process in which they read selections from what we write – sometimes in the original "scholarly" versions, more often in versions intended for practitioners. In this way, a kind of "canon" of texts on psychological principals of learning and instruction has been developed and most practitioners in the field can remember the names of a few major theorists and their claims. However, the links between these theoretical findings and what educators and trainers actually do in their work are very thin. As I go into schools and classrooms today I find very little practice that matches the principles of learning and instruction that are being taught in teacher-preparation programs.

This is not for lack of sophisticated trying to get better at the telling process. Let me use as an example the way in which the psychological research community has worked over the past 10 years or so to communicate the most important general findings of cognitive science research to American policy makers and practitioners of education. The story begins with the convening of a National Research Council (NRC) Committee on Learning in 1996. The committee was chaired by one of our most distinguished cognitive psychologists, John Bransford, and included a distinguished roster of members. The group met repeatedly over a period of three years and produced an important scholarly book entitled *How People Learn* (Bransford, Brown, & Cocking, 1999). This quickly became the point of reference for learning scholars concerned with possible educational applications across the USA and in many other countries as well.

The 319-page volume was a scholars' report, written for scholars with all of the paraphernalia of references and, more important, shadings of opinion and differences of interpretation. The NRC leadership knew from the start that if the committee's work was to have an impact on educational practice some direct efforts to communicate with practitioners would be needed. Within a few months a version for educators, written in a more accessible style, appeared (Donovan, Bransford, & Pellegrino, 1999). The NRC sponsored workshops and meetings to present the findings to practitioners and conducted discussions with them about the implications for teaching practice. This was the beginning of a serious effort to carry the principles of *How People Learn* into classroom use. Most recently, a new volume has been published that includes detailed examples of how to apply the principles in teaching history, science and mathematics (Donovan & Bransford, 2005). These are sophisticated attempts by scholarly leadership in psychology to tell education practitioners what the research says and to make the telling as closely related to practice as possible. The books are coming into wide use among scholars, in the USA and beyond, and are used to some degree in university programs that prepare education practitioners. However, it is possible to go even further toward effective *telling* by building study tools for educators that teams of professionals can use "on the job" to learn psychological principles directly relevant to their work.

Training and tools for professional learning communities

Over the past 12 years, I have been working directly "in the field" of education practice, bringing my own immersion in cognition and learning research along with me. Working with a growing team of highly accomplished professionals in the Institute for Learning at the University of Pittsburgh's Learning Research and Development Center, we have formed alliances with leading school districts – the large "urban" ones that in the USA contain the preponderance of poor, minority and immigrant students; those most in need of a strong science of learning. Educators there were hungry to learn what the cognitive research of the past 25 years or so could offer them in the way of guidance. But they wanted this knowledge to come to them in forms that were tightly tied to their own work, not forcing them first to learn a bulky theory and only later focus on educational practice. They wanted to become skilled "reflective practitioners" (Schon, 1987), not (once again) novice university students studying for exams. We began with an analysis of the kinds of professional knowledge and skills that educators would need in order to lead the kind of "knowledge-based constructivist" (Resnick & Hall, 1998) learning environments that psychological research now tells us we need to construct. From there, we went on to build a series of study tools for professionals – learning much along the way about how to make them truly usable in practice, and what organizational supports would be needed to make them truly powerful in use.

Tools for learning core principles in a community of practice

A first step in building professional practice communities (see Wenger, 1998), we knew, was to build a common base of understanding and to begin a regular practice of professional *talk* about practice. To support this kind of learning practice, we have built a series of CD-ROMs around nine Principles of Learning distilled from 25-plus years of cognitive research on teaching and learning.[2] These might best be construed as a practitioner-friendly version of the theoretical ideas presented in the NRC's recent reports on the science of learning and cognitive assessment, joined with a small set of organizational practices aimed at creating equitable opportunities to learn for the full spectrum of students populating today's schools.

The CDs are intended for use by study groups of about six people, possibly including an expert facilitator. Containing a browser-accessible website of text, images, and media clips, the CDs set forth the rationale and substance of the principles and illustrate how they play out in classrooms. They use the affordances of the medium to: (a) enliven and illustrate expositions of the Principles; (b) teach the meaning of key concepts of learning and teaching through multiple examples of instructional practice that can be compared, contrasted and intensively analyzed, using support tools built into the CDs; (c) engage groups of educators in intensive case studies of particular examples of practice; and (d) simulate some aspects of live communities of practice in more socially protected settings.

An introductory CD, *Principles of Learning: Study Tools for Educators* (Resnick, Hall et al., 2001) is mainly designed to set forth the core theories and build common ways of using the language of teaching and learning. The "e-book" section of the CD introduces and illustrates the Principles of Learning. Audio segments expand upon some of the background for the Principles, and video segments provide classroom examples that illustrate points made in the text.

Another section of the *Principles of Learning* CD presents an *Instruction and Learning Profile*. This section allows users to study a particular principle in greater depth. The Profile sets forth an encapsulated definition of each principle. The features of classroom activity that reflect use of each principle are presented, along with indicators that can be watched for when observing classroom practice. The Profile provides multiple video examples, from a mix of grade levels and subject areas, to help users build their understanding of how the principle might look when enacted in schools and classrooms. When a video is selected, it is accompanied by a written transcript to assist people in following the language and a set of suggested discussion questions to guide users' consideration of how the segment exemplifies the principle.

Yet another section of the CD provides extended case studies designed to help study groups detect several principles in an ongoing flow of instruction. Suggested study activities are organized to help groups conduct discussions in which they combine information from several points of view. The group begins by watching a video (typically 15 minutes in length) together. Individuals or subgroups next select a Principle of Learning as their lens for further, detailed observation. The group then splits up, each printing out an observation sheet that provides a transcript of the entire video and coding information specific to the Principle that they have chosen. Individually or in small groups, users watch the video again, with as many starts and stops as they wish, and use the observation sheet to record instances of "their" principle. Next the participants reconvene and develop a group composite observation sheet that constitutes their shared interpretation of the episode as a whole.

Additional CDs focusing on individual Principles of Learning – *Clear Expectations: Putting Standards to Work in the Classroom* (Resnick & Bill, 2001) and *Accountable Talk: Classroom Conversation that Works* (Michaels, O'Connor, & Hall, 2002) – provide study groups with the means of further developing a shared theory of instruction and learning. Each CD set presents an overview of the Principle, either in text format or as an extended video presentation, as well as materials for in-depth study of specific aspects of the Principle. Each also contains extended case studies. All are supported by suggested activities for individuals and study groups, along with observation sheets (which can be printed out) to help ground the conversation and provide a record of issues discussed.

Evaluations of our study tools, as used in three different school districts, have made it clear that providing good tools and time for study is not enough to ensure that our psychological "gifts" will be well-received. During the 2001–2002 school year, the *Principles of Learning* CD was given a trial run in three medium-size school districts in the USA. When evaluators visited each district to examine how well the experiment was working, their interviews and observations led to radically different assessments in the three districts. In one of the districts, the evaluators were able to observe active study groups using the CDs in some schools and heard reports from principals and teachers in many schools about successful use of the CDs. There was considerable – although not universal – enthusiasm for the CD as a powerful tool for initiating or supporting teacher study of the Principles. Few complaints about technical flaws were heard. In the two other districts, by contrast, the CDs were rarely used. Indeed, principals and others throughout these districts often reported that the CD was technically flawed – that it couldn't be opened, that navigation through the different parts of the CD was not smooth or didn't work at all, that videos wouldn't play or that sound was inadequate.

After checking out various possible explanations, the evaluators determined that technical and individual skill differences in the three districts did not account for the differences in receptivity. Instead, it appeared that the differences were due to organizational differences in how the Principles of Learning study tools were situated in the "official" and ongoing work of the district. In the high-use district, participants were given "homework assignments" in which they were asked to go back to their schools and lead study sessions using the CD and its printable activity sheets. They were expected to collect "artifacts" from these sessions – filled-out activity sheets, for example – that would be shared and discussed at the next principals' meeting. Several cycles of assignments and artifact discussion ensued, making it highly likely that even the initially reluctant principals would find a way to launch the CD project in their schools. None of this social facilitation and demand was present in the two low-use districts. There, at the end of the introductory sessions, principals were told that the CDs could help in their efforts to establish ongoing professional development in their schools; but no particular expectations for use were established and there was no follow-up.

Protocols for professional practice

Transcripts, videos and tailored study protocols can open an avenue to reflective practice. However, in the real world, no example of teaching ever neatly illustrates a particular principle or practice. If one observes a classroom for longer than a few minutes, one sees multiple things happening. Teachers may pose problems and start discussions, but – with rare exceptions – matters do not unfold according to a script. Students' responses may lead in a direction not anticipated by a teacher, efforts to make expectations clear to students may appear to interfere with a goal of students managing their own learning, a complex and academically rigorous lesson may become much less demanding in the teacher's attempt to help weak or shy students, different students may react differently to the same teacher-proposed activities.

This variety and complexity means that it cannot be enough to teach educators about specific features of effective learning and teaching – even when these are well illustrated by carefully selected examples from practice. Educators also need to learn how to analyze the "messy" instructional practice of the real world – deciding which principles of learning are illustrated (or violated) and learning how to discuss examples of practice that may be headed toward, but still somewhat distant from, the "best practices" that we are aiming for. They also need to learn how to function "in community" – that is, how to treat discussion of instructional cases as legitimate opportunities for comparing ideas and sharpening concepts rather than as evaluations of teaching practices. This shift in attitude toward analysis and reflection and away from evaluative judgment turns out to be a substantial challenge, given the traditions of the school systems within which today's teachers work.

One approach to building communities of instructional practice is for groups of educators to visit classrooms together and then confer about what they have seen. Shared classroom observations provide an anchor for discussion. A skilled facilitator can guide the discussion, and shared protocols for observation can help to direct the initial observations – including examination of students' work and, sometimes, conversations with students – in productive directions. At the Institute for Learning, we have developed a structured set of protocols for this kind of communal, interactive classroom visitation, which we have dubbed the LearningWalk[SM] (Goldman, Resnick, Bill, Johnston, Micheaux, & Seitz, 2004). We have trained educators in a number of US school districts in the processes of facilitating these professional visits. LearningWalks[SM] are organized visits to a series of classrooms using the Principles of Learning to focus on the instructional core. The "walkers" (who can be principals and other administrators, teachers, parents, curriculum specialists, etc.) observe interactions between students and teachers, examine "artifacts" (displayed student work, student notebooks, written assignments . . .) and talk directly with students – all guided by a semistructured protocol. After each classroom visit, the walkers gather in the school hall and use another protocol to discuss and analyze what they have seen, always focused on trying to understand, rather than evaluate, what they have seen. The LearningWalk[SM] helps build professional learning communities by focusing participants on teaching and learning, breaking down classroom isolation, developing insight into what students are learning, and providing a basis for designing professional development for the school members.

LearningWalks[SM] have been enthusiastically embraced by senior managers of schools and districts. When used as intended by principals and supervisors, they are associated with functional professional learning communities in schools. However, for people with little experience of new forms of community building, there is a tendency to assimilate the LearningWalk[SM] into a form of classroom visitation with which they are more familiar: evaluation of teacher performance. When this happens, we almost universally encounter resistance from teachers who are used to "professional privacy" inside their classrooms and when this happens the entire process may be shut down for a period by the actions of teachers' unions. Thus, it requires constant attention to matters of *organizational design* and functioning to maintain the professional learning intention of the LearningWalk[SM] protocol in practice.

From tools and protocols to organizational design

The limits of psychology

Psychology provides articulated theories of learning and some demonstrations that these theories work for education when faithfully applied. However, as the examples I have given above from my own Institute's work in school systems illustrate, when we try to apply our theories, programs, and tools in a more systemic manner, we encounter blockages. Our ideas and practices seem to gain a toehold among people whom we have met and worked with personally, but the new ideas and processes do not become the standard way of doing things. We have partial success at most, and only rare experiences of sustainability – i.e., continued use of our concepts, tools and programs after the initiators leave. To create more sustainable use, to guard against our psychological "gifts" being stashed away in the closet after the externally funded party is over, we need to understand what causes the blockages.

Psychologists have a favorite set of blockage explanations, all focused on the *individuals* within the organizations we are trying to influence. We point, for example, to difficulties of *motivation*. The new ideas are difficult at first and people don't want to put out the extra effort it would take to apply them. This analysis calls for using various motivational techniques to build loyalty to the new processes and programs and keep people working in the new ways. Incentives may be offered for persistence – out-and-out rewards or merely the camaraderie of participating with others.

Other blockages, according to psychologists' analyses, come from participants *beliefs*. These may be beliefs about the nature of teaching and learning, which can lead teachers to resist modifications to established educational programs. For example, American teachers have been heavily schooled in the ideas of "mastery learning" – students should keep working on a new skill or concept until they master it, and only then go on to the next topic. Carefully designed reading and mathematics programs that rely instead on a principle of "spiral learning" (Bruner, 1960) – returning again and again to a concept so that full mastery is built only over repeated, separate exposures – run against the grain of this belief and teachers may distort such programs or reject them entirely. The psychologist's remedy for this kind of disbelief is likely to be training programs in which the theory of spiral learning is taught to teachers, along with training in the details of how to implement a particular curriculum. These are both solutions aimed at what individuals know and believe, not, for example, at how spiral curricula fit into the overall distribution of time, personnel and material resources within a school or school district.

Teachers may also have strong beliefs about which students can learn what kind of material; which students are "ready" for investments in learning. Beliefs about who can learn what run deep in our schooling systems and our societies. Despite substantial research showing that ability to learn can be acquired, most Western countries continue to believe that intelligence and aptitude set the limits on learning and we invest heavily in tests to detect that aptitude. Many psychologists' response to belief blockages is to try to intervene directly on the belief systems of educators, and even of students themselves.

Psychologists may also attribute blockages to lack of *expertise* on the part of some actors in the system. So, for example, psychologists (along with some economists interested in *human capital*) may argue that the reason that students don't learn mathematics better in school is that their teachers are not expert enough in mathematics and so cannot adequately explain mathematical concepts. On this theory, education reformers, including psychologists, aim to select better teachers (here is the aptitude argument in a new form) or to provide more training to teachers – on the mathematics knowledge and on expert methods of teaching it.

All these blockage analyses and potential responses are *psychological* explanations and potential solutions. They focus on what individuals in education systems know, believe or have the individual capacity to learn. Such explanations and solutions are certainly part of the picture. But they are almost certainly not the whole story. To find powerful solutions to the education and learning problems that face us we are going to have to look beyond individuals, and thus beyond what psychology alone can offer. Perhaps paradoxically, if we really want to give psychology away, we are going to have to first receive wisdom, ideas and practice from other fields. Our psychological explanations, focused on individuals, need to be matched with explanations and interventions that take account of the social groups and organizations in which people live and work. Other social sciences can offer complementary explanations that will help build *organizational* as well as individual capacity. Let us briefly examine a few interdisciplinary resources.

Anthropology and sociocultural theory

Of all the social sciences, probably the best known one to psychologists is that particular branch of anthropology that has become known as "sociocultural" theory (see Cole, Engestrom, & Vasquez, 1997; Lave & Wenger, 1991) or, in its variants closest to psychology, "situated learning" (Greeno, Collins, & Resnick, 1996). In the 1970s, driven partly by the rediscovery of the work of Vygotsky (1978) and partly by tentative and then growing collaborations of learning, developmental and instructional psychologists with anthropologists, a new way of thinking about learning began to develop (see Hutchins, 1995; Resnick, Levine, & Teasley, 1991; Rogoff, Goodman-Turkanis, & Bartlett, 2001). The new theories of situated cognition treated learning not as simply a matter of individual brains at work acquiring new knowledge or skills, but as persons coming to function effectively in specific, socially defined situations. Cognition came to be viewed as a social activity, "stretched over" individuals, tasks and tools (especially language). Mind and motivation, skills and self-concepts were linked in an essentially "sociocognitive" theory of learning and development.

This sociocognitive stance has become increasingly influential among psychologists of development, cognition and instruction. For learning and instructional psychologists, it introduces, or reinforces, a stance that goes beyond individual minds acquiring personal skills and knowledge. However, with only rare exceptions (e.g., Engeström & Middleton, 1999), sociocultural analyses are largely silent on the *organizations* within which interactive groups function. It is as if the broad societal *culture* – long, and still, the purview of anthropology as a discipline – is carried by individuals into their interactive groups, without an institutional or organizational mediation. For more help in designing learning organizations, we will have to turn to three other fields of research, each with origins in the discipline of sociology.

Institutional theory

Beginning with Max Weber in the 19th century, sociologists have sought to understand how formally constituted organizations work and why they come into being. Weber focused on explaining how bureaucratic structures (governmental and private) were efforts to rationalize and make more efficient the work and accountability of large organizations, where personal relationships could not sufficiently govern actions (Weber, 1947). Weber's theories were taken up by students and colleagues all over the world; variants of this rationalist theory dominated social-science thinking about organizations throughout the first half of the 20th century. They were used to prescribe organizational designs in both public (government) agencies and private businesses. In the USA, bureaucratic principles traveled from business into education along with the general principles of scientific management that were applied to industrial production (Tyack, 1974). In other countries, similar principles of rational management came into educational practice by extension from governmental agencies.

For multiple reasons the Weberian rationalist analysis lost favor among sociologists in the 1960s and 1970s. But more recently a "new institutionalism" theory has developed (Meyer & Rowan, 1977; Powell & DiMaggio, 1991) that has much to offer those (such as psychologists) interested in seeing their ideas used. This research tells us that organizations operate within a set of "taken-for-granted" (institutionalized) beliefs, practices, and structures. Organizations mostly conform to these, adopting ritualistic forms and structures that compete with efficiency; this is how organizations survive over time. Organizations can also challenge these ritualized practices, in order to become more effective in meeting reform goals. But changes of this kind lessen the likelihood of organizational survival.

Among the institutionalized practices for public-service organizations (such as education systems) are professions that control entry and advancement, labor agreements, expectations for transparency and consultation outside the organization, and avoidance of evaluation and the *decoupling* of the technical core from management and policy. Many analyses of education reform efforts show how institutionalization limits effective change in established organizations. Of particular note is the way in which new processes that we might bring in, informed by psychological research, are treated as temporary "pilot" studies and not allowed to enter the core policy of the organization. In this way, education organizations can appear very "progressive" while in fact maintaining institutionalized practices that prevent new practices from penetrating beyond a few "experimental" sites.

Organizational resources: Human and social capital

For several decades, social scientists have been trying to extend the power of resource analysis from purely financial forms of capital to other kinds of resources that can make a difference to what organizations are able to accomplish. Economists tend to be especially interested in "human capital" – what people in the organization know and know how to do. Human capital is measured by credentials, performance observations, and individual outputs. Reformers promote programs – usually of salary incentives and hiring policies – that they believe will attract and hold the most qualified and productive professionals in educational jobs. I am not aware of active efforts to link such incentives experiments to the kinds of training and instructional programs promoted by psychologists.

"Social capital" is a term introduced by sociologists (Becker, 1964; Coleman, 1988) referring to the opportunities that some people have, and that organizations can create, for acquiring knowledge from others. The term has been broadened to include social networks, trustful relationships, and co-construction of knowledge and practices (Adler & Kwon, 2002; Nahapiet & Ghoshal, 1998). A small "movement" of scholars studying processes of education reform has begun to document links between social capital (for example, groups of teachers professionally engaged with one another within a school) and the forms of knowledge-based constructivism that the NRC reports espouse and that our Institute for Learning Principles embody (e.g., Bryk & Schneider, 2002; Gamoran, Anderson, Quiroz, Secada, Williams, & Ashmann, 2003; McLaughlin & Talbert, 2001; Newman, 1996).

Organizational theory: Bounded rationality

A very particular, and influential, response to the observed limits of Weberian rationalism has been the "Carnegie School" of organizational theory, developed by James March and Herbert Simon (March & Simon, 1993). Because it was founded on an analysis of the limits of individual cognitive rationality in decision making, March and Simon's theory seems particularly accessible to psychologists. March and Simon argued that people cannot manage fully rational or reasoned decision making. They *satisfice* (a form of tradeoff between intuition and reason) rather than optimize.

Organizations, too, do not literally follow the strictures of even their own formal plans. Instead, groups and individuals develop action routines (*standard operating procedures* or *SOPs*) that constitute the normal ways in which work gets done. These SOPs are not necessarily what the organizations' official manuals say *should* be done. Rather, they are inventions by organization members that allow them to perform satisfactorily, in terms of the judgments of clients and supervisors and also in terms of self-satisfaction. They often involve adaptation of institutional constraints of the kind discussed above and may also recruit the power of informal "below the radar" work groups of the kind that sociocognitive theorists have documented (e.g., Orr, 1996; Suchman, 1996), although there seems to be relatively little communication between these groups of scholars. The concept of organizational routines gives us yet another powerful point of view for thinking about organizational change. In the March and Simon tradition, what systems "know" is their routines of action (SOPs). *Organizational learning* is a change in these routines. To help an organization learn, then, we would need to help an organization analyze its routines, including their sources of authority and control, and pick initial targets for changes in SOPs that are both likely to succeed quickly and likely to impact other routines and thus exercise leverage on the organization as a whole.

Creating learning organizations

How might we actually apply the theories and insights of the sociocultural, institutional and organizational perspectives to the task of redesigning education (and perhaps other) organizations to make them more receptive to psychology's gifts? I offer, in closing, a few principles.

Map routines and standard operating procedures

Those who want to change organizations will find it useful to begin by attempting to understand the routines and SOPs of those organizations. They will need to know not only what the SOPs are (a task of some breadth, since working SOPs are often hidden from official view), but also who is invested in them. They will need analyses of which SOPs are blocking change in organizational performance and which might provide support for the new processes that they want to introduce.

Introduce a small number of "kernel" routines and procedures

Care must be taken to establish leadership for them together with incentives for taking the risks associated with organizational change. Select for first attention routines and procedures likely to win early allegiance from many different actors in the organization and in which people are likely to experience early success. Create rituals that make their successes visible. Build alliances – both inside the organization and among "stakeholders" outside the organization – that allow as broad a band of people as possible to join the effort and take some "credit" for successes.

Build social capital by distributing leadership and knowledge in all directions

This includes extending technical knowledge and expertise "upward" in the organization, in order to end, or at least limit, the decoupling of technical expertise from management/political activity. In school systems, for examples, principals might participate in activities such as new forms of classroom visitation, direct teaching of students, or coaching of teachers – activities that had formerly been crowded out by the management aspects of their jobs.

Leadership and authority should also be extended "downward" so that those who are the first to practice new processes can play a role in spreading them upward and laterally in the organization. The various ways in which distributed leadership can function to build new organizational processes and then stabilize them within the organization have been extensively studied by James Spillane and his colleagues (e.g., Spillane, Halverson, & Diamond, 2002).

Create learning opportunities for everyone in the organization

In a period of organizational change everyone in the organization will be challenged to change their practices. They need opportunities to learn the new practices – including time and supportive teaching and coaching. Training and professional development in a transforming organization will require substantial resources of money and, perhaps most important, of time. A significant portion of members' *working time* will need to be devoted to learning.

Establish two-way accountability

This should apply to every level/unit in the organization. As the organization changes its practices, members will be responsible for behaving in new ways. But we cannot expect them to learn the new ways without organizationally sponsored opportunities. Accountability in a transforming organization thus needs to flow in two directions at once – members of a work group (for example, teachers) are accountable to their supervisors for taking on and learning the new practices. At the same time, they have the right to hold their supervisors accountable for providing working conditions, learning opportunities and resources that enable the new ways of working. Keep in mind that two-way accountability will probably require two-way monitoring systems – evaluations of supervisors by those they supervise, as well as the other way around. In this and other ways, two-way accountability and distributed leadership strategies are intimately related.

Use external partners to help manage the change process

Even well-managed organizational shifts will involve periods of pain and disorder within the organization. Mistakes are inevitable, as are the aroused emotions that can block successful adaptations. External partners can help in three ways. First, they can often gather information about what is really going on more quickly and more reliably than senior management itself (because outsiders can talk to everyone and will often hear a more honest version of events and relationships than even a well-liked insider). Second, because they have encountered similar changes in other organizations, experienced outsiders can advise senior managers through the difficult choices associated with transformational shifts. These are both what we might call "friendly" functions. But there is a third function that many managers of change welcome but rarely discuss: the possibility, if things go badly wrong, of "blaming" the outsider, dismissing him or her, and making a fresh start. Such "sacrifices" of people are well known in organizations. In biblical times, "scapegoating" – laying the sins of a community on a sacrificial animal that was then sent into the wilderness – gave communities a chance to purify themselves and begin again. Individuals and groups who serve as outside partners to organizations that are transforming themselves should be prepared to play this kind of function occasionally.

The principles that I have just sketched out are inferences from the social-science theories described above. The organizational-change principles do not carry the weight of the Principles of Learning with which I began this chapter, not having been tested over decades in multiple laboratories nor crafted in extended discourse between scholars and practitioners. Yet they can, I believe, serve as a starting point for psychologists who want to try to help build organizations better suited to receiving the gifts of psychology. Perhaps in a few years, it will be possible to provide empirical documentation for a revised and tested set of organizational principles. There is little chance that we psychologists will be able to do this new form of work alone. Instead, we will have to enter into new alliances and develop forms of collaboration that may make us uneasy – because we won't be on completely secure ground even as we are offering our most expert knowledge to others. We will have to build new routines and procedures for ourselves, as well as for our clients and collaborators. I have been working in this way for some time and can speak from experience about what to expect: It is hard, it is doable, it works (sometimes), and it is our only serious chance to successfully give psychology away.

Notes

1 The National Research Council (NRC) is the "working arm" of the United States National Academies of Science, Engineering and Medicine. NRC takes on projects in which the cumulated scientific knowledge can be applied to current problems of policy and research direction. Its typical way of working is to assemble "consensus panels" of scholars and practitioners who review multiple literatures and attempt to arrive at a common view of what the literature says on the problem under review. Its reports use these literature reviews to arrive at recommendations for policy and/ or further research in a field. Reports are reviewed in detail by the relevant National Academy before being released, usually in book form, to the public.
2 For a description of the Principles of Learning, see the Appendix below or the following page at the Institute for Learning website: http://www.instituteforlearning. org/develop.html.

References

Adler, P. S., & Kwon, S. (2002). Social capital: Prospects for a new concept. *Academy of Management Review, 27*(1), 17–40.

Becker, G. (1964). *Human capital: A theoretical and empirical analysis, with special reference to education.* New York: Columbia University Press for the National Bureau of Economic Research.

Bransford, J. D., Brown, A. L., & Cocking, R. R. (1999). *How people learn: Brain, mind, experience, and school.* Washington, DC: National Academy Press. (Available online at http://www.nap.edu/html/howpeople1/)

Bruner, J. (1960). *The process of education.* Cambridge, MA: Harvard University Press.

Bryk, A. S., & Schneider, B. (2002). *Trust in schools: A core resource for improvement.* New York: Russell Sage.

Cole, M., Engestrom Y., & Vasquez, O. (Eds.). (1997). *Mind, culture, and activity.* Cambridge, UK: Cambridge University Press.

Coleman, J. S. (1988). Social capital in the creation of human capital. *The American Journal of Sociology, 94,* S95–S120.

Donovan, S., & Bransford, J. (2005). *How students learn: History, mathematics, and science in the classroom.* Washington, DC: National Academy Press.

Donovan, S., Bransford, J., & Pellegrino, J. (1999). *How people learn: Bridging research and practice.* Washington, DC: National Academy Press.

Engeström, Y., & Middleton, D. (Eds.). (1999). *Cognition and communication at work.* Cambridge, UK: Cambridge University Press.

Gamoran, A., Anderson, C. W., Quiroz, P. A., Secada, W. G., Williams, T., & Ashmann, S. (2003). *Transforming teaching in math and science: How schools and districts can support change.* New York: Teachers College Press.

Goldman, P., Resnick, L. B., Bill, V., Johnston, J., Micheaux, D., & Seitz, A. (2004). Learning Walk[SM] sourcebook, Version 2.0. Available from the Institute for Learning, Learning Research & Development Center, University of Pittsburgh, Pennsylvania.

Greeno, J. G., Collins, A., & Resnick, L. B. (1996). Cognition and learning. In D. C. Berliner & R. C. Calfee (Eds.), *Handbook of educational psychology* (pp. 15–46). New York: Macmillan.

Hutchins, E. (1995). *Cognition in the wild.* Cambridge, MA: MIT Press.

Lave, J., & Wenger, E. (1991). *Situated learning: Legitimate peripheral participation.* Cambridge, UK; New York: Cambridge University Press.

March, J. G., & Simon, H. A. with the collaboration of Guetzkow, H. (1993). *Organizations* (2nd ed.). Cambridge, MA: Blackwell.

McLaughlin, M. W., & Talbert, J. E. (2001). *Professional communities and the work of high school teaching.* Chicago, IL: University of Chicago Press.

Meyer, J., & Rowan, B. (1977). Institutional organizations: Formal structure as myth and ceremony. *American Journal of Sociology, 83,* 340–363.

Michaels, S., O'Connor, M. C., & Hall, M. W. with Resnick, L. B. (2002). *Accountable Talk[SM]: Classroom conversation that works* [CD-ROM Set, Beta version 2.0]. Pittsburgh, PA: Institute for Learning, Learning Research and Development Center, University of Pittsburgh.

Nahapiet, J., & Ghoshal, S. (1998). Social capital, intellectual capital and the organizational advantage. *Academy of Management Review, 23,* 242–266.

Newmann, F. M. (1996). *Authentic achievement: Restructuring schools for intellectual quality.* San Francisco, CA: Jossey-Bass.

Orr, J. (1996). *Talking about machines.* Ithaca, NY: Cornell University Press.

Powell, W. W., & DiMaggio, P. J. (Eds.). (1991). *The new institutionalism in organizational analysis* (pp. 63–82). Chicago, IL; & London: University of Chicago Press.

Resnick, L. B., & Bill, V. L. (2001). *Clear expectations: Putting standards to work in the classroom* [CD-ROM, Beta version 1.0]. Pittsburgh, PA: Institute for Learning, Learning Research and Development Center, University of Pittsburgh.

Resnick, L. B., & Hall, M. W. (1998). Learning organizations for sustainable education reform. *Daedalus, 127*(4), 89–118.

Resnick, L., Hall, M. W., & Fellows of the Institute for Learning (2001). *The Principles of Learning: Study tools for educators* [CD-ROM]. Pittsburgh, PA: Institute for Learning, Learning Research and Development Center, University of Pittsburgh.

Resnick, L. B., Levine, J. M., & Teasley, S. D. (Eds.). (1991). Perspectives on socially shared cognition. Washington, DC: American Psychological Association.

Rogoff, B., Goodman-Turkanis, C. G., & Bartlett, L. (2001) *Learning together. Children and adults in a school community*. New York: Oxford University Press.

Schon, D. (1987). *Educating the reflective practitioner*. San Francisco, CA: Jossey-Bass.

Spillane, J. P., Halverson, R., & Diamond, J. B. (2002). Toward a theory of leadership practice: A distributed perspective. *Journal of Curriculum Studies, 35*, 1–32.

Suchman, L. (1996). Constituting shared workspaces. In Y. Engeström & D. Middleton (Eds.), *Cognition and communication at work* (pp. 35–60). Cambridge, UK: Cambridge University Press.

Tyack, D. (1974). *The one best system: A history of American urban education*. Cambridge, MA: Harvard University Press.

Vygotsky, L. (1978). *Mind in Society*. Boston, MA: Harvard University Press.

Weber, M. (1947). *The theory of social and economic organization*. London: Free Press.

Wenger, E. (1998). *Communities of practice: Learning meaning and identity*. New York: Cambridge University Press.

Appendix

Principles of Learning

The Principles of Learning are condensed theoretical statements summarizing decades of learning research. The statements are linked to several explanatory points about particular features of each principle. Some of the features are further elaborated by a series of indicators that schools and classrooms are functioning in accord with the principle. They are designed to help educators analyze the quality of instruction and opportunities for learning that they offer to students.

Organizing for effort

An effort-based school replaces the assumption that aptitude determines what and how much students learn with the assumption that sustained and directed effort can yield high achievement for all students. Everything is organized to evoke and support this effort, to send the message that effort is expected and that tough problems yield to sustained work. High minimum standards are set and assessments are geared to the standards. All students are taught a rigorous curriculum, matched to the standards, along with as much time and expert instruction as they need to meet or exceed expectations.

Clear expectations

If we expect all students to achieve at high levels, then we need to define explicitly what we expect students to learn. These expectations need to be communicated clearly in ways that get them "into the heads" of school professionals, parents, the community and, above all, students themselves. Descriptive criteria and models of work that meets standards should be publicly displayed, and students should refer to these displays to help them analyze and discuss their work. With visible accomplishment targets to aim toward at each stage of learning, students can participate in evaluating their own work and setting goals for their own effort.

Fair and credible evaluations

If we expect students to put forth sustained effort over time, we need to use assessments that students find fair; and that parents, community, and employers find credible. Fair evaluations are ones that students can prepare for: therefore, tests, exams and classroom assessments – as well as the curriculum – must be aligned to the standards. Fair assessment also means grading against absolute standards rather than on a curve, so students can clearly see the results of their learning efforts. Assessments that meet these criteria provide parents, colleges, and employers with credible evaluations of what individual students know and can do.

Recognition of accomplishment

If we expect students to put forth and sustain high levels of effort, we need to motivate them by regularly recognizing their accomplishments. Clear recognition of authentic accomplishment is a hallmark of an effort-based school. This recognition can take the form of celebrations of work that meets standards or intermediate progress benchmarks en route to the standards. Progress points should be articulated so that, regardless of entering performance level, every student can meet real accomplishment criteria often enough to be recognized frequently. Recognition of accomplishment can be tied to opportunity to participate in events that matter to students and their families. Student accomplishment is also recognized when student performance on standards-based assessments is related to opportunities at work and in higher education.

Academic rigor in a thinking curriculum

Thinking and problem solving will be the "new basics" of the 21st century. But the common idea that we can teach thinking without a solid foundation of knowledge must be abandoned. So must the idea that we can teach knowledge without engaging students in thinking. Knowledge and thinking are intimately joined. This implies a curriculum organized around major concepts that students are expected to know deeply. Teaching must engage students in active reasoning about these concepts. In every subject, at every grade level, instruction and learning must include commitment to a knowledge core, high thinking demand, and active use of knowledge.

Accountable Talk^SM

Talking with others about ideas and work is fundamental to learning. But not all talk sustains learning. For classroom talk to promote learning it must be accountable – to the learning community, to accurate and appropriate knowledge, and to rigorous thinking. Accountable talk seriously responds to and further develops what others in the group have said. It puts forth and demands knowledge that is accurate and relevant to the issue under discussion. Accountable talk uses evidence appropriate to the discipline (e.g., proofs in mathematics, data from investigations in science, textual details in literature, documentary sources in history) and follows established norms of good reasoning. Teachers should intentionally create the norms and skills of accountable talk in their classrooms.

Socializing intelligence

Intelligence is much more than an innate ability to think quickly and stockpile bits of knowledge. Intelligence is a set of problem-solving and reasoning capabilities along with the habits of mind that lead one to use those capabilities regularly. Intelligence is equally a set of beliefs about one's right and obligation to understand and make sense of the world, and one's capacity to figure things out over time. Intelligent habits of mind are learned through the daily expectations placed on the learner. By calling on students to use the skills of intelligent thinking – and by holding them responsible for doing so – educators can "teach" intelligence. This is what teachers normally do with students they expect much from; it should be standard practice with all students.

Self-management of learning

If students are going to be responsible for the quality of their thinking and learning, they need to develop – and regularly use – an array of self-monitoring and self-management strategies. These metacognitive skills include noticing when one doesn't understand something and taking steps to remedy the situation, as well as formulating questions and inquiries that let one explore deep levels of meaning. Students also manage their own learning by evaluating the feedback they get from others; bringing their background knowledge to bear on new learning; anticipating learning difficulties and apportioning their time accordingly; and judging their progress toward a learning goal. These are strategies that good learners use spontaneously and all students can learn through appropriate instruction and socialization. Learning environments should be designed to model and encourage the regular use of self-management strategies.

Learning as apprenticeship

For many centuries most people learned by working alongside an expert who modeled skilled practice and guided novices as they created authentic products or performances for interested and critical audiences. This kind of apprenticeship allowed learners to acquire complex interdisciplinary knowledge, practical abilities, and appropriate forms of social behavior. Much of the power of apprenticeship learning can be brought into schooling by organizing learning environments so that complex thinking is modeled and analyzed, and by providing mentoring and coaching as students undertake extended projects and develop presentations of finished work, both in and beyond the classroom.

2 Which should be the contribution of psychology to education?

Emilio Ribes-Iñesta

Two main assumptions have biased the relations between psychology and education from its very beginnings. The first one is that the school is an institution that provides the necessary and sufficient conditions for the optimal delivery of education. The second one is that education is a matter of teaching through the appropriate techniques, and that psychology is the science that may provide this knowledge to improve learning by individuals. I argue that both assumptions are incorrect. To do so, I will not review the current literature on educational psychology, but rather base myself in historical, sociological, and conceptual considerations.

How can psychology and education be related?

Educational psychology may be seen as a special multidisciplinary field devoted to the ways in which psychology contributes to the improvement and understanding of education. Almost one hundred years ago, Thorndike (1910), in the first issue of the *Journal of Educational Psychology*, stated that:

> Psychology is the science of the intellect, characters and behavior of animals including man. Human education is concerned with certain changes in the intellects, characters, and behavior of men, its problems being roughly included under these four topics: aims, materials, means and methods. Psychology contributes to a better understanding of the aims of education by defining them, making them clearer, by limiting them, showing us what can be done and what can not; and by suggesting new features that should be made parts of them.
>
> (p. 5)

In this seminal text, Thorndike enumerated the contributions of psychology to education. Psychology: (a) makes ideas of educational aims clearer by requiring us to put them in terms of the exact changes to be made; (b) helps to measure the probability that an aim is attainable; (c) enlarges and refines the aim of education; (d) provides the field of education with knowledge about the material in which it works, since the art of education depends upon physiology and psychology, specially with reference to the intellect, character, and behavior; and (e) contributes to understanding the means of education, by deducing methods outright from the laws of human nature, by explaining why actual working experiences are successful, and by providing methods of measuring knowledge and skill. If Thorndike's terms were adapted to contemporary psychological jargon, we would agree that this is still a fair description of the field of educational psychology.

My purpose here is to challenge this conception about the relation between psychology and education, and to suggest new possibilities of reciprocal enrichment between both fields. For economic reasons, I will use the term education to refer either to pedagogy, to the process of educating, to its outcome, or to the three aspects at the same time.

Psychology and education have had a deep and long relationship. Intelligence, instruction, learning, development, language, and evaluation are some of the issues in which both disciplines share a common interest. Psychometrics, programmed instruction, classroom management, verbal learning and memory are some of the outstanding areas encompassed by the integrated endeavor known as educational psychology. However, it is important to point out to important differences in the nature of problems being dealt with and in the goals to be met by both disciplines. Psychology, as a basic science, is committed to the knowledge of its subject matter. Psychology, irrespective of the diversity of existing epistemological positions, has to do with the *individual acting* in relation to its natural and social environment. Psychology is interested in the identification of properties, parameters, relations and processes accounting for a wide variety of individual phenomena referred to in ordinary language as knowing, perceiving, remembering, learning, feeling, thinking, and so on. At the same time, psychology attempts to extend its knowledge to relevant areas of natural and social settings by developing techniques and procedures to evaluate the effectiveness of intervention variables on individual behavior and its outcomes.

Education is a complex, social endeavor, through which culture is reproduced and expanded. Education takes place through a variety of institutions, some of them formally established to accomplish educational goals (e.g., schools, workshops), and others that develop education through an informal, but equally effective, social role (e.g., the family, the church, the factory or work place, etc.). The *school*, as a generic term, constitutes the educational institution *par excellence*. The main functions exerted by the school, but not all of them, are related to enabling individuals to incorporate to and participate in different levels of the complex social structure of labor division. Schooled education (using Ivan Illich's term) extends from the preparation for alphabetization and motor development (kindergarten) to the formation of highly specialized technologists and researchers (doctoral programs). Schooled education is organized in distinctive cycles, with different sequenced goals directly or indirectly enabling for the social division of labor.

The school, being the institution responsible for education in society, has promoted the training of professionals dedicated to teach in the different educational cycles, and the emergence of a discipline especially dedicated to the study of education as its subject matter. However, education as a subject matter is not comparable to psychology or to any other science. Education deals with a human enterprise pursuing goals and effects on society, while psychology attempts to know about individuals interacting with other individuals, things and events in their surroundings.

At the same time, professionals in psychology are mostly knowledgeable about psychology, while educators must know something about teaching and something about what they teach about. In fact, education has to do with the education of somebody on something, or with the contributions that specific sciences make to the understanding of some aspect of the educational problem: economics, sociology, philosophy, psychology or anthropology of education. In brief, psychology is a science with a specific subject matter to be known and explained, whereas education may be conceived as an interdiscipline, indissolubly linked to the school institution, and its specific social assignment. Psychology deals with the abstract individual. Education deals with populations and their social and cultural backgrounds. Problems in psychology are problems of understanding and analysis. Problems in education are problems of intervention and decision taking.

Educational psychology (or psychological pedagogy) is an area of intersection. On the one hand, psychology may contribute to the process of education since learners, ultimately, are individuals acting with regard to their teachers, materials and situations. It could be said that psychology is deeply involved in the individual process of learning, the core of the educational enterprise. On the other hand, education is not restricted to a single individual and to the process of learning. Education has to do with social values and interests, politics, economics, demography, culture, language, art, technology, and many other aspects interwoven in the reproduction and expansion of social systems and their forms of life. Psychology may feed the educational enterprise with specific knowledge, but the contribution of psychology, contrary to common belief, is not univocal. The ways in which psychology may contribute to education depend upon how the goals of education are conceived, in general, and the functions of the school, in particular. As a first step to clarify the role of psychology in education, we need to reflect on the relation between the school and the model of society that we aspire to. Knowledge about the history of education and the school cannot be considered superfluous.

The school as educational institution

The structure of school, as we know it nowadays, can be partly traced back to the renaissance and the end of feudalism, and is connected with changes brought out by geographic discoveries, technological invention, commerce expansion and diversification, and the growing of the bourgeoisie as a new social class. In the classical antiquity period, where most of Western institutions originated, education was not restricted to a special institution.

The school probably appeared in Athens where children and youngsters received basic instruction in physical education, music and literary arts, including writing. Collective and individual preceptors were the model of advanced education for a limited sector of the population (Marrou, 1948). Science was equated with wisdom and the exercise of mathematics, natural science, logic, rhetoric, politics, and poetics, among other disciplines. Writers were *magisters*. With the fall of the Roman Empire, educational traditions were kept in monasteries and churches, excepting the Caliphates of Damascus and Cordoba, where reading, commenting and teaching of the Classics was conserved until the pre-Renaissance. In this period, the Carolingian Empire promoted the founding of the first universities, with special emphasis on physics, engineering, and medical studies, and also began the emergence of corporative unions of artisans and trades. It was in the 14th century that schooled education consolidated in the form of *curricula* developed by different monastic orders to deal with pre-university education (Esteban, 2002). The invention of the printing press by Gutenberg expanded the limits of education and instruction within and beyond school, and the teaching of reading became a public concern.

The modern school, however, can trace its origins, but not its spirit, back to the idea of public instruction driven by the encyclopedic movement preceding the French Revolution in the 18th century. Condorcet (2001, Spanish translation) claimed that the State should take care of public instruction but not of education. The family should take care of education, which involves opinions, beliefs and religion. The State should provide primary instruction "in which is taught what every individual needs to conduct himself and to enjoy of the plenitude of his/her rights". The school could not provide a complete education, because education was conceived as an all-or-nothing affair. If education was incomplete, it became harmful. Public instruction could not teach opinions as if they were truths, nor should associate the teaching of morals with that of religion. Public instruction could not be delegated in perpetual corporations, and could not consist of a compulsory doctrine. Women should receive the same instruction as men, and both sexes should be grouped together for primary instruction. Basic instruction included reading and writing, arithmetic, natural sciences, history and geography, as well as the study of languages, specially the classic ones.

With the French Revolution the school, as the agency of public instruction, is seen as the instrument for making men and women actual citizens. Instruction should make possible the exercise of the rights and obligations formally established in the Constitution. Contrary to previous historical periods, instruction and education were not seen as instruments to incorporate and dissolve individuals into the State, but as a mean to promote the growth of individuals and their equality despite their beliefs, religion, language, or social class. Instruction should catalyze education and liberty.

With the ideology of progress subordinated to the development of technologies for the production of goods and financial benefits, the role and conception of schools have changed. The modern school has become a complex, stratified institution. Valid education has been confined to that provided by certified schools, and evaluation of schools and programs has become a major issue in contemporary societies. School has monopolized education in spite of its proved inefficacy, low coverage, and increasing costs. Public and private power agencies have dealt with this situation by adding new financial controls, educational options and branches, efficiency criteria, curriculum requirements, and evaluations for admission and graduation. The outcome of this state of affairs was keenly described by Ivan Illich:

> Many students, especially those who are poor, intuitively know what the schools do for them. They school them to confuse process and substance. Once these become blurred, a new logic is assumed: the more treatment there is, the better are the results; or, escalation leads to success. The pupil is thereby "schooled" to confuse teaching with learning, grade advancement with education, a diploma with competence, and fluency with the ability to say something new. His imagination is "schooled" to accept service in place of value. Medical treatment is mistaken for health care, social work for the improvement of community life, police protection for safety, military poise for national security, the rat race for productive work. Health, learning, dignity, independence, and creative endeavor are defined as little more than the performance of the institutions which claim to serve these ends, and their improvement is made to depend on allocating more resources to the management of hospitals, schools, and other agencies in question.
>
> (1972, p. 1)

Schooled education is based on several highly questionable assumptions:

1 Successful and pertinent learning only can be attained under the expertise and supervision of professional teachers in the school.
2 Cultural, ideological, and knowledge diversity are well represented by a universal, homogeneous curriculum of basic, intermediate, and higher education.
3 Formal education and instruction provide the basic skills and knowledge for effective and independent life, irrespective of specific communities' conditions and social needs and aspirations.
4 The school, as a generic institution, is rationally designed to provide effective educational services.
5 School facilities are the most appropriate for the learning and acquisition of knowledge, skills, and social competencies.
6 Teaching procedures and strategies are optimally suited for the promotion of learning.

7 Successful exercise is preceded by the acquisition of knowledge, or phrasing it in different words, knowing how follows knowing that (Ryle, 1949).
8 Basic instruction provides equal opportunities for the development of skills and interests other than those related to expertise directed to economic gains and consumption.
9 Social roles, cultural values, and living competencies are an automatic outgrowth or byproduct of formal education and the circumstances in which it takes place.
10 As a general rule, group instruction and media-assisted teaching are sufficient for individual learning.
11 The certification of learning requires an additional step consisting of the evaluation of the outcomes of teaching.

Illich (1972) has shown the inconsistency of most of these assumptions, and the intimate relation that the school institution has with an economic and political system based on benefits, consumption, rank, and inequity. The inequality related to school ranking applies both to individuals in a society as well as among nations. On the one hand, schooled education is not as effective as is usually claimed. The school system is more than imperfect. It is poorly suited to providing the conditions necessary for learning competencies and knowledge that may be pertinent to all individuals. On the other hand, the public school system has failed in its aspiration to erase social differences and provide equal opportunities to every individual, irrespective of origin, social class, beliefs, and race, because it has subordinated instruction to certification. The school system has created social and national castes according the certification of instructional ranking: the individual's and nation's labor and merits are objects of retribution according to their educational certification and background.

Some comments by Illich (1972) are illuminating in this regard:

> Neither learning nor justice is promoted by schooling because educators insist on packaging instruction with certification. Learning and the assignment of social roles are melted into schooling. . . . Learning frequently is the result of instruction, but selection for a role or category in the job market increasingly depends on mere length of attendance.
>
> (p. 16)

> Curriculum has always been used to assign social rank. . . . Universal schooling was meant to detach role assignment from personal life history: it was meant to give everybody an equal chance to any office. Even now many people wrongly believe that school ensures the dependence of public trust on relevant learning achievement. However, instead of equalizing chances, the school system has monopolized their distribution.
>
> (p. 17)

A second major illusion on which the school system rests is that most learning is the result of teaching. Teaching, it is true, may contribute to certain kinds of learning under certain circumstances. But most people acquire most of their knowledge outside school, and in school only insofar as school, in a few rich countries, has become their place of confinement during an increasing part of their lives.

(p. 18)

Contemporary education, in rich and poor countries, has fallen behind in satisfying criteria of quantity, quality, and pertinence. A large percentage of people in the world is out of the scope of school educational services. Only a very small portion of those that gain entry to the various levels of schooled education enjoy quality instruction. And, finally, it is difficult to establish the pertinence of this educational offer to meet the communities' diversity of needs, physical and cultural conditions, and welfare. Schooled education has failed not only in regard to the quality, pertinence and extension of professionalized instruction, but also in providing citizens with instruments for a better social life, as the increases in poverty, pollution, delinquency, health problems, addictions, moral noncommitment, and political indifference clearly show.

Education from the viewpoint of the learner

The meaning of education as a process depends on two referents: the learner, and the social group that originates and uses knowledge to be learned. The school, the teacher, instructional materials and media, must be seen as elements to be adapted to the conditions and criteria of both of education's referents. Otherwise, as it is happening, ends become subordinated to means.

Education can be sensibly conceived as a process through which an individual pertaining to a given social group learns a set of practical and theoretical activities *considered* to be meaningful for the well-being, survival and conservation of all the individuals of that social group. Ultimately, education can be summarized as the process through which an individual learns what a social group determines as important. The crucial aspect to be approached about education is what happens while the individual learns (how he/she learns) what the social group has established as important (what is learned and what for/why is learned). Indisputably, the study of individual learning concerns psychology. Psychology should approach the identification of the conditions that facilitate and allow for learning according to different criteria of what is being learned and the ultimate purposes of this learning; that is, how, where, when, and with whom what has been learned has to be performed.

I have argued elsewhere (Ribes, 2002) that learning is not a psychological process. Learning is rather a social or interpersonal process in which the learner has to do something "novel" in order to satisfy a criterion in the form of outcomes, results or forms of behavior. Nevertheless, when an individual learns, a diversity of psychological processes occur that must be taken into account to ensure that the learning episode involving acts and outcomes will take place. Psychological processes taking place during learning are the same as those that occur when learning does not occur. The differences between learning and nonlearning consist in the fact that for learning to be identified it is necessary to meet predetermined criteria related to achievements and outcomes. Learning situations usually consist of circumstances especially designed to facilitate the behaviors and outcomes required to meet specific criteria. Learning occurs as a specific behavioral episode in context. The specificity of the learning episode requires a functional correspondence between what is learned (acts) and the situation and materials delimiting how and where learning is taking place. Nobody can learn a motor skill if the materials to be manipulated are not provided, nor can speech be acquired if the person is not required to talk or to listen to others. If learning is expected, it is necessary to provide the learner with a functional environment, in which what is learned has a performing value, both as a possibility of acting and in terms of outcomes and achievements (see, for instance, literacy training with adults when meaningful problems are presented through texts; Freire, 1984).

Psychology may contribute to education if, and only if, it examines the interpersonal process of learning from the viewpoint of the learner, and not from the traditional view of the teacher. Teaching may be conceived as the set of procedures, materials and conditions that promote learning. However, teaching is effective to the extent that learning takes place, and learning involves always acting or behaving in some way according to well-established criteria and outcomes. In the presence of ill-defined criteria learning cannot occur, since there is no standard allowing the judgment of the fitness or adequacy of the acts or behaviors that might take place. This is the reason why psychology has to focus first on two aspects of the learning episode: (1) the analysis of the actual behaviors and their outcomes; and (2) the social validation of their pertinence. These two aspects deal with *what* is learned and *why* (or what for) it is learned, the central issues of education. A further step consists of investigating the optimal conditions for the occurrence of learned acts and outcomes and their transfer to daily-life situations. This means that teaching has to be conceived and developed from the analysis of the learning situation and not the reverse. *How* to teach must depend on *what* is being learned and *where* it is being learned.

Human learning occurs in a linguistically structured environment. School learning is always mediated by teaching through language: gesturing and signaling, speaking or writing. Education begins by learning to understand through observing, listening, and reading. Basic education begins by establishing linguistic and motor behaviors that will permit the acquisition of new forms of acting. Initially, emphasis is made on learning understanding and communicative language skills, arithmetic skills and symbols, reading simple texts, and motor skills related to rhythm, displacement and manipulation.

Once these basic skills have been acquired, the possibilities and scope of new learning are expanded. Further learning is directed to the acquisition of theoretical or practical knowledge of natural and social sciences, different arts and crafts, physical education and recreation, as well as to the development of health-, moral- and civic-related practices. Learning can take place in direct relation to the circumstances where theoretical and practical knowledge is relevant: counting and distributing objects, solving arithmetic operations, looking at a microscope, mixing chemical substances, producing and measuring electricity, painting, performing on a musical instrument, playing with a ball, and so on. But learning can also occur without direct contact with the circumstances being known: how Darwin concluded that animals and plants evolved from extinct ancestors, why Copernicus formulated the heliocentric theory of the solar system, the influence of Greco-Roman culture on the beginning of the Renaissance period, the geopolitical consequences of Napoleon's defeat by the absolutist European monarchies, and so on.

In both learning situations, direct and indirect, the educational process is mostly guided by the teacher with the assistance of texts, audiovisual presentations, computer-assisted tasks, demonstrations, and apparatus. The student learns by reading texts, listening to instructions, explanations, descriptions, and narrations, by observing demonstrations and examples. The teacher's behavior and the social, ecological, or analogical validity of the situation where teaching takes place are the fundamental factors for learning to occur. The validity of the situation is related to the pertinence of what is being learned. Pertinence and transfer are closely related. It is very unlikely that somebody can learn about doing experiments in plant physiology when teaching is only verbalistic, and consists of illustrated narrations about the production of chlorophyll, without direct exposure to real plants and to a biological laboratory in which to observe and manipulate the variables related to plant growth and reproduction. The teacher's behavior is, unquestionably, the central factor for learning. But this importance does not depend on the histrionic or instrumental abilities of the teacher. The teacher's behavior is fundamental because it constitutes the analogical antecedent of what the student or pupil will learn. The teacher should master the theoretical and practical competencies to be learned by the student. The teacher should not only be able to perform practical activities. He/she should dominate, understand and show the application of the texts commended to the students, should be able to describe the course of the performed activities, the circumstances that determine this course, and the general factors that explain its characteristics and outcomes in relation to the diversity of things and concepts to be known.

Psychology should concentrate three fundamental aspects: (1) the identification and description of competencies to be learned in terms of actual behaviors shown by the students, pertinent situations in which those behaviors are relevant, and social criteria of relevance; (2) how the teacher's mastery of a field can be translated to actual behavior affecting what and how students learn; and (3) the design of teaching situations optimizing the relation between theoretical and practical knowledge and its transfer to valid social and ecological settings. This strategy means a radical shift in the way that psychology looks at education. Contrary to Thorndike's assertion, methods of teaching cannot be deduced outright from the laws of human nature. Methods of teaching have to be suited to what is learned, where it is learned, and why it is learned. Psychology has to look towards social criteria and to the behavior and achievements of the learner, instead of emphasizing assumed psychological processes and their relation with cognitive contents.

The need to change schooled education

I have argued about the need to shift the emphasis from psychological processes and teaching procedures to the learner's behavior and learning situations. The school should be conceived as an intelligent educational environment where varied and effective learning is likely to occur.

Present schooled education can be grossly characterized as follows (Ribes, 2004):

1 The learner's behavior and its outcomes are omitted in the planning and operation of the curriculum, the instructional system and related facilities.
2 The student is considered as a receptacle of cognitive contents provided through information and demonstration procedures.
3 It is assumed that learning "that" includes learning "how".
4 Teaching is conceived as the "transmission" of knowledge.
5 Evaluation takes place at a time different from that of teaching.
6 Learning is basically evaluated as repetition and recognition of what has been observed, read or listened to.
7 Knowledge is not identified on the basis of competent acts.
8 Teaching situations are generally restricted to verbal exposition, routine demonstration, media-assisted illustration, and drill-problem solving, taking place in the classroom or the "practical" laboratory.
9 Teaching goals (instead of learning goals) are specified in terms of disciplinary contents that must be repeated, recognized or performed by the student, without correspondence with mastery criteria referred to theoretical and practical competences in the corresponding discipline.
10 Teaching is imparted to groups, assuming that the "transmission" of knowledge is uniform and equivalent in all students.
11 Teaching is scheduled according to administrative criteria, and prevents each student from progressing at his/her own pace according to mastery-based criteria.
12 Most of competences acquired are not functional outside the classroom situation.

In what direction should the school environment change? Schools should be learning-oriented instead of teaching-oriented. Learning involves three aspects: (1) satisfying an achievement requirement in terms of an activity, and outcome, or an effect; (2) the behaviors or activities that must occur in order to satisfy such requirement; and (3) the circumstances in which those activities and achievements become functional. What is being learned? It is learned to know how to do something or to know about something. The activities performed, the outcomes or effects of those activities, and the criteria to be satisfied will depend on what is attempted to know how to do it or to know about it. To know how to do something or to know about something constitutes a set of performances involving linguistic and nonlinguistic behaviors in different measure, satisfying criteria of pertinence, functionality, and achievement in different circumstances or situations. Planning, design and application of educational strategies and procedures should adapt to and subordinate to the nature of what the student has to learn.

Given that learning is learning of knowing how and knowing about, four general types of learning may be identified (in this case, I take "saying" as representative of the three active modes of language behavior: speech, signaling/gesturing, writing):

1 Learning how to do and to say.
2 Learning how to say as a doing.
3 Learning how to say about doing.
4 Learning how to do as a saying.

Psychology should approach the experimental and applied study of the conditions related to these four general types of learning. The potential knowledge about these types of learning should be used to design intelligent educational environments for the new school, concerned with:

1 The identification of knowledge as competent acts.
2 The design of situations that are relevant to the competencies to be learned.
3 The specification of teaching goals in terms of the acquisition or learning of linguistic and nonlinguistic competencies.
4 The evaluation of learning as equivalent to the occurrence of the learned act.
5 Teaching as a demonstration of mastering the competency that the learner should acquire.
6 Programming learning as a self-paced process in which the student's progress is based on mastery criteria that differ in different dominions of knowledge.
7 The pertinence of the competencies learned by the student, which should be functional in daily-life situations.

Schooled education must be reinvented. Otherwise, both psychology and education will continue, inadvertently, helping to perpetuate an institution that has cut its ties with the search for social equality and progress.

References

Condorcet, J.-A.-N., Marqués de (Jean-Antoine-Nicolas de Caritat). (2001). *Cinco memorias sobre la instrucción pública y otros escritos*. Madrid: Ediciones Morata. (Spanish translation)

Esteban, L. (2002). *La educación en el renacimiento*. Madrid: Síntesis.

Freire, P. (1984). *La importancia de leer y el proceso de liberación*. México: Siglo XXI. (Spanish translation)

Illich, I. (1972). *Deschooling society*. New York: Harper & Row.

Marrou, H. I. (1948). *Histoire de l'education dans l'Antiquité. 1. Le monde grec. 2. Le monde romain*. Paris: Editions du Seuil.

Ribes, E. (2002). El problema del aprendizaje: Un análisis conceptual e histórico. In E. Ribes (Ed.), *Psicología del aprendizaje*. México: El Manual Moderno.

Ribes, E. (2004). Psicología, educación y análisis de la conducta. In S. Castañeda (Ed.), *Educación, aprendizaje y cognición. Teoría en la práctica*. México: El Manual Moderno.

Ryle, G. (1949). *The concept of mind*. New York: Barnes & Noble.

Thorndike, E. L. (1910). The contribution of psychology to education. *The Journal of Educational Psychology*, *1*, 5–12.

3 Activating historical and conceptual links in the realm of instruction in Latin America

Alfonso Orantes

Origins

The original purpose of this chapter was to update a review of the area of educational psychology in Latin America (Orantes, 1993).

Educators have had a prominent place in Latin America. In the UNESCO series *100 Thinkers on education* (available at: http://www.ibe.unesco.org/International/Publications/Thinkers/thinhome.htm) seven Latin American educators are included. Educators have also played an important role since the time of independence, for example: Andres Bello; Simon Rodriguez, mentor of Simon Bolivar the "Libertador" of six countries; national heroes such as Jose Marti in Cuba; presidents such as Benito Juarez in Mexico, Domingo Sarmiento in Argentina and, more recently, Pedro Aguirre Cerda in Chile, Manuel Prado y Ugarteche in Peru, and Juan Jose Arevalo in Guatemala; and presidential candidates such as Luis Beltran Prieto in Venezuela. It has also produced educators suitable for export such as Paulo Freire, author of *Pedagogy of the oppressed*, whose outstanding pupil is the current President of Brazil.

Latin America occupies a vast region of the American continent. It includes more than 20 countries and in area it is twice the size of Europe. Latin American countries by no means constitute a coherent unit. They differ in territorial extension – Brazil could hold within its expanse all the other countries in Latin American while El Salvador has a bare twenty thousand square kilometers. They also differ in the wealth and economic development. They include regions as different as Patagonia, in the Antarctic region, the warm beaches of the Caribbean Sea, and the Mexican deserts in the North. While some countries have four seasons, others enjoy an eternal spring or an exhausting summer. At least four international languages are spoken in Latin America: Spanish, Portuguese, French, and English. Aboriginal languages, such as quechua, catchiquel or aymara reflect deep ancestral roots, which differ from one country to another. There are also deep differences in the conception of their political systems, the role of the state and distribution of wealth. Ironically, underdevelopment, an euphemism for poverty, is perhaps the only common denominator, that is apart from having been colonized and forced to speak a foreign language while living under cultural and ideological subjugation by either Spain or Portugal or, on a smaller scale, England, France or Holland.

The real purpose

However, for some reason still not clear to me, I was attracted by a fascinating character who led a crusade offering elementary educational opportunities to the poor in the 18th century at the beginning of the industrial revolution, a time depicted by Dickens in *Oliver Twist*, when there was no public education and no teacher colleges. Joseph Lancaster, inspired by a clever solution devised by the Scottish educationalist Andrew Bell, developed the *Monitorial System* or *Mutual Teaching* method, also known as the Lancaster Method, the Lancasterian Method, and Education of Mutual Progress. Here, Mutual Teaching is used as a generic term.

Instead of reviewing the contributions in the area of educational psychology, I have chosen to reflect on the implications of this teaching method to current conceptions of instruction and trends in educational psychology.

This monitorial method offered a mechanism for mass elementary education, by changing the conventional dynamics of the classroom into a refined system directed to the optimization of educational efforts. The core of the method was to use the students who had already acquired the three basic tools of literacy (i.e., reading, writing, and arithmetic) with Bible reading as a moral complement, to help others who knew less, thus evoking the essential process of learning a trade and transforming the classroom into a beehive of mutual help. Thus, a single teacher could handle a school with hundreds of students.

The system soon spread over England and then to all of Europe, the United States, the emerging Latin American republics, still at war, and regions as remote as Australia (Vaughan, 1989) and became the prevailing pedagogical approach during the 19th century. Considering the magnitude of its dissemination, it was the biggest pedagogic enterprise of the 19th century and probably of the whole history of education, and promised an educational panacea, which was called "the best of all possible methods" by Lopez and Narodowski (1999). It is perhaps equivalent to the promise offered by Programmed Instruction in the 1960s (Glaser, 1965), seen by some teachers as a threat, and nowadays to the application of Information and Communication Technologies (ICTs) to education, which perhaps has better opportunities for success.

Never before has an educational innovation achieved such broad dissemination, nor produced such a resounding failure.[1] Neither has an educational failure ever received – and still receives[2] – so much attention. As an example of the spell exerted by the method, Foucault (1977) considered it the paradigm of order and social control that announced modernity. It still attracts the interest of historians (Vaughan, 1989) and specialists in organizational analysis (Hassard & Rowlinson, 2002) as well as those interested in the development of technologies in education (Harris, 1987). Within the context of Latin America, it has captured the attention of educational research groups in Germany (Caruso, 2003), Argentina (Lopez & Narodowski, 1999), Brazil (Camara Bastos, 1999), Guatemala (Samayoa, 1953), Mexico (Roldan, 2004) and Venezuela (Canchica, 1970; Fernandez Heres, 1984).

In the present journey through the development of this method, an attempt will be made to paint a portrait of the main characters involved, point out salient historical events and indicate the peculiar features of the method. Finally, the method will be related to present approaches to instruction in order to explore its implications for this area of psychology.

Starting the search

Having limited access to references on the development of the Mutual Teaching Method (MTM), the author took advantage of current facilities in global communication. The process of obtaining information became an exciting experience and, thanks to the Internet, it was possible to trace sources of information and contact specialists. The search also drew upon the generosity of many people in different countries willing to provide comments, materials, papers and books. As a group, too large to enumerate, they constitute a vast network of virtual Samaritans.

A homework timeline

To acquire an overview of the development and dissemination of the MTM in Latin America a series of papers was prepared, using a timeline of three columns to register the information obtained. This resource has been used to summarize, analyze and organize historical events (Orantes, 1993). The main column contained a brief description of events related to the method, preceded by three columns corresponding to the year, the historical periods of Latin America (e.g., Colonial) and general events (e.g., innovations, inventions, educational developments and key thinkers) – information that was taken from Asimov (1989).

The purpose of the first paper was to summarize the preliminary information about Lancaster's life and his visit to Caracas (Orantes, 2003). The next paper presented the information collected on Latin America in a timeline of 170 entries (Orantes, 2004a), which can be reduced to 40 entries by considering only the movements of the actors from one country to another in order to spread the method. An overview of the achievements and difficulties encountered by the method was also prepared, with the aim of trying to figure out why this impressive enterprise has left no traces in current educational practices (Orantes, 2004b).

The historical links

The beginning

The points of departure are the concurrent efforts of Andrew Bell (1753–1832), and Joseph Lancaster (1778–1838), two diametrically opposed characters. The first came from a Scottish middle-class family, received a degree in mathematics and natural philosophy and took orders in the Anglican Church. He had great economic and social success, for he knew how to take advantage of opportunities and simultaneously administer several sources of income in order to increase his personal assets. The second, who had only elementary education, grew up in a poor neighborhood of London and, as an adolescent, felt a call to help the needy and joined the Quakers, a dissident congregation of the official church. A man of contrasts and impulsive character, and a bad administrator, he frittered away his resources, was ungrateful to his benefactors, was almost maniacal in his planning of school activities and was able to advance his projects by appealing to influential figures for support (Salmon, 1932).

The story began in 1779 when the young Andrew Bell was sent to India as an army chaplain and appointed superintendent of an asylum for the orphans of British soldiers (Dickson, 1986). Facilities were scarce: not enough qualified teachers, poor pay and a total lack of resources such as paper or individual slates. One day, Bell observed a very clever boy of the group helping other children to write. He decided to prepare him to teach the alphabet to others, and it occurred to him to use boxes with sand in the bottom so that pupils could write the letters; this became a distinctive feature of the method. The procedure was so successful that he taught other children to teach reading and other subjects to their less-able peers. In this way the *Supervised Mutual Teaching* or *Mutual Teaching* method was born (Dickson, 1986).

In 1797, after returning to London, Bell published *Experiments in education – made at the male asylum at Egmore, near Madras*, with his reflections on the potential of this new method to satisfy the educational demands of children from poor neighborhoods. He also founded the *National Society to Promote the Education of the Poor* in 1811, becoming the leader of a movement for public education. By the time that Bell died, in 1832, the society had established twelve thousand schools in Great Britain (Dickson, 1986).

The thread of this history continued when a copy of Bell's pamphlet fell into the hands of Joseph Lancaster in 1798. He was then a young lad in his twenties – the son of an army pensioner who manufactured sieves to supplement his earnings – who decided to provide education to the poor children of his neighborhood. As a very young man, he felt a call to became a missionary, left home at 14 and went to Bristol where he tried to board ship to Jamaica in order to teach the Bible to poor children. Unable to afford the ticket, he returned home, entered the community of Quakers and worked for a time as an usher in two schools (Hassard & Rowlinson, 2002). He became so excited by that experience that he soon wanted to have his own school. He obtained his father's support and, in his own words:

> Joseph Lancaster commenced a school in his father's house, in London, in the first month, 1793. Here, under the protecting hand of a pious parent, he, undesignedly, formed the outline of a system of education . . . which has since extended its ramification over the circumference of the globe.
>
> (Dickson, 1986)

With his own hands, he built the tables and benches, using old boards, and put a notice in the door offering free education to those could not pay for it; soon students flocked in. Not having funds to hire enough teachers he found the solution when Andrew Bell's *Experiment in education* fell into his hands. Soon he got so involved in this venture that he started to develop his own version of the method using a meticulous approach of military precision. In 1808 he published *Improvements in education*, describing his approach as the Monitorial System or Lancaster Method, which soon became an educational landmark.

The industrial age

It is surprising how meticulous Lancaster's descriptions were. Procedures, routines, and the breakdown of the subject matter of reading, writing, counting and elementary mathematics were carefully described, as well as the set of orders and signs, which for some look like choreography (Caruso, 2003), but also resembled military procedures. The origin of this military style that Lancaster stamped on the method, is not considered in the literature found.[3]

Kaestle (1973) has captured the spirit of the system in the phrase: "schools like factories, schools like regiments". However, the mechanical was an acceptable metaphor in the days of the industrial revolution. Foucault (1977) has even considered the method to be an indicator of the beginning of modernity, pointing to the social mechanisms of submission to the control of the collective, according to his perspective, in factories, jails and schools.

The royal patronage

Lancaster soon became famous and was even was invited to the palace to meet George III, receiving his royal patronage and full support and generating jealousy in officials of the official Anglican Church who saw a danger in the preponderance acquired by a member of a nonconformist religious denomination. In 1808, the *Society for Promoting the Lancasterian System for the Education of the Poor* was formed with Lancaster as chairman. However, his difficult personality, his squandering of resources, and his bad manners created such insurmountable problems that he was dismissed from office.

In 1813, the society became the British and Foreign School Society (BFSS), which still exists.

Dissemination in Latin America

During the 19th century, the use of the system spread throughout England, Europe and the United States. It also spread to the emerging Latin American republics. The first related event occurred when a delegation from Caracas traveled to London in 1810, seeking support from the British government. Joseph Lancaster met the group and, after a period in the USA, he went to Caracas to try to set up his system, but failed. The method spread though Mexico, Rio de Janeiro, Buenos Aires and Bogota, to become the official method of elementary instruction in most Latin American countries. However, economic, cultural and religious obstacles prevented its consolidation, and it gradually fell into disuse. It was used in Mexico until 1890, when the Lancasterian Company was dissolved (Roldan, 1999).

The method

The method was created as a reaction against the traditional system of one teacher in charge of a classroom, attending to students one at a time while the rest remained idle. Lancaster reacted against this teaching mode and, when facing the problem of having too many students and a lack of teachers, developed a system that used advanced students as monitors to help the others learn the basic skills of reading, spelling and writing. His idea was to prevent idle learners.

The rigid pedagogical system comprised a complex, comprehensive set of elaborate rules, routines, commands, and teaching devices and was founded on progressive achievement, rewards and punishments. The core of this comprehensive approach was the instructional process based on a sort of tutorial typical of trade apprenticeships.

An outline of the method

A comment published in the magazine *Westminster Review*, at the beginning of 1824 (Vaughan, 1989), points to some of the key aspects of the teaching procedures used by the method:

> The manner in which the lessons are said is similar to that in which they are learned. Each boy takes precedence of him whose error he is able to correct; hence as a high place in the class can be obtained only by great attention, so it can be maintained only by uniform vigilance. Each lesson as soon as said, is marked in the monitor's book; and the sum of these daily lessons, and of the other daily tasks, together with the individual proficiency of each scholar, are entered in a register book.

It was also claimed that the efficiency of the method compared to the traditional class reflected the knowledge required for performing the given tasks and that the level of the language used by the student teachers was more appropriate for understanding. This idea evokes the distinction between public and private codes proposed by Bernstein (1962).

> In the first place, it is evident that on this system children are better taught than on the old, because from the sympathy they take in each other, they learn every thing communicable by one to the other more easily and perfectly. Whatever a child has been taught, he will communicate to his companions better than a master; because his manner of teaching, and the words he employs, will be suited to the capacity of his pupil; he knows where this difficulty lies, and how to remove it

The guidelines

- A teacher for a thousand students;
- No idle learners;
- Order and discipline;
- A *monitor* for every 10 students. Using pupils who know a little to teach others who know less;
- If small groups are used, no one gets bored;
- Constant evaluation and ranking of the students according to achievement;
- Emulation. Prizes such as merit badges and tokens (for books, pencils, etc.) were awarded for excellence.

The components

From the perspective of Alec Rodger's framework for analyzing jobs and occupations (Rodger & Cavanagh, 1968), aimed at fitting the man to the job through *selection procedures, guidance, and training*, and fitting the job to the man by means of *norms and procedures, ergonomic aspects, emulation and rewards*, the Lancaster system can be seen in terms of: *selection procedures, instructional modes and teaching devices, norms and procedures, ergonomic aspects, emulation and rewards* (and also punishments).

Selection procedures

Students and monitors were selected by practical assessment. The best, most advanced students were promoted to monitors. On admission into school, students were ranked according to achievement into eight classes or levels in relation to each content area (spelling, reading, writing, and mathematics). Eight progressive levels of proficiency were considered in content areas such as reading, spelling, writing and arithmetic. Pupils whose proficiency was nearly equal were grouped in a class, assuming that they would perform better. They were examined by the master and assigned to a particular class and promoted from one class to another according to a set of cumulative rules such as whether the pupil knew the alphabet, whether he could write, read and repeat all the lessons.

Instructional devices

- *Sand boxes*. These devices, taken from Bell, were the most emblematic. They were used to learn how to write the alphabet. The bottom of the box was painted black, so letters traced in the sand could be seen better.
- *Slates* for individual use as a substitute for paper.
- *Pasteboards* instead of books for semicircle activities. These hung on the walls and were printed in a type three-times larger than the common size.
- *Telegraph*. When the groups were large the instructions were presented on a rectangular board (called the telegraph) placed on high to display commands by means of keys (e.g., SS = show slates).
- *Whistle* for commands.

Instructional modes

All modes were supervised by monitors. Groups contained about 10 pupils.

Semicircles

A typical mode. Students were grouped in semicircle before a lesson written on a pasteboard. They would correct each other's mistakes. The following steps constituted the routine:

- The monitor points to one word from the lesson for the day.
- The first boy then repeats the word pointed at.
- If he commits any mistake, the next boy is required to rectify it without being told what the mistake is.
- The boy who corrects the mistake, takes precedence and receives his insignia of precedence.
- Students change their position in the semicircle in accordance with the number of correct answers they have given.

The teaching script

In Lancaster's own words the motto was: "It is not the monitor's business to teach, but to see that the boys in his class, or division, teach each other." This meant that the monitor had to "move up and down the desks, and examine the performance and progress of the boys in writing on their slate." Lancaster believed that "any boy who can read, can teach" (Dickson, 1986).

The script for monitors prescribed that "he first makes a letter on the sand the child is then required to retrace the same letter till he can make the letter himself, without the monitor's assistance." This routine resembles the three steps of Gilbert's model (1962) for teaching any skill: *Demonstration, prompt and release.*

Norms and procedures

The whole system relied on a complex set of norms to control the activities and duties of monitors and sequences such as classroom formation, taking off hats and roll calls (where each student had to stand next to his number written on the wall).

There were detailed procedures to mechanize teaching the progressive steps for learning the alphabet, reading and writing of letters words and sentences, and elementary arithmetic operations. The system evokes the structured approach of programmed instruction in the 1960s. Though the conceptual and technical resources were different, the procedures were similar in that they attempted to reconcile an empirical attempt to solve a problem and one based on scientific research.

Ergonomy

Importance was given to the physical conditions of the teaching environment to such an extent that the building of Borough Road was erected according to Lancaster's requirements. The rooms had to be rectangles or parallelograms, with the floor on an inclined plane with an elevated platform at the lower end for the master's desk. Details were important, such as tables and desks being firmly fixed in the ground, with their corners rounded off to avoid hurting pupils.

Emulation

The system combined supervision of performance with competition among students. Numbers were assigned to the pupils inside the group in accordance with progress, thus creating a closed emulation system. Every boy was placed "next to one who can do as well or better than himself: his business is to excel him, in which case he takes precedence of him." Also, badges of merit were awarded for reading, spelling, etc., but these could be lost when another pupil surpassed the owner. In addition "price" badges were given, as tokens of different value, to be exchanged for goods worth twopence, threepence, or sixpence.

Some modes of punishment

As well as emulation, several types of punishment were used. Corporal punishment was a common practice in those days. Lancaster was opposed to these practices and designed an alternative system of sanctions:

- *The pillory.* A wooden log around the pupil's neck.
- *Shackles.* The legs of offenders were fastened together with a piece of wood, about a foot long, tied to both legs, which made walking difficult.
- *The single shackle.* Pieces of wood about a foot long tied to each leg.
- *The basket.* The offender was put in a sack, or in a basket, suspended from the roof of the school.
- *Labels of disgrace.* A label was attached to the pupil, on which there was a description of the fault.
- *Confinement.* After school hours. So as to avoid the need for supervision, the boy can be tied to a desk.

Looking at these "Instruments and modes of punishment" it is difficult not to ask if it would not have been better to keep to the previous practices.

The conceptual links

The initial reflection

After this brief revision it is important to recall Piaget's (1957/1993) warning, that:

> Nothing is easier, or more dangerous, than to treat an author of 300 years ago as modern and claim to find in him the origins of contemporary or recent trends of thought. . . . The real problem is to find what makes the vital unity behind the contribution in theory and practice; and to compare this with what we know and want today.

Therefore, it becomes appropriate to reflect on the meaning of the *Mutual Teaching* method for present-day conceptions of instruction and trends in educational psychology.

The method poses the central question of whether it is better to group students by age or by achievement. But it also encourages us to reflect on the basic notions underlying instruction. In this attempted journey toward the sources of instruction as a discipline, some of the essential properties of the method of Mutual Teaching can be considered as points of departure.

A journey towards instruction

The concept of Mutual Teaching acts as a centripetal force uniting a number of notions underlying some present-day trends in educational psychology, such as the notion of *cognitive apprenticeship* (Collins, Brown, & Newman, 1989), which blends the long-term accumulative practice common to workplaces with a tutorial relationship with someone who gives help and supervision while the learner tries to perform a task. Other modern notions such as *reciprocal teaching* (Brown & Palincsar, 1989), *cooperative learning* (Slavin, 1996), and even *collaborative learning within the Internet* (Teles, 1993), and *one-to-one tutorials* based on complex interactions, where student construction is elicited through scaffolding given by tutors, as research has pointed out (Chi, Siler, Jeong, Yamauchi, & Hausmann, 2001). It can be inferred from Lancaster's practice that this was an idea that he guessed at.

Instruction as an essential category

Instruction has been defined as the process of facilitating learning (Skinner, 1954/1968), but its role as an essential and irreplaceable basic mechanism of social transmission and replication has received little attention. It is the natural medium for transmitting the values, norms, and skills of a culture to new members of the social group, and thus guaranteeing their survival within the culture and therefore the permanence of the culture itself.

In our urban society, teaching becomes a basic competence, which embraces infinite domains and multiple levels. The challenge of understanding the long-term complex processes of social transmission has traditionally been assumed by social psychology. Now instructional psychology can also assume this challenge and offer an account of the internal mechanisms of social transmission.

The aims of instructional psychology

The discipline of instruction deals with the processes of acquiring competences. If the goal of teaching is to facilitate learning, then the function of education is to analyze society's goals and provide suitable environments for developing the competences necessary for reaching them. In consequence, the aims of instructional psychology are to decipher the complexity of the mechanisms that guarantee the replication of competences and to improve the efficiency of the teaching process.

Nowadays, knowledge is considered a central category and skills are seen as the result of long-term deliberate practice. Thus, the purpose of instructional psychology can be seen as the search for tools for analyzing, representing and multiplying socially valued competences.

A soft and appropriate technology

Instructional developments can reflect either theoretical conceptions, as occurs nowadays with constructivist approaches, or they can consist of solutions to practical problems (Ofiesh, 1968). It is often said that necessity is the mother of invention. This applies to the case of the Mutual Teaching method. It was a practical solution that became a success and was in agreement with the prevailing mechanical metaphor during the industrial revolution.

Mutual Teaching is clearly the first known example of a soft educational technology that required no hardware. It became an efficient solution and generated a series of innovations tailored to the available resources, so it is a good example of an appropriate technology (Schumacher, 1973). Perhaps, in the future, developing countries should try to learn from the Lancasterian approach.

Lancaster's dream

Finally, perhaps Lancaster's dream of multiplying tutorials has come to pass. Thanks to the Internet, the emergence of online courses allows students to ask questions, receive information and to have their work continually assessed. In addition, the structured nature of the *rubrics* now used in evaluation resembles Lancaster's systematic approach. Perhaps technology has come to the rescue of this forgotten instructional dream.

The Lancaster method became the greatest educational enterprise ever known, but it only lasted about a hundred years, after which it faded away and finally disappeared. Fortunately, historians have rescued this enterprise, but few psychologists have had the opportunity of analyzing its innovations or of considering the fundamental questions it poses.

The questions posed

The success and fall of MTM, particularly in Latin America, is a historical enigma with more questions than available answers. Historians have been trying to unveil the reasons for the fate of this educational process and some tend to relate it to the complexity of individual and social factors involved in the transmission and appropriation of knowledge in which different conceptions, in this case about education, are supplanted by new practices representing practical advantages. Originally, MTM offered an attractive mechanism for a quick and cheap elementary education (Roldan, 2004) reflecting the philosophy of modernism as Foucault (1977) has pointed out. However, in the case of Latin America, despite the fact that the method was officially prescribed, the practice faced many problems of different kinds. On the one hand, derived from the required infrastructure, not always available in those days in these emerging nations; such as clocks for keeping precise timetables and a printing press for preparing the teaching boards required for semicircle teaching. On the other hand, the technical requirements involved in the teaching decisions and routines for the elementary content being taught (reading, writing and counting) meant a great effort for teachers; it was an unusual method completely different to the usual teaching practices. But also important was the religious opposition by the Catholic church to a method that avoided indoctrination in school, and reduced religious education to reading the Bible. Finally, there was the fear of reduced job opportunities for teachers.

One of the contentions of this chapter is about the role of instruction as a basic social mechanism for the transmission of values, norms and skills of a culture to cast new members of a social group. Instruction becomes an adaptive mechanism of cultural supervision that guarantees the development of socially valuable skills as a product of long-term practice. It is interesting that Vygotsky's sociocultural theory is one of the first theories of instruction based on the role of social mores to encourage learners to achieve higher levels of performance. The function of instruction is to facilitate this process, reducing learning time and effort, but also to guarantee the acquisition of otherwise unattainable knowledge.

During this process the new knowledge acquired by the learner is translated into personal representations or declarative knowledge and gradually converted into procedural knowledge as the individual generates and adjusts routines and, after repeated practice, develops competent performance in a given content, as John Anderson (1982) has pointed out.

Also, the MTM is a hardly known antecedent to later teaching innovations that considered that all students should achieve the same levels of performance, allowing different time to each one according to individual differences, such as the Keller Plan (Keller, 1968) and Mastery Learning (Bloom, 1974), which itself was inspired by Washburne's Winnetka Plan developed in 1931. The MTM had very precise levels of proficiency for each subject and students were grouped in classes accordingly. This was achieved using advanced students as monitors to help others who were less able to achieve the necessary level of performance. Thus, posing an important question: Is it better to group students by age or by achievement? Can advanced students teach those who are less advanced? Can a single teacher manage a class of a hundred students? Can we respond to the needs of present-day society by developing soft instructional technologies that use available resources?

Only time will tell.

Notes

1 The method was officially abolished in Chile (1832), Ecuador (1860), Costa Rica (1880), and in Mexico in 1890 (Vaughan, 1989).
2 In August 2001 the Lancasterian Society (http://www.constitution.org), was resurrected in Texas and a defense of the method has been made (Roland, 1998) attributing the decline in the quality of American education and its increasing costs to the

displacement of the Lancaster method in schools when the Educational Boards were created.

3 For Hector Mago (December 2003, personal communication), this reflects the influence of Lancaster's father, who fought as a member of the Queen's Regiment on Foot, and then in North America. At least his father's advice can be inferred from the military conception of discipline, appropriate for dealing with large contingents of students. His father may have helped him develop the procedures, on the basis of orders for activating routines, for example for sitting in the correct manner, or for placing the hat on the rack.

Acknowledgements

I am in debt to my colleague Robin Urquhart for revising the English text and her suggestions; also to the anonymous reviewer who made very sharp and pertinent comments valuable for corrections in this final version.

References

Anderson, J. R. (1982). Acquisition of cognitive skills. *Psychological Review, 89*, 369–406.

Asimov, I. (1989). *Cronologia de los descubrimientos* [Chronology of science and discovery]. Barcelona: Ariel. (Published in Spanish, 1990)

Bernstein, B. (1962). Social class, linguistic codes and grammatical elements. *Language and Speech, 5*, 221–240.

Bloom, B. (1974). An introduction to mastery learning. In J. H. Block (Ed.), *School, society, and mastery learning* (pp. 3–14). New York: Holt, Rinehart & Winston.

Brown, A. L., & Palincsar, A. S. (1989). Guided cooperative learning and individual knowledge acquisition. In L. B. Resnick (Ed.), *Knowing, learning and instruction. Essays in honor of Robert Glaser* (pp. 393–451). Hillsdale, NJ: Lawrence Erlbaum Associates, Inc.

Camara Bastos, M. H. (1999). O ensino mutuo no Brasil 1808–1827 [Mutual teaching in Brazil 1808–1827]. In M. E. Camara Bastos & L. Mendes de Faria (Eds.), *A escola elementar no seculo XIX. O metodo monitoria/mutuo* (pp. 95–118). Brazil: Universidade de Passo Fundo.

Canchica, A. (1970). *El sistema lancasteriano en Venezuela* [The Lancasterian system in Venezuela]. Unpublished manuscript. Escuela de Educacion, Universidad Central de Venezuela, Caracas.

Caruso, M. (2003). *La oficializacion del metodo lancasteriano. America Latina en el contexto del movimiento internacional por la educacion mutua* [Making official the Lancaster method in Latin America within the context of the international movement for mutual teaching]. Paper presented at VI Congreso Hispanoamericano de Historia de la Educacion Latinoamericana, San Luis Potosi, 19–13 Mayo.

Chi, M. T. H., Siler, S., Jeong, H., Yamauchi, T., & Hausmann, R. G. (2001). Learning from tutoring. *Cognitive Science, 25*, 471–533.

Collins, A., Brown, J. S., & Newman, S. E. (1989). Cognitive apprenticeship: Teaching the crafts of reading, writing and mathematics. In L. B. Resnick (Ed.), *Knowing, learning and instruction. Essays in honor of Robert Glaser* (pp. 453–494). Hillsdale, NJ: Lawrence Erlbaum Associates, Inc.

Dickson, M. (1986). *Teacher extraordinary: Joseph Lancaster*. London: The Book Guild.

Fernandez Heres, R. (1984). *Sumario sobre la Escuela Caraqueña de Lancaster* [A summary about Lancaster's school in Caracas]. San Cristobal: Coleccion Sumario, Universidad Catolica del Tachira.

Foucault, M. (1977). *Discipline and punish: The birth of the prison*. Harmondsworth, UK: Penguin. (First published as *Surveiller et punir: Naissance de la prison* by Editions Gallimard, 1975)

Gilbert, T. F. (1962). Mathetics: The technology of education. *The Journal of Mathetics*, *1*, 7–73. (Reproduced in *RECALL*, London: Longman, 1969)

Glaser, R. (Ed.). (1965). *Teaching machines and programmed learning II: Data an directions*. Washington, DC: Department of Audiovisual Instruction. National Education Association of the USA.

Harris, D. (1987). *Educational technology and the "colonisation" of academic work*. Paper presented to the British Sociological Association Annual Conference, Leeds, UK.

Hassard, J., & Rowlinson, M. (2002). *Researching Foucault's research: Organization and control in Joseph Lancaster's monitorial schools*. Paper presented at the Critical Management Workshop, Academy of Management Conference, Denver, Colorado, August.

Kaestle, C. F. (1973). *Joseph Lancaster and the monitorial school movement. A documentary history*. New York: Teacher College Press.

Keller, F. (1968). "Good Bye Teacher . . .". *Journal of Applied Behavior Analysis*, *5*, 79–89.

Lopez, C., & Narodowski, M. (1999). El mejor de los metodos posibles [The best of possible methods]. In M. E. Camara Bastos & L. Mendes de Faria (Eds.), *A escola elementar no seculo XIX. O metodo monitorial/mutuo* (pp. 45–72). Brazil: Universidade de Passo Fundo.

Ofiesh, G. D. (1968). Tomorrow's educational engineers. *Educational Technology*, *8*, 5–9.

Orantes, A. (1993). Panorama y perspectivas de la psicologia aplicada a la educacion en Latinoamerica [Psychology applied to education in Latin America: Overview and perspectives]. *Papeles del Psicologo. Revista del Colegio Oficial del Psicologos*, *Epoca II*, No. 55, 31–40. Madrid.

Orantes, A. (2003, March). *Activando vinculos historicos de la enseñanza mutua* [Activating mutual teaching historical links]. Unpublished manuscript. Universidad Central de Venezuela.

Orantes, A. (2004a). *El metodo de enseñanza mutua de Lancaster en America Latina. Reconstruyendo su historia con una hoja de ruta* [Lancaster's mutual teaching method in Latin America. Reconstructing its history through a timeline]. Paper presented at X Jornadas de Investigacion Educativa, Universidad Central de Venezuela, Caracas, May 26–28.

Orantes, A. (2004b, July). *Enseñanza mutua: Lo bueno, lo malo y lo feo* [Mutual teaching: The good, the bad and the ugly]. Unpublished manuscript. Universidad Central de Venezuela.

Piaget, J. (1993). Jan Amos Comenius (1592–1670). *Prospects* (UNESCO, International Bureau of Education), *23*(1/2), 173–196.

Rodger, A., & Cavanagh, P. (1968). Personal selection and vocational guidance. In A. T. Welford, M. Argyle, & D. V. Glass (Eds.), *Society, psychological problems and methods of study* (pp. 90–109). London: Routledge & Kegan Paul.

Roland, J. (1998). *My grandfather on public education.* (Retrieved 19 September 2003 from: http://www.constitution.org/col/one_room_schoolhouse.htm)

Roldan, E. (1999). The monitorial system of education and civic culture in early independent Mexico. In *Paedagogica Historica: International Journal of the History of Education, 35*(2), 297–331.

Roldan, E. (2004). El niño enseñante: Infancia, aula y estado en el metodo de enseñanza mutua en Hispanoamerica independiente [The child teacher: Infancy, classroom and the state on the mutual teaching method in independent Hispanic America]. In B. Potthast & S. Carreras (Eds.), *Entre familia, sociedad y estado: Niños y jovenes en America Latina.* Berlin: Vervuert/Iberoamericana.

Salmon, D. (Ed.). (1932). *The practical parts of Lancaster's improvements and Bell's experiment.* London: Cambridge University Press.

Samayoa, H. H. (1953). Apuntes para la historia del metodo Lancasteriano en Guatemala [Notes for the history of the Lancaster method in Guatemala]. *Antropologia e historia de Guatemala, V*(2), 32–62.

Schumacher, E. F. (1973). *Small is beautiful: Economics as if people mattered.* New York: Harper & Row.

Skinner, B. F. (1968). The science of learning and the art of teaching. In *Technology of teaching* (pp. 29–58). New York: Appleton Century. (Originally published in 1954)

Slavin, R. E. (1996). Research on cooperative learning and achievement: What we know, what we need to know. *Contemporary Educational Psychology, 21,* 43–69.

Teles, L. (1993). Cognitive apprenticeship on global networks. In L. Harasim (Ed.), *Global networks. Computers and international communications* (pp. 271–281). Cambridge, MA: MIT Press.

Vaughan, E. (1989). *Joseph Lancaster en Caracas (1824–1827).* Tomo I y II. Caracas: Ediciones del Ministerio de Educacion de Venezuela.

Washburne, C. (1931). La Escuela individualizada. Sistema de Winnetka [The Winnetka individualized school system]. In L. Luzuriaga (Ed.), *Métodos de la Nueva Educación* (pp. 237–309). Buenos Aires, Argentina: Losada. (Published in Spanish, 1952)

4 English classes without English teachers: The Pan Deng English learning program

Qi Dong, Sha Tao, Beilei Li,
Wenjing Wang, and
Chuansheng Chen

Humans live in a world with languages. Their possession of languages distinguishes them from other animals. Moreover, many individuals have a mastery of two or more languages, which not only demonstrates the great plasticity of the human brain but also empowers humans in many ways (Kim, Relkin, Lee, & Hirsch, 1997; Perani et al., 1996). For decades, second-language learning has drawn much attention in multiple areas of scientific studies such as psychology, linguistics, anthropology, and sociology (Ellis, 1985; Hakuta & Pease-Alvarez, 1992). Previous studies have deepened our understanding of the mechanisms of second-language learning and human development in general.

Studies on second-language learning, however, are not only of great academic interest, they also have significant practical implications. Economic globalization, increasing international social and cultural exchanges, and rapid development of the Internet have brought all parts of the world into much closer contact and the world is metaphorically becoming a smaller place (Caragata & Sanchez, 2002). As a result, to master a second language is likely to be a necessity, rather than a luxury, for people in the 21st century. Beyond individuals, a nation's social development and economic competitiveness, especially in the case of developing countries including the People's Republic of China (PRC), may depend to a great extent on the second-language abilities of its general population.

There is now a special urgency in second-language learning in China because of its recent entry into the World Trade Organization (WTO) and its impending hosting of the 2008 Olympic Games (Lin, 2002). As the lingua franca of the world, English is also the most popular second language in China. Recently, the Chinese government has put more emphasis on English education from primary schools to colleges. For primary schools, a new national curriculum for English was issued by the Ministry of Education of PRC in 2002, which required that all the primary-school students should start to take English courses no later than grade 3 (PRC Ministry of Education,

2001). For college and university students, English proficiency is one of the graduation requirements. Bachelor degrees cannot be granted until students pass College English Test Band 4 or 6[1] in some universities.

The elevated status of English learning in China at present raised a great need for English education and attracted a huge amount of investment from families, governments, and societies. According to some estimates (PRC Ministry of Education, 2003b), there were more than 234 million students who were either getting or were in need of English instruction in school in 2003. More than 10 billion renminbi (RMB) were spent per year on English learning in China (Mo, 2002). Another way to view the magnitude of this investment and market is that, from primary school through college, English classes take up at least 100 minutes per week of in-school instruction time (PRC Ministry of Education, 2001).

Despite the huge amounts of financial and time investment in English learning, the outcome is disappointing for many Chinese students. They fall far below the expectation of becoming proficient in English. Although some students have learned English very well, and even obtained very high scores on TOEFL (Test of English as a Foreign Language, managed by Educational Testing Service, USA), GRE (Graduate Record Examinations, managed by Educational Testing Service, USA), and IELTS (International English Language Testing System, jointly managed by University of Cambridge ESOL Examinations [Cambridge ESOL], the British Council and IDP Education Australia [IELTS Australia]), a large number of students and their parents have complained about the slow progress of English learning and pointed out the prevalent weaknesses in their listening and speaking skills – thus dubbed as "deaf and dumb" English (Li, 2004). Moreover, several national and regional surveys have shown that English was rated as the most difficult subject by students. Students, especially the low-achieving ones, reported high levels of learning anxiety (Wang & Ding, 2001; Zhang & Chang, 2004).

Taken together, the current status of English learning in China is that the need for English learning is urgent, the investment great, but the outcome unsatisfactory. The only way to get out of this conundrum is to improve English instruction both in and outside school. In the following sections, we analyze the major challenges for English learning in Chinese primary schools and describe the Pan Deng English Learning Program (PDELP) that successfully answered those challenges by taking advantage of research advances in cognitive science, developmental and educational psychology and educational technology. We also discuss the implications that our program has for future research, the practice of teaching English as a second language (ESL), and policy making about second-language learning.

Major challenges facing English learning in China

English learning in China faces a multitude of challenges. Here we will highlight five of them.

Severe shortage of (qualified) English teachers

Teacher shortage is the first and foremost challenge for English education in China. Take 2002 (the most recent year for which statistics are available) as an example (PRC Ministry of Education, 2003a), 121.57 million pupils (3.53 million classes) were enrolled in 456.9 thousand primary schools in China. However, there were only 140.16 thousand English teachers. That means each English teacher had to teach 867.37 students in 25.19 classes in 3.26 primary schools. If we assume that one English teacher can manage to teach 5 classes in primary schools, we had a shortage of more 565.84 thousand English teachers. Furthermore, the severity of teacher shortage is uneven across China, much worse in the underdeveloped western areas and mountainous areas than in the coastal urban areas. It is expected that the shortage of English teachers will last for an extended period of time because: (1) colleges and universities have a limited capacity to increase the number of English teachers they can train; and (2) compared to teaching in primary and secondary schools, careers in large companies (especially international corporations that operate in China) are a bigger draw for college graduates with English language skills.

Even among the 140,160 existing English teachers in primary schools, many of them are not as qualified as one desires. Some teachers had not majored in English and had only short-term pre-service or in-service training in English teaching (PRC Ministry of Education, 2003a). These teachers' oral English is especially poor, and consequently they serve as poor models for students in terms of aspects such as pronunciation. Another group of teachers may have been adequate in their oral English because they majored in English, but they often did not have training in effective teaching. Even for those who had learned about how to teach English, their training is outdated because traditional English-teacher training focused on grammar, vocabulary, and reading, whereas the new curriculum has a comprehensive emphasis on listening, speaking, reading, and writing. A final problem is that few of teachers have taken advantage of the new information technology to assist their teaching, even though the past decades have witnessed major advances in information technology applicable to English teaching in the classroom. In sum, many of the existing English teachers need further training and must update their teaching techniques to meet the need of today's students.

Lack of English environment

The availability of opportunities for using a second language, or even just being exposed to it, would be a key factor in second-language learning. However, unlike the case in India and the Philippines, where English is one of the official languages, Chinese students' English learning occurs in a largely non-English environment. It is common, even in big cities, that the only time students can hear English is during the English classes. Apart from the

English classes, Chinese students have few opportunities to use English in their daily life. Their homework and in-class exercises usually include reciting their textbooks or remembering what they have been taught in order to pass examinations. In such an environment, students typically associate English learning with repetitive and boring exercises, rather than with its utility as a second language. Consequently, many students have a low level of motivation and confidence in English learning.

Limitations in learning resources

Limited learning resources are another significant problem that has seriously impeded the progress of English education in China. There are few high-quality instructional resources and learning materials. Teachers and students mainly rely on textbooks. Furthermore, many of the existing materials are outdated. The limited recent materials have typically been directly transplanted from abroad, thus their contents may be too far removed from Chinese students' daily life to sustain their interest. Finally, even with good materials that are up-to-date and relevant to Chinese students' daily life, they still need to be well organized for teaching and learning purposes. However, most of the English teachers lack training in how to organize teaching materials and make them more adaptive to their students' needs.

Neglect of developing positive feelings and attitudes toward English learning

There are three main types of anxiety about English learning among Chinese primary students. They are afraid of attending English classes, taking English examinations, and communicating in English (Hu, 2005). These negative feelings and attitudes toward English learning may have roots in the way English is taught in the classroom. In traditional English classes, teachers put much emphasis on English grammar and require students to memorize many grammatical rules in addition to the rote memory of vocabulary and sentences. Students are also evaluated based on their performance on a final paper-and-pencil examination that is heavily tilted towards vocabulary and grammar. Such practices have dampened students' interest in English learning.

Great regional disparity

China is a large country with a vast territory and a huge population. Great economic disparity among the different regions has consequentially led to imbalanced development of English education across regions and made it a significant challenge to have high-quality English education across the country. The aforementioned challenges to English learning in China such as a shortage of funds, limited learning resources, and the lack of an English environment are particularly serious in underdeveloped regions (Zhang, 1999). There are few teaching materials designed for rural students and their English teachers (Feng, 2003).

To meet the various challenges to English learning in China, new and creative strategies are needed. These new strategies should be effective in solving the problem of teacher shortage, providing rich English environments, offering useful resources for teachers and students, introducing innovative teaching and learning procedures to elicit more positive attitudes from students, and reducing the regional inequality in English education.

The Pan Deng English Learning Program

In the past five years, with support from various government foundations (i.e., Ministry of Science and Technology of China, Ministry of Education of China, Beijing Municipal Government), we have designed a comprehensive English learning program as a possible solution to the English learning difficulty in China and have implemented this program with more than 20,000 students from 117 schools in 24 cities, towns and counties. Our program – the Pan Deng English Learning Program – uses various types of equipment such as VCRs, VCD/DVD machines and recorders to provide students with a rich English learning environment where English teachers are not needed.

The Pan Deng English Learning Program (PDELP) was initiated in 2000. The initial support came from the National Pan Deng Research Plan directed by the Ministry of Science and Technology of PRC. Continuing support has been provided by the Research Foundation on Humanities and Social Sciences directed by the Ministry of Education of PRC and by the National Curriculum Reform (Basic Education) Grant as well as by provincial governments such as Beijing Municipal Government. So far, more than 406 classes in 117 schools from the urban and rural areas in Beijing, Anhui Province, and Shandong Province have been involved in the PDELP.

Based on the analysis of the critical challenges to English learning and teaching in China and recent advances in various research fields, we designed this program: (1) to provide high-quality English learning experiences for primary-school children in urban and rural areas without the need for additional English teachers; (2) to develop children's interests and positive attitudes toward English learning; (3) to improve children's ability to use English, especially their speaking and listening abilities; and (4) to promote the overall collaboration among teachers, schools, and parents by involving all of them in the children's learning process.

Compared to many other English-learning programs, the most salient feature of the PDELP is "English classes without English teachers." In this program, teachers do not play the traditional role of modeling as English speakers. They are merely the organizers and facilitators for children's English learning. Therefore, they do not need to be English teachers as traditionally defined. The idea of "English classes without English teachers" is not only to meet the major challenges facing English learning in China, but also to take advantage of the recent research advances in language learning and child development. In the following sections, we discuss the relevant research advances in multiple areas first, and then describe the main features of the PDELP.

Research advances relating to children's second-language learning

Much attention has been paid to second-language learning in several areas, including brain science, cognitive psychology, developmental psychology, applied linguistics, pedagogy, and educational technology. The important findings revealed in three particular areas were of interest to us during the development of this English-training program for Chinese children.

The importance of early language exposure

It has been proved that there are advantages to learning a second language in early childhood. In a functional magnetic resonance imaging (fMRI) study (Chee et al., 1999), it was found that proficient bilinguals exposed to both languages early in life utilize common neuroanatomical regions during the conceptual and syntactic processing of the two languages irrespective of their differences in surface features. The remarkable brain plasticity in early development has also been documented in many studies showing that only child learners are capable of acquiring the native accent of a second language (Bongaerts, Planken, & Schils, 1997; Snow & Hoefnagel-Hohle, 1977). Moreover, children usually experience less language anxiety during second-language learning. Therefore, being exposed to a second language in child-hood could be very helpful. More and more researchers and practitioners in China (e.g., Wang, 2001) have recognized the importance of childhood exposure to a second language (e.g., English) and have called for new strategies.

Children's language-learning potential

Despite the popular idea that children can learn languages easily, more and more studies have found that children's advantages in language learning are closely related to specific learning approaches, which should be taken into account in the design of training programs. On the one hand, *constructivism*, one of the modern learning theories, proposes that students don't passively accept all presented stimuli but actively seek for what they want and thus develop through their own active construction (Steffe & Gale, 1995). It is therefore important to set up a child-centered learning environment and enhance peer interaction and child–environment interaction. In learning English as a second language, it is of particular importance to provide children with plenty of opportunities to use and practice English in a variety of situations. On the other hand, it has been documented that there are great differences in information-processing mechanisms between adults and children. Children often learn incidentally and unintentionally, while adults often adopt a planned, procedural, analytical and logical method of learning (Cronin, Farrell, & Delaney, 1999; Huckin & Goady, 1999). An effective learning program should pay adequate attention to children's incidental learning in addition to intentional learning activities.

The trend of integrating information technology into children's learning

Modern information technology (IT) brings a tremendous transformation to children's learning, and deeply affects the approaches, processes and pedagogical strategies of children's language learning (Brett, 1995; Brown, 1997). Multimedia technology can provide knowledge about language, society and culture, which can set good models for students to imitate and learn from. As a result, it decreases the pressure on teachers' own language abilities in English classes and allows them to become better organizers in classes. At the same time, multimedia technology can create a favorable environment for children's English learning and practicing through the provision of plentiful multimodality language information and interesting real-life situations.

The relevant research advances discussed above provided insightful cues for us to develop the Pan Deng English Learning Program for Chinese children. This program is unique in five aspects:

1   it uses non-English teachers as the qualified organizers and facilitators for children's English learning;
2   it enriches the learning environment by making the best use of educational technology;
3   it provides meaningful and user-friendly language resources;
4   it constructs a learning community in school and at home; and
5   it develops a positive learning attitude and motivation among children by reforming the assessment of English learning.

Non-English teachers as the qualified organizers and facilitators for children's English learning

As discussed above, because the shortage of English teachers in China is a persistent problem, a practical solution would have to function without English teachers. In the PDELP, we use teachers who are otherwise teaching subjects such as Chinese, mathematics, music, or physical education. These teachers have a very low level of English proficiency. Their main roles are to organize and facilitate students' English-learning activities.

The main requirements for teachers in the PDELP are a passion for facilitating children's English learning, advanced class-management skills, and basic skills in using educational technology (e.g., VCD/DVD and sometimes computers). English proficiency is not a prerequisite for becoming an "English teacher" in this program. According to these requirements, it is much easier to find "English teachers" in many primary schools in the cities, towns or even in villages.

In order to prepare the non-English teachers for their job as qualified teachers for children's English learning, we conduct intensive teacher training. The three specific aims of the training are to change these teachers' beliefs about teaching in order to prepare them for the nontraditional approach to teaching English, to modify their class-management skills in the face of this nontraditional class, and to improve their skills in using educational technology. The training sessions include lectures, discussions, and demonstrations. We typically use school-based field training so that teachers can apply what they learn in real contexts. Training is conducted by an expert team in the PDELP who were involved in the design of this program. The expert team usually visits the school and the classrooms, offers face-to-face training and instruction to teachers, and provides suggestions and encouragement.

Additionally, teacher support groups have also been set up within schools. These support groups consist of school administrators, traditional English teachers (if there are any), and PDELP "English teachers." Such support groups promote information sharing and help to reduce non-English teachers' anxiety about teaching a new course.

Creating a rich English environment with multimedia technology

Multimedia teaching resources provide a combination of English stimuli with sounds, written words, photographs, cartoons, and videos. These stimuli are often lively and fun. They are organized into learning activities. In fact, equipments, learning materials, and organized activities are the three necessary requirements for a rich English environment.

In terms of equipment, at the very minimum a VCD/DVD player with a hand-held controller and a TV monitor are needed. With these pieces of equipment, children and teachers can use the learning materials recorded in VCD/DVD format. Supplemental materials are also available on audio CDs and tapes and even computer disks. In most cases children are learning English from VCD/DVD recorders and, sometimes, computers rather than from teachers. Organized activities for such learning include role-playing, dramatic acting, games, etc. All these activities were developed to integrate what children have learned. They provide children with ample opportunities to listen to English, to speak English, and even to play in English.

Providing meaningful and user-friendly English resources

Resources for children's English learning were selected and designed to meet three goals: (1) to develop children's interest in learning English;

(2) to offer substantial English input; and (3) to promote children's use of English in daily life. The PDELP provides teachers with activities and games for each unit of the course as well as tips for organizing additional learning activities. As an example of such activities, the "Songs and Chants" part of each unit has four sections "Watch & Listen," "Listen & Repeat," "Follow," and "Perform." Teachers are also provided with detailed suggestions about how best to use different sections. With such guidance, teachers feel confident about how to teach, which should facilitate children's learning.

Constructing a learning community in school and at home

Because class time is limited, it is crucial for children to practice speaking English after class. Turning peer groups and home into active learning communities is a practical and effective way of providing additional learning opportunities. A "No Chinese" game is introduced to children's peer groups and home in order to help children to practice their English after class. The DPELP has a large number of game materials supporting the "No Chinese" game. During this game, children are encouraged to communicate with their peers, teachers, and parents in English and to role-play in English. Because most parents do not speak English, their role is mainly to encourage children to perform in English and to be a patient audience. The "No Chinese" game provides a situation in which children have to put aside their fear of speaking English and focus on communicating with others. Gradually, children feel more and more comfortable with spoken English.

Developing a positive learning attitude and motivation among children by reforming the assessment of English learning

Assessment plays an important role in learning. The PDELP develops a system of assessment that motivates children to learn English. This assessment system follows three principles: tolerance of mistakes; process orientation; and participation by children.

The principle of tolerance of mistakes states that teachers should understand and tolerate language errors made by children at the beginning of their learning in order to create a harmonious and comfortable learning environment. This principle should help children to develop their interest and confidence in learning English by focusing on the positives. This principle is similar to the general tolerance of mistakes in native language acquisition during infancy and early childhood.

Our assessment is also process-orientated. Distinct from the summative assessment commonly used in traditional English classes, process-orientated assessment is included in every learning session to document and encourage any sign of progress. This kind of assessment keeps teachers, children, and parents well informed about the children's learning progress and allows them to adjust the subsequent learning schedule. Individualized learning schedules could be implemented with process-orientated assessment.

Finally, children are included in the assessment process. Their participation is helpful in cultivating self-regulated learning. In this program, children are not only encouraged to assess their peers and themselves, but also instructed to give advice to their peers and themselves based on information available in the school portfolio, family portfolio and semester report cards. Such opportunities allow children to reflect on their own learning experience in comparison with that of their peers and to make adjustments to their own learning schedule if necessary.

Because the teachers involved in this program usually have only very limited English proficiency, four strategies are applied in practice. The first, which is the most salient one, is to prepare a series of learning activity record cards for teachers to use in class and parents to use at home. The focus of this assessment is about tracking children's learning activities and their efforts in English learning. The second strategy is to develop peer monitoring and correcting procedures. All students are encouraged to be other students' "Little teacher". When learning new information and reviewing information already learned, there is always a step of peer monitoring and correcting activities, sometimes for the whole class, sometimes in small groups, and sometimes even in pairs. The third strategy is to train teachers in weekly or monthly seminars. The training is not to teach all the course content to teachers, but to show what sentences, words and stories the children will be exposed to in the next week and to help teachers to catch the key points. In order to make sure that children get accurate feedback on their English, proficient teachers are encouraged to observe children's English activities once a week, sum up the common errors and give specific feedback during whole-class activities.

Empirical evidence of the effectiveness of the PDELP

The Pan Deng English Learning Program attempts to explore the possibility of providing high-quality English instruction to Chinese primary-school children without teachers who are proficient in English. Can children learn English in this program? How much can they achieve in English learning? How do children feel about learning English in this program? In July 2004, an empirical evaluation study was conducted to try to answer these questions.

The framework of program evaluation

Goals

As mentioned above, the PDELP has a broad goal of providing children with high-quality English instruction without English teachers. To accomplish that, we introduced new ideas in beliefs about teaching, in instructional strategies, and in school-based education reform. Therefore, the present evaluation aimed to reveal the comprehensive outcomes of the program. Three clusters of outcomes were included: (1) children's achievement in English (i.e., listening, speaking, and reading abilities); (2) children's learning attitude, anxiety, and self-concept; and (3) perceived impacts on teachers, parents, and schools.

Participants

Children involved in the evaluation came from 10 primary schools in Beijing City and its suburbs. The majority of these children's parents were factory workers and peasants. These schools were rated as average by their respective districts' educational committees in terms of teachers' quality, school facilities, and students' school achievement. There were 140 children (69 boys, 71 girls, M_{age} = 8.06 years, SD = 1.03) in the experimental group. A majority of them (85 children) had just finished their first grade, whereas the rest (55 children) had just finished their third grade. All of them began to take English classes in the PDELP scheme starting at first grade. None of the children had been taking after-school English classes other than the PDELP.

There were 126 children (72 boys, 54 girls, M_{age} = 9.69 years, SD = 1.63) in the control group. About half of them (57 children) had just finished their first grade, 34 had just finished their third grade, and 35 had just finished their fifth grade. The third graders started taking English when they were in first grade and the fifth graders started when they were in third grade. In other words, both third and fifth graders had undertaken three years of English lessons. According to teachers' report, half of children in the control group had taken various after-school English classes.

The control group was not exactly matched to the experimental group in terms of grade level because of logistical difficulties in securing cooperation from schools not participating in the PDELP. Additional subjects from fifth-grade classes were included assuming that they would give the control group an advantage (i.e., to present a more conservative test of the program's effects). To exclude gross biases in the selection of the two samples, both experimental and control groups (one child did not take the test) were given the Chinese version of Raven's Progressive Matrix (revised by Zhang & Wang, 1985). There was no significant difference in their scores on that test: $M_{Experimental\ group}$ = 34.02, SD = 10.30; $M_{Control\ group}$ = 32.34, SD = 11.62; t = 1.25, df = 263, p > .05.

Measures

In addition to Raven's test, individual and group tests of English proficiency were administered. Interviews with children, teachers, and parents were conducted.

ENGLISH PROFICIENCY ASSESSMENTS

Six tests were developed to assess children's achievement in English in terms of listening, speaking, and reading abilities. Test items for vocabulary and sentence structures came from two sources: English textbooks used by students in the control group and the PDELP materials. Half of the test items appeared in both the English textbooks and the PDELP materials; one fourth appeared only in the English textbooks; and another fourth only in the PDELP materials. A spelling test was not given because it is only a requirement for fourth and higher grades according to the National Curriculum of English.

There were two tests of listening comprehension. The word comprehension test required children to listen to a word and to select the correct picture out of four alternatives. The test had 60 words. For the sentence comprehension test, children were read a sentence and asked to select the correct picture out of four. There were 20 sentences. These tests were administered in groups. Cronbach alpha coefficients were .77 or higher.

Children's speaking proficiency was assessed with two individual tests. In the picture-naming test, children were asked to name 60 pictures one at a time. In the picture-narration test, children were presented with a picture of a birthday party and asked to say what happened at the party. They were asked to say as much as they wanted. The mean length of each utterance (MLU) was used to indicate the complexity of children's speech, and the mean length of each run of utterance (MLR) was used to indicate the fluency.

Children's reading abilities were assessed by individual tests of word recognition and sentence comprehension (third and fifth graders only). The word-recognition test involved the presentation of a list of words one at a time then the children were asked to read the words out loud. Performance was measured as the total number of words read correctly in one minute. (Because subjects completed different numbers of words, no Cronbach alpha coefficients were calculated for this test.) Sentence comprehension was assessed by asking children to select a picture from four alternatives after having been read a sentence. There were 25 sentences. The Cronbach alpha for this test was .85.

MEASURES OF ATTITUDES, ANXIETY, AND SELF-CONCEPT

Third and fifth graders completed a questionnaire that included a measure of attitudes toward English learning, a scale of English learning anxiety, and a self-description scale. The measure of attitude toward English learning consisted of 20 items tapping children's general attitude toward English learning, attitude toward English classes, and the general self-efficacy about English learning. The scale of English-learning anxiety was based on the "Foreign Language Classroom Anxiety Scale" (Horwitz, Horwitz, & Cope, 1986). There were 31 items and five dimensions. The five dimensions are: oral communication anxiety; class input anxiety; class output anxiety; general class anxiety; and English subject anxiety. Finally, the Chinese version of the Self-Description Questionnaire (Wang, 1993) was used. It had 20 items along four dimensions: general; English; Chinese; and mathematics self-concepts. All the instruments used 5-point Likert scales. Cronbach alpha coefficients were .87 or higher.

PERCEIVED IMPACTS ON TEACHERS, PARENTS, AND SCHOOLS

Interviews were conducted to examine the influence of the PDELP on teachers' beliefs about teaching and their teaching strategies, parent–child interactions, and schools in general.

Major results from the evaluation study

Children's English abilities

As Table 4.1 shows, children in the PDELP attained a high level of English performance even though they did not have an English teacher. They were superior to their control group in terms of listening, speaking, and reading abilities. Specifically, children in the experimental group gave 64–79% correct responses in listening, speaking, and reading tests, much higher than their

Table 4.1 Average proportion of correct responses and the mean raw scores (and *SD*) on English tests for the experimental and control groups

		Experimental group		Control group	
		Correct responses (%)	Mean (SD)	Correct responses (%)	Mean (SD)
Listening	Word comprehension	76	36.76 (10.79)	54	27.98 (10.34)
	Sentence comprehension	72	14.38 (2.75)	45	8.96 (3.53)
Speaking	Picture naming	64	31.04 (12.58)	30	15.46 (12.42)
	Narration – MLU		4.77 (1.50)		1.41 (2.00)
	Narration – MLR		5.42 (1.35)		0.91 (1.38)
Reading	Word recognition in 1 minute		35.24 (18.93)		19.83 (21.09)
	Sentence comprehension	79	19.72 (3.73)	57	14.29 (4.94)

Note: MLU = mean length of utterances; MLR = mean length of each run before any pause longer than 1.5 s within any sentence.

peers in the control group (30–57%). These differences were statistically significant, $ts > 4.05$, $ps < .001$. The advantage of the program is especially remarkable in children's speaking ability. Children in the experimental group correctly named more than 64% of pictures while those in the control group named only 30% correctly. Similarly, there were sharp contrasts between the two groups in MLU and MLR of picture narration, favoring the experimental group. On average, children in the experimental group produced sentences that were 4.77 words long (MLU) and spoke continuously for more than 5.42 words before any pauses longer than 1.5 s (MLR). In contrast, children in the control group could only produce sentences that were 1.41 words long and had short runs of utterances (0.91 words). In fact, some of them said only one or two individual words during the assessment. As for reading ability, the experimental group shows superiority in both word recognition and sentence comprehension even though reading instruction had not yet been implemented in the PDELP. It is worth noting that there was a large standard deviation of 21.09 in the word-recognition test for the control group. Further analysis found that individual scores ranged from 0 to 77, with 14.3% of the students scoring 0 and 47.1% lower than 10. The median and mode for the scores were 11 and 0 respectively. In contrast, none of students in the experimental group got 0 and only 7.3% scored lower than 10. Individual scores in the experimental group ranged from 6 to 90, with a median of 36 and the mode of 13.

Further analysis on the effect size in each measure indicated that the advantages of the experimental group were obvious and consistent (Figure 4.1). All effect size coefficients were above 0.7. Children in the experimental group gained more in speaking relative to listening and reading abilities, and more at the sentence level than at the word level.

Children's attitude, anxiety, and self-concept

As shown in Table 4.2, compared to children in the control group, children in the experimental group liked English learning much more ($t = 5.76$, $df = 120$, $p < .001$), had far less anxiety ($ts - 3.28$ to $- 4.27$, $df = 120$, $ps < .001$), and rated themselves more positively in English ($t = 4.18$, $df = 120$, $p < .001$) and slightly more positively in general academic performance ($t = 1.11$, $df = 120$, $p > .05$). Most of the size of the positive effects of the program ranged from medium to large (effect size coefficients > 0.5) (Figure 4.2). It seems that the PDELP not only improved children's English proficiency, but also generated positive feelings about the English experience.

Perceived impacts on teachers, parents, and school-based education reform

Although the primary purpose of the PDELP is to create English-learning opportunities when English teachers are in short supply, the implementation

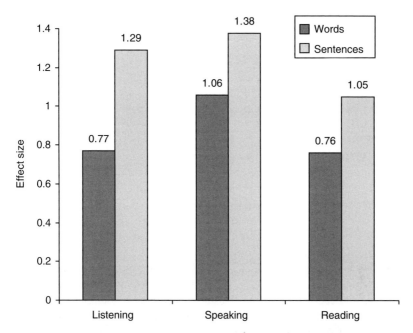

Figure 4.1 Effect size (*d*) of the experiment according to the English tests: (1) listening to words; (2) listening to sentences; (3) speaking – word level (picture naming); (4) speaking – sentence level (picture narration); (5) reading – word level (1 minute word recognition); (6) reading – sentence level.

Table 4.2 Means (and *SD*) of children's attitudes, anxiety, and self-concept

		Experimental group Mean (SD)	*Control group Mean (SD)*
Attitude toward English learning		4.64 (0.40)	3.95 (0.81)
English learning anxiety	Oral English anxiety	1.70 (0.64)	2.26 (0.76)
	Class output anxiety	1.57 (0.69)	2.06 (0.78)
	English class anxiety	1.72 (0.70)	2.17 (0.82)
	English subject anxiety	1.47 (0.68)	1.91 (0.79)
Self-concept	English self-concept	4.26 (0.79)	3.57 (1.00)
	Chinese self-concept	4.20 (0.79)	4.25 (0.77)
	Math self-concept	4.17 (0.81)	4.17 (0.76)
	General academic self-concept	4.12 (0.67)	3.89 (0.89)

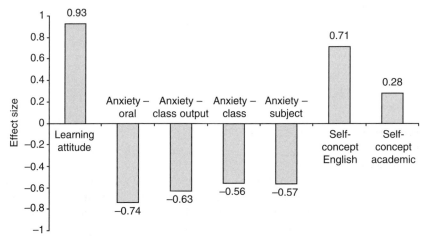

Figure 4.2 Effect size of the experiment in terms of children's attitudes, anxiety, and self-concept: (1) attitude toward English learning; (2) anxiety – oral: children's anxiety about oral communication; (3) anxiety – class output: children's anxiety about the output requirements and activities in class; (4) anxiety – class: children's anxiety about taking an English class; (5) anxiety – subject: children's anxiety about the school subject of English; (6) self-concept English: children's self-concept in English; (7) self-concept academic: children's general academic self-concept.

of the program has involved, and thus impacted, the larger learning contexts. Changes have been documented in terms of teacher–children interactions, parent–child interactions, and school-based education reform. However, these qualitative data have yet to be analyzed. Here we only summarize the general impressions from a preliminary review of the data.

TEACHERS

Teachers in the program appeared to report that their confidence and trust in students' learning potential were increased, and they were more comfortable with using the IT to assist teaching. Interviews with the school principals showed that all teachers in the PDELP applied much more encouragement and positive feedback in class management than did their colleagues who were not in the program. Children reported that they liked their teachers more than before.

PARENTS

Although most parents did not know English, they gradually learned to encourage their children and to help them to practice English at home. Parents recognized that English learning is a long-term process and they should respect their children's own pace. Children reported that their parents enjoyed the English "shows" they put on at home and liked to learn English from the children. Through this program, parents learned to become supporters and facilitators as well as monitors of children's learning.

SCHOOLS

Support from the schools' administration has played an important role in this program. This program also contributed to the schools in terms of supporting school-based education reform. First, the program provided a vivid demonstration of the uses of computers and video and audio equipment for education and a demonstration of the importance of administrative support for IT-based learning and teaching. Second, the program provided an opportunity to conduct teacher training by involving teachers themselves in the problem-based pedagogical innovation. Third, the program helped the schools to integrate the potential resources from students, teachers, and parents. The establishment of a learning community based on peer groups offers opportunities for children to practice English after class. The close connections between teachers and parents provide an understanding and supportive context for school, teachers, and children alike. The teacher–administrator support groups maximize the available human resources and improve teaching quality.

Implications

The PDELP has been implemented in more than 117 schools in 24 cities, towns and counties. More schools are considering its implementation. The preliminary evaluation study showed that this program is effective in facilitating Chinese children's English learning without English teachers. This program represents a new approach to teaching a second language in the context of teacher shortages. The implications of the PDELP for future research, practices, and policy making regarding second-language education are discussed below.

The responsibilities of psychologists and other researchers in improving educational practices

The PDELP was initiated by a group of research psychologists. The success of this program shows once again that psychologists can make significant contributions to improving the quality of education by actively engaging in research on important practical issues. In China, a developing country with a population of more than 1.3 billion people, the responsibilities for solving important real-life problems through scientific studies need to be borne by academicians. We believe that applied research will not only facilitate educational and social development, but also benefit the basic research in psychology because real-life problems involve many fundamental laws of human behavior.

Integrating information technology into education

The success of the PDELP shows the bright prospect of integrating IT into educational practice. It is clear that educational technology provides a practical and effective solution to the crisis of English education in China, especially in the western and rural areas. Teachers and school administrators should pay attention to the development of new technology and use it in their classrooms and beyond. At the same time, the government should increase the investment required to supply the basic equipment to every classroom. Researchers should also continue to investigate new ways to use educational technology to enhance students' learning and teachers' instruction.

Teachers' professional development through participation in school-based research and educational reform

This program also provides a new way of facilitating teacher's professional development. First, teachers should be involved in school-based curriculum research and be encouraged to become active researchers. Through participation in school-based research and educational reform, teachers will be motivated to learn about new educational and psychological theories that can be used in their profession. Second, through participatory research, teachers can also obtain training in new class-management skills and instruction strategies. Such training will help teachers to become better at organizing, facilitating, and evaluating students' learning. Third, school administrators should recognize that teachers' professional development needs support from their peers in addition to experts. In the PDELP, the teacher–principal team is a support system that plays a crucial role in program implementation and teachers' development.

Policy issues about second-language education

The PDELP provides a possible approach to narrowing the gap in educational opportunities between developed and underdeveloped areas by taking advantage of IT. When a severe inequity in human resources (in our case English teachers) exists, IT is a great equalizer. Governments, especially those of developing countries like PRC, should invest in educational technology to offset the regional imbalance in economic development. Governments should also support large-scale applied research projects that introduce new ideas and strategies to education reform. The PDELP is a clear example of how research can be successfully integrated into second-language education. Future efforts should aim to expand this program to other subject areas (e.g., arts education) that also experience a shortage of teachers.

Note

1 College English Test, which includes Band 4 and Band 6, is a nationally standard-ized single-subject test that has been administered by the Department of Higher Education of China's Ministry of Education since 1987.

References

Bongaerts, T., Planken, B., & Schils, E. (1997). Age and ultimate attainment in the pronunciation of a foreign language. *Second Language Research, 19,* 447–465.

Brett, P. (1995). Multimedia for listening comprehension: The design of a multimedia-based resource for developing listening skill. *System, 23*(1), 77–85.

Brown, J. D. (1997). Computers in language testing: Present research and some future directions. *Language Learning and Technology, 1*(1), 44–59.

Caragata, L., & Sanchez, M. (2002). Globalization and global need: New imperatives for expanding international social work education in North America. *International Social Work, 45*(2), 217–238.

Chee, M. W. L., Caplan, D., Soon, C. S., Sriram, N., Tan, E. W. L., Thiel, T. et al. (1999). Processing of visually presented sentences in Mandarin and English studied with fMRI. *Neuron, 23,* 127–137.

Cronin, V., Farrell, D., & Delaney, M. (1999). Environmental print and word recogni-tion. *Journal of Research on Reading, 22,* 271–282.

Ellis, R. (1985). *Understanding second language acquisition.* Oxford, UK: Oxford University Press.

Feng, Z.-K. (2003). How wide is the gap between laggard rural English teaching and new curriculum standards? *Chinese Teachers,* February 12.

Hakuta, K., & Pease-Alvarez, L. (1992). Enriching our views of bilingualism and bilingual education. *Educational Researcher, 21,* 4–6.

Horwitz, E., Horwitz, M., & Cope, J. (1986). Foreign language classroom anxiety. *Modern Language Journal, 70,* 125–132.

Hu, X.-Y. (2005). English learning anxiety in primary school students. *English Coaching (Primary School), Issue 24,* p. 2.

Huckin, T., & Goady, J. (1999). Incidental vocabulary acquisition in a second lan-guage: A review. *Studies in Second Language Acquisition, 21,* 181–193.

Kim, K. H. S., Relkin, N. R., Lee, K.-M., & Hirsch, J. (1997). Distinct cortical areas associated with native and second languages. *Nature, 388,* 171–174.

Li, X. (2004). Knowing deaf and dumb English. *Journal of Liaoning Educational Administration Institute, 21*(7), 61–62.

Lin, Y. (2002, July 19). English ability: First step to deal with WTO. *Chinese Educa-tion,* p. 3.

Mo, M. (2002, April 13). English fervor "burned" 10 billion RMB. *Chinese Journal of Water Resources,* p. 6.

Perani, D., Dehaene, S., Grassi, F., Cohen, L., Cappa, S. F., Dupoux, E., et al. (1996). Brain processing of native and foreign languages. *NeuroReport, 7,* 2439–2444.

PRC Ministry of Education. (2001). MOE guidelines for furthering English curric-ulum in primary schools. No. 2 Document of 2001 from Department of Basic Education. Beijing, China: MOE.

PRC Ministry of Education. (2003a). Educational background of subject teachers in elementary schools. In Editorial Department of China Education Yearbook,

China education yearbook of 2003 (p. 101). Beijing, China: People's Education Press.

PRC Ministry of Education. (2003b). Statistical bulletin for national educational development in 2002 released by MOE on May 13, 2003. In Editorial Department of China Education Yearbook, *China education yearbook of 2003* (pp. 79–81). Beijing, China: People's Education Press.

Snow, C., & Hoefnagel-Hohle, M. (1977). Age differences in the pronunciation of foreign sounds. *Language and Speech, 20*, 357–365.

Steffe, L. P., & Gale, J. (Eds.). (1995). *Constructivism in education.* Hillsdale, NJ: Lawrence Erlbaum Associates, Inc.

Wang, C.-M. (2001). Age factor in foreign language learning. In Y.-P. Dong & C.-M. Wang (Eds.), *Linguistics in China: Research and application* (pp. 100–105). Shanghai, China: Shanghai Foreign Language Education Press.

Wang, Q., & Ding, X.-S. (2001). A study of students' English language anxiety in the rural regions of western China. *Journal of Northwest Normal University (Social Science), 38*(5), 68–73.

Wang, X.-D. (Ed.). (1993). Handbook of mental health assessments. *Chinese Journal of Mental Health, Suppl.,* 310–314.

Zhang, H.-C., & Wang, X.-P. (1985). *Chinese version of Raven's standard progressive matrix test (for urban areas).* Beijing, China: Beijing Normal University.

Zhang, X.-C., & Chang, M.-H. (2004). A survey of non-English majors' anxiety in learning English. *Journal of Zhejiang Education Institute,* Issue 5, 82–87.

Zhang, Z.-Y. (1999). Overcoming difficulties to improve English teaching in rural primary schools. *Tianjin Education,* Issue 10, 35.

5 Rules and tools of intelligence: How IQ became obsolete

J. P. Das

I begin with a saying that has been going around for the last 2000 years:

> From untruth, lead me to truth
> From darkness, lead me to light
> From death, lead me to immortality.

We speak about what's true and what's practical, for intelligence has both sides, as will become quite clear in the next few paragraphs. The major trouble with the concept of IQ is that it started as something convenient to classify children into those who need special education and those who do not, but somehow, somewhere along the way, Binet's intention was hijacked, as it were. As we review the entire evolution of intelligence as a concept and end up by defining, ridiculously, intelligence or IQ as what IQ tests measure, I am reminded of a line of poetry written by Omar Khayam:

> And the first morning of creation wrote
> What the last dawn of reckoning shall read.

So, what did the first morning of creation write that, in retrospect, made intelligence almost useless? Binet had no intention of raising his eclectic test based on school achievement to the status of a general cognitive ability. In fact he was very critical of Spearman's early attempt to define intelligence in terms of factor analysis. Spearman reported the hierarchy of abilities thus: Classics, of course, came first, then French, English, and math, pitch, and music. The hierarchy of abilities consisted of classroom marks obtained by children attending grammar school in Britain in Spearman's time. The idea of the famous "general factor" was reported on only 22 children. No one will accept it today as a creditable study, and many will object to the then "new" method of factor analysis that Spearman used. But factor analysis has been criticized seriously in many scholarly articles as well as popular writings (Gould, 1981). Complaints, such as "you get what you put in" and that the method of factor analysis is engineered in such a way that it would give a general factor, are quite common. And on this controversial method rested the theory of general intelligence, or *g*. From the very beginning, Alfred Binet was derogatory about Spearman's general intelligence, *g*.

Binet's test became the fountainhead of American intelligence tests. Wechsler Sattler worked with Wechsler and has written a definitive textbook on measuring intelligence. During one of my rare meetings with Sattler in San Diego I was told that Binet's test was liberally used by Wechsler to make Wechsler's first test, and it has not changed much over the years. Comparing the early Wechsler with Binet the similarity is astounding. Though I do not want to belabor this obvious point, although Binet never conceived his tests as tests of intelligence, the IQ tradition stems from his early measures to separate children with special needs from those who should stay in regular classes.

Why did scientists object to the foundation of IQ? The foundation was built on the notion of a general ability derived from Galton. His most famous book, often associated with the concept of intelligence, is *Hereditary Genius*. Darlington (1962), a famous scientist, wrote an introduction to Galton's *Hereditary Genius* nearly one hundred years after its publication, and this is what he had to say:

> Experts today may still want to follow a one-dimensional scale of merit or intelligence. The measurement of merit, the quantitative as opposed to the qualitative method of study, leads to simple assessments of superiority and inferiority. Hence it justifies simple policies of opposition, of exclusion, and of oppression. These are all the more dangerous in ignorant hands for they contain an element of truth. They have a conditional validity.
>
> (p. 18)

I do not need to continue quoting old statements like this, which raise serious doubt about the validity of the concept of IQ. Instead let us review some of the contemporary researchers who are genuinely concerned about schooling and intelligence and how certain sections of society, which receive inferior schooling, may also turn out to be low in IQ tests. Ceci (2003) concludes from the results of a series of studies that schooling may directly influence an IQ score: "Each additional month a student remains in school may increase the student's IQ score above what would be expected if the student dropped out" (p. 855).

I am now running a study on Canadian Native children in a reserve school near Edmonton, Alberta, many of whom are very poor in reading. Such children may face the lack of a literacy environment, possible parental neglect and abuse, perhaps even some amount of malnutrition, but the major reason the children do not learn to read appears to be because they do not come to school regularly.

Ceci also showed how volatile IQ scores can be. Several independent studies have documented, with large samples, the systematic decline in IQ and related cognitive ability measures that occur over summer months.

Thus by looking at children's performance as a function of time away for vacations we once again find evidence for a causal relationship between schooling and IQ.

"We cannot dismiss how IQ has been misused and how it has seriously affected the lives of countless millions of people in the 20th century," wrote Richardson (1986). He continues, ". . . and it's no joke that largely because of IQ theory a substantial proportion of people, perhaps a majority, have left and are still leaving school throughout the world convinced they are incapable of learning anything very serious" (p. 579).

Do we have enough ammunition, then, to say that IQ has been a harmful idea? Some sane voices in the field of intelligence research should be heard. Leona Tyler (1986), reviewing a collection of papers on general ability, concluded that: "the greatest weakness is its reliance on correlational research exclusively. We must take in consideration research in special education, rehab, mental retardation, and other specialized areas that has demonstrated that individuals at many *g* levels can do productive work" (p. 449).

Very recently, Nisbett (2003) commented on the reason why even ordinary children and adults may have different intelligences, different styles of solving intellectual problems, in a fascinating book called *The Geography of Thought*:

> So long as economic forces operate to maintain different social structures, different social practices and children-rearing will result in people focusing on different things in the environment and focusing on different things will produce different understandings about the nature of the world. Different worldviews will in turn reinforce differential attention and social practices. The different world views will also prompt differences in perception, reasoning processes, which will tend to reinforce world views.
>
> (p. 38)

Nisbett was contrasting and attempting to reflect on the prototypic Chinese–Japanese versus Greco–European ways of thinking, both of which are valid, and whose origins are very different due to the specific social and cultural history of the two regions.

So what are we left with now, after saying that general intelligence has done more harm than good and intelligence is inextricably integrated with social-cultural history? Here is an opinion expressed by Flynn (2003) on *g*, the famous Flynn of the Flynn effect, which can be paraphrased as follows: Flynn suggests that *g* lacks a sociological dimension and cannot explain cognitive trends over time, neither can it assess their significance. He said let us pretend that Jensen's ideal of a purely physiological *g* has been realized. Flynn does this in order to show that the closer we approach that ideal, the more the *g* concept suffers from a peculiar limitation, namely, that it becomes sociologically blind. The symptoms are most evident when we take a look at the evolution of cognitive skills over time.

I will end this tirade against *g* with a final insightful quotation. I ask you not to look at the source of the quotation and to imagine who, in 1934, could have said this:

> The mind is not a complex network of general capabilities, such as observation, attention, memory, judgment, and so forth, but a set of specific capabilities, each of which is, to some extent, independent of others and is developed independently. Learning is more than the acquisition of the ability to think. It is the acquisition of many specialized abilities for thinking about a variety of things. Learning does not alter our overall ability to focus attention, but rather develops various abilities to focus attention on a variety of things.
>
> (Vygotsky, 1986, p. 83)

Who else but Vygotsky would have such foresight about intelligence? The quotation is taken from a book published in 1986, but he wrote it around 1934. So the plea here is for looking at specific abilities that develop in a diverse manner. Consider how Chris Frith (1997), a contemporary neuropsychologist, reframes the same idea: why we should look at specific rather than general abilities.

> The brain consists of a great many modules that process information more or less independently of each other. It seems likely that it will be easier to discover how one of those modules works than to explain the functioning of the brain as a whole.
>
> (p. 5)

The quotation questions the validity of the notion that there is a general factor of intelligence. Contemporary thinking is in line with Vygotsky, Luria, and even before them, with Pavlov: much as the organs of the body are specific and diverse in their functions, the brain, although admittedly working as a whole, cannot be conceived to have one general intelligence function.

Even factor analytic statistics do not necessarily support a *g* or general ability. Some who have attempted to support a *g* factor typically regard the first unrotated factor as *g*. However, I present the results of a study we carried out some years ago (Das & Dash, 1983).

Notice, in Table 5.1, that the first unrotated factor has a higher loading on short-term memory tests, serial recall and visual short-term memory (STM), than it has on progressive matrices. The matrices are typically regarded as a solid test of *g* whereas short-term memory is at the bottom of the pole in representing *g*! Next, a hierarchical analysis yields a *g* but again the two tests of STM have much higher loading on this than the progressive matrices. So the tests that are selected and the individuals who take the tests determine what is *g*.

Table 5.1 Hierarchical factor solution of simultaneous–successive battery for grade 4 sample ($N = 104$)

Variable h^2	Unrotated principal axes loadings				Schmid–Leiman hierarchical orthogonalization			
					Second order	First order		
					G	Succ.	Simult.	Speed
Colored progressive matrices	.502	−.309	.185	.382	.367	.016	.497	.041
Figure copying	.509	−.344	.059	.380	.390	.091	.461	−.071
Memory for designs	.476	−.455	.281	.513	.320	−.073	.637	.004
Serial recall	.675	−.032	−.116	.471	.573	.297	.221	.057
Visual short-term memory	.716	.130	−.426	.711	.664	.519	−.027	−.038
Digit span	.464	.148	−.275	.313	.434	.346	−.063	.018
Word reading	.520	.559	.184	.617	.441	.164	−.115	.610
Color naming	.313	.370	.518	.504	.207	−.135	.101	.666

Table 5.2 Confirmatory factor analytic results for ages 11–13 years

Subtest	Scale			
	Planning	Simultaneous	Attention	Successive
Matching numbers	.738			
Planned codes	.558			
Planned connections	.765			
Nonverbal matrices		.671		
Verbal–spatial relations			.719	
Figure memory		.663		
Expressive attention			.580	
Number detection			.761	
Receptive attention			.778	
Word series				.752
Sentence repetition				.860
Sentence questions				.813

Note: Confirmatory factor analysis is utilized in this table to assess the three-factor and the four PASS-factor solutions; the latter had the best fit.

Table 5.3 Confirmatory factor analytic results for ages 14–17 years

Subtest	Scale			
	Planning	*Simultaneous*	*Attention*	*Successive*
Matching numbers	.697			
Planned codes	.529			
Planned connections	.777			
Nonverbal matrices		.639		
Verbal–spatial relations			.742	
Figure memory		.682		
Expressive attention			.652	
Number detection			.705	
Receptive attention			.719	
Word series				.720
Sentence repetition				.857
Sentence questions				.773

Note: Confirmatory factor analysis is utilized in this table to assess the three-factor and the four PASS-factor solutions; the latter had the best fit.

Does factor analysis support the four PASS (planning, attention, simultaneous, successive) cognitive factors rather than the hypothesis that only one general factor explains the variance in cognitive abilities? Confirmatory factor analysis can answer that question, and it does, clearly rejecting a one-factor, one-ability solution (Naglieri & Das, 1997). The PASS theory with its four processes is consistent with this claim. The theory is briefly described below.

To conclude the above section on the advocacy of *g*, some of the prominent persons are Galton, Spearman, Cyril Burt, Eysenck, and Jensen. Jensen has promoted *g* doggedly and has done much more for *g*, or psychometric *g*, as it is called nowadays, than Spearman ever did. He was a postdoctoral fellow with Eysenck, who himself was a student of Cyril Burt.

However, if one is not in the *g* camp there are alternatives to the notion of *g*. The alternatives are supplied by people who are followers of information-processing theories, who look at intelligence measures as tasks, as an opportunity for observing mental functions. The pioneer in this area is Broadbent. William Estes, the learning theorist, an experimental psychologist par excellence, analyzed the relationship between intelligence tasks and learning, as did Earl Hunt. Hunt is very active in the twin fields of computational modeling and experimental psychology, which influence his views on intelligence.

Then there are the even more popular figures of Gardner and Sternberg, who defied the *g* crowd and attractively proposed multiple intelligences. Still following an information theory bias, they analyze mental functions into multiple components and categories. Other researchers such as Ceci and

Flynn have raised serious doubts about the stability and immutability of *g*. The notion of *g* may need not to be eliminated but superseded, which has happened as neuropsychologists using old and new tools have advanced the study of intelligence as cognitive functions.

Luria (1966) was a pioneer in neuropsychology and one of its few founding fathers. Following his research and clinical work in the field and integrating it with contemporary ideas on cognitive psychology, my colleagues and I (Das, Naglieri, & Kirby, 1994) have proposed a theory of cognitive processes consisting of planning, attention, simultaneous, and successive processing (PASS), all encased within knowledge base, and each one relating to a functional organization in the brain. PASS theory is rooted in Pavlov and in Luria's three blocks of the brain. Our use of factor analysis, which was reinforced by experiments on cognitive processes, arose from Luria's syndrome analysis. I will not go into great detail here, as the PASS theory has been discussed in numerous articles and books (Das & Naglieri, 2001; Das, Naglieri, & Kirby, 1994).

Core components of PASS theory

In this brief review of the PASS theory, the basic division of Input, Processing, and Output proposed in 1975 has been retained (Das, Kirby, & Jarman, 1975, 1979). People receive information, that is, input, from external sources through their senses and internal organs. When that sensory information is sent to the brain for analysis, central processes become active. However, internal cognitive information in the form of images, memory, and thoughts becomes a part of the input as well. The external information may be presented serially, that is, one after another, for instance, "Listen to these words: cow, hot, wall, man, key," or concurrently, for instance, in dichotic listening when two different words are presented simultaneously, one to each ear. No such presentation mode can exist for internal input, however. "Automatic," "learned," and "effortful" describe the ways in which internal inputs are accessed.

The four components of the central processing mechanisms, that is, Planning (P), Attention–Arousal (A), and Simultaneous (S) and Successive (S) processing, together make up "PASS" (Figure 5.1). An important addition is knowledge: one's knowledge base is a part of each of the components. The base of past experiences, learning, emotions, and motivations provides the background as well as the source for the information to be processed.

Thus, the four processes must be active in the context of an individual's knowledge base. It is as if PASS processes were floating on a sea of knowledge; without seawater they would sink. In other words, they cannot operate outside the context of knowledge. "Cognitive processes rely on (and influence) the base of knowledge, which may be temporary (as in working memory) or more long term (that is, knowledge that is well learned)" (Naglieri & Das, 1997, p. 145). Knowledge can also be tacit (e.g., spontaneous, experiential, or nonconscious) or explicit (e.g., formal or instructed).

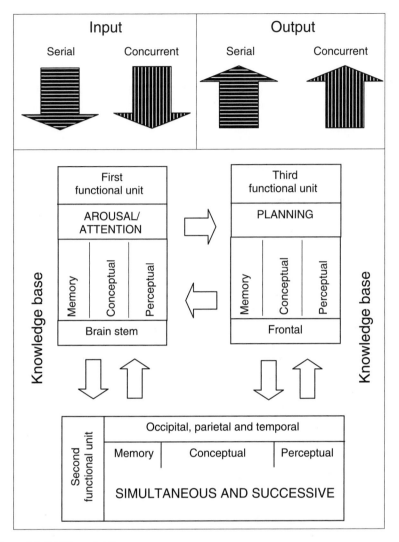

Figure 5.1 PASS model figure.

The final component of the PASS model is Output, or action and behavior. Simply by changing the output demand, a change in performance may become evident. For instance, individuals who may be able to recognize but not recall items from memory can often recall them with a little prompting. In many cases, recognition improves retrieval where recall has failed. Therefore, how we measure output becomes important in measuring performance as an indicator of "intelligence".

Planning

Planning is a mental process by which the person determines, selects, and uses efficient solutions to problems:

- problem solving;
- formal mental representations;
- impulse control;
- retrieval of knowledge;
- imaging studies demonstrate selective activation of the prefrontal cortex during planning tasks.

Attention–arousal

Attention is a mental process by which the person selectively attends to some stimuli and ignores others:

- focused cognitive activity;
- selective attention;
- resistance to distraction;
- orienting response;
- vigilance;
- reticular formation as substrate;
- under/over arousal implicated in AD/HD.

Simultaneous processing

Simultaneous processing is a mental process by which the person integrates stimuli into groups:

- stimuli are seen as a whole or gestalt;
- each piece must be related to others;
- simultaneous processing is not necessarily nonverbal;
- associated with the integrity of the parieto-occipital-temporal regions.

Successive processing

Successive processing is a mental process by which the person integrates stimuli in a specific serial order:

- stimuli form a chain-like progression;
- successive processing is not necessarily verbal;
- associated with the fronto-temporal regions.

Input is of two kinds: external and internal. External input may be visual, auditory, etc. These can be presented all at once (concurrently) or one after another (sequentially). Internal inputs are images, thoughts, and their emotional contexts as accessed from knowledge base.

Output can be in two modes as well: concurrent and sequential. An individual may use three tools for output (Donald, 1991). These are:

- movements: fine and gross;
- mimetic: gestures, dance, music;
- language: oral, written, sign language.

Knowledge base comprises implicit (tacit, experiential, and spontaneous) knowledge, and explicit (formal, instructed) knowledge. The sources of know-ledge are integrated from at least three kinds of stores, which are long-term memory, books and media, and the computer.

The vexing question of "Who knows?" or "Is there a homunculus?" in the brain–mind has not been answered yet.

I have presented a quick view of the PASS theory. Its operationalization in the tests of the Das Naglieri Cognitive Assessment System or CAS (Naglieri & Das, 1997) is briefly illustrated below. The CAS has tests that pre-eminently measure one or the other of the four PASS processes. The tests yield a psychometric profile as a result of assessment. An example of test protocol is given in Figure 5.2.

	CAS Subtests	Raw Scores	Scaled Scores (Appendix A)			
Record Form	Matching Numbers	4	6			
	Planned Codes	25	8			
	Planned Connections	412	6			
	Nonverbal Matrices	13		10		
	Verbal-Spatial Relations	14		9		
Recording of raw scores and calculation of standard scores	Figure Memory	9		10		
	Expressive Attention	28			9	
	Number Detection	34			10	
	Receptive Attention	37			12	
	Word Series	10				10
	Sentence Repetition	8				11
	Speech Rate/ Sentence Questions	9				10
	Sum of Subtest Scaled Scores		20	29	31	31	111
			PLAN	SIM	ATT	SUC	FS
	PASS Scale Standard Scores		79	98	102	102	93

Figure 5.2 Record form.

This protocol shows that the child's planning is 79 (100 is the mean, as in IQ tests), which is the lowest here. The child's strength is equal in simultaneous processing, attention, and successive processing. The child was referred to us for poor school achievement in spite of a healthy-looking score in three out of the four processes. The process that was pulling the child down in school was planning. He was disorganized, couldn't manage time, could not reflect and think through a plan, did not evaluate feedbacks well, and all of these contributed to his poor achievement (see Naglieri, 1999, for clinical interpretations).

Planning processes are required when an individual makes decisions such as how to solve a problem, carry out an activity, or compose a narrative. It involves goal setting and within it, anticipating and monitoring feedback. Planning comprises the programming, regulation, and verification of behavior (Luria, 1966). An individual adopts a set of decisions and strategies and modifies these while solving a problem and planning. Planning processes are closely connected with attention, on the one hand, and with simultaneous and successive processing, on the other. In assessing an individual's information processes, planning processes are needed when a test requires that the individual make decisions about how to solve a problem, execute an approach, activate attentional, simultaneous, and successive processes, monitor the effectiveness of the approach, and modify the approach as needed. Instead of being a hierarchical and linear process, planning is often nonlinear and revisionary in nature, and the formation and execution of a plan can occur simultaneously (Das, Kar, & Parrila, 1996).

The planning tasks in the CAS require strategies, which are coded from the examiner's observations and verbalizations of the individual child. In the case of the particular child whose planning score is low it would be easy to guess why his school achievement was poor.

The PASS theory is not universally accepted as a substitute for intelligence. However, whenever practitioners have used the tests that stem from the PASS theory, the CAS (Naglieri & Das, 1997), they have appreciated it, if for nothing else than that they can talk about what they find in testing a child who was referred to them. They can talk about the child's cognitive processes, not only to the teachers but also to the parents and concerned guardians. This is not possible when they try to explain, for example, WISC.

In concluding the above discussion, I present the following statements that summarize the rules of intelligence:

- intelligence is not IQ but cognitive processes;
- intelligence changes due to learning and cultural demands – it is not immutable or fixed;
- modules in the mind likely exist for the explicit purpose of categorizing and otherwise dealing with information processing of a certain kind;
- some aspects of intelligence are domain general while some other aspects are domain specific.

Tools of intelligence

Process-based measures such as CAS are useful tools to understand and apply cognitive processes to important topics such as reading (Das, 2000; Das, Naglieri, & Kirby, 1994), but I would like to draw your attention to two other tools. They are interrelated and quite closely associated not only with cognition but also with neuropsychology. I refer here first to mental chronometry (Posner & Rueda, 2002). For those of you who might not have had a very clear idea of what mental chronometry is, here is a quotation from Posner:

> It is a field that seeks to measure the time course of mental operations in the human nervous system. We draw upon diverse methods, such as neuroimaging, electrical recording, and reaction time to illustrate the use of chronometry in conjunction with anatomy and genetics to approach both normal individual differences and pathologies.
>
> (p. 968)

Obviously, mental chronometry does not refer mechanically to reaction time but uses reaction time as a tool to understand cognitive processes. It has nothing to do with speed of processing, a general and, I think, useless idea, because, as I will discuss in a later section, the concept of speed of processing, which has replaced the concept of *g*, is a surrogate, a blanket term. "Speed" stands for a host of specific cognitive strategies.

Here is one of the experiments from mental chronometry that goes against the view that the faster you are in processing speed, the more intelligent you are. I am using the conclusion from a recent experiment on event-related potentials, an offshoot of EEG measurement, and the P300 (Houlihan, Stelmack, & Campbell, 1998). Houlihan et al. hypothesized that if high-IQ individuals normally process information faster than lower-IQ individuals, then P300 latency will be faster for the high-IQ group, thus providing a measure that would directly evaluate the relation between speed of processing and intelligence. However, contrary to predictions, higher-IQ participants had longer latency than lower-ability participants. The longer latency for higher-ability participants, I think, may be due to the adoption of a response strategy: that is, they might be devoting more time to stimulus encoding and planning of future events. These strategies for encoding and planning are signs of real intelligence. The intelligent person is not indiscriminately fast, preferring to be slow and reflective when giving a response. I think a quest for "speed" of neural conduction as a biological index of intelligence is unproductive; the track record shows the correlation between IQ and nervous conduction speed to be near zero (Wahlsten, 2002).

Besides such amazing techniques as PET scan and functional MRI (fMRI), and sophisticated measures of event-related potential, which have become interesting toys in the hands of cognitive psychologists, there is the old-fashioned componential analysis of behavior.

Componential analysis of naming speed

In spite of Jensen's claim that speed of processing is a basic component of intelligence, several studies have raised doubt about such a connection (Das, 2004). The vast literature on speed is mainly divided into two points of view: (1) speed represents cognitive strategies that are specific to specific tasks; and, in contrast, (2) speed is a general ability, a generic explanation for intelligence. What I suggest is that speed is not a good measure of IQ unless we understand the cognitive processing that is measured by speed. This domain-specific view has two advantages: it defines processing in terms of certain kinds of tasks, and goes a step further as it is informative in regard to the specific cognitive processes involved in performing those tasks. How might a domain-specific view of speed help in understanding naming speed, a correlate of reading?

I turn now to componential analyses of naming speed or naming time. It is a measure frequently used in relation to reading speed. Naming time for words can be considered as a composite of phonological coding time, articulatory programming of speech, and the reaction time for speech activation (McRae, Jared, & Seidenberg, 1990). A slow naming time is a distinguishing mark of the slow, though phonologically accurate, reader. These readers can be distinguished from those who are slow in naming as well as deficient in phonological coding. The slow-but-accurate readers present a viable group of dyslexics who compel us to understand the processes behind naming time. Although there are minor differences in how we present naming-time tasks, the overwhelming evidence in favor of its positive relationship with reading ability cannot be ignored. Denckla and Rudel (1976, pp. 471–479) clearly showed that rapid automatized naming, or RAN, can differentiate between dyslexics and nondyslexics. The RAN paper is also important in relation to IQ and speed. The authors pointed out quite clearly that those who were slow in naming colors were not necessarily less intelligent than those who were fast. Speed of naming, they observed, varies with the type of material to be named, even among those with dyslexia; many dyslexic children were slow in color naming time but not in their naming time for pictures and objects. Thus, in their very early work, Denckla and Rudel made two points relevant to the question of whether speed equates with general intelligence: that speed of naming is not uniform across stimulus materials, there being little correlation between color naming and object naming time for some of their samples; and that IQ had nothing to do with it because many dyslexics in fact had a higher IQ and slower naming time compared to nondyslexics.

In a typical rapid naming time task, 40 or 50 randomly sequenced colors, pictures, numbers, or letters appear on a page in rows of 8 or 10 items. Note that the typical experiment that connects naming time to serial recall and to reading competence (and dyslexia) uses rapid naming, not confrontational reading of a picture, object, or color-patch. Is a theoretical model needed, then, to explain the connection? I think it is, as I reason below, tracing the research through the past 25 years to contemporary reports of experiments (Baddeley, 1981; Das, Mok, & Mishra, 1993; Das & Siu, 1989).

Let me delve a little deeper into understanding naming time itself and its connection to successive processing. There is now ample evidence to show that successive processing difficulty is generally associated with reading difficulties in specifically reading disabled children rather than in "garden variety" poor readers. Successive processing is clearly measured through serial word recall, one of the tests in the Cognitive Assessment System, and it is also involved in naming time. Typically naming time procedure requires: (1) first a search for the name of the color, object, or picture in the semantic lexicon, which is a conceptual system related to comprehension; and, then, (2) a name for the color, object, or picture may be found. From that point onwards reading a written word quickly, which is a form of naming time, and the phonological coding of the name found from the conceptual system, share essentially common pathways. Both then lead to assembling pronunciation, and articulation of the word whose pronunciation has been assembled. An articulation is essential when oral reading is required.

However, this simple procedure for naming time includes (1) speed of lexical access in naming, which is confounded with (2) the serial repetition of the colors, objects, pictures, or words presented in a matrix (8×5 for 40 stimuli) typical of a naming-time task. Although both articulation of the names and reading off the names on a sheet of paper are successive processing activities, there might not be individual differences in articulation but in lexical access to the phonological or the semantic store for the stimulus item.

Articulation itself is pre-eminently tested by the CAS test Speech Rate. In this test, three given words are repeated over and over again ten times, such as *egg bus leaf, egg bus leaf, egg bus leaf,* and so on. The dyslexics are usually slower in speech rate. However, among the dyslexics it should be possible to distinguish between those who are slow in naming time but not in speech rate, that is, slow in articulation speed but not in the processes preceding the stage of articulation. Remember now that both are measures of speed but the processes that precede articulation comprise the time for lexical access or sublexical phonological coding and, therefore, can be separated from articulation time.

Most dyslexics have a relatively short memory span (Torgesen, 1982). Furthermore, individual differences in memory span can be theoretically related to articulation rate (Baddeley, 1981; Hulme, Thomson, Muir, & Lawrence, 1984). Memory span is roughly equivalent to the number of words an individual can read in 2 seconds irrespective of age. The 2 second time determines the efficiency of rehearsal in short-term memory tasks for measuring memory span.

I propose that short-term memory performance that requires rehearsal includes a set of processing operations separate from naming time, although these are interdependent processes that together influence reading. I discuss below how articulation, a core process that determines naming speed, may take the same time for dyslexic or poor readers and normal readers, but the other processes involved in naming time distinguish between the slow vs. normal readers.

A very recent study separated the processes involved in naming a series of colors, these have been illustrated in Figure 5.3 (Georgiou & Parrila, 2004).

Notice that in the diagram two major components are shown: articulation (the wavy marks) and pause time. In this case a child is naming colors *red, yellow, green, blue*. The pauses between the color naming and the articulation of the color name itself are distinctly visible in the diagram. Recent research has shown that the major difference between dyslexic and nondyslexic readers exists in the pauses, rather than in the articulation time. In other words the dyslexic reader is not slow in articulation, but has longer pauses.

How can we explain pauses in terms of cognitive processes? The first component of the pause is disengagement of attention. The child has to give up what he has just said and get ready to say the name of the next color. Then the remainder of the gap time could be broadly named *encoding*, which ends after finding a name for the next color, assembling the pronunciation for the color name, and formation of a motor program for articulation. Encoding simplistically is suggested to involve all three different processes, and each one could contribute to the gap time. Remember also that typically 5 color patches, objects, pictures, or letters to be repeated in a naming-time test number about 40 or 50. It is suggested that while repeating the stimuli over and over again, some amount of reactive inhibition may build up due to the continuous demand on fast reading. Reactive inhibition is expected to arise during massed practice (Eysenck, 1967). As a consequence of accumulation of reactive inhibition, involuntary rest pauses, a temporary condition of pauses, must occur for dissipation of reactive inhibition. Therefore, perhaps towards the middle of the naming-time task, reactive inhibition would be sufficiently strong to depress the gap time; I am not sure if it would also depress the articulation time. Then the child automatically takes an involuntary rest pause, becomes refreshed when the reactive inhibition has been dissipated, and comes back rejuvenated to resume a faster naming speed. I could go on and try to make more speculative statements in regard to the various processes that contribute to the gap.

Instead, here is an experiment by Georgiou and Parrila (2004) on kindergarten children who were observed longitudinally(Figure 5.4).

The children were first tested in kindergarten, again in the fall term of grade 1, and last in the spring term of grade 1, separated by about 6 months. The top line shows the pause time and the bottom line shows the articulation time. As the children get older and get into school at grade 1, we see that the articulation time hardly changes. The pause time, however, is the longest in kindergarten, has decreased substantially, by about 35%, 6 months later, and then by springtime it has decreased further, though not so spectacularly. The child is perhaps now able to encode faster, to disengage attention more

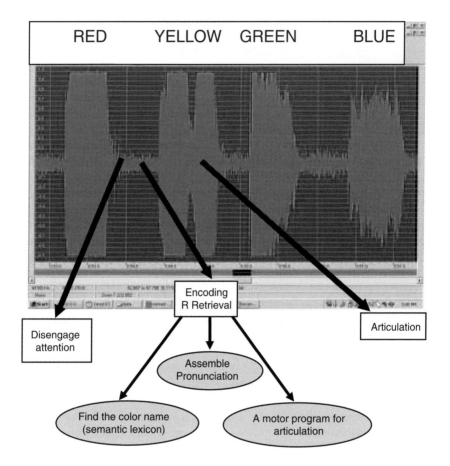

Reaction inhibition slows down all processes

Figure 5.3 Explaining the gap. *Note*: This diagram, reproduced from Georgiou's MEd thesis (Georgiou & Parrila, 2004), may help to explain the processes leading to the abandonment of a stimulus item that has been responded to and the shift to the next item in a series of items to be named. The speed with which items are identified had been suggested as a major contributor to individual differences in memory span (Case, Kurland, & Goldberg, 1982; Dempster, 1981). But the diagram goes a step further in explaining the sequence of shift in attention and then encoding, the steps within it and finally retrieval of the semantic label (Encoding R). Encoding is defined as "the initial stage during which information arrives in the brain following sensory analysis or via imagination and input and comprehension of this information occurs . . . as well as to the transformation of the experience into memory" (Paller, 2004, p. 50). I have added the essential components within encoding as well as the component of reactive inhibition that can depress the speed of all processes, represented by the gap when the task demands repetitive responses. Retrieval from semantic lexicon (R) must precede articulation.

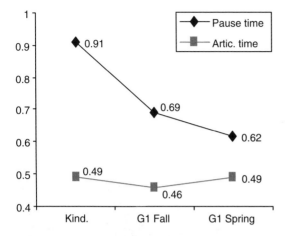

Figure 5.4 Pause time/articulation time graph. *Note*: Pause time decreases with children's development, but articulation speed does not. The speed of articulation is unrelated to pause time.

efficiently, and to prepare for articulation by assembling a pronunciation that has become easier as he/she has grown older.

This is a very interesting graph showing two things: that speed of articulation is not the critical variable in individual differences between children, be they poor readers or good readers. At least, it is not developmentally sensitive, but the pause time does decrease with development. This is a very simple way of getting back to componential analysis of speed. It emphasizes the fact that speed is not a blanket term – that it is not so domain-general, for even within the same task, the speed of articulation is unrelated to the pause time. A general speed of processing, like its predecessor, IQ, is noninformative.

Conclusion

I will complete this chapter with one last quotation, from my own writing (Das, 2004). We think about intelligence in terms of Galton and *g*, and many intelligent researchers on intelligence who must pride themselves on having very high intelligence still seek the true IQ of a child. But then there is time to pause and reflect.

The world has changed since Galton suggested a general intelligence based on inheritance, as people now know that the vast majority of the world's children lack schooling and health care and have disrupted childhoods due to wars and other disasters. We see this on our television screen every day; in Sudan, in Rwanda, in Palestine, and so on and so forth. Disrupted childhood due to wars, poverty, and other man-made disasters, much of which can be prevented by privileged nations. This is my belief. The question is this: should science still look for the true score in intelligence testing, or promote the human values of compassion and lack of greed for ensuring an equitable distribution of intelligence?

(p. 20)

References

Baddeley, A. D. (1981). Cognitive psychology and psychometric theory. In M. P. Friedman, J. P. Das, & N. O'Connor (Eds.), *Intelligence and learning*. New York: Plenum.

Case, R., Kurland, D. M., & Goldberg, J. (1982). Operational efficiency and the growth of short-term memory span. *Journal of Experimental Child Psychology, 33*, 386–404.

Ceci, S. J. (2003). Cast in six ponds and you'll reel in something: Looking back on 25 years of research. *American Psychologist, 58*, 855–864.

Darlington, C. D. (1962). *Introduction to F. Galton, hereditary genius*. London: William Collins.

Das, J. P. (2000). *Reading difficulties and dyslexia* (Rev. ed.). Deal, NJ: Sarka Educational Resources.

Das, J. P. (2004). Theories of intelligence: Issues and applications. In G. Goldstein & S. R. Beers (Eds.), *Comprehensive handbook of psychological assessment* (Vol. 1). New York: Wiley.

Das, J. P., & Dash, U. N. (1983). Hierarchical factor solution of coding and planning process. Any new insights? *Intelligence, 7*, 27–37.

Das, J. P., Kar, B. C., & Parrila, R. K. (1996). *Cognitive planning*. New Delhi, India: Sage Publications.

Das, J. P., Kirby, J. R., & Jarman, R. F. (1975). Simultaneous and successive synthesis: An alternative model. *Psychological Bulletin, 82*, 87–103.

Das, J. P., Kirby, J. R., & Jarman, R. F. (1979). *Simultaneous and successive cognitive processes*. New York: Academic Press.

Das, J. P., Mok, M., & Mishra, R. K. (1993). The role of speech processes and memory in reading disability. *The Journal of General Psychology, 12*(2), 131–146.

Das, J. P., & Naglieri, J. A. (2001). The Das–Naglieri Cognitive Assessment System in theory and practice. In J. J. W. Andrews, D. H. Saklofske, & H. L. Janzen (Eds.), *Handbook of psychoeducational assessment: Ability, achievement, and behavior in children* (pp. 34–64). San Diego, CA: Academic Press.

Das, J. P., Naglieri, J. A., & Kirby, J. R. (1994). *Assessment of cognitive processes*. Needham Heights, MA: Allyn & Bacon. (In Chinese: Dongdaixinkukexue East China Normal University, 1999)

Das, J. P., & Siu, I. (1989). Good and poor-readers' word naming time, memory span, and story recall. *Journal of Experimental Education, 57*(2), 101–114.

Dempster, F. M. (1981). Memory span: Sources of individual and developmental differences. *Psychological Bulletin, 89*(1), 63–100.

Denckla, M. B., & Rudel, R. G. (1976). Rapid automatized naming: Dyslexia differentiated from other learning disabilities. *Neuropsychologia, 14*, 471–479.

Donald, M. (1991). *Origins of the modern mind: Three stages in the evolution of culture and cognition*. Cambridge, MA: Harvard University Press.

Eysenck, H. J. (1967). *The biological basis of personality*. Springfield, IL: Thomas.

Flynn, J. R. (2003). Movies about intelligence: The limitations of *g*. *Current Directions in Psychological Science, 12*(3), 95.

Frith, C. (1997). Linking brain and behavior. In R. S. J. Frackowiack, K. J. Friston, R. J. Dolan, & J. C. Mazziotta (Eds.), *Human brain function* (pp. 3–23). San Diego, CA: Academic Press.

Georgiou, G., & Parrila, R. (2004). *RAN components and reading acquisition*. Paper presented to SSSR, Amsterdam, 28 June 2004.

Gould, S. (1981). *The mismeasure of man*. New York: Norton.

Houlihan, M., Stelmack, R., & Campbell, K. (1998). Intelligence and the effects of perceptual processing demands, task difficulty and processing speed on P300, reaction time and movement time. *Intelligence, 26*, 9–25.

Hulme, C., Thomson, N., Muir, C., & Lawrence, A. (1984). Speech rate and the development of short-term memory span: *Journal of Experimental Child Psychology, 38*, 241–253.

Luria, A. R. (1966). *Higher cortical functions in man*. New York: Basic Books

McRae, K., Jared, D., & Seidenberg, D. (1990). On the roles of frequency and lexical access in word naming. *Journal of memory and language, 29*, 43–65.

Naglieri, J. A. (1999). *Essentials of CAS assessment*. New York: Wiley.

Naglieri, J. A., & Das, J. P. (1997). Intelligence revised. In R. Dillon (Ed.), *Handbook on testing* (pp. 136–163). Westport, CT: Greenwood Press.

Nisbett, R. E. (2003). *The geography of thought*. New York: The Free Press.

Paller, K. A. (2004). Electrical signals of memory and the awareness of remembering. *Current Directions in Psychological Science, 13*, 49–55.

Posner, M. I., & Rueda, M. R. (2002). Mental chronometry in the study of individual and group differences. *Journal of Clinical Experimental Neuropsychology, 24*(7), 968–976.

Richardson, K. (1986). Theory? Or tools for social selection? *Behavioral and Brain Sciences, 93*, 579–581.

Torgesen, J. (1982). The use of rationally defined subgroups in research on learning disabilities. In J. P. Das, R. Mulcahy, & R. E. Walls (Eds.), *Theory and research in learning disabilities*. New York: Plenum.

Tyler, L. (1986). Back to Spearman? *Journal of Vocational Behavior, 29*, 445–450.

Vygotsky, L. S. (1986). *Thought and language* (A. Kozulin, Ed. and Trans.). Cambridge, MA: MIT Press.

Wahlsten, D. (2002). The theory of biological intelligence: History and a critical appraisal. In R. J. Sternberg & E. L. Grigorenko (Eds.), *The general factor of intelligence: How general is it?* (pp. 245–280). Mahwah, NJ: Lawrence Erlbaum Associates, Inc.

6   A combined emic–etic approach to cross-cultural personality test development: The case of the CPAI

Fanny M. Cheung

Interest in cross-cultural personality studies has a long history. Marsella, Dubanoski, Hamada, and Morse (2000) reviewed the historical background of anthropological and psychological studies of personality across cultures. The early studies in culture and personality may be dated to the 1930s when cultural anthropologists and psychoanalysts described the "basic personality type" found in different cultures. During World War II, "national character" studies in countries including China, Germany, Japan, Romania, Russia, and Thailand became part of the allied war effort to delineate national personality structures.

Psychological approaches to cross-cultural personality studies focus on individual differences and measurement, instead of typical or modal personality, which have been criticized as stereotypical. Kaplan's (1961) edited volume on cross-cultural personality, *Studying Personality Cross-culturally*, was one of the earliest books on methodology in cross-cultural personality measurement. The classic volume on *Cross-cultural Research Methods* by Brislin, Lonner, and Thorndike published in 1973 has since become the standard reference for cross-cultural research in psychology. Interest in cross-cultural comparisons of personality traits have been revived in the 1990s by the studies of McCrae and Costa (1996, 1997) and their associates, who argued for the universality of the Five Factor Model across cultures.

With the revived interest in personality measurement across cultures, cross-cultural psychologists have come forward with warnings on the methodological problems that may be neglected in cross-cultural studies of personality. Marsella and Leong (1995) highlighted two major errors in validity due to ethnocentrism: The "error of omission" refers to the failure to conduct cross-cultural comparisons, resulting in generalizations about human behavior based on a culturally selective or biased sample. The "error of commission" refers to the application of concepts and measures based on one culture to another culture without consideration of their relevance or equivalence for the groups under study. In cross-cultural studies of personality, it is very common to find Western personality constructs and assessment tools applied directly to another cultural group under the assumption that they are valid for all cultures.

The challenge to the ethnocentrism of Western psychology has resulted in the development of indigenous psychology movements in different countries. Psychologists in Asian countries have identified indigenous concepts that are relevant to the study of personality in their own countries, such as the Chinese concepts of harmony and face, the Japanese concept of *amae* (sweet indulgence), the Korean concept of *chong* (affection), and the Indian concept of the selfless self (Cheung, 2004; Cheung, Cheung, Wada, & Zhang, 2003). Despite the long history of indigenous psychology movements in Asia, there are few personality measures developed to cover the broad range of personality dimensions found in Western personality inventories. Most Asian psychologists have translated and adopted personality scales developed in the West, taking for granted that the personality constructs measured in these scales are universally applicable.

Berry (1969, 1989) distinguished two basic approaches in cross-cultural psychology. The *etic* approach assumes methodologies and concepts developed in one culture to be universally applicable in other cultures On the other hand, the *emic* approach uses locally developed methodologies and concepts, which emphasize the examination of a phenomenon from the perspectives of the local culture and its members. The terms "etic" and "emic" were originally proposed by Pike (1967) to understand two different approaches to language and culture. According to Pike, both the etic and the emic approaches have their values. For example, the etic approach may provide a broad and unified framework to understand similarities and differences of a phenomenon across different cultures. The emic approach, on the other hand, may provide a perspective highly relevant to members of a culture in terms of attitudes and personality. Taken together, these two approaches provides a "tri-dimensional understanding" of the same phenomenon, viewing the same phenomenon from the etic "lens" and the emic "lens" (Pike, 1967, p. 41).

Berry (1969, 1989) further described the *imposed etic* approach, in which foreign instruments or concepts are applied to another culture, and they are assumed to be valid in comparing the same phenomenon between the two cultures. Stanley Sue (1983) challenged the "cultural imperialism" in the use of these "imposed" etic measures. However, Berry (1969, 1989) argued that the imposed etic approach may serve as the starting point for the development of emic theories and instruments in a culture. The emic theories in the local culture can then be compared to the emic theories in the culture of origin of the imported theories and instruments. The parts universal to these cultures can be then viewed as *derived etic*, universal only for the sets of cultures being compared. The parts unique to each culture can be viewed as truly emic concepts for that culture.

On the theoretical level, the etic and emic approaches can be viewed as complementary; in reality psychologists usually take either the etic approach or the emic approach, as if the universal and culture-specific personality characteristics are distinct dimensions competing for truism. In the context of personality psychology, some cross-cultural psychologists attempted to explain the two approaches as different ways to "cut the social perceptual world" (Yik & Bond, 1993). Yang and Bond (1990) acknowledged that both etic and emic approaches might produce true realities, even though they represent different theories of the local reality. Marsella et al. (2000) provided a point of convergence by concluding that "it may well be that there are a limited number of biologically or socially determined behavior dimensions . . . but cultural variations may shape (1) their display patterns (2) situations in which they are elicited (3) the interpersonal responses to them (4) their utility or value in behavioral description, and (5) the meanings they are assigned" (p. 60).

Van de Vijver and Leung (1997) proposed the adoption of a convergence approach in cross-cultural psychology. They considered indigenously derived measures to be maximally relevant for particular cultures. However, if culturally diverse instruments yield similar results, these results are likely to be universal. In the combined emic–etic approach, the measurement of culture-specific personality characteristics would provide within-culture relevance, whereas the measurement of universal personality characteristics would allow cross-cultural comparisons of similar constructs. Given the predominance of Western personality research, existing models of personality may be considered imposed etics, i.e., the personality characteristics found in Western models of personality are presumed to be universal and relevant in other cultures. In this sense, emic personality characteristics derived from Western cultures may become imposed etics in another culture.

Development of the Chinese Personality Assessment Inventory

The Chinese Personality Assessment Inventory (CPAI) was developed with the intent of providing a comprehensive personality inventory suited to the local needs while retaining the psychometric standards of established assessment measures. A combined emic–etic approach was adopted to include both indigenous and universal personality constructs that would be relevant to describing person characteristics and predicting behaviors in the Chinese cultural context. Personality constructs were derived from a review of contemporary Chinese literature as well as research on Chinese personality, and empirical surveys of everyday-life experiences. A detailed description of the development of the CPAI is found in Cheung, Leung, Fan, Song, Zhang, and Zhang (1996). Scale construction was based on the psychometric properties of items and scales using large-scale samples. The original CPAI was standardized using representative norms from different regions of China and Hong Kong.

The CPAI consisted of 22 normal personality scales, 12 clinical scales and 3 validity scales. Four factors were extracted from the normal personality scales: Dependability, Interpersonal Relatedness, Social Potency, and Individualism. To examine how the CPAI differed from existing personality measures in the West, the CPAI factors were compared to the Five Factor Model. In a joint factor analysis between the NEO-PI-R and the CPAI (Cheung et al., 2001), it was found that three of the CPAI factors converged with four of the Big Five factors. However, none of the NEO-PI-R facets loaded on the CPAI Interpersonal Relatedness factor. The Interpersonal Relatedness factor may be considered an indigenous factor (Table 6.1). In other cross-cultural samples in which the CPAI was jointly factor analyzed with the NEO-FFI, similar results were obtained (Cheung, Cheung, Leung, Ward, & Leong, 2003). The Interpersonal Relatedness factor was distinct from the Big Five factors even in non-Chinese samples.

On the other hand, none of the CPAI scales loaded on the Openness factor of the NEO-PI-R. In the indigenously derived scales of the CPAI, none of the scales could be aligned along the structure of the Openness factor in the Five Factor Model. Thus, the Big Five Openness factor may be considered an etic factor imposed upon the Chinese culture.

How can we account for the absence of the Openness factor in the CPAI? One of the possible explanations is the irrelevance of Openness as defined by the Five Factor Model for person descriptions in the Chinese culture. However, in studies using the NEO-PI-R or NEO-FFI with Chinese samples, the Openness factor was consistently extracted although its psychometric properties tend to be weaker than the other Big Five factors. It may be argued that even if the Openness factor was identified in these studies, it may still be an imposed etic construct with questionable relevance to the Chinese context.

Alternatively, there is the possibility that the absence of Openness from the CPAI may be due to the oversight of the researchers who have excluded intellect-related constructs from the initial list of indigenously derived personality constructs. The Openness factor has previously been interpreted as "Intellect" (Goldberg, 1993). The exclusion of person descriptions such as "clever" and "intelligent" in the construct selection phase of the CPAI development may have limited the extraction of an openness dimension. Despite its absence from the original CPAI when it was first developed in the early 1990s, the rapid changes in globalization and information technology (IT) may warrant a re-examination of the Openness construct in Chinese culture in the new millennium.

CPAI-2

The original CPAI was revised in 2000 to accommodate several changes: development of a new set of openness scales for normal personality assessment, and the lengthening of the clinical scales to increase their validity in clinical assessment. Here, I will focus on the changes in the normal personality scales, especially the development of openness scales for the CPAI-2.

Table 6.1 Joint factor analysis between the NEO-PI-R and the CPAI (Cheung et al., 2001)

Factor	NEO-PI-R facets	CPAI scales
Neuroticism (16.0%)	N1 Anxiety N3 Depression N6 Vulnerability N4 Self-consciousness O5 Ideas[-]	Adventurousness[-] Inferiority vs. Self-acceptance External vs. Internal Locus of Control Leadership[-] Emotionality
Conscientiousness (9.7%)	C5 Self-discipline C6 Deliberation C2 Order C4 Achievement Striving C3 Dutifulness N5 Impulsiveness[-] C1 Competence	Responsibility Meticulousness Practical Mindedness
Agreeableness (9.5%)	A4 Compliance A2 Straightforwardness A1 Trust N2 Angry Hostility A3 Altruism	Graciousness vs. Meanness Veraciousness vs. Slickness Family Orientation
Extraversion (7.0%)	E2 Gregariousness E1 Warmth E4 Activity E3 Assertiveness E6 Positive Emotions	Introversion vs. Extraversion[-] Self vs. Social Orientation[-]
Interpersonal Relatedness (4.2%)		Optimism vs. Pessimism Renqing (Relationship Orientation) Flexibility[-] Defensiveness (*Ah Q* Mentality) Harmony Face Logical vs. Affective Orientation
Openness (3.5%)	O3 Feelings O2 Aesthetics O1 Fantasy A6 Tender-mindedness	

Note: Facets and scales are organized by their primary factor loadings. Figures in parentheses are the variance explained by the factors. [-]The facet or scale loaded negatively on the factor.

Development of openness scales for CPAI-2

As in the development of the original CPAI, a combined emic–etic approach was adopted to derive the new set of openness scales. Research on openness-related concepts in Chinese and Western cultures was reviewed. We conducted informal interviews and focus group discussions with diverse groups of participants to generate the lexicons that are associated with openness in the Chinese culture. We collected descriptions of people who were considered to be open using different Chinese terms, including *kaifeng, kaitong,* and *kaiming,* which were terms that respondents in the preliminary interviews associated with the concept of openness. We asked the focus-group participants to describe the traits, thoughts, feelings and behaviors of these people, and to illustrate these with behavioral examples in daily life.

We extracted 18 constructs from the focus groups and literature review, and generated close to 300 items for the preliminary study. Based on item analyses using large samples, we finalized six openness-related scales for the re-standardization study: Novelty, Diversity, Divergent Thinking, Aesthetics, Interpersonal Tolerance, and Social Sensitivity. The revised CPAI-2 consisted of 28 personality scales, 12 clinical scales and 3 validity scales. It was re-standardized in 2001, using the same representative sampling methods in different regions of Mainland China and Hong Kong. The valid normative sample consisted of 1911 adults ranging in age from 18 to 70.

Factor structure of CPAI-2

Although we expected that the addition of the six openness-related scales would result in a fifth factor among the normal personality scales of the CPAI-2, we only extracted the four factors that were most interpretable. The four factors were Social Potency, Dependability, Accommodation, and Interpersonal Relatedness, similar to the factor structure of the original CPAI. There was no separate factor for openness. Four of the openness scales, Novelty, Diversity, Divergent Thinking, and Aesthetics, loaded with Leadership, Extraversion, Logical Orientation, and Enterprise to form an expanded Social Potency factor. Interpersonal Tolerance loaded on the Accommodation factor, and Social Sensitivity loaded on the Interpersonal Relatedness factor, together with Harmony, Renqing (relationship orientation), Traditionalism and Discipline (Table 6.2).

Joint factor analysis between the CPAI-2 and NEO-FFI

If there is no separate Openness factor on the CPAI-2, how would the CPAI-2 scales load on the Big Five Openness factor?

In a study involving 962 college students from Mainland China, Hong Kong and Taiwan, the CPAI-2 scales and the NEO-FFI factors were submitted to a joint factor analysis. A six-factor solution was most interpretable.

Table 6.2 Four-factor solution of the CPAI-2

Factor	CPAI scales
Social Potency (16.7%)	Novelty[a]
	Diversity[a]
	Divergent Thinking[a]
	Leadership
	Logical vs. Affective Orientation
	Aesthetics[a]
	Extraversion vs. Introversion
	Enterprise
Dependability (16.5%)	Responsibility
	Emotionality[(-)]
	Inferiority vs. Self-acceptance[(-)]
	Practical Mindedness
	Optimism vs. Pessimism
	Meticulousness
	Face[(-)]
	Internal vs. External Locus of Control
	Family Orientation
Accommodation (12.2%)	Defensiveness (*Ah Q* Mentality)[(-)]
	Graciousness vs. Meanness
	Interpersonal Tolerance[a]
	Self vs. Social Orientation[(-)]
	Veraciousness vs. Slickness
Interpersonal Relatedness (10.0%)	Renqing (Relationship Orientation)
	Social Sensitivity[a]
	Discipline
	Harmony
	Thrift vs. Extravagance
	Traditionalism vs. Modernity

Note: Scales are organized by their primary factor loadings. Figures in parentheses are the variance explained by the factors. [(-)]The scale loaded negatively on the factor; [a]Openness-related scales.

With the addition of the six openness scales in CPAI-2, the Big Five Openness factor is now loaded by five of the scales from the Social Potency factor. The Social Sensitivity scale from the CPAI-2 Interpersonal Relatedness factor loads on the Big Five Extraversion factor, while the Interpersonal Tolerance scale of the CPAI-2 Accommodation factor loads on the Big Five Agreeableness factor. Four of the CPAI-2 Interpersonal Relatedness scales, Traditionalism, Thrift, Discipline, and Renqing (Relationship Orientation) remained as a distinct factor not loaded by any of the Big Five factors (Table 6.3).

Examination of the Interpersonal Relatedness factor and the Openness factor in different cultural contexts provides an illustration of the emic–etic approach to cross-cultural personality assessment.

From the joint factor analysis of a combined emic–etic measure and an etic

Table 6.3 Joint factor analysis of the NEO-FFI and the CPAI-2: The correspondence between the CPAI-2 scales and the factors extracted

Factor	*CPAI scales*
Neuroticism (13.1%)	Dependability Scales Optimism vs. Pessimism[-] Inferiority vs. Self-acceptance Face Emotionality Practical Mindedness[-] Internal vs. External Locus of Control[-] Social Potency Scale Enterprise[-]
Extraversion (9.9%)	Social Potency Scales Extraversion vs. Introversion Leadership Interpersonal Relatedness Scale Social Sensitivity[a]
Openness (9.9%)	Social Potency Scales Novelty[a] Diversity[a] Divergent Thinking[a] Aesthetics[a] Logical vs. Affective Orientation
Consciousness (9.0%)	Dependability Scales Responsibility Meticulousness
Agreeableness (8.9%)	Accommodation Scales Defensiveness (*Ah Q* Mentality)[-] Graciousness vs. Meanness Veraciousness vs. Slickness Self vs. Social Orientation[-] Harmony Interpersonal Tolerance[a]
Interpersonal Relatedness (5.0%)	Interpersonal Relatedness Scales Renqing (Relationship Orientation) Discipline Thrift vs. Extravagance Traditionalism vs. Modernity

Note: Scales are organized by their primary factor loadings. Figures in parentheses are the variance explained by the factors. [-]The scale loaded negatively on the factor; [a]Openness-related scales.

measure, we were able to show the overlap in content between the indigenously derived openness scales of the CPAI-2, such as Novelty, Diversity, Divergent Thinking, and Aesthetics, and the etic facets of openness from the Five Factor Model, such as Aesthetics, Actions and Ideas. By including these indigenous concepts of openness, the contents of the openness facets have become more relevant to the Chinese culture.

On the other hand, from the factor structure of the CPAI-2 itself, it appears that openness is not commonly used as a distinct dimension in the taxonomy of personality traits in the Chinese culture. All six indigenously derived openness-related scales were aligned with other personality characteristics. In particular, the alignment of some of the openness scales with the other CPAI-2 factors illustrates the social or interpersonal implications of these characteristics.

What is the implication from the discrepant findings in the conceptualization of openness in Chinese culture? Cheung and Leung (1998) argued that "imposing" an etic construct in understanding Chinese personality may find a structurally equivalent construct, but it cannot guarantee that this construct is culturally relevant. If openness was indeed an important and distinct factor in Chinese personality, the CPAI-2 Openness items should be as salient in connotation as the NEO-FFI Openness items. From an emic perspective, although openness-related aspects could be found, they did not emerge as a distinct Openness factor as has been found in Western culture.

CPAI-2 Cross-cultural factor congruence

In the past, we have used Western models of personality as the basis for defining salient personality dimensions. If personality research originated in Chinese culture, how would we have constructed the taxonomy of personality?

Using the 2001 Chinese normative sample as the target to extract the four CPAI-2 personality factors, we compared the factor congruence in a number of cross-cultural samples. The samples included college students from Mainland China, Taiwan, Korea, Japan, as well as Asian American and Caucasian American students from the USA. The total factor congruence coefficients for all the samples were above .94. Even for the Caucasian American students, the factor congruence for the Interpersonal Relatedness factor reached .90 (Table 6.4). The convergence of the factor structure led us to reconsider the

Table 6.4 Congruence coefficients in replication samples with respect to the normative structures

	PRC	Taiwan	Korea	Japan	US Asians	US Caucasians
Social Potency	.94	.97	.98	.98	.96	.97
Dependability	.91	.95	.96	.96	.96	.96
Accommodation	.96	.95	.92	.92	.93	.94
Interpersonal Relatedness	.97	.94	.92	.93	.95	.90
Total congruence	.94	.95	.95	.95	.95	.95

cross-cultural relevance of the CPAI-2, which was originally intended to be an indigenous personality measure for Chinese culture. We have since renamed the CPAI-2 as the Cross-cultural Personality Assessment Inventory.

Discussion

It is not our intention to impose the CPAI-2 factor structure on other cultures. Instead, cross-cultural research on the CPAI-2 poses a challenge for us to re-examine the controversy of etic vs. emic approaches. An important test of the usefulness of any personality factor lies in the ability of the factor to predict behaviors (Ashton & Lee, 2001). While there has been ample evidence of the usefulness of etic personality traits, the usefulness of the indigenously derived personality domains would illustrate the value of emic characteristics. Here, I cite a few examples of recent studies on the validity and utility of the CPAI-2.

With the CPAI-2 normative sample, we examined the pattern of relationship between the personality scales and various indices of life satisfaction, including those related to the job, physical, mental, and family domains. The emic personality scales, such as Family Orientation, Defensiveness, Face, and Harmony, demonstrated strong correlations with many of these domains of life satisfaction, comparable to those obtained by the etic scales, such as Extraversion, Emotionality, Inferiority, and Optimism (Table 6.5).

Similarly, indigenous personality scales are also useful in characterizing the personality profile of psychiatric patients in Mainland China and Hong

Table 6.5 Correlations between various indices of life satisfaction and selected CPAI-2 scales

CPAI-2 scales	Indices of life satisfaction				
	Job	*Physical*	*Mental*	*Family*	*Overall life satisfaction*
Etic scales					
Extraversion	.13***	.13***	.15***	.10***	.18***
Emotionality	−.20***	−.14***	−.28***	−.18***	−.29***
Inferiority	−.20***	−.18***	−.32***	−.21***	−.32***
Optimism	.20***	.23***	.36***	.22***	.36***
Diversity	.01	.09**	.01	.00	.06**
Interpersonal Tolerance	.11**	.08**	.16**	.10**	.15*
Emic scales					
Family Orientation	.21***	.15***	.26***	.37***	.37***
Defensiveness	−.15***	−.08***	−.15***	−.16***	−.20***
Face	−.10***	−.07**	−.18***	−.11***	−.17***
Harmony	.14***	.06**	.16***	.14***	.19***

Note: *Significant at $p < .05$; **Significant at $p < .01$; ***Significant at $p < .001$.

Kong. For example, profiles of patients with depression, neurotic disorders, and substance abuse showed that scores on Defensiveness, Face, Family Orientation, Self vs. Social Orientation, and Harmony characterize the interpersonal aspects of emotional disturbance in Chinese culture, beyond those related to Emotionality, Pessimism, and Inferiority (Figure 6.1). A combination of the etic and emic personality scales is also useful in characterizing the disturbance of Chinese patients during the manic and depressive phases of their bipolar disorders (Figure 6.2).

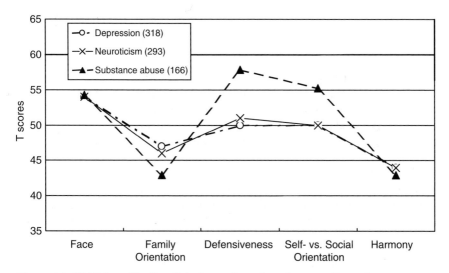

Figure 6.1 CPAI-2 profiles for clinical samples: selected personality scales.

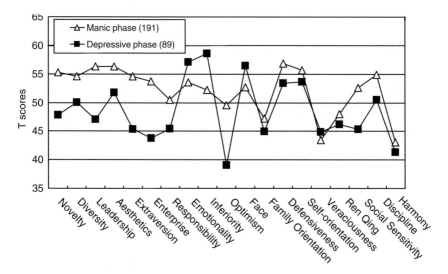

Figure 6.2 Bipolar disorders (manic vs. depressive) selected personality scales.

Other studies are underway to examine the behavioral correlates of the Openness and Interpersonal Relatedness factors across cultures. We are also using the CPAI-2 to predict job performance of employees and senior managers in Chinese work settings. We expect the indigenous CPAI-2 scales to be particularly relevant to the interpersonal domains of performance.

Conclusions

In the review on the debate over universality versus cultural specificity of personality structure, similar to positions held by Pike (1967) and Berry (1969, 1989), Marsella et al. (2000) concluded that there is no substantive proof to support conclusions regarding either approach. They proposed a better question to address the etic vs. emic approach: ". . . under what conditions . . . might people from different cultural contexts evidence similarities and differences in behavior . . .?" (p. 60).

In this address, I have attempted to show the usefulness of a combined emic–etic approach using the CPAI-2 as an illustration. The CPAI-2 provides a measure that is sensitive to the indigenous cultural context, allows cross-cultural comparison of the meaning of etic or imposed etic traits, and extends the interpretation of indigenous traits in a broader cultural context. The original intention of providing a culturally relevant personality measure for the Chinese context has led us to uncover many broader theoretical issues of cross-cultural personality assessment.

Acknowledgements

Correspondence concerning this article and permission for the use of the Cross-Cultural (Chinese) Personality Assessment Inventory-2 scales should be addressed to Fanny M. Cheung, Department of Psychology, The Chinese University of Hong Kong, Hong Kong (e-mail: fmcheung@cuhk.edu.hk).

The projects presented in this article were partially supported by the Hong Kong Government Research Grants Council Earmarked Grants CUHK4333/00H and CUHK 4326/01H, and CUHK Direct Grants #2020662 and #2020745. Collaborators on these projects include Lynn Alden, Shu-fai Cheung, Jeung Ryeul Cho, Kyum Koo Chun, Virginia Kwan, Kwok Leung, Frederick Leong, Shu Chun Yang, Kuang Huei Yeh, Sayuri Wada, and Zeqing Wang. I thank Shu-fai Cheung for his assistance in preparing this article.

References

Ashton, M. C., & Lee, K. (2001). A theoretical basis for the major dimensions of personality. *European Journal of Personality, 15*, 327–353.
Berry, J. W. (1969). On cross-cultural comparability. *International Journal of Psychology, 4*, 119–128.

Berry, J. W. (1989). Imposed etics–emics–derived etics: The operationalizations of a compelling idea. *International Journal of Psychology, 24*, 721–735.

Brislin, R. W., Lonner, W. J., & Thorndike, R. M. (1973). *Cross-cultural research methods.* New York: Wiley.

Cheung, F. M. (2004). Use of western and indigenously developed personality tests in Asia. *Applied Psychology: An International Review, 53*, 173–191.

Cheung, F. M., Cheung, S. F., Leung, K., Ward, C., & Leong, F. (2003). The English version of the Chinese Personality Assessment Inventory: Derived etics in a mirror position. *Journal of Cross-Cultural Psychology, 34*, 433–452.

Cheung, F. M., Cheung, S. F., Wada, S., & Zhang, J. X. (2003). Indigenous measures of personality assessment in Asian countries: A review. *Psychological Assessment, 15*, 280–289.

Cheung, F. M., & Leung, K. (1998). Indigenous personality measures: Chinese examples. *Journal of Cross-Cultural Psychology, 29*, 233–248.

Cheung, F. M., Leung, K., Fan, R., Song, W. Z., Zhang, J. X., & Zhang, J. P. (1996). Development of the Chinese Personality Assessment Inventory (CPAI). *Journal of Cross-Cultural Psychology, 27*, 181–199.

Cheung, F. M., Leung, K., Zhang, J. X., Sun, H. F., Gan, Y. G., Song, W. Z. et al. (2001). Indigenous Chinese personality constructs: Is the Five-Factor Model complete? *Journal of Cross-Cultural Psychology, 32*, 407–433.

Goldberg, L. (1993). The structure of phenotypic personality traits. *American Psychologist, 48*, 26–34.

Kaplan, B. (Ed.). (1961). *Studying personality cross-culturally.* New York: Harper & Row.

Marsella, A. J., Dubanoski, J., Hamada, W. C., & Morse, H. (2000). The measurement of personality across cultures: Historical, conceptual, and methodological issues and considerations. *American Behavioral Scientist, 44*, 41–62.

Marsella, A. J., & Leong, F. T. L. (1995). Cross-cultural issues in personality and career assessment. *Journal of Career Assessment, 3*, 202–218.

McCrae, R., & Costa, P. (1996). Toward a new generation of personality theories: Theoretical contexts for the Five-Factor Model. In J. Wiggins (Ed.), *The Five Factor Model of personality: Theoretical perspectives* (pp. 51–87). New York: Guilford.

McCrae, R., & Costa, P. (1997). Personality trait structure as a human universal. *American Psychologist, 52*, 509–516.

Pike, K. L. (1967). *Language in relation to a unified theory of the structure of human behavior.* The Hague, The Netherlands: Mouton.

Sue, S. (1983). Ethnic minority issues in psychology: A re-examination. *American Psychologist, 38*, 583–592.

Van de Vijver, F., & Leung, K. (1997). *Method and data analysis for cross-cultural research.* Thousand Oaks, CA: Sage.

Yang, K. S., & Bond, M. H. (1990). Exploring implicit personality theories with indigenous or imported constructs: The Chinese case. *Journal of Personality and Social Psychology, 58*, 1087–1095.

Yik, M. S., & Bond, M. H. (1993). Exploring the dimensions of Chinese person perception with indigenous and imported constructs: Creating a culturally balanced scale. *International Journal of Psychology, 28*, 75–95.

7 Chinese personality: Structure and measurement

Dengfeng Wang and Hong Cui

Presuppositions on exploring Chinese personality structure

The most significant progress in understanding personality was the emergence of "Big Five" personality structure model proposed by many researchers (e.g., Goldberg, 1990; John, 1990; Norman, 1963) according to the lexical hypothesis of personality structure (Allport & Odbert, 1936; John, Angleitner, & Ostendorf, 1988). Several scales and questionnaires measuring the Five Factor Model (FFM) have been established (Costa & McCrae, 1989; Goldberg, 1990; John, Donahue, & Kentle, 1991) and widely applied in Western and other culture backgrounds. For example, NEO PI-R, the most widely used questionnaire of FFM, had been modified by Chinese psychologists and applied in many researches (Yang et al., 1999).

However, FFM can only be applied where it comes from, that is, where the individuals use English as their native language because as Piedmont (1998) indicated, "different cultures may emphasize certain qualities over others, or may not exhibit various characteristics that are apparent in other cultural contexts. Thus, word-based models [of personality] may lack of generalizability" (p. 22). Some researchers have argued that cultural differences lead to differences in personality (e.g., Shweder, 1991) because people in different cultures face different survival pressures. However, others believed that both environment and heredity affect personality, considering personality to be the product of the interaction between environment and heredity. Psychologists should explore the common characteristics of personality across cultures; however, they should also acknowledge the uniqueness of different cultures (Maccoby, 2000; Triandis & Suh, 2002). Nevertheless, some researchers insisted that although cultures are different, human beings face similar survival pressures, hence they should have similar personality structures. For instance, McCrae and Costa (1997) maintained that the Big Five personality structure is applicable to all human beings.

How can we know about the similarities and/or differences of personality structure among different cultures? Berry (1969, 1989) proposed two strategies of cross-cultural studies, *imposed-etic* or *derived-etic*. The *imposed-etic* approach applied personality questionnaires that were developed in one culture (e.g., NEO PI-R in Western culture) to another culture (e.g., Chinese culture). The modified Western personality scales that are currently used in China (e.g., Chen, 1983; Gong, 1983; Li, 1981; Qian, Wu, Zhu, & Zhang, 2000; Song, 1984; Yang et al., 1999) adopted the Western personality structure completely. This approach was convenient; however, it posed significant threats to the validity of the measures. The characteristics of Chinese personality measured by these scales may not reflect the real personality of Chinese people.

According to the *derived-etic* strategy, to compare the similarities and differences of the Chinese and Western personality structure, the best approach should be to establish Chinese personality concepts and questionnaires, then compare the results from those to the Big Five structure and the results from NEO PI-R. Based on the *derived-etic* model, the personality structures will likely be different in different cultures. Church (1987) proposed that personality structure was composed of two parts, the *etic*-component, which can be found the same in all cultures, and the *emic*-component, which was unique and only can be found in one specific culture.

Cross-cultural comparison of personality structure has been controversial. Many researchers found the same FFM in different cultures (Caprara, Barbaranelli, Bermudez, Maslach, & Ruch, 2000; McCrae, & Costa, 1997; Rolland, Parker, & Stumpf, 1998; Trull & Geary, 1997; Yang et al., 1999), while others found quite different personality structures in different cultures (Bond, Nakazato, & Shiraishi, 1975; Caprara, Barbaranelli, Hahn, & Comrey, 2001; Chen & Piedmont, 1997; Church, Katigbak, & Reyes, 1996; Guthrie & Bennett, 1971). Therefore, in order to find out whether Western personality questionnaires can accurately reflect and measure the personality of Chinese people, we need to ascertain the Chinese personality first.

Indigenous study exploring Chinese personality structure

In fact, the indigenous study on Chinese personality had demonstrated Chinese personality structure and the significant differences between Chinese and Western personality structures. Systematic lexical research on Chinese personality has indicated that Chinese personality consists of seven factors (Cui & Wang, 2003; Wang & Cui, 2000, 2001, 2003, 2004; Yang & Wang, 1999), which was different from the Western FFM personality structure. According to the lexical hypothesis, if all Chinese adjectives that are used to describe human behavior are selected and evaluated by subjects, the personality structure of the Chinese should emerge, which was the same way Western psychologists found the FFM of personality. In 1995, Wang and his/her colleagues published the selection results of Chinese personality adjectives (Wang, Fang, & Zuo, 1995). Seven thousand seven hundred ninety-four personality adjectives were selected from *The Modern Chinese Dictionary* and its supplements (Institute of Linguistics, Chinese Academy of Social Sciences, 1988), Chinese textbooks in primary and middle schools, newspapers, magazines, novels, and vocabularies that college students used to describe themselves and people that they knew.

To explore the personality structure of the Chinese systematically, Yang and Wang (1999) combined the personality adjectives describing stable personality traits collected in Taiwan and the adjectives collected by Wang and his/her colleagues (1995). One thousand five hundred twenty adjectives were evaluated on favorableness, meaningfulness, familiarity, and foreignness, and 410 adjectives were selected. Subjects from mainland China and Taiwan were asked to evaluate the degree to which each adjective describes him/herself or others. Seven dimensions and 15 subfactors resulted from factor analyses. This result was significantly different from the Western FFM personality structure in both quality and quantity, and it provided evidence that Chinese and Westerners had both similarities and differences in personality structure (Wang & Cui, 2000, 2003).

Cui (2002) reduced the 410 adjective list to 273 by removing synonyms, based on the results from Yang and Wang (1999). One thousand five hundred eleven subjects evaluated the degree to which these adjectives described themselves, and repeated the previous process; the seven dimensions and 15 subfactors were confirmed, and confirmatory factor analysis also proved the results (Cui, 2002). All these results affirmed the personality structure for the Chinese (see Table 7.1).

Furthermore, the response patterns of Chinese subjects to the items and facets of NEO PI-R did not yield the five-factor structure; instead, the seven-factor structure emerged (Wang, Cui, & Zhou, 2005). This result indicated that the Big Seven model of Chinese personality is stable, and that Western personality questionnaires could not accurately measure the personality of Chinese people. The same results emerged in Italian personality structure; Di Blas and Forzi (1998) systematically collected and rated Italian personality adjectives and found three factors of personality. Recently, Caprara et al. (2001) asked both American and Italian subjects to complete the NEO PI-R; as expected, five factors emerged for American subjects, and three factors emerged for Italian subjects.

The compilation of the Chinese Personality Scale (QZPS)

The establishment of Chinese seven-factor personality structure and the adjectives selected in those researches provided theoretical foundation and empirical materials for the compilation of the personality scale for the Chinese. Although adjective rating scales are useful to measure Chinese personality (the Chinese Adjective Rating Scale, QZPAS, had been established and validated, see Cui & Wang, 2004a, 2004b), adjectives have higher variances when measuring personality and are sometimes hard to handle. So, a questionnaire is more useful to measure personality characteristics (Piedmont, 1998). Two important principles of establishing the Chinese personality scale are: (1) the structure of the scale should reflect the Big Seven model of Chinese

Table 7.1 The Big Seven personality structures of Chinese (QZPS; Wang & Cui, 2003)

1. Extraversion (WX)

It reflects active, initiative, positive, easy to communicate, easy going and mild characteristics in socialization, happy and positive mood. People with high scores are active, positive, sociable, communicative, well-liked, happy and emotionally positive; lower scores mean passive, restrictive, unapproachable, depressive and dejected.

WX1 – Active Active and sociable. Higher scores mean active, positive, lively, natural, with high coordination skills; lower scores mean quiet and reserved.

WX2 – Gregariousness Affinity. Higher scores mean cordial, gentle, and well-liked; lower scores mean unapproachable and not well-liked.

WX3 – Optimistic Happy and positive. Higher scores mean positive and energized; lower scores mean depressed and dejected.

2. Kindness (SL)

The "good person" portrait in Chinese culture, including honest, forgiving, caring, trustworthy, righteous, and affectionate characteristics. Higher scores mean honest, kind, caring, trustworthy, and affectionate; lower scores mean false, dishonest, and selfish.

SL1 – Altruistic Friendly and caring about others. Higher scores mean forgiving, friendly, and caring about others; lower scores mean angry, selfish, and use all means to achieve personal goals.

SL2 – Honest Honest and credible. Higher scores mean honest and as good as their word; lower scores mean false and deceiving.

SL3 – Affectionate The degree to which one emphasizes feelings versus personal interests. Higher scores mean affectionate and righteous; lower scores mean goal-oriented and selfish.

3. Behavior Styles (XF)

The way one behaves and one's attitude. Higher scores mean serious, meticulous, thoughtful, clear about goals, practical, obeying rules, and cooperative; lower scores mean impetuous, trying to be different, not obeying rules, impractical and hard to deal with.

XF1 – Rigorous The characteristics in work attitudes and self-constraints. Higher scores mean serious, steady and rigorous; lower scores mean careless, impractical, uncooperative, and hard to deal with.

XF2 – Self-constrained Cooperative and law-abiding. Higher scores mean self-constrained, law-abiding, cooperative, uninterested in fame and wealth; lower scores do not abide by laws and behave differently from others.

XF3 – Composed Composed. Higher scores mean meticulous and thoughtful; lower scores mean careless and impulsive.

4. Talents (CG)

The ability and work attitudes of an individual. Higher scores mean not afraid of difficulties, persistent, involved, and are not afraid to use their brains; lower scores mean hesitant, slack in their work, reluctant to make decisions, and avoidant of difficulties.

CG1 – Decisive The ability to make a decision. Higher scores mean not afraid of difficulties, decisive, quick thinking, and with colorful character; lower scores mean hesitant, nervous, anxious, and reluctant to make a decision.

CG2 – Persistent Persistent in work. Higher scores mean have clear goals, abide by principles and persistent; lower scores mean not persistent and tend to slack off in work.

CG3 – Alert and Resourceful Assertiveness and alertness. Higher scores mean involved with work, dare to do what they think is right, active and quick; lower scores mean always avoid difficulties and are not willing to take chances.

5. Emotionality (QX)

The stability of one's emotion in working and interpersonal situations. Higher scores mean impetuous and impulsive, can not control their emotion easily; lower scores mean stable, mild, and in control.

QX1 – Patient The control and expression of one's emotion. Higher scores mean emotionally stable and mild, can control their emotion well; lower scores mean impetuous, impulsive, tempestuous, and hard to control.

QX2 – Candid Candid characteristics of emotion. Higher scores mean frank and outspoken, impetuous, and have difficulty controlling their emotion; lower scores mean tactful and reserved with their emotion

6. Human Relations (RG)

The basic attitude on human relations. Higher scores mean friendly and mild, altruistic, and easy to communicate with; lower scores view human relations as a means for achieving personal goals, are self-centered, indifferent, stingy, and sluggish.

RG1 – Generous The basic attitude toward human relations. Higher scores mean mild, friendly, generous, and self-content; lower scores mean stingy, impetuous, angry, indifferent, and self-centered.

RG2 – Warm The characteristics of human relations. Higher scores mean active, positive, mature, and persistent in communication; lower scores mean passive, sluggish, and without a goal.

7. Ways of Life (CT)

The fundamental attitude of the individual toward life and career. Higher scores mean goal-oriented, persistent, have clear visions of the future, assertiveness about the future, and aspiring to excellence; lower scores mean satisfied with current situations, have no clear goals and no strong ambition for the future.

CT1 – Assertiveness The seeking of career. Higher scores mean assertiveness about life and future and work actively toward goals; lower scores have no clear goals, are sluggish and do not like to think.

CT2 – Not Seeking Fame and Wealth The attitudes toward achievement and success. Higher scores mean satisfied with current situations and have no clear goals or ambitions toward the future, leads peaceful life without secular desires; lower scores mean always unsatisfied, always seeking excellence and longing for success.

personality; and (2) the items should reflect the personality structure of the Chinese and their daily life experiences (Wang & Cui, 2003). Based on dimensions and subfactors of Chinese personality structure, the main challenge in constructing a scale is to write a sufficient number of sentences or items that reflect Chinese personality characteristics, and then to conduct psychometric tests. Because Chinese personality dimensions are defined by personality trait adjectives, writing sentences that reflect the meanings of the adjectives should form sufficient items that reflect Chinese personality characteristics (Wang & Cui, 2003).

The writing of the items was based on each of the personality trait adjectives used to explore the Chinese personality structure. Professors and graduate students in the personality and social psychology area wrote the items. The writing principle was that, assuming somebody had the personality characteristic that was defined by a target adjective (for example, "shy"), use four or more sentences to describe: (a) behaviors of the "shy" person; (b) internal experiences of the "shy" person; (c) the motivations of the "shy" person; and (d) the degree to which the "shy" person has or doesn't have the personality trait. After this procedure, 1861 sentences or items were created. Then, all the items were categorized into seven dimensions and their corresponding subfactors. According to the meaning of each subfactor and dimension, respectively, each of the items was rewritten. After these rewritings, we combined and removed some similar items and items that did not relate to the dimensions. This resulted 1635 items.

To make it easy for a subject to evaluate and for us to select items, we compiled four questionnaires out of the 1635 items, and asked four groups of subjects to evaluate them. We conducted factor analyses separately on the 13 subfactors of dimensions 1 through 5 and dimensions 6 and 7 in order to select items that measured these 13 subfactors and two dimensions (referred to as 15 subfactors). Based on these analyses, we selected 718 items and used 409 items to represent the seven dimensions and 15 subfactors. Each subfactor comprised about 30 items.

Then the new scale was tested with 3200 subjects. Principal component factor analysis was conducted on the 409 items. Based on the variances explained and the scree test, it was reasonable to retain a seven-factor solution. After extracting seven factors and using varimax rotation, and removing items with loadings lower than .25 and commonality lower than .15, the remaining items explained 30.09% of the variance. After conducting factor analysis within each dimension, we revealed 3, 3, 2, 2, 3, 3, and 2 subfactors within dimensions 1 through 7 with total items of 180. The dimensions and subfactors of QZPS are listed in Table 7.1.

Three secondary factors were also developed on the basis of secondary factor analysis applied to the 18 subfactors of QZPS, and were named as Self-oriented, Other-oriented, and Object-oriented characteristics (abbreviated as SELF, OTHER, and OBJECT, respectively). SELF was composed of six subfactors of QZPS, they are CG3, CT1, XF2, CT2, RG1 and WX3.

OTHER was composed of six subfactors of QZPS, they are SL1, WX1, SL2, RG2, CG1 and SL3. OBJECT was composed of six subfactors of QZPS, they are QX1, QX2, XF1, CG2, XF3 and WX2 (Wang & Cui, 2002).

Chinese–Western personality differences and its cultural origins

Comparative characteristics of Chinese and Western personality models

The "big five" model of Western personality reflects five independent aspects of Western behavioral and personality characteristics. For example, Neuroticism is an independent dimension of emotionality, which comprises almost all emotional characteristics of emotion. And every one of the five dimensions is the objective description of behavior and experiences, although evaluative meaning of behavior and experiences are included. Each dimension reflects classifications of behavior only; the meanings of behavior are the behavior per se, no references are needed to understand the signification of the behaviors in each of the five dimensions, neither for inner characteristics (e.g., Openness) nor for behavior descriptions (e.g., Extraversion, Neuroticism). Furthermore, the five dimensions are mutually independent, and each dimension has its own integrity of meanings. That is, behaviors described in every one of the five dimensions are seldom superimposed on one another and are mutually independent. For example, Neuroticism is an independent dimension about an individual's emotional stability; the other four dimensions are seldom involved in it. The only exception is the Positive Emotions facet of Extraversion, but it is more an exterior rather than an interior characteristic as Neuroticism is.

Chinese big seven personality structure is more complex than Western personality structure. As shown in Table 7.1, two of the seven dimensions (Talents and Ways of Life) are about an individual's intrinsic characteristics, four of them (Extraversion, Kindness, Emotionality, and Human Relations) are about interpersonal relations, and one of them (Behavior Styles) is about object-oriented characteristics. Emotionality, Talents and Ways of Life also partly reflect an individual's object-oriented characteristics.

A comprehensive view of Chinese personality reveals at least two significant specialties. First, each of the seven dimensions is mainly evaluative of behavioral characteristics instead of objective description. No matter whether they refer to characteristics that are intrinsic (e.g., Kindness, Talents, and Ways of Life) or extrinsic (e.g., Extraversion, Behavior Styles, and Emotionality), each dimension reflects the classification and significant evaluative and social judgment of behavior; the behavior per se seemed less important. Second, behavior superposition across dimensions is very significant, each dimension is relatively integral in meaning, but not entirely. For example, although there is a dimension of "Emotionality", it only reflects emotional characteristics in working and interpersonal situations, instead of the whole meaning of emotionality. The contents of Western Neuroticism are distributed through-out the rest of the six dimensions of Chinese personality (Wang & Cui, 2005a; Wang et al., 2005).

Therefore, differences between Western and Chinese personality are mainly manifested as the different degree of description and evaluation of the behaviors under consideration. Meanwhile, Western personality structure is relatively simplistic and perspicuous for the behaviors included in each of the five dimensions, while Chinese personality structure is relatively complex and each dimension has independent meanings, instead of whole meanings, for some aspects of behavior characteristics. So, the deep cultural reasons for the Western–Chinese personality differences deserve further discussion.

Cultural origins of Chinese–Western personality differences

Chinese and Western cultures view evaluation of behavior differently, and this may be the reason why Chinese and Western personality structures are different. Furthermore, the different emphasis each culture puts on evalu-ation must have deeper reasons. According to Li (2003), culture serves as the camouflage for human consciousness of sin or human nature. The funda-mental differences between cultures are embodied in their views of human nature. Chinese and Western cultures view human nature in exactly opposite ways. The dominant view in Chinese culture is that human nature is good (although other views reckon human nature as evil, as neither good nor evil, etc.), but the dominant view in Western culture is that human nature is evil, although human nature has also been proposed as good in Western culture. Therefore, if a Westerner behaves evilly sometimes, he/she does not need to defend him/herself as much as a Chinese person will, because he/she believes that human nature is evil while the Chinese believe that human nature is good. On the other hand, if a Chinese person behaves evilly, in order to maintain his/her self-respect and good social adaptation, he/she has to strongly defend his/her behavior by saying that he/she does not intend to behave evilly.

The origins of the word *culture* are also different in Chinese and Western languages. In Chinese, the word *culture* is composed of two characters: *wen* (grain, vein), and *hua* (change). In Chinese *Word Source* (The Commercial Publishing House, 1979) and *Sea of Words* (Shanghai Dictionary Press, 1999), *Wen* originated from veins and grain, *hua* originated from change, and also means flower and glamour. These two words combined together as *wen-hua* mean to put grains and veins on the surface to change or to beautify the object. It emphasizes decoration and beautification on the surface. In English, the word *culture* originated from a Latin word *colere*, which means tillage, cultivation, farming, and fostering. From cultivation of plants to edu-cation of people, the word implies that human nature can be educated or changed (Li, 2003, p. 5).

The emphasis on "decorating and tailoring" or "cultivation and fostering" reveals the differences between Chinese and Western cultures. In Chinese culture where human nature is believed to be good, the role of culture is to decorate and beautify human behavior, to hide the real objectives of human behavior, and to make human behavior more acceptable (good or perfect). That is, a Chinese person will pay much attention to the surface or exhibition of the behavior to avoid displaying weakness. Therefore, a Chinese person may restrain his/her behavior or avoid showing off in order to hide his/her weakness or reduce the opportunities of showing his/her weakness. Selfishness, greed, and rudeness are not in accord with human nature, therefore an individual will make a great effort to hide the evil side of his/her nature. He/she may change his/her behavior slightly according to his/her beliefs on human nature. As a result, his/her words or behaviors are camouflaged. Even if his/her behavior does not show evilness, he/she will decorate his/her words and behaviors with glorified human nature. For example, a Chinese person tends to defend him/herself regardless of success or failure, but in different ways. In the face of failure, he/she will defend him/herself so that his/her behavior "does not look so evil". In the face of success, he/she will say that he/she "is not that good." The goal is not to show conceit, so that he/she can defend him/herself more effectively when he/she acts evilly (Wang, 1992).

In a society that believes human nature is evil, the role of culture is to cultivate and foster good behavior, in order to change the level of current behavior. The goal is to reduce the evilness in human behavior in order to achieve goodness and perfection. Therefore, a Westerner is candid because he/she does not face the pressure to defend him/herself as much as a Chinese person. A Westerner is proud because he/she uses success to show his/her distance from evilness. Western culture also has a tendency to beautify; however, it uses strategies to change rather than hide. In believing human nature is evil, Western culture achieves its goals by changing rather than hiding. In other words, Western culture acknowledges that selfishness, greed, and rudeness need beautification, but it rationalizes them and does not face the pressure to defend them. The emphasis is on cultivation and fostering, rather than hiding. In contrast with the Chinese, a Westerner only defends him/herself when facing failure (Basgall & Snyder, 1988). When he/she succeeds, he/she does not defend him/herself; rather, he/she will fortify his/her success to distance him/herself from the evilness of human nature.

The beautification characteristics of Chinese culture will influence the control of an individual over his/her words and behavior and his/her cognition of other people's words and behavior. First, before revealing his/her wishes and needs, a Chinese person needs to evaluate the "individual effect" of his/her words and behavior. More importantly, he/she needs to evaluate the "social effect" of his/her words and behavior at the same time. In many situations, although an individual wants very much to satisfy his/her own needs through revealing his/her wishes or acting upon a wish, he/she has to give up or use other implicit or covert ways to express his/her wishes, because this action may violate social norms or others' expectations, or incur negative opinions from others. Often, the words or behavior of a Chinese person are not what he/she really intends to say or do; rather, they are modified by cultural beliefs. Therefore, a Chinese person rarely expresses his/her wishes or opinions without inhibition. Even if he/she thinks his/her opinion is correct, he/she will not say anything out of fear that others may think he/she is too conceited. This is even more the case when he/she is not sure that he/she is correct. In Chinese culture, expressing one's wishes, demands, and views directly is often viewed as immature and childish.

In addition, if the social role of an individual is different, the degree to which he/she modifies his/her behavior is also different. In general, one who is more knowledgeable needs to hide his/her weakness more. As a public servant, a clerk may need to hide more. In contrast, an intellectual may need to hide less. Furthermore, factory workers and farmers may hide their words and behavior less. Unfortunately, there is little research on this topic. Some indirect evidence from research on people with different occupations supported our arguments. In the seven dimensions of Chinese personality structure, Extraversion, Kindness, and Ways of Life reflect characteristics of individual social interaction, personal character, and career motivation. As a result, when an individual evaluates him/herself on these three personality dimensions, he/she will be influenced by the "beautifying" tendency of the culture. In contrast, public servants will put highest emphasis on these three dimensions, and their beautification tendency should be the highest. Research results have supported this hypothesis. Public servants scored significantly higher than factory workers, farmers, and intellectuals (Wang & Cui, 2005b).

Second, when an individual realizes that his/her words and behavior need beautification and he/she can not express them directly, he/she will use the same strategy to understand other people's words and behavior. He/she will not take other people's words and behavior at face value; rather, he/she will try to remove the camouflage and reveal the real intention. In Chinese culture it is widely believed that knowing a person is difficult because one not only needs to know what a person says or does, but also know what the person really thinks, and the latter is more critical. In other words, a Chinese individual's words do not necessarily reflect what he/she thinks; even his/her behavior may not reflect what he/she really thinks. Even Confucius stated, "I seldom feel harassment if people do not know me, but I do feel harassed if I do not know them". Perhaps Chinese culture is considered "broad and profound" because of this.

Compared to the indirect and complicated Chinese ways of expressing self and judging other people, Westerners are more direct and candid. The Chinese pay more attention to evaluation and connection; therefore it is hard to make a correct reading of a person based on observable information only. Westerners pay more attention to observable information because they believe that what the heart thinks the tongue speaks. In other words, Westerners do much better than Chinese people with respect to the consistency between internal wishes and needs and external words and behaviors.

Personality characteristics of the Chinese

To illustrate the validity of QZPS and the characteristics of Chinese personality, Wang & Cui (2005b) compared personality characteristics of about 2000 subjects. A 2 (Sex) × 3 (Age Groups) × 2 (Marital Status) × 3 (Occupation Groups) analysis of variance (ANOVA) was conducted on seven dimensions (including 18 subfactors) and three secondary factors of QZPS, respectively. For the three occupation groups, 700 of them were factory workers and farmers (FWF), 617 administrators (ADM), and 356 educators, researchers, and health workers (ERH). Personality characteristics of different subject groups are discussed briefly below.

Extraversion

ADM had significantly higher Extraversion scores than FWF and ERH. FWF and ERH participants did not different from each other. For the sub-factor of Activeness, males had higher scores than females. The interaction between sex, age, and occupation was significant. For Gregariousness, females were more gregarious than males, ADM were more gregarious than both FWF and ERH. The interaction between sex and age was significant. For Optimism, married participants were more optimistic than single participants, ADM were more optimistic than both FWF and ERH.

Kindness

Females were kinder than males, younger participants were kinder than other age groups, and ADM were kinder than both FWF and ERH. The interaction between age and occupation was significant for FWF and ADM, the scores increased from younger to median age groups, but tapered off in older group; for ERH the scores decreased from the younger to the median age group, and increased from the median to the older age group. For the subfactor of Altruism, females were more altruistic than males, ADM had significantly higher scores in altruism than FWF and ERH. The interaction between age and occupation was significant, the pattern was similar to Kindness. For Honesty, females were more honest than males, older participants were more honest than median participants, who, in turn, were more honest than younger participants. The interaction between age and occupation was significant, with a pattern similar to Kindness. The interactions among sex, occupation, and marital status, and among age, occupation, and marital status were also significant. For Affection, females were more affectionate than males. Older participants having higher scores than younger participants. FWF had lower scores than other occupations. The interaction between age, marital status, and occupation was significant.

Behavioral Styles

Males had lower Behavioral Styles scores than females; scores decreased from older to median to younger age groups; and scores increased from FWF to ADM to ERH. The interaction between age and occupation was significant, for FWF and ADM scores increase along with the increase in age; for ERH, however, older age groups have higher scores than both median and younger groups, but there was no difference between median and younger groups. For the subfactor of Rigor, males had lower scores than females; the scores increased from younger to median to older age groups; and ADM had higher scores than FWF and ERH groups. For Self-constraint, males showed more self-constraint than females; scores increased from younger to median to older participants. For Composure, males were more composed than females; and younger participants scored lower than older participants. The interaction between sex, age, and occupation was significant in male participants.

Talents

Talents scores increased from younger to median to older age groups and all differences were significant; FWF scored lower than ADM and ERH groups, singles have higher scores than married participants. For the subfactor of Decisiveness, males were more decisive than females; FWF scored lower than both ADM and ERH groups. For Persistency, scores increased significantly from younger to median to older age groups; FWF scored lower than both ADM and ERH groups. The interaction between age and occupation was significant. For Alertness and Resourcefulness, FWF scored lower than ADM and ERH groups; single participants scored higher than married participants. The interaction between age and occupation was significant.

Emotionality

For Emotionality, FWF score higher than ADM and ERH groups. The interaction between sex, age, and marital status was significant for married younger and older age groups, females had higher emotionality than males. It was exactly the opposite in the median group. For single participants sex difference only existed in the older age group, where females scored higher than males. For the subfactor of Patience, younger participants scored lower than other age groups; FWF scored lower than both ADM and ERH groups. The interaction between sex, age, and marital status was significant. For Candidness, males scored lower than females; younger participants scored lower than the other two age groups. The interaction between sex, age, and marital status was significant, this pattern was similar to that in Emotionality.

Human Relations

For Human Relations, the FWF group scored lower than both the ADM and ERH groups. The interaction between age and occupation was significant, in younger and median age groups ADM scored significantly higher than other two groups. In the older age group ERH had the highest scores. For the subfactor of Generosity, females had higher scores than males; FWF scored lower than both the ADM and ERH groups. The interaction between age and occupation was significant, the pattern was similar to that of Human Relations. For Warmth, single participants scored higher than married participants; males scored higher than females.

Ways of Life

Median and older age groups scored lower than the younger group in Ways of Life; single participants scored higher than married participants. The interaction between age and occupation was significant in younger and median age groups, ADM scored higher than both the FWF and ERH groups. However, in the older age group, ERH had the highest scores, FWF had the lowest scores, with the ADM group in the middle, and all differences were significant. For the subfactor of Assertiveness, single participants scored higher than married participants. The interaction between age and occupation was significant, the pattern was similar to that in Ways of Life. For Not Seeking Fame and Wealth, males scored lower than females; younger participants scored lower than the other two groups.

SELF, OTHER and OBJECT

For SELF, males scored higher than females; single participants scored higher than married participants; younger participants scored higher than the other two age groups. The interaction between sex, age, and occupation was significant, in younger male participants, the scores decreased significantly from ADM to ERH to FWF groups; in median male participants ERH had lower scores than ADM and FWF groups; in older male participants the FWF group had lower scores than the ADM and ERH groups. In younger female participants the scores decreased significantly from the ADM to ERH to FWF groups; in median-age female participants ADM had higher scores than the ERH and FWF groups; in older-age female participants the ADM group had lower scores than the FWF and ERH groups. For OTHER, females scored higher than males; younger participants scored lower than other age groups. The interaction between age and occupation; sex, age, and occupation; sex, marital status, and occupation were significant. In younger male participants the ADM group scored lower than both the FWF and ERH groups; in median male participants the scores decreased significantly from the FWF to ADM to ERH groups; in older male participants FWF

scored lower than the ADM and ERH groups. In younger female participants the FWF group scored lower than both the ADM and ERH groups; in
median female participants the scores decreased significantly from the ADM
to FWF to ERH groups; in older female participants ADM scored lower
than the FWF and ERH groups. For OBJECT, scores increased significantly
from younger to median to older age groups; FWF scored lower than both
the ADM and ERH groups.

Conclusions and future research directions

The seven factor model of Chinese personality was developed and validated
through lexical research on Chinese personality trait adjectives; it displayed
significant differences from the five factor model of Western personality
structure. Just as FFM reflects the realm of Western personality, the seven
factor model reveals the personality structure of the Chinese in accordance
with Chinese culture. The QZPS score distribution among subjects with different age, sex, occupation, and marital statues indicates good validation of
the Chinese personality structure. The behavior classification hypothesis of
personality structure was supported by comparisons of Chinese and Western
personality structure, and differences between Chinese and Western cultures
served as the main origins of differences in personality structure. Generally
speaking, Chinese culture is rooted in the belief that human nature is good; it
encourages individuals make great efforts to beautify their actions and
behaviors in order to maintain their good self-image and their good-person
standing in the eyes of others. Therefore, individuals pay great attention to
the inner or deeper meanings of their own or others' behaviors, instead of to
the behavior per se; in other words, the classification of behaviors was based
mainly on the implications of behaviors. Westerners, in contrast, would classify behaviors mainly on their objective qualities, because Western culture
proposes that human nature is evil and individuals are under less defensive
pressure than the Chinese.

Along with the development and validation of Chinese personality scales
(e.g., QZPS), the characteristics of Chinese personality can be clarified and
applications can be made in many psychological areas. For example, psychological counseling and human resources are two of most popular areas in
China at present. These two areas of psychology rely on personality theory
and measurement. However, currently the theoretical and instrumental foundations of almost all areas of applied psychology in China are Western
personality theories, questionnaires and scales. The seven factor model of
Chinese personality and the corresponding scale (QZPS) could serve as
a new alternative, and exciting results can be expected because of the
cultural concordance of the model. Meanwhile, psychosocial mediators of
Chinese–Western personality differences also deserve further investigation.

Acknowledgments

This research was supported by a grant from National Natural Science Foundation (30270469) to the first author.

The authors are grateful to Professors Qicheng Jing and John Berry for their helpful comments on an earlier version.

References

Allport, G. W., & Odbert, H. S. (1936). Trait names: A psycho-lexical study. *Psychological Monographs*, *41*(1). (Whole No. 211)

Basgall, J. A., & Snyder, C. R. (1988). Excuses in waiting: External locus of control and reactions to success – failure feedback. *Journal of Personality and Social Psychology*, *54*, 656–662.

Berry, J. W. (1969). On cross-cultural comparability. *International Journal of Psychology*, *4*, 119–128.

Berry, J. W. (1989). Imposed etics–emics–derived etics: The operationalisation of a compelling idea. *International Journal of Psychology*, *24*, 721–735.

Bond, M., Nakazato, H., Shiraishi, D. (1975). Universality and distinctiveness in dimensions of Japanese person perception. *Journal of Cross-Cultural Psychology*, *6*, 346–357.

Caprara, G. V., Barbaranelli, C., Bermudez, J., Maslach, C., & Ruch, W. (2000). Multivariate methods for the comparison of factor structures in cross-cultural research – An illustration with the Big Five questionnaire. *Journal of Cross-Cultural Psychology*, *31*(4), 437–464.

Caprara, G. V., Barbaranelli, C., Hahn, R., & Comrey, A. L. (2001). Factor analysis of the NEO PI-R inventory and the Comrey Personality Scales in Italy and the United Stated. *Personality and Individual Differences*, *30*(2), 217–228.

Chen, M. C., & Piedmont, R. L. (1997). Development and validation of the NEO PI-R for a Taiwanese sample. *Symposium on Five-Factor Personality Structure in Asia at the 2nd Conference of the Asian Association of Social Psychology*. Kyoto, Japan.

Chen, Z. (1983). The item analysis on Eysenck Personality Questionnaire. *Acta Psychologica Sinica*, *15*(2), 211–218. (in Chinese)

Church, A. (1987). Personality in a non-Western culture: The Philippines. *Psychological Bulletin*, *102*(1), 272–292.

Church, A. T., Katigbak, M. S., & Reyes, J. A. S. (1996). Toward a taxonomy of trait adjectives in Filipino: Comparing personality lexicons across cultures. *European Journal of Personality*, *10*(1), 3–24.

Costa, P. T., McCrae, R. R. (1989). *Revised NEO Personality Inventory (NEO PI-R) and NEO Five-Factor Inventory (NEO-FFI)*. Lutz, FL: Psychological Assessment Resources, Inc.

Cui, H. (2002). *The Lexical Study and Adjective Evaluation Scale of Chinese Personality*. Unpublished Doctoral Dissertation, Peking University. (in Chinese)

Cui, H., & Wang, D. (2003). The re-validation of Chinese personality structure and the results from adjectives evaluation. *Psychology and Behavioral Research*, *1*(2), 89–95. (in Chinese)

Cui, H., & Wang, D. (2004a). Development and availability of the "big five" personality model. *Psychological Science*, *27*(3), 545–548.

Cui, H., & Wang, D. (2004b). Reliability, validation, and norm for Chinese Personality Adjective Rating Scale (QZPAS). *Psychological Science, 27*(1), 185–188.

Di Blas, L., & Forzi, M. (1998). An alternative taxonomic study of personality-descriptive adjectives in the Italian language. *European Journal of Personality, 12*(2), 75–101.

Goldberg, L. R. (1990). An alternative "descriptive of personality": The big five structure. *Journal of Personality and Social Psychology, 59*, 1216–1229.

Gong, Y. (1983). *The manual for modified Eysenck Personality Questionnaire.* Changsha, China: Hunan Medicine College. (in Chinese)

Guthrie, G. M., & Bennett, A. B., Jr. (1971). Cultural differences in implicit personality theory. *International Journal of Psychology, 6*, 305–312.

Institute of Linguistics, Chinese Academy of Social Sciences (1988). *Modern Chinese dictionary.* Beijing: The Commercial Publishing House.

John, O. P. (1990). The "big five" factor taxonomy: Dimensions of personality in the natural language and in questionnaires. In L. Pervin (Ed.), *Handbook of personality: Theory and research* (pp. 66–100). New York: Guilford Press.

John, O. P., Angleitner, A., & Ostendorf, F. (1988). The lexical approach to personality: A historical review of trait taxonomic research. *European Journal of Personality, 2*, 171–203.

John, O. P., Donahue, E. M., & Kentle, R. L. (1991). *The Big Five Inventory – Versions 4a and 54.* Technical Report, Institue of Personality and Social Research, University of California, Berkeley, CA.

Li, S. (1981). *The manual for 16PF.* Liaoning Educational Science Institute. (in Chinese)

Li, M. (2003). *Why Chinese so stupid? – How to get clever for Chinese in 21st century.* Beijing: Hualing Press. (in Chinese)

Maccoby, E. E. (2000). Parenting and its effects on children: On reading and misreading behavior genetics. *Annual Reviews of Psychology, 51*, 1–27.

McCrae, R. R., & Costa, P. T. (1997). Personality trait structure as a human universal. *American Psychologist, 52*(5), 509–516.

Norman, W. T. (1963). Toward an adequate taxonomy of personality attributes: Replicated factor structure in peer nomination personality ratings. *Journal of Abnormal and Social Psychology, 66*, 574–583.

Piedmont, R. L. (1998). *The Revised NEO Personality Inventory: Clinical and research applications.* New York and London: Plenum Press.

Qian, M., Wu, G., Zhu, R., & Zhang, S. (2000). Development of the Revised Eysenck Personality Questionnaire Short Scale for Chinese (EPQ-RSC). *Acta Psychologica Sinica, 32*(3), 317–323. (in Chinese)

Rolland, J. P., Parker, W. D., & Stumpf, H. (1998). A psychometric examination of the French translation of the NEO PI-R and NEO-FFI. *Journal of Personality Assessment, 71*(2), 269–291.

Shanghai Dictionary Press (1999). *Sea of words.* Shanghai, China: Shanghai Dictionary Press.

Shweder, R. A. (1991). Rethinking culture and personality theory. In R. A. Shweder (Ed.), *Thinking through cultures: Expeditions in cultural psychology* (pp. 269–312). Cambridge, MA: Harvard University Press.

Song, W. (1984). *Manual of the revised Chinese version of MMPI.* Beijing, China: Institute of Psychology, Chinese Academy of Sciences. (in Chinese)

The Commercial Publishing House (1979). *Word source.* Beijing, China: The Commercial Publishing House.

Triandis, H. C., & Suh, E. M. (2002). Cultural influences on personality. *Annual Reviews of Psychology*, *53*, 1–32.

Trull, T. J., & Geary, D. C. (1997). Comparison of the Big Five factor structure across samples of Chinese and American adults. *Journal of Personality Assessment*, *69*(2), 324–341.

Wang, D. (1992). Blaming and excuse-making as a function of internal versus external locus of control: Further evidence. *Acta Psychologica Sinica*, *24*(2), 314–321. (in Chinese)

Wang, D., & Cui, H. (2000). Culture, language, and personality. *Journal of Peking University (Humanities and Social Sciences Edition)*, *37*(4), 38–46. (in Chinese)

Wang, D., & Cui, H. (2001). The theoretical considerations on constructing the Chinese Personality Scale (QZPS). *Journal of Peking University (Humanities and Social Sciences Edition)*, *38*(6), 48–54. (in Chinese)

Wang, D., & Cui, H. (2002). The object-oriented, others-oriented, and self-oriented characteristics of Chinese. *Journal of Peking University (Humanities and Social Sciences Edition)*, *39*(4), 79–85. (in Chinese)

Wang, D., & Cui, H. (2003). The constructing process and the preliminary results of Chinese Personality Scale (QZPS). *Acta Psychologica Sinica*, *35*(1), 127–136. (in Chinese)

Wang, D., & Cui, H. (2004). Reliabilities and validities of the Chinese Personality Scale (QZPS). *Acta Psychologica Sinica*, *36*(3), 347–358.

Wang, D., & Cui, H. (2005a). Is neuroticism an independent dimension of Chinese personality structure? *Journal of Southwest Normal University*, *31*(3), 25–30. (in Chinese)

Wang, D., & Cui, H. (2005b). Personality characteristics as a function of age, sex, occupation, and marital statues. In D. Wang & H. Cui (Eds.), *Explorations of Chinese personality* (pp. 356–372). Beijing, China: Social Sciences Press.

Wang, D., Cui, H., Zhou, F. (2005). Measuring the personality of Chinese: QZPS versus NEO PI-R. *Asian Journal of Social Psychology*, *8*(1), 97–122.

Wang, D., Fang, L., & Zuo, Y. (1995). The lexical research on Chinese personality. *Acta Psychologica Sinica*, *27*(4), 420–427. (in Chinese)

Yang, J., McCrae, R. R., Costa, P. Y., Dai, X. Y., Yao, S. Q., Cai, T. S. et al. (1999). Cross-cultural personality assessment in psychiatric populations: The NEO PI-R in the People's Republic of China. *Psychological Assessment*, *11*(3), 359–368.

Yang, K., & Wang, D. (1999). *The personality dimensions of Chinese*. Paper presented at the Third Chinese Psychologists Convention, Beijing. (in Chinese)

Section II

Health psychology

8 Effects of stress, emotion, and Type-A behavior on heart disease and psychological disorders

Charles D. Spielberger

Stress is an integral part of the natural fabric of life, and coping with stress is an everyday requirement for normal human growth and development. Hurricanes, floods and wars are examples of catastrophic stressors that exert tremendous pressures on large masses of people. City dwellers must adjust to noise, pollution, and crowded living conditions. Taking tests, giving speeches, job pressures and deadlines at work, marriage and family relationships. Retirement and old age must also be included among the ubiquitous sources of stress in human life. Even holidays and vacations, which are usually regarded as positive events, can be extremely stressful for some people.

In the introduction to his classic book, *Stress and the Heart*, Robert S. Eliot (1974), observed that human distress and the incidence of death from coronary disease showed parallel increases during the 20th century. Also more than a quarter century ago, S. Leonard Syme (1975) reviewed research evidence from an epidemiological point of view bearing on psychosocial and behavioral risk factors in heart disease, and concluded that consistent findings have "begun to emerge linking coronary heart disease to increased socio-cultural mobility, Behavior Pattern A, and, perhaps, stressful life events" (1975, p. 19).

During the past 40 years, the pioneering work on Type-A behavior of two San Francisco cardiologists, Meyer Friedman and Ray H. Rosenman (1974), has stimulated a great deal of research and public interest in the effects of social and personality factors on cardiovascular disease. Although this research was immediately challenged by leading medical authorities (e.g., Jeremiah Stamler, Chief of Preventive Medicine, Northwestern University, and Richard S. Ross, Chief of Cardiology, Johns Hopkins University, cited in Brody, 1975), the importance of personality variables as risk factors for heart disease was strongly supported by the findings of Friedman, Rosenman, and their associates (Rosenman, Brand, Jenkins, Friedman, Straus, & Wurm, 1975). Based on the results of the Western Collaborative Group Study (WCGS), an eight year prospective epidemiological study initiated in 1960–1961, these researchers have reported impressive evidence that the Type-A behavior pattern must be considered, along with smoking habits, serum cholesterol and hypertension, as a critical risk factor for heart disease.

Persons classified as Type-A in the WCGS were more than twice as likely to suffer heart attacks as Type-Bs, even when other major risk factors such as cholesterol and smoking were controlled (Friedman & Rosenman, 1974; Matthews, Glass, Rosenman, & Bortner, 1977)

Over the past 40 years, the role of anxiety in the etiology of cardiovascular disorders has also received increasing attention. The State–Trait Anxiety Inventory (STAI: Spielberger, 1983; Spielberger, Gorsuch, & Lushene, 1970) has been used in a number of studies in which relations between anxiety, essential hypertension, and coronary heart disease have been investigated. Significant positive correlations of trait anxiety with systolic blood pressure have been consistently found for hypertensive individuals (Banahan, Sharpe, Baker, Liao, & Smith, 1979; Whitehead, Blackwell, DeSilva, & Robinson, 1977).

Practical considerations in psychological assessment are guided by theories of personality and psychopathology that identify fundamental emotional states and personality traits, and by combinations of these dimensions that define major diagnostic syndromes. The nature of anxiety, anger/hostility and Type-A behavior, and the relation of emotions and personality to cardiovascular disease are reviewed in this chapter. The procedures employed in measuring anxiety and anger as psychological constructs are also described in detail. The chapter concludes with a discussion of emotional vital signs of psychological distress that should be carefully assessed and continuously monitored in diagnostic evaluations of persons with cardiovascular disease, and in studies of treatment outcome.

Anxiety in cardiovascular disease

Anxiety has been recognized as a central problem and a predominant theme of modern life, as was noted by the French author, Albert Camus, who referred to the 20th century as "The Century of Fear." The importance of anxiety (fear) was clearly recognized by Charles Darwin (1872/1965), who considered this emotion to be a product of evolution in both humans and animals. Darwin also observed that fear and anxiety varied in intensity, from mild apprehension or surprise, to an extreme "agony of terror." In his classic book, *The Meaning of Anxiety*, Rollo May (1950/1977) cogently described the pervasive impact of anxiety in literature, music, art and religion, along with its importance in psychoanalysis, psychiatry, and psychology. May documented the historical antecedents of current concerns with fear and anxiety in the philosophical work of Pascal, Nietzsche, Schopenhauer and, especially, Kierkegaard, who considered fear to be a state of mind characterized by the expectation that something painful or unpleasant might happen.

According to Sigmund Freud (1895/1924), anxiety consists of a unique combination of phenomenological and physiological qualities, with behavioral manifestations similar to those that Darwin attributed to fear. Freud described anxiety as "something felt," an unpleasant emotional state characterized by subjective feelings of chronic apprehension, and by ". . . all that is covered by the word 'nervousness' " (1895/1924, p. 79). He was concerned primarily with identifying the sources of stimulation that precipitated anxiety reactions, rather than analyzing the properties of such states. Fear was regarded by Freud as "objective anxiety," in which the intensity of the emotional reaction was proportional to the external danger; the greater the danger, the stronger the perceived threat, and the more intense the resulting anxiety reaction. He distinguished objective anxiety (fear) from neurotic anxiety, in which the danger resulted from unacceptable internal impulses that were punished in childhood and subsequently repressed (Spielberger, 1972, 1979). In both objective and neurotic anxiety, the perceived presence of danger evokes an emotional state that warns the individual that some form of adjustment is necessary.

In contemporary psychiatry and psychology, anxiety refers to at least two related, yet logically different, constructs. As described by Freud, anxiety is an unpleasant emotional state (S-Anxiety) that varies in intensity. S-Anxiety is characterized by subjective feelings of tension, apprehension, nervousness and worry, and by activation (arousal) and discharge of the autonomic nervous system. The physiological changes that occur in anxiety states include increased heart rate (palpitations, tachycardia), muscular tension, irregularities in breathing (hyperventilation), dilation of the pupils, vertigo (dizziness), nausea, and muscular skeletal disturbances, such as tremors and tics. Trait anxiety (T-Anxiety) refers to relatively stable individual differences in the disposition or proneness to experience anxiety as an emotional state. Persons high in T-Anxiety tend to see the world as more dangerous or threatening, and are therefore more vulnerable to stress. Consequently, they experience S-Anxiety more frequently, and with greater intensity, than persons who are low in T-Anxiety. Individuals who are high in T-Anxiety are generally aware of their negative feelings, and can report the intensity of these unpleasant emotional reactions.

The concepts of state and trait anxiety introduced by Cattell (1966), and subsequently refined and elaborated by Spielberger (1966, 1972, 1983), provided the conceptual framework for constructing the State–Trait Anxiety Inventory (STAI; Spielberger et al., 1970). In developing the STAI, the initial goal was to identify a single set of items that could be administered with different instructions to assess the intensity of S-Anxiety and individual differences in T-Anxiety. However, given the difficulties encountered in measuring state and trait anxiety with the same items, 20 items that were stable over time, with the best concurrent validity as indicated by the highest correlations with other anxiety measures, were selected for the T-Anxiety scale (Spielberger et al., 1970). The 20 items with the best construct validity when given with state instructions, as indicated by higher and lower scores under stressful and nonstressful conditions, were selected for the S-Anxiety scale. Factor analyses of the 40 STAI items have consistently identified distinct state and trait anxiety factors (Spielberger, 1983; Spielberger et al., 1970).

Over the past 35 years, the State–Trait Anxiety Inventory (Spielberger, 1983; Spielberger et al., 1970) has been frequently used to assess anxiety in research and clinical practice. Since the STAI was first published in 1970, this inventory has been translated and adapted in 66 languages and dialects, and cited in more than 16,000 archival studies. In three studies of patients with a documented history of myocardial infarction (Hiland, 1978; Roskies, Spevack, Surkis, Cohen, & Gilman, 1978; Spielberger, 1976), the mean STAI state and trait anxiety scores for the cardiovascular patients were higher than the means for a normative sample of working adults of similar age (Spielberger, 1983). However, the anxiety scores of these patients did not differ significantly from the control groups in two of the three studies (Roskies et al., 1978; Spielberger, 1976).

The myocardial infarction patients in the Hiland (1978) study had significantly higher S-Anxiety and T-Anxiety scores than the control group, but these patients also tended to be higher in socioeconomic status, which is inversely related to trait anxiety (Spielberger, 1983). Although the anxiety scores of Hiland's cardiovascular patients were not elevated as compared with the general population, their T-Anxiety scores were higher than would be expected on the basis of their socioeconomic status. Byrne (1979) also reported interesting findings for anxiety in patients with acute chest pains who were admitted to a coronary care unit. In this study, state anxiety was assessed with visual analog scales; trait anxiety was measured with Eysenck's Neuroticism scale. The results indicated that patients with documented myocardial infarction were higher in S-Anxiety than patients for whom an infarction could not be confirmed.

The STAI and the State–Trait Personality Inventory (STPI) were used in several recent investigations of anxiety in patients with angina pectoris and coronary artery disease (Elias, Robbins, Blow, Rice, & Edgecomb, 1982; Greene, 1988; Schocken, Greene, Worden, Harrison, & Spielberger, 1987). The results in these studies were remarkably consistent in demonstrating that patients with angina pectoris, but no angiographically documented coronary artery disease, scored higher on both state and trait anxiety than patients with both conditions. Thus, although high T-Anxiety was not associated with coronary artery disease, it seems to be a risk factor for referral for angiography.

Taken together, the research findings suggest that individuals with hypertension, or with a documented history of myocardial infarction, are slightly higher in anxiety than people of similar socioeconomic status who do not have cardiovascular problems. However, anxiety does not appear to be related to the Type-A behavior pattern. The finding that anxiety was more predictive of angina pectoris than coronary artery disease suggested that patients with chest pains who are referred for coronary angiography and found to have clean arteries were likely to be higher in T-Anxiety than patients whose chest pain was caused by coronary artery disease.

Anger/hostility, hypertension and heart disease

Both fear and rage were recognized by Darwin (1872/1965) as universal characteristics of both humans and animals that evolved through a process of natural selection because these emotions facilitated successful adaptation and survival. Darwin observed that rage was reflected in facial expression (e.g., reddened face, clenched teeth, dilated nostrils), and in accelerated heart rate, muscular tension, and aggressive or violent behavior. He regarded rage as intense anger that motivated "... animals of all kinds, and their progenitors before them, when attacked or threatened by an enemy ..." to fight and defend themselves (Darwin, 1872/1965, p. 74). For Darwin, anger was a state of mind that differed "... from rage only in degree, and there is no marked distinction in their characteristic signs" (1872/1965, p. 244).

In Freud's (1933/1959) psychoanalytic theory, aggression is considered a fundamental instinctual drive that involves angry feelings that motivate aggressive behavior. Freud conceptualized aggression as resulting from a biologically determined "death instinct" (thanatos) that motivated people to destroy themselves. Because thanatos was generally inhibited by a more powerful life instinct (libido), the energy associated with this self-destructive drive was redirected and expressed in aggressive behavior towards other persons or objects in the environment. However, when aggression could not be directly expressed because it was unacceptable and evoked intense anxiety and guilt, it was turned back into the self, resulting in depression and other psychosomatic manifestations (Alexander & French, 1948).

Anger, hostility and aggression are now recognized as fundamental concepts in most contemporary theories of personality and psychopathology, and as important contributors to the etiology of the psychoneuroses, depression, and schizophrenia. However, angry feelings are generally confounded with hostile attitudes and the expression of aggressive behavior, and these terms are frequently used interchangeably in the research literature. Consequently, definitions of anger, hostility and aggression remain somewhat ambiguous, leading to conceptual confusion and overlapping measurement operations of questionable validity (Biaggio, Supplee, & Curtis, 1981).

Given the substantial overlap in the prevailing definitions of anger, hostility, and aggression, we have referred collectively to these constructs as the AHA! Syndrome (Spielberger, Johnson, Russell, Crane, Jacobs, & Worden, 1985), and have endeavored to identify relatively independent and meaningful definitions for each concept. Anger refers to an emotional state that varies in intensity from mild irritation or annoyance to intense fury or rage, with associated activation or arousal of the autonomic and neuroendocrine systems (Spielberger, 1988, 1999). Hostility generally involves the experience of intense angry feelings, but this concept also has the connotation of complex attitudes and behaviors that include being mean, vicious, vindictive, and often cynical. As a psychological construct, the term aggression is traditionally used to describe destructive or punitive behaviors directed towards other persons or objects in the environment.

Physiological correlates of hostility and behavioral manifestations of aggression have been investigated in numerous studies. However, until the 1980s, anger was largely neglected in psychological research. Recent research on anger, hostility, and aggression, as well as observations of violence in daily life, provide strong evidence that anger-related problems are ubiquitous. In a series of studies, Deffenbacher and his associates (Deffenbacher, Story, Stark, Hogg, & Brandon, 1987) found that persons high in anger as a personality trait experienced angry feelings across a wide range of situations, and were more likely to engage in aggressive behavior. Anger, hostility, and aggression have also been found to contribute to the pathogenesis of hypertension (Crane, 1981), and to coronary heart disease (Spielberger & London, 1982).

Substantial evidence that anger motivates hostility and a wide range of aggressive behaviors makes clear the need to evaluate the intensity of anger as an emotional state, and how frequently this emotion is experienced. The State–Trait Anger Scale (STAS) was constructed to assess the intensity of feelings of anger, and individual differences in anger proneness as a personality trait (Spielberger et al., 1985). The results of a study in which hypertensive patients were compared with general medical and surgical patients with normal blood pressure demonstrated the importance of differences in trait anger assessed by the STAS T-Anger Temperament and Reaction subscales (Crane, 1981). The significantly higher STAS T-Anger scores that were found for the hypertensives, as compared with patients with normal blood pressure, were due entirely to their substantially higher scores on the T-Anger Reaction subscale; no differences in T-Anger Temperament were found.

As our research on anger has progressed, the critical importance of differentiating between the *experience* and *expression* of anger became increasingly apparent. The 20-item Anger EXpression (AX) Scale (Spielberger et al., 1985) included items that described the inhibition or suppression of angry feelings and the expression of anger directed toward other persons or objects in the environment. Respondents were informed that everyone feels angry or furious from time to time, and then instructed to report ". . . how often you generally react or behave in the manner described *when you feel angry or furious*" (Spielberger, Reheiser, & Sydeman, 1995, p. 58). The expanded 24-item AX Scale (Spielberger, Krasner, & Solomon, 1988) included 8-item AX/In, AX/Out and AX/Con scales.

The AX Scale was combined with the 20-item STAS to form the State–Trait Anger Expression Inventory (STAXI). An entirely new 8-item subscale was subsequently added to assess how often a person tries to control anger-in (AX/Con-In) by reducing the intensity of suppressed anger (Spielberger, 1999). The revised 57-item STAXI-2 also includes an expanded 15-item S-Anger scale, with three factorially derived subscales that assess Feeling Angry, Feel Like Expressing Anger Verbally, and Feel Like Expressing Anger Physically.

The STAXI has proved useful for assessing the experience, expression and control of anger in normal and abnormal individuals (Deffenbacher et al., 1987; Moses, 1992), and for evaluating relations between the components of anger with a variety of disorders, including alcoholism, hypertension, coronary heart disease, and cancer (Spielberger, 1988, 1999). Research with the STAXI and its subscales provides encouraging evidence of the utility of this inventory for assessing anger in diagnoses, treatment planning, and the evaluation of treatment outcomes (Spielberger et al., 1995).

Moses, Daniels and Nickerson (1956) investigated the relationship of anger and anxiety to blood pressure (BP) during psychotherapy for patients whom they followed for up to 5 years. They observed that hypertensive patients reacted to frustration with excessive and continuous rage and anxiety. Persistent BP elevations were most directly associated with "repressed" anger, whereas transient BP elevations were more often associated with anxiety. Employing a similar methodology, Wolf, Pfeiffer, Ripley, Winter, and Wolff (1948) found that hypertensive patients were more anxious and hostile than a normotensive control group; the hypertensive patients also showed a greater rise in BP than the controls at times when they experienced anger and anxiety. Similar findings were reported by van der Valk (1957).

Suppressed anger and hostility were also predominant features of the hypertensive cases reported by Hambling (1952) and Engel, Hamburger, Reiser, and Plunkett (1953). Tucher (1949) and Binger, Ackerman, and Cohn (1945) also observed that hostility and dependency were characteristics of hypertensive patients. In addition, Tucher (1949) described his patients as hard driving, ambitious, and always striving for success and recognition in their work. It is interesting to note that these characteristics were subsequently incorporated in the definition of the Type-A personality (Friedman & Rosenman, 1974).

The findings in most clinical case studies are strikingly consistent in describing hypertensive patients as experiencing high levels of anger and anxiety, and as having difficulty in expressing anger (Alexander, 1939; Binger et al., 1945; Kalis, Harris, Bennett, & Sokolow, 1961; Moses et al., 1956; Saul, 1939; Schnieder & Zangari, 1951; Tucher, 1949; van der Valk, 1957; Wolf et al., 1948). Although several investigators have reported that hypertensive patients "suppressed" their hostility (Alexander, 1939; Engel et al., 1953; Hambling, 1952), others described them as "inhibiting" anger (Binger et al., 1945; Saul, 1939; van der Valk, 1957) or "restraining" their angry feelings (Wolf et al., 1948). The results of clinical case studies provide strong support for Alexander's (1939) specificity hypothesis.

Type-A behavior and heart disease

The research of Freidman and Rosenman (1974) has stimulated the scientific study of nonphysical risk factors in heart disease. They noticed that many of their patients who had suffered heart attacks were uncommonly ambitious, striving, competitive, and hard driving prior to their being diagnosed with cardiovascular disease. Describing such persons as Type A, Freidman and Rosenman contrasted them with relaxed Type B individuals, and this A–B distinction struck a cord in the minds of many clinicians and researchers. Subsequently, using different tests and interviews, the connection between Type-A behavior and heart disease has been verified in numerous studies in which three major components of Type-A Behavior have been identified:

1   A competitive, hard-driving way of life.
2   A sense of time urgency that combines speed, impatience and obsessive concern with doing more and more in less and less time.
3   Excessive involvement in one's job.

Probing deeper, Friedman and Rosenman (1974) and other researchers (Matthews et al., 1977) identified 44 specific Type-A characteristics. However, only 7 of the 44 Type-A characteristics proved to be related to coronary heart disease (CHD), as was noted by Spielberger and London (1982). The specific characteristics that were each related to heart disease were:

1   Potential for hostility (as judged by original interviewer).
2   Gets angry more than once a week.
3   Anger directed outward (toward others rather than at oneself).
4   Irritability at having to wait in lines (queues).
5   Competitiveness in games with peers.
6   Explosive voice modulation (such as the tendency to talk in loud, staccato bursts).
7   Vigorous responses to interview questions (rather than calm, deliberate answers).

Anger was the single thread that wove through the seven deadly Type-A characteristics. Manifestation of anger in hostility, irritability, impatience, and explosive behavior added up to plain and fancy versions of the hothead. These findings made it clear that anger was the major lethal component of Type-A behavior, and suggested that anger and hostility were the key elements contributing to heart disease.

Psychological vital signs

The contribution of emotional and personality factors, especially anger, to the etiology of hypertension and coronary heart disease has been suggested by a number of investigators (Alexander, 1939; Spielberger, 1976; Spielberger et al., 1995). It is therefore essential to evaluate and monitor emotional vital states in diagnosis and treatment just as physicians in medical examinations routinely measure pulse rate, blood pressure, and temperature, the vital signs that provide essential information about physical health. When a physician detects an abnormal pulse during a physical examination, this signals a potentially significant problem in the functioning of the cardiovascular system. Running a high fever may indicate that the immune system is not protecting the person from harmful viruses.

Intense anxiety and anger are analogous to elevations in pulse rate and blood pressure, while the presence of a fever, as indicated by abnormally high body temperature, may be considered as roughly analogous to depression. Elevations in temperature that define a fever are interpreted by physicians as a strong indication of the presence of an infection or metabolic problem that requires immediate attention (Guyton, 1977). Similarly, anxiety, anger and symptoms of depression often indicate the presence of pervasive unresolved conflicts that result in an emotional fever.

The effects of intense feelings of anxiety and anger on an emotional fever are readily apparent. However, depression is more complex in that it often involves angry feelings that evoke anxiety and defense mechanisms that cause the anger to be turned inward, toward the self, resulting in feelings of guilt and sadness. While fevers in patients with colds or the flu can usually be reduced by aspirin or acetaminophen (paracetamol), the emotional conflicts that contribute to clinical depression are not likely to be relieved by either drugs or simple behavioral interventions. Because the threshold for seeking psychological treatment tends to be higher than for using medication to alleviate pain or fever, the problems that cause the emotional fever resulting from anxiety, anger and depression are more likely to persist to a point of crisis before help is sought.

Anxiety, anger, and depression are the psychological vital signs that are most critical to an individual's well-being. Variations in the intensity and duration of these emotional states provide essential information about a person's mental health, and can help to identify recent events, as well as long-standing conflicts, that have particular meaning and impact on an individual's life. Assessing emotional vital signs and providing timely and meaningful feedback during treatment will enhance a patient's awareness and understanding of her/his feelings. Helping patients to cope more effectively with their feelings early in treatment will also facilitate their dealing with the underlying mental and physical problems, and contribute to a more favorable treatment outcome.

Symptoms of anxiety are typically found in almost all emotional disorders. From a psychoanalytic perspective, Freud (1936, p. 85) regarded anxiety as the "fundamental phenomenon and the central problem of neurosis." The implication of Freud's theory was clearly noted by de la Torre (1979, p. 379), who concluded that: "The ubiquitousness of anxiety among psychiatric patients demands a careful assessment and diagnosis." According to de la Torre (1979), helping people to cope with their feelings of anxiety should be a major priority in all forms of psychotherapy, especially in crisis intervention and dynamic treatments that focus on the specific problems of a patient or client, and should be given priority in working with patients with medical problems.

Recent research findings, as well as observations of daily life, suggest that problems with anger are also ubiquitous. In a series of studies, Deffenbacher (1992) and his associates (Deffenbacher, Demm, & Brandon, 1986; Deffenbacher et al., 1987; Hogg & Deffenbacher, 1986) found that persons high in anger as a personality trait experienced angry feelings across a wide range of situations. As previously noted, anger and hostility contribute to hypertension and cardiovascular disease (Crane, 1981; Matthews et al., 1977; Spielberger & London, 1982). Treatments designed to assist clients reduce their anger by engaging in relaxation exercises help them to function more effectively, and to make better use of problem-solving techniques and social skills that are disrupted by their angry feelings. Consequently, careful assessment of the experience, expression and control of anger is essential in treatment planning (Sharkin, 1988).

The World Health Organization (WHO, 2001) estimates that 340 million people currently suffer from some form of clinical depression. Consequently, depression has been described as "the common cold of mental health problems that strikes the rich and poor as well as the young and the old" (Rosenfeld, 1999, p. 10). Symptoms of depression vary in severity, from feeling sad or gloomy for a relatively short period of time, to deep despair, extreme guilt, frequent crying, hopelessness, and thoughts of death that could result in suicide (Rosenfeld, 1999). Clearly, depression is a complex, multifaceted syndrome that is composed of a number of underlying dimensions. Like anxiety and anger, the assessment of depression is essential in treatment planning and outcome assessment.

Measuring anxiety, anger/hostility, and depression as psychological vital signs is of critical importance in the diagnosis and treatment of psychological disorders, and can provide patients with timely feedback that can contribute to the prevention and treatment of hypertension and cardiovascular disease. Assessing a patient's emotional vital signs can also facilitate treatment by directly linking intense emotional feelings to the events and experiences that give rise to them. In conclusion, anxiety, anger, and depression are important indicators of psychological distress and lack of well-being that should be carefully assessed in diagnostic evaluations, continuously monitored in counseling and psychotherapy, and assessed as outcome measures in behavioral interventions.

References

Alexander, F. (1939). Psychoanalytic study of a case of essential hypertension. *Psychomatic Medicine*, *1*, 139–152.

Alexander, F. G., & French, T. M. (Eds.). (1948). *Studies in psychosomatic medicine: An approach to the cause and treatment of vegetative disturbances.* New York: Ronald.

Banahan, B. F., Sharpe, T. R., Baker, J. A., Liao, W. C., & Smith, M. C. (1979). Hypertension and stress: A preventive approach. *Journal of Psychosomatic Research*, *23*, 69–75.

Biaggio, M. K., Supplee, K., & Curtis, N. (1981). Reliability and validity of four anger scales. *Journal of Personality Assessment, 45*, 639–648.

Binger, C. A. L., Ackerman, N. W., & Cohn, A. E. (1945). *Personality in arterial hypertension* (Psychosomatic Medicine Monographs). New York: American Society for Research in Psychosomatic Problems.

Brody, J. E. (1975, January 23). "Type A" theory challenged. *St. Petersburg Times.*

Byrne, D. G. (1979). Anxiety as state and trait following survived myocardial infarction. *British Journal of Social and Clinical Psychology, 18*, 417–423.

Cattell, R. B. (1966). Patterns of change: Measurement in relation to state dimension, trait change, liability, and process concepts. In *Handbook of Multivariate Experimental Psychology*. Chicago: Rand McNally.

Crane, R. S. (1981). The role of anger, hostility, and aggression in essential hypertension. Doctoral dissertation, University of South Florida, Tampa, FL. *Dissertation Abstracts International, 42*, 2982B.

Darwin, C. (1965). *The expression of emotions in man and animals.* Chicago: University of Chicago Press. (Originally published 1872)

de la Torre, J. (1979). Anxiety states and short-term psychotherapy. In W. E. Fann, I. Karacan, A. D. Polorny, & R. L. Williams (Eds.), *Phenomenology and treatment of anxiety* (pp. 377–388). Jamaica, NY: Spectrum Publications, Inc.

Deffenbacher, J. L. (1992). Trait anger: Theory, findings, and implications. In C. D. Spielberger & J. N. Butcher (Eds.), *Advances in personality assessment* (Vol. 9, pp. 177–201). Hillsdale, NJ: Lawrence Erlbaum Associates, Inc.

Deffenbacher, J. L., Demm, P. M., & Brandon, A. D. (1986). High general anger: Correlates and treatment. *Behavior Research and Therapy, 24*, 480–489.

Deffenbacher, J. L., Story, D. A., Stark, R. S., Hogg, J. A., & Brandon, A. D. (1987). Cognitive-relaxation and social skills interventions in the treatment of general anger. *Journal of Counseling Psychology, 34*, 171–176.

Elias, M. F., Robbins, M. A., Blow, F. C., Rice, A. P., & Edgecomb, J. L. (1982). A behavioral study of middle-aged chest pain patients physical symptoms reporting anxiety and depression. *Experimental Aging Research, 8*, 45–51.

Eliot, R. S. (Ed.). (1974). *Stress and the heart.* Mount Kisco, NY: Futura Publishing Company.

Engel, G., Hamburger, W., Reiser, M., & Plunkett, J. (1953). Electroencephalographic and psychological studies of a case of migraine with sever preheadache phenomena. *Psychosomatic Medicine, 19*, 337–348.

Freud, S. (1924). *Collected papers* (Vol. 1). London: Hogarth Press. (Originally published 1895)

Freud, S. (1936). *The problem of anxiety.* New York: W. W. Norton.

Freud, S. (1959). Why war? In J. Strachey (Ed.), *Collected papers* (Vol. 5). London: Hogarth Press. (Original work published 1933.)

Friedman, M., & Rosenman, R. H. (1974). *Type A behavior and your heart.* Greenwich, CT: Fawcett Publications, Inc.

Greene, A. F. (1988). *Coronary heart disease in anxious angry hearts.* Unpublished doctoral dissertation, University of South Florida, Tampa, FL.

Guyton, A. C. (1977). *Basic human physiology: Normal function and mechanism of disease.* Philadelphia: W. B. Saunders.

Hambling, J. (1952). Emotions and symptoms in essential hypertension. *British Journal of Medical Psychology, 24*, 242–253.

Hiland, D. N. (1978). Type A behavior, anxiety, job satisfaction and life stress as risk factors in myocardial infarction. Doctoral dissertation, University of South Florida, Tampa, FL. *Dissertation Abstracts International, 39*, 3516B.

Hogg, J. A., & Deffenbacher, J. L. (1986). Irrational beliefs, depression and anger in college students. *Journal of College Student Personnel, 27*, 349–353.

Kalis, B., Harris, R., Bennett, L., & Sokolow, M. (1961). Personality and life history factors in persons who are potentially hypertensive. *Journal of Nervous and Mental Disorders, 132*, 457–468.

Matthews, K. A., Glass, D. C., Rosenman, R. H., & Bortner, R. W. (1977). Competitive drive, Pattern A, and coronary heart disease: A further analysis of some data from the Western Collaborative Group Study. *Journal of Chronic Diseases, 30*, 489–498.

May, R. (1977). *The meaning of anxiety*. New York: W. W. Norton. (Originally published 1950)

Moses, J. A. (1992). State–Trait Anger Expression Inventory, Research Edition. In D. J. Keyser & R. C. Sweetland (Eds.), *Test critiques* (Vol. IX, pp. 510–525). Austin, TX: PRO-ED, Inc.

Moses, L., Daniels, G., & Nickerson, J. (1956). Psychogenic factors in essential hypertension: Methodology and preliminary report. *Psychosomatic Medicine, 18*, 417–485.

Rosenfeld, I. (1999). When the sadness won't go away. *Parade Magazine, September, 19*, 10.

Rosenman, R. H., Brand, R. J., Jenkins, C. D., Friedman, M., Straus, R., & Wurm, M. (1975). Coronary heart disease in the Western Collaborative Group Study: Final follow up experience of 8½ years. *Journal of the American Medical Association, 233*, 872–877.

Roskies, E., Spevack, M., Surkis, A., Cohen, C., & Gilman, S. (1978). Changing the coronary prone (Type A) behavior pattern in a nonclinical population. *Journal of Behavioral Medicine, 1*, 201–216.

Saul, L. J. (1939). Hostility in cases of essential hypertension. *Psychosomatic Medicine, 1*, 153–161.

Schneider, R. A., & Zangari, J. M. (1951). Variations in clotting time, relative viscosity and other physiochemical properties of the blood accompanying physical and emotional stress in the normotensive and hypertensive subjects. *Psychosomatic Medicine, 13*, 288–303.

Schocken, D. D., Greene, A. G., Worden, T. J., Harrison, E. E., & Spielberger, C. D. (1987). Effects of age and gender on the relationship between anxiety and coronary artery disease. *Psychosomatic Medicine, 49*, 119–126.

Sharkin, B. S. (1988). Treatment of client anger in counseling. *Journal of Counseling and Development, 66*, 361–365.

Spielberger, C. D. (1966). Theory and research on anxiety. In C. D. Spielberger (Ed.), *Anxiety and behavior* (pp. 3–20). New York: Academic Press.

Spielberger, C. D. (1972). Current trends in theory and research on anxiety. In C. D. Spielberger (Ed.), *Anxiety: Current trends in theory and research* (Vol. 1, pp. 3–19). New York: Academic Press.

Spielberger, C. D. (1976). Stress and anxiety and cardiovascular disease. *Journal of the South Carolina Medical Association* (Suppl.), 15.

Spielberger, C. D. (1979). *Understanding stress & anxiety*. London: Harper & Row.

Spielberger, C. D. (1983). *Manual for the State-Trait Anxiety Inventory: STAI (Form Y)*. Palo Alto, CA: Consulting Psychologists Press.

Spielberger, C. D. (1988). *Manual for the State-Trait Anger Expression Inventory (STAXI)*. Odessa, FL: Psychological Assessment Resources, Inc.

Spielberger, C. D. (1999). *Professional manual for the State-Trait Anger Expression Inventory-2 (STAXI-2)*. Odessa, FL: Psychological Assessment Resources, Inc.

Spielberger, C. D., Gorsuch, R. L., & Lushene, R. D. (1970). *STAI: Manual for the State–Trait Anxiety Inventory*. Palo Alto, CA: Consulting Psychologists Press.

Spielberger, C. D., Johnson, E. H., Russell, S. F., Crane, R. J., Jacobs, G. A., & Worden, T. J. (1985). The experience and expression of anger: Construction and validation of an anger expression scale. In M. A. Chesney & R. H. Rosenman (Eds.), *Anger and hostility in cardiovascular and behavioral disorders* (pp. 5–30). New York: Hemisphere/McGraw-Hill.

Spielberger, C. D., Krasner, S. S., & Solomon, E. P. (1988). The experience, expression and control of anger. In M. P. Janisse (Ed.), *Health psychology: Individual differences and stress* (pp. 89–108). New York: Springer Verlag.

Spielberger, C. D., & London, P. (1982). Rage boomerangs: Lethal Type-A anger. *American Health, 1*, 52–56.

Spielberger, C. D., Reheiser, E. C., & Sydeman, S. J. (1995). Measuring the experience, expression, and control of anger. In H. Kassinove (Ed.), *Anger disorders: Definitions, diagnosis, and treatment* (pp. 49–76). Washington, DC: Taylor & Francis.

Syme, S. L. (1975). Social and psychological risk factors in coronary heart disease. *Modern Conceptions of Cardiovascular Disorders, 44*, 17–21.

Tucher, W. I. (1949). Psychiatric factors in essential hypertension. *Diseases of the Nervous System, 10*, 273–278.

van der Valk, J. M. (1957). Blood pressure changes under emotional influences in patients with essential hypertension and control subjects. *Journal of Psychosomatic Research, 2*, 134–146.

Whitehead, W. E., Blackwell, B., DeSilva, H., & Robinson, A. (1977). Anxiety and anger in hypertension. *Journal of Psychosomatic Research, 21*, 383–389.

WHO. (2001). *Depression/depression1.htm*. World Health Organization. (Available at: www.who.int/mental_health/Topic_Depression/depression1.htm)

Wolf, S., Pfeiffer, J., Ripley, M., Winter, O., & Wolff, H. (1948). Hypertension as a reaction pattern to stress: Summary of experimental data on variations in blood pressure and renal blood flow. *Annals of Internal Medicine, 29*, 1056.

9 Temperament as a predictor of maladaptive behavior under extreme stress: The Polish studies of natural disasters

Jan Strelau, Magdalena Kaczmarek, and Bogdan Zawadzki

Introduction

The aim of the study was to investigate the role of temperament as a predictor of maladaptive behavior under the experience of extreme stress. Although previously the role of personality was usually not mentioned or was underestimated in this context (see Lauterbach, 2005) current studies and the literature highlight the role of personality and individual differences, beside objective features of the event, as crucial determinants of the intensity of pathological reactions to extreme stress. Regarding personality, temperamental traits are especially worth taking into consideration. One reason is that temperament is described as a variable moderating stress phenomena (Strelau, 1995).[1] The second one is that temperament is present and may be measured beginning from early life. Hence, studies should be conducted comparing people's reaction to extreme stressors depending on their age from early childhood onwards.

The role of temperament in stress phenomena

Figure 9.1 shows the model of relationships between temperament and stress phenomena. Temperament is defined as personality traits that are present from early childhood, and can be observed not only in human behavior but also in animals, and refers rather to formal aspects of behavior (Strelau, 1998). Formal characteristics of behavior can be considered in terms of energetic and temporal patterns in behavior. Temperamental traits, being more or less unspecific, penetrate all kinds of behavior, whatever the content or direction of this behavior. Following the regulative theory of temperament (RTT), formulated by Strelau and described in details in several publications (Strelau, 1996, 1998) temperament plays a regulatory role, which consists of modifying (moderating) the stimulatory and temporal value of situations and behavior, according to the individual-specific temperamental traits. This role is especially evident in difficult situations and extreme behaviors. The state of stress is understood here as a result of lack of equilibrium (occurrence of

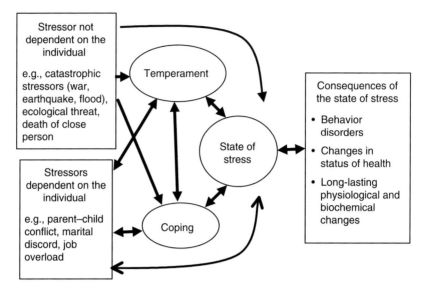

Figure 9.1 The model of relationships between temperament and stress phenomena.

discrepancy) between demands and the individual's capability (capacity) to cope with them (see Krohne & Laux, 1982; McGrath, 1970; Strelau, 1995, 1998). Temperament is one of the factors moderating the relationships between demands and capacities, independent of whether they exist objectively or are perceived by the individual.

As shown in Figure 9.1 the "temperament–stress" phenomena constitute a system of complex and reciprocal relationships. Beside the role of temperament in moderating the intensity of the state of stress, studies indicate some further relationships inside the model. Temperament: (1) co-determines the intensity of stressors and, in case of stressors dependent on the individual, also the probability of their occurrence; (2) moderates the coping efforts; and (3) contributes to the psychophysiological and/or psychological costs of the state of stress (Strelau, 1998). In most of the cases, the arrows on the ends of connecting lines are turned in both directions; thus indicating the transactional nature of relationships between temperament and stress phenomena.

In Figure 9.1 stressors are divided into two groups: dependent and non-dependent on the individual. Stressors of the latter type were especially investigated in this study. Natural disasters as well as human-made disasters may be regarded as experiences that can be defined as unexpected, uncontrolled by their victims, usually violent, highly disruptive for material property, and dangerous to human life and health (see Green, 1998). Disasters, such as natural catastrophes, can be defined as universal stressors. They lead to the state of stress in all individuals regardless of age, and result in stress not only in humans but also in other animals (Strelau, 1995). In terms of Lazarus' theory (see Folkman & Lazarus, 1988) they are relatively independent from individual differences. One may say that primary appraisal does not vary among individuals.[2] Hence, the more severe and long-lasting the stressor, the more intense is the state of stress being experienced. According to our view the intensity of reactions to such stressors is moderated by, among other things, temperamental traits. The conclusion is that, on the basis of the described model, two main characteristics influence the intensity of experienced stress: (1) the objective features of the extremely stressful event; and (2) individual differences, which in our study are limited to temperamental characteristics.

The state of stress is understood here as a state characterized by strong negative emotions, such as fear, anxiety, anger, hostility, or other emotional states evoking distress, accompanied by physiological and biochemical changes that evidently exceed the baseline level of arousal (Strelau, 1995). Depending on the intensity of such experiences some psychophysiological and/or psychological costs may be paid by the individual. In this study in terms of psychological costs the intensity of symptoms of posttraumatic stress disorder were considered.

Symptoms of post-traumatic stress disorder

Post-traumatic stress disorder (PTSD) is a set of symptoms described in DSM-IV (APA, 1994) and defined as a possible sequel of the experience of a traumatic event. Following the definition of traumatic event, the core feature of such an event is the threat to life or health (see APA, 1994). From this point of view, a disaster, such as a natural catastrophe, meets the definition of a traumatic event. The symptoms of PTSD are defined by means of three diagnostic criteria, each composed of similar kinds of symptoms. In short, the PTSD manifests as: (1) symptoms of re-experiencing the event, such as intrusive thoughts or dreams; (2) symptoms of numbness, expressed as emotional coldness or decreased activity, together with avoidance of stimuli associated with the traumatic event; and (3) symptoms of the state of hyperarousal, e.g., expressed as difficulties in concentrating or falling asleep. To meet the diagnosis of PTSD, the level of intensity and duration of symptoms must reach a threshold defined in DSM-IV. Regardless of the clinical approach to PTSD, which is focused on identifying the occurrence of a psychiatric disease, the dimensional approach to intensity of PTSD symptoms may be applied. In this approach the full range of intensity of symptoms is taken into consideration. Such a strategy provides an opportunity not only to look for the risk factors of the pathological level of symptoms, but also to identify determinants of resilience to such experience (Bonanno, 2004; Ruscio, Ruscio, & Keane, 2002). The general idea of such an approach is exemplified in Figure 9.2.

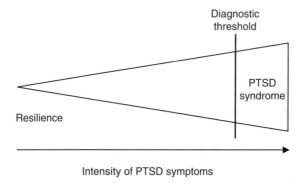

Figure 9.2 The dimensional approach to the intensity of PTSD symptoms.

Hypotheses

As already mentioned, two main groups of determinants of the intensity of PTSD symptoms were considered: characteristics of the event and temperamental traits. In our study both of them have been taken into account with respect to different age groups: children, youths, and adults.

Disaster is considered as an extreme stressor comprising several features that influence trauma. Generally, as the number of features of the stressor increases, the level of impairment in functioning grows (see Norris, Friedman, Watson, Byrne, Diaz, & Kaniasty, 2002). This relationship, called the "dose–response" effect, was revealed in a wide range of studies on disaster with regard to children, youths, and adults. Studies also show that threats to life and health are the most important features of such stressors (see Norris et al., 2002; Ozer, Best, Lipsey, & Weiss, 2003). Moreover, losses and damage to property, and the further economic troubles caused by them, which are typical in the aftermath of a natural disaster, may be significantly related to the intensity of pathological symptoms in the future (see Green, 1998; Norris et al., 2002). However, the impact of such characteristics is not so evident in younger participants, who are dependent on caregivers.

Temperamental traits have rarely been studied in the context of psychological consequences of disaster. According to Lauterbach (2005) such a state of affairs might be caused by the severe and universal nature of disaster itself. The widely observed stressful reactions to the event may obscure the role of individual personality differences within the range of such reactions. In one of the first studies in this domain, however, McFarlane (1988) found that neuroticism and introversion measured by the Eysenck Personality Inventory were higher in groups in which participants (firefighters) manifested chronic PTSD compared with groups of non-PTSD participants. The role of neuroticism in predicting the level of impairment in the aftermath of traumatic events was confirmed in studies conducted by Lauterbach (2005; Lauterbach & Vrana, 2001). In these studies neuroticism was investigated according to the Eysenckian model of PEN (Eysenck & Eysenck, 1985) and the Big Five model of personality elaborated by Costa and McCrae (1992). As well as neuroticism and introversion, such temperamental traits as, e.g., trait-anxiety and sensation seeking were also studied (Dekel, Solomon, Ginzburg, & Neria, 2005; Fairbank, Klaric, O'Dekirk, Fairbank, & Costello, 2005; Zeidner & Ben-Zur, 1994). Most parts of these studies were conducted on samples consisting of adult victims. However, there is some empirical evidence (see Fairbank et al., 2005) and theoretical expectation (see Gordon & Wraith, 1993) leading to the conclusion that temperament may play a similar role under extreme stress in children as in adults. The common feature of the temperamental traits mentioned above – anxiety, introversion, neuroticism, and low sensation seeking – is that they have roots in a high level of chronic arousal (arousability) although the mechanism responsible for regulating arousal is specific to different temperament traits (see Strelau, 1998). High arousability regarded as a trait (trait-arousal) is related to poor functioning under highly demanding (stimulating) conditions. One may say that traits referring to the construct of arousability are related to the energetic aspect of behavior. Beside this, the temporal aspect of behavior may be considered because both refer to the formal characteristics of behavior. Temporal characteristics describe how fast individuals react to changes in the environment, and how fast they are able to stop reacting to stimuli that have disappeared. For this reason, temporal aspects of behavior may be related to the process of adaptation after a stressful experience and, as a consequence, related also to the intensity of PTSD symptoms. According to the RTT, on which this study is based, six temperamental traits have been distinguished (Strelau & Zawadzki, 1993) as follows: (1) briskness; (2) perseveration; (3) emotional reactivity; (4) sensory sensitivity; (5) endurance; and (6) activity (1 and 2 refer to the temporal characteristics of behavior, while 3 to 6 cover the energetic aspect of behavior). From these traits briskness, perseveration and emotional reactivity were selected for this study. According to the RTT these three temperamental traits are defined as follows:

- *Briskness* (BR): a tendency to react quickly, to keep a high tempo in performing activities, and to shift easily in response to changes in the surroundings from one behavior (reaction) to another.
- *Perseveration* (PE): a tendency to continue and to repeat behavior and experience emotional states after cessation of the stimuli (situations) evoking this behavior or states.
- *Emotional reactivity* (ER): a tendency to react intensively to emotion-generating stimuli, expressed in high emotional sensitivity and low emotional endurance.

Taking into account the aim of our study two hypotheses were formulated:

1 The characteristics of the event, such as threats to life and health, losses

and damages to property (trauma characteristics), and any further economical consequences resulting from them (trauma consequences), and emotional reactivity understood as a temperament trait related to high arousability, will allow us to predict the general PTSD level as well as its components regardless of the age of the victims.

The role of temporal characteristics – briskness and perseveration – regarded as predictors of PTSD is more specific.

2   Briskness, underlying the ability to adapt to new environments, serves mainly as a predictor of symptoms of avoidance. In turn, perseveration, understood as the tendency to continue and repeat behavior and emotions, is primarily related to symptoms of intrusion. These relationships are comparative regardless of age.

Method

Subjects

The data analyzed in this chapter were obtained from three independent samples of flood victims. All participants were witnesses of the event and suffered from it. They lived in distinct parts of Poland in places of different sizes – from a small village (Budzów) to a big city (Gdańsk). In all groups trauma characteristics, and the prolonged objective consequences, temperament, and PTSD symptoms were assessed during one session in two to three years after the flood. Demographic characteristics of these groups are presented in Table 9.1.

The first sample (A) was composed of 124 children (65 girls and 59 boys) ranging in age from 8 to 13 years and 214 of their parents (117 mothers and 97 fathers) aged from 27 to 66. Subjects survived the flood in 2001 and were investigated two years later at their homes in southern Poland (Maków Podhalański and Budzów; 97 families) and in Gdańsk, a city located in the northern part of Poland (27 families). All parents were asked about the event characteristics, its consequences, the intensity of PTSD symptoms and temperament via self-report assessment. In children all of these variables were measured via parent-rating instruments. The ratings of temperament and the intensity of PTSD symptoms were obtained from 90 couples. In case of 34 children only one parent was investigated, due to the fact that the second parent was temporarily or continually absent from home.

The second sample (B) was composed of 267 subjects, split into two groups: 196 adults (109 females and 87 males) aged from 22 to 75 and 71 youths (49 females and 22 males) aged from 14 to 21. All participants had also survived the 2001 Polish flood and all of them were investigated two years after the disaster at their homes in Gdańsk.

The third sample (C) was composed of 276 subjects: 198 adults (104 females and 94 males) aged from 22 to 75 and 78 youths (40 females and 38 males) aged from 14 to 21. These subjects survived the 1997 Polish flood and were

Table 9.1 Demographic characteristics of the investigated samples with time of investigation after disaster and basic statistics (means and standard deviations) of applied scales of intensity of PTSD symptoms (general score and subscales)

Sample	Time of investigation after trauma	Age group (source of the diagnosis)	N	Gender	Age M (SD)	Range of age	PTSD	Intrusion	Avoidance
A	Two years	Children (parent-rating)	124	65F/59M	10.31 (1.50)	8–13	14.48 (8.98)	8.07 (5.04)	6.40 (5.98)
		Adults (self-report)	214	117F/97M	39.76 (6.69)	27–66	18.57 (15.57)	11.03 (9.13)	7.54 (7.77)
B	Two years	Youths (self-report)	71	49F/22M	16.97 (2.27)	14–21	14.29 (13.11)	9.38 (9.23)	4.91 (5.81)
		Adults (self-report)	196	109F/87M	44.18 (9.73)	22–75	29.02 (16.42)	19.27 (10.01)	9.75 (8.31)
C	Three years	Youths (self-report)	78	40F/38M	17.17 (1.77)	14–21	34.55 (19.75)	20.39 (11.15)	14.16 (10.62)
		Adults (self-report)	198	104F/94M	44.01 (9.19)	22–75	22.86 (17.90)	15.45 (11.45)	7.41 (7.96)

Note: F, females; M, males; PTSD, total score of PTSD-F and PTSD-F(C); Intrusion, scores of Intrusion/Hyperarousal from PTSD-F and PTSD-F(C); Avoidance, scores of Avoidance/Numbing from PTSD-F and Passive Avoidance/Hyperarousal from PTSD-F(C). For detailed description of the scales see text.

investigated three years after the disaster at their homes in Racibórz (a town in southern Poland).

The group of youths was appointed on the bases of Levinson's (1990) concept of life stages. The individuals forming these groups are more mature than children and more similar to adults with respect to their psychological functioning. However, all the children and a large number of the participants classified as youths lived with their parents as their financial dependants. Most of the youths, similar to the children, attended schools and had not set up their own families yet.

Measures

In order to measure the intensity of PTSD symptoms in adults and youths, a new instrument known as the PTSD-Factorial Version (PTSD-F) inventory was developed by Strelau and coworkers (Strelau, Zawadzki, Oniszczenko, & Sobolewski, 2002). The PTSD-F is designed to assess the intensity of PTSD symptoms along the whole dimension describing the range of intensity of PTSD symptoms observed in flood victims (as discussed in the introduction). Apart from a total score, PTSD-F comprises two scales corresponding to two basic PTSD factors – Intrusion/Hyperarousal and Avoidance/Numbing. The PTSD-F total score correlates highly (.71, $p < .01$) with the Polish translation of the Revised Civilian Mississippi Scale (RCMS) developed by Norris and Perilla (1996). Detailed data showing convergent and discriminant validity of the PTSD-F inventory are presented elsewhere (Strelau et al., 2002). In all reported studies the total score as well as both scales of the PTSD-F inventory were taken into account. The total score, reflecting the general intensity of PTSD symptoms, was calculated as a sum of answers to all 30 items, scoring from 0 to 3 points each. The scores in both scales were calculated as a sum of answers to a set of 15 items. They reflect the empirically found dimensions grouped into particular PTSD symptoms and their names describe the kinds of symptoms included.

For the assessment of the symptoms of PTSD in children (sample A), another instrument, called the PTSD-Factorial Version for Children, PTSD-F(C), inventory was developed by Kaczmarek (see Kaczmarek & Zawadzki, 2005). The PTSD-F(C) is constructed in the form of parent-rating. Similarly to the PTSD-F, this inventory is designed to assess the intensity of PTSD symptoms along the whole dimension. Apart from a total score, PTSD-F(C) comprises two scales corresponding to two basic factors grouping the particular symptoms – Intrusion/Avoidance and Passive Avoidance/Hyperarousal. The PTSD-F(C) total score correlates highly (.76, $p < .01$) with the Polish translation of the Children's Post-traumatic Disorder Reaction Index, Parent Version, Revision 1 developed by Rodriguez, Steinberg and Pynoos (1999). The intensity of PTSD in children was measured by means of the total score of the PTSD-F(C) inventory. It reflects the general intensity of PTSD symptoms. The total score was calculated as the sum of answers to all 20 items, scoring from 0 to 3 points for each. Also scores of both scales were taken into account and calculated as the sum of answers to sets of 11 items for Intrusion/Avoidance and 9 items for Passive Avoidance/Hyperarousal. The score of the intensity of PTSD symptoms for each child was either the mean of scores rated by both parents or the score rated by one parent only (if only one parent was investigated).

Trauma intensity was assessed in samples A and B by an interview comprising seven questions referring to: (a) threat to life during flood (2 items); (b) injuries to the body (2 items); and (c) material damage (3 items). The total trauma index comprises all three aspects. In sample C the preliminary version of the interview was used: trauma intensity was assessed by four questions referring to: (a) threat to life during flood (1 item); and (b) material damage (3 items). The total trauma index comprises both aspects.

The prolonged trauma consequences were assessed by eight items asking about: (d) financial problems (3 items); (e) problems with housing (2 items); and (f) decline in SES after flood (3 items). The total index of prolonged trauma consequences comprises all three aspects.

Temperament was assessed in all samples of adults and youths by the Formal Characteristics of Behavior – Temperament Inventory (FCB-TI; Strelau & Zawadzki, 1993, 1995) composed of six scales: Briskness, Perseveration, Sensory Sensitivity, Endurance, Emotional Reactivity and Activity. All scales contain 20 items each scored in "Yes–No" format (the scores range from 0 to 20 points). In children a version of this inventory was applied in the form of parent-rating (Temperament Inventory for Children [TIC]; see Oniszczenko & Radomska, 2002). All scales of TIC contain 5 items each scored in "Yes–No" format (the scores range from 0 to 5 points). Similarly to the assessment of the intensity of PTSD symptoms, the mean of rate of both parents was calculated (or the score rated by one parent was applied). For the purpose of the analyses presented in this chapter the Emotional Reactivity, Briskness and Perseveration scales from FCB-TI and TIC were taken into account.

Procedure

All participants were surveyed in their homes. They were appointed by the local social welfare officers, who classified the participants as primary victims of the event who had experienced substantial property damage. All family members were asked to take a part in the study – in the case of children written permissions from the parents were required – and, if they agreed, they were asked to fill out the set of inventories. All families participating in the study were paid in cash.

Results

In all samples the analysis was started by calculating the basic statistics of the applied scales of the intensity of PTSD symptoms (see Table 9.1) as well as the correlations between trauma characteristics, trauma consequences, temperamental traits, and the intensity (total and dimensions) of the PTSD symptoms. Factorial scales were classified into "intrusion" and "avoidance" according to the main content covered by the factor and correlations with criteria symptoms B, C, and D category from the RCMS and Children's Posttraumatic Disorder Reaction Index. Thus, Intrusion/Hyperarousal from PTSD-F and Intrusion/Avoidance from PTSD-F(C) were classified into "intrusion" and Avoidance/Numbing and Passive Avoidance/Hyperarousal into "avoidance", respectively. It should be noted, however, that the factorial scales cover a broader content than the one that strictly refers to the above mentioned two criteria of PTSD symptoms. Nevertheless, the differences between the empirically found structure of PTSD symptoms in children and in adults are congruent with other investigations (see Anthony, Lonigan, & Hecht, 1999). Next, the correlations between trauma characteristics, trauma consequences, temperamental traits, and the intensity of PTSD symptoms measured by means of total score and scores of factorial scales grouping intrusion and avoidance symptoms are displayed in Table 9.2.

The findings indicate that almost all coefficients of correlations were significant, which suggests that trauma and temperament really predict the intensity of PTSD symptoms. The correlations of trauma intensity with the PTSD total score ranged from .11 to .43 (.10 to .41 for intrusion symptoms and .10 to .38 for avoidance symptoms). For trauma consequences, slightly higher values of correlations with the intensity of PTSD symptoms were found: from .18 to .47 (.24 to .44 for intrusion symptoms and .08 to .42 for avoidance symptoms). Moreover, it seems that in adults both aspects of the event – trauma characteristics and its consequences – are more strongly related to the intensity of PTSD symptoms than they are in children and youths. Regarding the correlation of trauma characteristics and consequences, and subsets of PTSD symptoms – avoidance and intrusion – no crucial differences between the matrixes were found. These results partially support our first hypothesis. The unexpected finding shows relatively low relationships between trauma characteristics and consequences and measures of the intensity of PTSD symptoms in children and in youths.

Regarding the magnitudes of coefficients of correlations, temperament is as much related to the intensity of PTSD symptoms as to the characteristics of the disaster and its consequences. The main predictor of PTSD intensity is emotional reactivity, which explains almost to the same degree the total score (.26 to .49), as both factorial scores (.23 to .46 for intrusion and .25 to .47 for avoidance). The relationships with emotional reactivity are strong and comparable to the scores among investigated samples differing in age. The described findings support our first hypothesis.

The correlations with briskness and perseveration are lower in respect of the total score (ranging from −.20 to −.48 for briskness and .12 to .40 for perseveration). These traits are more strongly related to the intensity of the subset of PTSD symptoms: briskness correlates more highly than

Table 9.2 Correlations between temperamental traits, trauma characteristics and their consequences, and PTSD intensity (total and dimensions)

PTSD symptoms intensity – total

Variable	Children (sample A)	Youths (sample B)	Youths (sample C)	Adults (sample A)	Adults (sample B)	Adults (sample C)
TR	.43*	.11	.11	.36*	.38*	.36*
CO	.22*	.18	.35*	.28*	.32*	.47*
ER	.45*	.26*	.39*	.35*	.49*	.49*
BR	−.42*	−.23*	−.33*	−.20*	−.48*	−.27*
PE	.40*	.12	.19	.30*	.38*	.34*

Intrusion symptoms intensity

Variable	Children (sample A)	Youths (sample B)	Youths (sample C)	Adults (sample A)	Adults (sample B)	Adults (sample C)
TR	.41*	.10	.10	.36*	.32*	.38*
CO	.25*	.24*	.27*	.24*	.26*	.44*
ER	.27*	.23*	.40*	.36*	.46*	.46*
BR	−.25*	−.06	−.29*	−.12	−.36*	−.24*
PE	.33*	.12	.26*	.37*	.44*	.34*

Avoidance symptoms intensity

Variable	Children (sample A)	Youths (sample B)	Youths (sample C)	Adults (sample A)	Adults (sample B)	Adults (sample C)
TR	.28*	.10	.10	.29*	.38*	.26*
CO	.10	.08	.36*	.27*	.32*	.42*
ER	.47*	.25*	.24*	.25*	.43*	.45*
BR	−.45*	−.38*	−.28*	−.24*	−.51*	−.26*
PE	.31*	.10	.03	.15*	.24*	.27*

Note: *Correlations significant at $p < .05$ (two-tailed). TR, trauma characteristics; CO, prolonged consequences of disaster; BR, Briskness; PE, Perseveration; ER, Emotional Reactivity.

perseveration with avoidance symptoms (−.24 to −.51 against .03 to .31), while perseveration correlates more highly than briskness with intrusion symptoms (.12 to .44 against −.06 to −.36). This observation is also valid if the correlations of given temperament traits with both PTSD factors are compared – briskness correlates more highly with avoidance symptoms than with intrusion symptoms and, vice versa, perseveration correlates more highly with intrusion symptoms than with avoidance symptoms. Such findings support the second hypothesis.

In the next stage, regression analyses were performed with all independent variables introduced to the model (Pedhazur & Pedhazur-Schmelkin, 1991). These analyses were conducted mainly to answer the question about the discriminative role of temperamental variables. In Table 9.3 the multiple correlations and proportions of explained variance as well as partial correlations for each predictor of general intensity of PTSD symptoms and of both subsets of PTSD symptoms are presented.

The results confirmed our expectations described in the first hypothesis. In the case of emotional reactivity, four partial correlations were significant for the prediction of the general intensity PTSD symptoms as well as for the prediction of the intensity of avoidance symptoms, and three for predicting the intensity of intrusion symptoms. Briskness only marginally predicts the total score (two significant effects) and does not predict the intrusion symptoms (no significant effects). The role of briskness is very clear in the model of predictors of the intensity of avoidance symptoms: four significant effects were found. The reverse pattern of relationships was found with respect to perseveration: no significant effects for avoidance symptoms and two effects for intrusion (similar to briskness the only marginal impact on the total score – one significant effect).

Based on these findings and in congruence with expected relationships, the next stage of regression analyses (enter method) was conducted. The results indicate the crucial role of emotional reactivity as a temperamental predictor of intensity of PTSD symptoms regardless of the measure of PTSD symptoms. For this trait, all six partial correlations were significant in the analysis of the general intensity PTSD symptoms and four partial correlations in the analysis of each subset of symptoms. Moreover, briskness allows us to predict the intensity of avoidance symptoms (four significant effects), while perseveration predicts the intensity of intrusion symptoms (two effects). Trauma characteristics and trauma consequences are also significant predictors of the intensity of PTSD symptoms. However, the strength and significance of the partial correlations vary among samples and the set of PTSD symptoms taken into account. Based on these findings, the last regression analysis was performed via the stepwise method.[3] The results are presented in Table 9.4.

The findings indicate that emotional reactivity seems to be the best predictor of the general intensity of PTSD symptoms (total score). For all six groups covering the whole range of investigated differences in age, this trait significantly predicted intensity of symptoms. The role of this trait is also important in the case of subsets of symptoms (four significant effects), but only with respect to adults. Only one significant effect was found in the group of children (avoidance symptoms) and only one in groups of youths (intrusion symptoms). The main temperamental predictor of avoidance symptoms is briskness (five significant effects). Perseveration allows us to substantially predict the intensity of intrusion symptoms: three effects were found (in children and in two groups of adults).

Similar differences were found regarding the trauma indices. Trauma characteristics predict the general intensity of PTSD symptoms in adults and in

Table 9.3 The results of regression analysis with trauma characteristics, its consequences and temperamental traits as predictors of PTSD intensity (total and dimensions) – enter method

PTSD symptoms intensity – total

Statistics	Children (sample A)	Youths (sample B)	Youths (sample C)	Adults (sample A)	Adults (sample B)	Adults (sample C)
R	.61*	.34	.50*	.52*	.66*	.63*
R^2	.38	.12	.25	.27	.43	.40
TR	.26*	.11	.01	.31*	.30*	.22*
CO	.08	.18	.30*	.15*	.26*	.32*
ER	.27*	.10	.20	.20*	.19*	.28*
BR	−.29*	−.14	−.17	−.06	−.24*	−.06
PE	.09	.01	−.02	.10	.15*	.08

Intrusion symptoms intensity

Statistics	Children (sample A)	Youths (sample B)	Youths (sample C)	Adults (sample A)	Adults (sample B)	Adults (sample C)
R	.49*	.33	.46*	.53*	.60*	.61*
R^2	.24	.10	.21	.28	.36	.37
TR	.25*	.09	.02	.31*	.23*	.25*
CO	.11	.20	.21	.10	.22*	.29*
ER	.10	.17	.21	.21*	.18*	.24*
BR	−.12	.05	−.10	.04	−.10	−.04
PE	.11	−.01	.05	.17*	.25*	.11

Avoidance symptoms intensity

Statistics	Children (sample A)	Youths (sample B)	Youths (sample C)	Adults (sample A)	Adults (sample B)	Adults (sample C)
R	.58*	.41*	.46*	.43*	.63*	.55*
R^2	.34	.17	.21	.19	.40	.30
TR	.12	.12	.00	.24*	.30*	.12
CO	−.01	.12	.33*	.16*	.24*	.29*
ER	.34*	.03	.10	.13*	.16*	.26*
BR	−.34*	−.32*	−.22	−.15*	−.33*	−.06
PE	.02	−.01	−.12	−.01	.00	.03

Note: R, multiple correlation; R^2, explained variance. *Correlations significant at $p < .05$ (two-tailed). For each independent variable the partial correlation is presented. For other abbreviations see Tables 9.1 and 9.2.

Table 9.4 The results of regression analysis with trauma characteristics, its consequences and selected temperamental traits as predictors of PTSD intensity (total and dimensions) – stepwise method

PTSD symptoms intensity – total

Statistics	Children (sample A)	Youths (sample B)	Youths (sample C)	Adults (sample A)	Adults (sample B)	Adults (sample C)
R	.54*	.26*	.48	.51*	.62*	.63*
R^2	.29	.07	.23	.26	.39	.39
TR	.35*	–	–	.33*	.31*	.23*
CO	–	–	.31*	.14*	.28*	.32*
ER	.38*	.26*	.35*	.35*	.47*	.43*

Intrusion symptoms intensity

Statistics	Children (sample A)	Youths (sample B)	Youths (sample C)	Adults (sample A)	Adults (sample B)	Adults (sample C)
R	.45*	.24*	.40*	.52*	.59*	.60*
R^2	.20	.06	.16	.27	.35	.36
TR	.32*	–	–	.35*	.24*	.27*
CO	–	.24*	–	–	.23*	.28*
ER	–	–	.40*	.23*	.25*	.40*
PE	.19*	–	–	.17*	.25*	–

Avoidance symptoms intensity

Statistics	Children (sample A)	Youths (sample B)	Youths (sample C)	Adults (sample A)	Adults (sample B)	Adults (sample C)
R	.57*	.38*	.45*	.43*	.63*	.54
R^2	.33	.14	.20	.19	.40	.29
TR	–	–	–	.24*	.30*	–
CO	–	–	.36*	.16*	.24*	.33*
ER	.39*	–	–	.15*	.19*	.38*
BR	-.36*	-.38*	-.28*	-.15*	-.33*	–

Note: For all abbreviations see Table 9.3.

children. Moreover, in adults they predict the intensity of both subsets of symptoms, whereas in children they do not. Trauma characteristics seem to have no impact on the intensity of PTSD symptoms in youths, regardless of the predicted variable being considered – neither on the total score nor on any factorial subdimensions. Additionally, regarding adult groups, trauma characteristics show greater influences on intrusion symptoms than on avoidance symptoms (four effects against two). Trauma consequences also predict the general intensity of PTSD symptoms (total score), but only in adults and in youths. In children trauma consequences do not predict the intensity of any kind of post-traumatic symptoms. Contrary to trauma characteristics, trauma consequences exhibit greater influence on avoidance symptoms than on intrusion symptoms (four effects against three).

Regarding the subset of PTSD symptoms, the results may be summarized as follows. Trauma characteristics influence intrusion symptoms to a greater extent, while trauma consequences influence avoidance symptoms more (with a similar effect of both trauma aspects on the general intensity of PTSD symptoms). Similar conclusions hold true for temperamental traits – briskness influences avoidance symptoms more, while perseveration influences intrusion symptoms more. Emotional reactivity is, however, the main predictor of each measure of the intensity of PTSD symptoms in adults. In children and in youths the role of emotional reactivity seems to be weaker. Although most recorded effects were in line with our hypotheses, some findings were not expected and thus should be carefully verified in future studies.

Discussion

The aim of the study was to investigate the role of temperament as a predictor of maladaptive behavior under the experience of extreme stress. Two hypotheses were formulated. It was expected that the temperamental trait known as emotional reactivity, and trauma characteristics and trauma consequences would be related to and predict the intensity of PTSD symptoms (considered in terms of costs of stress evoked by disaster) regardless of the set of symptoms taken into account and regardless of the age of the investigated sample. Furthermore, we expected that temperamental traits referring to temporal characteristics of behavior would predict the intensity of PTSD symptoms regardless of age but dependent on the set of PTSD symptoms. Taking into account the described range of symptoms of PTSD (APA, 1994) and the role of particular temperamental traits in stress phenomena, it was hypothesized that briskness, defined mainly as the ability to fit behavior to changes in the environment, would predict symptoms of avoidance, whereas perseveration, understood as the tendency to continue and repeat behavior and emotions, would predict symptoms of intrusion.

Both hypotheses were generally supported by the empirical findings. The characteristics of the event (trauma intensity) and its consequences as well as temperamental traits proved their predictive value regarding the prolonged intensity of PTSD symptoms. With respect to the role of trauma characteristics, the so called "dose–response" effect was revealed in analyses. Such findings are congruent with the majority of studies conducted in the field of extreme stress phenomena (see Norris et al., 2002). On the other hand, temperamental traits seem to be another factor comparable to the intensity of stressors influencing the amount of costs when individuals are under extreme stress. Emotional reactivity, which describes the tendency to react intensively to emotion-generating stimuli, expressed in high emotional sensitivity and in low emotional endurance was found as the universal – in the sense of sets of symptoms and age of victims – predictor of the intensity of PTSD symptoms. Emotional reactivity, as well as such basic temperamental traits as neuroticism, introversion, trait-anxiety or sensation seeking tendency are crucial predictors of the risk of maladaptive behavior under extreme stress. Furthermore, the traits describing behavior in temporal terms – briskness and perseveration – are also important, symptom-specific predictors of functioning under such conditions. This remark seems to be worth highlighting due to the lack of extreme stress investigations in which such categories are included among individual features.

Such findings give support to Lauterbach's conceptualization of a multivariable model of determinants of the intensity of PTSD symptoms (see Lauterbach, 2005; Lauterbach & Vrana, 2001). As was postulated, personal factors, such as temperamental traits, together with features of the traumatic event allow us to explain about 40% of the variance of the intensity of PTSD symptoms. Based on this model in almost all age groups and symptom categories it was possible to substantially predict PTSD intensity. The interesting pattern, however, was found while analyzing the relationship between both factors with PTSD intensity throughout the age groups. It seems that in adults this model is fully valid: both external (trauma) and personal (temperament) factors playing a crucial role in influencing the intensity of PTSD symptoms. For these age groups the multiple-correlation coefficients were the highest. In children trauma consequences seem to be less important, although trauma characteristics are crucial. Conversely, in youths trauma characteristics are less important, whereas trauma consequences do influence the intensity of PTSD symptoms. Another interesting finding may be drafted for temperamental traits. In adults all traits influence the intensity of PTSD symptoms regardless of the kinds of symptoms, while traits of temporal characteristics (briskness and perseveration) are more important for children and youths than emotional reactivity. Such results are present especially when the subsets of symptoms are taken into account. Moreover, the whole model allows us to explain the greater percentage of variance in the intensity of PTSD symptoms in children and in adults compared to youths.

As was mentioned, trauma characteristics and their consequences are more weakly related to the intensity of PTSD symptoms in younger individuals than in adults. Only trauma characteristics, but not trauma consequences, influence the general intensity of PTSD symptoms as well as the intensity of intrusive symptoms in children, whereas only trauma consequences, but not trauma characteristics, predict the intensity of PTSD symptoms in youths. One reason may be that younger participants, due to their stage of cognitive development, do not perceive such features in terms of material and financial losses or comprehend the future consequences of them. However, such a conclusion seems to be more valid in the case of school-age children than it is in youths. Another reason may result from a feature common in both younger groups: the fact of being financially dependent on their caregivers. Thus, the economical troubles do not influence them directly, but rather do so indirectly through changes in the functioning of the caregivers and the family system. The family system and behavior of caregivers may buffer the impact of disaster on the younger family members. Detailed investigation of the determinants of the intensity of PTSD symptoms in children provides support to such expectations. Using path analysis, Kaczmarek and Zawadzki (2005) found that in school-age children trauma characteristics and trauma consequences influence the general intensity of PTSD symptoms indirectly – via the intensity of PTSD symptoms in both parents and via such family climate characteristics as organization and conflicts. Also other studies investigating the relationships between intensity of pathological symptoms in children and adolescents and family climate, psychological functioning of caregivers, and style of upbringing show that younger victims are specially vulnerable to external – "family" – factors under extreme stress (see Green et al., 1991; McFarlane, 1987a, 1987b).

A further remark refers to the differences in the impact of trauma characteristics and trauma consequences on the successive subsets of symptoms – avoidance and intrusion. On the whole, trauma characteristics influence the intensity of intrusive symptoms more, whereas trauma consequences predict the symptoms of avoidance better. Such findings, as well as the differences in the determinative role of briskness and perseveration, provide evidence for heterogeneous mechanisms of PTSD symptom development. The last remark refers to the role of temporal characteristics of temperament as determinants of the intensity of PTSD symptoms. The role of such traits, especially briskness, is more evident in younger victims than in adults. The reason for such differences may lie in the differences in the process of self-regulation between the groups of children, youths, and adults. The self-regulative mechanisms develop and change through life. In younger subjects they may be rooted to a greater extent in the basis of personality – temperamental mechanism. Thus, the role of briskness, which describes the ability to adapt to new circumstances and to shift from one activity to another in response to changes in the environment, emerges as the essential determinant of the intensity of PTSD symptoms in children and decreases in adults.

In conclusion, characteristics of the traumatic event and temperamental traits are important and widespread determinants of the psychological costs of being under extreme stress evoked by natural disaster. However, some differences in detailed patterns of determinants with respect to age of victims and the set of symptoms emerged. As already mentioned, the results of our study may serve for selection purposes in professions involving a high risk of trauma experience.

Acknowledgements

This project was supported by grants from the National Committee for Scientific Research (PBZ-KBN 001/H01 and H01F 067 27) and by Subsidies for Scientists (NP.-2/1988) awarded to Jan Strelau by the Foundation of Polish Science. We would like to express our gratitude to Professor Włodzimierz Oniszczenko, Dr Adam Sobolewski, Piotr Pawłowski, MA and Ewa Kobyłka, MA who took part in collecting the data.

Notes

1   In this context, the term "moderating" means, according to Folkman and Lazarus (1988), that temperamental traits constitute antecedent conditions that influence other conditions.
2   However, with respect to the perceived personal resources, the second appraisal varies among victims.
3   On the penultimate stage the model with interactions between trauma characteristics, its consequences and temperamental traits were also tested. All interactions were calculated as products of simple variables (Pedhazur & Pedhazur-Schmelkin, 1991). Taking into account that significant interactions were found in only a few analyses and at each time the interactions between different variables were recorded, the model was finally abbreviated to the simple variables only.

References

Anthony, J. L., Lonigan, C. L., & Hecht, S. A. (1999). Dimensionality of post-traumatic stress disorder symptoms in children exposed to disaster: Results from confirmatory factor analyses. *Journal of Abnormal Psychology*, *108*, 326–336.

APA (1994). *Diagnostic and statistical manual of mental disorders* (Version IV). Washington, DC: American Psychiatric Association.

Bonanno, G. (2004). Loss, trauma, and human resilience. *American Psychologist*, *59*, 20–28.

Costa, P. T., Jr., & McCrae, R. R. (1992). *Revised NEO Personality Inventory (NEO-PI-R) and NEO Five Factor Inventory (NEO-FFI): Professional manual.* Odessa, FL: Psychological Assessment Resources.

Dekel, R., Solomon, Z., Ginzburg, K., & Neria, Y. (2005) Coping with war captivity: The contribution of personality resource. In J. Strelau & T. Klonowicz (Eds.), *People under extreme stress: An individual differences approach.* New York: Nova Science Publishers, Inc.

Eysenck, H. J., & Eysenck, M. W. (1985). *Personality and individual differences: A natural science approach.* New York: Plenum Press.

Fairbank, J. A., Klaric, J. S., O'Dekirk, J. M., Fairbank, D. W., & Costello, E. J. (2005). Environmental vulnerabilities and posttraumatic stress disorder (PTSD) among children with different personality styles. In J. Strelau & T. Klonowicz (Eds.), *People under extreme stress: An individual differences approach.* New York: Nova Science Publishers, Inc.

Folkman, S., & Lazarus, R. S. (1988). Coping as a mediator of emotion. *Journal of Personality and Social Psychology*, *54*, 466–475.

Gordon, R., & Wraith, R. (1993). Responses of children and adolescents to disaster.

In J. P. Wilson & B. Raphael (Eds.), *International handbook of traumatic stress syndromes* (2nd ed., pp. 561–575). New York: Plenum Press.

Green, B. L. (1998). Psychological responses to disaster: Conceptualization and identification of high-risk survivors. *Psychiatry and Clinical Neurosciences, 52*, S67–S73.

Green, B. L., Korol, M., Grace, M. C., Vary, M. G., Leonard, A. C., Gleser, G. C. et al. (1991). Children and disaster: Age, gender, and parental effects on PTSD symptoms. *Journal of the American Academy of Child and Adolescent Psychiatry, 30*, 945–951.

Kaczmarek, M., & Zawadzki, B. (2005). Temperamental and environmental determinants of the intensity of PTSD symptoms in children two years after a flood. In J. Strelau & T. Klonowicz (Eds.), *People under extreme stress: An individual differences approach.* New York: Nova Science Publishers.

Krohne, H. W., & Laux, L. (Eds.). (1982). *Achievement, stress, and anxiety.* New York: Hemisphere/McGraw-Hill.

Lauterbach, D. (2005). Personality, trauma exposure, and posttraumatic stress disorder severity: Moving beyond the monovariable predictor model. In J. Strelau & T. Klonowicz (Eds.), *People under extreme stress: An individual differences approach.* New York: Nova Science Publishers, Inc.

Lauterbach, D., & Vrana, S. (2001). The relationship among personality variables, exposure to traumatic events, and severity of posttraumatic stress symptoms. *Journal of Traumatic Stress, 14*, 29–45.

Levinson, D. J. (1990). A theory of life structure development in adulthood. In N. C. Alexander & E. J. Langer (Eds.), *Higher stages of human development* (pp. 35–54). New York: Oxford University Press.

McFarlane, A. C. (1987a). Posttraumatic phenomena in a longitudinal study of children following a natural disaster. *Journal of the American Academy of Child and Adolescent Psychiatry, 26*, 764–769.

McFarlane, A. C. (1987b). Family functioning and overprotection following a natural disaster: The longitudinal effects of post-traumatic morbidity. *Australian and New Zealand Journal of Psychiatry, 21*, 210–218.

McFarlane, A. C. (1988). The aetiology of post-traumatic stress disorders following a natural disaster. *British Journal of Psychiatry, 152*, 116–121.

McGrath, J. E. (Ed.). (1970). *Social and psychological factors in stress.* New York: Holt, Rinehart & Winston.

Norris, F. H., Friedman, M. J., Watson, P. J., Byrne, C. M., Diaz, E., & Kaniasty, K. (2002). 60,000 disaster victims speak: Part I. An empirical review of the empirical literature, 1981–2001. *Psychiatry, 65*, 207–239.

Norris, F. H., & Perilla, J. L. (1996). The Revised Civilian Mississippi Scale for PTSD: Reliability, validity, and cross-language stability. *Journal of Traumatic Stress, 9*, 285–298.

Oniszczenko, W., & Radomska, A. (2002). Kwestionariusz Temperamentu dla Dzieci (KTD) oparty na Regulacyjnej Teorii Temperamentu – wersja eksperymentalna [Temperament Inventory for Children regarding to Regulative Theory of Temperament – experimental version]. *Psychologia – Etologia – Genetyka, 5*, 85–98.

Ozer, E. J., Best, S. R., Lipsey, T. L., & Weiss, D. S. (2003). Predictors of posttraumatic stress disorder and symptoms in adults: A meta-analysis. *Psychological Bulletin, 129*, 52–73.

Pedhazur, E. J., & Pedhazur-Schmelkin, L. (1991). *Measurement, design, and analysis: An integrated approach.* Hillsdale, NJ: Lawrence Erlbaum Associates, Inc.

Rodriguez, N., Steinberg, A., & Pynoos, R. S. (1999). *UCLA PTSD Index for DSM IV (Revision 1). Instrument information: Child Version, Parent Version, Adolescent Version.* Los Angeles: UCLA.

Ruscio, A. M., Ruscio, J., & Keane, T. M. (2002). The latent structure of posttraumatic stress disorder: A taxonomic investigation of reactions to extreme stress. *Journal of Abnormal Psychology, 111,* 290–301.

Strelau, J. (1995). Temperament and stress: Temperament as moderators of stressors, emotional states, coping and costs. In C. D. Spielberger & I. G. Sarason (Eds.), *Stress and emotion: Anxiety, anger, and curiosity* (Vol. 15, pp. 215–254). Washington, DC: Hemisphere.

Strelau, J. (1996). The regulative theory of temperament: Current status. *Personality and Individual Differences, 20,* 131–142.

Strelau, J. (1998). *Temperament: A psychological perspective.* Washington, DC: Plenum Press.

Strelau, J., & Zawadzki, B. (1993). The Formal Characteristics of Behaviour – Temperament Inventory (FCB-TI): Theoretical assumptions and scale construction. *European Journal of Personality, 7,* 313–336.

Strelau, J., & Zawadzki, B. (1995). The Formal Characteristics of Behaviour – Temperament Inventory (FCB-TI): Validity studies. *European Journal of Personality, 9,* 207–229.

Strelau, J., Zawadzki, B., Oniszczenko, W., & Sobolewski, A. (2002). Kwestionariusz PTSD – wersja czynnikowa (PTSD-C). Konstrukcja narzędzia do diagnozy głównych wymiarów zespołu stresu pourazowego [The factorial version of the PTSD Inventory (PTSD-F): The development of a questionnaire aimed at assessing basic dimensions of post-traumatic stress disorder]. *Przegląd Psychologiczny, 45,* 149–176.

Zeidner, M., & Ben-Zur, H. (1994). Individual differences in anxiety, coping, and post-traumatic stress in the aftermath of the Persian Gulf War. *Personality and Individual Differences, 16,* 459–476.

10 The involvement of psychological processes in immunocompetence

Wenjuan Lin

Introduction

The issue of whether psychological processes can influence immune competence is controversial. The notion that stress makes you sick and belief makes you well has been part of popular culture for thousands of years. In ancient Chinese culture, a medicine book named *Nei Jing* asserted that loss of the control of emotion, such as anger or sadness, resulted in damage to the gut and then the occurrence of the disease (Li, 1989). The Greek physician Galen also around 200 AD described the phenomenon that depressed women are more susceptible to breast cancer than optimistic women (Dunn, 1989). So the idea that psychological events can influence physical events is actually universal throughout all cultures. That is to say, there is a link between the mind and the body. However, until very recently there has been no convincing scientific evidence to demonstrate such a link. For a long time most scientists have even rejected the concept that mental events or processes can affect physiological events. Recently, a new field of psychoneuroimmunology has focused on research on the interactions between behavior, the nervous system, the endocrine system, and the immune system. It emphasizes that psychological or behavioral factors can influence immune function and therefore influence health and susceptibility to disease. So the immune system is one of the important links between the mind and the body. However, although many data indicate that the central nervous system (CNS) is capable of influencing immune function, many physiologists still believe that the immune system is mainly self-regulated. The issue is actually concerned with a longstanding problem in medicine, namely the separation between the mind and the body. Some have argued that the evidence for direct links between psychological processes and immune function is unconvincing. So the issue as to whether and how psychological processes affect immune functions is still controversial (Greer, 2000). This chapter is concerned with the examination of the role of psychological processes in the modulation of immune function and the related mechanisms. I do not intend to review the evidence or data published in the literature, but mainly to introduce the work conducted in our own laboratory. These studies include conditioned enhancement of immunity, effect of emotional stress, and psychological intervention in cancer patients.

Studies on psychoneuroimmunomodulation

Conditioned enhancement of immunity

Since Ader and Cohen (1975) initially reported their conditioned immuno-suppression paradigm, the conditioned immunosuppression paradigm has been studied and replicated extensively (e.g., Exton et al., 2002; Lin, Wei, Guo, Tang, & Liu, 1998). In this paradigm, a novel taste solution, such as saccharin solution, as the conditioned stimulus (CS) was paired with an immunosuppressive agent as the unconditioned stimulus (UCS). After CS/UCS pairings were made, re-exposure of animals to the CS alone resulted in significant conditioned taste aversion and conditioned attenuation of the immune response. The conditioned immunosuppression paradigm reveals that the associative learning process, a psychological process, is capable of modulating immune function. Certainly, this conditioned immunomodulation should be bidirectional. That is to say, immune responses should be regulated by Pavlovian conditioning principles in the two dimensions: conditioned immunosuppression and conditioned immunoenhancement. However, evidence for conditioned enhancement of immunity is limited. We previously first reported a conditioned enhancement of the antibody production paradigm in which an antigen ovalbumin (OVA) was used as the UCS and saccharin as the CS, the conditioned enhancement of antibody response can be invoked by re-exposure to the CS alone, via a single conditioning trial (Husband, Lin, Madsen, & King, 1993). However, the magnitude of conditioned antibody production induced by the CS alone was relatively small, since the value of statistical significance between the conditioned and unconditioned groups was marginal. So we further examined conditioned enhancement of antibody response by using two kinds of conditioned stimuli. One was saccharin and the other was electro-acupuncture.

Using saccharin as the conditioned stimulus

In the studies using saccharin as the conditioned stimulus, the animals were allowed to drink the saccharin solution and then were injected with the antigen ovalbumin. Re-exposure of animals to the CS alone resulted in significant conditioned immunoenhancement of antibody conduction. In our previous work, presentation of the CS was during the rapid rise of the primary antibody response, the magnitude of conditioned enhancement therefore was small. In a further experiment, re-exposing animals to the CS was during the declining phase of primary antibody response (Chen et al., 2004). This procedure placed the conditioned response on a lower basis of primary response and therefore might magnify the conditioned antibody production. Indeed, it was found that re-exposure of the animal to the CS during the declining phase of primary antibody response resulted in very significant changes in antibody production. The statistical significance p value between the conditioned group and all other controls reached less than .01 or .001 levels.

A pattern of kinetic changes of conditioned antibody production was further found. That is, the CS gradually induced the conditioned antibody production and this antibody production then achieved a peak level, finally attenuating down to baseline. This pattern in the kinetic changes of conditioned antibody production was similar to the regular antibody production pattern induced by the antigen itself. These findings not only demonstrate that immune function can be enhanced by associative learning processes but also may have potential significance in clinical practice.

Using electro-acupuncture as the conditioned stimulus

When considering clinical application in human beings, sweet drinks can easily be encountered in daily activities and thus saccharin solution might not be available as an effective novel CS. Thus we considered whether a peripheral electric stimulation (PES), a kind of somatic-sensory signal, could be used as a CS to induce immune response. To determine whether a kind of PES could be used to enhance specific immune responses, each rat was put into a plastic holder with its hind legs out, and two stainless steel needles were inserted about 5 mm into the leg muscle. To minimize the experimental error, the traditional Chinese acupoint Zusanli was chosen as the stimulation site. Therefore, peripheral electrical stimulation could be also called electro-acupuncture (EA). In this experiment two kinds of intensities (2 volt and 4 volt) of EA were used as conditioned stimuli (Huang, Lin, & Chen, 2004).

After EA was paired with injection of OVA, animals were re-exposed to the EA alone. Blood samples were collected by tail vein incisions 10, 17, 24, and 31 days after re-exposure to the EA. The results showed that the levels of anti-OVA IgG production of the conditioned groups, for both 2 volt and 4 volt stimulating intensity of EA, were significantly greater than all the controls at the days 10 and 17 after re-exposure to EA. The EA/OVA pairing could be made even during deep sleep induced by anesthesia. In this case, the holder was not used on the conditioning day because the animals were under anesthesia. It was found that the animals could associate a single CS with UCS under anesthesia and an antibody response upon subsequent re-exposure to the CS was induced. No effect of EA on normal antibody production was found. These results reinforce the view that the enhancement of antibody production can be induced by single-trial Pavlovian conditioning where the CS alone is sufficient to induce immune response. These results also demonstrate for the first time that EA could be used as an effective CS in inducing conditioned immune response, which may have potential practical significance in the clinic.

Brain areas involved in conditioned immunomodulation

Although it has been demonstrated that both conditioned immunosuppression and conditioned immunoenhancement could be induced by Pavlovian conditioning techniques, to date the neurocircuitry underlying the conditioned immunity is largely unknown (Lin, 1997). Using c-fos protein production as a marker of neuronal activation (Kaczmarek, 2002), we found that re-exposure to CS alone significantly increased c-fos production in many brain regions throughout cortical, and limbic to brain stem areas (Chen, 2002). There are some nuclei that should be emphasized in particular. In both conditioned immunosuppression and immunoenhancement paradigms, re-exposure conditioned animals to CS induced extensive c-fos expression in the insular cortex, the central amygdala nucleus, and the paraventricular nucleus of the hypothalamus (Chen, 2002; Chen et al., 2004; Li, Lin, & Zheng, 2004; Lin, Li, Zheng, Wang, & Chen, 2004). These results demonstrate that conditioned immune responses are associated with changes in brain activities. However, it is should be noted that in our c-fos studies as well as the other neurocircuitry studies, the conditioned stimulus commonly used was saccharin (e.g., Chen et al., 2004; Ramirez-Amaya, Alvarez-Borda, & Ormsby, 1996; Ramirez-Amaya & Bermudez-Rattoni, 1999). Since we have demonstrated that the EA is also an effective conditioned stimulus for introducing conditioned immune response and the activation model of brain areas induced by EA is dissimilar from that induced by saccharin (Guo, Tian, Wang, Fang, Hou, & Han, 1996), so re-examining the brain activities by using EA as conditioned stimulus may provide new and more conclusive information on the brain mechanism involved in conditioned immunity.

Stress and immunity

Although the notion that stress can induce alteration of immune function has been supported by increasing evidence in the literature, most investigations dealing with the effects of stress on the immune system in animals employed restraint or electric foot-shock as stressors, which include components of physiological stress (Demetrikopoulos, Keller, & Schleifer, 1999). In order to observe the effect of emotional stress or emotions such as anger or anxiety on behavioral, neuroendocrine and immunological responses, our laboratory developed a new animal model of emotional stress (Shao, Lin, Wang, Washinton, & Zheng, 2003). In this model, animals were trained to drink water at two set times each day before the experiment. Then they were injected with OVA antigen to challenge the immune system to produce specific anti-OVA antibodies. Then all animals were divided into one of the three groups, that is, the emotional stressed group (ES), and two control groups (control 1 and control 2). Rats in the ES group were given empty water bottles during one of the two watering periods for two weeks to induce emotional stress. Rats in the control 2 group had no empty water bottles and no water during the same watering periods as the ES group. This group was used to control for the possible physiological effect of no water during watering time. Rats in the control 1 group were given water during all watering periods. After the completion of the experiment, blood samples and the spleen and thymus were taken to determine neuroendocrine and immune functioning. The results we found were very interesting. First emotional stress induced significant behavioral responses, namely attacking behavior and exploring behavior. Second, it was found that emotional stress significantly increased the level of plasma corticosterone, norepinephrine, and epinephrine, which means that the emotional stress significantly induced both hypothalamo–pituitary–adrenal axis (HPA) activation and sympathetic activation. Third, emotional stress significantly decreased the count of white blood cells (WBC) as well as the level of anti-OVA antibody production, which means that emotional stress suppresses the immune function. It was further found that there was a negative correlation between catecholamine level and antibody levels and a negative correlation between the catecholamine levels and spleen weights. In contrast, physiological stress, that is, lack of water, only evoked exploring behavior, increased the corticosterone level and decreased WBC counts (Lin, Wang, & Shao, 2003). Physiological stress had no effect on attacking behavior and no effect on specific antibody production.

Collectively, the results suggest that emotional stress has a great influence on behavioral and immunological responses and that the sympathetic nervous system (SNS) is involved in mediating the effects of emotional stress on humoral immune function.

To confirm the role of the SNS in the mediating emotional stress-induced antibody suppression, in a subsequent study, using pharmacological manipulations we separately suppressed the HPA activation and the SNS activation and found that chemical sympathectomy, that is to say, inhibition of the SNS, but not inhibition of HPA function, completely blocked the stress-suppressive effects on the antibody production. We further found that in the SNS system β_2 adrenergic receptor (β_2-ADR), not β_1-ADR, mediated this emotional stress-induced immunomodulation (Wang, 2004).

In the literature, most often, stress has been reported to suppress immune response and this suppression has been mainly attributed to an increase in adrenal cortical hormone, that is to say, to the HPA activation. But in our experiment, we demonstrated that the sympathetic system, not the HPA system, plays a major role in the emotional stress-induced humoral immunosuppression.

Behavioral intervention

Since psychological factors such as emotion or conditioning, as mentioned above, can induce immunological as well as behavioral reactions in animals, we then wondered whether psychobehavioral intervention could affect immune function in cancer patients. Studies have proven that cancer is a disease that affects the entire body, by incorporating emotional/psychological factors (Edelman & Kidman, 1997). For this reason, we carried out two experiments with cancer patients to examine the effect of behavioral intervention. In the first experiment, 40 hospitalized breast-cancer patients undergoing radio-therapy were assigned to either a month-long psychobehavioral intervention group or a control group. Subjects in the two groups were basically matched in age, education, cancer stage, medical treatments, etc. The intervention group was given a kind of imagination training after progressive muscle relaxation, in which the subjects imagined themselves walking on a beach, feeling the sunshine on their faces and the seawater under their feet, etc. The procedure then went on to guide the subjects to imagine how the immune cells destroyed the cancer cells and how the dead cancer cells were washed away with the seawater. Before and after the intervention, saliva and blood samples were taken from all subjects in the two groups to determine the level of natural killer (NK) cell activity. It was found that psychobehavioral intervention significantly increased the level of NK activity. The percentage of the patients who had to take medication to increase the level of white blood cells decreased as a side effect to radiotherapy was significantly less in the intervention group than that in the control group (Liu, Lin, Liu, & Zhang, 2001). These results suggested that the function of recovering or compensation of the immune system was better in the intervention group than in the control group.

In a second experiment, 120 hospitalized cancer patients undergoing chemotherapy were assigned to either a three-month psychobehavioral intervention group or a control group. Subjects in the two groups were also basically matched. The same procedure of intervention as described in experiment 1 was used. Saliva and blood samples were taken before and after the intervention for determination of immunological parameters including WBC, NK, immunoglobulin G (IgG), immunoglobulin M (IgM), and immunoglobulin A (IgA). Data showed that psychological intervention improved the levels of all the immunological parameters measured when compared with the control group (Wang, Lin, Leung, & Lin, 2002). In the meantime, the quality of life was improved while the symptoms caused either by cancer or the medical therapy were ameliorated in the intervention group (Wang, Lin, & Sun, 2002). For both breast-cancer and lung-cancer patients the scores of their quality of life, including physical function, role function, emotional function, cognitive function and social function, were increased in the intervention group compared to the control group. The scores of the symptoms, including fatigue, vomiting, pain, loss of appetite, etc., were decreased in the intervention group. It was further found that the patients whose mood status, physical function, and quality of life were improved applied more active cognitive methods and fewer avoidant methods to cope with the cancer disease after psychological intervention (Wang, Lin, Leung, & Lin, 2003). The results from experiments 1 and 2 are basically the same, demonstrating that psychological intervention does contribute to the immune function in cancer patients.

Concluding remarks

Based on the three lines of experimental evidence provided from our own laboratory, we conclude that psychological processes, such as associative learning, emotion, and behavioral imagination, do influence immune functions although the mechanisms of the mind–body interactions remain largely unknown.

Acknowledgements

Preparation of this article was supported by a grant (NSF30370482) from the National Natural Science Foundation of China and a grant (KSCX2-2-03) from the Chinese Academy of Sciences.

References

Ader, R., & Cohen, N. (1975). Behaviorally conditioned immuno-suppression. *Psychosomatic Medicine, 37*, 333–340.

Chen, J. (2002). *Conditioned enhancement of antibody response and c-fos expression in brain.* Unpublished doctoral thesis, Institute of Psychology, Chinese Academy of Sciences, Beijing, China.

Chen, J., Lin, W., Wang, W., Shao, F., Yang, J., Wang, B. et al. (2004). Enhancement of antibody production and expression of c-*Fos* in the insular cortex in response to a conditioned stimulus after a single-trial learning paradigm. *Behavioral Brain Research, 154*(2), 557–565.

Demetrikopoulos, M. K., Keller, S. E., & Schleifer, J. (1999). Stress effects on immune function in rodents. In M. Schedlowski & U. Tewes (Eds.), *Psychoneuroimmunology* (pp. 259–275). New York: Kluwer Academic/Plenum Publishers.

Dunn, A. J. (1989). Psychoneuroimmunology for the psychoneuroendocrinologist: A review of animal studies of nervous system–immune system interaction. *Psychoneuroendocrinology, 14*, 251–274.

Edelman, S., & Kidman, A. (1997). Mind and cancer: Is there a relationship? A review of evidence. *Australian Psychologist, 32*, 79–85.

Exton, M. S., Gierse, C., Meier, B., Mosen, M., Xie, Y., Frede, S. et al. (2002). Behaviorally conditioned immunosuppression in the rat is regulated via noradrenalin and beta-adrenoceptors. *Journal of Neuroimmunology, 131*, 21–30.

Greer, S. (2000). Neuroimmunology or psychoneuroimmunology? *Annals of New York Academy of Sciences, 917*, 568–574.

Guo, H. F., Tian, J., Wang, X., Fang, Y., Hou, Y., & Han, J. (1996). Brain substrates activated by electroacupuncture of different frequencies (I): Comparative study on the expression of oncogene c-*fos* and genes coding for three opioid peptides. *Brain Research Molecular Brain Research, 43*(1–2), 157–166.

Huang, J., Lin, W., & Chen, J. (2004). Antibody response can be conditioned using electroacupuncture as conditioned stimulus. *NeuroReport, 15*(9), 1475–1478.

Husband, A. J., Lin, W., Madsen, G., & King, M. G. (1993). A conditioning model for immunostimulation: Enhancement of the antibody response to ovalbumin by behavioral conditioning in rats. In A. J. Husband (Ed.), *Psychoimmunology: CNS-immune interactions* (pp. 139–147). Boca Raton, FL: CRC Press.

Kaczmarek, L. (2002). C-*Fos* in learning: Beyond the mapping of neuronal activity. In L. Kaczmarek & H. A. Robertson (Eds.), *Handbook of chemical neuroanatomy: Immediate early genes and inducible transcription factors in mapping of the CNS function and dysfunction* (pp. 189–215). Edinburgh, UK: Elsevier Health Sciences.

Li, J., Lin, W., & Zheng, L. (2004). Study on conditioned immunosuppression and the expression of c-*fos* in the hypothalamic nuclei. *Acta Psychologica Sinica, 36*(2), 201–207.

Li, X. (1989). Ancient Chinese thoughts of medical psychology. In X. Li (Ed.), *Medical psychology* (pp. 19–22). Beijing, China: People's Hygiene Publisher.

Lin, W. (1997). Review and research ideas on psychoneuroimmunology. *Acta Psychologica Sinica, 29*(3), 301–305.

Lin, W., Li, J., Zheng, L., Wang, W., & Chen, J. (2004). Expression of c-*fos* in amygdala and conditioned immunosuppression. *Acta Psychologica Sinica, 36*(4), 500–505.

Lin, W., Wang, W., & Shao, F. (2003). A new animal model of emotional stress: Behavioral, neuroendocrine and immunological consequences. *Chinese Science Bulletin, 15*, 1561–1571.

Lin, W., Wei, X., Guo, Y., Tang, C., & Liu, Y. (1998). Study on conditioned immuno-suppression and conditioned taste aversion. *Acta Psychologica Sinica, 30*(4), 418–422.

Liu, Y., Lin, W., Liu, X., & Zhang, J. (2001). The effect of psychobehavioral interven-tion on the emotional reaction and immune function in breast cancer patients undergoing radiotherapy. *Acta Psychologica Sinica, 33*(5), 437–441.

Ramirez-Amaya, V., Alvarez-Borda, B., & Ormsby, C. E. (1996). Insular cortex lesions impair the acquisition of conditioned immunosuppression. *Brain Behavior and Immunity, 10*, 103–14.

Ramirez-Amaya, V., & Bermudez-Rattoni, F. (1999). Conditioned enhancement of antibody production is disrupted by insular cortex and amygdala but not hippocampal lesions. *Brain Behavior and Immunity, 13*, 46–60.

Shao, F., Lin, W., Wang, W., Washinton, W., & Zheng. L (2003). The effect of emo-tional stress on the primary humoral immunity of rats. *Journal of Psychopharma-cology, 17*(2), 153–157.

Wang, J., Lin, W., Leung, F., & Lin, X. (2002). Effects of psychological intervention on immunological function in cancer patients. *Chinese Journal of Clinical Oncology, 29*(12), 841–844.

Wang, J., Lin, W., Leung, F., & Lin, X. (2003). The mediating effects of the coping styles and related factors on psychological intervention in cancer patients. *Chinese Journal of Clinical Psychology, 10*(3), 176–178.

Wang, J., Lin, W., & Sun, H. (2002). The effects of psychological intervention on cancer patients. *Chinese Journal of Clinical Oncology, 29*(5), 305–309.

Wang, W. (2004). *The role of sympathetic nervous system in humoral immunosuppres-sion induced by emotional stress in rats.* Unpublished doctoral thesis, Institute of Psychology, Chinese Academy of Sciences, Beijing, China.

11 Self-regulatory processes in health behavior change

Ralf Schwarzer, Urte Scholz, Sonia Lippke, Falko F. Sniehotta, and Jochen P. Ziegelmann

Many health conditions are caused by risky behaviors such as problem drinking, substance use, smoking, reckless driving, overeating, and unprotected sexual contact. Fortunately, human beings have, in principle, control over their conduct. Health-compromising behaviors can be eliminated by self-regulatory efforts, and health-enhancing behaviors. For instance, physical exercise, weight control, preventive nutrition, dental hygiene, or condom use, can be adopted. The adoption of health-promoting behaviors is often viewed rather simplistically as a response to a threat to health. According to this view, individuals who become aware that their lifestyle puts them at risk for a threatening disease may make a deliberate decision to refrain from risky behaviors. This commonsense view of behavioral change is based on the questionable belief that humans are rational beings who respond to a perceived risk in the most reasonable manner. However, many studies show that perception of a risk, by itself, is a poor predictor of behavioral change. This state of affairs has encouraged health psychologists to identify other alterable variables that may play a role in changing health-related behaviors and to design more complex models of the processes of change (for reviews, see Conner & Norman, 2005; Schwarzer, 1992; Wallston & Armstrong, 2002; Weinstein, Rothman, & Sutton, 1998).

Goal setting: Motivation to change

Before people change their habits, they need to become motivated to do so. This is a process leading toward an explicit intention (e.g., "I intend to quit smoking this weekend"). Three variables are considered to play a major role in this process: (1) risk perception; (2) outcome expectancies; and (3) perceived self-efficacy.

Perceiving a health threat seems to be the most obvious prerequisite for the motivation to end a risky behavior. People who are not aware at all of the risky nature of their actions will not develop the motivation to change them. Scaring people into healthy behaviors, however, has not been shown to be effective. In general, the initial perception of risk seems to put people on track for developing a motivation to change, but later on other factors are more influential.

People not only need to be aware of the existence of a health threat, they also need to understand the contingencies between their actions and subsequent outcomes. These *outcome expectancies* are among the most influential beliefs in the motivation to change. A smoker may find more good reasons to quit smoking (e.g., "If I quit smoking, then I will save money") than to continue smoking. This imbalance does not directly lead to action, but it can help developing an intention to quit. Although the pros and cons, which represent a number of positive and negative outcome expectancies, typically play a role in rational decision making, they need not be explicitly worded and evaluated – they can also be rather diffuse mental representations, loaded with emotions. Outcome expectancies can also be understood as methods, or means–ends relationships, indicating that people know proper strategies to produce desired effects.

The efficacy of a method has to be distinguished from individuals' belief in their personal efficacy in applying the method. *Perceived self-efficacy* refers to individuals' beliefs in their capabilities to exercise control over challenging demands and over their own functioning (Bandura, 1997). These beliefs are critical when people approach novel or difficult situations or try to adopt strenuous self-regimens. People attribute capabilities to themselves when they forecast that they will change their behavior (e.g., "I am certain that I can quit smoking even if my friend continues to smoke"). Such optimistic self-beliefs influence the goals that people set for themselves, what courses of action they choose to pursue, how much effort they invest in given endeavors, and how long they persevere in the face of barriers and setbacks. Some people harbor self-doubts and cannot motivate themselves. They see little point in even setting a goal if they believe they do not have what it takes to succeed. Thus, the intention to change a habit that affects health depends to some degree on a firm belief in one's capability to exercise control over that habit.

Health interventions that focus on arousing fear of disease, informing about health-compromising habits, or increasing perceived personal vulnerability are less effective than health interventions that raise belief in personal efficacy. Perceived self-efficacy operates in concert with risk perception, outcome expectancies, and other factors in influencing the motivation to change. There is a large body of evidence documenting the influence of such predictors on the development of an intention to change behavior (Ajzen, 2002; Bandura, 1997; Schwarzer & Renner, 2000; Sutton, 2001). Because most studies are based on cross-sectional research designs, little is known about the causal sequence and interplay of these factors. It is assumed that initial risk perception sets the stage for the development of an intention to change behavior, whereas outcome expectancies and perceived self-efficacy may play a more important role later. At the point in the process when studies typically measure behavioral intentions, the latter two factors emerge as the major predictors, whereas risk perception often seems only weakly related to behavioral intentions.

Goal pursuit: Self-regulatory processes

Unfortunately, research on behavioral intentions is more prevalent than research that addresses whether behaviors actually change (Bandura, 1997; Schwarzer & Fuchs, 1995). After people have adopted a goal of behavioral change, they need to take action and, later, maintain the changes in the face of obstacles and failures. Thus, goal setting and goal pursuit can be understood as two distinct processes, the latter of which requires a great deal of self-regulatory effort.

Entrenched habits seldom yield to a single attempt at change. Renewed efforts are needed in order to achieve success. Strong self-beliefs can keep people on track and help them to persevere when temptations to resort to previous behaviors arise.

The pursuit of a goal of behavioral change can be subdivided into a sequence of activities, such as planning, initiation, maintenance, relapse management, and disengagement, although these are not clearly distinct categories. The importance of *planning* was recently emphasized by Gollwitzer (1999), who reviewed research on what he called "implementation intentions" (see also Leventhal, Singer, & Jones, 1965). These plans specify the when, where, and how of a desired action and have the structure: "When situation S arises, I will perform response R". They form cognitive links between situational circumstances or opportunities and the goal behavior. Gollwitzer argued that goals do not induce actions directly, but that they may lead to highly specific plans, which in turn induce actions. For example, the pursuit of goals for promoting health, such as strenuous physical exercise, and preventing disease, such as cancer screening, is facilitated by mental simulation (e.g., by imagining success scenarios).

If the appropriate opportunity for a desired action is clearly defined in terms of how, when, and where, the probability for procrastination is reduced. People take *initiative* when the critical situation arises and they give the action a try. This requires that they firmly believe they are capable of performing the action. People who do not hold such beliefs see little point in even trying.

A health-related behavior is adopted and then *maintained* not through an act of will, but rather through the development of self-regulatory skills and strategies. In other words, individuals embrace a variety of means to influence their own motivation and behaviors. For example, they set attainable subgoals, create incentives for themselves, draw from an array of options for coping with difficulties, and mobilize support from other people. Processes they can use to control their actions include focusing attention on the task while ignoring distractors, resisting temptations, and managing unpleasant emotions. Perceived self-efficacy is required in order to overcome barriers and stimulate self-motivation repeatedly.

Individuals who can get themselves started on the path towards change are quickly confronted with the problem of whether they can be resolute. Adherence to a self-imposed healthy behavior is difficult because performance fluctuates, and improvements may be followed by plateaus, setbacks, and failures. Competent *relapse management* is needed to recover from setbacks. Some people rapidly abandon their newly adopted behavior when they fail to get quick results. When entering high-risk situations (e.g., a bar where people smoke), they cannot resist temptation because they lack a strong belief in their self-efficacy. The competence to recover from a relapse is different from the competence enlisted for commencing an action. Restoration, harm reduction, and renewal of motivation are constantly needed within the context of health self-regulation.

Disengagement from the goal can be evidence for lack of persistence and, thus, can indicate self-regulatory failure. But in the case of repeated failure, disengagement or scaling back the goal might become adaptive, depending on the circumstances. For example, if the goal was set too high, or if the situation has changed and become more difficult than before, it is seldom worthwhile to continue the struggle. In the case of health-compromising behaviors, however, giving up is not a tenable option. Instead, the individual needs to develop improved self-regulatory skills and adopt new approaches to the problem. Failure can be a useful learning experience and may lead to increased competence, if the individual interprets the episode optimistically and practices a constructive self-talk to renew the motivation (Baumeister & Heatherton, 1996).

Models of changing health behavior

In summary, changing health-related behaviors involves an initial motivation process that results in setting goals and a subsequent self-regulation processes that address the pursuit of these goals. Health psychologists are attempting to model these processes in order to understand how people become motivated to change their risky behaviors, and how they become encouraged to adopt and maintain healthy actions. In the past, the focus of such models was on identifying a parsimonious set of variables that would predict people's success in changing their behavior. These variables included constructs such as attitudes, social norms, personal vulnerability, and behavioral intentions. The most prominent approaches were the health belief model (Becker, 1974), the theory of planned behavior (Ajzen, 2002), and protection motivation theory (Rogers, 1983; for an overview and critique of these and other models, see Conner & Norman, 2005; Schwarzer, 1992; Wallston & Armstrong, 2002; Weinstein et al., 1998).

Models of health behavior change consider beliefs and actions that may improve motivation and eventually lead to sustained behavior change. A distinction between continuum models and stage models is made.

In so-called continuum models, individuals are placed along a continuum that reflects the likelihood of action. Influential predictor variables are identified and combined in one equation. The goal of an intervention is to move the individual along this continuum towards action. Apart from limitations at the empirical level, researchers have suggested two major theoretical deficiencies. First, a single prediction rule for describing behavior change implies that cognitive and behavioral change occur in a linear fashion, and that a "one-size-fits-all" intervention approach is suitable for all individuals engaging in unhealthy behaviors. Consequently, it excludes qualitative changes during the course of time, such as stage transitions or recycling through phases. According to continuum models, it is not important whether an intervention approach is targeted towards changing perceived vulnerability, perceived consequences, or perceived self-efficacy first. Hence, interventions are not required to be progressed in a certain sequence. Rather, they could be applied in any order, or even simultaneously. Second, continuum models typically do not account for the post-intentional phase where goals are translated into action. The segment between intentions and behaviors is a black box. Theorizing about health behavior change, then, is reduced to the motivation phase only, while omitting the decisive action phase.

Stage models can be seen as superior to continuum models if empirical evidence emerges that attests to the discontinuity between stages and to the successful tailoring of interventions to subgroups of individuals who have been identified at such stages. Moreover, factors that move people from one stage to another need to be demonstrated.

The *health action process approach* (HAPA; Luszczynska & Schwarzer, 2003; Schwarzer, 1992, 2001; Schwarzer & Fuchs, 1995; Schwarzer & Renner, 2000) pays particular attention to post-intentional mechanisms, and it conveys an explicit self-regulation perspective. It suggests a distinction between (a) pre-intentional motivation processes that lead to a behavioral intention and (b) post-intentional volition processes that lead to actual health behavior. This volition phase can be subdivided into a post-intentional pre-actional phase and an actional phase. In the three phases, different patterns of social-cognitive predictors should emerge (see Figure 11.1 for a schematic of this model).

In the initial *motivation phase*, a person develops an intention to act. Risk perception, which may include not only the perceived severity of possible health threats, but also one's personal vulnerability to fall prey to them, is merely a distant antecedent in this phase. Risk perception in itself is insufficient to enable a person to form an intention. Rather, it sets the stage for further elaboration of thoughts about consequences and competencies. Thus, outcome expectancies and perceived self-efficacy, operating in concert, contribute substantially to the development of an intention to change.

This pattern of influence changes after goal setting, when people enter the *self-regulation phase*, in which they pursue their goal by planning the details, trying to act, investing effort and persistence, possibly failing, and finally recovering or disengaging. According to the HAPA, progressing through this

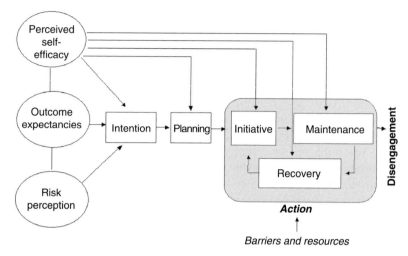

Figure 11.1 Health action process approach (Schwarzer, 1992).

phase consists of moving from one substage to the next, and this movement is facilitated by perceived self-efficacy. Thus, at each point there are two predictors of success, namely, the successful completion of the previous substage and an optimistic sense of control over the next one. Risk perception and outcome expectancies no longer exert much influence once goals have been set, although there may be other influential variables in the self-regulation phase that have not yet been identified.

In the remainder of this chapter, we will describe two studies that deal with the promotion of physical activity, inspired by the HAPA model (Lippke, Ziegelmann, & Schwarzer, 2004a, 2004b, 2005; Sniehotta, Scholz, & Schwarzer, 2005; Sniehotta, Schwarzer, Scholz, & Schüz, 2005; Ziegelmann, Lippke, & Schwarzer, in press).

Study I: Physical exercise in orthopedic rehabilitation

Study I includes orthopedic patients (N = 509) enrolled in exercise therapy in an out-patient rehabilitation center. The sample had a mean age of 45 years (range 18–80 years), and consisted of 317 (62%) women and 192 (38%) men. Their medical problems were mainly back pain (53%), damage of intervertebral discs (48%), and arthritis and arthropathy (28%). Prior to exercise therapy (Baseline), patients were handed out the first questionnaire. At the end of the three-week rehabilitation period, the second questionnaire was administered (Wave 1). Patients who completed Baseline and Wave 1 questionnaires were scheduled for an additional interview at two weeks (Wave 2) and four weeks after discharge (Wave 3). Questionnaires and interviews contained several psychometric scales, in addition to demographic information.

Risk-perception was measured at Baseline with the following three items: "Compared to other persons of your age and gender, how do you estimate the likelihood that you will ever (a) suffer from chronic pain, (b) suffer from movement limitations, and (c) get a severe disease?" Responses were given on 5-point scales, anchored at *much below average* (1), *below average* (2), *average* (3), *above average* (4), and *much above average* (5).

Perceived *self-efficacy* at Baseline was composed of three items. Participants reported how certain they were that they could exercise regularly, even when facing barriers. The stem "I am able to . . ." was followed by ". . . change my lifestyle to an active one," ". . . exercise at least once per week," and ". . . exercise at least twice per week for at least twenty minutes." Answers were scored on a 4-point scale from *not at all true* (1), *not true* (2), *a little true* (3), to *exactly true* (4).

For the assessment of *outcome expectancies* at Baseline, the stem: "If I would engage in physical exercises on two or more days for at least 20 minutes, . . ." was followed by six items on positive outcome expectancies, ". . . then I would feel better afterwards," ". . . then I would be doing something good for my health," ". . . then I will cope better with daily hassles," ". . . then I will be in better shape," ". . . then I can meet new friends," and ". . . then I will enjoy the company of others."

Intentions to perform physical activities were assessed with three items: "I intend to exercise for 20 minutes or longer on at least two days per week on a regular basis," "I intend to exercise for 20 minutes or longer on at least two days per week sometimes (at least once a month)," and "I intend to exercise fitness and muscle strengthening activities." Answers were scored on a 4-point scale with *not at all true* (1), *not true* (2), *a little true* (3) and *absolutely true* (4).

Action plans were measured with the question: "How precisely did you plan your exercising on two or more days per week, for at least 20 minutes?" The participants had to rate the five statements: "I already planned precisely . . . which physical activity I will perform; when; where; with whom; and how I will exercise." To rate these items a 4-point Likert scale was provided with the anchors: *not at all true* (1), *not true* (2), *a little true* (3), and *absolutely true* (4). Intentions and action plans were assessed at all measurement points in time.

Three domains of *physical activity* were taken into consideration: (1) fitness activities; (2) exercises to train muscle strength; and (3) sports such as volleyball or golf. Individuals were asked how many days they performed the activity in question during the last week and for how many hours and minutes per session. For each domain, the amount of physical activity was computed by multiplying the sessions per week by the minutes per session. The three domains were added to a sum score. Physical activity was assessed at the beginning of the rehabilitation (Baseline) and at Wave 3. Details of data analysis are described in Lippke et al. (2004a, 2004b).

The results are summarized in Figure 11.2. The best predictors of physical activity were intentions (.25) and planning (.23). Self-efficacy and outcome expectancies at Baseline were joint predictors of intentions at Wave 1 (16%

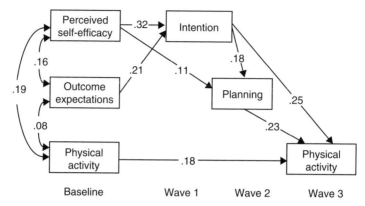

Figure 11.2 Planning as a mediator between social-cognitive variables and subsequent physical activity.

explained variance), but only self-efficacy predicted planning at Wave 2 (6% of explained variance). When considering direct and indirect effects of all predictors on physical activity at Wave 3, the following rank order of standardized total effects was given: intentions (.29), planning (.23), baseline physical activity (.18), self-efficacy (.12), and outcome expectancies (.06).

In this study, behavior was not related to risk perception, and no relationship between risk perception and any other social-cognitive variable was found, except Baseline self-efficacy ($r = -.16$), and planning at Baseline ($r = -.09$), and Wave 1 ($r = -.12$).

The fact that risk perception was only weakly related to any of the variables under study, as opposed to the other social-cognitive variables, raises general questions about how health behaviors can be modified. The fear-appeal approach has focused on using risk communication to let people recognize how much they are at risk for illness or injury. This traditional intervention strategy has not been successful. The present findings would emphasize a different strategy by making people aware of their resources, that is, their skills and strategies to change a refractory behavior. Resource communication would be more appropriate than risk communication. People should not be threatened by what they may lose, but rather should be challenged by what they could gain. Further, interventions should be tailored to fit the needs of the recipients. For those who are in the pre-intentional (goal setting) phase, it would be most promising to improve perceived self-efficacy and outcome expectancies, whereas for their counterparts in the post-intentional (goal pursuit) phase it would be more suitable to focus on action plans. Brief planning interventions are particularly suitable for rehabilitation patients since most of them have already been moved to a post-intentional stage by illness experience and medical treatment. They want to change but need help to translate their intentions into actions (Lippke et al., 2004a, 2004b, 2005; Ziegelmann et al., in press).

Study II: Physical exercise in cardiac rehabilitation

Study II included a total of 437 in-patients with coronary heart disease (CHD) who had a medical recommendation to exercise. Participants were recruited from three cardiac rehabilitation centers in Germany. The mean age of participants was 59 years (*SD* = 9.98) with a range from 31 to 82 years, and 245 (79.8%) of the participants were men. The first point of measurement took place during patients' stay in the rehabilitation centers. Two follow-up questionnaires were sent to patients by ordinary mail two and four months after discharge. Longitudinal data collected during all three waves were available from 307 persons (70.3% of the participants).

The Wave 1 questionnaire included the HAPA variables that belong to the motivational phase (i.e., risk awareness, outcome expectancies, task self-efficacy, and intentions). The Wave 2 questionnaire assessed action planning and maintenance self-efficacy, whereas the Wave 3 questionnaire assessed physical exercise.

Risk awareness was measured by three items assessing vulnerability to coronary health problems with the stem: "If I keep my lifestyle the way it was prior to the acute treatment, . . ." followed by three statements concerning probable future coronary events and coronary health problems, such as, ". . . I will suffer from coronary health problems." The three items were used as indicators for risk awareness.

Task self-efficacy was assessed by four items, for example, "I am confident that I can adjust my life to a physically active lifestyle," or "I am confident that I can be physically active at least once a week."

Outcome expectancies regarding the behavior change were assessed with eight items. All items had the stem: "If I exercise on a regular basis, . . ." followed by positive consequences such as ". . . then I would feel balanced in my daily life," or ". . . it would be good for my blood pressure."

Behavioral intentions were assessed for the time after discharge from the rehabilitation centre. Participants were asked to reply to six intentional statements regarding exercise and physical activity. The stem: "I intend to . . ." was followed by the recommended activities, for example, ". . . be physically active regularly for a minimum of 30 minutes at least three times a week."

Maintenance self-efficacy was assessed in accordance with Luszczynska and Schwarzer (2003) and Luszczynska (2004): "After having started engaging in physical activity, it is important to maintain this behavior on a long-term basis. How confident are you that you will succeed in doing so?" The item stem: "I am confident of engaging in physical activity regularly *on a long-term basis*, . . ." was followed by four items concerning typical barriers that might hamper the maintenance of the behavior, such as, ". . . even if I cannot see any positive changes immediately," or ". . . even if I am together with friends and relatives who are not physically active."

Action planning was assessed using the item stem: "I have made a detailed plan regarding . . ." followed by the items (a) ". . . when to do my physical exercise," (b) ". . . where to exercise," (c) ". . . how to do my physical exercise," and (d) ". . . how often to do my physical exercise."

To assess *physical exercise*, participants were asked to indicate how often per week they engaged in different exercise activities. The latent construct was composed of two indicators. Since all patients were strongly advised to engage in vigorous exercise, a check list consisting of endurance sports, such as swimming, running, power walking, biking, etc., was summed up to an endurance sports score indicating the average workout frequency per week. The second indicator referred to activities of a similar strain as the training program in the rehabilitation centre. The daily exercise program in these centers consisted of bicycle-ergometer training at an individual level of strain (measured in kilowatts) according to the previously assessed exercise stress test for each patient. Participants were asked to report how often on average per week they had trained at a strain level that corresponded in intensity to their individual level of strain in the rehabilitation centre. Details of data analysis are described in Sniehotta, Scholz, & Schwarzer (2005).

Results indicate that intentions at Wave 1 were a significant predictor of action planning at Wave 2, $\beta = .21$, $p < .01$, while action planning predicted exercise at Wave 3, $\beta = .28$, $p < .01$ (see Figure 11.3). The direct path from intentions to exercise turned out to be no longer significant, $\beta = .08$, $p = .30$, while it had been significant when action planning was not included in the model ($\beta = .33$, $p < .01$). Thus, the effect of intentions on exercise was fully mediated by action planning. Maintenance self-efficacy at T2 was predicted by task self-efficacy at T1, $\beta = .47$, $p < .01$. Maintenance self-efficacy, in turn, was a significant predictor of action planning, $\beta = .41$, $p < .01$, and of exercise behavior, $\beta = .25$, $p = .01$. The amount of explained exercise

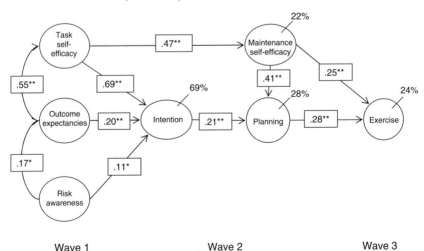

Wave 1   Wave 2   Wave 3

Figure 11.3 Prediction of physical exercise by planning and maintenance self-efficacy. *$p < .05$, **$p < .01$.

variance was 24%, whereas intentions alone explained only 11% of variance in behavior.

Special attention has been paid to the mediation of the intention–behavior relationship that has guided health behavior research for many years. It could be shown that the predictive power of intentions was weakened when post-intentional processes were taken into consideration. Furthermore the inclusion of maintenance self-efficacy and planning led to a notable increase in explained variance. Results of this study again underline the importance of strengthening positive self-beliefs, such as self-efficacy. Self-efficacy is especially important in persons who already have high intentions of changing their behavior. Thus, interventions with post-intentional persons should address both enhancing the positive self-beliefs to maintain a certain behavior (i.e., maintenance self-efficacy) and enhancing planning skills to foster health behavior change (Sniehotta, Scholz, & Schwarzer, 2005; Sniehotta, Schwarzer, Scholz, & Schüz, 2005).

Conclusions

The major models of health behavior specify variables that predict behavioral intentions and actual behaviors. These models share several common predictors, among them outcome expectancies and perceived self-efficacy. The names for these factors are different in different theories, however. For example, behavioral beliefs can be equated to outcome expectancies, and perceived behavioral control is more or less the same as perceived self-efficacy. Communication among theorists and among researchers has been undermined by lack of conceptual clarity, on the one hand, and use of different names for similar constructs, on the other. A consensus in specifying and labeling constructs is required.

Although these models assume underlying processes, most studies have used cross-sectional designs in which intentions and self-reported behaviors are predicted by other variables. However, such static prediction does not reflect changes over time, for example, transition from one stage to the next or recycling through phases. Most important, only a few of these models account for the post-intentional phase, in which goals are translated into action.

The present studies provide evidence in favor of health behavior models that distinguish between a goal-setting and a goal-pursuit phase. The present findings replicate the results of Luszczynska and Schwarzer (2003) and Renner and Schwarzer (2003). They are also perfectly in line with the theoretical assumptions of the HAPA (Schwarzer, 1992, 2001).

The HAPA model outlines the complex mechanisms that operate when individuals become motivated to change their habits, when they adopt and maintain a new habit, and when they attempt to resist temptations and recover from setbacks. The model applies to all health-compromising and health-enhancing behaviors and could even be adjusted to apply to behavior change more generally. Longitudinal research is needed so that changes can be assessed more precisely. Moreover, there is a need for applied research on matching intervention strategies to stages of change.

References

Ajzen, I. (2002). Perceived behavioral control, self-efficacy, locus of control, and the theory of planned behavior. *Journal of Applied Social Psychology, 32*(4), 665–683.

Bandura, A. (1997). *Self-efficacy: The exercise of control.* New York: Freeman.

Baumeister, R. F., & Heatherton, T. F. (1996). Self-regulation failure: An overview. *Psychology Inquiry, 7*(1), 1–15.

Becker, M. H. (Ed.). (1974). *The health belief model and personal health behavior.* Thorofare, NJ: Slack.

Conner, M., & Norman, P. (Eds.). (2005). *Predicting health behavior: Research and practice with social cognition models* (2nd ed.). Buckingham, UK: Open University Press.

Gollwitzer, P. M. (1999). Implementation intentions: Strong effects of simple plans. *American Psychologist, 54*, 493–503.

Leventhal, H., Singer, R., & Jones, S. (1965). Effects of fear and specificity of recommendation upon attitudes and behavior. *Journal of Personality and Social Psychology, 2*, 20–29.

Lippke, S., Ziegelmann, J. P., & Schwarzer, R. (2004a). Initiation and maintenance of physical exercise: Stage-specific effects of a planning intervention. *Research in Sports Medicine, 12*, 221–240.

Lippke, S., Ziegelmann, J. P., & Schwarzer, R. (2004b). Behavioral intentions and action plans promote physical exercise: A longitudinal study with orthopedic rehabilitation patients. *Journal of Sport and Exercise Psychology, 26*, 470–483.

Lippke, S., Ziegelmann, J. P., & Schwarzer, R. (2005). Stage-specific adoption and maintenance of physical activity: Testing a three-stage model. *Psychology of Sport & Exercise, 6*, 585–603.

Luszczynska, A. (2004). Change of breast self-examination: The effects of intervention on enhancing self-efficacy. *International Journal of Behavioural Medicine, 11*, 95–103.

Luszczynska, A., & Schwarzer, R. (2003). Planning and self-efficacy in the adoption and maintenance of breast self-examination: A longitudinal study on self-regulatory cognitions. *Psychology and Health, 18*, 93–108.

Renner, B., & Schwarzer, R. (2003). Social-cognitive factors predicting health behavior change. In J. Suls & K. Wallston (Eds.), *Social psychological foundations of health and illness* (pp. 169–196). Oxford, UK: Blackwell.

Rogers, R. W. (1983). Cognitive and physiological processes in fear appeals and attitude change: A revised theory of protection motivation. In J. R. Cacioppo & R. E. Petty (Eds.), *Social psychology: A sourcebook* (pp. 153–176). New York: Guilford.

Schwarzer, R. (1992). Self-efficacy in the adoption and maintenance of health behaviors: Theoretical approaches and a new model. In R. Schwarzer (Ed.), *Self-efficacy: Thought control of action* (pp. 217–243). Washington, DC: Hemisphere.

Schwarzer, R. (2001). Social-cognitive factors in changing health-related behavior. *Current Directions in Psychological Science, 10*, 47–51.

Schwarzer, R., & Fuchs, R. (1995). Changing risk behaviors and adopting health behaviors: The role of self-efficacy beliefs. In A. Bandura (Ed.), *Self-efficacy in changing societies* (pp. 259–288). New York: Cambridge University Press.

Schwarzer, R., & Renner, B. (2000). Social-cognitive predictors of health behavior: Action self-efficacy and coping self-efficacy. *Health Psychology, 19*, 487–495.

Sniehotta, F. F., Scholz, U., & Schwarzer, R. (2005). Bridging the intention–behaviour gap: Planning, self-efficacy, and action control in the adoption and maintenance of physical exercise. *Psychology & Health, 20*(2), 143–160.

Sniehotta, F. F., Schwarzer, R., Scholz, U., & Schüz, B. (2005). Action planning and coping planning for long-term lifestyle change: Theory and assessment. *European Journal of Social Psychology, 35*, 565–576.

Sutton, S. (2001). Health behavior, psychosocial theories of. In N. J. Smelser & P. B. Baltes (Eds.), *The international encyclopedia of the social and behavioral sciences.* Oxford, UK: Elsevier.

Wallston, K., & Armstrong, C. (2002). Theoretically-based strategies for health behavior change. In M. P. O'Donnell (Ed.), *Health promotion in the workplace* (3rd ed., pp. 182–201). Albany, NY: Delmar.

Weinstein, N. D., Rothman, A. J., & Sutton, S. R. (1998). Stage theories of health behavior: Conceptual and methodological issues. *Health Psychology, 17*, 290–299.

Ziegelmann, J. P., Lippke, S., & Schwarzer, R. (in press). Adoption and maintenance of physical activity: Planning interventions in young, middle-aged, and older adults. *Psychology & Health.*

12 Violence against women: A global health issue

Nancy Felipe Russo

> In all countries and cultures, women have frequently been the victims of abuse by their intimates. They have been battered, sexually abused and psychologically injured by persons with whom they should enjoy the closest trust. This maltreatment has gone largely unpunished, unremarked, and has even been tacitly, if not explicitly condoned.
>
> (United Nations, 1989, p. 11)

Age-old proverbs from around the world provide a window into our human culture in which men have been advised:

> Women, like drums, should be beaten regularly (United States, England);
> Clubbing produces virtuous wives (China);
> A woman who is beaten is going to be a better wife (Korea);
> Beat your wife regularly; even if you don't know why, she will (Middle East);
> The nails of a cart and the head of a woman, they only work when they are hit hard (India);
> A woman, a dog and a walnut tree – the harder you beat them, the better they be (Europe);
> For the man who beats his wife, God improves the food (Russia).

Although some might argue that these proverbs are mere remnants of an unenlightened past, they do remind us that male violence against women is not a recent phenomenon. They also suggest that such violence has roots in gender-related beliefs and norms of the cultural context – beliefs and norms that present women as a threat to men's power and manhood, and that offer violence as the "natural" way to control women and preserve their virtue. For centuries, such beliefs and norms have rendered male violence against women unchallenged and left victims to suffer in silence.

In the 1970s, with the rise of what has become a global women's movement, male violence against women became recognized as a social problem. Today, male gender-based violence against women is globally recognized as a health, economic development, and human rights concern (Amnesty

International, 2004; Koss, Heise, & Russo, 1994b; National Center for Injury Prevention and Control, 2003; Russo, Koss, & Goodman, 1995; United Nations General Assembly, 1993). There is now a large and growing body of interdisciplinary research on such gender-based violence that is being applied in public education programs, reflected in criminal justice and health care systems, and influencing new laws and policies cross-nationally (Heise, Ellsberg, & Gottemoeller, 1999; Jasinski & Williams, 1998; Koss, Bailey, Yuan, & Lichter, 2003; Koss, Goodman, Browne, Fitzgerald, Keita, & Russo, 1994a; Renzetti, Edleson, & Bergen, 2001; Russo, Koss, & Ramos, 2000; World Health Organization, 2002, 2004).

The term "gender-based" is used because such violence reflects women's gender roles and status in society. Gender inequality and a disadvantaged status for women support and perpetuate gender-based violence. Cultural values, beliefs, norms, and social institutions often legitimize gender-based violence and provide little recourse for its victims (Koss et al., 1994a).

My goals for this chapter are to highlight some of the major findings of that literature and to illustrate how they are being applied in public-education programs in diverse countries. I also want to draw attention to some sources of information about international efforts on the issue of violence against women, as it is impossible to do justice here to the enormous amount of activity going on around the world.

Gender-based violence defined

In the Platform for Action of the United Nations World Conference on Women in Beijing (Beijing Conference), gender-based violence was defined as "any act that results in, or is likely to result in physical, sexual, or psychological harm or suffering to women, including threats of such acts, coercion or arbitrary deprivation of liberty, whether occurring in public or private life" (United Nations, 1995, Platform for Action, Section D.113). The Beijing Conference definition represents international consensus on how to conceptualize the dynamics of gender-based violence.

Research on violence against women that simply counts physically violent acts (e.g., hitting, shoving, stabbing) is helpful, but does not provide a complete view of the dynamics of gender-based violence encompassed in the Beijing Conference definition. There are five aspects of the Beijing definition that have important implications for the conduct of research aimed at understanding the causes, levels, and consequences of gender-based violence in women's lives.

First, a behavior does not actually have to result in harm. A *threat* is sufficient, and an act only needs to be *likely* to result in harm. Just because throwing a woman across a room does not result in a broken bone does not exclude it from an assessment of a women's exposure to violence by this definition.

Second, harm needs to be assessed at *multiple levels* – physical injuries are not the only outcomes to be assessed. Psychological and sexual outcomes, such as depression and sexual dysfunction, are equally important.

Third, threat, coercion, abuse, intimidation, and force used by men to control women are recognized as forms of violence that provide a context of meaning for specific violent acts. This includes situations that involve a threat of violence such as stalking (Kurt, 1995) and sexual terrorism (Sheffield, 1995). Specific acts of aggression are part of an overall pattern of behaviors in which men attempt to exert power and control over women (APA Intimate Partner Abuse and Relationship Violence Working Group, 2004).

Fourth, coercion and arbitrary *deprivation of freedom to act*, such as threatening to lock a woman in a closet or denying her access to friends and family are recognized as playing an important role in the dynamics of violence.

Fifth, and finally, acts occurring in the "private" context of the family are not exempt from this definition and are considered legitimate targets for public-policy-related research and intervention.

Obviously, a particular behavior may reflect more than one of these aspects. For example, a husband who threatens to kill children or pets if not obeyed is using a coercive threat likely to result in psychological distress in order to deprive his wife of freedom to act. So even while the focus is on findings in one area (e.g., physical assault), it must always be kept in mind that obtaining a full picture of the dynamics of gender-based violence and its effects on physical and mental health requires attention to all of these dimensions.

Gender-based violence is a special category of violence. It does not encompass every violent act a woman may happen to experience (e.g., being threatened by a weapon during a robbery, for example). Such violence is:

- a reflection of gender roles and status in society;
- supported and perpetuated by gender inequality, which confers male entitlement and a disadvantaged status for women;
- typically perpetuated by men against women;
- legitimized by cultural values, beliefs, norms, and social institutions; and
- associated with little support or recourse for its victims (Koss et al., 1994b, 2003).

Gender-based violence against women is pervasive – found in streets, homes, schools, and workplaces around the globe (Koss et al., 1994b; Russo et al., 1995; Heise et al., 1999). As seen in Table 12.1, gender-based violence is manifested in many forms over the life cycle (Heise et al., 1999; Koss et al., 1994a; Shane & Ellsberg, 2002).

Findings from the enormous body of research that has been conducted on these various forms of violence inform a wide variety of public-education programs around the world, from youth poster competitions in the Caribbean to bus advertisements in South Africa.[1]

Table 12.1 Gender-based violence over the life span

Life period	Abuse
Prenatal	Sex selection
Infancy and childhood	Child physical and sexual abuse and neglect
	Female genital mutilation
	Female infanticide
	Malnutrition
Adolescence	Forced early marriage
	Forced prostitution
	Peer sexual harassment
	Psychological abuse
	Rape
	Sex trafficking
Reproductive years	Dowry killings
	Forced abortion and sterilization
	Homicide
	Honor killings
	Marital rape and intimate partner violence
	Rape and sexual harassment
	Sex work and trafficking
	Stalking
Elder years	Elder/widow abuse

The many forms of gender-based violence must be kept in mind for they are not independent experiences. For example, women experiencing childhood sexual abuse report higher rates of partner violence (Russo & Denious, 2001). Further, dividing rape and intimate partner violence into distinct and separate categories may obscure the overlapping nature of rape and battery in women's experiences (Russo et al., 1995; Koss et al., 2003; Krug, Dahlberg, Mercy, Zwi, & Lozano, 2002). Similarly, distinguishing violence in the home from violence in the workplace is an artificial distinction – partner violence accounts for a sizable proportion of women's workplace deaths (Younger, 1994). The primary focus here is on intimate partner violence.

Gender-based intimate partner violence

In keeping with the Beijing Conference definition, gender-based intimate partner violence (IPV) has been defined as acts performed by a husband or intimate male partner that include physical, sexual, and emotional abuse, including physical assault, verbal abuse, forced intercourse and other forms of sexual coercion, and a variety of controlling behaviors aimed at restricting women's freedom of action (e.g., isolation from family and friends).

Challenges to researchers who seek to study IPV arise from methodological and ethical as well as conceptual issues (Desai & Saltzman, 2001;

Ellsberg, Heise, Pena, Agurto, & Winkvist, 2001; Schwartz, 2000; White, Smith, Koss, & Figueredo, 2000). In addition to the private and sensitive nature of the information, the confidentiality and safety of research participants must be preserved and referral information that identifies places to go for help made available to them. Interviewers require special training and sensitivity if they are to conduct interviews in the nonjudgmental and empathic way needed to obtain disclosure of violent events. To assist researchers, the World Health Organization (WHO) has developed guidelines for research that address ethical and safety issues (World Health Organization, 2001).

Community-based survey research is being used to document the prevalence of violence in Asia, Africa, the Middle East, Latin America, Europe, and North America (Kishor & Johnson, 2004). Not all dimensions of gender-based violence are typically measured in national surveys, so such studies only present a slice of the picture. In particular qualitative research is needed to illuminate the meanings of violence and coercive acts in the cultural contexts in which women experience them (World Health Organization, 2001). The WHO is conducting a multicountry study of women's health and partner violence that combines qualitative and quantitative approaches and provides a model for the conduct of such research. When completed, that work will provide the most comprehensive information on the prevalence and health consequences of intimate violence in eight countries (Garcia-Moreno, Watts, Jansen, Ellsberg, & Heise, 2003). To date, most survey research has focused on physical assault and rape by intimate partners.

Physical assault and rape by intimate partners

A transnational review of population-based survey data found the lifetime proportion of women experiencing physical assault by an intimate partner to range from 10–69% (Krug et al., 2002). With regard to the USA, the National Violence against Women Survey (NVWS) estimated one out of five (22.1%) women to be physically assaulted in their lifetime; about one in thirteen (7.7%) to be raped by an intimate partner. The rates for the 12 months preceding the study were 1.3% and 0.2%, respectively. In other words, an estimated 1.3 million women experienced physical assault and more than 201,394 women experienced rape at the hands of an intimate partner in the previous year (Tjaden & Thoennes, 2000). These lifetime figures of rape and physical assault are comparable to those found in community surveys (Bureau of Justice Statistics, 1998; Finkelhor & Yllo, 1985; Russell, 1990).

The definition of physical assault used in the NVWS covered a range of 12 behaviors that included threat associated with a weapon but not other forms of physical aggression. "Pushed, grabbed, and shoved" was the most frequently reported category of assault (18.1%), followed by "slapped, hit" (16%). These were followed by "pulled hair" (9.1%), "beat up" (8.5%), "threw something that could hurt" (8.1%), "choked, tried to drown" (6.1%), "kicked, bit" (5.5%), "hit with object" (5.0%), "threatened with gun" (3.5%), "threatened with knife" (2.8%), "used knife" (0.9%), and "used gun" (0.7%). These items, which are from the Conflict Tactics Scales (Strauss, 1979), reflect the recommendations of the WHO protocol for research on domestic violence that advises asking about the experience of particular specific acts and avoiding the use of "loaded" words such as "abuse," "rape," or "violence" (World Health Organization, 2001).

A recent multicultural study based on the WHO recommendations (Kishor & Johnson, 2004) has identified similarities and differences in exposure to intimate partner violence across cultures. That research also documents the relationship of intimate violence to men's attempts to control women by restricting their freedom of action cross-culturally. As can be seen in Figure 12.1, rates of intimate partner violence vary by country, but in all countries studied, a substantial proportion of married women reported being physically assaulted by their husbands. Note that direct comparisons across countries should be made with caution as the questionnaire wording and sampling approach differed in some cases (see Kishor & Johnson, 2004, pp. 3 and 12 for more detail).

Feminists have emphasized that IPV has been legitimized as a means of social control for women, as evidenced by the lack of sanctions and public

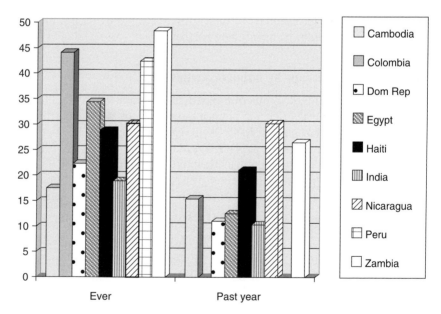

Figure 12.1 Percentage of ever-married women age 15–49 experiencing IPV ever and in the past year, by country. *Notes*: Dom Rep = Dominican Republic; 12-month figures for Colombia and Peru not available. Ns = 2403; 7602; 6807; 7123; 2347; 90,303; 8507; 17,369; 3792, respectively (Source: Kishor & Johnson, 2004, p. 12).

interventions for male partner violence (Koss et al., 1994b; Marin & Russo, 1999). Men who connect masculinity with being able to control and dominate their partners are more likely to be abusive (Goodrum, Umberson, & Anderson, 2001). Kishor and Johnson (2004) provide cross-cultural evidence for the link between male intimate partner violence and other socially controlling behaviors, specifically:

• becoming jealous or angry if she talks with another man;
• frequently accusing her of being unfaithful;
• not permitting her to meet girlfriends;
• limiting her contact with her family;
• insisting on knowing where she is all the time; and
• not trusting her with money.

Figure 12.2 shows the increase in the percentage of women experiencing intimate partner violence by the number of these marital control behaviors. As can be seen, the link between intimate partner violence and other forms of controlling behavior is strong. The risk for violence increases with the number of behaviors exhibited, and the association is found across diverse cultures. More needs to be known about the meanings of violence or threat of violence as it is used to control women in specific contexts.

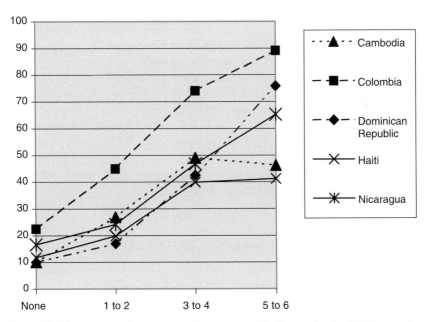

Figure 12.2 Percentage of ever-married women age 15–49 experiencing IPV by number of kinds of marital control behaviors experienced, by country. *Notes:* *N*s = 2403; 7602; 6807; 2347; 8507, respectively (Source: Kishor & Johnson, 2004, p. 70).

Mahoney (1991) has offered the concept of "separation assault" to focus attention on the way that intimate male partners use violence to keep women from leaving violent relationships. Examination of affidavits that women have filed to obtain restraining orders suggests that intimate partners use violence to attain specific objectives: (1) to keep the woman in the relationship; (2) as punishment, coercion, or retaliation for challenging his authority with regard to the children; (3) coercion or retaliation related to her pursuing court or police remedies, such as a restraining order; and (4) punishing her for challenges to a variety of perceived male entitlements, including the right to drink and demand sex (Ptacek, 1997).

These finding are congruent with US studies that report a strong link between abuse of alcohol and other drugs and intimate partner violence (Hotaling & Sugarman, 1986). Further, men with substance-abuse problems (alcohol or drugs) are not only more frequently violent – they are more likely to injure their partners, sexually assault them, and be violent outside the home. Just because men who are frequently drunk are violent does not mean that they are violent only when they are drunk (Browne, 1997).

Research has documented the use of alcohol as a means to disavow male responsibility for violent actions. Men claim: "I couldn't help myself"; "I didn't know what I was doing"; "I didn't mean it." And women forgive: "He really loves me – it's the drink"; "He can't help it." The alcohol–violence connection has been a target for public education campaigns attacking the cultural myths about alcohol use that underlie such statements.

As Figure 12.3 shows, there is a strong relationship between male violence and drunkenness, but it is complex. There is not a great deal of difference in the proportion of women experiencing partner violence among women whose partners "don't drink" versus "never get drunk," and in the three countries for which there is information, the proportion of women experiencing partner violence was lowest in the "never get drunk" category. Being with a man who was "drunk occasionally" raised the risk somewhat, but being with a man who was "drunk frequently" was the category that stood out from the other groups (except for the case of Cambodia, where the categories are virtually undistinguishable). More needs to be known about the causal dynamics of the relationship of IPV to alcohol and other forms of substance abuse.

How does culture affect responses to gender-based violence?

Gender-based violence is shaped by cultural norms and expectations that influence the meanings of and responses to violence, including:

- silencing and underreporting (whether the woman will tell anyone at all);
- help seeking (including to whom she will turn and what kind of help she will seek);
- responses of friends, family, and community (whether the man will be

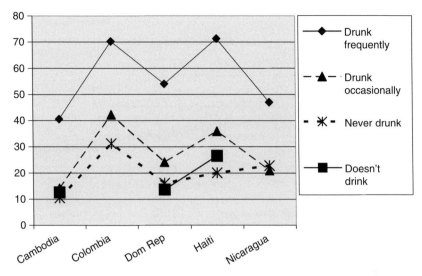

Figure 12.3 Percentage of ever-married women age 15–49 ever experiencing IPV, by partner alcohol use and country. *Notes*: Dom Rep = Dominican Republic; "Doesn't drink" figures not available for Colombia or Nicaragua. *N*s = 2403; 7602; 6807; 2347; 8507, respectively (Source: Kishor & Johnson, 2004, p. 33).

    punished; whether the women will receive support or be rejected and stigmatized); and
- emotional responses of victims (including depression, guilt, and shame).

Most women do not seek help, but the proportion varies widely across cultures, as do the reasons for not seeking help. One review of studies from nine countries found the proportion of women experiencing physical abuse who never told anyone to range from a high of 70% in Bangladesh to a low of 30% in Canada (Heise et al., 1999). Examining data from seven countries on help seeking in response to violence by anyone, including partners, Kirshor and Johnson (2004) found the largest proportion of women to seek help in Nicaragua (59.5%) and the smallest in Cambodia (22.5) – with Egypt (47.2%), Peru (42.2%), the Dominican Republic (41.2%), Colombia (38%), and Haiti (31.3%) falling in between. Among women who did not seek help, at the top of the list of reasons why are: (1) the belief that it would be of no use; and (2) embarrassment (although specific reasons varied by country; see Figure 12.4). These findings suggest that despite progress in recognizing that IPV is pervasive, the silencing and underreporting of such violence continue to be a severe problem.

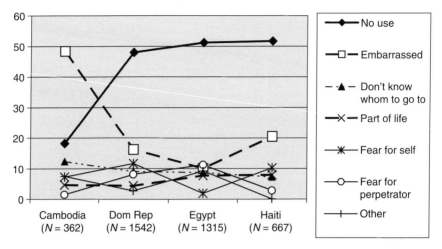

Figure 12.4 Reasons given for not seeking help by women experiencing violence from
anyone, by country. *Notes*: Dom Rep = Dominican Republic (Source:
Kishor & Johnson, 2004, p. 12).

Gender-based violence is destructive

Gender-based violence has a host of negative physical and mental health
effects (Coker, Smith, Bethea, King, & McKeown, 2000; Goodman, Koss, &
Russo, 1993; Heise et al., 1999; Koss & Heslet, 1992; Koss, Koss, & Woodruff,
1991; Krug et al., 2002), with concomitant social and economic costs. In the
USA alone, the costs of intimate violence are estimated to exceed $5.8 billion
each year. More than two-thirds of that cost ($4.1 billion) goes for direct
medical and mental health care service delivery (National Center for Injury
Prevention and Control, 2003). Then there is the negative impact of exposure
to gender-based violence on children, which has also been documented (for
reviews, see Geffner, Jaffe, & Sudermann, 2000; Holden, Geffner & Jouriles,
1998; Koss et al., 2003).

Negative physical, mental, and behavioral health outcomes associated with
victimization include:

- pregnancy complications and higher risk for having a low birthweight
  infant;
- infant and child mortality;
- chronic pain and gynecological problems;
- gastrointestinal problems;
- stress, depression, and anxiety;
- injury, suicide and death;
- drug and alcohol abuse;
- sexual risk-taking, STIs, HIV/AIDS; and
- unintended pregnancy and unsafe abortion.

A link between exposure to intimate violence and unwanted pregnancy would be expected for a variety of reasons (see Russo & Denious, 1998). Among them is the fact that violent partners are more likely to demand unprotected sex and refuse to use a condom (Russo & Denious, 2001). Having a child also increases a women's dependency on her partner and, for him, is an additional point of leverage to exercise control via threats to harm the child (Ptacek, 1997).

The strong association between violence and unintended and unwanted pregnancy found in US women is seen in the change in the proportion of mothers of newborns experiencing violence in the 12 months preceding the birth by type of pregnancy intendedness – intended, mistimed, and unwanted (see Figure 12.5). The positive association is strongest among unmarried women, reminding us that national surveys that focus solely on married women underestimate the prevalence of intimate partner violence in women's lives (Gazmararian et al., 1995). Further, focus on pregnancy intendedness among mothers of newborns does not encompass what are arguably the most unwanted of pregnancies, i.e., those terminated by abortion.

Figure 12.6 presents the proportion of women who report experiencing a history of various forms of intimate violence by whether or not they reported having an abortion. Women who reported having an abortion were more likely to experience childhood physical and/or sexual abuse, to be a victim of rape (by someone other than the intimate partner), to have a violent partner, or to have a partner who refused to wear a condom (Russo & Denious, 2001).

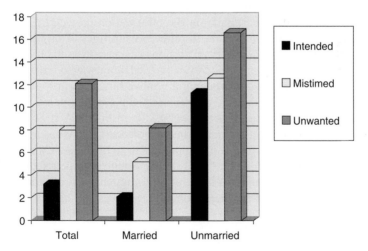

Figure 12.5 Physical violence by pregnancy intendedness and marital status among mothers of newborns, USA. *Notes*: Each woman was asked if her "husband or partner physically hurt [her] during the 12 months before delivery" (p. 1032). $N = 12,612$ mothers of newborns (Source: CDC Pregnancy Risk Assessment Monitoring System data; Gazmararian et al., 1995).

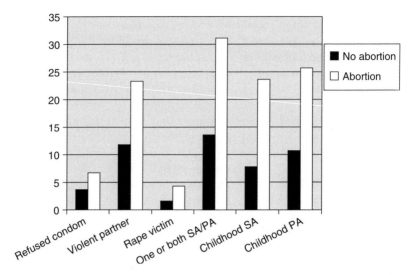

Figure 12.6 Percentage of women experiencing types of intimate violence by history of abortion, USA. *Notes*: SA = sexual abuse; PA = physical abuse; *N* = 2525 (Source: Commonwealth Fund Women's Health Survey data; Russo & Denious, 2001).

Similarly, Kishor and Johnson (2004) found that in all nine countries studied, except for Haiti, experiencing partner violence was consistently associated with a higher likelihood of having an unwanted birth (see Figure 12.7). Unfortunately, the proportion of unwanted pregnancies terminated by abortion is not possible to ascertain from the information provided. Differential access to abortion may contribute to differences in rates of unwanted pregnancies ending in births across countries, making comparisons problematic. However, it was found that among ever-married women who had ever had a birth the percentage of women having a nonlive birth/abortion was consistently higher in women who had experienced violence compared to women who had not experienced violence (Kishor & Johnson, 2004, p. 86), which is congruent with a pregnancy intendedness–violence link. More needs to be known about the use of forced pregnancy as a tactic to keep women from leaving a violent relationship, as well as the extent to which such a tactic contributes to the persistence of high rates of unintended pregnancy around the globe, even in countries where women have access to effective forms of birth control.

Emergent themes

As can be seen by this selective overview of the enormous literature related to gender-based violence against women, the past 30 years have been productive. Multiple forms of intimate gender-based violence have been identified

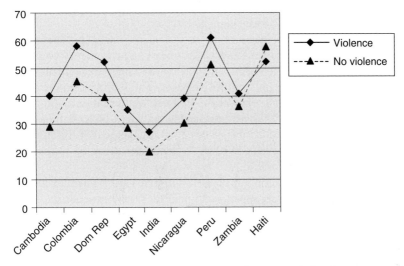

Figure 12.7 Percentage of births in last five years that were mistimed or unwanted by experience of IPV and country. *Notes*: Dom Rep = Dominican Republic; India data from last three years only; women currently pregnant are included. Ns = 414/1654; 1908/2631; 1020/3450; 2350/3835; 7341/31,769; 2145/5098; 4736/7446; 2198/2248; 603/1719 for partner violence and no partner violence by country, respectively (Source: Kishor & Johnson, 2004, p. 78).

and a multiplicity of physical, mental, and behavioral health outcomes are being examined. Each of the forms of gender-based violence over the life cycle has unique aspects that need to be studied in their cultural contexts. However, several emerging themes cut across the forms as well.

Gender-based violence is:

- manifested in multiple forms over the life cycle;
- a pervasive experience that crosses lines of culture and national origin;
- destructive – to the woman, her family, and society;
- most likely to be perpetuated by men against women and supported by cultural myths; and
- a reflection of men's attempts to exert power and control over women, implicating revisions in male entitlements and gender-role constructions as the key to predicting and permitting such violence.

Conclusion

Gender-based violence is a complex, multifaceted phenomenon, one that takes multiple forms and that is rooted in patriarchal social structures and cultural roles of women and men. Such violence has widespread and enduring physical, mental, and behavioral health effects on women and men, their families, and society. Given that the various forms of gender-based violence have common roots, those roots must be targeted by prevention and intervention efforts. Such efforts need to be informed by research that identifies gender-related factors that lead men to be violent against women (e.g., beliefs about a male entitlement that generate anger when confronted with a woman's insubordination) and trigger violent behaviors. The Beijing Conference Platform defines violence as a global health concern and reminds us that society cannot afford to define intimate partner violence as a private issue. Public education efforts in diverse countries designed to change cultural norms and male attitudes supporting gender-based violence are affirming that view, but much more needs to be done.

Priorities for specific action should be tailored to the particular cultural context. I want to underscore two broad priorities for future efforts.

First, conduct cross-cultural research that will: (a) identify the mechanisms underlying gender-based violence; and (b) articulate how the broad range of physical, mental, and social effects of the many forms of such violence over the life cycle vary with cultural context.

Second, develop culturally appropriate public policies and programs to prevent intimate violence and ensure protection and treatment for its victims. Laws that are consistently enforced in culturally appropriate ways by police officers trained to intervene in domestic disputes are a first step towards preventing intimate violence. Legal strategies will not be sufficient to eliminate such violence, however. They must be accompanied by a change in the traditional attitudes and practices that underlie women's unequal status in the family and society, and that legitimize violence as a means for enforcing that status. Public-education programs that challenge such attitudes and teach males of all ages to value women as equal partners in the family and society are critical if gender-based violence is to be truly eliminated and not merely suppressed.

Note

1   These illustrations, and other images used in public education campaigns, which illustrate points made throughout the chapter but are not be reproduced here, can be found at the Johns Hopkins University Media and Materials Communication Center. The Johns Hopkins University media/materials database provides access to a large collection of health communication materials, including posters and videos designed to reduce violence against women. For information, contact M/MC Librarian, Johns Hopkins Bloomberg School of Public Health/Center for Communication Programs, Media/Materials Clearinghouse, 111 Market Place, Suite 310, Baltimore, MD 21202, USA (http://www.hcpartnership.org/mmc/mmc_search.php).

References

Amnesty International (2004). *It's in our hands: Stop violence against women.* London: Amnesty International.

APA Intimate Partner Abuse and Relationship Violence Working Group (2004). *Intimate partner abuse and relationship violence.* Washington, DC: American Psychological Association.

Browne, A. (1997). Violence in marriage: Until death do us part? In A. P. Cardarelli (Ed.), *Violence between intimate partners: Patterns, causes, and effects* (pp. 48–69). Needham Heights, MA: Allyn & Bacon.

Bureau of Justice Statistics. (1998). *Bureau of Justice Statistics sourcebook of criminal justice – 1997.* Washington, DC: US Department of Justice, Bureau of Justice Statistics, NCJ 171 147:198.

Coker, A. L., Smith, P. H., Bethea, L., King, M., & McKeown, R. E. (2000). Physical health consequences of physical and psychological intimate partner violence. *Archives of Family Medicine, 9*, 451–457.

Desai, S., & Saltzman, L. E. (2001). Measurement issues for violence against women. In C. M. Renzetti, J. L. Edleson, & R. K. Bergen (Eds.), *Sourcebook on violence against women* (pp. 35–52). Thousand Oaks, CA: Sage.

Ellsberg, M. C. L., Heise, L., Pena, R., Agurto, S., & Winkvist, A. (2001). Researching domestic violence against women: Methodological and ethical considerations. *Studies in Family Planning, 32*, 1–16.

Finkelhor, D., & Yllo, K. (1985). *License to rape: Sexual abuse of wives.* New York: Holt, Reinhardt, & Winston.

Garcia-Moreno, C., Watts, C., Jansen, H., Ellsberg, M., & Heise, L. (2003). Responding to violence against women: WHO's multicountry study on women's health and domestic violence. *Health and Human Rights, 6*(2), 113–127. (Available at: http://www.who.int/gender/documents/en/vawhealthandhumanrights.pdf)

Gazmararian, J. A., Adams, M. M., Saltzman, L. E., Johnson, C. H., Bruce, F. C., Marks, J. S. et al. (1995). The relationship between pregnancy intendedness and physical violence in mothers of newborns. *Obstetrics & Gynecology, 85*, 1031–1038.

Geffner, R., Jaffe, P. G., & Sudermann, M. (2000). *Children exposed to domestic violence: Current research, interventions, prevention, & policy development.* New York: Haworth Press.

Goodman, L. A., Koss, M. P., & Russo, N. F. (1993). Violence against women: Physical and mental health effects. Part I: Research findings. *Applied & Preventive Psychology: Current Scientific Perspectives, 2*, 79–89.

Goodrum, S., Umberson, D., & Anderson, K. L. (2001). The batterer's view of the self and others in domestic violence. *Sociological Inquiry, 71*, 221–241.

Heise, L., Ellsberg, M., & Gottemoeller, M. (1999, December). Ending violence against women. *Population Reports*, Series L (11), pp. 1–45.

Holden, G., Geffner, R., & Jouriles, E. (Eds.). (1998). *Children exposed to marital violence: Theory, research, and applied issues.* Washington, DC: American Psychological Association.

Hotaling, G. T., & Sugarman, D. B. (1986). An analysis of risk markers in husband to wife violence: The current state of knowledge, *Violence and Victims, 1*, 101–124.

Jasinski, J. L., & Williams, L. M. (Eds.). (1998). *Partner violence: A comprehensive review of 20 years of research.* Thousand Oaks, CA: Sage Publications.

Kishor, S., & Johnson, K. (2004). *Profiling domestic violence: A multi-country study.* Calverton, MD: ORC Macro.

Koss, M. P., Bailey, J. A., Yuan, N. P., & Lichter, E. (2003). Depression and PTSD in survivors of male violence: Research and training initiatives to facilitate recovery. *Psychology of Women Quarterly, 27*, 130–142.

Koss, M. P., Goodman, L. A., Browne, A., Fitzgerald, L., Keita, G. P., & Russo, N. F. (1994a). *No safe haven: Male violence against women at home, at work, and in the community*. Washington, DC: American Psychological Association.

Koss, M. P., Heise, L., & Russo, N. F. (1994b). The global health burden of rape. *Psychology of Women Quarterly, 18*, 509–530.

Koss, M. P., & Heslet, L. (1992). Somatic consequences of violence against women. *Archives of Family Medicine, 1*, 53–59.

Koss, M. P., Koss, P. G., & Woodruff, W. J. (1991). Deleterious effects of criminal victimization on women's health and medical utilization. *Archives of Internal Medicine, 151*, 342–357.

Krug, E. G., Dahlberg, L. L., Mercy, J. A., Zwi, A. B., & Lozano, R. (2002). *World report on violence and health*. Geneva, Switzerland: World Health Organization.

Kurt, J. (1995). Stalking as a variant of domestic violence. *Bulletin of the American Academy of Psychiatry and the Law, 23*, 219–230.

Mahoney, M. R. (1991). Legal images of battered women: Redefining the issue of separation. *Michigan Law Review, 1*, 43–49.

Marin, A. J., & Russo, N. F. (1999). Feminist perspectives on male violence against women: Critiquing O'Neil and Harway's model. In J. M. O'Neil & M. Harway (Eds.), *New perspectives on violence against women* (pp. 18–35). Thousand Oaks, CA: Sage Publications.

National Center for Injury Prevention and Control (2003) *Costs of intimate partner violence against women in the United States*. Atlanta, GA: Centers for Disease Control and Prevention.

Ptacek, J. (1997). The tactics and strategies of men who batter: Testimony from women seeking extreme orders. In A. P. Cardarelli (Ed.), *Violence between intimate partners: Patterns, causes, and effects* (pp. 104–123). Needham Heights, MA: Allyn & Bacon.

Renzetti, C. M., Edleson, J. L., & Bergen, R. K. (Eds.). (2001). *Sourcebook on violence against women*. Thousand Oaks, CA: Sage Publications.

Russell, D. E. H. (1990). *Rape in marriage*. Bloomington, IN: Indiana University Press.

Russo, N. F., & Denious, J. (1998). Understanding the relationship of violence against women to unwanted pregnancy and its resolution. In L. J. Beckman & S. M. Harvey (Eds.), *The new civil war: The psychology, culture, and politics of abortion* (pp. 211–234). Washington, DC: American Psychological Association.

Russo, N. F., & Denious, J. E. (2001). Violence in the lives of women having abortions: Implications for public policy and practice. *Professional Psychology: Research and Practice, 32*, 142–150.

Russo, N. F., Koss, M. P., & Goodman, L. (1995). Male violence against women: A global health and development issue. In L. L. Adler & F. L. Denmark (Eds.), *Violence and the prevention of violence* (pp. 121–127). Westport, CT: Praeger.

Russo, N. F., Koss, M. P., & Ramos, L. (2000). Rape: A global health issue. In J. Ussher (Ed.), *Women's health: Contemporary international perspectives* (pp. 129–142). London: British Psychological Society.

Shane, B., & Ellsberg, M. (2002, September). Violence against women: Effects on reproductive health. *Outlook, 20*(1), 1–8.

Schwartz, M. S. (2000). Methodological issues in the use of survey data for measuring and characterizing violence against women. *Violence Against Women, 6*, 815–838.

Sheffield, C. J. (1995). Sexual terrorism. In J. Freeman (Ed.), *Women: A feminist perspective* (5th ed., pp. 1–21). Mountain View, CA: Mayfield Publishers.

Strauss, M. A. (1979). Measuring intrafamily conflict and violence: The Conflict Tactics (CT) scales. *Journal of Marriage and the Family, 41*, 75–88.

Tjaden, P., & Thoennes, P. (2000). *Full report of the prevalence, incidence, and consequences of violence against women: Findings from the National Violence against Women Survey.* Washington, DC: National Institute of Justice/Centers for Disease Control and Prevention. (Available at: http://www.ojp.usdoj.gov/nij)

United Nations General Assembly. (1993, December 20). *Declaration on the elimination of violence against women.* Proceedings of the 85th Plenary Meeting, Geneva, Switzerland.

United Nations (1989). *Violence against women in the family.* New York: United Nations.

United Nations (1995). *Report of the fourth world conference on women, Beijing 4–15 September 1995.* New York: United Nations.

White, J. W., Smith, P. H., Koss, M. P., & Figueredo, A. J. (2000). Intimate partner aggression – what have we learned? Comment on Archer (2000). *Psychological Bulletin, 126*, 690–696.

World Health Organization (2001). *Putting women first: Ethical and safety recommendations for research on domestic violence against women.* Geneva, Switzerland: Department of Gender and Women's Health.

World Health Organization (2002). *World report on violence and health.* Geneva, Switzerland: WHO.

World Health Organization (2004). *Gender-based violence.* (Available at: http://www.who.int/gender/violence)

Younger, B. (1994). Violence against women in the workplace. *Employee Assistance Quarterly, 9*, 113–133.

13 Professional psychology around the world: A fifty-year progress report

Raymond D. Fowler

Overview

For the purposes of this chapter, the term "professional psychology" is used to mean the application of psychological principles to human health and mental health. The specialties of clinical, counseling, school and health psychology are examples of the professional areas considered here. There are, of course, many other applied areas of psychology such as industrial, organizational, environmental, and traffic psychology, but these are beyond the scope of this chapter.

This chapter examines the history of professional practice and its evolution from academic psychology. Developments in the United States are described, followed by a description of the status of professional practice in some other countries. Finally, some possible developments in the future are discussed.

Origins of psychological practice

It is often said that psychological practice has a long past, but a short history. Throughout history, methods to modify behavior and attitudes, including punishment, rewards and instruction have been developed.

Long before there was a science of psychology there were psychological practitioners. As in the field of medicine, practice emerged long before there was a scientific foundation for the procedures developed.

Psychological practice without psychologists

In the 19th century many individuals around the world provided psychological services, including what we would now call intellectual evaluation, diagnosis, hypnosis and psychotherapy. The early practitioners were called by a variety of names, including: phrenologists; physiognomists; characterologists; psychics; mesmerists; spiritualists; mental healers; and graphologists. Some practitioners began to be called psychologists, and that name gradually prevailed.

American Psychological Association and professional practice:1892–1941

For the first 60 years after its founding, the major focus in the American Psychological Association (APA) was on psychology as an academic discipline. The APA was small, exclusive and inward looking, with little interest in psychology as a profession. In fact, those psychologists interested in applying psychological principles to human problems were looked down upon by those whose primary interest was psychology as a science.

The new practitioners

Despite the general lack of interest by their colleagues, some of the early psychologists in the United States were interested in applying scientific psychology to the solving of human problems. For example, James McKeen Cattell, one of the first PhD-level psychologists, developed the concept of mental testing and promoted it as a major psychological technique. Lightner Witmer, another early psychologist, founded the first psychological clinic, and is often referred to as the founder of both clinical psychology and school psychology. Many other psychologists began to follow the lead of Cattell and Witmer, and soon the new practitioners began the development of a scientifically based practice of psychology.

The status of professional psychology prior to World War II

Before the United States entered World War II in 1941, almost a half century after the founding of APA, the practice of psychology was still held in low esteem by most academic psychologists, and there had been little development of psychology as an organized profession. Less than half of the states had a state psychological association. No state had passed a psychology licensing law, and only one state had even tried.

To make matters worse, there was no consensus on what constituted adequate training for a professional psychologist, and almost no university department offered good clinical training.

After World War II

With the beginning of World War II, hundreds of psychology professors left their universities for military service, and many were assigned to provide diagnostic and treatment services for military personnel. The good work done by those psychologists helped to improve the image of professional psychologists, both within the profession and with the public in general. Psychologists were respected for their wartime service, and many veterans of military service and others were attracted to psychology as a career.

In the years immediately following World War II, thousands of students, including many veterans, majored in psychology and proceeded to graduate school. Most of the new students were professionally oriented, and psychology departments had to move rapidly to recruit new professionally oriented faculty. Psychology departments grew rapidly to accommodate the influx of new graduate students.

Substantial government funds supported the development of professional psychology. Most of the veterans had their tuition and expenses paid through legislation known as the "GI Bill" that was passed by congress to assure that veterans had an opportunity for higher education. In addition, government agencies, especially the Veteran's Administration and the National Institute of Mental Health, made funds available in the form of training grants and internships.

Professional psychology in the United States

Why did professional psychology thrive in the United States in comparison with countries in Europe and Asia? A major factor was the great interest in psychology that the American public has always shown. Many newspapers carried columns by psychologists that were eagerly read by the public, and books on self-understanding were quite popular. Teachers welcomed advice and assistance by psychologists and some prominent psychologists, including William James, gave lectures to teachers. The public's respect for psychology was greatly heightened by the service psychologists provided in World Wars I and II.

Another factor that permitted psychology to flourish in the post-war years was that the USA had minimal war damage. Many countries in Europe and Asia had severe damage during the war, and required many years to rebuild their economies and their education systems. By contrast, the US economy boomed during and after the war, and there were adequate resources to provide financial assistance to universities and to students. Without those favorable conditions, it is doubtful that psychology would have developed as rapidly in the USA. Many countries in Europe and Asia are now experiencing the kind of accelerated growth in psychology that the USA experienced 50 years ago.

1949: Boulder Conference

Recognizing that it was important for the field of psychology to have a consensus on how psychology students should be trained to provide clinical services and who should be recognized as psychologists, leaders in psychology convened a conference in Boulder, Colorado. That conference, usually referred to as the Boulder Conference, developed a model for training and practice in psychology that has become known as the Boulder Model. Although variations on that model have developed, the general principles established at the Boulder Conference have been dominant for over half a century and are still widely accepted by US psychologists. Some key aspects of the Boulder Model are as follows:

- Training in professional psychology includes training in research as well as practice.
- The training includes a one-year internship to provide direct clinical experience.
- Practice in Clinical Psychology requires a doctoral degree.
- One postdoctoral year of supervision is required prior to independent practice.
- Psychologists should be licensed to practice.

Current status of professional psychology in the USA

Psychology is now recognized by law and by the public as a healthcare profession. There are currently 117,000 psychologists in the United States, 75,000 (64%) of whom are in professional practice. All states and territories have licensure laws that regulate the practice of psychology and prohibit non-psychologists from presenting themselves as psychologists. Licensure, and the title *psychologist*, requires a doctoral degree in most states. As a result of the rapid growth of professional psychology, psychology is now the largest doctoral level provider of mental health services in the United States.

Professional practice of psychology around the world

Psychologists practice in most countries in the world, but countries vary greatly in numbers, scope of practice, legal recognition, regulation and licensure, and training resources. Since it is impossible to review practice in all countries in the limited space available, what follows is a brief survey of practice in representative countries in Europe, Asia, Africa, the Middle East and South America. This survey draws heavily from the *Handbook of International Psychology* (Stevens & Wedding, 2004).

Europe

Europe has a long tradition of academic psychology. The first psychology laboratories were in Europe, and psychology traces its origins to Wundt's laboratory in Germany. Psychology was negatively impacted by the devastation of two world wars, and professional psychology, as well as psychology in general, languished for many years, but there has been rapid growth since the 1970s. One of the most important developments was the formation in 1981 of a strong European Federation of Psychology Associations (EFPA). All of the major European countries participate in EFPA, which coordinates the work of the national associations of psychology, and most European countries have legal regulation and licensure. Currently, EFPA is working toward the development of a European Diploma of Psychology.

United Kingdom

The professional practice of psychology in the United Kingdom (UK) primarily developed after World War II. The UK recognizes the doctoral degree as the entry level for clinical practice. Despite an active professional community, the UK has no legal recognition or licensure of psychologists. The British Psychological Society has developed a system to recognize qualified practitioners, and there are currently 10,000–11,000 Chartered Psychologists. Most psychologists in the UK work for government agencies, where licensure is not as essential as it is in independent practice. The British Psychological Society accredits training programs, and recognizes those that reach a satisfactory level of excellence.

Most major therapeutic approaches have advocates in the UK, but the dominant approach is cognitive/behavioral. The UK has taken a leadership position in working toward European Diploma for Psychology.

Germany

In general, education in Germany is free, and psychology is popular among German students. At present, 2000–3000 psychology diplomas are awarded each year. The BA and MA are not traditional in Germany. The doctorate takes 4–5 years.

Since 1999, licensure has been mandatory for national health insurance reimbursement. Reimbursement of psychologists is on parity with physicians. Behavior therapy, psychoanalysis and depth psychotherapy are currently recognized for reimbursement. Private practice is still relatively rare.

Asia/Pacific

Psychology in Asia has a long history, but professional practice by psychologists is relatively recent in some countries. Professional practice is well established in some countries, for instance Japan, Australia, New Zealand and Singapore but hardly exists in some of the poorer countries. Most psychologists in Asia are employed in the public sector. Training standards vary from country to country, and are in a state of flux in many countries. There are no recognized standards for recognition as a psychologist throughout most of the region.

China

China was one of the first Asian countries to include psychology in its education system, and scholars from China went to study in North America and

Europe in the early 1900s. Psychology departments developed slowly but steadily during the 20th century, but progress was often impeded by wars that destabilized the country's education system. After World War II, China's psychology orientation was influenced by Russian psychology. In the 1970s, the cultural revolution resulted in severe damage to colleges and universities, and psychology was a particular target of attack.

In subsequent years, psychology has slowly rebuilt and is now well established. Psychology is now a popular subject throughout China with an annual production of 1000 BA graduates and 500 masters and doctoral graduates. Psychology graduates find jobs relatively easily. There are now approximately 10,000 psychologists in China. Professional practitioner psychologists are still relatively rare: there are only 1300 clinical psychologists for a population of well over a billion. There is essentially no independent practice of psychology in China at the present time: most psychologists work in the public sector.

Africa

Except for South Africa psychology is not well developed in Africa, particularly in sub-Saharan Africa. Most African countries are quite impoverished and their educational systems are, for the most part, quite poor. Most of Africa has few psychologists and even fewer practitioners. The need for professional psychology is great in Africa, a continent that has high levels of stress and deprivation as a result of poverty, violence, HIV/AIDS and poor availability of health and mental-health services.

Nigeria

Psychology in Nigeria, with its large population, is somewhat more developed than in most African countries, but the status of professional practice is quite poor. There are increasing demands for services, but few psychologists to provide service and few resources to provide training. At the present time there are no established procedures for licensing or certification. Independent clinical practice is rare. Most psychologists work in the public sector, where reimbursement is much below that of the medical professions, including nursing. As a result, there is a brain drain, with qualified psychologists migrating to other countries where opportunities are better. Few people in Nigeria have access to psychological services.

Middle East

There is great variability in the status of psychology in the Middle East. Egypt and Iran have a long tradition of psychology, and psychology in Israel is on a par with Europe and North America, but with those exceptions psychology is poorly developed in most of the region. In some countries, fundamentalist Muslim clerics oppose psychology, which makes progress difficult. A recent conference held in Dubai resulted in the formation of a regional association of psychologists in the Middle East and North Africa (MENA). This nascent development holds promise for coordination and mutual support for psychologist in the region.

Iran

In Iran, there is growing interest in psychology and rapid growth in the training of professional psychologists. There are currently over 5400 individuals with training in psychology, mostly at the BA level but there are 389 with MA degrees and 25 at the PhD level. Psychiatry is well established in Iran, with 735 psychiatrists. Psychologists in Iran primarily work in public and private hospitals and counseling centers in urban areas. There is little independent practice, and supervision by psychiatrists is required. New laws will regulate psychological practice and permit practice without psychiatric supervision.

South and Central America

As in most regions of the world, psychology is very variable in South and Central America. It is reasonably well developed in some countries including Chile, Mexico, Brazil and Argentina, but there are relatively few psychologists in smaller countries and poorer countries. There is a regional psychological association: the Interamerican Psychological Society (SIP). Its membership includes North Americans, but the focus is on psychologists from South and Central America.

Brazil

With its large population, and relative affluence, Brazil has a well-developed system for training psychologists and regulating their practice. At the present time, Brazil has 140,000 licensed psychologists; more than any other country in the world. Of those, only 900 have doctoral degrees, but there are 70,000 psychology students of whom over 10,000 graduate annually. Licensure requires five years of training plus a two-year internship. There is no single unitary psychological association, but many professional societies represent psychologists of different persuasions. Most psychologists work in public facilities, in private clinics or in independent practice. In general, psychologists in Brazil feel that they are well respected as professionals. The growth of psychology in Brazil is rapid and the outlook for future development is quite positive.

And what of the future?

With the great diversity of psychologists in the world, it is difficult to make reliable predictions for the future. The growing interest in psychology and the large number of students suggest that there will be substantial growth world-wide. North America, once the home of most of the world's psychologists, now represents only about 20% of psychologists and that percentage is likely to drop still further.

Licensure and legal regulation, well developed in North America and Europe, are barely beginning in many countries, but are a trend that will surely be followed in most countries as the numbers of practitioners increase. The standards for training are still quite variable, but there is some movement toward the doctoral level or its equivalent as the entry level for practice, particularly in the more developed countries. The advent of major international and regional associations facilitates the development of common standards, greater communication and sharing of ideas. The trend is toward increasing similarity with useful variations. With its rapid growth and the growing need for its services, psychology may well become the healthcare profession of the 21st century.

Reference

Stevens, M. J., & Wedding, D. (2004). *Handbook of international psychology*. New York: Brunner-Routledge.

Section III

Social and cultural psychology

14 Cognition and perception: East and West

Richard E. Nisbett

I would like to argue that, for the past 2500 years at least, Asians and people of European culture have had very different ways of understanding – even of seeing – the world around them (Nisbett, 2003; Nisbett, Peng, Choi, & Norenzayan, 2001). Western perception and cognition from the ancient Greeks forward has been *analytic*: the focus is on some central object (which could be a person) with respect to which the individual has some goal. The attributes of the object are attended to with the intention of categorizing it so that rules can be applied that will allow for prediction and control. Eastern perception has been *holistic*: the object or person is seen in a broad context or field and behavior is understood in terms of relationships and similarities rather than generalized categories and rules.

Ancient Greek and Chinese philosophy and science illustrate the dramatic differences in thought and perception (Cromer, 1993; Fung, 1983; Lloyd, 1990, 1991; Munro, 1969; Nakamura, 1964/1985). Aristotle's physics focused almost exclusively on the object. A stone placed in water falls because it has the property of gravity; a piece of wood floats because it has the property of levity. In contrast, Chinese conceptions of action took into account the interaction between the object and the surrounding field. The concept of action at a distance was understood by the Chinese almost 2500 years before it was understood in the West. For example, the Chinese had substantial knowledge of magnetism and acoustics and understood the true reason for the tides (which escaped even Galileo).

Most Greek philosophers and scientists regarded objects as being composed of particles or atoms, whereas the Chinese saw matter as substances in wave form. Because the Greeks had a belief in rules governing categories of objects, they had a sense of control over the world. In contrast, the Chinese did not have an elaborate set of rules to explain the behavior of objects and did not experience the world as being as controllable as did the Greeks.

What might explain these radical differences in thought and perception? In my view it has to do with the nature of Chinese vs. Greek societies. Chinese society was based on agriculture and required substantial cooperation at the family and village level. Substantial interdependence or collectivism was the result. Confucian philosophy both codified and encouraged the following of elaborate rules governing social existence, which was hierarchically arranged. Greek society was based on occupations such as herding, fishing and trade that allowed for more independence or individualism.

Why might these social differences have prompted different views of the world? This could be because the Chinese social system encouraged viewing the world as complex and dependent on relationships whereas the Greek social system allowed for focus on objects (including of course social objects) with respect to which the individual had goals. The Chinese and Greeks were attending to different aspects of the social world and this might have prompted different cognitions and perceptions about it – holistic in the case of the Chinese and analytic in the case of the Greeks. The different under- standings of the social world would have resulted in different understandings of the physical world, because, as Markus and Kitayama put it, if "one perceives oneself as embedded within a larger context of which one is an interdependent part, it is likely that other objects or events will be perceived in a similar way" (Markus & Kitayama, 1991b, p. 246).

If this social-origins account of divergent Chinese vs. Greek thought is correct, then it has implications for cultural differences in the cognition of ordinary people today. East Asians in general remain much more interdepend- ent in their social lives than are Americans and other Westerners (Fiske, Kitayama, Markus, & Nisbett, 1998; Hsu, 1953, 1981; Markus & Kitayama, 1991a, 1991b; Triandis, 1989, 1995). Anthropologist Edward T. Hall (Hall, 1976) used the concept of "low context" vs. "high context" societies to describe differences in social relations. Westerners regard themselves as pos- sessing traits, abilities, and preferences that are unchanging across social contexts. But East Asians view themselves as being so connected to others that who they are depends on the context. As philosopher Donald Munro put it, East Asians understand themselves "in terms of their relation to the whole, such as the family, society, Tao Principle, or Pure Consciousness" (Munro, 1985; Shih, 1919). If an important person is removed from the individual's social network, that individual literally becomes a different person.

These differences in self-perception are captured by self-descriptions. When Americans and Canadians are asked to describe themselves, they mention their personality traits and attitudes more than do Japanese, who are more inclined to mention relationships (Cousins, 1989; Kanagawa, Cross, & Markus, 2001). North Americans tend to overestimate their distinctiveness and to prefer uniqueness in themselves and in their possessions (Markus & Kitayama, 1991b). In one clever study, Koreans and Americans were given a choice among different colored pens to have as a gift. Americans chose the rarest color whereas Koreans chose the most common color (Kim & Markus, 1999).

Socialization for independent vs. interdependent roles begins very early. Western babies often sleep in a different bed from their parents (or even in a different room), but this is rare for Asian babies. Adults from several gener- ations often surround the Chinese baby, and the Japanese baby is almost always with its mother. When American mothers play with their children, they tend to focus their attention on objects and their attributes ("See the truck; it has nice wheels"), whereas Japanese mothers emphasize feelings and relationships ("When you throw your truck, the wall says, 'Ouch'") (Fernald & Morikawa, 1993). Koreans are better able to judge an employer's true feelings about an employee from ratings of the employee than are Americans (Sanchez-Burks, Lee, Choi, Nisbett, Zhao, & Jasook, 2003). And when Masuda and Nisbett (2001) showed participants videos of fish, they found that Japanese were more likely to see emotions in the fish than were Americans.

These social differences, along with their implications for a sense of control, have been pointed out by L.-H. Chiu (Chiu, 1972):

> Chinese are situation-centered. They are obliged to be sensitive to their environment. Americans are individual-centered. They expect their environment to be sensitive to them. Thus, Chinese tend to assume a passive attitude while Americans tend to possess an active and conquering attitude in dealing with their environment.
>
> (p. 236)

> [The American] orientation may inhibit the development of a tendency to perceive objects in the environmental context in terms of relationships or interdependence. On the other hand, the Chinese child learns very early to view the world as based on a network of relationships; he is *socio-oriented*, or *situation-centered*.
>
> (p. 241)

If contemporary Asian and Western societies are different in their emphasis on relationships vs. independent action, then it might be the case that Asians and Westerners differ in their cognitive and perceptual habits along the lines of the holistic vs. analytic stance characteristic of ancient Chinese vs. ancient Greek science and philosophy. (By Asia I mean those East Asian countries in the Confucian tradition originating in China including China, Japan and Korea. By the West I mean Europe and many of the present and former members of the British Commonwealth including the USA, Canada, Australia and New Zealand.) For the past several years, my colleagues and I have been examining the possibility of cultural differences in a number of cognitive and perceptual domains.

Cognitive differences

We find that East Asians and Westerners differ in the way they make causal attributions and predictions, in categorization based on rules vs. family resemblance and in categorization based on shared taxonomic labels vs. relationships.

Causal attribution

We might expect that Westerners, like ancient Greek scientists, would be inclined to explain events by reference to properties of the object and that East Asians would be inclined to explain the same events with reference to interactions between the object and the field. There is much evidence indicating that this is the case (for reviews see Choi, Nisbett, & Norenzayan, 1999; Norenzayan, Choi, & Nisbett, 1999; Norenzayan & Nisbett, 2000). Morris and Peng (1994) and Lee, Hallahan, and Herzog (1996) have shown that Americans are inclined to explain murders and sports events respectively by invoking presumed traits, abilities, or other characteristics of the individual, whereas Chinese and Hong Kong citizens are more likely to explain the same events with reference to contextual factors, including historical ones. Cha and Nam (1985) and Choi and Nisbett (1998) found that East Asians used more contextual information than did Americans in making causal attributions. The same is true for predictions.

Explanations are different even for events involving animals and inanimate objects. Morris and Peng (1994) showed participants cartoon displays of an individual fish moving in relation to a group of fish in various ways. Chinese participants were more likely to see the behavior of the individual fish as being produced by external factors, namely the other fish, than were Americans, whereas American participants were more inclined to see the behavior as being produced by factors internal to the individual fish. Peng and Knowles (2003) showed that for ambiguous physical events involving phenomena that appeared to be hydrodynamic, aerodynamic, or magnetic, Chinese were more likely to refer to the field when giving explanations (e.g., "the ball is more buoyant than the water") than Americans were. The differences in causal attribution therefore probably reflect deep metaphysical differences that transcend specific rules about particular domains that are taught by the culture. In many of the causal attribution studies, incidentally, it could be shown that the East Asian tendency to prefer context was more likely to result in a correct analysis than was the American preference for the object.

Categorization

East Asians have been found to classify objects and events on the basis of relationships and family resemblance whereas Americans classify on the basis of rule-based category membership. Liang-Hwang Chiu (1972) showed triplets of objects like those in Figure 14.1 to Chinese and American children and asked them to indicate which of the two objects went together. American children put the chicken and the cow together and justified this by pointing out that "both are animals." Chinese children put the cow and the grass together and justified this by saying that "the cow eats the grass." Our research group has found the same sort of differential tendency in college students given word triplets to read (Ji, Zhang, & Nisbett, 2004). For

Figure 14.1 "Which two go together?" Item from Chiu (1972) test.

example, Chinese and American participants were asked to indicate which two of the following three go together: notebook, magazine, pen. Americans tended to put the notebook and the magazine together because both have pages. Chinese tended to put the pen and the notebook together because the pen writes on the notebook. Norenzayan and his colleagues asked participants to report whether a target object like that at the bottom of Figure 14.2 was more similar to the group of objects on the left or the group on the right (Norenzayan, Smith, Kim, & Nisbett, 2002).The target object bears a strong family resemblance to the group of objects on the left, but there is a rule that allows placing the object in the group on the right, namely, "has a straight stem." Figure 14.3 shows that East Asians were inclined to think that the object was more similar to the group with which it shared a family resemblance, whereas European Americans were more likely to regard the object as similar to the group to which it could be assigned by application of the rule. Asian Americans, though closer to East Asians, showed no overall preference. (In several of our studies we have included Asian Americans. They were always intermediate in their responses and most typically closer to the European Americans than to the East Asians.)

Attention and perception differences

Differences between East Asians and Westerners extend beyond cognition to encompass many tasks that are attentional and perceptual in nature. Asians

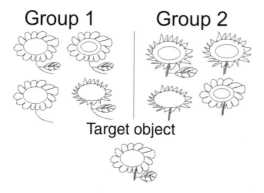

Figure 14.2 "Which group does the target object belong to?" Target bears a strong family resemblance to group on the left but can be assigned to group on the right on the basis of a rule.

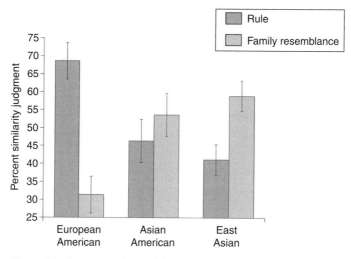

Figure 14.3 Percent of participants basing similarity judgments on family resemblance vs. rule.

appear to attend more to the field and Westerners to attend more to salient objects.

Detection of covariation

If East Asians pay more attention to the field, we would expect them to be better at detecting relationships between events. Ji, Peng, and Nisbett (2000) presented arbitrary objects like those in Figure 14.4 to Chinese and American participants. One of the objects on the left appeared on the left side of a split computer screen followed rapidly by one of the objects on the right appearing

Figure 14.4 Sample of arbitrary objects shown in covariation detection task.

on the right side of the screen. The participants' task was to judge the strength of relationship between one object appearing on the left and a corresponding object appearing on the right. The actual strength ranged from zero – that is, the probability of a particular object on the right appearing was independent of which object appeared on the left – to a relationship equal in strength to a correlation of. 60. The Chinese participants saw more covariation than did American participants; they were more confident about their judgments; and their confidence was better correlated with the actual degree of covariation. At any rate, all of this was true in the setup just described. When some control over the setup was given to participants by giving them a choice as to which object to present on the left and how long an interval to have before presentation of the object on the right, American performance was entirely similar to Chinese performance.

Field dependence: Difficulty in separating an object from its surroundings

If East Asians are inclined to focus their attention simultaneously on the object and the field, then we might expect them to find it more difficult to make a separation between an object and the field in which it appears. Such a tendency is called "field dependence" (Witkin, Lewis, Hertzman, Machover, Meissner, & Karp, 1954). One of the ways of examining it is the Rod and Frame test shown in Figure 14.5. The participant looks down a long box at the end of which is a rod whose orientation can be changed, and a frame around the rod that can be moved independently of the rod. The participant's task is to judge when the rod is vertical. Participants are deemed "field dependent" to the extent that their judgments of verticality of the rod are influenced by the orientation of the frame. Ji et al. (2000) found that Chinese participants were more influenced by the position of the frame than were American participants. And, although Chinese and Americans were equally confident of their judgments in the setup just described, when participants were given control in the form of being able to position the rod as they wished, the Americans became more confident than the Chinese (and the actual performance of American males improved).

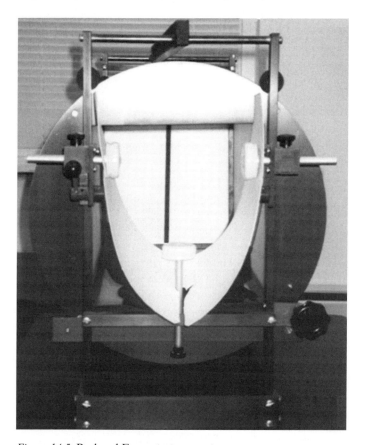

Figure 14.5 Rod and Frame test apparatus.

Attention to the field

Masuda and Nisbett (2001) presented 20-second animated vignettes of underwater scenes to Japanese and American participants. A still photo from one of the videos is presented in Figure 14.6. After seeing each video twice, participants were asked to report what they had seen. The first sentence was coded as to whether a participant initially mentioned one of the salient objects (with "salience" defined as being larger, faster moving and more brightly colored than the other objects) or the field (e.g., color of the water, floor of the scene, inert objects). American participants started their statements by mentioning salient objects far more frequently than Japanese participants did. In contrast, Japanese participants began by mentioning information about the field almost twice as often as Americans did. Overall, Japanese actually made 65% more observations about the field than did Americans. And Japanese participants mentioned almost twice as many relations between objects and the field as did American participants.

After participants had seen 10 vignettes, they were presented with still photos of 45 objects that they had seen before and 45 that they had not seen. The 45 previously seen objects were shown either against the original background, no background or a novel background, as seen in Figure 14.7. The prediction was that, since they attend to objects in relation to the field, Japanese participants would be more thrown off by presentation of the object against the novel field than would Americans. And this was in fact the case. Whereas American performance was literally unaffected by the background manipulation, the Japanese made substantially more errors when the object

Figure 14.6 Still photo from animated underwater vignette.

| Fish with original background | Fish with no background | Fish with novel background |

Figure 14.7 Focal fish previously seen viewed against previously seen background (left), no background (middle) or novel background (right).

was seen against a novel background than when it was seen against the original background.

Change blindness

Perceptual psychologists have recently been studying a phenomenon called "change blindness" (Simons & Levin, 1997). When a picture of a scene and a somewhat altered version of it are presented sequentially, with just a brief pause in between, people can find it very difficult to detect changes that are completely obvious when the two versions are shown side by side. This seems to be produced by an automatic tendency of the nervous system to render two highly similar scenes into a single consistent picture, something that the visual system is constantly doing in order to maintain a coherent view of the world. If it is the case that East Asians attend to the field more than do Westerners, then changes in the field, including relationships between objects, should be easier for them to detect. If Westerners focus more on objects and their attributes, then it should be changes in salient objects that would be easier for them to detect. Masuda and Nisbett (2005) presented Japanese and American participants with scenes like those in Figures 14.8 and 14.9, which are stills from 20-second animated vignettes. The scene in Figure 14.8 is intended to mimic the object-salience of a Western city and that in Figure 14.9 to mimic the field salience, complexity and interpenetration characteristic of East Asian cities. Other vignettes included an object-salient American farm scene and a field-salient Japanese farm scene. Finally, two scenes were intended to be neutral with respect to culture – a construction scene and an airport scene.

Sensitivity to change was measured by asking participants, after they had seen two versions of the same scene, which had changes in both salient foreground objects as well as in relationships between objects and less-salient background objects, to tell us which aspects of the scene had changed from

Figure 14.8 Still photo from animated "American" city vignette in change blindness study.

the first version of the vignette to the second. An example of an object change in Figure 14.8 is a change in the front car's hubcaps. An example of a relationship change in Figure 14.8 is relocation of the buildings in the background. An example of a background object change is a change in the type of houses in the background. Figure 14.10 shows the differences in changes perceived by Americans and Japanese. It can be seen that American participants were more likely to detect changes in salient objects than were Japanese participants, whereas Japanese participants were more likely to detect relationship and environment (context) changes than were Americans.

"Affordances" in the environment

As it happens, the different environments themselves had an effect on the perception of both Americans and Japanese. As may be seen in Figure 14.11, when the scenes were intended to resemble American environments, both Americans and Japanese found it easier to detect object changes than field changes. When the scenes were intended to resemble Japanese environments, both Americans and Japanese found it easier to detect field changes than object changes. These findings indicate that environmental factors, known as the "affordances" to perception, may contribute to people's habit-

Figure 14.9 Still photo from animated "Japanese" city vignette in change blindness study.

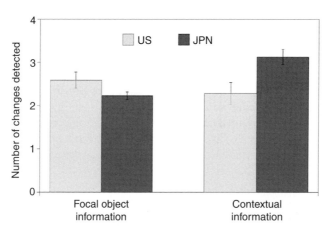

Figure 14.10 Focal object and contextual changes detected by Americans (US) and Japanese (JPN).

ual patterns of attention and perception. When the environment affords mostly salient, distinctive objects, it may be that people attend to them more closely than to the field. When objects are more numerous, more complex and more interpenetrating, the distinction between object and field may

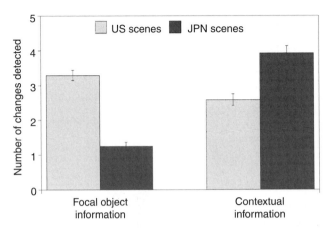

Figure 14.11 Focal object and contextual changes detected in "American" (US) and "Japanese" (JPN) environments.

become blurred and relationships and background elements may become relatively salient.

Of course, these generalizations would be valid only if the scenes that we composed actually captured real differences in Eastern and Western environments. In order to examine this question, Yuri Miyamoto and Nisbett (2005) took photographs in front of, to each side of, and behind three kinds of buildings – post offices, schools, and hotels – in towns of three different sizes in Japan and America. Total populations were defined for each type of building in pairs of towns that were comparable in many respects across the two nations – New York and Tokyo, the towns of Ann Arbor, MI, and its "sister city" Hikone, Japan, and the villages of Chelsea, MI, and Torahime, Japan. Buildings were selected at random from the populations of each type. American and East Asian college students were questioned about the photographs and both groups reported finding Japanese scenes to have more objects and more ambiguous boundaries for objects. Each picture was schematized and assessed for number of objects using the NIH Image Program for Macintosh. An example of a schematized picture is shown in Figure 14.12. The number of objects in each picture was assessed based on the number of edges. The more the edges, the more the objects. The average number of objects defined in this way was 32% greater for Japanese scenes than for American scenes. The differences between Japanese and American scenes were marked at each city size but were especially great for the smaller towns.

In order to show that the affordance differences of the environment were the reason for the differences in perception of object vs. field found by Masuda and Nisbett (2005), Miyamoto and Nisbett presented Japanese and American participants with pictures taken either in Japan or in the USA and then asked them to report on the changes that they saw in the neutral, con-

Figure 14.12 Schematized rendering of a Japanese street scene for the purpose of
assessing number of objects.

struction site and airport vignettes drawn from the Masuda and Nisbett
(2005) study. They found, as expected, that participants who were primed
with Japanese scenes were relatively more likely to be able to report changes
in the field and participants who were primed with American scenes were
more likely to be able to report changes in salient objects. This was true both
for Japanese and American participants.

Perception of everyday-life events

The experiments reported to this point all used materials that, to one degree
or another, depart from everyday-life objects and events. In a final study to be
reported, Chua and Nisbett (2005) studied more naturalistic materials. They
asked American and Taiwanese college students to describe some personal
events (e.g., their first day of the current term), to read some narratives (e.g.,
about a day in the life of a woman in which everything seemed to prevent her
from getting to work) and then summarize what they had read, and to watch
videos of silent comedies and summarize them. Taiwanese were randomly
selected to write either in Mandarin or in English. The anticipations were that
the Americans would make more mentions of the central character than
would the Taiwanese and would make more "intentional" statements, that is

statements that indicated that the central character had control over a situation or had a desire to achieve control. Taiwanese were expected to make more comments about the emotional states of various characters. The differences between Americans and Taiwanese were the same regardless of whether personal stories, summarized narratives or descriptions of the videos were examined. Thus we added all three of these together for purposes of analysis. It may be seen in Figures 14.13 to 14.15 that all of the predictions were borne out and that the results were the same whether the Taiwanese answered in Mandarin or in English. This latter finding is consistent with the results of several other studies showing that language used, and facility of Asians in English when the testing language is English, are not generally predictive of results (Norenzayan et al., 2002).

Discussion

We have seen that there are substantial differences in the cognitive processes of East Asians and Westerners. These include categorization, causal attribution, and reliance on rules. In our view these cognitive differences derive in good part from perceptual differences – in particular differences in what is attended to. Westerners pay more attention to focal objects and East Asians pay more attention to the field. Attention to the object encourages categorization of it, application of rules to it, and causal attribution in terms of it.

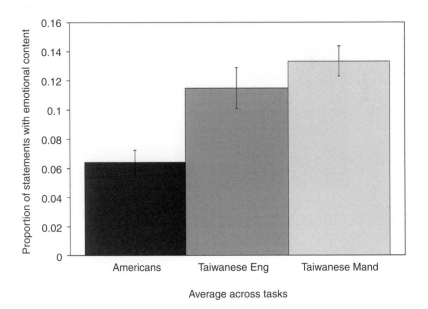

Figure 14.13 Number of statements referring to central figures minus number of statements referring to others by Americans and Taiwanese tested either in English or in Mandarin.

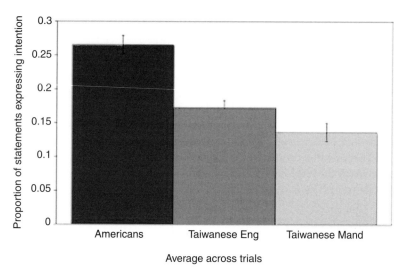

Figure 14.14 Proportion of statements with intentional content by Americans and Taiwanese tested either in English or in Mandarin.

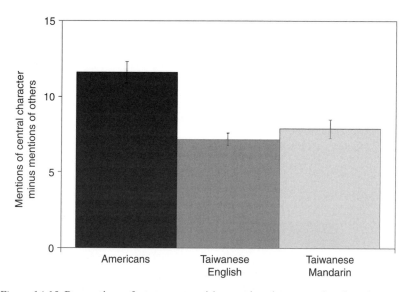

Figure 14.15 Proportion of statements with emotional content by Americans and Taiwanese tested either in English or in Mandarin.

Attention to the field encourages noticing relationships and similarities, and prompts causal attribution to take into account context and distal forces. In addition, attention to the field could be expected to make it difficult to segregate a particular object from a field in which it is embedded.

I believe that the differences in attention, perception and cognition are driven by differences in social structure and social practices that prompt Asians to look to the environment and allow Westerners the luxury of attending to some focal object and their goals with respect to it. Sometimes, though not always, these differences may be caused or enhanced by economic factors. I endorse the speculation by others that East Asians emphasize role relations and social harmony as much as they do, in part, because, since ancient times and until quite recently, they have been primarily farmers, and farmers need to get along with one another (Nakamura, 1964/1985; Needham, 1954). In addition, irrigated agriculture, characteristic of much of East Asia since ancient times, requires effective hierarchies, adding more vertical constraints to the vertical and horizontal constraints within the family and village. Such an emphasis on social concerns might possibly have sustained itself, in part out of sheer inertia, for an indefinite period of time up to the present.

The economy of ancient Greece was quite different from that of East Asia. Greece, consisting substantially of mountains descending to the sea, did not lend itself to large-scale agriculture. Common occupations such as hunting, fishing, trading, and keeping kitchen gardens did not require extensive social collaboration. In the absence of substantial social constraints, attention to a focal object and one's goals in relation to it were luxuries that the Greeks could afford. Many aspects of Western industrial and post-industrial economies in the last 200 years are also characterized by relatively few social constraints, at least for those in middle-class and professional occupations.

Thus, I believe that there is a causal chain running from economy and social structure to social practice to attention to cognition. In support of this view, Knight, Varnum and Nisbett (2005) examined categorization by Eastern Europeans and Western Europeans, asking them to group items on the basis of taxonomic category or relationships. Eastern Europeans are in general more collectivist than Western Europeans (Triandis, 1995), and thus we might expect that Eastern Europeans would categorize more like East Asians than would Western Europeans, and this is what was found. Similarly, we compared the categorization of Southern Italians and Northern Italians. Southern Italians are more collectivist than Northern Italians (Gramsci, 1957; Putnam, 1993) and thus we would expect them to categorize in a fashion more nearly resembling that of East Asians than do Northern Italians; and this is what was found. Finally, working-class people are more collectivist than middle-class people (Kohn & Schooler, 1969; Triandis, McCusker, & Hui, 1990) and we would therefore expect working-class people to categorize in a fashion more like that of East Asians than would middle-class people. This was tested with the Italian sample and was found for Southern Italians but not for Northern Italians.

It seems likely that the affordances of the built environment in Asia vs. the West underlie some of the habitual attention differences. Just why there should be such affordance differences between East and West is not clear. One plausible explanation of the greater complexity of Eastern environments is that the esthetic preferences match the perceptual focus of each group.

Easterners focus broadly on the field and attend to a large number of elements – and they construct environments with a large number of elements. Westerners focus more narrowly on a smaller number of elements and they seem to prefer environments with a smaller number of elements. The work presented here suggests that these differences operate in such a way as to intensify each other – the environments influence perception and the resulting perceptual preferences prompt people to produce different environments.

Acknowledgments

This material is based upon work supported by the National Science Foundation under Grant Nos. SBR 9729103 and BCS 0132074, grant AG15047 from the National Institute of Aging, the Russell Sage Foundation, and a John Simon Guggenheim Fellowship. An earlier version of this article appeared in the *Proceedings of the National Academy of Sciences of the United States*.

References

Cha, J.-H., & Nam, K. D. (1985). A test of Kelley's cube theory of attribution: A cross-cultural replication of McArthur's study. *Korean Social Science Journal, 12*, 151–180.

Chiu, L.-H. (1972). A cross-cultural comparison of cognitive styles in Chinese and American children. *International Journal of Psychology, 7*, 235–242.

Choi, I., & Nisbett, R. E. (1998). Situational salience and cultural differences in the correspondence bias and in the actor–observer bias. *Personality and Social Psychology Bulletin, 24*, 949–960.

Choi, I., Nisbett, R. E., & Norenzayan, A. (1999). Causal attribution across cultures: Variation and universality. *Psychological Bulletin, 125*, 47–63.

Chua, H., & Nisbett, R. E. (2005). Culture and the perception of everyday life events. *Personality and Social Psychology Bulletin, 31*, 925–934.

Cousins, S. D. (1989). Culture and self-perception in Japan and the United States. *Journal of Personality and Social Psychology, 56*, 124–131.

Cromer, A. (1993). *Uncommon sense: The heretical nature of science*. New York: Oxford University Press.

Fernald, A., & Morikawa, H. (1993). Common themes and cultural variations in Japanese and American mothers' speech to infants. *Child Development, 64*, 637–656.

Fiske, A. P., Kitayama, S., Markus, H. R., & Nisbett, R. E. (1998). The cultural matrix of social psychology. In D. T. Gilbert, S. T. Fiske, & G. Lindzey (Eds.), *Handbook of social psychology* (4th ed., pp. 915–981). Boston, MA: McGraw-Hill.

Fung, Y. (1983). *A history of Chinese philosophy* (D. Bodde, Trans., Vols 1–2). Princeton, NJ: Princeton University Press.

Gramsci, A. (1957). *La questione meridionale*. Rome: Editori Riuniti.

Hall, E. T. (1976). *Beyond culture*. New York: Anchor Books.

Hsu, F. L. K. (1953). *Americans and Chinese: Two ways of life*. New York: Schuman.

Hsu, F. L. K. (1981). *Americans and Chinese: Passage to differences*. Honolulu, HI: University of Hawaii Press.

Ji, L., Peng, K., & Nisbett, R. E. (2000). Culture, control, and perception of relationships in the environment. *Journal of Personality and Social Psychology, 78*, 943–955.

Ji, L., Zhang, Z., & Nisbett, R. E. (2004). Is it culture or is it language? Examination of language effects in cross-cultural research on categorization. *Journal of Personality and Social Psychology, 87*, 57–65.

Kanagawa, C., Cross, S. E., & Markus, H. R. (2001). "Who am I?" The cultural psychology of the concept of self. *Personality and Social Psychology Bulletin, 27*, 90–103.

Kim, H., & Markus, H. R. (1999). Deviance or uniqueness, harmony or conformity?: A cultural analysis. *Journal of Personality and Social Psychology, 77*, 785–800.

Knight, N., Varnum, M. E. W., & Nisbett, R. E. (2005). *Culture and class effects on categorization.* Ann Arbor, MI: University of Michigan.

Kohn, M. L., & Schooler, C. (1969). Class, occupation, and orientation. *American Sociological Review, 34*, 657–678.

Lee, F., Hallahan, M., & Herzog, T. (1996). Explaining real life events: How culture and domain shape attributions. *Personality and Social Psychology Bulletin, 22*, 732–741.

Lloyd, G. E. R. (1990). *Demystifying mentalities.* New York: Cambridge University Press.

Lloyd, G. E. R. (1991). The invention of nature. In G. E. R. Lloyd (Ed.), *Methods and problems in Greek science.* Cambridge, UK: Cambridge University Press.

Markus, H. R., & Kitayama, S. (1991a). Cultural variation in the self-concept. In J. Strauss & G. R. Goethals (Eds.), *The self: Interdisciplinary approaches.* New York: Springer-Verlag.

Markus, H. R., & Kitayama, S. (1991b). Culture and the self: Implications for cognition, emotion, and motivation. *Psychological Review, 98*, 224–253.

Masuda, T., & Nisbett, R. E. (2001). Attending holistically vs. analytically: Comparing the context sensitivity of Japanese and Americans. *Journal of Personality and Social Psychology, 81*, 922–934.

Masuda, T., & Nisbett, R. E. (2005). *Culture and change blindness.* Sapporo, Japan: Hokkaido University.

Miyamoto, Y., & Nisbett, R. E. (2005). *Perceptual affordances in Japan and America.* Ann Arbor, MI: University of Michigan.

Morris, M. W., & Peng, K. (1994). Culture and cause: American and Chinese attributions for social and physical events. *Journal of Personality and Social Psychology, 67*, 949–971.

Munro, D. (1985). Introduction. In D. Munro (Ed.), *Individualism and holism: Studies in Confucian and Taoist Values* (pp. 1–34). Ann Arbor, MI: Center for Chinese Studies, University of Michigan.

Munro, D. J. (1969). *The concept of man in early China.* Stanford, CA: Stanford University Press.

Nakamura, H. (1985). *Ways of thinking of eastern peoples.* Honolulu, HI: University of Hawaii Press. (Originally published 1964)

Needham, J. (1954). *Science and civilisation in China* (Vol. 1). Cambridge, UK: University Press.

Nisbett, R. E. (2003). *The geography of thought: How Asians and Westerners think differently . . . and why.* New York: The Free Press.

Nisbett, R. E., Peng, K., Choi, I., & Norenzayan, A. (2001). Culture and systems of thought: Holistic vs. analytic cognition. *Psychological Review, 108*, 291–310.

Norenzayan, A., Choi, I., & Nisbett, R. E. (1999). Eastern and western perceptions of causality for social behavior: Lay theories about personalities and social situations. In D. Prentice & D. Miller (Eds.), *Cultural divides: Understanding and overcoming group conflict* (pp. 239–272). New York: Sage.

Norenzayan, A., & Nisbett, R. E. (2000). Culture and causal cognition. *Current Directions in Psychological Science, 9,* 132–135.

Norenzayan, A., Smith, E. E., Kim, B. J., & Nisbett, R. E. (2002). Cultural preferences for formal versus intuitive reasoning. *Cognitive Science, 26,* 653–684.

Peng, K., & Knowles, E. (2003). Culture, ethnicity and the attribution of physical causality. *Personality and Social Psychology Bulletin, 29,* 1272–1284.

Putnam, R. D. (1993). *Making democracy work: Civic traditions in modern Italy.* Princeton, NJ: Princeton University Press.

Sanchez-Burks, J., Lee, F., Choi, I., Nisbett, R. E., Zhao, S., & Jasook, K. (2003). Conversing across cultural ideologies: East–West communication styles in work and non-work contexts. *Journal of Personality and Social Psychology, 85,* 363–372.

Shih, H. (1919). *Chung-kuo che-hsueh shi ta-kang* [*An outline of the history of Chinese philosophy*]. Shanghai, China: Commercial Press.

Simons, D. J., & Levin, D. T. (1997). Change blindness. *Trends in Cognitive Sciences, 1,* 261–267.

Triandis, H. C. (1989). The self and social behavior in differing cultural contexts. *Psychological Review, 96,* 269–289.

Triandis, H. C. (1995). *Individualism and collectivism.* Boulder, CO: Westview Press.

Triandis, H. C., McCusker, C., & Hui, C. H. (1990). Multimethod probes of individualism and collectivism: Cross-cultural perspectives on self-in group relationships. *Journal of Personality and Social Psychology, 59,* 1006–1020.

Witkin, H. A., Lewis, H. B., Hertzman, M., Machover, K., Meissner, P. B., & Karp, S. A. (1954). *Personality through perception.* New York: Harper.

15 Cross-cultural psychology: An ecocultural approach

John B. Berry

Behavior and culture

Cross-cultural psychology attempts to understand similarities and differences in human behavior in their cultural contexts (Berry, Poortinga, Segall, & Dasen, 2002). As such, it takes culture seriously as a factor in the development and display of individual behavior.

As a discipline, psychology tends to be both "culture-bound" and "culture-blind." By and large, it has ignored the most all-encompassing habitat of human life (a person's culture), and how this relates to behavior. Psychology has also remained mostly an activity of one culture area (the Euro American), both in terms of its theoretical orientations and its empirical data; its findings have thus been bound to one small part of the world. One way of viewing the field of cross-cultural psychology is to see it as a way to reduce these two problems.

When we recognize these problems, and decide to break out of this limited frame of reference, we need to arm ourselves with concepts and methods that will enable us to achieve our goals. Three goals have been identified by Berry and Dasen (1974): (1) to transport and test our current psychological knowledge and perspectives by using them in other cultures; (2) to explore and discover new aspects of the phenomena being studied in the local indigenous terms of other cultures; and (3) to integrate what has been learned from these first two approaches in order to gain a more complete knowledge and universal understanding, one that has pan-human validity. The existence of universals in other disciplines (e.g., biology, linguistics, sociology, anthropology) provides some basis for the assumption that we should be able to work our way through to this third goal of achieving a universal psychology with some success.

From cultural anthropology, we have gained valuable insights into the various meanings of the concept of "culture." Earlier conceptions saw culture as a shared way of life of a group of socially interacting people, with culture being transmitted from generation to generation by the processes of enculturation and socialization. That is, culture was viewed as a "given," that preceded in time the life of any individual member (see Munroe & Munroe, 1997).

This longstanding view of culture continues to have a major influence on thinking in cross-cultural psychology. The main task is to understand how an established cultural context influences the psychological development of individuals, and guides their day-to-day behaviors. In recent years, along with the emergence of more cognitive approaches in many branches of psychology, individuals have come to be viewed, not as mere pawns or victims of their cultures, but as cognizers, appraisers and interpreters of them. Thus, individuals are now widely considered to experience different aspects of their culture, and in different ways.

In sharp contrast to this established perspective on the nature of culture is one advanced by those adopting a "social constructivist" perspective (Gergen & Gergen, 2000; Miller, 1997). From this perspective, culture is not something that is given, but that is being interpreted and created daily through interactions between individuals and their social surroundings. This view is one espoused by those identifying with "cultural psychology," which has been defined as "a designation for the comparative study of the way culture and psyche make up each other" (Shweder & Sullivan, 1993, p. 498).

This emphasis on the individual as an active agent who creates and interprets culture may be recent, but the notion of interactive relationships has been part of cross-cultural psychology for a long time. There are numerous examples of interactions between context and person (e.g., the use of technology to alter the ecosystem, for better or for worse), and of reactions to, even rejection of, external cultural influence (as one form of adaptation associated with acculturation; e.g., Berry, 1976). The reciprocal relationship between person and culture, leading to modification and creation of new cultural forms, has been of longstanding interest in the field (Segall, Dasen, Berry, & Poortinga, 1999).

Theoretical perspectives

Three broad theoretical perspectives on behavior–culture interaction have been discerned: *absolutism*, *relativism*, and *universalism* (Berry et al., 2002). The absolutist position is one that assumes that human behavior is basically the same (qualitatively) in all cultures: "honesty" is "honesty," and "depression" is "depression," no matter where one observes it. From the absolutist perspective, culture is thought to play a limited or even no role in either the meaning or display of human characteristics. Assessments of such characteristics are made using standard instruments (perhaps with linguistic translation) and interpretations of differences are straightforward, without alternative culturally based views taken into account. As a general orientation, absolutism amounts to an imposition of a uniform (Euro American) mold on all of humanity. Following the well-known distinction between etic (culture-general) and emic (culture-specific) approaches, this orientation can be said to resemble an *imposed etic* approach (Berry, 1969).

In sharp contrast, the relativist approach assumes that human behavior is culturally defined. This approach seeks to avoid cultural imposition (and ethnocentrism) by trying to understand people "in their own terms." Explanations of human diversity are sought in the cultural context in which people have developed. Assessments are typically carried out employing the values and meanings that a cultural group gives to a phenomenon. Comparisons are judged to be problematic and ethnocentric, and are thus often avoided. Thus, this orientation resembles an *emic* approach.

A third perspective, one that combines some aspects of the first two positions, is that of universalism. Here it is assumed that basic human psychological processes are common to all members of the species (i.e., constituting a set of psychological givens), and that culture influences the development and display of them (i.e., culture plays different variations on these underlying themes). This universalist perspective has become rather widely accepted in many fields of psychology, such as leadership (Bass, 1998). From this perspective, assessments are based on the presumed underlying process, but measures are developed in culturally meaningful versions. Comparisons are made cautiously, employing a wide variety of methodological principles and safeguards, while interpretations of similarities and differences are attempted that take alternative culturally based meanings into account. This orientation can be said to resemble a *derived etic* approach (Berry, 1969).

While few today advocate a strictly absolutist (or imposed etic) view, the relativist/emic position has given rise to numerous approaches, often referred to as "indigenous psychology" (see Kim & Berry, 1993), and to some extent "cultural psychology" (Shweder & Sullivan, 1993). And the derived etic view has given rise to a "universalist psychology" (Berry et al., 2002). A mutual compatibility between the emic and derived etic positions has been noted by many: for example, Berry et al. (2002, p. 384), Berry and Kim (1993) and Enriquez (1990) have claimed that indigenous psychologies, while valuable in their own right, serve an equally important function as useful steps on the way to achieving a universal psychology; they provide the diverse chips or building blocks that are necessary to complete the mosaic.

The "culture-comparative" approach is rooted in the universalist perspective, and employs the "derived etic" method. It argues that cultural contexts are important factors in human behavioral development, and need to be thoroughly examined. However, remaining within a single culture will not allow us to discover what may be human, in its broadest meaning. Thus, the culture-comparative approach is both "cultural" and "cross," generating the term "cross-cultural" that is often employed to refer to this way of thinking about culture–behavior relationships.

The ecocultural framework

Over the years, an attempt has been made to incorporate many of the foregoing ideas and issues into a working framework for cross-cultural psychological research (Berry, 1966, 1976; Berry et al., 1986; Mishra, Sinha &

Berry, 1996). This *ecocultural framework* is a kind of map that lays out the categories of variables that need to be examined in studies seeking to understand human behavioral diversity, both in context and comparatively.

This ecocultural perspective has evolved through a series of research studies devoted to understanding similarities and differences in perception, cognition and social behavior (Berry, 1976; Berry et al., 1986; Mishra, Sinha, & Berry, 1996; Berry, Denny, & Bennett, 2000) to a broad approach to understanding human diversity. The core ideas have a long history (Jahoda, 1995), and have become assembled into conceptual frameworks (Berry, 1975, 1995) used in empirical research, and in coordinating textbooks in cross-cultural psychology (Berry et al., 2002; Segall et al., 1999). Similar ideas and frameworks have been advanced both by anthropologists (e.g., Feldman, 1975; Whiting, 1974) and psychologists (e.g., Bronfenbrenner, 1979), who share the view that human activity can only be understood within the context in which it develops and takes place.

The ecocultural perspective is rooted in two basic assumptions. The first (the "universalist" assumption) is that all human societies exhibit commonalities, both cultural ("cultural universals") and psychological. This latter perspective holds that basic psychological *processes* are shared, species-common characteristics of all human beings on which culture plays variations during the course of development and daily activity. The second (the "adaptation" assumption) is that *behavior* is differentially developed and expressed in response to ecological, sociopolitical and cultural contexts. This view allows for comparisons across cultures (on the basis of the common underlying process), and makes comparison worthwhile (using the surface variation as basic evidence). In the social sciences, like cultural anthropology (e.g., Murdock, 1975) or sociology (e.g., Aberle, Cohen, Davis, & Sutton, 1950), there is substantial evidence that groups everywhere possess shared cultural attributes. For example, all peoples have language, tools, social structures (e.g., norms, roles) and social institutions (e.g., marriage, justice). It is also evident that such commonalities are expressed by groups in different ways from one time and place to another. Similarly, there is parallel evidence, at the psychological level, for both underlying similarity and surface variation (Berry et al., 1997). For example, all individuals have the competence to develop, learn and perform speech, technology, role playing and norm observance. At the same time, there are obviously group and individual differences in the extent and style of expression of these shared underlying processes. As we have noted, this combination of underlying similarity with surface expressive variation has been given the name "universal" by Berry et al. (2002) to distinguish it both from "absolutism," which tends to ignore cultural influence on behavioral development and expression, and from "relativism," which tends to ignore the existence of common underlying psychological processes. Of course, while variations in behavioral expression can be directly observed, underlying commonalities are a theoretical construction and cannot be observed directly (Troadec, 2001). Paradoxically, this search for our common humanity can only be pursued by observing our diversity. And this dual task is the essence of cross-cultural psychology (Berry, 1969, 2000).

Following is an outline of our current ecocultural thinking about how people adapt culturally (as a group) to their longstanding ecological and sociopolitical settings. It continues with a selective review of studies that show how people develop and perform (as individuals) in adaptation to their ecocultural situation.

Ecological and cultural adaptation

One continuing theme in cultural anthropology is that cultural variations may be understood as adaptations to differing ecological settings or contexts (Boyd & Richerson, 1983). This line of thinking usually known as "cultural ecology" (Vayda & Rappoport, 1968), "ecological anthropology" (Moran, 1982; Vayda & McKay, 1975), or the "ecosystem approach" to anthropology (Moran, 1990) has a long history in the discipline (see Feldman, 1975). Its roots go back to Forde's (1934) classic analysis of relationships between physical habitat and societal features in Africa, and Kroeber's (1939) early demonstration that cultural areas and natural areas co-vary in Aboriginal North America. Unlike earlier simplistic assertions by the school of "environmental determinism," the ecological school of thought has ranged from "possibilism" (where the environment provides opportunities, and sets some constraints or limits on the range of possible cultural forms that may emerge) to an emphasis on "resource utilization" (where active and interactive relationships between human populations and their habitat are analyzed).

Of particular interest to psychologists was Steward's (1955) use of what was later called the "cognized environment"; this concept refers to the features of the environment that are perceived as being of greatest relevance to a population's subsistence. With this notion, ecological thinking moved simultaneously away from any links to earlier deterministic views, and towards the more psychological idea of individuals actively perceiving, appraising, and changing their environments.

The earlier ecological approaches have tended to view cultures as relatively stable (even permanent) adaptations (as a state), largely ignoring adaptation (as a process), or adaptability (as a system characteristic) of cultural populations (Bennett, 1976). However, it is clear that cultures evolve over time, sometimes in response to changing ecological circumstances, and sometimes due to contact with other cultures. This fact has required the addition of a more dynamic conception of ecological adaptation as a continuous, as well as an interactive process (between ecological, cultural, and psychological variables). It is from this most recent position that I have developed my ecocultural framework. This is a view that is consistent with more recent general changes in anthropology, away from a "museum" orientation to culture (collecting and organizing static artifacts) to one that emphasizes cultures as constantly changing, and being concerned with creation, metamorphosis, and recreation.

As is well known, over the years ecological thinking has influenced not only anthropology, but also psychology. The fields of ecological and environmental psychology have become fully elaborated (see Werner, Brown & Altman, 1997), with substantial theoretical and empirical foundations. In essence, individual human behavior has come to be seen in its natural setting or habitat, both in terms of its development, and its contemporary display. The parallel development of cross-cultural psychology (see Berry et al., 1997) has also "naturalized" the study of human behavior and its development. In this field, individual behavior is accounted for to a large extent by considering the role of cultural influences on it. Ecological as well as cultural influences are considered as operating in tandem, hence I have used the term "ecocultural approach" (Berry, 1976).

The current version of the ecocultural framework (see Figure 15.1) proposes to account for human psychological diversity (both individual and group similarities and differences) by taking into account two fundamental sources of influence (ecological and sociopolitical), and two features of human populations that are adapted to them: cultural and biological characteristics. These population variables are transmitted to individuals by various "transmission variables" such as cultural transmission (enculturation, socialization), genetics, and acculturation. Our understanding of both cultural and

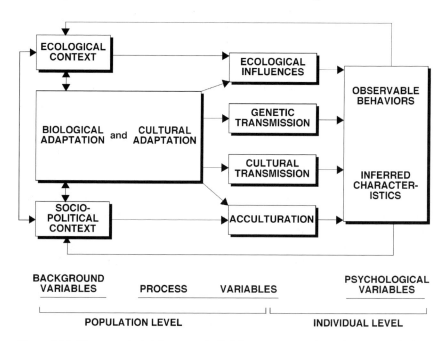

Figure 15.1 The ecocultural framework, linking contexts, adaptation, transmission, and behavior.

genetic transmission has been greatly advanced by recent work on culture learning (e.g., Tomasello, Kruger, & Ratner, 1993) and on the human genome project. The essence of both these domains is the fundamental similarity of all human beings (at a deep level), combined with variation in the expression of these shared attributes (at the surface level). Work on the process and outcomes of acculturation has also been advancing (e.g., Chun, Balls-Organista, & Marin, 2003; Sam & Berry, 2006), necessitated by the dramatic increase in intercultural contact and change.

To summarize, the ecocultural framework considers human diversity (both cultural and psychological) to be a set of collective and individual adaptations to context. Within this general perspective, it views cultures as evolving adaptations to ecological and sociopolitical influences, and views individual psychological characteristics in a population as adaptive to their cultural context. It also views (group) culture and (individual) behavior as distinct phenomena at their own levels that need to be examined independently in order to be able to examine their systematic relationships.

Within psychology the early ecological research, and the findings of the burgeoning field of environmental psychology (Werner et al., 1997), have attempted to specify the links between ecological context and individual human development and behavior. Cross-cultural psychology has tended to view cultures (both one's own, and others that one is in contact with) as differential contexts for development, and view behavior as adaptive to these different contexts.

The ecocultural approach offers a "value neutral" framework for describing and interpreting similarities and differences in human behavior across cultures (Berry, 1994). As adaptive to context, psychological phenomena can be understood "in their own terms" (as the anthropologist Malinowski insisted), and external evaluations can usually be avoided. This is a critical point, since it allows for the conceptualization, assessment and interpretation of culture and behavior in non-ethnocentric ways. It explicitly rejects the idea that some cultures or behaviors are more advanced or more developed than others (Berry, Dasen, & Witkin, 1983; Dasen, Berry, & Witkin, 1979). Any argument about cultural or behavioral differences being evaluated or ordered hierarchically requires the adoption of some absolute (usually external) standard. But who is so bold, or so wise, to assert and verify such a standard?

Finally, the sociopolitical context brings about contact among cultures, so that individuals have to adapt to more than one context. When many cultural contexts are involved (as in situations of culture contact and acculturation), psychological phenomena can be viewed as attempts to deal simultaneously with two (sometimes inconsistent, sometimes conflicting) cultural contexts (Berry, 2003). These attempts at understanding people in their multiple contexts is an important alternative to the more usual pathologizing of colonized or immigrant cultures and peoples. Of course, these intercultural settings need to be approached with the same non-ethnocentric perspective as cross-cultural ones (Berry, 1985).

Selected studies using the ecocultural framework

Initially (Berry, 1966) the link between ecology, culture, and behavior was elaborated into a framework in order to predict differential development of some perceptual and cognitive abilities between hunting-based and agriculture-based peoples. The first step was to propose that the "ecological demands" for survival that were placed on hunting peoples asked for a high level of certain perceptual-cognitive abilities, in contrast with people employing other (particularly agricultural) subsistence strategies. Second, it was proposed that "cultural aids" (such as socialization practices, linguistic differentiation of spatial information, and the use of arts and crafts) would promote the development of these abilities. As predicted, empirical studies of Inuit (then called Eskimo) in the Canadian Arctic and Temne (in Sierra Leone) revealed marked differences in analytic, disembedding and spatial abilities. Further studies were carried out, and during the course of this empirical work, the ideas became further elaborated into the ecocultural framework presented in Figure 15.1. In each case, a consideration of ecological and cultural features of the group were taken as a basis for predicting differential psychological outcomes in a variety of domains. That is, features of the ecosystem and culture were employed in the research design and hypotheses, and in the culture sampling and behavior sampling. For example (Berry, 1967, 1979), differential degrees of reliance on hunting, and variations in social stratification (ranging from "loose" to "tight"; Pelto, 1968) and in child socialization practices (ranging from emphases on "assertion" to "compliance"; Barry, Child, & Bacon, 1959) were used to predict variations in the development of these abilities considered to be functional in their respective contexts.

Further work on perceptual and cognitive abilities (aligned in part to the theory of psychological differentiation, particularly the cognitive style of field dependence–field independence; Witkin & Berry, 1975) resulted in three volumes (Berry, 1976; Berry et al., 1986; Mishra, Sinha, & Berry, 1996) reporting results of studies in the Arctic, Africa, Australia, New Guinea and India. The ecocultural framework has also been used to understand sources of variation in perceptual-cognitive development (Dasen, 1975; Nsamenang, 1992), in part linked to Piagetian perspectives.

While most use of the ecocultural framework has been in the study of perception and cognition, it equally applies to the exploration of social behavior. For example, studies of social conformity (Berry, 1967, 1979) have shown that greater conformity to a suggested group norm is likely to occur in cultures that are structurally tight (with high norm obligation). The relationship is robust, whether examined at the level of individuals, or by using the group's mean score as the variable related to ecology (see Bond & Smith, 1996, for a review). A further example shows how ecocultural indicators are related to the currently popular concepts of "individualism" and "collectivism." Using a distinction proposed by Lomax and Berkowitz (1972), it is suggested (Berry, 1993) that individualism may be related to "differentiation" in a society (structural complexity), with greater differentiation being predictive of greater personal individualism. However, collectivism is proposed to be related more to "integration" (structural tightness), with greater integration predictive of greater collectivism. It is further suggested that whenever individualism and collectivism are found to be at opposite ends of one psychological dimension, it is because data are usually obtained in societies (such as industrial urban ones) where the two cultural dimensions (differentiation and integration) are strongly distinguished; if data were to be collected over a broader range, in other types of societies (e.g., hunting or agricultural) where the two dimensions coincide, then this apparent opposition or incompatibility between individualism and collectivism may not be observed. If such studies were carried out, we would be able to enjoy the benefits of extending the range of ecocultural variation, and using the comparative method.

Recent work (Georgas & Berry, 1995; Georgas, van de Vijver, & Berry, 2004) has further extended this interest in social aspects of behavior. The first study sought to discover ecological and social indicators that might allow societies to be clustered according to their similarities and differences on six dimensions: ecology, education, economy, mass communications, population, and religion. The second study further examined ecosocial indicators across cultures, and then sought evidence of their relationships with a number of psychological variables (such as values and subjective well-being). Results showed that many of the indicators came together to form a single economic dimension (termed "Affluence"), and this was distinct from "Religion" in the pattern of relationships with the psychological variables. Specifically, across cultures, a high placement on Affluence (along with Protestant Religion) was associated with more emphasis on individualism, utilitarianism, and personal well-being. In contrast, for other religions, together with low Affluence, there was an emphasis on power relationships, loyalty, and hierarchy values.

Process variables

Up to this point in the description of the ecocultural framework, I have concentrated on the background contexts, and some behavioral outcomes. The transmission processes involved in allowing these "ecological demands" or "constraints" to manifest themselves in behavior are now considered. In Figure 15.1, these intermediate process variables identify the numerous ways in which contexts become incorporated into behavioral repertoires. Here, we are particularly concerned with two of these: "cultural transmission" and "acculturation."

As we have seen, various features of a society become established in adaptation to the ecological context; within these societal arrangements, the process of cultural transmission (including both enculturation and socialization) is central. Many of these activities take place in the family, which serves as the core institution for cultural transmission. It is well established that features of family and marriage are closely related to ecocultural features of a society, especially to settlement pattern, role differentiation and social stratification. These relationships were already noted in a public lecture by the anthropologist Tylor in the 1880s. He proposed that nomadic societies (mainly hunting and gathering-based peoples) tended to have nuclear families and monogamous marriages, in contrast to sedentary societies (mainly agricultural peoples), who tended to have extended families and polygamous marriages. Tylor suggested that these family and marriage types allowed for efficient economic functioning in their respective habitats: hunters operate best in small units, with symbiotic relationships between two spouses and their direct offspring; agriculturalists require larger working units, facilitated by multiple spouses and a larger network of kin and offspring.

Since these early observations, many empirical studies have demonstrated their validity, and have expanded the network of relationships. For example *role differentiation* (the number of specialized tasks that are distinguished within the society) and *social stratification* (the hierarchical arrangement among these roles, leading to variations in status) are now important elements of these complex patterns. Nimkoff and Middleton (1960) divided societies into categories of "great" or "little" social stratification, and into four exploitive patterns; they found that most societies classed as "agriculture present" are also classed as "highly stratified," whereas among the societies classed as "hunting or gathering," most were in the "low stratification" category.

The ecology element of the framework proposes that human organisms interact with their physical environments in ways that seek to satisfy their needs. Because of variations in environmental features (e.g., temperature, rainfall, and soil quality), there will emerge variations in economic possibilities that may satisfy these needs. A well-established dimension of varying economic pursuits is that of "exploitive subsistence pattern" (Murdock, 1969), where pre-industrial societies may be classified as gathering, hunting, pastoral, fishing, and varieties of agriculture. Two demographic patterns vary as a function of these economic patterns. For Murdock, "settlement patterns" may be classified as fully nomadic, seminomadic, semisedentary, and fully sedentary; and the size of local populations units may be arranged from small camps or settlements up to large towns. Both settlement pattern and population unit size are empirically related to exploitive pattern (Murdock, 1969), with hunting and gathering societies being predominantly nomadic or seminomadic with small population units, and agricultural and pastoral societies being predominantly sedentary or semisedentary with much larger population units.

To summarize, the evidence for the ecology element of the framework shows that knowledge of physical environmental features allows prediction of the economic opportunities (exploitive pattern and food accumulation), which in turn allows prediction of the demographic distribution (settlement patterns and size of population units). The relationships are all probabilistic or correlational, rather than deterministic. Nevertheless, they are extant and are of sufficient strength to make predictions from ecological factors to the cultural adaptation element of the model.

In Figure 15.1, there are four "transmission" or "process" variables shown; these variables allow us to study how cultural features of the population become incorporated into individual behavior. Using terms advocated by Triandis (2004), cultural features of a population are both "material" (e.g., technology, food, dress) and "subjective" (e.g., language, values, religion), while cultural features transmitted to individual members are largely "subjective." Here, we focus on two of these variables: "cultural transmission" and "acculturation." With respect to *cultural transmission*, a distinction is commonly made between *enculturation* and *socialization*. The first process refers to a general, pervasive "enfolding" of developing individuals, leading to an individual's adoption of the norms and values of their society, and their incorporation into the cultural group. The second is a more specific process involving deliberate teaching, and reinforcement, so that particular characteristics and skills are acquired by developing individuals. Both these forms of cultural transmission have been proposed as adaptive to ecological context. Specifically, Barry, Child, and Bacon (1959) were able to demonstrate a clear relationship between type of ecological (exploitive) pattern and socialization. More specifically, training of children for "responsibility" and "obedience" appeared more in agricultural and pastoral societies, whereas training for "achievement," "self-reliance," and "independence" was more frequent in hunting and gathering societies. Thus, on the basis of their study, we have evidence that an exploitive subsistence pattern is a reasonably good predictor of socialization emphases.

Overall for cultural transmission, there is a broad ecological dimension running from hunting and gathering to agricultural interactions with the environment. Associated with the latter end of the dimension are a sedentary lifestyle, high population density, high sociocultural stratification, polygamy, extended families, and socialization emphases on compliance; associated with the former end of the dimension are a nomadic lifestyle, low population density, low stratification, monogamy, nuclear families, and practices emphasizing assertion. Societies that range along this ecological dimension also vary concomitantly on these other ecological and cultural variables. When this ecological dimension is extended to include contemporary industrial and post-industrial societies, a more complex pattern becomes apparent (Lomax & Berkowitz, 1972; Berry, 1993). With the increasing high density of cities, we observe a reduction in pressures toward compliance as a result of loss of community cohesion, and the increase in anonymity afforded by these large cities. There is also a reduction in the frequency of extended families, and a parallel increase in proportion of nuclear families, which is accompanied by a further reduction in pressures toward compliance. Thus, an increase in stratification, compliance and conformity from hunting through to agrarian societies changes course to become a decrease in these ecocultural features as societies experience a change from agrarian to industrial and post-industrial arrangements.

In addition to the role of the ecological context, the sociopolitical context has introduced the need for a second transmission or process variable, that of "acculturation." This process has played an important role in shaping both cultural, process and behavioral features of the framework. Particularly, the colonization of Asia by Indian and Chinese societies, and of Africa and the Americas by European societies has brought about societal changes that have altered cultural patterns, including family arrangements and emphases in cultural transmission. Colonization also introduced new religions and forms of education (particularly formal schooling) in most of these societies. The much increased availability of telemedia continues to promote change from outside by portraying alternative lifestyles and consumer goods. Their impact has led to a shift in numerous aspects of culture and behavior, as diverse as consumer behavior, diet and disease, parent–child relations and societal and personal values. These acculturative influences are mainly emanating from contemporary Western societies through domination of the "Majority World." However, there is evidence of resistance and retaliation, so that cultural and behavioral homogenization is not the inevitable result of these sociopolitical influences. Human diversity is apparently here to stay; and this is good news for cross-cultural psychology!

Conclusion

Cross-cultural psychology attempts to describe and understand the many varieties of human behavior within the cultural contexts in which it develops and is currently displayed. To assist in this rather grandiose task, the ecocultural framework has been developed as a concrete guide, taking on the dual task of viewing people in their own terms, and doing so comparatively. Research using this framework began with studies of perception and cognition, continued with some social behaviors, and is now being used to consider the origins of the distribution of values and well-being. It has served both as a source of research ideas, and as a tool for pursuing them. It seems to be a sufficiently valuable approach that we may anticipate its continued development and further use.

References

Aberle, D. F., Cohen, A. K., Davis, A., & Sutton, F. X. (1950). Functional prerequisites of society. *Ethics*, *60*, 100–111.

Barry, H., Child, I., & Bacon, M. (1959). Relations of child training to subsistence economy. *American Anthropologist*, *61*, 51–63.

Bass, B. M. (1998). *Transformational leadership*. Mahwah, NJ: Lawrence Erlbaum Associates, Inc.

Bennett, J. (1976). *The ecological transition*. London: Pergamon.

Berry, J. W. (1966). Temne and Eskimo perceptual skills. *International Journal of Psychology*, *1*, 207–229.

Berry, J. W. (1967). Independence and conformity in subsistence-level societies. *Journal of Personality and Social Psychology*, *7*, 415–418.

Berry, J. W. (1969). On cross-cultural comparability. *International Journal of Psychology*, *4*, 119–128.

Berry, J. W. (1975). An ecological approach to cross-cultural psychology. *Nederlands Tijdschrift voor de Psychologie*, *30*, 51–84.

Berry, J. W. (1976). *Human ecology and cognitive style: Comparative studies in cultural and psychological adaptation*. New York: Sage/Halsted.

Berry, J. W. (1979). A cultural ecology of social behavior. In L. Berkowitz (Ed.), *Advances in experimental social psychology* (Vol. 12, pp 177–206). New York: Academic Press.

Berry, J. W. (1985). Cultural psychology and ethnic psychology. In I. Reyes Lagunes & Y. Poortinga (Eds.), *From a different perspective* (pp. 3–15). Lisse, The Netherlands: Swets & Zeitlinger.

Berry, J. W. (1993). Ecology of individualism and collectivism. In U. Kim, H. C. Triandis, C. Kagitcibasi, S.-C. Choi, & G. Yoon (Eds.), *Individualism and collectivism* (pp. 77–84). London: Sage.

Berry, J. W. (1994). An ecological approach to cultural and ethnic psychology. In E. Trickett (Ed.), *Human diversity* (pp 115–141). San Francisco: Jossey-Bass.

Berry, J. W. (1995). The descendants of a model. *Culture & Psychology*, *1*, 373–380.

Berry, J. W. (2000). Cross-cultural psychology: A symbiosis of cultural and comparative approaches. *Asian Journal of Social Psychology*, *3*, 197–205.

Berry, J. W. (2003). Conceptual approaches to acculturation. In K. Chun, P. Balls-Organista, & G. Marin (Eds.), *Acculturation: Advances in theory, measurement and applied research* (pp. 3–21). Washington, DC: APA Books.

Berry, J. W., & Dasen, P. R.(Eds.). (1974). *Culture and cognition*. London: Methuen.

Berry, J. W., Dasen, P. R., & Witkin, H. A. (1983). Developmental theories in cross-cultural perspective. In L. Alder (Ed.), *Cross-cultural research at issue* (pp. 13–21). New York: Academic Press.

Berry, J. W., Denny, J. P., & Bennett, J. A. (2000). *Ecology, culture and cognitive processing*. Unpublished manuscript, Queen's University, Kingston, Canada.

Berry, J. W., & Kim, U. (1993). The way ahead: From indigenous psychologies to a universal psychology. In U. Kim & J. W. Berry (Eds.), *Indigenous psychologies* (pp. 277–280), Newbury Park, CA: Sage

Berry, J. W., Poortinga, Y. H., Pandey, J., Dasen, P. R., Saraswathi, T. S., Segall, M. H. et al. (1997). *Handbook of cross-cultural psychology* (3 vols). Boston: Allyn & Bacon.

Berry, J. W., Poortinga, Y. H., Segall, M. H., & Dasen, P. R. (2002). *Cross-cultural psychology: Research and applications*. (2nd ed.). New York: Cambridge University Press.

Berry, J. W., van de Koppel, J. M. H., Sénéchal, C., Annis, R. C., Bahuchet, S., Cavalli-Sforza, L. L. et al. (1986). *On the edge of the forest: Cultural adaptation and cognitive development in Central Africa*. Lisse, The Netherlands: Swets & Zeitlinger.

Bond, R., & Smith, P. (1996). Culture and conformity: A meta-analysis. *Psychological Bulletin*, *119*, 111–137.

Boyd, R., & Richerson, P. (1983). Why is culture adaptive? *Quarterly Review of Biology*, *58*, 209–214.

Bronfenbrenner, U. (1979). *The ecology of human development.* Cambridge, MA: Harvard University Press.

Chun, K., Balls-Organista, P., & Marin, G. (Eds.). (2003). *Acculturation: Advances in theory, measurement and applied research.* Washington, DC: APA Books.

Dasen, P. R. (1975). Concrete operational development in three cultures. *Journal of Cross-Cultural Psychology, 6,* 156–172.

Dasen, P. R., Berry, J. W., & Witkin, H. A. (1979). The use of developmental theories cross-culturally. In L. Eckensberger, W. Lonner, & Y. Poortinga (Eds.), *Cross-cultural contributions to psychology* (pp. 69–82). Lisse, The Netherlands: Swets & Zeitlinger.

Enriquez, V. (Ed.). (1990). *Indigenous psychologies.* Quezon City, The Philippines: Psychology Research and Training House.

Feldman, D. A. (1975). The history of the relationship between environment and culture in ethnological thought. *Journal of the History of the Behavioral Sciences, 110,* 67–81.

Forde, D. (1934). *Habitat, economy and society.* New York: Dutton.

Georgas, J., & Berry, J. W. (1995). An ecocultural taxonomy for cross-cultural psychology. *Cross-Cultural Research, 29,* 121–157.

Georgas, J., van de Vijver, F., & Berry, J. W. (2004). The ecocultural framework and psychological variables in cross-cultural research. *Journal of Cross-Cultural Psychology, 35,* 74–96.

Gergen, M. M., & Gergen, K. J. (2000). Qualitative inquiry: Tensions and transformations. In N. K. Denzin & Y. Lincoln (Eds.), *Handbook of qualitative research* (2nd ed., pp. 1025–1046). Thousand Oaks, CA: Sage.

Jahoda, G. (1995). The ancestry of a model. *Culture & Psychology, 1,* 11–24.

Kim, U., & Berry, J. W. (Eds.). (1993). *Indigenous psychologies.* Newbury Park, CA: Sage.

Kroeber, A. (1939). *Cultural and natural areas of native North America.* Berkeley, CA: University of California Press.

Lomax, A., & Berkowitz, W. (1972). The evolutionary taxonomy of culture. *Science, 177,* 228–239.

Miller, J. G. (1997). Theoretical issues in cultural psychology. In J. W. Berry, Y. H. Poortinga, & J. Pandey (Eds.), *Handbook of cross-cultural psychology. Vol. 1. Theory and method* (pp. 85–128). Boston: Allyn & Bacon.

Mishra, R. C., Sinha, D., & Berry, J. W. (1996). *Ecology, acculturation and psychological adaptation: A study of Advasi in Bihar.* Delhi, India: Sage Publications.

Moran, E. (1982). *Human adaptability: An introduction to ecological anthropology.* Boulder, CO: Westview Press.

Moran, E. (Ed.). (1990). *The ecosystem approach in anthropology.* Ann Arbor, MI: University of Michigan Press.

Munroe, R. L., & Munroe, R. H. (1997). A comparative anthropological perspective. In J. W. Berry, Y. H. Poortinga, & J. Pandey (Eds.), *Handbook of cross-cultural psychology. Vol. 1. Theory and method* (pp. 171–213). Boston: Allyn & Bacon.

Murdock, G. P. (1969). Correlations of exploitive patterns. In D. Damas (Ed.), *Ecological essays. National Museum of Canada Bulletin No. 230, Anthropological Series No. 86.*

Murdock, G. P. (1975). *Outline of cultural materials.* New Haven, CT: Human Relations Area Files

Nimkoff, J., & Middleton, R. (1960). Types of family and types of economy. *American Journal of Sociology, 66,* 215–225.

Nsamenang, B. (1992). *Human development in cultural context*. Newbury Park, CA: Sage.

Pelto, P. (1968). The difference between "tight" and "loose" societies. *Transaction, 5,* 37–40.

Sam, D. L. & Berry, J. W. (Eds.). (2006). *Cambridge handbook of acculturation psychology*. Cambridge, UK: Cambridge University Press.

Segall, M. H., Dasen, P. R., Berry, J. W. & Poortinga, Y. H. (1999). *Human behavior in global perspective: Introduction to cross-cultural psychology* (2nd ed.) Boston: Allyn & Bacon.

Shweder, R. A., & Sullivan, M. A. (1993). Cultural psychology: Who needs it? *Annual Review of Psychology, 44,* 497–527.

Steward, J. (1955). The concept and method of cultural ecology. *Theory of culture change*. Urbana, IL: University of Illinois Press.

Tomasello, M., Kruger, A., & Ratner, H. (1993). Culture learning. *Behavioral and Brain Sciences, 16,* 495–552.

Triandis, H. C. (2004). Subjective culture. In C. Spielberger (Ed.), *Encyclopedia of applied psychology* (Vol. 3, pp. 507–509). San Diego, CA: Elsevier.

Troadec, B. (2001). Le modèle écoculturel: Un cadre pour la psychologie culturelle comparative. *International Journal of Psychology, 36,* 53–64.

Vayda, A. P., & McKay, B. (1975). New directions in ecology and ecological anthropology. *Annual Review of Anthropology, 4,* 293–306.

Vayda, A. P. & Rappoport, R. (1968). Ecology, cultural and non-cultural. In J. Clifton (Ed.), *Cultural anthropology* (pp. 477–497). Boston, MA: Houghton Mifflin.

Werner, C., Brown, B. & Altman, I. (1997). Environmental psychology. In J. W. Berry, M. H. Segall, & C. Kagitcibasi (Eds.), *Handbook of cross-cultural psychology. Vol. 3: Social behavior and applications* (pp 253–290). Boston, MA: Allyn & Bacon.

Whiting, J. W. M. (1974). A model for psychocultural research. In *Annual report*. Washington, DC: American Anthropological Association.

Witkin, H., & Berry, J. W. (1975). Psychological differentiation in cross-cultural perspective. *Journal of Cross-Cultural Psychology, 6,* 4–87.

16 Some metatheoretical issues in culture, parenting, and developmental science

Marc H. Bornstein

Parent–child relationships are at the heart of the microsystem of interaction in the ecological view of human development. However, a singular focus on dyadic relationships involving parent and child fails to recognize that parent–child relationships are embedded in a mesosystem of broader contexts, like peers, schools, and neighborhoods. In turn, each of these situations shapes and is shaped by a community of exosystem influences, including the extended family, work place, and media, in which they are embedded. In its turn, a macrosystem of values, laws, social class, and *culture* influences exosystem institutions and so indirectly supports and encourages parenting principles and practices as well as child development. Thus, human beings do not grow up, and adults do not parent, in isolation, but in multiple physical and social contexts (Bronfenbrenner & Morris, 1998). Figure 16.1 shows these several nested ecological settings in which parenting and child development take place. Notably, cultural prescriptions and proscriptions help to determine, to a great extent, the goals parents have for their children and parents' cognitions, the practices of parents, and ultimately the experiences that children have. Culture plays an overarching role in organizing and directing the ecology of parenthood and childhood. This chapter is concerned with some metatheoretical issues in culture, parenting, and developmental science.

The childrearing principles and practices of one's own culture seem "natural," of course, but some may actually be rather unusual in an absolute sense. Even family structures take different forms depending on culture; nuclear families represent only one of a variety of social ecologies in which parents and children are found. Children in many cultures are tended by a variety of nonparental care providers, whether in their own homes, daycare centers, or wheat fields. Rogoff, Mistry, Göncü, and Mosier (1991) pointed out that in most places in the world young children are tended by multiple caregivers, and that, while important, the well-studied dyadic case of mother-and-child is not the rule. Furthermore, few nations in the world are characterized by social homogeneity; ethnic differences within countries equally emphatically color childrearing principles and practices. Thus, a cultural perspective enriches our understanding of the nature of parenting

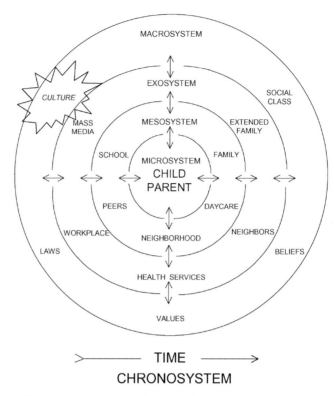

Figure 16.1 The contextual ecological view of development.

and child development: In acknowledging multiple views, we admit to a global – and more comprehensive and accurate – understanding of parenting and child development.

Studies in culture, parenting, and development derive originally from ethnographic accounts and today also encompass the disciplines of cross-cultural and cultural psychology. Some research has sought to understand how parenting and child development work as part of a cultural system, whereas other research has focused on why parenting and child development vary across cultures. As Harkness and Super (2002) pointed out, these two lines of investigation recognize that the care and rearing of children routinely take place within different settings that instantiate cultural themes of importance to parents, and in this way communicate central cultural messages, and so are key to understanding parents' cultural construction of child life and child development.

Culture is frequently used as a means of understanding relations between physical and social environments on the one hand and individual psychological structures on the other. Geertz (1973, p. 44) interpreted culture as a "set of control mechanisms – plans, recipes, rules, instructions . . . – for the governing of behavior." Every psychological construct, structure, function, and process has cultural underpinnings. Thus, cultures (and subcultures) consist of distinctive patterns of affiliation as well as norms, ideas, values, and assumptions about life that are shared by a group of people and that guide and regulate specific behaviors and inculcate valued competencies (Cole, 2005). Variations in physical and social settings, customs and practices, and the psychology of childcare and childrearing constitute the cultural contexts of parenting and child development. All societies prescribe certain characteristics that their members are expected to possess, and proscribe others that they must not do, if they are to function adequately as members of their society. Some of these prescriptions and proscriptions may be universal across cultures, such as the requirement that parents (or surrogates) nurture and protect children. Other standards and values vary greatly from one cultural setting to the next. In all societies, training children occurs to ensure that children are socialized in such a way that each new generation acquires its culturally prescribed and proscribed patterns of beliefs and behaviors.

The cultural perspective on parenting and child development raises some enduring questions: What is the nature and extent of variability in normative parenting? What are the social, historical, or economic causes of cultural differences in parenting and child development? How are cultural beliefs and values related to parenting principles and practices? What are the effects on children of different cultural approaches to parenting, both in the immediate sense and over the longer course of development? In considering these several questions, we must first define the parameters of the intersection of culture and parenting and next set parenting in the context of the several forces that shape it, with culture as an ultimate distal antecedent. Culture is a crucial desideratum in parenting and child development.

Parenting and culture

Biological parents contribute directly to the genetic makeup of their children, but parents (and caregivers of all kinds) also directly shape children's experiences. Although behavior genetics argues that a host of different characteristics of offspring reflect inheritance in some degree (e.g., Plomin, 1999), the strength and expression of genetic inheritance for a particular characteristic clearly depend on the environmental or cultural "niche" in which the child is reared. Thus parents influence children directly through the experiences they provide and environments they choose. All prominent theories of psychology and development put experience in the world as either the principal source of individual growth or as a major contributing component (Wachs, 2000). Evidence of heritability neither negates nor diminishes equally compelling evidence for the direct and indirect effects of parent-provided experiences (Collins, Maccoby, Steinberg, Hetherington, & Bornstein, 2000).

Human children do not and cannot grow up as solitary individuals;

parenting constitutes the initial and all-encompassing ecology of child development. Much empirical research attests to the short- and long-term influences of parent-provided experiences on child development. Parents influence child development both by their beliefs and by their behaviors (Okagaki & Bingham, 2005), and they do so according to different mechanisms and following different models (Bornstein, 2002). Moreover, culture perfuses all of these parental considerations. In the natural course of things, the two sorts of direct effects are confounded: The parents who endow their child genetically also surround their child with a climate of beliefs, engage in actions towards their children, and structure their child's world and experiences.

Parents also influence their children indirectly by virtue of one's influence on the other and their associations with larger social networks. In many societies, children spend much or even most of their time with significant others, including siblings, nonparental relatives, or nonfamilial caregivers, and the various responsibilities of parenting are distributed across the various members of the culture. In some, the mother is the principal caregiver; in others, multiple care giving is more the norm. In the minds of many observers, however, the mother is still unique, the role of mother universal, and motherhood unequivocally principal to children's development. The ultimate responsibility for young children within the context of the nuclear or extended family usually, if not universally, falls to the mother. Cross-cultural surveys attest to the primacy of biological mothers = care giving (e.g., Leiderman, Tulkin, & Rosenfeld, 1977), and on average mothers spend between 65 and 80% more time than fathers do in direct one-to-one interaction with their young children (Parke, Dennis, Flyr, Morris, Leidy, & Schofield, 2005).

Historically Western fathers' social and legal claims and responsibilities on children were pre-eminent (French, 2002), and fathers are neither inept nor uninterested in child caregiving. Indeed, Western industrialized nations have witnessed increases in the amount of time fathers spend with their children. In reality, though, fathers typically assume little responsibility for childcare and rearing, and fathers are primarily helpers (Cabrera, Tamis-LeMonda, Bradley, Hofferth, & Lamb, 2000). Mothers and fathers also tend to interact with and care for children in complementary ways; that is, they divide the labor of care giving (Parke, 2002).

Indirect effects are more subtle and less noticeable than direct effects, but perhaps no less meaningful. One type of indirect effect is marital support and communication (Cowan & Cowan, 1992). Effective co-parenting bodes well for child development (Fincham & Hall, 2005; McHale, Khazan, Rotman, DeCourcey, & McConnell, 2002), and mothers who report supportive relationships with "secondary parents" (husbands or lovers or grandparents) are more competent and sensitively responsive to their children than are women lacking such relationships (Grych, 2002). Both direct and indirect effects vary in their form and function by culture.

Central to a concept of culture is the expectation that different peoples possess different beliefs and behave in different ways with respect to parenting.

Furthermore, it is the special and continuing task of parents (and children's other caregivers) to enculturate children, that is to prepare them for socially accepted physical, economic, and psychological situations that are characteristic of the culture in which they are to survive and thrive (LeVine, 2003). Actively or passively, to a greater or lesser degree, intentionally or unwittingly parents pass their culture on to their offspring and reciprocally children become enculturated. Parenting is a principal reason why individuals in different cultures are who they are and often differ so much from one another.

What are the chief processes of enculturation? As culture is organized information, parenting consists of mechanisms for transmitting that information, and childhood of processing and assimilating that information. Both parent and child "select, edit, and refashion" cultural information. So, minimally, enculturation involves bidirectional processes in which adult and child alike play active roles. Not yet well worked out, however, are functional or theoretical connections between culture and parenting. How do components of culture relate to parenting attitudes and actions and in turn to the developmental differentiation and enculturation of children?

How to care for children, how to rear them, how to apprentice them into the culture are, as Benedict (1938) observed, perennial concerns of parents in every society. Although much of what is known about parenting and child development derives from studies of parents and children from middle-socioeconomic-status (SES) families living in modern industrialized and Western countries, particularly the United States and Western Europe (Tomlinson & Swartz, 2003), more earnest efforts are underway to understand the impact of culture on parenting and child development on a larger worldwide stage. Cross-cultural comparisons show that virtually all aspects of parenting children – whether principles or practices – are shaped by cultural habits. Cultures provide their members with implicit or explicit models or ethnotheories of childrearing. They include: when and how to care for children; what child characteristics are desirable; which parenting practices are accepted or expected; as well as normative orientations toward extended family, employment, and childcare. In Morelli and Tronick's (1991) view, social participation in a culture structures a child's reality and experience in ways that increase the likelihood that the child will acquire an image of the society and develop into a culturally adjusted member of the society.

Adults in different cultures adopt some similar, as well as some different, approaches to parenting. Parenting and child development are each influenced by culture, but each also influences culture. Thus, how parenting is culturally constructed can lead to parents expressing one or another kind of affect, thinking, or behavior in childrearing. How parents construe parenthood or childhood functions in the same way. How parents see their own children has its cultural connotations and specific consequences as well.

Parents' cognitions – their ideas, knowledge, beliefs, values, goals, and attitudes – hold a consistently popular place in the study of parent–child relationships (e.g., Goodnow, 2002; Holden & Buck, 2002; Sigel & McGil-licuddy-De Lisi, 2002). Parental cognitions are conceived to serve many functions; they may generate and shape parental behaviors, mediate the effectiveness of parenting, or help to organize parenting and, in a larger sense, they may contribute to the "continuity of culture" by helping to define culture and the transmission of cultural information across generations. Increasing interest in cultural parental cognitions has helped focus attention on the formation, expression, and developmental consequences of culture within the family system. Research in diverse cultural settings suggests that the relations between sociocultural context and parental cognitions are complex, however (Okagaki & Bingham, 2005). For example, Welles-Nyström (1988) described a high level of parental anxiety about child survival among Swedish mothers even though Sweden has one of the lowest mortality rates in the world.

Significantly, parents in different cultures harbor different cognitions about their own parenting as well as children (e.g., Bornstein et al., 1996; Goodnow, 2002). Differences in cultural ideology also make for subtle, but potentially meaningful, differences in patterns of child–parent interaction (Pomerleau, Malcuit, & Sabatier, 1991). Indeed, cultural differences in some parenting cognitions appear to persist even among parents born and reared in one culture but who later live in another culture with different childrearing norms (Bornstein & Cote, 2004). More salient in the phenomenology of the child are parents' practices, the actual experiences parents provide to children. Cultural messages perfuse daily interactions between parents and children (Dunn & Brown, 1991). Cultures help to "construct" children by influencing parental cognitions about childrearing and about the developmental capacities of children, which in turn influence parents' actions and further children's development.

One perennial theme in cultural approaches to parenting turns on the question of culture-specific versus culture-universal parenting principles and practices. Certain aspects of parenting recur across cultures, even very different ones. *Why*? Parents even in different cultures must show some similarities in interacting with their children. All must nurture and promote the physical growth of children if their children are to survive, for example (Bornstein, 2002; LeVine, 2003). Whether converging patterns of parenting reflect factors indigenous to children and their biology, biological bases of parenting and caregiving, the historical convergence of parenting styles, the fact that economic or ecological determinants are shared, or the increasing prevalence of migration or dissemination via mass media is difficult to determine. In the end, different peoples (presumably) wish to promote similar general competencies in their young. Some do so in some qualitatively and quantitatively similar ways.

That said, some principles and practices of parents are culturally unique and specifically contextualized. Certain culturally consistent biological characteristics of children, such as constitutionally based characteristics of temperament, promote parental activities and/or attitudes that vary systematically across cultures. Adults in different cultures also parent differently because of their own biological characteristics, for example their differential threshold sensitivity or attention to child signals. Finally, ecological or economic conditions specific to a given cultural setting promote parental cognitions and actions indigenous to that culture, ones evolved differentially to optimize adjustment and adaptation of offspring to the circumstances of the local situation. Of course, culture-specific patterns of childrearing can be expected to be adapted to each specific society's settings and needs.

Parents' principles and practices influence child development via different paths. A common assumption in parenting is that the overall level of parental involvement or stimulation affects the child's overall level of development (Maccoby & Martin, 1983). Increasing evidence suggests, however, that more sophisticated processes need to be brought to bear to explain parenting effects adequately. First, the specificity principle states that specific parent-provided experiences at specific times exert specific effects over specific aspects of development in specific children in specific ways (Bornstein, 2002). Obviously, many parent-provided experiences are culturally specific. Second, the transaction principle recognizes that an individual's characteristics shape her or his experiences and, reciprocally, experiences shape characteristics of the individual through time (Sameroff, 1983). By virtue of their unique characteristics and propensities children actively contribute to producing their own development. Children affect which experiences they will be exposed to and how they interpret those experiences, and so determine how those experiences affect them (Scarr & McCartney, 1983). Child and parent bring distinctive characteristics to, and each is believed to change as a result of, every interaction; both then enter the next round of interaction as different individuals. Vygotsky (1978) contended that, as a central feature of this transactional perspective, the more-advanced partner (the parent) raises the level of competence or performance in the less-advanced partner.

In brief, parents influence their children directly via their genes, principles, and practices as well as indirectly via their influences on one another and selection of the multiple contexts in which they live. Mothers typically take responsibility for and caregive more than do fathers, but fathers play complementary and signal roles in caregiving. Parent-provided experiences affect children via different mechanisms of action, but tend to follow principles of specificity and transaction. Parents' effects on child development can be influenced indirectly by social-environmental supports and stressors; development does not take place in a social vacuum. Moreover, relationships, like individuals, change over time. As the dynamics of the culture change, changes in relationships between the two parents, and between each parent and the child, are expectable.

The place of culture among the ecological antecedents of parenthood and childhood

A critical step on the path to fully understanding parenting principles and practices and children's development is to evaluate forces that shape them. The origins of variation in parental beliefs and behaviors and children's growth are multivariate and extremely complex, but certain factors seem to be of paramount importance; they may be arranged into classes of antecedents that accord with a bioecological perspective (Belsky, 1984; Bornstein, 2002; Bronfenbrenner & Morris, 1998). They include: biological processes and personality attributes of parents, actual and perceived characteristics of children, and contextual influences, including notably family structure, socioeconomic status, and culture. Here I focus on culture.

Cross-cultural study shows that virtually all aspects of parenting and child development are ultimately influenced by culture. For example, the timetables for child development in new mothers from Australia versus Lebanon are shaped by culture much more than by experiences observing their own children, directly comparing them to other children, and receiving advice from friends and experts (Goodnow, Cashmore, Cotton, & Knight, 1984). Culture influences who parents children, the extent to which parents permit children freedom, how nurturant or restrictive parents are, which behaviors parents promote, and so forth (Benedict, 1938; Bornstein, 1991; Erikson, 1950; Whiting, 1981). For example, Japan and the USA maintain reasonably similar levels of modernity and living standards and both are child-centered societies, but the two differ dramatically in terms of childrearing goals (e.g., Azuma, 1986; Bornstein, 1989). For example, Japanese mothers expect early mastery of emotional maturity, self-control, and social courtesy in their offspring, whereas American mothers expect early mastery of verbal competence and self-actualization in theirs. American mothers promote autonomy and organize social interactions with their children so as to foster physical and verbal assertiveness and independence, and they promot children's interest in the external environment; by contrast, Japanese mothers organize social interactions with children so as to consolidate and strengthen closeness and dependency within the dyad, and they tend to indulge children.

In a systems view, the development of a construct, structure, function, or process, like parenting or child development, can be expected to be the product of continuing interactions among multiple antecedents, including the environment and experience as well as genetics and biology. Parenting and child development thus stand at the confluence of many complex tributaries of influence; some arise within the individual, whereas others have macro-level determinants. Generally speaking, however, more distal variables, like culture, are thought to influence more proximal variables, like parenting principles and practices, and thereby to affect child development.

Theory and methodology in culture, parenting, and developmental science

The description of parenting or child development measured in a given way at a given time in a given sample has served parenting and developmental science adequately in the past. To understand both more deeply, however, one wants to understand various perspectives on and dimensions of parenting and child development (*multimethod*); one wants to understand how those perspectives and dimensions present and develop across various ages or stages in the life course (*multi-age*); and one wants to understand how those different perspectives and dimensions at different developmental periods manifest themselves in different settings (*multiculture*). First, no single approach to measurement trumps all others, and researchers today advocate multiple assessments from multiple perspectives or reporters and employing converging operations targeted on the same phenomenon. Second, developmental science is interested in aspects of phenomena that implicate time and growth. Comparative longitudinal or cross-sectional designs are critical to an onto-genetic field of study and are at the core of the field's unique contributions to human knowledge. Specifically, developmental research is concerned with continuity of group average performance across time, stability of individual variation about the average across time, and predictive validity of individual variation at one time for individual variation at a later time. Third, limitations imposed by monocultural investigation include narrow generalization about its nature and scope and restricted understanding of its origins and ontogeny. It is requisite, therefore, for parenting and developmental science to explore their phenomena in multiple cultural settings. In consequence, assessments with two or more converging measures longitudinally or cross-sectionally at two or more developmental periods in two or more different cultures promote confidence in reliability and validity, permit strong developmental inferences, and rule out both monocultural bias and oversimplified cultural contrasts. The larger the number of methods, ages, or cultures studied, the more compelling is the conclusion that observed findings can be validly attributed to the theoretical dimension of interest.

The scope of developmental science embraces both description and explanation of the nature of human behavior over the life span. Among the many perspectives from which to pursue these twin charges, the cross-cultural developmental method of comparison occupies a privileged position because it encompasses the full spectrum of human variation across a worldwide context and over a lifespan ontogeny. A pervading critique of contemporary parenting and developmental science is that, traditionally, research in the field has tended to describe the constructs, structures, functions, and processes of socialization and child growth in accordance with ideals appropriate to normal, middle-class, industrialized and developed, Western societies (Bornstein, 2002; Tomlinson & Swartz, 2003). However, as Luria (1930/1978, p. 45) observed long ago, ". . . no psychological function can be understood except in terms of its development (the genetic approach) and its particular social conditions (the sociological approach)." In the past, developmental scientists have tended to arrive at species-general conclusions from person- or situation-specific results without paying adequate attention to limitations imposed by ecology and culture. In actuality, three cultural limitations have constrained the scope of prevailing psychological theories of parenting and child development: a narrow participant data base, a biased sampling of world cultures in its authorship, and a corresponding bias in the audience to which it is addressed. In response to such criticism, cultural context is achieving greater recognition in mainstream psychology (Serpell, 1990).

People are always curious about parenting and child development in other cultures, and anthropologists, sociologists, and psychologists have long sought to compare and contrast parenting children of different ages from different regions of the world. Insofar as cultural descriptions of parenting and child development encompass the widest spectrum of human variation, they are also the most comprehensive in science. They are vital to delimiting the full range of human experience, and in this sense they are also critical to establishing realistic and valid developmental norms. Psychological science has long been concerned with description in the service of defining normality and identifying abnormality. Yet "normal" is a relative and situation-specific concept – that is, what is normal to me might or might not be normal to you. Before the advent of cross-cultural study, the relativity of normal was acknowledged in psychological and developmental science in only small degree. To the extent that cross-cultural developmentalists attempt to describe the widest spectrum of human variation, their accounts document the full range of human experience and establish valid developmental norms while permitting an unconfounding of variables thought to influence human behavior. Needless to say, awareness of alternative modes of development also enhances understanding of the nature of our own culture.

The examination of culture also uniquely facilitates the quest to understand forces at work in parenting and child development by exposing variables that may be influential but are "invisible" from a monocultural perspective. The rationale for submitting parenting and child development in different cultures to psychological analysis derives from the extraordinary and unique power cross-cultural comparisons furnish the science. Cross-cultural developmental study helps to explain the origins and contingent developmental course of the widest possible variety of constructs, structures, functions, or processes in parenting and children's development. This type of analysis also helps to distinguish those phenomena that emerge and evolve in a culture-dependent fashion from those that transcend or are independent of culture. Crossing cultures can aid uniquely in the quest to understand what forces contribute to parenting and child development and how those forces contribute to their ontogeny and effectiveness.

Finally, understanding an activity and its meaning often depends on examining that activity in the context of culture (Bornstein, 1995). A given parenting activity or expression of development can have the same meaning in different cultures, just as it can have different meanings in different cultures. Conversely, different activities or expressions can have similar or different meanings depending on culture. Culture is a prime context for determining relations between activity and meaning (Bornstein, 1995).

Historical antecedents of culture, parenting, and developmental science

Cultural orientations to parenting and child development have their origins in many academic disciplines, including philosophy, history, biology, sociology, and anthropology, and they range from the legendary Athenian idealization of Spartan childrearing practices to romantic philosophical fancies, like Rousseau's "noble savage," and epistemological inquiry in Bacon and Descartes to history and sociological commentary, such as that of De Toqueville, Spengler, Compte, and Huizinga. Historically, however, anthropology contributed more to the theory and study of culture, parenting, and child development than any other discipline. First, via ethnographic study anthropologists systematically and single-handedly enlarged cultural knowledge about parenting and family life. In classic anthropological reports, detailed documentation of more formal developmental practices, such as birth rituals, naming ceremonies, and rites of passage, are often interwoven with descriptions of cultural customs. Second, anthropologists documented cultural dimensions of human personality and cognition. Anthropology thus sensitized psychology to culture and to the limitations that challenge a monocultural science.

Cultural variation in childrearing exerts significant and differential influences over mental, emotional, and social development of children, just as cultural variation clearly dictates the language children eventually speak. Whiting and Child (1953) developed this essential idea in their seminal study *Child Training and Personality*, arguing that modal developmental behaviors could be linked to different cultural treatments if it could be assumed that consistent individual relations mediate society-wide effects.

In brief, a primary concern of anthropological studies is to understand how cultural patterns are expressed in childrearing and the actual processes through which culture is transmitted from one generation to the next in parenting practices. Benedict (1932, p. 24) imagined culture as "individual psychology thrown large upon the screen, given gigantic proportions and a long time span," and she conceived that cultural environments "communicate" ways of thinking, feeling, and behaving to the growing child. According to LeVine (1973, p. 54):

> The transmission of culture from generation to generation is, in Mead's (1935) view, a process of communication in which many aspects of the growing individual's cultural environment relay the same messages to

him, messages reflecting the dominant configurations of his culture. He acquires his "cultural character" by internalizing the substance of these consistent messages. The first set of messages is transmitted to him by his parents in childhood and early childhood.

Conclusions

The human child is totally dependent on parents for survival. Children have many of the same biological needs and must meet and succeed at the same developmental tasks and challenges, and their parents have the same responsibilities to guide children to survival and adaptation to their physical and social environment and culture. It is the continuing task of parents to parent their children as well as to enculturate their children by preparing them for the physical, psychosocial, and educational situations that are characteristic of their environment and culture. For this reason, many social theorists have asserted that the family generally, and the parent–child relationship specifically, constitute the effective crucible for the early (and perhaps eventual) development of the individual and promote continuity in culture. The parent and the family are shaped by their ecological and cultural context, just as the parent and family shape their culture. Every culture promotes unique ways of adapting to its ecology and environment and has developed traditions and ethnotheories to achieve the common goals of childrearing. As a consequence, even in the face of shared goals, parenting children varies dramatically across cultures. The cultural contexts of parenthood and childhood are therefore of increasing interest to both parenting and developmental science.

A still major task of developmental science is to explain *how* contexts and settings help to shape socialization and development. Yet, after approximately a century of study, the vast majority of the literatures in parenting and developmental science, and consequently our understanding of them, still derives from studies conducted in Western industrialized and developed nations, and where there are exceptions precious little standardization has been brought to bear on comparative examinations of even the most basic constructs, structures, functions, or processes in parenting or child development. Parenting researchers need to recognize the subtleties, complexities, and uniquenesses that manifestly reflect the richness of each culture they study, while trying to determine and understand the similarities in beliefs and behaviors that equally clearly exist across cultures.

The long-standing issues of developmental science are:

- What are the universals of child development and childcare in our species?
- How do children participate in and shape the environments of child development?
- How do parents parent and organize the effective environments of childhood?

- What are the contributions of culture to parenting, childhood, and parent–child relationships?

No study of a single society (even in comparison with populations previously studied) can address these broad questions. It is possible, however, to learn lessons from different societies that will shed new light on these questions and perhaps lead to meaningful reformulations. The child perspective provides an indispensable basis for assessing the impact of caregiving on development; the parental perspective provides the social and cultural context that affects those responsible for organizing childcare; and the cultural perspective tells us about the principles and practices of the society and how they are instantiated.

We cannot fathom parenthood or childhood fully unless we know more about the multiple ecologies in which parents parent and children develop. Cultural variation in patterns of childrearing exert important influences on the ways in which children are reared and what is expected of them as they grow up. These variations merit study because they illustrate the limits of what we know about development, because they serve to highlight the too narrow perspective scientists too often bring to their research, and because they identify important factors that are often discounted or overlooked completely.

More data on cultural beliefs, practices, and the settings of parents and children promise to inform studies of parenting, development, and culture alike. This task requires paradigms traditionally associated with different disciplines and so challenges researchers. Moreover, culture is not a static entity, but rather a dynamic system that is constantly in the process of reconstruction.

Socialization researchers once depicted parents as "molding" children to function adequately in a society; however, contemporary views point to multiple roles for parents that no longer imply such single-minded determinism. Children play signal roles in their own development, seeking out and interpreting their experiences. The expression of heritable traits depends on experiences, including specific parental cognitions and actions, as well as predispositions and age-related factors in the child. Contemporary research also shows the interrelated effects of parenting, nonfamilial influences, and the roles of the broader contexts in which families reside. Socialization research today is guided by an ecological perspective on human development. Families have important influences on children, but their impact is revealed in light of the simultaneous influences of the several ecological spheres in which they are embedded. These influences occur within broad contexts (e.g., neighborhood, culture, historical epoch) that add to, shape, and moderate the nature of the family. The ecological perspective emphasizes the potential significance of extra-familial influences on parenting and child development, but also stresses the interactive and synergistic nature of the links among culture, parenting, and developmental science.

Acknowledgements

This chapter summarizes selected aspects of my research, and portions of the text have appeared in previous scientific publications cited in the references. I thank C. Varron for assistance.

References

Azuma, H. (1986). Why study child development in Japan? In H. Stevenson, H. Azuma, & K. Hakuta (Eds.), *Child development and education in Japan* (pp. 3–12). New York: W. H. Freeman.

Belsky, J. (1984). The determinants of parenting: A process model. *Child Development, 55,* 83–96.

Benedict, R. (1932). Configurations of culture in North America. *American Anthropologist, 34,* 1–27.

Benedict, R. (1938). Continuities and discontinuities in cultural-conditioning. *Psychiatry, 1,* 161–167.

Bornstein, M. H. (1989). Cross-cultural developmental comparisons: The case of Japanese–American infant and mother activities and interactions. What we know, what we need to know, and why we need to know. *Developmental Review, 9,* 171–204.

Bornstein, M. H. (Ed.). (1991). *Cultural approaches to parenting.* Hillsdale, NJ: Lawrence Erlbaum Associates, Inc.

Bornstein, M. H. (1995). Form and function: Implications for studies of culture and human development. *Culture & Psychology, 1,* 123–137.

Bornstein, M. H. (2002). Parenting infants. In M. H. Bornstein (Ed.), *Handbook of parenting.* Mahwah, NJ: Lawrence Erlbaum Associates, Inc.

Bornstein, M. H., & Cote, L. R. (2004). Mothers' parenting cognitions in cultures of origin, acculturating cultures, and cultures of destination. *Child Development, 75,* 221–235.

Bornstein, M. H., Tamis-LeMonda, C. S., Pascual, L., Haynes, O. M., Painter, K., Galperín, C. et al. (1996). Ideas about parenting in Argentina, France, and the United States. *International Journal of Behavioral Development, 19,* 347–367.

Bronfenbrenner, U., & Morris, P. A. (1998). The ecology of developmental processes. In R. M. Lerner (Ed.), W. Damon (Series Ed.), *Handbook of child psychology: Vol. 1. Theoretical models of human development* (5th ed., pp. 993–1028). New York: Wiley.

Cabrera, N. J., Tamis-LeMonda, C. S., Bradley, R. H., Hofferth, S., & Lamb, M. E. (2000). Fatherhood in the twenty-first century. *Child Development, 71,* 127–136.

Cole, M. (2005). Culture in development. In M. H. Bornstein & M. E. Lamb (Eds.), *Developmental psychology: An advanced textbook* (5th ed., pp. 45–101). Mahwah, NJ: Lawrence Erlbaum Associates, Inc.

Collins, W. A., Maccoby, E. E., Steinberg, L., Hetherington, E. M., & Bornstein, M. (2000). Contemporary research on parenting: The case for nature and nurture. *American Psychologist, 55,* 218–232.

Cowan, C. P., & Cowan, P. A. (1992). *When partners become parents.* New York: Basic Books.

Dunn, J., & Brown, J. (1991). Becoming American or English? Talking about the social world in England and the United States. In M. H. Bornstein (Ed.), *Cultural approaches to parenting.* Hillsdale, NJ: Lawrence Erlbaum Associates, Inc.

Erikson, E. H. (1950). *Childhood and society*. New York: Norton.

Fincham, F. D., & Hall, J. H. (2005). Parenting and the marital relationship. In T. Luster & L. Okagaki (Eds.), *Parenting: An ecological perspective* (2nd ed., pp. 205–233). Mahwah, NJ: Lawrence Erlbaum Associates, Inc.

French, V. (2002). History of parenting: The ancient Mediterranean world. In M. H. Bornstein (Ed.), *Handbook of parenting. Vol. 2. Biology and ecology of parenting* (2nd ed., pp. 345–376). Mahwah, NJ: Lawrence Erlbaum Associates, Inc.

Geertz, C. (1973). *Interpretation of cultures*. New York: Basic Books.

Goodnow, J. J. (2002). Parents' knowledge and expectations: Using what we know. In M. H. Bornstein (Ed.), *Handbook of parenting* (2nd ed.). Mahwah, NJ: Lawrence Erlbaum Associates, Inc.

Goodnow, J. J., Cashmore, R., Cotton, S., & Knight, R. (1984). Mothers' developmental timetables in two cultural groups. *International Journal of Psychology, 19*, 193–205.

Grych, J. H. (2002). Marital relationships and parenting. In M. H. Bornstein (Ed.), *Handbook of parenting. Vol. 4. Applied parenting* (2nd ed., pp. 203–225). Mahwah, NJ: Lawrence Erlbaum Associates, Inc.

Harkness, S., & Super, C. M. (2002). Culture and parenting. In M. H. Bornstein (Ed.), *Handbook of parenting. Vol. 2. Biology and ecology of parenting* (2nd ed., pp. 253–280). Mahwah, NJ: Lawrence Erlbaum Associates, Inc.

Holden, G. W., & Buck, M. J. (2002). Parental attitudes toward childrearing. In M. H. Bornstein (Ed.), *Handbook of parenting. Vol. 3. Status and social conditions of parenting* (2nd ed., pp. 537–562). Mahwah, NJ: Lawrence Erlbaum Associates, Inc.

Leiderman, P. H., Tulkin, S. R., & Rosenfeld, A. (Eds.). (1977). *Culture and infancy: Variations in the human experience*. New York: Academic Press.

LeVine, R. A. (1973). *Culture, behavior, and personality*. Chicago: Aldine.

LeVine, R. A. (2003). *Childhood socialization*. Hong Kong, China: The University of Hong Kong.

Luria, A. R. (1978). [A child's speech responses and the social environment] (M. Vale, Trans.). In M. Cole (Ed.), *The selected writings of A. R. Luria*. New York: M. E. Sharpe. (Original work published 1930)

Maccoby, E. E., & Martin, J. A. (1983). Socialization in the context of the family: Parent–child interaction. In M. Hetherington (Ed.), *Handbook of child psychology* (Vol. 10, pp. 1–103). New York: Wiley.

McHale, J., Khazan, I., Rotman, T., DeCourcey, W., & McConnell, M. (2002). Co-parenting in diverse family systems. In M. H. Bornstein (Ed.), *Handbook of parenting. Vol. 3. Status and social conditions of parenting* (2nd ed., pp. 75–107). Mahwah, NJ: Lawrence Erlbaum Associates, Inc.

Mead, M. (1935). *Sex and temperament in three primitive societies*. New York: Morrow.

Morelli, G. A., & Tronick, E. Z. (1991). Parenting and child development in the Efe foragers and Lese farmers of Zaire. In M. H. Bornstein (Ed.), *Cultural approaches to parenting*. Hillsdale, NJ: Lawrence Erlbaum Associates, Inc.

Okagaki, L., & Bingham, G. E. (2005). Parents' social cognitions and their parenting behaviors. In T. Luster & L. Okagaki (Eds.), *Parenting: An ecological perspective* (2nd ed., pp. 3–33). Mahwah, NJ: Lawrence Erlbaum Associates, Inc.

Parke, R. D. (2002). Fathers and families. In M. H. Bornstein (Ed.), *Handbook of parenting. Vol. 3. Status and social conditions of parenting* (2nd ed., pp. 27–73). Mahwah, NJ: Lawrence Erlbaum Associates, Inc.

Parke, R. D., Dennis, J., Flyr, M. L., Morris, K. L., Leidy, M. S., & Schofield, T. J. (2005). Fathers: Cultural and ecological perspectives. In T. Luster & L. Okagaki (Eds.), *Parenting: An ecological perspective* (2nd ed., pp. 103–144). Mahwah, NJ: Lawrence Erlbaum Associates, Inc.

Plomin, R. (1999). Behavioral genetics. In M. Bennett (Ed.), *Developmental psychology: Achievements and prospects* (pp. 231–252). Philadelphia: Psychology Press.

Pomerleau, A., Malcuit, G., & Sabatier, C. (1991). Child-rearing practices and parental beliefs in three cultural groups of Montréal: Québécois, Vietnamese, Haitian. In M. H. Bornstein (Ed.), *Cultural approaches to parenting* (pp. 45–68). Hillsdale, NJ: Lawrence Erlbaum Associates, Inc.

Rogoff, B., Mistry, J., Göncü, A., & Mosier, C. (1991). Cultural variation in the role relations of toddlers and their families. In M. H. Bornstein (Ed.), *Cultural approaches to parenting*. Hillsdale, NJ: Lawrence Erlbaum Associates, Inc.

Sameroff, A. J. (1983). Developmental systems: Contexts and evolution. In W. Kessen (Ed.), P. H. Mussen (Series Ed.), *Handbook of child psychology: Vol. 1. History, theory, and methods* (pp. 237–294). New York: Wiley.

Scarr, S., & McCartney, K. (1983). How people make their own environments: A theory of genotype–environment effects. *Child Development, 54,* 424–435.

Serpell, R. (1990). Audience, culture and psychological explanation: A reformulation of the emic–etic problem in cross-cultural psychology. *Quarterly Newsletter of the Laboratory of Comparative Human Cognition, 12,* 99–132.

Sigel, I. E., & McGillicuddy-De Lisi, A. S. (2002). Parental beliefs and cognitions: The dynamic belief systems model. In M. H. Bornstein (Ed.), *Handbook of parenting. Vol. 3. Status and social conditions of parenting* (2nd ed., pp. 485–508). Mahwah, NJ: Lawrence Erlbaum Associates, Inc.

Tomlinson, M., & Swartz, L. (2003). Imbalances in the knowledge about infancy: The divide between rich and poor countries. *Infant Mental Health Journal, 24,* 547–556.

Vygotsky, L. (1978). *Mind in society*. Cambridge, MA: Harvard University Press.

Wachs, T. D. (2000). Necessary but not sufficient: The respective roles of single and multiple influences on individual development. Washington, DC: American Psychological Association.

Welles-Nyström, B. (1988). Parenthood and infancy in Sweden. In R. A. LeVine, P. M. Miller, & M. M. West (Eds.), *Parental behavior in diverse societies*. New Directions for Child Development, Vol. 40. San Francisco: Jossey-Bass.

Whiting, J. W. (1981). Environmental constraints on infant care practices. In R. H. Munroe, R. L. Munroe, & B. B. Whiting (Eds.), *Handbook of cross-cultural human development* (pp. 155–179). New York: Garland STPM Press.

Whiting, J. W. M, & Child, I. L. (1953). *Child training and personality: A cross-cultural study*. Cambridge, MA: Harvard University Press.

17 Dealing with norm and meta-norm violators: Cultural differences in thoughts or motivated actions?

Ramadhar Singh

Building on the observations of Durkheim (1925/1976), Tetlock (2002) proposed that people live in a highly interdependent world characterized by constant accountability demands: "who must answer to whom, for what, and under what ground rules" (p. 453). Depending upon whether they are responding to the accountability demands of others, placing accountability demands on others, or defending the accountability procedure itself, people navigate themselves through complex role-rule structures to affirm a positive self-image and make their society a safe place to live, love, and work.

While responding to the accountability demands of others, people act as *intuitive pragmatic politicians*. The goal of intuitive politicians is to maintain positive social identity vis-à-vis their significant constituencies, for example, teachers, voters, or customers. So, people in this mindset engage themselves in an *internalized dialogue*, anticipating objections to their plans and actions and crafting arguments in ways that could enable them to make a positive self-presentation. Counterfactual thinking (Junid, 2003), pre-emptive self-criticism (Lerner & Tetlock, 1999), and defensive bolstering (Tetlock, Skitka, & Boettger, 1989) often serve as coping strategies. The seemingly *inflated claims* of one's performance in appraisal and admission applications and the *central tendency* effects in evaluations of one's constituency members are thus not errors and biases, but self-serving adaptive responses (Tetlock, 2000).

People defend legitimate regimes (Tetlock, 2002), and follow the norms and laws of the collective they belong to (Peters, 1960). The pressures for doing so come from people's sentiments of attachment to the collective and respect for its authority, symbols, and rules (Durkheim, 1925/1965, 1925/1976). While putting accountability demands on others, the goal shifts from pursuing self-interests to upholding social order. Thus, people act as *intuitive prudent prosecutors*. In this mindset, thought is directed at detecting "cheaters and free riders who seek the benefits but shirk the responsibilities of membership in the collective" and action at closing "the loopholes in the accountability" procedures (Tetlock, 2002, p. 452). To achieve these purposes, intuitive prosecutors analyze the causes behind the shirking of responsibility (e.g., internal versus external, person versus situation, Kelley, 1972; association, negligence, foreseeability, intention, and mitigating factors, Heider,

1958) and match the normative sanctions with the norm violated. While doing the latter, they may adopt an across-the-board hard-line stance if the prevailing law-and-order situations demand so (Durkheim, 1925/1976). The so-called *severity bias* – the greater the severity of consequence, the greater the moral responsibility (see, e.g., Burger, 1981, for a review and meta-analysis) – and the *fundamental attribution error* – more emphasis on personal than situational causation (Ross, 1977) – are, therefore, not errors and biases but motivated tightening of the accountability procedure (Tetlock et al., 2006).

Common to these mindsets is the legitimization of the accountability procedure itself. Existential needs require people to believe that "the rules governing their social world are not just the preferences of currently domin-ant interest groups but rather are anchored in sacred values that confer legit-imacy on collective practices" (Tetlock, 2002, p. 452). Any encroachment on sacred values by secular ones, for example, market pricing for lives or rela-tionships, triggers the mindset of *intuitive principled theologians*. Thoughts and actions are directed at protecting sacred values from secular encroach-ments (Tetlock, Kristel, Elson, Green, & Lerner, 2000). Consequently, people show *moral outrage* consisting of heightened anger, lower threshold of internal attribution, and harsher punitive actions, and make *moral cleansing responses* not only to those who compromised with the sacred values (i.e., norm violators) but also to those who were close to the social circle of the norm violators. Family, friends, organization, and country of the indi-vidual norm-violator could have prevented him/her from making the viola-tion. As errors of omission, negligence, or commission (Lickel, Schmader, & Hamilton, 2003) on their parts resulted in the taboo trade-off, they become *meta-norm violators*. Collective punishment for failing to assume *vicarious responsibility* is thus justified under the theologian mindset.

East–West differences

The goals of pursuing self-interests, upholding social order, and protecting accountability procedure in the foregoing social-functionalist mindsets require motivated reasoning (Kunda, 1999). How can motivated reasoning operate uniformly across the globe when Easterners and Westerners think differently. As Nisbett (2003, p. 100) noted:

> . . . to the Asian, the world is a complex place, composed of continuous substances, understandable in terms of the whole rather than in terms of the parts, and subject more to collective than to personal control. To the Westerner, the world is a relatively simple place, composed of discrete objects that can be understood without undue attention to context, and highly subject to personal control. Very different worlds indeed.

Stated simply, Easterners are *holistic* and see similarity between an object and its context. In contrast, Westerners are *analytic* and see a difference between an object and its context (see, e.g., Nisbett, Peng, Choi, & Norenzayan, 2001, for a review and integration).

The consequences of such difference in thought systems seem to be profound. Westerners insist on "a cause, rather than a number of causes" sought by Easterners (Nisbett, 2003, p. 205). Westerners see agency in the individual person, but Easterners see agency in a person's groups (see, e.g., Morris, Menon, & Ames, 2001, for a discussion). Westerners make dispositional attributions to the individual person; Easterners make dispositional attributions to groups or situations (see, e.g., Choi, Nisbett, & Norenzayan, 1999, for a review and discussion).

The author takes the position that the holistic-versus-analytic division of the world (Nisbett, 2003) may be confined to automatic thinking about physical stimuli. With motivated reasoning about norm and meta-norm violators, Easterners and Westerners think alike about causal forces but differ in their ways of enforcing their country-specific norms. This position was suggested by three lines of evidence. First, Americans are as indirect as are East Asians in social situations (Sanchez-Burks, Lee, Choi, Nisbett, Zhao, & Koo, 2003). Second, exposures to the media and access to the Internet have enabled university students to develop multicultural minds. So, activation of constructs pertaining to social order may activate a uniform *frame switching* (Hong, Morris, Chiu, & Benet-Martinez, 2000) but culture-specific ways of adapting to them. Finally, cultures condition actions more than emotions and cognitions (Rozin, 2003).

Causal versus implicational analysis

In the model of *intuitive scientists* (Ross, 1977), people are believed to be *rational* decision makers. They gather information about *consistency* (i.e., would the actor behave in the same way over time?), *distinctiveness* (i.e., would the actor behave in the same way with similar stimuli?), and *consensus* (i.e., would other people also behave like this actor?) of the event. From the pattern in responses to these basic factors (Kelley, 1972), causation is attributed to the person, the situation, or both.

Jones and Thibaut (1958) suggested that the *causal-genetic set* is not the rule. The *situation-matching set* – a concern "with the appropriateness of the stimulus person's behavior . . . to the present behavior setting" (p. 159) – renders causal analyses irrelevant. Doubts on correspondence between causal attributions and assignments of responsibility have thus been expressed (e.g., Fincham & Jaspars, 1980; Hamilton, 1978, 1979). In fact, adult-like responses emerged by 10 years of age in assignments of blame, but not in causal attributions (e.g., Fincham & Jaspars, 1979). In the present author's view, people can respond to events as scientists, prosecutors, or both. It is important to specify the circumstances that activate causal analysis of the scientist mindset over implicational analysis of the prosecutorial mindset.

In the scientist mindset, people are motivated in seeking *social explanations* (Hamilton, 1978). The important questions to them are: (a) Why did those involved behave in that way? (b) Were they those kinds of people? and (c) Were they under some kinds of external pressure? The inferences are backward-looking, from acts to dispositions (Jones & Davis, 1965). Dispositional attributions are gratifying to intuitive scientists, for they can now "predict the behaviors of others" (Gilbert & Malone, 1995, p. 34).

In the prosecutorial mindset, by contrast, people are motivated by social control. They consider implications that the event might have for social order. The questions that dominate their thoughts are: (a) How do acts of others disturb or promote the existing social order? (b) What are the implications of those acts for people's lives, properties, and liberties? and (c) What ought to be done to deter or encourage the actor and his associates? These questions are *sanctioning inquiries* (Hamilton, 1979), and the answers help close the "loopholes" in the exploited accountability procedure (Tetlock, 2002). The adaptive responses of scientists and prosecutors can be termed as *causal* and *implicational* analyses, respectively.

Singh et al. (2004) collected headlines news that fell into the four categories of: (1) *good–unusual* (e.g., Mahathir [Prime Minister] defends use of English [in Malaysia]); (2) *good–social control* (e.g., Kofi Annan [the UN Secretary General] for restraint against military strike on Iraq); (3) *bad–unusual* (e.g., Step-dad accused of raping girl 3 times); and (4) *bad–social order* (e.g., Bashir [the Jemaah Islamiah leader in Indonesia] aided planned attacks on embassies). Participants inferred the likelihood of their first responding to the news from both the causal and implicational angles. As predicted by the motive of social control, the good and the social-order-related news triggered a stronger inclination to undertake implicational than causal analysis. The unusual news, in contrast, evoked a stronger inclination to undertake causal than implicational analysis as predicted by the motive of social explanation. The likelihood of undertaking both the causal and implicational analyses of the bad news was the same. Obviously, implicational analysis is as prevalent and important as is causal analysis, and equating implicational responses to everyday events with their causal explanations might have caused the East–West differences in thought systems (Nisbett, 2003).

Social-functionalist accounts of motivated actions

This section has two objectives. One is to review the key findings of some studies claiming that Easterners and Westerners have different theories about agency of collectives and individual persons and so think differently about person and groups. Another is to provide the social-functionalist interpretations of the so-obtained cultural differences in attributions and thoughts.

Greater agency of person in the West than the East

Menon, Morris, Chiu, and Hong (1999, Pilot study) asked participants from Singapore and America to endorse some statements expressing beliefs in the agency of a individual person or a group (e.g., "Individuals [Organizations] set a course for themselves independent of the influences surrounding them"; "The rules and laws in my society say that individuals [organizations] should take control of the situations around them and exercise free will"). Singaporeans endorsed beliefs in collective autonomy ($M = 3.98$) more than those in individual autonomy ($M = 3.50$). By contrast, Americans endorsed beliefs in individual autonomy ($M = 4.10$) more than those in collective autonomy ($M = 3.74$). Similar cross-cultural differences were obtained with participants from Hong Kong and America. It was concluded, therefore, that cultures differ in their "theories about the relative autonomy of individuals and collectives" (p. 712). Such differences in the perceived autonomy of individuals and groups were later equated with the *dispositions* of persons and groups (Morris et al., 2001).

In Menon et al. (1999), there was no test of difference between cultures at the levels of agency of either the individual person or the collective. From nearly equal endorsements of autonomy of the collective in America ($M = 3.74$) and Singapore ($M = 3.98$), the locus of the Culture × Agency effect appears to be in a greater autonomy of the individual person in America than in Singapore. So, the emphasis that the social-functionalist frameworks lay on high interdependency in the collectives across cultures is also supported by the results reported.

Dispositional attribution to group or respondeat superior?

For the attempted assassination of the Chinese emperor, the penalty was death for the assailant and his entire family (Menon et al., 1999). In accord with the 746 BC system of *yuan zuo*, responsibility for a wrongdoing by an individual person within work and neighborhood settings was also extended to his boss and parents (Chiu & Hong, 1992). Such cases and results led to the hypothesis that the Chinese see greater agency or disposition in groups than in an individual person (Chiu, Morris, Hong, & Menon, 2000; Menon et al., 1999). The measures of agency or disposition were inferred likelihood of internal versus external causes of the events or trait-ascriptions.

Giving internal explanations for a negative act – either along a rating scale (Morris & Peng, 1994) or by generating descriptions (Chiu et al., 2000; Miller, 1984) – may overlap considerably with the assignment of blame or moral responsibility. Asking for the internal and external causes of an event may yield answers generated for the angle of either explaining or sanctioning the act. That makes use of such measures in any causal analysis unsatisfactory (Gilbert & Malone, 1995). In particular, results from such measures cannot allow a decision about whether participants made dispositional attributions to the person and group actors or merely passed moral judgments on them. Besides, the legal principle *respondeat superior* ("let the superior answer"), or *vicarious responsibility* is as prevalent in the West (Lickel et al., 2003) as in the East (Chiu et al., 2000). Hence, the finding of a greater agency of group than person could have been an instance of *respondeat superior* or *moral outrage* of principled theologians (Tetlock et al., 2000).

Menon et al. (1999, Study 2) sought explanations for the "rogue trader" scandals in the banks in America and Japan. In both settings, an individual person was the norm violator and his organization was the meta-norm enforcer. All scandals involved multimillion-dollar losses and threatened the existence of the collective itself. Explanations for these scandals had appeared in both the Japanese and American newspapers. References to the norm-violator and meta-norm enforcer in the reports served as the dependent variable. Japanese made more references to the meta-norm enforcer than the norm violator; Americans made nearly the same number of references to them in the case of in-group American scandals, but more references to the norm violator than the meta-norm enforcer for the out-group Japanese scandals. While the results were seemingly supportive of the hypothesis of a greater disposition of groups rather than persons in the East, more attention to the meta-norm enforcers than the norm violator in three of the four cases is also consistent with the model of principled theologians.

In Chiu et al. (2000, Pilot study, Study 1), there was a threat to the lives of more than 100 Hong Kong children due to a medicine mix-up. Negative responses to both the pharmacy worker (person) and the health-care organization (group) were sought. More negative description of the group than the person agreed with the prediction of the model of principled theologians (Lim & Singh, 2003). There was no difference between evaluations of person and group by Americans who were visiting Hong Kong. Inclusion of a moderator variable of need for closure, moreover, led the authors to state that "the Culture × Agent interaction in Menon et al.'s (1999) studies (as well as the one in the pilot study and the present study) resulted mainly from the high-NFC [Need for Cognition] participants' responses" (p. 254). Apparently, dispositional attribution to groups is a phenomenon that cannot be generalized, even within a culture.

When shirking of responsibility was not value-encroaching, as in Studies 2 and 3 of Menon et al. (1999), there was no difference between dispositional attribution to the individual and group actors by Chinese (see Figure 4, p. 709; Figure 5, p. 713). The only evidence for a greater dispositional attribution to group rather than individual person by the Chinese was, therefore, in the high-time-pressure condition of Chiu et al.'s (2000) Study 3. As the vignette pertained to animals and the results conflict with those of Menon et al., evidence for an implicit theory of a greater perceived agency of group than person among Chinese is weak.

Person- versus situation-centered theorists or pragmatic politicians?

Morris and Peng (1994) tested the hypothesis that Westerners and Easterners have person- and situation-centered theories of behavior, respectively. The former explain an act by making more internal attributions; the latter explain it by making an external or situational attribution. Comparisons of attributions by Americans and Chinese supported the hypothesis.

Morris and Peng's conclusion would have been different had they included the measures of internal and external attributions as a repeated-measurement factor in their data analyses (Hewstone, 1990). Reorganizations of their four means from Study 1 in the Culture × Attribution format showed that both the high-school and graduate students had made more external than internal attributions in the compulsion and connection display sets, but the reverse in the collection display set, regardless of their cultural theories. The hypothesized cultural difference had held in the compulsion display. However, American high-school students made a similar attribution to the internal and external forces. So, support for the hypothesized differences in theories across cultures was equivocal.

Explanations of a murder by an in-group or out-group actor were sought from American and Chinese graduate students in Study 2. Americans made more dispositional and fewer situational attributions to an out-group murderer Lu than to an in-group murderer McIlvane (Figure 8, upper panel, p. 965). There was no such Categorization × Attribution effect on explanations by Chinese (Figure 8, lower panel, p. 965). In spite of the nonsignificant interaction effect, two intriguing patterns in their results are notable. First, dispositional attribution to Lu ($M = 2.32$) was lower than that to McIlvane ($M = 3.22$) and also lower than situational ($M = 2.86$) attribution to Lu by the Chinese. Second, the Chinese saw the operation of personal and situational forces to be equal in case of McIlvane. Stated simply, Chinese people gave more situational than personal explanations for an in-group murder but more personal explanations for an out-group than in-group murderer. Such patterns of differences illustrate the *ultimate attribution error*, a tendency to explain negative acts of out-group members by disposition but of in-group members by situation (Hewstone, 1990; Pettigrew, 1979), even by Chinese. Evidence for the ultimate attribution error by both Americans and Chinese is more consistent with the model of people as pragmatic politicians (Junid, 2003) than differences in the person- versus situation-centered theories across cultures.

Lee, Hallahan, and Herzong (1996) analyzed attributions in sports articles and editorials of newspapers published in Hong Kong and the United States. The cultural difference in attributions was more marked in sports articles than in editorials. More interestingly, there were situational attributions in the editorials. So, the cultural difference was not as orderly as predicted by the hypothesis of thought systems.

Choi, Dalal, Kim-Prieto, and Park (2003, Study 4) sought internal and external explanations for a murder from Americans and Koreans. The former made more internal attributions (M = 4.39) than did the latter (M = 3.87). However, both cultural groups made similar external attributions (Ms = 4.04 and 4.25 for Americans and Koreans, respectively, p < .10). Results from tests of significance of difference between attributions by each cultural group were not reported. From their means, both internal and external attributions seem to be equally prevalent in each culture. If this interpretation is correct, then more internal attributions by Americans than Koreans indicate a stronger moral outrage at the murderer in the former than the latter group of participants (Tetlock et al., 2000). Because participants in all four studies considered more than one cause of the event, regardless of whether it was murder or help to a car accident victim, evidence against the "either/or" requirement of the analytic thought system (Nisbett, 2003) is present even in this study. Such use of multiple standards is, however, predicted by the model of people as pragmatic politicians (Tetlock, 2002).

Summary

Three points emerge from the literature just reviewed. First, the measures of internal attribution – asking whether the cause is internal or endorsing a negative description – reflect more on the moral judgment of those implicated (implicational analysis) than on dispositional attributions to them (causal analysis). Second, evidence for implicit theories of a greater agency of person in the West, but of group in the East, is equivocal. Finally, harsher actions against the meta-norm enforcer than the norm violators in the East and the ultimate attribution type-error may be outcomes of the respective social-functionalist mindsets of principled theologians and pragmatic politicians.

Cultural differences in thoughts or motivated actions?

This section reports results showing that the measures of attributions in the past research overlapped with those of moral actions, and hence country or cultural differences in ways of norm-enforcements were erroneously interpreted as East–West differences in thought systems. Norms are enforced across the globe in informal, private ways (e.g., gossip, assignments of blame, praise, or moral responsibility, social distancing and coming closer) as well as in formal, legal ways (e.g., assignments of demerit or merit points, fines, canning, imprisonment, capital punishment). By separating the measures of dealing with norm violations (i.e., actions from the angles of implications of the act for society) from those of attribution (i.e., causal analyses), it is possible to show that cultures differ more in *actions* against than in thoughts about the norm- and meta-norm violators. Besides, the *fundamental attribution error*, *ultimate attribution error*, and *collective punishment* operate more at the level of actions than cognitions of prudent prosecutors, pragmatic politicians, and principled theologians.

People as prudent prosecutors

Cultural and developmental differences in accountability demands

Singh et al. (2003, Experiment 1) regarded assignments of blame for a negative act, but of praise for a positive act, as moral actions, and tested the hypothesis that the social circle of responsibility is wider in the East than the West. So, Singaporeans, relative to Americans, should blame the person less but his group more. This hypothesis was tested by describing a negative behavior of an individual person to the participants, and asking them to assign blame to the *person* and his *family, friends, school, organization*, and *country* along rating scales. When the behavior was positive, participants assigned praise to the person and his five groups. Participants were university students from Singapore, the UK, and the USA. Three results are notable.

First, assignments of blame or praise decreased from the person to his country in all three countries. Informal actions were thus guided by social closeness between the person and his groups, and not by the "either/or" logic of analytic thought (Nisbett, 2003). Second, the person was blamed more in the USA than in either the UK or Singapore. However, there was no such country difference in assignments of praise to the person. Finally, assignments of blame or praise to the groups were greater in number in Singapore than in either the UK or the USA.

The foregoing findings made two points convincingly. First, the social circle of responsibility is wider in Singapore than either the UK or the USA. Second, and no less important, blaming the person for failing against the standard of morality of duty is a typically American phenomenon (Fuller, 1969).

The same task was also used with Chinese aged 8, 12, and 16 years in Singapore (Singh et al., 2004, Experiment 3). In addition to assigning blame or praise to the person and his groups, participants distributed 20 demerit or 20 merit points among them. The order of measurement of the two forms of action was counterbalanced over half of the participants of each age group. The arcsin transformations of proportions of points allocated served as the measure of formal action. Four results are relevant.

First, children as young as eight held the person, relative to his groups, more accountable for his behavior. Second, the family and friends of the person were blamed more for his negative behavior by the older rather than the younger participants. Third, assignments of praise to the person and his groups were more indiscriminate than those of blame to them. Finally, the person received more merit or demerit points for his good or bad act from the older rather than the younger participants. Stated simply, the accountability demands on the person increased with age in the formal action. These results jointly indicate that, in Singapore, formal actions, such as assignments of points, represent responsibility of the person better, but informal actions, such as assignments of blame and praise, represent responsibility of groups better. In addition, people closer to the person's social circle, such as family and friends, are held more morally accountable for his negative behavior by adolescents and adults than children. So, the social circle of responsibility is indeed wider in the East than the West.

Cultural differences in moral and legal actions, not in attributions

Singh et al. (2003) further pursued the hypothesis of more cultural differences in moral than in legal actions. They presented a vignette of crime committed by an individual person in front of his group of friends in a public place. The person had allegedly snatched the handbag of an elderly lady in spite of warnings by his friends (an *exacerbating circumstance*), without any clue of his intention to commit the crime to his friends (a *control circumstance*), or because of provocation by his friends (an *extenuating circumstance*). The crime was unsuccessful, and the perpetrator was caught by passers-by and handed over to the police. Nevertheless, the lady was hurt *slightly* (low severity of consequence) or *seriously* (high severity of consequence) when she resisted the theft. Participants were university students from Singapore and America, and they assigned blame or moral responsibility to the person and his friends and also recommended duration of imprisonment for them.

The assigned blame to the person was greater in America ($M = 8.00$) than Singapore ($M = 7.44$), and more in the exacerbating and control circumstances ($Ms = 7.92$ and 7.96) than the extenuating circumstance ($M = 5.25$). The recommended duration of imprisonment for the person had neither the main effect of country nor of the circumstance of the crime. Obviously, formal legal actions against the perpetrator were uniform across cultures, as the results of the developmental study (Singh et al., 2004). More importantly, the rigidity in imprisonment across circumstances was not a *fundamental attribution error* but a prudent way of enforcing the norm. This interpretation of rigidity in imprisonment across circumstances was justified because assignments of blame to the person were extenuation-sensitive.

In both countries, the effect of severity of consequence was on the recommended imprisonment for the person, but not on the blame assigned to him. This severity effect was also a prudent way of sending signals to the perpetrator and the public that the dangers they pose to the social order could rebound on them as well.

The levels of both assigned blame and recommended imprisonment for the group were higher in Singapore ($Ms = 5.29$ and 2.90) than in America ($Ms = 4.39$ and 2.29). Such vicarious responsibility agrees with the hypothesis of a wider social circle of responsibility in the East than the West, but not with the hypothesis of a greater disposition of groups than persons.

Distinguishing attributions from actions

To substantiate the interpretation just made, Singh et al. (2003) included new measures of causal attribution (i.e., why did the crime happen?) and dispositional attribution (i.e., would the people involved in the crime commit new crimes in the future?). Causal attributions asked for responses to two counterfactuals:

1   How likely is it that crime would have occurred if someone else had been in the perpetrator's place? (High response = Situational attribution); and
2   How likely is it that crime would have occurred if the perpetrator had not been with this group of friends? (High response = Person attribution).

Notably, the counterfactual thinkings were directed at cognitions of the crime committed (Roese, 1997), and asked for its causes, *situation* or *person*.

Dispositional attributions were tapped by Kelley's (1972) basic factors of *consistency*, *distinctiveness*, and *consensus*:

1   How likely is it that the person (or his group of friends) would do the same in similar situations in the future? (High response = High consistency);
2   How likely is it that the person (or his group of friends) would do the same in any crime situation? (High response = Low distinctiveness); and
3   How likely is it that other persons (or other groups of his friends) would do the same in the situation described? (High response = High consensus).

The average of high consistency and low distinctiveness responses represents dispositional attribution, whereas the average of responses to the consensus for the person and the group represents the base rate. Dispositional attribution would hold if the former was higher than the latter.

The foregoing measures of causal and dispositional attributions did not overlap with either the moral or legal action against the norm and the meta-norm violators. Consequently, responses to these new measures of attribution and of actions from the same participants were better suited for tapping the loci of the East–West differences in thoughts (Nisbett, 2003).

As predicted, the person was a more likely cause of the crime in the exacerbating and control circumstances (Ms = 6.91 and 5.48) than in the extenuating circumstance (M = 3.02). In contrast, the situation was a more likely cause of the crime in the extenuating circumstance (M = 5.38) than in the exacerbating and control circumstances (Ms = 3.77 and 3.88). Dispositional attributions to the person were stronger in the exacerbating and control circumstances (Ms = 6.06 and 5.84) than in the extenuating circumstance (M = 4.84). Dispositional attributions to the group were, by contrast, stronger in the extenuating and exacerbating circumstances (Ms = 5.95 and 5.31) than in the control circumstance (M = 4.58). No difference between dispositional attributions to the group of the extenuating and exacerbating circumstances imply that the former would provoke crime but the latter would advise against it, as they had in fact done previously. Most important, both causal attributions and dispositional attributions were uniform across cultures.

Summary

The preceding patterns of differences in attributions across circumstances indicate that attributions are made as they ought to be, and that the causal roles of the norm and meta-norm violators are never lost sight of in either country. However, Americans and Singaporeans differ in their ways of placing accountability demands on the norm and meta-norm violators. Intuitive prosecution of the norm violator is the same across countries, but moral pressures on him are greater in America than in Singapore. Even though Singaporeans, compared to Americans, place greater accountability demands on the groups of the norm-violator, the country differences are more a matter of degree than of kind. Considered from this angle, then, assignments of collective responsibility is another prudent way of sending message to people that what anyone of their social circle does is very much their business (Tetlock et al., 2006).

People as principled theologians

Lim and Singh (2003) tested the hypothesis that more negative trait ascriptions to the pharmacy than to the medical worker in Hong Kong (Chiu et al., 2000) were moral outrage against the more responsible company instead of a greater dispositional attribution to the group than to the person in the East. Chinese participants in Singapore read a vignette describing either a taboo trade-off (a decision to spend hospital resources on infrastructure development instead of providing a child with a dialysis machine) or a tragic trade-off (allocating one dialysis machine between two children). Participants expressed their emotions, made attributions, and recommended punitive actions against the individual norm violator and his hospital management board.

As in Chiu et al. (2000), there was an encroachment of the sacred value of human life by the secular economic consideration in the condition of taboo trade-off. So, internal attribution, anger, and punitive actions should be higher in the taboo rather than the tragic trade-off condition. More importantly, recommended punitive action should be harsher against the meta-norm enforcer than the individual norm violator. Results supported the predictions: people in the mindset of principled theologians placed greater accountability demands on the more responsible meta-norm enforcers than the individual norm violator.

Lim and Singh (2003) manipulated encroachment of the sacred value of marital fidelity by the secular value of freedom in romantic relations. A man brought his wife or a date to a party but either neglected or intervened when the woman started flirting with another man. Participants expressed greater anger with and took harsher punitive action against the norm-violator, relative to the meta-norm enforcer, when the man had intervened. When he had ignored the woman's misconduct, outrage with both the norm violator and meta-norm enforcers was equal. Also, ignoring the misconduct of one's wife, compared to a date, led to a greater outrage.

Findings of these studies indicate that greater responsibility is allocated to the group than to the individual person in the medicine mix-up case in pharmacy (Chiu et al., 2000) and in rogue-trader scandals in banks (Menon et al., 1999) are interpretable as instances of moral outrage with the meta-norm enforcers for failing to act otherwise. Similarly, collective punishment for the attempted assassination of the Chinese emperor might have been an outcome of moral outrage of principled theologians rather than activation of the theory of a greater agency of group than person in China (Morris et al., 2001).

People as pragmatic politicians

The *ultimate attribution error* (Pettigrew, 1979) may also be more a behavioral than a cognitive response of people in the mindset of pragmatic politicians. Politicians perceive the situations realistically, but protect people who could be significant in promoting a positive identity (Tetlock, 2002). Singh, Lim, and Tan (2005) presented instances of acts showing in-group favoritism equally, in-group favoritism unequally, or fairness by a female or male leader. Participants were Chinese male and female adolescents in Singapore who made causal attributions to and endorsed the leader's decision.

Attributions were stereotypical, a greater dispositional attribution to a male than to a female leader, not the ultimate attribution error-type relying on the out-group versus in-group categorization. For an in-group favoring decision, however, endorsement was higher for an in-group than for an out-group leader.

Even when the participants were adults and a decision favoring the out-group was included, dispositional attributions to leaders were independent of their acts: there was no in-group serving or out-group derogating attribution. For an in-group favoring decision, however, endorsement of the in-group leader was higher than that of the out-group one. Evidently, the *ultimate attribution error* (Pettigrew, 1979) is a pragmatic action by people in the mindset of intuitive politicians. The same in-group favoring act that makes the in-group leader attractive makes the out-group one repulsive. The politician interpretation is justified because the leader making a fair decision was always endorsed more than the one making either an in-group or an out-group favoring decision. It is the in-group favoring act of the leader that activates the mindset of politicians.

Lessons, limitations, and future prospects

The key message from this review is that the goals of self-interest, social order, and moral order pursued under the respective mindsets of politicians, prosecutors, and theologians trigger similar analytic thoughts across the globe. When measures of attributions are separated from those of actions, causal analyses are circumstance-specific everywhere. With motivated reasoning, Easterners are analytic in their thoughts as are Westerners. It is premature, therefore, to draw any geographical line between the East and the West vis-à-vis their thought systems (Nisbett, 2003). The motivated formal actions of Easterners and Westerners can also be alike. It is the informal moral way of norm-enforcement that distinguishes Easterners from Westerners. In particular, the social circle of responsibility is wider in Singapore than America.

The studies testing the model of people as prudent prosecutors (Singh et al., 2003, Tetlock et al., 2006) showed the main effects of culture on actions. Punitive actions against persons are greater in America than Singapore but those against groups are greater in Singapore than America. Such a wider social circle of responsibility in the East than the West is also illustrated when the main effect of culture is confined to actions against groups. As Japan has a tight system of social control (Hamilton & Sanders, 1992), actions by Americans and Japanese against the norm-violator should be uniform. The level of responsibility assigned to groups by the former may, however, be less than by the latter, causing the main effect of culture. A nonsignificant main effect of culture on action against the person and a significant effect on action against the group show that moral responsibility is limited to the person in the West but is also extended to his groups in the East. With the evidence for the multicultural minds (Hong et al., 2000) and their differential accessibility in intuitive prosecution, it is even possible to reverse the patterns in the main effects on assigned responsibility and recommended imprisonment across countries.

The person and the group of the crime vignettes used in the studies reviewed were confounded with their respective roles of *agent* and *accomplice*. This confounding did not pose any threat to the test of the hypothesis of a wider social circle of responsibility in the East than in the West. Nevertheless, it is unclear whether the obtained East–West difference in dealing with meta-norm violators is an accomplice- or group-linked phenomenon. Also, the person and his group in the extenuating circumstance (Singh et al., 2003) were confounded by the criminal act of the former but the criminal intention of the latter (i.e., the group was the brain behind the crime). The smaller difference between actions against the norm and meta-norm violators in the extenuating circumstance in Singapore rather than America may be an equating of the group with the person (e.g., Menon et al., 1999) or of criminal intention with criminal act.

These ambiguities can be removed in future research by having the person and his group in the roles of both agent and accomplice. A crime by just two individuals – one as agent and the other as accomplice – can be particularly informative, for it can show how Easterners and Westerners use information about criminal intentions and acts. Because behavior engulfs the field in America (Heider, 1958), it is likely that Americans may weight the criminal act of the person much more than his criminal intention, whereas Singaporeans may weight them equally. The importance of such a study would lie in choosing between the person-versus-group and act-versus-intention representations.

Another lesson is that the *fundamental attribution error, severity bias, collective punishment,* and *ultimate attribution error* of the model of people as intuitive scientists (Ross, 1977) should not be perceived as such, but as adaptive responses to the immediate goals activated by the social-functionalist mindsets. It is important, therefore, to always keep in mind whether people are undertaking causal analyses of the incident or implicational analyses for social control. Motivated tightening of the accountability demands for upholding social and moral order is an adaptive response in the mindsets of prosecutors and theologians, as is the motivated use of double-standard in dealing with the in-group and out-group leaders favoring their respective in-group (Pettigrew, 1979; Singh et al., 2005).

If a uniform imprisonment across circumstances is a way of tightening the accountability procedure, then extenuation-sensitive recommendations for imprisonment are possible in countries where the formal social control and legal systems are far from satisfactory. In some of these countries, excuses and justifications of the norm violator may be discarded in assignments of responsibility to him. Such rigidity would hopefully tighten the moral accountability procedure. Tetlock et al. (2006) in fact showed that intuitive prosecution is sensitive to exacerbation in a condition of bad social control but to extenuation in a condition of good social control. Accordingly, it can be predicted that participants from a country with a good system of social control (e.g., Malaysia, Singapore) may tighten the legal accountability but loosen the moral one. Since the formal system is strict, the public does not have to be so strict. By contrast, participants from a country with a bad system of social control (e.g., India, Indonesia) may tighten the moral accountability but loosen the legal one. Because the formal system is loose, at least the public has to be strict. The same person who takes a strict moral position may be liberal with regard to the use of the laws and vice versa. Inconsistency between the moral and legal positions taken with regard to the same incident may make intuitive prosecutors appear as "fair-but-biased" and as people who are in contact with the social reality. In this way, the social-functionalist "research programs are an integral part of a societal social psychology that must ultimately be consistent with, but is not reducible to, the intrapsychic levels of analysis at which most theory is now pitched" (Tetlock, 2002, p. 453).

Two conclusions can be drawn from the literature reviewed. First, the social circle of responsibility is wider in the East than the West. Second, the locus of the East–West difference lies in ways of enforcing norms instead of thought systems (Nisbett, 2003). These conclusions and the evidence for multicultural minds (Hong et al., 2000) jointly offer great prospects for analyzing cultural differences in terms of social-functionalist models of people as *politicians, prosecutors,* and *theologians* and how and when people shift from one to another mindset.

Acknowledgements

The preparation of this report, a revised version of the author's state-of-the-art lecture at ICP 2004, was supported in part by Grants R-107–000–030–112 and R-107–000–045–112 from the National University of Singapore. The author thanks Lakshmi L. Jayashree, Sanjana Kiran, George Thornton, and an anonymous reviewer for their comments on an earlier version.

References

Burger, J. M. (1981). Motivational biases in the attribution of responsibility for an accident. A meta-analysis of the defensive-attribution hypothesis. *Psychological Bulletin, 90*, 496–512.

Chiu, C. Y., & Hong, Y. Y. (1992). The effects of intentionality and validation on individual and collective responsibility attribution among Hong Kong Chinese. *Journal of Psychology, 120*, 291–300.

Chiu, C. Y., Morris, M. W., Hong, Y. Y., & Menon, T. (2000). Motivated cultural cognition: The impact of implicit cultural theories on dispositional attributions varies as a function of need for closure. *Journal of Personality and Social Psychology, 78*, 247–259.

Choi, I., Dalal, R., Kim-Prieto, C., & Park, H. (2003). Culture and judgment of causal relevance. *Journal of Personality and Social Psychology, 84*, 46–59.

Choi, I., Nisbett, R. E., & Norenzayan, A. (1999). Causal attribution across cultures: Variation and universality. *Psychological Bulletin, 125*, 47–63.

Durkheim, E. (1965). *Moral education.* Glencoe, IL: Free Press. (Original work published 1925)

Durkheim, E. (1976). *The elementary forms of the religious life* (2nd ed.) London: Allen & Unwin. (Original work published in 1925)

Fincham, F. D., & Jaspars, J. M. (1979). Attribution of responsibility to the self and other in children and adults. *Journal of Personality and Social Psychology, 37*, 1589–1602.

Fincham, F. D., & Jaspars, J. M. (1980). Attribution of responsibility. From man the scientist to man as lawyer. In L. Berkowitz (Ed.), *Advances in experimental social psychology* (Vol. 13, pp. 81–138). New York: Academic Press.

Fuller, L. (1969). *The morality of law* (2nd ed.). New Haven, CT: Yale University Press.

Gilbert, D. T., & Malone, P. S. (1995). The correspondence bias. *Psychological Bulletin, 117*, 21–38.

Hamilton, V. L. (1978). Who is responsible? Toward a social psychology of responsibility attribution. *Social Psychology, 41*, 316–328.

Hamilton, V. L. (1979). Intuitive psychologist or intuitive lawyer? Alternative models of the attribution process. *Journal of Personality and Social Psychology, 39*, 767–772.

Hamilton, V. L., & Sanders, J. (1992). *Everyday justice: Responsibility and the individual in Japan and the United States.* New Haven, CT: Yale University Press.

Heider, F. (1958). *The psychology of interpersonal relations.* New York: Wiley.

Hewstone, M. (1990). The ultimate attribution error? A review of the literature on intergroup causal attribution. *European Journal of Social Psychology, 20*, 311–335.

Hong, Y., Morris, M. W., Chiu, C., & Benet-Martinez, V. (2000). Multicultural minds: A dynamic constructivist approach to culture and cognition. *American Psychologist, 55*, 709–720.

Jones, E. E., & Davis, K. E. (1965). From acts to dispositions: The attribution process in person perception. In L. Berkowitz (Ed.), *Advances in experimental social psychology* (Vol. 2, pp. 219–266). New York: Academic Press.

Jones, E. E., & Thibaut, J. W. (1958). Interactional goals as bases of inference in interpersonal perception. In R. Tagiuri & L. Petrol (Eds.), *Person perception and interpersonal behavior* (pp. 151–178). Stanford, CA: Stanford University Press.

Junid, F. B. (2003). *Judging others from nationality and race: Are people intuitive pragmatic politicians?* Unpublished master's thesis. Singapore: Department of Social Work and Psychology, National University of Singapore.

Kelley, H. H. (1972). Attribution in social interaction. In E. E. Jones, D. E. Kanous, H. H., Kelley, R. E. Nisbett, S. Valins, & B. Weiner (Eds.), *Attribution: Perceiving the causes of behavior* (pp. 1–26). Morristown, NJ: General Learning Press.

Kunda, Z. (1999). *Social cognition: Making sense of people.* Cambridge, MA: MIT Press.

Lee, F., Hallahan, M., & Herzong, T. (1996). Explaining real-life events: How culture and domain shape attributions. *Personality and Social Psychology Bulletin, 22*, 732–741.

Lerner, J. S., & Tetlock, P. E. (1999). Accounting for the effects of accountability. *Psychological Bulletin, 125*, 255–275.

Lickel, B., Schmader, T., & Hamilton, D. L. (2003). A case of collective responsibility: Who else was to blame for the Columbia High School shootings? *Personality and Social Psychology Bulletin, 29*, 194–204.

Lim, C. S. M., & Singh, R. (2003). *Protecting values: People as intuitive principled theologians.* Unpublished paper. Singapore: Department of Social Work and Psychology, National University of Singapore.

Menon, T., Morris, M. W., Chiu, C. C., & Hong, Y. Y. (1999). Culture and the construal of agency: Attribution to individual and group dispositions. *Journal of Personality and Social Psychology, 76*, 701–717.

Miller, J. G. (1984). Culture and the development of everyday social explanation. *Journal of Personality and Social Psychology, 46*, 961–978.

Morris, M. W., Menon, T., & Ames, D. R. (2001). Culturally conferred conceptions of agency: A key to social perception of persons, groups, and other actors. *Personality and Social Psychology Review, 5*, 169–182.

Morris, M. W., & Peng, K. (1994). Culture and cause: American and Chinese attributions for social and physical events. *Journal of Personality and Social Psychology, 67*, 949–971.

Nisbett, R. E. (2003). *The geography of thought: How Asians and Westerners think differently . . . and why.* New York: Free Press.

Nisbett, R. E., Peng, K., Choi, I., & Norenzayan, A. (2001). Culture and systems of thought: Holistic versus analytic cognition. *Psychological Review, 108*, 291–310.

Peters, R. S. (1960). *The concept of motivation* (2nd ed.). London: Routledge & Kegan Paul.

Pettigrew, T. F. (1979). The ultimate attribution error: Extending Allport's cognitive analysis of prejudice. *Personality and Social Psychology Bulletin, 5*, 451–476.

Roese, N. J. (1997). Counterfactual thinking. *Psychological Bulletin, 121*, 133–148.

Ross, L. (1977). The intuitive psychologist and his shortcomings: Distortions in the attribution process. In L. Berkowitz (Ed.), *Advances in experimental social psychology* (Vol. 10, pp. 174–220). New York: Academic Press.

Rozin, P. (2003). Five potential principles for understanding cultural differences in relation to individual differences. *Journal of Research in Personality, 37*, 273–283.

Sanchez-Burks, J., Lee, F., Choi, I., Nisbett, R., Zhao, S., & Koo, J. (2003). Conversing across cultures: East–West communications styles in work and nonwork contexts. *Journal of Personality and Social Psychology, 85*, 363–372.

Singh, R., Kaur, J., Ong, P., Ramasamy, M., Chang, A., Chong, D. et al. (2004). *Development of intuitive prosecution: A social-functionalist analysis*. Working Paper No. 80. Singapore: Department of Social Work and Psychology, National University of Singapore.

Singh, R., Lim, H. K., & Tan, S. P. (2005). *Responding to in-group and out-group leaders: Are people intuitive pragmatic politicians?* Unpublished manuscript. Singapore: Department of Social Work and Psychology, National University of Singapore.

Singh, R., Tetlock, P. E., Bell, P. A., Crisp, R., May, J., Tay, A. Y. L. et al. (2003). *Intuitive prudent prosecution of person and group: East–West differences in holistic-analytic thoughts or schema usage?* Working Paper No. 78. Singapore: Department of Social Work and Psychology, National University of Singapore.

Tetlock, P. E. (2000). Cognitive biases and organizational correctives: Do both disease and cure depend on the political beholder? *Administrative Science Quarterly, 45*, 293–326.

Tetlock, P. E. (2002). Social-functionalist frameworks for judgment and choice: The intuitive politician, theologian, and prosecutor. *Psychological Review, 109*, 451–471.

Tetlock, P. E., Kristel, O., Elson, B., Green, M., & Lerner, J. (2000). The psychology of the unthinkable: Taboo trade-offs, forbidden base rates, and heretical counter-factuals. *Journal of Personality and Social Psychology, 78*, 853–870.

Tetlock, P. E., Skitka, L., & Boettger, R. (1989). Social and cognitive strategies for coping with accountability: Conformity, complexity, and bolstering. *Journal of Personality and Social Psychology, 57*, 632–640.

Tetlock, P. E., Visser, P., Singh, R., Polifroini, M. Scott, A., Elson, B. et al. (2006). People as intuitive prosecutors: The impact of social-control goals on punitiveness and attributions of responsibility. Submitted for publication.

18 Culture and psychology: A SWOT analysis of cross-cultural psychology

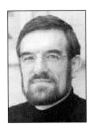

Fons J. R. van de Vijver

The current paper attempts to provide a SWOT analysis of cross-cultural psychology. A SWOT analysis (acronym for an analysis of Strengths, Weaknesses, Opportunities, and Threats) is a well-known management tool to gain insight into, among other things, the current state of an organization, initiative or field.

The history of cross-cultural psychology as an empirical endeavor is relatively short. With some alleged arbitrariness, it could be argued that the field has grown with the strong interest in visual illusions (Segall, Campbell, & Herskovits, 1966), field independence (Berry 1976), and Piagetian psychology, notably the cross-cultural study of conservation (e.g., Dasen, 1972). Since those days thousands of studies have been published. At least two different kinds of factors have contributed to this growth. The first was the scientific success of the field. The cross-cultural studies of visual illusions provide a strong demonstration of the pervasive influence of culture on perception as well as a theoretical framework to understand the cross-cultural patterning of the differences. A similar argument holds for cross-cultural studies of field independence and conservation. These studies showed clear cross-cultural differences and demonstrated convincingly that Western data and theories apparently neglected the cultural factor. The second and independently contributing force was formed by the processes of migration and globalization. Cross-cultural encounters became more common, businesses discovered that good managers in the home office were not always the successful managers when they were sent to a foreign branch; classrooms became multicultural. In short, societies were confronted with new problems, which were studied in cross-cultural psychology.

The following sections describe the main strengths, weaknesses, opportunities, and threats of cross-cultural psychology. Each of these aspects is illustrated. Instead of giving an overview of all pertinent, major research initiatives (which would be beyond the scope of this work), exemplars are chosen, which are described in more detail in order to highlight their relevance to the current chapter. The final sections describe recommended areas of growth and draw conclusions.

Strengths: Interest in cross-cultural differences and similarities

In order to gain insight in trends in cross-cultural psychology an analysis was carried out of the publications dealing with this topic in PsycInfo. Starting in 1978 and ending in 2003, every five years the number of cross-cultural publications was determined using *(cross-cultural in de or ethnic in de or accult* in de) and py = 1978* as the instruction. The results are presented in Figure 18.1. In the top panel it can be seen that the number of publications has increased dramatically over these 25 years (from 557 to 1398). As this change

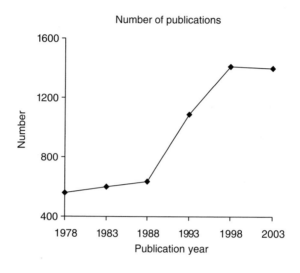

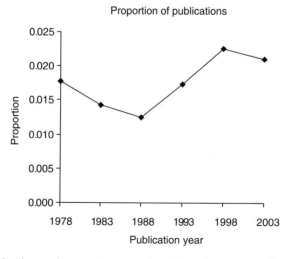

Figure 18.1 Number and proportion of publications about cross-cultural and ethnic issues from 1978 to 2003.

is also a reflection of the overall increase in the number of publications in psychology (and in PsycInfo), the proportion of studies dealing with cross-cultural issues was also computed. The bottom panel of Figure 18.1 provides an overview. The proportion of publications dealing with cross-cultural issues shows an increase over time, although the trend is less spectacular than for the number of publications. It can be concluded that one of strongholds of cross-cultural psychology is the widely shared interest in its object of study. It is very difficult to extrapolate the current trend and to foresee the developments in psychology; yet, the globalization and international migration, which undoubtedly have contributed to the growth in scientific interest, are very likely to continue in the foreseeable future. Therefore, attention and resources for the topic will continue for at least some time.

Weaknesses: Biases in the field

It is argued here that the main weaknesses of cross-cultural psychology are the field's conceptual biases. The first one is the focus on cross-cultural differences at the neglect of similarities; cross-cultural psychology is remarkably poor at striking a balance between similarities and differences. The second one refers to a problem that is inherited from mainstream psychology: cross-cultural psychology has not been successful in overcoming the dualism of individual and culture. It appears to be difficult to develop theories and carry out studies that deal with the interface of individual and cultural factors. The two biases are now explored in more detail.

Brouwers, Van Hemert, Breugelmans, and Van de Vijver (2004) carried out a content analysis of the first 35 volumes (starting from 1970) of the *Journal of Cross-Cultural Psychology*. From the 1150 available articles a random sample of 200 was drawn. Various characteristics were rated. The first analysis involved the domain of the studies. A classification was used that was developed by Poortinga and Van de Vijver (Poortinga, Kop, & Van de Vijver, 1990; Van de Vijver & Poortinga, 1990), which distinguishes between the psychophysi(ologi)cal, perceptual, cognitive, personality, and social domains. The authors also coded whether cross-cultural differences or similarities were expected using some theoretical framework (such as individualism–collectivism) and whether authors explained cross-cultural similarities or differences by substantive factors (genetic, ecological, ecocultural, or sociocultural) or by methodological factors (bias or the design of the study). An overview of the latter is given in Figure 18.2. Cross-cultural psychology has always shown a strong interest in the social domain; about two-thirds of all cross-cultural studies published in the *Journal of Cross-Cultural Psychology* deal with a topic from this domain.

An analysis of trends showed a shift in topics of the published studies. In the early days of the journal there was relatively more interest in perceptual and cognitive topics (such as Piagetian conservation, visual illusions, and cognitive style), while nowadays there is more emphasis on the social domain.

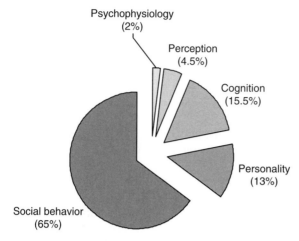

Figure 18.2 Proportion of studies in 35 volumes of the *Journal of Cross-Cultural Psychology* per domain.

Moreover, more recent studies tend to be less exploratory and more hypothesis testing, to use self-reports (the common data collection method in social psychology), and to more explicitly motivate the choice of cultures. This trend reflects a broad change from skill-based tests administered in the First and Third World to social-psychological studies in which the USA and Japan are compared on some psychological characteristics such as the independent and interdependent self (the comparison between the USA and Japan is the one most frequently found in the *Journal of Cross-Cultural Psychology*). The shift in focus in the 35 volumes towards social behavior can be seen as both a weakness and a strength of cross-cultural psychology. It constitutes a weakness in that in the study of cross-cultural similarities and differences, social behavior constitutes one domain, next to several others that are as relevant as social behavior for cross-cultural psychology. The strength of the focus on social behavior is its influence on mainstream psychology. The relevance of a cross-cultural perspective is probably more widely accepted in mainstream social psychology than in other fields of psychology.

Another analysis involved the success with which authors predicted the occurrence of cross-cultural differences and similarities. This analysis involved the set of 89 studies in which hypotheses about similarities and differences were specified. Table 18.1 presents the relationship between expected and obtained results. Two findings emerge from the table. The first is that only in 58% of the studies' expectations were borne out. The second and more important finding involves the patterning of the remaining 42%. In nearly all studies the same problem occurred: expected differences were not found. The reverse error (similarities were expected while differences were found) almost never occurred. Two reasons can be envisaged why more similarities are found than expected. The first is methodological; significant

Table 18.1 Relationship between expected and obtained findings in studies published in the *Journal of Cross-Cultural Psychology*

	Found differences	*Found both similarities and differences*
Expected differences	28%	41%
Expected similarities and differences	1%	30%

Note: The numbers in the cells refer to the proportion of studies pertaining to the category; for example, in 28% of the sample of 200 studies authors expected and found cross-cultural differences.

differences in the population may lead to nonsignificant observed differences when working with small samples or with instruments with a low reliability. However, because of the pervasiveness of the error methodological issues are unlikely to be the only problem. It is more likely that the error points to the presence of a strong bias in the field towards the observation of cross-cultural differences; cross-cultural psychology is "difference focused" (see Van de Vijver & Leung, 2000). Cross-cultural psychology owes its existence to the presence of cross-cultural differences. The focus on differences could well be so engrained that we find it difficult to strike a balance between similarities and differences.

There may have been a need to document the presence of cross-cultural differences in some psychological functioning in the early days of cross-cultural psychology. However, it is safe to conclude after 40 years of empirical cross-cultural psychology that the field has identified so many cross-cultural differences that we need to abandon the implicit agenda; the one-sided focus on differences can easily become counterproductive. It could even be argued that fields like cognitive testing have found so many significant differences that similarities of scores obtained in groups with a widely different cultural background are more informative than differences. In summary, a balanced treatment of similarities and differences is necessary in cross-cultural psychology in order for it to mature as a science.

Opportunities: overcoming the duality of individual and culture

It is in the nature of studies in cross-cultural psychology to have both individual- and culture-level variables included in a research design. The former are usually scores derived from some psychological instrument. The emphasis in psychology on good measurement properties (reliability and validity) is also present in cross-cultural psychology. However, the strict measurement criteria are often less applied to culture-level factors. The variability in kind and quality of culture-level variables is considerable. In so-called psychological differences studies (Van de Vijver & Leung, 1997) an instrument is administered to individuals from various cultural groups in an exploratory way. Because of the absence of a theoretically guided search, culture is then treated as a nominal-level variable. Other studies use country-level information that is more precise, specific, and metric. These data are often obtained from the literature (Hofstede's, 2001, work is often used) or public sources on the Internet (such as GDP figures from www.worldbank.org). This country-level information is often correlated with psychological variables. In still other studies cultural information is derived from individual scores. For example, individuals are asked to report on norms in their environment. These scores can be used at individual level or, when aggregated across all participants, at culture level.

Despite the availability of theoretical models to link cultural and individual factors such as the ecocultural framework (Berry, Poortinga, Segall, & Dasen, 2002), the link between the two levels of variables is usually weak in empirical studies. Finding that cultures differ with regard to some target variable does not yet explain the mechanisms behind the difference. It could indeed be argued that our focus on experimental designs with analysis of variance or *t*-tests as the statistical procedure to test the significance of cross-cultural differences has not been conducive to linking individual and cultural factors.

Let us take a look at a hypothetical study to examine how the individual–culture relationship often takes shape in cross-cultural studies. It is popular nowadays to study psychological differences of individualist and collectivist countries. Suppose that we are interested in independent and interdependent self-construals (Markus & Kitayama, 1991) in an Eastern and a Western culture and administer Singelis's (1994) scale to measure these concepts. Furthermore, suppose that we find the expected differences and that independent self-construals are higher in the Western country and the interdependent self-construals in the Eastern country. The study seemingly supports the theory that the differences in self-construal are due to individualism–collectivism differences of the countries.

Is this conclusion methodologically compelling? Clearly not. Donald Campbell has repeatedly argued that comparisons based on two countries are difficult to interpret, because they are open to multiple interpretations (see Berry et al., 2002). In our example confounding sample differences could be age, gender, socioeconomic status, and education. Concurrent country differences could also challenge our interpretation. Since no information about confounding variables is available in our study, the link between self-construals and individualism–collectivism can only be based on a big inferential leap. The reasoning shows a methodological loophole that threatens many cross-cultural studies: alternative interpretations are not included in the design. When concurrent explanations have been measured (such as religiosity and social desirability), it becomes possible to bolster findings against alternative interpretations. It can be concluded that our hypothetical study cannot establish a close link between individual and culture.

In the next sections three methodologically based tools are presented, which in combination with appropriate theorizing can establish firm links between individual and cultural factors.

Use of mediation and moderation models

Since the publication of the paper by Baron and Kenny in 1986, the interest in mediation and moderation has grown considerably in psychology. The underlying conceptual scheme, presented in Figure 18.3, is relevant to cross-cultural psychology, because it provides a template to link individual and cultural variables. The intervening variable (the box with the letter M in the Figure) defines the link. M is moderating the relationship between the cultural factor (C in Figure 18.3) and the individual-level outcome (I in Figure 18.3), if all three effects (x, y, and z) are significant; if x and y are significant while z is not significant, M mediates the relationship. Moderation means that culture has both a direct and an indirect effect. For example, individualism–collectivism (C) may have an influence on conformity (I) (Bond & Smith, 1996), individualism–collectivism may influence social desirability (M) which in turn may influence conformity, a negative influence on self-esteem. If all relations were to be positive and significant, we would have a relation between individualism–collectivism and conformity that is strengthened by social desirability. Alternatively, suppose that the introduction of social desirability renders the direct relationship (i.e., path coefficient) between individualism–collectivism and conformity nonsignificant. In that case the relationship between the latter two can be entirely accounted for by social desirability, which means that social desirability mediates the relationship. It may be noted that the three variables have to be measured at individual level (so, an individual-level measure of individualism–collectivism has been administered) or at country level (in which case many countries are needed).

The C–M–I scheme is popular in acculturation research (e.g., Ward, Bochner, & Furnham, 2001). The three aspects refer to background conditions (such as the presence of institutions for the ethnic group), acculturation orientations and adjustment outcomes (such as stress, mental health, and proficiency in the majority language, respectively). A recent example can be found in a study by Ait-Ouarasse and Van de Vijver (2004). The influence of the perceived acculturation context of young Moroccan Dutch adults (C)

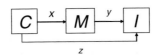

Figure 18.3 Conceptual scheme of a mediation and moderation relationship.
Note: C = culture or a cultural factor; M = mediating or moderating variable; I = individual outcome variable (e.g., psychological test score); x, y, and z denote effects. M moderates the effect of C on I if x, y, and z differ from zero. M mediates the effect of C on I if x and y differ from zero, while $z = 0$.

on their contacts with Moroccan conationals and Dutch majority group members (*M*) and on school success, work success, and stress (*I*) was tested. The authors tested the appropriateness of a moderation scheme. They found that the background as perceived by the immigrants was split up into four relatively independent factors: integration by the mainstream (focus on the development of a bicultural identity), tolerance by the mainstream, permissiveness of the Moroccan community to adjustment, and the vitality of the Moroccan community. The path diagram (which showed a good fit) is shown in Figure 18.4. As can be seen in the figure, a moderating relationship was supported. The background had both a direct and an indirect influence on the outcome variables. The perceived home background factors showed stronger relationships with school success, while the mainstream context mainly influenced school success.

Mediating and moderating variables referred to focal explanations (such as social contacts) in the previous acculturation study. Mediating and moderating variables can also refer to nuisance variables, which inadvertently have not been controlled in experiments. Statistical tools are then needed to eliminate the influence of variables that ideally should have been included in the design as a variable that was controlled by randomization or matching across conditions (such as social desirability in the above example). Both when used as focal and nuisance factors, mediating and moderating variables provide a conceptually vital link between distal (cultural) and proximal (individual) variables. These are the very mechanisms that are needed in cross-cultural psychology to overcome the dualism between individual and cultural factors.

Use of models of psychological variables at country level

In cross-cultural psychology there is a growing interest in the study of psychological constructs at country level. Studies of values (Schwartz, 1992) and personality (McCrae & Allik, 2002) are good examples of this trend. The interest in the study of personality at cultural level has a long history. In the 1920s there was a huge interest in psychodynamic theories, which were broader than psychiatry and clinical psychology. Many important anthropologists of those days found that psychodynamic theory was the first scientific theory of the human psyche that could help them to understand the psyche of non-Western people. The application of psychodynamic theories to the characterization of the modal personality of cultures became very popular (a good overview can be found in Bock, 1988; see also Piker, 1998). Initially dubbed culture-and-personality, the approach became known later as psychological anthropology. The enthusiasm for the approach has never spread to cross-cultural psychology. Scientists (like most cross-cultural psychologists) who are trained in a positivist tradition and have solid measurement as one of their canons do not tend to feel attached to the studies and conclusions of psychological anthropology, which often have a shallow empirical basis in positivist eyes.

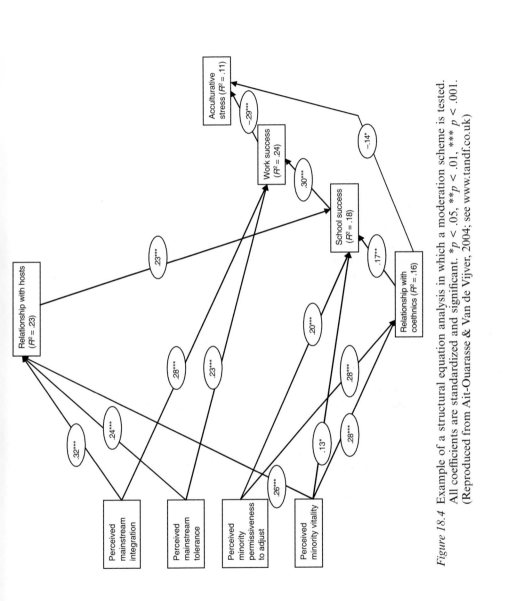

Figure 18.4 Example of a structural equation analysis in which a moderation scheme is tested. All coefficients are standardized and significant. *$p < .05$, **$p < .01$, ***$p < .001$. (Reproduced from Ait-Ouarasse & Van de Vijver, 2004; see www.tandf.co.uk)

In recent years the issue of the personality of a culture has received attention from cross-cultural psychology. Remarkably, there are no references to its intellectual ancestors. This absence may be due to the completely different background from which the interest emerges. Like psychological anthropology, the new studies start from a psychological model (such as the five-factor model of personality). The remainder of this section illustrates issues that have been addressed in recent studies of personality at country level.

The first question involves multilevel equivalence: Do individual and country scores have the same meaning (Muthén, 1994; Van de Vijver & Poortinga, 2002a)? If a Big-Five inventory is administered to different persons, we take it for granted that individual differences in scores reflect underlying differences in the factors of the Big Five. Similarly, a country comparison of scores on the Big Five should ideally reflect differences in these factors. How can we be sure that differences in mean Big-Five scores of two countries reflect the intended five factors and nothing but these factors? Do personality factors apply at country level? The authors argue that factors have the same meaning at individual and country level if the factor structures are identical at both levels. An instrument shows multilevel equivalence if it measures the same construct(s) at each level. In operational terms it means that we consider two data matrices: individual-level data (from which cross-cultural differences in score levels have been eliminated) and country-level data (in which each country is represented by a single row in the data matrix, which requires data sets involving many countries). The similarity of structure across levels is not a foregone conclusion. Both substantive and methodological reasons may create a difference. Examples of the latter are response tendencies (which are stronger in one country than in another) and inadequate items or scales (which could make the factor structure at individual and country level different).

A few studies have addressed the similarity of psychological instruments at individual and country level. McCrae (2002) found that the Big Five structure applies to both levels. This implies that the Big Five factors are equally appropriate to describe individual and country differences. Van de Vijver and Watkins (2006) administered the ASSEI, a self-esteem questionnaire to measure the independent and interdependent self, in 19 countries. A two-factor solution based on factors interpreted as representing the independent and interdependent self was highly similar at individual and country level, supporting the structural equivalence. Interestingly, the expected and obtained structure deviated at both levels in the same way from expectation. The independent self involved both intrapersonal and interpersonal skills, while the interdependent self was narrowed down to unselfishness and being a good member of the family, community, and society. It was found that these independence and interdependence factors have the same meaning at individual and country level.

The second question in the study of personality at country level involves the "geography of personality": what does a map of the world look like if personality factors are used to define the dimensions instead of altitude and latitude? One of the 2004 issues of the *Journal of Cross-Cultural Psychology* contained a number of contributions on multilevel issues. In one of these Allik and McCrae (2004) used scores on the Big Five to design a two-dimensional map of 36 cultures. The result of their multidimensional scaling is given in Figure 18.5. The horizontal dimension is mainly a split of European and American cultures (positive scores) and Asian and African cultures (negative scores). The vertical dimension is more difficult to interpret. Furthermore, the figure makes a fairly clear split in religious denominations. The upper right quadrant mainly contains Roman Catholic countries, the lower right quadrant Protestant countries, the lower left quadrant Muslim, and the upper left quadrant the Hindu and Buddhist countries. In order to see to what kind of patterning the Eysenck Personality Questionnaire would yield, the country-level data collected by Van Hemert, Van de Vijver, Poortinga,

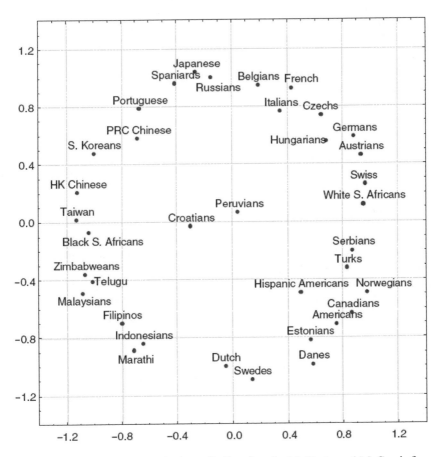

Figure 18.5 The "geography of personality" as found with Costa and McCrae's five-factor model (reproduced from Allik & McCrae, 2004).

and Georgas (2002) were reanalyzed. A factor analysis of the four scales (Extraversion, Psychoticism, Neuroticism, and Lie Scale/Social Desirability) was carried out for 38 countries. Although it could be argued that a sample of 38 observations is not sufficient for a factor analysis, it may be noted that the ratio of observations to input variables is acceptable (viz. 9.5:1) and that country-level data tend to be very stable. Based on a scree plot, two factors were extracted, which together explained 66.4% of the variance. The factor loadings are given in Table 18.2. The horizontal dimension was bipolar with social desirability at the negative end and extraversion at the positive end. The vertical dimension was unipolar and showed high loadings for psychoticism and neuroticism. Positive scores on the horizontal dimension seem to reflect aspects of personality that are typically positively valued in Western cultures (high scores refer to extraversion and low scores to social desirability), while the vertical dimension refers to the negative aspects.

The factor loadings of Table 18.2 and the multidimensional scaling solution of Figure 18.5 are based on arbitrary rotations. In order to compare the solutions a target rotation should be carried out in order to maximize the agreement. This was not done as the number of countries that are present in both data sets is limited, which would challenge the cross-sample stability of the results. Furthermore, the need was more apparent than real, as the next analysis shows. Table 18.3 presents correlations between Eysenck's

Table 18.2 Factor loadings in country-level analysis of Eysenck's scales (varimax rotated)

Scale	Horizontal dimension	Vertical dimension
Psychoticism	−.10	.80
Neuroticism	.05	.81
Extraversion	.71	−.34
Lie/Social Desirability	−.83	−.20

Table 18.3 Country correlations of Hofstede's (2001) dimensions and gross national product with the two country dimensions found with Eysenck's personality scales and the five-factor model

	Eysenck		Allik & McCrae	
	Horizontal	Vertical	Horizontal	Vertical
Individualism	.75**	−.16	.78**	−.35
Masculinity	−.18	.63**	−.18	.64*
Power Distance	−.61**	.42	−.71**	.38
Uncertainty Avoidance	.17	.35	.20	.82**
Gross National Product	.61**	.11	.60**	−.22

$*p < .05; **p < .01.$

dimensions and Allik and McCrae's (2004) dimensions on the one hand and the four Hofstede dimensions (Individualism, Masculinity, Power Distance, and Uncertainty Avoidance) and Gross National Product on the other hand. The patterning of the correlations is remarkably similar. The horizontal dimension shows positive and significant correlations with Individualism and Gross National Product and a significant, negative correlation with Power Distance. In both data sets the vertical dimension shows a positive correlation with Masculinity; however, Uncertainty Avoidance is strongly correlated with the vertical dimension in the data set by Allik and McCrae while a positive, though nonsignificant correlation was found in the Eysenck data set.

Social desirability defined one end of the horizontal dimension. The presence of this variable complicates the interpretation of the dimension. There is a discussion in the literature about whether social desirability is a stable personality trait that is related to agreeableness and conformity (McCrae & Costa, 1983) or a face-saving mechanism that threatens the validity of measures of personality dimensions (as found in Eysenck's work). There is evidence in favor of both interpretations. In a meta-analysis of studies employing Asch's paradigm, Bond and Smith (1996) concluded that "collectivist countries tended to show higher levels of conformity than individualist countries" (p. 111), which is in line with the first interpretation, while the significant correlation between Gross National Product and the Lie Scale, reported by Van Hemert et al. (2002), supports the second interpretation. Current country-level data cannot tell the interpretations apart. As a consequence, it is not clear to what extent country differences on the first dimension are influenced by differences in response styles. Smith (2004) compared acquiescence and social desirability (Lie Scale) across a number of large crosscultural studies and found positive correlations between the response style indicators. It is clear that response tendencies are stable country characteristics that require further scrutiny in order to clarify their nature further.

It can be tentatively concluded that two widely used instruments show important, though incompletely overlapping, information about the "geography of personality". One dimension involves aspects of personality that are typically seen as negative (such as neuroticism) and which are essentially unrelated to other country characteristics. The other dimension involves the personality aspects such as extraversion, which are valued in Western countries and which, probably not surprisingly, show relationships with affluence. The latter dimension might involve both "style and substance".

Use of multilevel models

In the literature the term "multilevel modeling" refers to a set of statistical techniques developed since the 1980s (Bryk & Raudenbush, 1992; Goldstein, 2003). The techniques are relevant to cross-cultural psychology as they address the study of phenomena at different levels of aggregation. Suppose that we are interested in individual and cross-cultural differences in social desirability scores and that we administer a social desirability questionnaire in various countries. Suppose, furthermore, that data are also obtained about presumably relevant predictors both at individual level (e.g., conformity and education) and country level (e.g., Gross National Product). Multilevel modeling allows us to address two kinds of questions. The first involves the proportion of variance accounted for by individual and country level. The second involves the role of individual- and country-level predictors. Whereas classical regression models would treat the individual and country variation in separate analyses, multilevel models enable a joint analysis of both levels, addressing the relevance of predictors at both levels as well as the interaction of these levels.

An example can be found in a study on cross-cultural differences in inductive reasoning of primary and secondary school pupils from Zambia, Turkey, and the Netherlands (Van de Vijver & Brouwers, 2006; see also Van de Vijver, 2002). Examples of items of the two tests that were administered are given in Figure 18.6. In Inductive Reasoning Figures the first eight figures in each row are identical while the final four are different. In one of the five rows the final four are a valid continuation of the first eight. In the test instruction the pupils were told what made a continuation valid. The item of Figure 18.6 consists of sets of four figures in which subsequent figures in a set contain one element more than the previous one. This rule is consistently applied only

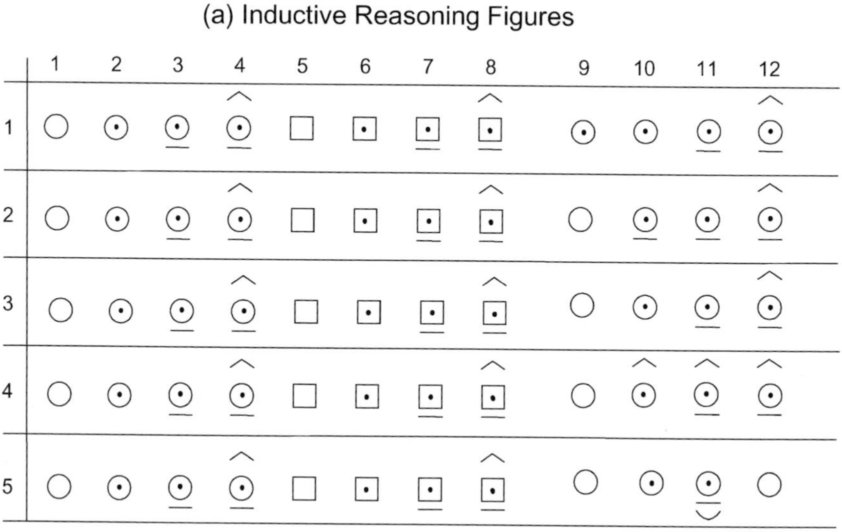

(a) Inductive Reasoning Figures

(b) Inductive Reasoning Letters

| BBBBBB | LLLLLL | JJJJJJ | PPPPPP | ZZZTZZ |

Figure 18.6 Examples of inductive reasoning items.

in the third row (which makes "Row 3" the correct answer). In Inductive Reasoning Letters the pupils had to indicate the "odd one out" (i.e., to mark the group of letters that did not follow the rule of the other items). As all boxes contain only identical letters except for the final box, "the last box" is the right answer. Information was also collected about school quality indicators, such as number of learning books in the school.

The first question addressed the relative proportions of variance at country ($N = 3$), school ($N = 38$), and individual ($N = 2213$) level. It was found that these sources explained 12%, 21%, and 67% of the variation, respectively. So, lower levels of aggregation explained more variation. However, even at country level 12% of the variation is explained, which according to Cohen (1988) constitutes a large effect size. Scores of Zambian pupils were the lowest, followed by the Turkish pupils, while the highest scores were obtained by the Dutch pupils.

The second analysis involved the prediction of scores at individual and school level (country was left out as a separate level because of the small number of countries involved). A socioeconomic status indicator was used at individual level, which was based on the number of siblings, parental educational level, father's professional level, and the number of books at home (these variables were found to load on a single factor). School quality was measured by a combination of the number of pupils per teacher, number of books in the library, number of textbooks per pupil, average age of teachers, and average educational level of the teachers (which yielded a single factor). Three predictors were used, namely pupil's socioeconomic status at individual-level, the "school's socioeconomic status" (the school means of the pupils' socioeconomic status scores), and school quality.

A first analysis examined whether the predictors were fixed or random. A predictor is fixed if its intercept varies across all individuals (or schools) while its regression coefficient is identical. In a random model the regression coefficient differs across individuals (or schools). A good fit was found for a model in which pupils' socioeconomic status and school quality had fixed effects, while the school's socioeconomic status had a random effect. Pupil-level socioeconomic status was found not to contribute much to the score variation; the school's socioeconomic status and school quality were more powerful predictors. The regression model explained 87% of the variation at school level and 85% at country level. The influence of the predictors went in the expected direction, with higher socioeconomic status and school quality being associated with higher inductive reasoning scores. The relatively small influence of socioeconomic status at individual level might seem unexpected. It is a probably a consequence of the fairly large cross-cultural differences in this variable (the Zambian pupils obtained the lowest and the Dutch the highest scores) as well as the considerable within-country variation in Zambia. As a consequence, the major differences in scores at school and country level were better picked up by the predictors at school level.

The example shows that multilevel models allow us to compare different levels of aggregation in great detail, thereby bringing individual and culture much closer to each other than can be achieved in classical regression models, which consider individual- and country-level variation in separate analyses. Multilevel models help to narrow the gap between individual and cultural factors.

Threats: Long-term viability of cross-cultural psychology

In the last 30 to 40 years cross-cultural psychology has grown and flourished. However, at some point in the future the growth will stop and the interest may even decrease. What can be said about the long-term viability of the field? The chapter is based on a concern about the long-term viability of cross-cultural psychology as a science. At least four long-term scenarios of cross-cultural psychology can be envisaged (apart from continuation of current practice). The first would be when the major goals of cross-cultural psychology have been achieved. This would be the case when new theories and models have been developed with cultural variations fully integrated in them and when it becomes routine practice to test new theories in a cross-cultural context. Walter Lonner calls this the "death wish of cross-cultural psychology." When the "cultural factor" is fully integrated in psychology, there is no need for cross-cultural psychology as a separate discipline.

The second scenario would occur if mainstream psychology lost interest in cross-cultural issues and worked with theories and models that were parochial from a cross-cultural perspective. Such a situation would be more likely to arise if cross-cultural psychology did not have much to offer to mainstream psychology. If cross-cultural psychology was not able to generate valuable insights that matter in mainstream psychology, it would become theoretically sterile, self-centered in its research, and eventually would eradicate itself. It seems to me that the long-term viability of cross-cultural psychology as a science is best ensured by making a lasting contribution to theory formation in psychology.

The third scenario is related to globalization. Some of the globalization literature seems to be based on the assumption that cross-cultural differences will vanish as a result of the globalizing economy. In my view globalization will not have the pervasive impact on existing cultures that is sometimes ascribed to it. Indeed, globalization is often accompanied by opposite developments at national and regional level in which more room is left for local cultures; so, globalization seems to generate its own counterforces. There is no reason in my view to expect cross-cultural differences to decrease substantially in the foreseeable future.

In a final scenario the field of cross-cultural psychology will eventually vanish because the study of cross-cultural differences and similarities will be taken over by new fields with their own orientations and approaches. Some would like to argue that the fields of cultural psychology (e.g., Miller, 1997) and indigenous psychology (Sinha, 1997) are heirs to the cross-cultural throne. Compared to cross-cultural psychology the latter fields are less comparative and borrow more from ethnography, combining it with a more culture-specific perspective. However, compared to ethnography, these new fields employ more psychological theories and assessment models. In my view these new fields are compatible (and hardly competing) with a more comparative approach in psychology (contrary to what is sometimes claimed, e.g., Greenfield, 1997), as they are well positioned to study cultural specifics in human functioning (Van de Vijver & Poortinga, 2002b). It is unlikely in my view that a field of study that emphasizes cultural specifics takes over cross-cultural psychology, in which there is more emphasis on the building of comparative models. Obviously, it is impossible to predict whether new developments in psychology, which are better able to understand human–culture interactions than cross-cultural psychology does, will not take over the latter field.

Where can the field of cross-cultural psychology grow?

The question of whether cross-cultural psychology can retain its level of interest is difficult to answer in general terms. However, it is quite possible to delineate factors that can be expected to contribute to the generation of new insights and, hence, to the long-term interest and viability of the field (see Van de Vijver & Leung, 2000). The first set of factors is related to the implicit biases of the field, described before. In order to mature as a science, we should critically evaluate and abandon our implicit biases. A first bias involves our focus on cross-cultural differences; we need to consider both cross-cultural similarities and differences. In our studies we should be more geared to a balanced treatment of similarities and differences, both in our theories and methods. Another bias involves our emphasis on documenting cross-cultural differences; we need to shift from documenting to explaining cross-cultural differences (and similarities). We should become increasingly critical of studies in which cross-cultural differences are merely reported and only post hoc interpretations of these differences are offered.

The long-term viability of cross-cultural psychology will also be served by an increasing sophistication in its theories, data collection, and data analysis methods. The current chapter has proposed various methodological tools in which the dualism between individual and culture can be reduced or even overcome, such as the usage of moderation and interaction models.

The above points can be summarized as pointing to the need for a change in basic attitudes toward cross-cultural studies. Trained as psychologists, we are often inclined to focus on individual-level differences; however, in cross-cultural psychology individual differences are often used to understand differences and similarities at cultural level. We need to "enrich" our models and designs in ways described before so as to better cover both individual and cultural differences.

Conclusion

We live in an era of cross-cultural encounters. Migration and globalization make their mark on many societies. These developments influence psychology; the number of cross-cultural studies continues to increase. It is argued here that in order to make a lasting influence on psychology, cross-cultural psychology should make substantive contributions to the larger field of psychology. Cross-cultural psychology focuses on the interplay of individual and culture. However, in our studies we tend to focus on psychological factors. Many cross-cultural studies are more advanced in their psychological component than in their cultural component. Bringing together individual and cultural factors in single theoretical models is a major challenge for the coming period. It is my contention that cross-cultural psychology will be more successful and innovative when it can bring individual and cultural determinants of individual behavior closer to each other. This chapter has described and illustrated three methodological tools that can be employed to overcome the traditional dualism of individual and cultural factors, namely mediator and moderator models, psychological variables at country level, and multilevel models. These three tools are not meant to constitute an exhaustive list, but merely to illustrate a way of thinking about cross-cultural studies. In the early days we were interested in documenting cross-cultural differences as they legitimized our endeavors. We have moved beyond that stage, we now have to deal with a whole new set of issues such as the patterning and explanation of cross-cultural differences. In order to successfully address these issues we need to broaden our psychological scope and to focus more on the interface of individual and culture. An additional advantage of this broadened scope will be the increased relevance of cross-cultural psychology to related disciplines such as ethnography and sociology, which also deal with the individual–culture interface.

References

Ait-Ouarasse, O., & Van de Vijver, F. J. R. (2004). Structure and function of the perceived acculturation context of young Moroccans in the Netherlands. *International Journal of Psychology*, *39*, 190–204.

Allik, J., & McCrae, R. R. (2004). Toward a geography of personality traits: Patterns of profiles across 36 cultures. *Journal of Cross-Cultural Psychology*, *35*, 13–28.

Baron, R. M., & Kenny, D. A. (1986). The moderator–mediator variable distinction in social psychological research: Conceptual, strategic and statistical considerations. *Journal of Personality and Social Psychology*, *51*, 1173–1182.

Berry, J. W. (1976). *Human ecology and cognitive style. Comparative studies in cultural and psychological adaptation*. Beverly Hills, CA: Sage.

Berry, J. W., Poortinga, Y. H., Segall, M. H., & Dasen, P. R. (2002). *Cross-cultural psychology. Research and applications* (2nd ed.). New York: Cambridge University Press.

Bock, P. K. (1988). *Rethinking psychological anthropology: Continuity and change in the study of human action*. New York: Freeman.

Bond, R., & Smith, P. B. (1996). Culture and conformity: A meta-analysis of studies using Asch's (1952b, 1956) Line Judgment Task. *Psychological Bulletin, 119*, 111–137.

Brouwers, S. A., Van Hemert, D. A., Breugelmans, S. M., & Van de Vijver, F. J. R. (2004). A historical analysis of empirical studies published in the Journal of Cross-Cultural Psychology. *Journal of Cross-Cultural Psychology, 35*, 251–262.

Bryk, A. S., & Raudenbush, S. W. (1992). *Hierarchical linear models: Applications and data analysis*. Newbury Park, CA: Sage.

Cohen, J. (1988). *Statistical power analysis for the behavioral sciences* (2nd ed.). Hillsdale, NJ: Lawrence Erlbaum Associates, Inc.

Dasen, P. R. (1972). Cross-cultural Piagetian research: A summary. *Journal of Cross-Cultural Psychology, 3*, 23–39.

Goldstein, H. (2003). *Multilevel statistical models*. London: Arnold.

Greenfield, P. M. (1997). You can't take it with you: Why ability assessments don't cross cultures. *American Psychologist, 52*, 1115–1124.

Hofstede, G. (2001). *Culture's consequences* (2nd ed.). Newbury Park, CA: Sage.

Markus, H. R., & Kitayama, S. (1991). Culture and the self: Implications for cognition, emotion, and motivation. *Psychological Review, 98*, 224–253.

McCrae, R. R. (2002). NEO-PI-R from 36 cultures: Further intercultural comparisons. In A. J. Marsella (Series Ed.), R. R. McCrae & J. Allik (Eds.), *The five-factor model across cultures* (pp. 105–125). New York: Kluwer Academic/Plenum Publishers.

McCrae, R. R., & Allik, J. (Eds.). (2002). *The five-factor model across cultures*. New York: Kluwer Academic/Plenum Publishers.

McCrae, R. R., & Costa, P. T. (1983). Social desirability scales: More substance than style. *Journal of Consulting and Clinical Psychology, 51*, 882–888.

Miller, J. G. (1997). Theoretical issues in cultural psychology. In J. W. Berry, Y. H. Poortinga, & J. Pandey (Eds.), *Handbook of cross-cultural psychology* (2nd ed., Vol. 1, pp. 85–128). Boston: Allyn & Bacon.

Muthén, B. O. (1994). Multilevel covariance structure analysis. *Sociological Methods & Research, 22*, 376–398.

Piker, S. (1998). Contributions of psychological anthropology. *Journal of Cross-Cultural Psychology, 29*, 9–31.

Poortinga, Y. H., Kop, P. F. M., & Van de Vijver, F. J. R. (1990). Differences between psychological domains in the range of cross-cultural variation. In P. J. D. Drenth, J. A. Sergeant, & R. J. Takens (Eds.), *European perspectives in psychology* (Vol. 3, pp. 355–376). Chichester, UK: Wiley.

Schwartz, S. H. (1992). Universals in the content and structure of values: Theoretical advances and empirical tests in 20 countries. In M. Zanna (Ed.), *Advances in experimental social psychology* (Vol. 25, pp. 1–65). Orlando, FL: Academic Press.

Segall, M. H., Campbell, D. T., & Herskovits, M. J. (1966). *The influence of culture on visual perception*. Indianapolis, IN: Bobbs-Merrill.

Singelis, T. (1994). The measurement of independent and interdependent self-construals. *Personality and Social Psychology Bulletin, 20*, 580–591.

Sinha, D. (1997). Indigenizing psychology. In J. W. Berry, Y. H. Poortinga, & J. Pandey (Eds.), *Handbook of cross-cultural psychology* (2nd ed., Vol. 1, pp. 131–169). Boston: Allyn & Bacon.

Smith, P. B. (2004). Acquiescent response bias as an aspect of cultural communication style. *Journal of Cross-Cultural Psychology, 35*, 50–61.

Van de Vijver, F. J. R. (2002). Inductive reasoning in Zambia, Turkey, and the Netherlands: Establishing cross-cultural equivalence. *Intelligence, 30,* 313–351.

Van de Vijver, F. J. R., & Brouwers, S. A. (2006). *Inductive reasoning across cultures: A multilevel analysis.* (In preparation)

Van de Vijver, F. J. R., & Leung, K. (1997). *Methods and data analysis for cross-cultural research.* Newbury Park, CA: Sage.

Van de Vijver, F. J. R., & Leung, K. (2000). Methodological issues in psychological research on culture. *Journal of Cross-Cultural Psychology, 31,* 33–51.

Van de Vijver, F. J. R., & Poortinga, Y. H. (1990). A taxonomy of cultural differences. In F. J. R. Van de Vijver & G. J. M. Hutschemaekers (Eds.), *The investigation of culture. Current issues in cultural psychology* (pp. 91–114). Tilburg, The Netherlands: Tilburg University Press.

Van de Vijver, F. J. R., & Poortinga, Y. H. (2002a). Structural equivalence in multilevel research. *Journal of Cross-Cultural Psychology, 33,* 141–156.

Van de Vijver, F. J. R., & Poortinga, Y. H. (2002b). On the study of culture in developmental science. *Human Development, 45,* 246–256.

Van de Vijver, F. J. R., & Watkins, D. (2006). Assessing similarity of meaning at individual and country level: An investigation of a measure of independent and interdependent self. *European Journal of Psychological Assessment.* (In press)

Van Hemert, D. A., Van de Vijver, F. J. R., Poortinga, Y. H., & Georgas, J. (2002). Structural and functional equivalence of the Eysenck Personality Questionnaire within and between countries. *Personality and Individual Differences, 33,* 1229–1249.

Ward, C., Bochner, S., & Furnham, A. (2001). *The psychology of culture shock* (2nd ed.). Philadelphia: Routledge.

19 Mind and body in Japanese culture

Hayao Kawai

Mind and body in modern science

Modern science was established on the premise that clear distinctions exist between mind and body and between subject and object. Modern medicine is based on the same premise, so that a doctor can observe and examine patients' bodies objectively. As we know, modern medicine has been making enormous progress. Thanks to its contributions, many diseases have become curable through medical treatment.

We very much appreciate modern medicine's fruitful results. However, at the same time, I would like to point out that the modern medical method is not sufficient to cover medical practice as a whole in these current times. Psychotherapists, including myself, often face clients who have psychosomatic diseases. We know that modern medicine is somewhat effective in some cases, but not so in others. This is because the definition of psychosomatic disease, in itself, does not allow for a distinct separation of mind and body.

In order to compensate for the limitations of modern medicine, our present medical practice needs another method or point of view. In Japan we have a long history of an East-Asian medicine that is different from the Western model, although the main trend in medicine has become completely westernized since Japan established contact with Western culture. As you know, East-Asian medicine sees disease as a loss of balance within the whole being and does not consider body and mind to be separate. I think traditional East-Asian medicine, which is actually a mixture of medicine and psychology in the Western sense, could help to compensate for the shortcomings of modern medicine. Attempts to use Asian traditional medicine in this way have been made with some degree of success. Pursuing ideas about body/mind continuity in East Asia would be meaningful for both *medicine and psychotherapy* today. Since I am Japanese, I am going to consider "Mind and Body" in Japanese culture. However, I am quite aware that such Japanese ideas are influenced by both Chinese and Korean culture.

The two ways of cognition

I have been studying ego-consciousness, as a means to describe the difference between Westerners and Asians, in comparative studies on fairytales, mythology, and within my clinical practice. I was not quite sure how fully I could convey my idea to people both in the West and in Asia. Therefore, I was very glad when I heard that cognitive psychologists had found results similar to mine through their own experiments and questionnaires. These results are fully described in the book *The Geography of Thought* by Richard E. Nisbett (Nisbett, 2003). Let me introduce some of the impressive results contained in this valuable book.

In order to show the cognitive differences between Americans and Japanese, the following experiment was designed. Researchers showed the same color animated underwater scene to groups of Japanese and American students. Afterwards the students were asked about their memories of the things that impressed them.

I will summarize the results that Nisbett records in his book. The first statement by Americans usually referred to a large fish in the foreground. They would say something like, "There was what looked like a trout swimming to the right." The first statement by Japanese usually referred to background elements, e.g., "There was a lake or a pond." According to Nisbett, the Japanese made about 70% more statements than Americans about background aspects of the environment, and 100% more statements about relationships with inanimate aspects of the environment.

Both American and Japanese students mentioned the outstanding fish to almost the same degree, but there were distinct differences between Japanese and American students when they mentioned stones, bubbles, weeds, and other less impressive fish. They perceived things very differently regarding the environment within which the big fish was contained.

The author of the book noticed some differences in American and Chinese newspapers. When they wrote about murder, American newspapers tended to focus on the characteristics of the criminals to help find the "causes" of the murders. Chinese papers tended to stress factors relating to the whole situation.

To continue their research, American and Chinese students were presented with two murder cases (one by an American and one by a Chinese) and asked what they thought the important factors (causes) of the murders were. The results were as the researchers had presumed. The Chinese tried to find the causes of the crimes by examining the whole context, whereas the Americans tried to find the causes within the criminals' personalities.

The author's conclusion is that there are two types of cognition of phenomena. East-Asian thought is "holistic"; it is drawn to the perceptual field as a whole and to relations among objects and events within that field. Conversely, Westerners focus on salient objects or people, use attributes to assign them to categories, and apply rules of formal logic to understand their behavior. In comparison to Western modes of reasoning, East-Asian thought relies far less on categories or on formal logic, and it is fundamentally dialectic, seeking a "middle way" between opposing thoughts.

For East Asians, Chinese, Japanese and Koreans, all phenomena are complex and everything is understood to be interrelated. Americans can find important cause-and-effect relationships in any situation. Nisbett adds, however, that one cannot judge which type of cognition is right or wrong, or good or bad. Due to the fact that the Americans' method resulted in military, economic, and political dominance, people tend to think that it represents the correct method of cognition. The author is quite against this opinion and stresses the compensational character of the two means of cognition. I quite agree with him. I am glad to know that cognitive scientists accomplished this research, which, I think, supports the ideas that I have come to through my studies of depth psychology.

Body and mind in Japanese Buddhist priests

As mentioned above, you can see a difference in the approach to the body–mind continuum issue between the East and the West. Buddhism, while seeking ways to enlightenment, also had to face this problem due to influences from China and Korea. In the original Japanese ways of thinking, there was no clear distinction between mind and body. The Japanese word "mono" meant both psyche and matter. For example, unlike Westerners, Japanese priests did not separate body from mind. They did not analyze body and mind independently and approached human beings as a whole by their practice called "Shu-gyo." Shu-gyo can be translated as "practice" or "training." However, we should not forget that Japanese "Shu-gyo" is based on the idea that body and mind are inseparable.

As an example, I would like to talk about the Japanese Buddhist priest Myoe who lived from the 12th to the 13th century. Myoe was an extraordinary person who kept a dream diary during his life. He knew the importance of dreams for his religious life. I was so very impressed by his personality, as it was revealed in his dream diary, that I wrote a book about him and his dreams. It is titled *The Buddhist Priest Myoe: A Life of Dreams* (Kawai, 1992). I will focus on his attitude towards body and mind. Sexuality is an important and difficult matter for religion. Since it is really in between body and mind, it has complex meanings for human beings. In Christianity, there is a strong tendency to separate things quite distinctly. Sexuality and spirituality are completely separated and even seen as opposites. Sexuality has a very low evaluation. However, in ancient Babylonia for example, sexuality and spirituality were not separated. Therefore, there was an institution of sacred prostitution. In Buddhism, the situation is quite complex. As there is no clear-cut distinction between body and mind, sexuality *could* be valued highly. However, the priestly precepts of Buddhism (which came to Japan from China, Korea, and India) strictly forbade sexual contact between male and female.

Japan's Buddhist priests had, at that time, to face this contradiction. They found a rather simple way to solve their problem. They kept the precepts during the day. However, they forgot them from time to time at night and had relations with women secretly. It was a kind of "open secret" that everyone knew. Myoe could not stand this kind of deception. He strictly kept the Buddhist precepts. At the same time, he had good friendships with nuns and other women whom he respected and who respected him. According to the Buddhist teachings, body and mind are equally important and without a clear distinction between them. Myoe had to face the problem of sexuality. His answer was to gradually develop intimate relationships with women in his dream life. Outwardly he denied himself bodily contact with women, but, in his inner world, he had intimate relations with the feminine. I will not focus on it here, but Myoe's dreams reveal his inner development concerning his relationship with the feminine.

After he had come to this inner realization, he described an extraordinary experience that occurred during his Zen meditation:

> During an early meditation, I prayed for the extinction of sin and received the body which maintains the precepts. [He means that he could receive the body that maintains the precepts thanks to the graciousness of the Buddha.] I vowed to administer the precepts to everyone if I received an auspicious sign. My body and mind became quiescent in the midst of Samadhi. There was a pole made of lapis lazuli hanging from the sky, and I think it was hollow like a tube. I grabbed the end, and someone pulled me up. I maintained my hold and seemed to have reached the Tusita Heaven. My face suddenly became like a bright mirror. My entire body gradually became mirror-like. I felt completely whole, like a bead-jewel of quartz.
>
> I rolled and moved to another place. I was waiting for a voice and someone said, "All the Buddhas have entered. You have now attained purity." Following this my body expanded and I was adorned with a decoration made of the Seven Jewels. I emerged from meditation.

Here, Myoe experienced that his body and mind became quiescent. This is a wonderful attainment. I would like to stress here, what Myoe said was not based on any theory or dogma. Instead, it was what he experienced with his whole being. He reached the highest point of body and mind continuity through his constant Shu-gyo (practice).

There is another monk who lived in almost the same age as Myoe. Dogen was the founder of the Soto Zen sect in 13th century Japan. He bitterly criticized the Japanese Buddhism of that time. Priests were too much concerned with theoretical thinking and forgot about the essence of Shakamuni's original teaching. Dogen insisted on not using the intellect and concentrated instead on Zen practice; just sitting in the correct posture. Dogen said that if the ego believes itself to be a subject that examines and controls the environment, that belief is a delusion.

Forget about the ego, said Dogen. When the ego is weakened, the whole being becomes stronger and manifests its own true features. It is not the ego that recognizes the environment; rather it is the whole being that enlivens the ego. He described his experience of such a state with the famous words "dropping off body and mind". Here he experienced a state of consciousness that was beyond his personal body and mind.

I can imagine that what I have written above about the experiences of Japanese Buddhist priests and their original ways of perceiving cannot easily be understood by Western cognitive methods. I myself was influenced by Western modern science and could not understand Buddhism when I was young. The words of Buddhist priests were almost nonsense to me. It is not easy to attain such awareness. Only through the concentration of a practice like Shu-gyo can one reach such a point. However, during my long experience as a psychotherapist in Japan, I came to realize that there exists an altered state of consciousness in which it is possible to experience the fusion of mind and body. It is a state of mind quite unlike modern Western consciousness.

The practice of psychotherapy

The question may be, is what I am considering related to mind and body in Japanese tradition useful for psychotherapists in the Japan of today? My answer is "Yes." I would like to show how it serves my practice. When I meet clients who suffer from psychosomatic diseases, I do not talk about or treat their symptoms. However, while we are concentrating on dream analysis for their inner development, we often see their symptoms vanish or become very much weakened. When I engaged in dream analysis with an analysand who suffered from diabetes, his symptoms were very much relieved, even though he didn't recovered from diabetes completely. In the modern scientific point of view, diabetes and psychosomatic disease have no causality. However, modern medicine alone does not work in some situations. I think this is because when people have diseases, it is not only a problem of the physical self. We should consider all causality, including that of body and mind.

I think that the most important factor in my own practice is my attitude. I've learned this way of being from the Japanese traditional thinking that I've mentioned above. In the session, I try not to focus on the egos of clients, but rather to listen to what my clients say from the point of view of "their whole being." In other words, I try to lower the level of my consciousness without sacrificing clarity. This is exactly what Zen masters attempt to do in their practices.

However, at the same time, I have to add that I am different from Zen masters. I appreciate Buddhism but I also respect the Western way of observing phenomena. I know the advantage of the strong ego that modern society values so highly. I should not forget what I know. Therefore it is important to soften my ego and not to focus solely on a client's ordinary conscious state during the therapy process, but also without forgetting the importance of a strong ego in daily life. The role of therapists is to stand in this contradictory state. Fortunately, if a therapist is strong enough to hold the contradictions, a client will find a new way. That new way will be born not only from his ego, but also from his whole being. We should remember that a therapist does not cure a patient. A patient cures himself through the help of a therapist. In a sense, it is through the therapist's very existence.

References

Kawai, H. (1992). *The Buddhist priest Myoe: A life of dreams* (M. Unno, Trans. & Ed.). Venice, CA: The Lapis Press.

Nisbett, R. E. (2003). *The geography of thought: How Asians and Westerners think differently . . . and why*. New York: The Free Press.

20 The era of fluid culture: Conceptual implications for cultural psychology

Hiroshi Azuma

The era of fluid culture: Conceptual implications for cultural psychology

The world can no longer be viewed as a quilt of separate and distinct cultures. Each individual is a melting pot for an array of cultures. Barth (1993) proposed that culture is distributed, and that no individual represents the totality of his or her culture. For example, we can talk about the teenage culture, but no single teenager represent all aspects of this so-called teenage culture. The culture is distributed among group members in a differential and person-specific way. We may squeeze out a group culture using filter papers and catalysts, but it does not account for anyone's total cultural identity.

In the contemporary world, cultures cannot remain as uncontaminated as we tend to imagine they were in the past. People experience many different cultures through migration, traveling, reading, and media information. Cultures interact with and influence each other, and the well-circumscribed, distinct and static system envisioned by cultural anthropologists in the early 1900s is increasingly hard to come by. Since the aim of psychologists is to study the minds of living people, the focus of their interest in culture is not the culture found in literature or culture conceptualized as a sociological construct. It is rather the culture that surrounds each individual and actively participates in the formation of his or her mind. To distinguish it from the classical concept of traditional, demarcated and tightly knit culture, I will tentatively use the term *personal culture* to characterize the changing cultural environment of each living individual. The personal culture is unique to each individual, fluid and highly hybrid. It serves as the developmental niche (Super & Harkness, 1966) for an individual and provides the materials for her to weave together her personal culture. As psychologists take interest in personal culture, the boundary between cultural psychology and developmental psychology is bound to become more permeable.

Sociopolitical background of the change

Recent sociopolitical events have accelerated interest in personal culture. One such event was the end of the Cold War symbolized by the fall of the Berlin Wall. In mainstream psychology there used to be a tendency to believe in, or hope for, the self-contained lawfulness of psychology. The influences of education and culture were acknowledged but regarded as influences deriving from outside of the system, or as independent variables. Russian psychology, in contrast, had developed in a somewhat different direction insofar as it saw history, culture and education as forming the central core of the psyche. Russian perspectives had earlier been known in the USA and Western Europe through the works of Vygotsky, Luria and others, but the fall of the Berlin Wall was also the symbol of the removal of the invisible barrier that separated Russian psychology from the Western mainstream psychology. The influence of Russian thinkers was particularly strong in developmental and cultural psychology.

Traditional cross-cultural psychology sought to study and understand behavior in terms of the culture, and thus it regarded culture as a property of a group that could serve as a pseudo-experimental independent variable. The newer trend of cultural psychology, in contrast, viewed the human mind as an ever-growing open system in the formation of which history, education and social interaction were just as essential as genes and physiology. Cultural psychology has become an interdisciplinary science integrating various aspects of human development and artifacts.

Another political event that had a strong impact on the new direction of cultural psychology was the worldwide decolonization that took place after World War II (WWII). Until that time, the distinction between the civilized and the uncivilized, or between the developed and the underdeveloped world, had been taken for granted. Underlying this distinction was the implicit assumption that cultures could be rank-ordered on a unidimensional scale, with the Euro American civilization being the most highly valued (Rapport & Overing, 2003). As colonized nations attained independence after WWII and sent promising scholars abroad to be trained, they started to seek positive aspects inherent in their own traditions. This development led to a movement away from the unidimensional rank-ordering of cultures and toward Herder's classical view of cultures as separate and equally valuable. Many of those countries then gradually started to train social scientists and psychologists in their own countries.

In the cross-cultural studies conducted in the first half of the 20th century, native researchers participated mostly as informants, not as the principal investigators. During the last few decades, however, the number of cross-cultural studies directed or co-directed by researchers trained in non-Western countries has rapidly increased. This new breed of indigenous cultural psychologist came into existence around 1970.

These native psychologists argued that psychological theories needed indigenous input. Some of them even argued that mainstream psychology was not applicable to their cultural group. The majority stayed with mainstream psychology but was aware of the fact that there were indigenous psychological theories that might be universally useful but had not attracted the attention of Western researchers so far because they were foreign to the dominant mainstream thought. Non-Western folk psychology may have identified aspects of the human psyche that were overlooked due to the hegemonic role of Western assumptions. The concept of "amae," elaborated by the Japanese psychiatrist Takeo Doi (1973) based on his clinical experience, is one example.

For several years following 1972, my Japanese colleagues and I collaborated with a Stanford-based American group on a cross-cultural comparison of cognitive socialization. As a part of this study we asked American and Japanese mothers of four-year-old children what they would say if their child stubbornly refused to eat their supper dish. A number of Japanese mothers answered that an effective method to make the child eat was to say, "Okay then, you don't have to eat." This response was not found among the American mothers studied, although a few of them said that they would not force the child to eat the disliked dish because it was better to feed children food that they liked.

When coding the free response tape recordings, our American collaborators classified both responses as "don't force." Japanese colleagues, however, argued against this interpretation, because they felt that the response of the Japanese mothers was the strongest method of forcing their children to eat. To Americans this sounded odd, because the mothers clearly had told their children that they did not need to eat. It took one full month – this was before the age of e-mail – to settle the issue by time-consuming airmail letters and expensive international telephone calls. It was our reference to the "amae relationship" discussed in *The Anatomy of Dependence* by Takeo Doi (1973) that finally persuaded our American colleagues.

In this book, Doi notes willing maternal acceptance, on which the child's sense of security rests. The control technique used by the Japanese mothers implied a threat, namely that the amae relationship would be cut off because the child refused the mother's parental consideration. On the other hand, common American belief stresses independence as an important component of socialization. According to this dominant American view, socialization grounded in the acceptance of dependency was inconsistent (Azuma, 1994). So, for our American partners, this Japanese tactic needed further interpretation based on the Japanese-developed concept of amae. Later, after accepting our theory, our partners found that some American mothers used the same tactic. I also was told that Western psychotherapists use a variant of this acceptance technique (Gjerde, personal communication). The amae relationship, as well as the control technique based on it, had also existed in the USA. However, the repertoire of daily event scripts in American academic circles did not recognize this fact until a foreign concept had been introduced and accepted. Thus, reinterpretation of behaviors in terms of foreign indigenous concepts may, paradoxically, alleviate parochialism within psychology and make it a more global science.

Another sociopolitical influence on cultural psychology came from political, economic and informational globalization. For cultural anthropologists in the early 20th century, culture was a clearly circumscribed concept. For example, Kroeber and Kluckhorn (1963) stated, "A culture is a historically derived system of explicit and implicit designs for living, which lends to be shared by all or specially designed members of a group." It was a *system* of practices for living, *shared* by all members of a group. So was the Western Pacific culture for Malinowski (1927), Samoan culture for Margaret Mead (1928), and Japanese culture for Ruth Benedict (1946). The target of their investigation was, generally speaking, an ethnically and geographically circumscribed group that had rather limited interaction historically with mainstream Western culture.

In recent years, however, it has become increasingly difficult to find such "pure" culture and culture-pure people. In the present world of global mobility and interaction, culture is fluid and people are living multiculturally. For example, quite a few people hold double or triple nationality, or have spent their formative years moving through a number of regions of the world. Even without moving around, one may soak in different cultures through reading, schooling, TV and the Internet. Also, most cultures are becoming mixed and intermingled with each other. While I admit that the study of isolated cultures, to the limited extent that they exist, is exciting, reference to any coherent local group culture will account for rather little meaningful behavior of the individual member who is increasingly a citizen of the contemporary world. The history of his or her encounters with different cultures is essential in order to understand his or her behavior.

Finally, yet another issue makes adherence to pure cultures even more problematic. Gjerde (2004), for example, has pointed out that shared cultural forms may disguise an abundance of substantive discrepancies. Furthermore, seemingly homogeneous structures, often represented by a shared terminology, may yet be accorded a variety of personal meanings. The link between observable behavior and experiential meaning is therefore problematic.

Personal culture

The concept of culture as a group property that transcends individuals will fail to account for an important portion of variability in human behavior. An alternative position states that culture is the property of each individual. As I discuss later, this position does not deny the significance of group cultures. It simply proposes that instead of starting from the assumption of culture as a group property, we may start from the development and socialization of an individual person in constant interaction with cultural influences (Azuma, 2000). Those cultural influences constantly change as the result of both the change in the outside world and the physical and psychological locomotion of the person. No two persons will grow within an identical set of cultural influences, and thus personal culture necessarily becomes unique to each person. Preoccupation with the group culture will leave out the important wealth of personal cultures.

On the other hand, mankind is evolutionarily destined to live in groups. Members of any meaningful group will share certain cultural influences and the group will enhance this sharing in one way or another. We may eventually identify a group culture from commonalities across personal cultures, and personal cultures may be seen as branches shooting off from this stem. I don't see any *a priori* reason to prefer one approach to the other. In order to exploit the full meaning of man–culture interaction, we need both. A social group is a dynamic and functional concept. A collection of two or more people does not automatically make a social group, but as soon as there is some kind of interaction, visible or not, between those people, then we have a prototypical group. Within a group, interaction among members will be enhanced and the interpersonal overlap of cultural experiences will increase, eventually developing a common culture that is a prototypical group culture. As the group culture often survives beyond the life span of each individual group member, the group culture takes on an outlook that transcends individuals. This possibility being granted, we still need to pay attention to personal cultures inside a group and their function in changing and sometimes even destroying the group culture.

Recently, the relative impact of personal culture has rapidly increased in contrast to that of group culture, as the latter has become mixed and fluid. Moreover, the reference group of a person is becoming harder to identify, because it has become abstract and mixed. Indeed, the most important reference group for some people may exist only on a computer network. Under these circumstances, the advantage of starting by looking at a person, or at a person–culture interaction, is perhaps increasing.

From the moment of conception, any person is receptive and often even responsive to certain cultural stimuli. After birth, cultural stimuli literally soak the person and continue to act on him or her through his or her life. And he or she does not just stay receptive. Rather, he or she is selective in attending to, responding to, interacting with and incorporating incoming stimuli. Further, he or she may find, idiosyncratically, relationships or meanings among those stimuli that amount to the embryo of a personal culture. I will not explore the origin of this selectivity. It could be something in his or her genes, in his or her body structure, in his or her life history, or in all of them. But as human attention is intrinsically attuned to significant others, others' attitudes and beliefs are among the most important cultural stimuli around him or her. Since the assortment of significant people is person-specific, his or her personal history of encounters will be among the most important sources of his or her individuality. Cultural stimuli and his or her responses to them jointly weave out his or her personal culture around and inside of him or her.

Most readers of this chapter will be psychologists, and there is a set of human artifacts, such as psychological concepts, ethical codes, reporting standards, etc., shared by most of us. We may call this psychologists' culture. But do we think that we *belong* to a psychologists' culture? Perhaps we do not. Psychologists' culture constitutes a part of my culture, but at the same time many other cultures also constitute my culture. A personal culture is a homeostatic open system that is continually changing but allows one to conserve one's own identity as the agent for integrating one's cultural experience.

Group culture

The personal culture view, as noted above, does not entail denial of the importance of group culture. Each group displays a characteristic shape in the distribution of individual characteristics. In the contemporary world, we cannot take a group culture as a predestined superstructure for the mentality of the people born into it. A group culture may be seen as a statistical summary of the modal tendencies of a collection of personal cultures. The greater the similarity among the personal cultures in a group, the more representative that group culture is of its members. Because personal culture is formed through interaction with cultural stimuli, the culture of individuals who have been exposed to similar cultural stimuli will have a certain resemblance to each other. Hence the group culture can be a reasonably valid clue for approaching the probable personal culture, although we need to be vigilant of the risk of stereotyping. Just as the study of a personal culture must take into consideration the history of that person's encounter with various group cultures, studies of group cultures also lead us to divide subgroups into finer and finer elements, eventually reaching the individual.

In 1997 and 1998, in collaboration with David Crystal and Mayumi Karasawa, I studied how Japanese and American college and high-school students judged the acceptability of morally questionable acts such as cheating in an examination, injuring a teacher, breaking a promise, etc. (Azuma, 2001). Four groups of participants, each consisting of a little more than 100 students from several different schools and balanced for gender, participated. They were interviewed individually, and each was asked to rate how objectionable the act described was. The answer was made on a 6-point scale ranging from *highly objectionable* (1) to *not at all bad* (6). The initially provided description of the act was terse, indicating only who did what, without any contextual information. We called this the skeletal episode. Thus, the participant had to make a judgment with very limited knowledge. After this rating, the participant was allowed to ask questions about the context, for example, whether the person did the act with premeditation or not. For each question, a statistically controlled "answer" was provided, and the participant was asked to make the judgment again taking the new information into consideration.

As only two of the episodes, cheating on an exam and injuring the teacher, were common across both college and high-school participants, the results of other episodes were not very different and the results obtained with those two episodes will be presented. Table 20.1 shows the average ratings pooling across these two episodes, first without contextual information (before), and then with additional information supplied (after).

The design of the study was a cross-national comparison. Country effects, however, were dubious. The country main effect together with the interaction between nation and order, were significant for college students. American college students gave lower ratings, indicating stronger objections, to the skeletal episodes than Japanese college students. In other words, the average American judged the conduct to be less acceptable than the average Japanese. This difference narrowed in the last rating. Based on interview reports, our interpretation was that the Japanese moderated their ratings anticipating that unrevealed contextual information might include some acceptable motive for the "bad" act, while the Americans made categorical judgments, such that the "bad" act was simply seen as bad, unless contextual information had qualified the morally dubious behavior. As information accumulated, room for imagined justifiable reasons that might fill the information vacuum narrowed for the Japanese, while some of the information provided could have served as acceptable excuses for the Americans.

However, the high-school data revealed opposite results. Japanese high-school students rated the skeletal episodes to be more objectionable than their American counterparts. The difference grew wider as more information became available. Also, Japanese high-school students' ratings were significantly lower than those of the college students. Finally, American high-school students rated the act as more objectionable than American college students. Perhaps, we need to separate out age effects from country effects, and finer analysis may require more partitioning.

For the purpose of our present discussion, however, we do not need to go further into the interpretation of these data. The important point is that although our initial intention was to uncover straightforward cross-national differences, we discovered that this was not a simple task. It was confounded

Table 20.1 Average ratings before and after contextual information was supplied, with cheating and injury scenario scores pooled

Country	School level	Before	After
United States			
	College	2.39	2.58
	High school	2.84	3.09
Japan			
	College	3.20	3.04
	High school	2.73	2.88

by many interactions and a plausible interpretation will not come easily. The patterns found in Table 20.1 differed modestly between the USA and Japan, but the difference is not reducible to a general national stereotype. We may still, however, be interested in national differences, but it seems to me that we need to respect that Japan and the USA are heterogeneous societies, thus the point at which to start is at some subgroup level. Our participants can be subdivided not only in terms of nationality, but also in terms of age, gender, religion, class, etc. Without being preoccupied by the nation effects, we can start by partitioning the total variance into various sources of equal standing. As appreciation for the data deepens, we may find the need for further subdivision of participants. Depending on the development of the problem, we may also find the need to deal with intra-individual occasion-by-occasion variance. We may want to reach up to larger groups or even to humanity in general, but this needs to be preceded by analyses at the subgroup or even at the individual level, as suggested by Gjerde (2004), among others.

Cross-national study

Our study was aimed at national comparisons but ended up uncovering relations that suggest the limitations of cross-national comparison. This is not surprising because the nation is a surrogate for a collection of many different cultures. This means that the nation is a surrogate for a variety of subcultures divisible down to personal cultures. Is there any reason, then, to conduct cross-national studies? Don't such studies simply erase intra-national variability and build up erroneous stereotypes?

The problem of stereotyping is particularly serious when the basis of categorizing is beyond one's personal control, such as ethnicity, nationality, gender or class. Some of the cross-national comparisons have neglected this peril. But this does not mean that cross-national comparisons, although precarious, should categorically be excluded. When carefully interpreted, nationality comparisons may even serve to correct erroneous stereotyping. For example, a meta-analysis of cross-national studies by Takano and Osaka (1999) demonstrated persuasively that the common view that Japanese are collectivists has not been adequately supported.

We may cast doubt on the value of cross-national studies by arguing that defining nationality in terms of citizenship, birthplace or ethnicity is an artificial convention. But even artificially defined, nationality is not psychologically trivial. National institutions have the power to control and disperse information, to decide the content of education and even the cultural encounters among people. A geographical border born as the result of a pencil scratch on the table during a peace negotiation may make intermarriage between people belonging to two neighboring villages impossible for generations. Education is even more susceptible to national bordering. Comparing school textbooks of several Asian, American and European countries, Tomo, Mashima, and Nomoto (1998) found nation-specific tendencies in the selection of topics, specific avocation of interpersonal relationships, and content structure of stories. Similarly, newspapers, popular magazines, TV shows, and sometimes even the colors used to decorate streets reflect the direction advocated by those in power. The extent of direct influence of government policy will differ from country to country, but it is always there, significantly influencing the distribution of all cultural stimuli and eventually influencing the behaviors, attitudes and beliefs of individuals. In sum, an exclusive emphasis on the individual will remove the political and historical aspects from cultural studies. We always need to keep in mind who has the power to define culture and for whom it is defined.

Methodological problems

As I have discussed, the idea of personal culture is not incompatible with the group culture if the latter simply represents the fact that the member of a same group tends to maintain similar beliefs and exhibit similar behavior style. But the claim that the group culture is a tightly knit system needs to be toned down in order to be compatible with the approach from personal culture. Rather, a group culture would be viewed as a collection of more or less detachable elements.

Kosakai (2002), for example, views ethnic culture as a collection of culture elements. Among those elements he distinguishes the central elements and peripheral elements. The central group consists of the symbolic elements that produce the subjectively perceived intergroup differences and boundaries. The peripheral group, on the other hand, consists of the rest of the elements, which do not function as a basis for differentiating groups. He further discusses the fact that the basis for defining centrality is neither objective nor stable, and thus argues against the view of culture as a substantive reality that transcend individuals.

The traditional cultural psychology approach first picked up one or several existing societies defined in terms of geographic location, history, ethnicity, or any operationally definable marker. Then, the people of this society were observed. The patterns of behavior that were stably and uniquely shared by the members of this society, including beliefs and customs, were described. Finally, the conditions that had formed those behavior patterns were investigated. But when the culture is conceived as a tight and unitary system, the conditions that formed this culture also get lumped up as a whole and analytical investigation is difficult. Sometimes the explanation did not go much further than the markers that defined this society, such as Japanese behave like Japanese because they were born and raised in Japanese culture.

Some studies tried to get rid of this tautology by the effective use of socio-psychological constructs as mediation. For example, Markus and Kitayama (1991) assumed two groups of societies, collectivism societies and individualism societies. The naming suggests that each of them is a solid group culture. But, actually, neither collectivism nor individualism was meant to be a tight cultural system. Operationally, a collectivism society is the society where the collectivism response is seen more frequently. This is the common denominator of various "collectivism" cultures. A multiplicity of cultures such as Chinese, Japanese, Indian, Iranian or East European societies may be grouped together as collectivism societies. Pointing out a common denominator presupposes that elements can be partitioned in different ways, as Kosakai (2002) suggested. In this sense their position was a step forward toward the idea of the culture as a collection of elements some of which were subjectively perceived as central. Many groups may have had both collectivism and individualism as their cultural components. The argument of Markus and Kitayama, however, did not articulate this position and tended to invite the misunderstanding that the term collectivism, as well as individualism, defined a solid cultural system as defined by Kroeber and Kluckhorn (1963), and that a society is either collectivism or individualism and this variable determines whether people respond in one way or another.

When we want to work from the personal culture up, this dependent–independent variable scheme is not appropriate. While the culture of the society provides materials for shaping the personal culture, the person is selective about the materials used to weave out the personal culture. So, the personal culture is not separate from the person as an independent variable. Within the person–culture relationship, the influence of the person on the culture and of the culture on the person are inseparably circular.

Instead of assuming causal relationships between the two, we need to capture the dynamics of this twist. As a method to get closer to this person–culture twist, the narrative autobiography approach is obviously a strong candidate. The story of a person's history told by himself/herself will reveal his/her developmental niche in terms of his/her own conceptualization. But if we want to gain an insight applicable to somebody other than the informant himself/herself, autobiographical narratives are too idiosyncratic. There is a long way to go before arriving at a statement about his/her culture that has some generalizability. The value of in-depth understanding should be appreciated and, I personally believe that, any investigator who seeks to make a general statement about human mentality should have had the experience of struggling to understand the depths of some individual person's mind. But the duty of a scientific investigator is to come up with some statement beyond personal experience. For that, we need to reduce the narratives into general conceptual categories that cut through the dynamic person–culture twists.

Event script

When a person narrates any event, he or she has an implicit story grammar that he or she believes must be followed to make a story understandable to other people. To avoid an impression of claiming orthodoxy, I will call it an *event script* rather than grammar. This concept denotes the knowledge or belief about time-sequential processes, according to which an event will start, proceed and conclude. Each person will store a number of different event scripts and from this pool will be selected the one to be activated to deal with a given occasion. Event scripts constitute the framework for anticipation, imagination, judgment and evaluation of the actual process or story of the event. An event script may be specific to a class of events, e.g., love affairs, sibling rivalries or adventure stories. Another event script may describe more general and abstract levels that cut across stories on many different topics.

The group culture contains a great variety of event scripts. The accessibility of each script will depend on the kind and context of the event and the person who is trying to access it. The personal culture also includes a store of numerous event scripts. Most of the scripts have been taken from the group culture but selected by the person to add to his or her "personal store," tinted with personal color. Some of the scripts will come directly from the person's experience, thinking and ingenuity. The accessibility of each script partially reflects its accessibility in the group culture, but will also be influenced by the person's experience, attitude and intention.

My interest in event scripts started when we were trying to find an explanation for the finding quoted in the earlier section, in which Japanese judged morally questionable conduct more leniently than Americans when information about the context of the conduct was limited. The interview record revealed that many Japanese thought that there could have been some as-yet-unrevealed background information that could shed a more acceptable light on the conduct. Based on the shrinkage of the USA–Japan difference in later trials, with sufficient information and more interview data obtained, we surmised that the Japanese tended to fill the empty niche of information with an imagined acceptable reason. This activity amounts to authoring a story in its rudimentary form. In order to attain this goal, the author must use his/her knowledge or belief about how this kind of event could start and proceed. Further, the USA–Japan difference observed in this study suggests that there are cross-cultural differences in the stories produced.

Kawai (1982) discussed the possible link between the structure of the traditional folk tales of Japan and the in-depth dynamics of Japanese mentality. He found both culture-general and culture-specific aspects in the patterns of folk tales in Japan and in Europe. For example, many stories in both cultures have the "forbidden-room" motif: One person forbids another person to do something, for example peeping into a closed room, but the latter breaks the order and gets punished. Under this common motif, Japanese and European stories proceed differently. In the majority of Japanese stories, the party that forbids is female, the party forbidden is male, and the result of breaking the order is the disappearance of the first party. The story starts with no event, then an encounter, then an unrealistically happy life, then the promise is broken and things return to the original state of nothing in particular. In typical European stories, in contrast, the party that forbids is above the party forbidden in the power hierarchy, and the result of violating the order is either that the second party is severely punished, or that the second party is successfully avenged with the help of a "prince on a white horse." Kawai developed a Jungian-based theory of this difference, but in the present chapter I will restrict my discussion to the conscious cognitive level. Kawai's study, together with a number of studies including the aforementioned work by Tomo and colleagues (1998), *suggested that cultures might differ in the constitution of elements that constituted the central group of their stories and hence the most frequently activated event scripts.* Furthermore, not only group cultures differ, but also personal cultures will differ from each other in their event scripts.

Recently we have been studying national groups, the USA and Japan, with regard to the scripts that they use in writing up stories. In the first study, Japanese and American students were asked to write a story by adding short story frames of several sentences before and after the given brief description of the main event. The main event was a morally questionable act, such as "Susan lies to her mother about a recent grade on an important final exam." Comparing the stories written by students from the two nations, a number of significant USA–Japan differences were found. The typical beginning of Japanese stories is a harmonious state with a good mother–daughter relationship, close friends, etc. Then follows, quite accidentally, some annoying incident such as failure on an exam. This triggers the main event. Subsequent to the main event, some conflict may or may not take place, but somehow the story returns to its original harmonious state. In other words, a circular process is observed. American stories, on the other hand, start with a beginning that already suggests the forthcoming problem, such as a dominant mother, school absenteeism, etc. Then follows an intentional act that results in a negative incident like poor exam performance. The main event is followed by some consequence: punishment, successful cheating, victory, defeat, etc. Finally, the general state after the main event is not the same as the beginning. Thus, a linear process is observed and the finding corroborates Kawai's thesis. (Mashima, Yeh, Karasawa, & Azuma, 1995).

In another study that we are now analyzing, American, Chinese and Japanese participants were asked to write about: (a) their own experiences of working hard with some objective in mind; (b) a day in their lives seven years from now; and (c) a day in their lives twenty years from now. As we are still in the process of analyzing and writing up the results, I will mention here only that the results seem to be as equally informative as the first study. Cross-cultural and individual differences in frequently activated patterns of event scripts were detected more clearly with the use of three national groups and three different topics. For example, as compared to American and Chinese participants, Japanese writings tended to describe instrumental activities in detail without mentioning success, failure or achievement goals.

These findings suggest that the event script is one of the more useful intervening concepts that is acquired under the influence of social and personal culture and underlies each person's social expectations, judgments, evaluations and other aspects of social cognition. Ultimately, other researchers will develop equally effective intervening concepts, and all together they will prepare a seedbed for a theory that covers both the fluid and stable aspects of personal as well as group cultures.

Conclusion

In classical cross-cultural psychology, the culture transcended individuals. But in this era of fluid mobility, almost everyone becomes multicultural, and cultures themselves are always interacting inside each individual. The study of the cultural development of each person should focus first on that person's unique cultural environment, which we called personal culture. However, a personal culture has been formed by incorporating various levels of group cultures and therefore we eventually need to link personal cultures to multiple group cultures.

Assuming that the event script, or the knowledge as to how social events occur, proceed and end, is one of the central elements that link personal and group cultures, we are currently conducting a three-way cross-national study of event scripts. We believe that the empirical detection of groups of central elements stored in the group culture and internalized by member individuals to influence their cognitive activities, such as event scripts, will mediate this linkage.

Acknowledgements

The author is grateful to Per Gjerde of the University of California at Santa Cruz for his suggestions, comments and encouragement, to Lauren Shapiro of Williams College for her comments and careful editing, and Qicheng. Jing of the Chinese Academy of Sciences for important advice.

References

Azuma, H. (1994). *Nihonjin no shitsuke to kyoiku* [Socialization and education of the Japanese]. Tokyo: University of Tokyo Press.

Azuma, H. (2000). Indigenous to what? *International Society for the Study of Behavioral Development Newsletter*, 9–10.

Azuma, H. (2001). Moral scripts: A US–Japan comparison. In H. Shimizu & R. A. Levine (Eds.), *Japanese frames of mind: Cultural perspectives on human development*. Cambridge, UK: Cambridge University Press.

Barth, F. (1993). *Balinese lives*. Chicago: University of Chicago Press.

Benedict, R. (1946). *The chrysanthemum and the sword: Patterns of Japanese culture*. Boston: Houghton-Mifflin.

Doi, T. (1973). *The anatomy of dependence*. New York: Kodansha International.

Gjerde, P. (2004). Culture, power, and experience: Toward a person centered cultural psychology. *Human Development*, *47*, 138–157.

Kawai, H. (1982). *Mukashibanashi to nihonjin no kokoro* [Folk tales and Japanese mentality]. Tokyo: Iwanami Shoten.

Kosakai, T. (2002). *Minzoku to yuu kyoko*. [Ethnicity as afiction]. Tokyo: University of Tokyo Press.

Kroeber, A. L., & Kluckhorn, C. (1963). *Culture: A critical review of concepts and definitions*. New York: Vintage.

Malinowski, B. (1927) *Sex and representation in savage society*. London: Humanities Press.

Markus, H. R., & Kitayama, S. (1991). Culture and self: Implications for cognition, emotion and motivation. *Psychological Review, 98*, 224–253.

Mashima, M., Yeh, C., Karasawa, M., & Azuma, H. (1995). A US–Japan comparison of the process of completing imperfect moral episodes: The results of content analysis compared. *Human Developmental Research: Coder Annual Report, 11*, 80–87.

Mead, M. (1928). *Coming of age in Samoa*. New York: Morrow.

Rapport, N., & Overing, J. (2003). *Social and cultural anthropology: The key concepts*. London & New York: Routledge Key Guides.

Super, C. M., & Harkness, S. (1966). A conceptualization at the interface of child and culture. *International Journal of Behavior Development, 9*, 549–567.

Takano, Y., & Osaka, E. (1999). An unsupported common view: Comparing Japan and the US on individualism/collectivism. *Asian Journal of Social Psychology, 2*, 311–341.

Tomo, R., Mashima, M., & Nomoto, T. (1998). Content analysis of interpersonal coping behavior in Japanese and British textbooks. *Japanese Journal of Educational Psychology, 46*, 95–105.

21 Self-esteem in cultural contexts: The case of the Japanese

Susumu Yamaguchi, Chun-Chi Lin, and Sayaka Aoki

Self-esteem represents individualistic Western values such as self-confidence, self-reliance, and self-assertiveness. Indeed, one's self-esteem has been shown to be positively correlated with one's individualistic tendencies in both the USA and Japan (Carter & Dinnel, 1997; Waterman, 1984). Corresponding to this association of self-esteem with individualism, Japanese people have been shown to express lower self-esteem relative to people in North America (i.e., the USA and Canada), typically on Rosenberg's Self-Esteem Scale (for a review, see Heine, Lehman, Markus, & Kitayama, 1999). Heine et al.'s excellent review raises at least two interesting research questions. First, do Japanese really hold lower self-esteem than North Americans? Although this issue may seem to have been settled already, we believe this question has not yet been explored fully. For example, despite its low expression relative to North Americans, Japanese self-esteem is not negative. As will be elaborated below, the available evidence indicates that the Japanese on average have a positive (albeit only slightly) attitude towards the self. The second question is concerned with the importance of self-esteem for the Japanese. Heine et al. suggest that Japanese people may pursue something other than self-esteem. However, available evidence also indicates that self-esteem is important for the Japanese as well. Self-esteem is related to relevant variables such as persistence after failure and psychological well-being, as it is in the USA.

Definition of self-esteem

Self-esteem has been variously defined by previous researchers. Those definitions are largely similar but they are divided on the issue of emotional involvement. Some definitions emphasize the cognitive aspect (i.e., evaluation of the self), whereas others include emotion as an essential component of self-esteem. The majority of researchers apparently prefer a "cold" definition of self-esteem (e.g., Baumeister, Campbell, Krueger, & Vohs, 2003; Berkowitz, 1980; Coopersmith, 1967). For instance, "self-esteem is literally defined by how much value people place on themselves. It is the evaluative component of self-knowledge" (Baumeister et al., 2003, p. 2). As another example, Coopersmith (1967) defined self-esteem as "the evaluation that an individual makes and customarily maintains with regard to the self" (pp. 4–5). On the other hand, some researchers include an emotional component in self-esteem. For example, Rosenberg (1965), who developed the most popular self-esteem measure, stated that, "Self-esteem . . . is a positive or negative attitude toward a particular object, namely, the self" (p. 30). Because attitude contains both cognitive (evaluative) and affective components, as well as a behavioral component, the self-esteem construct as defined by Rosenberg contains both affective and cognitive aspects. A recent example of a definition that emphasizes an affective component is Kernis (2003), who defines global self-esteem as "an affective construct consisting of self-related emotions tied to worthiness, value, likeableness, and acceptance" (p. 3).

In this chapter, a definition of self-esteem with affective components would be more appropriate, because self-esteem and modesty represent opposite classes of emotions as classified by William James (1890). He made a distinction between two kinds of self-feelings. One set of feelings was "pride, conceit, vanity, self-esteem, arrogance, vainglory" and the other set was "modesty, humility, confusion, diffidence, shame, mortification, contrition, the sense of obloquy and personal despair." He referred to those classes as "two opposite classes of affection." Thus, Rosenberg's definition is adopted here: self-esteem is a positive or negative attitude, which involves both cognitive and affective components, toward the self.

Self-esteem as defined above needs to be distinguished from self-enhancement, which is defined as a "claim of self-superiority" (Sedikides, Gaertner, & Toguchi, 2003). People with high self-esteem may or may not express their high self-evaluations. Thus, self-enhancement cannot be considered an index of self-esteem. This distinction is more important when it comes to Asians, as will be elaborated later.

Japanese "lower" self-esteem

As stated already, there remains little question about Japanese expressed low self-esteem, as far as explicit measures are concerned. That is, Japanese express lower self-esteem on explicit measures such as Rosenberg's Self-Esteem Scale (RSE). However, because explicit measures are vulnerable to various sources of bias, the expressed low self-esteem is not readily attributable to actual low self-esteem. There are at least three sources of bias that need to be considered. First, it is well known that North Americans have an extreme response style relative to Asians. Chen, Lee, and Stevenson (1995) showed that Japanese and Chinese students were more likely to use the midpoint of the scale than North Americans. This response style was also shown to be connected to one's individualist tendencies, such that one's endorsement of individualism was positively related to the use of extreme values. Thus, the North America–Japan difference on the self-report measures of self-esteem can be a reflection of the difference in the response style rather than the level of self-esteem. Second, more recently, Heine, Lehman, Peng, and Greenholtz

(2002) argued that explicit measures are vulnerable to reference-group effect particularly when they are administered cross-culturally. The reference-group effect means that people make judgments based upon comparison with their reference group. In the case of cross-cultural studies, people's responses on a Likert scale, for example, are assumed to be based on how individuals compare with other people in their culture. Because high self-esteem is valued in North America and modesty is valued and practiced in Japan, North Americans may well elevate and Japanese may well lower their evaluations on self-report measures, as compared to when they make evaluations without a reference group. Consistent with this argument, Bachman and O'Malley (1984) showed that African Americans' high self-esteem (relative to Caucasian Americans) disappeared when their extreme response style was controlled by a truncated scoring method, which ignores the strength of agreement and all positive and negative responses were assigned a score of 3 and 1, respectively, with the midpoint being scored 2. Third, and most importantly, explicit measures are vulnerable to self-presentational concerns. In modern North America, high self-esteem has been valued extensively, except by some critiques in academia, such as Baumeister et al. (2003). A notable example is the state of California, which funded a movement for high self-esteem, expecting high self-esteem would solve social problems as well as personal ones. On the other hand, in the Japanese cultural context, modesty is valued more than self-assertiveness that often involves claim of self-worth (Lebra, 1976). Thus, inasmuch as modesty is valued in a culture, people in the culture must hesitate to express their high self-esteem even though they may have it in their mind. To the extent that a modesty norm is practiced in a culture, one's expression of self-esteem will be moderated.

Modesty and expression of self-esteem

It is well-known that people engage in impression management (Tedeschi, 1981). Self-presentation is a major tool for impression management: people express themselves or behave in ways designed to create a favorable impression among others. To create a favorable impression among others, it is obvious that individuals have to obey the prevalent norm in their society. In North America, self-assertive behavior is valued and encouraged. Notwithstanding the dominant cultural norm in the USA, it is interesting that even North Americans need to express modest self-views to create favorable impressions among others. For example, modest attribution about a group's performance created more favorable impressions than self-assertive attributions (Forsyth, Berger, & Mitchell, 1981). Specifically, individuals who made other-serving attributions regarding a group's success or failure (i.e., taking less responsibility for group success and more for group failure) were more liked than those who made self-serving attributions (i.e., taking more responsibility for group success and less for group failure). Also, Holtgraves and Srull (1989) suggest that people like modest individuals better than self-assertive individuals. In their experiment, they presented a fictitious conversation between two (same-sex) university students, in which the target person asserted positive self-statements such as, "My GPA is now 4.75," or "My IQ as a child was 133." When the subjects were asked to indicate their impressions of one of the interactants, they answered that they liked the target person less and perceived the target as more egotistical unless the positive self-assertions were made in an appropriate context in which the target person was asked specific questions about their competence (e.g., GPA or IQ). Furthermore, subjects in Miller and Schlenker's experiment (1985) expressed their egotistic attribution to a greater extent in private than in public, suggesting that publicly expressed attributions are moderated even in North America. Given those findings in North America, it appears quite reasonable that Japanese, who are supposed to subscribe to the modesty norm to a greater extent, show modesty to create favorable impressions among others. Our data (Murakami, Yamaguchi, & Ozaki, 2005) indicate that Japanese self-esteem expressed on self-report scales including RSE is negatively correlated with their score on the Modesty Responding Scale (MRS), which taps on one's tendency to be modest (Whetstone, Okun, & Cialdini, 1992). These findings indicate that expression of self-esteem is moderated by modesty. Expression of moderate self-esteem in East Asia, therefore, should not be taken at face value.

Middle of the road in expressing self-esteem

If modesty is valued in Japanese culture, would one benefit from expressing negative self-esteem? We don't think so. Self-respect is also valued by Confucius (unknown/1979). Excessive humility would be taken as a sign of one's lack of self-respect, which is against the Confucian value as well and thus will not result in favorable impressions even in East Asia. Thus, the two rather conflicting Confucian values, modesty and self-respect, will lead the Japanese to express moderate self-esteem. In responding to self-report measures, Japanese people would give scores close to the mid-point of the scale rather than negative scores below the mid-point. Indeed, previous research has shown that Japanese-expressed self-esteem on the Rosenberg's Self-Esteem Scale (RSE) is not negative, although it is lower than that of North Americans (Heine et al., 1999). A closer look at the data presented in Heine et al. reveals that the Japanese self-esteem score is slightly above the theoretical mean of RSE, meaning that the Japanese self-esteem score is slightly positive. Consistent with Heine's data, the average RSE score of 1225 Japanese university students (411 males and 814 females) from 10 universities was 25.3, which is slightly above the theoretical mid-point of the scale (a four-point scale was used in this study) (Oguchi, 2000). Thus, the empirical evidence indicates that Japanese people do indeed take the middle of the road in expressing self-esteem. As long as the Japanese subscribe to modesty with self-respect, the expression of moderate self-esteem makes sense logically.

Interpersonal benefit of expressing moderate self-esteem

So far, the expression of moderate self-esteem has been suggested to be beneficial in terms of creating favorable impressions among others in East-Asian cultural contexts. In order to test this hypothesis, our recent experiment examined the relationship between the expression of various degrees of self-esteem and interpersonal impressions. In this experiment, we adopted a distinction between *self-profitable* traits and *other-profitable* traits in person perception (Peeters, 1983). Self-profitable traits (e.g., intelligent, creative) have direct adaptive value for individuals who have these traits. If a person is intelligent or creative, the person will benefit from this in any situation. However, for other people, the fact that someone is intelligent or creative does not always have direct adaptive value. For example, if you have an enemy who is intelligent and creative you are likely to suffer from it. In the case of other-profitable traits (e.g., honest, kind), on the other hand, individuals who have those traits will not always benefit from them. If a person is excessively honest or kind, people around the person can benefit, although the person may be exploited by others. With this distinction between self-profitable and other-profitable traits, we hypothesized that expression of high self-esteem would create an impression among the University of Tokyo students that the stimulus person is high on self-profitable traits but low on other-profitable traits, whereas the expression of low self-esteem would lead to the opposite impression. In addition, we predicted that high self-esteem would be perceived as associated with egotistic tendencies such as competitiveness and stubbornness.

To test those predictions, we presented a copy of fictitious answers on RSE to undergraduate students at the University of Tokyo, who were randomly assigned to one of three conditions: average, high, and low (Yamaguchi, Lin, & Aoki, 2005). The fictitious answers on RSE were created based upon data from 40 undergraduate students. In the average condition, the average score of the 40 undergraduate students was marked on each item of RSE, which yielded a total score slightly above the neutral. On the other hand, in the high condition, the fictitious answers were higher than the average scores by 1 *SD*, whereas in the low condition, the fictitious answers were lower by 1 *SD*. Because the average score was close to the mid-point (i.e., 26.92), the average group was essentially shown a pattern of scores that hover around the neutral point, whereas the high/low group was shown positive/negative self-esteem. The subjects were asked to answer questions regarding impressions of the stimulus person who ostensibly gave the answers on the fictitious RSE. Specifically, participants were asked for impressions about the stimulus person's self-profitable traits (e.g., self-confident, intelligent), other-profitable traits (e.g., honest, kind), and egotistic tendencies (e.g., stubborn, competitive).

The results generally supported our hypothesis. The expression of higher self-esteem generated an impression that the stimulus person had higher self-profitable traits. In terms of the other-profitable traits, the low self-esteem stimulus person was perceived as higher on other-profitable traits than the other two stimulus persons but no significant difference was found between the high and average self-esteem persons. As to egotistic tendencies, as predicted, the low self-esteem student was perceived as lower on egotistic tendencies than the students with high or average self-esteem, with no significant difference between the high and average self-esteem students. In all, this study revealed that the expression of higher self-esteem can create an impression that one has self-profitable traits to a greater extent. However, the expression of high self-esteem suffers from an impression that the person has low other-profitable traits and higher egotistic tendencies as compared with the person who expresses low (and negative) self-esteem. On the other hand, persons who express low (and negative) self-esteem suffer from perceived lower self-profitable traits – individuals who express low self-esteem are not perceived as able people. The average self-esteem student was perceived as positive on the self-profitable traits and neutral on the other-profitable traits, although positive on egotistic tendencies (but lower than the high self-esteem student). Thus, we would suggest that somewhere between average and low self-esteem is desirable for self-presentation purposes, because one can avoid being perceived as egotistic while securing an impression that one is an able person. At the University of Tokyo one has to show moderate to low self-esteem to earn the impression that one has other-profitable traits and that one is not egotistical, because students know that they have high (and perhaps unexpressed) self-esteem in general. The findings of this study underscore the importance of the context within which people express their self-esteem. When among those who have supposedly high self-esteem, one needs to express lower self-esteem in order to create more favorable impressions.

Implicit self-esteem

Because explicit self-esteem is vulnerable to biases, as we have specified, one would reasonably attempt to measure the "real" self-esteem using implicit measures, which are difficult to fake by conscious effort. Implicit measures of attitudes can be used to measure self-esteem, which is defined as one's attitude toward the self (Figure 21.1). Indeed, several researchers have reported that the Japanese hold positive self-esteem at the implicit level (e.g., Hetts, Sakuma, & Pelham, 1999; Kitayama & Karasawa, 1997; Kitayama & Uchida, 2003; Kobayashi & Greenwald, 2003; Yamaguchi & Murakami, 2000). These workers unanimously report that the Japanese have a positive attitude towards the self at the implicit level. These findings are not surprising given the positive self-esteem on RSE among the Japanese, as we have seen in a previous section. Converging evidence indicates that Japanese self-esteem is positive at both the explicit and implicit levels.

Then, how about Japanese "low" self-esteem relative to North Americans? In our recent experiment, the Implicit Association Test (IAT) revealed that Japanese students have no less self-esteem compared to students in the USA

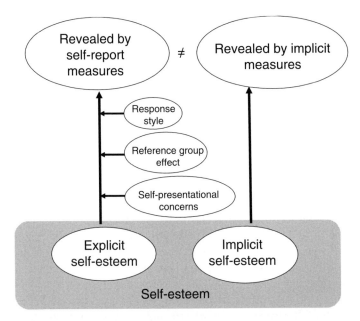

Figure 21.1 Relationship between implicit and explicit self-esteem.

(Yamaguchi et al., in preparation). The IAT is a procedure for measuring strengths of automatic associations between concepts (see Nosek, Greenwald, & Banaji, in press, for the validity of the IAT). In the case of implicit self-esteem, the IAT measures strength of associations between self and positive valence (Greenwald & Farnham, 2000). In this experiment, self was specifically contrasted with best friend and in-group. The results indicated that not only did the subjects more easily associate themselves with positive, compared to negative, attributes relative to their best friend or in-group, but also they associated themselves more easily with self-relevant, compared to other-relevant, traits relative to their best friend. More importantly, American subjects showed comparable or even lower implicit self-esteem as compared with the Japanese, indicating that Japanese implicit self-esteem is no lower than that of Americans.

Relationship between explicit and implicit self-esteem

The available evidence on Japanese explicit and implicit self-esteem can be summarized as follows. First, Japanese self-esteem is positive at both implicit and explicit levels. Namely, the Japanese have positive attitude towards the self. Second, compared to North Americans, Japanese express lower self-esteem at the explicit level but they have comparable or higher implicit self-esteem.

The second issue would entail further explanations. Which measures, implicit or explicit ones, can appropriately measure self-esteem? Because the self-report measures particularly, and explicit measures in general, are vulnerable to response biases, one could claim that only implicit measures, which are difficult to fake, can measure real self-esteem. On the other hand, if one questions the construct that implicit measures tap, one could also claim that "real" self-esteem can be measured only by explicit means, perhaps using unobtrusive measures. Another possibility is that both explicit and implicit self-esteem may be "real." According to Greenwald and Banaji's (1995) definition of implicit self-esteem, implicit self-esteem is "the introspectively unidentified (or inaccurately identified) effect of the self-attitude on evaluation of self-associated and self-dissociated objects" (p. 11). Thus, in theory, there can be both explicit self-esteem, which can be introspectively identified, and implicit self-esteem, which is difficult to identify introspectively. According to a recent review of evidence provided by research on IAT (Nosek, Greenwald, & Banaji, in press), it seems most appropriate to assume that there are two processes, each at the implicit and explicit levels (Figure 21.1). As to the difference between the implicit and explicit measures, Rudman (2004) suggests that early as well as affective experiences would influence implicit attitudes. According to this view, implicit self-esteem (i.e., implicit attitude toward the self) would be affected by one's experience of being accepted by care-takers (typically parents) in childhood. Previous research on Japanese childrearing practices provides evidence that unconditional acceptance of children by Japanese care-takers (i.e., parents and grandparents) is the norm. Caudill and Schooler (1973) found that Japanese mothers accept and encourage children's requests for indulgence to a greater extent than their Caucasian American counterparts. Such a finding indicates that Japanese children tend to be accepted unconditionally by care-takers, which can foster a strong sense of self-worth among children. This would explain why the Japanese hold as high a self-esteem as North Americans at the implicit level.

Relationship between self-esteem and relevant variables

Baumeister et al. (2003) reviewed the literature on self-esteem based on research conducted most extensively in North America. According to Baumeister et al., research in the USA has not proven that high self-esteem can cause positive outcomes and benefits as expected. High self-esteem does not cause high performance or attractiveness, although people with high self-esteem often make a claim for those. Thus, they concluded that the benefits of high self-esteem are rather limited to two categories: enhanced initiative and pleasant feelings. In the USA, people with high self-esteem tend to persist in the face of failure (e.g., McFarlin, Baumeister, & Blascovich, 1984). Also, males with high self-esteem tend to initiate romantic behavior such as asking for a date with a highly attractive confederate more than their low self-esteem counterpart (Kiesler & Baral, 1970). As to pleasant feelings, Diener and Diener (1995) showed that self-esteem is strongly related to life satisfaction.

If self-esteem serves similar functions in both North America and Japan, the benefits of high self-esteem among Japanese people must only be seen in the same two categories as they are in the USA (i.e., enhanced initiative and pleasant feelings). Indeed, Inoue (1986) found that Japanese 5th graders high in self-esteem tended to evaluate their academic performance highly, although their evaluation did not match their actual performance as evaluated by their teachers, as is the case in the USA. When it comes to initiative, on the other hand, Inoue reported that those with high self-esteem persisted more than their low self-esteem counterparts when they failed on a problem. Yagi (1996) also showed that Japanese undergraduate students high in self-esteem tended to choose a physically attractive opposite-sex student as their partner in an ostensive communication study, as compared to low self-esteem students. As to pleasant feelings, Diener and Diener (1995) collected data from 13,118 college students in 31 countries including the USA and Japan. The correlation between self-esteem and life satisfaction was positive in both the USA ($r = .60$) and Japan ($r = .44$). Self-esteem is also found to be positively correlated with satisfaction with physical fitness ($r = .57$ for males and $r = .67$ for females) (Shibata & Nobeji, 1990) and negatively correlated with shyness ($r = -.45$) (Aikawa, 1991). These findings indicate that Japanese self-esteem is positively related to enhanced initiative and pleasant feelings as it is in North America. Thus, despite Heine et al.'s (1999) suggestion that self-esteem may be unimportant for Japanese people, the benefits of self-esteem can be found in enhanced initiative and pleasant feelings, just as they are in the USA.

Conclusion and future directions

Hidden value seeps into psychology's research-based concepts. Self-esteem is no exception. Belief in positive outcomes of self-esteem has been prevalent in the USA, despite the fact that self-esteem is not always beneficial to those who strongly hold it. In this sense, William James (1890) appears to be right when he associated self-esteem with vanity and arrogance.

Available evidence indicates that at the explicit level relatively low Japanese self-esteem needs to be discounted due to the modesty norm prevalent in Japanese culture. Because self-respect is also valued (perhaps to a lesser extent than in the West), the Japanese tend to show moderate self-esteem at the explicit level. In cross-cultural comparisons of self-esteem, researchers need to pay attention to prevalent values and practice in each cultural context.

More importantly, recent development in the theory of self-esteem along with empirical evidence accumulated by cross-cultural comparisons poses a fundamental question: Is it important for individuals to claim high self-esteem at all? Logically, high self-esteem (which is defined as a highly positive attitude toward the self) will not entail its claim in public. With the prevalent modesty norm in Japanese culture, Japanese people with high self-esteem will not feel comfortable in expressing it. In future research, the expression of self-esteem needs to be separated from self-esteem in one's mind.

Acknowledgements

This work was supported by Grant-in-Aid for Scientific Research (c) (16244120) from the Japanese Society for the Promotion of Science.

We thank Emiko Kashima, Romin Tafarodi, Yohtaro Takano, and Yasuki Yagi for their critical comments on an earlier version of this manuscript.

References

Aikawa, A. (1991). Tokusei shyness shakudo no sakusei oyobi shinraisei to datousei no kentou ni kansuru kenkyuu [A study on the reliability and validity of a scale to measure shyness as a trait]. *Japanese Journal of Psychology, 62*, 149–155.

Bachman, J. G., & O'Malley, P. M. (1984). Black–White differences in self-esteem: Are they affected by response style? *American Journal of Sociology, 90*(3), 624–639.

Baumeister, R. F., Campbell, J. D., Krueger, J. I., & Vohs, K. D. (2003). Does high self-esteem cause better performance, interpersonal success, happiness, or healthier lifestyles? *Psychological Science in the Public Interest, 4*, 1–44.

Berkowitz, L. (1980). *A survey of social psychology* (2nd ed.). New York: Holt, Rinehart, & Winston.

Carter, K., & Dinnel, D. L. (1997, April). *Self-esteem conceptualization: A comparison of American and Japanese values.* Paper presented at the Annual meeting of the Western Psychological Association, Seattle, WA.

Caudill, W. A., & Schooler, C. (1973). Child behavior and child rearing in Japan and the United States: An interim report. *Journal of Nervous and Mental Disease, 157*, 323–338.

Chen, C., Lee, S.-Y., & Stevenson, H. H. (1995). Response style and cross-cultural comparisons of rating scales among East Asian and North American students. *Psychological Science, 6*, 170–175.

Confucius (1979). *The analects* (D. C. Lau, Trans.). London: Penguin Books.

Coopersmith, S. (1967). *The antecedents of self-esteem.* San Francisco: Freeman.

Diener, E., & Diener, M. (1995). Cross-cultural correlates of life satisfaction and self-esteem. *Journal of Personality and Social Psychology, 68*, 653–663.

Forsyth, D. R., Berger, R. E., & Mitchell, T. (1981). The effects of self-serving vs. other-serving claims of responsibility on attraction and attribution in groups. *Social Psychology Quarterly, 44*, 59–64.

Greenwald, A. G., & Banaji, M. R. (1995). Implicit social cognition: Attitudes, self-esteem, and stereotypes. *Psychological Review, 102*, 4–27.

Greenwald, A. G., & Farnham, S. D. (2000). Using the implicit association test to measure self-esteem and self-concept. *Journal of Personality and Social Psychology, 79*, 1022–1038.

Heine, S. J., Lehman, D. R., Markus, H. R., & Kitayama, S. (1999). Is there a universal need for positive self-regard? *Psychological Review, 106*, 766–794.

Heine, S. J., Lehman, D. R., Peng, K., & Greenholtz, J. (2002). What's wrong with cross-cultural comparisons of subjective Likert scales?: The reference-group effect. *Journal of Personality & Social Psychology, 82*, 903–918.

Hetts, J. J., Sakuma, M., & Pelham, B. W. (1999). Two roads to positive regard: Implicit and explicit self-evaluation and culture. *Journal of Experimental Social Psychology, 35*, 512–559.

Holtgraves, T., & Srull, T. K. (1989). The effects of positive self-descriptions on impressions: General principles and individual differences. *Personality and Social Psychology Bulletin, 15*, 463–472.

Inoue, N. (1986). Jidou no jisonsin to shippai kadai no taisho tono kanren [Relationship between child's self-esteem and response to unsuccessful problems]. *Japanese Journal of Educational Psychology, 34*, 10–19.

James, W. (1890). *The principles of psychology* (Vols. 1–2). New York: Dover.

Kernis, M. H. (2003). Toward a conceptualization of optimal self-esteem. *Psychological Inquiry, 14*, 1–26.

Kiesler, S. B., & Baral, R. L. (1970). The search for a romantic partner: The effects of self-esteem and physical attractiveness on romantic partner. In K. J. Gergen & D. Marlowe (Eds.), *Personality and social behavior* (pp. 155–165). Reading, MA: Addison-Wesley.

Kitayama, S., & Karasawa, M. (1997). Implicit self-esteem in Japan: Name letters and birthday numbers. *Personality & Social Psychology Bulletin, 23*, 736–742.

Kitayama, S., & Uchida, Y. (2003). Explicit self-criticism and implicit self-regard: Evaluating self and friend in two cultures. *Journal of Experimental Social Psychology, 39*, 476–482.

Kobayashi, C., & Greenwald, A. G. (2003). Implicit–explicit differences in self-enhancement for Americans and Japanese. *Journal of Cross-Cultural Psychology, 34*, 522–541.

Lebra, T. S. (1976). *Japanese patterns of behavior.* Honolulu, HI: East-West Center.

McFarlin, D. B., Baumeister, R. F., & Blascovich, J. (1984). On knowing when to quit: Task failure, self-esteem, advice, and nonproductive persistence. *Journal of Personality, 52*, 138–155.

Miller, R. S., & Schlenker, B. R. (1985). Egotism in group members: Public and private attributions of responsibility for group performance. *Social Psychology Quarterly, 48*, 85–89.

Murakami, F., Yamaguchi, S., & Ozaki, Y. (2005). *The effect of self-assertiveness on the expression of self-esteem: Using explicit and implicit measures.* Poster presented at the 6th meeting of the Society for Personality and Social Psychology, New Orleans.

Nosek, B. A., Greenwald, A. G., & Banaji, M. R. (in press). The Implicit Association Test at age 7: A methodological and conceptual review. In J. A. Bargh (Ed.), *Automatic processes in social thinking and behavior.* New York: Psychology Press.

Oguchi, T. (2000). Taimen bamen ni okeru shinriteki kojinsa scale no sougokankei no bunseki [Analyses of interrelationships among psychological individual difference scales in face-to-face situations]. In H. Nakamura (Ed.), *Taimen bamen ni okeru shinriteki kojinsa* (pp. 105–149). Tokyo: Brain Shuppan.

Peeters, G. (1983). Relational and informational patterns in social cognition. In W. Doise & S. Moscovici (Eds.), *Current issues in European social psychology,* (Vol. 1, pp. 201–237). Cambridge, UK: Cambridge University Press.

Rosenberg, M. (1965). *Society and the adolescent self-image.* Princeton, NJ: Princeton University Press.

Rudman, L. A. (2004). Sources of implicit attitudes. *Current Directions in Psychological Science, 13*, 79–82.

Sedikides, C., Gaertner, L., & Toguchi, Y. (2003). Pancultural self-enhancement. *Journal of Personality and Social Psychology*, *84*, 60–79.

Shibata, T., & Nobeji, M. (1990). Seinenki ni okeru shintai manzokudo to jison kanjyou no kanrensei [Relationship between satisfaction with physical fitness and self-esteem among adolescents]. In *Proceedings of the 54th conference of the Japanese Psychological Association* (p. 68). Tokyo, Japan: Japanese Psychological Association.

Tedeschi, J. T. (Ed.). (1981). *Impression management theory and social psychological research*. New York: Academic Press.

Waterman, A. S. (1984). *The psychology of individualism*. New York: Praeger.

Whetstone, M. R., Okun, M. A., & Cialdini, R. B. (1992). *The modest responding scale*. Presented at the Convention of the American Psychological Society, San Diego.

Yagi, Y. (1996). Self-esteem and self-envisagement in response to ego-threat and death-threat. Doctoral Dissertation submitted to the University of Tokyo.

Yamaguchi, S., Greenwald, A. G., Banaji, M. R., Murakami, F., Chen, D., Shiomura, K. et al. (in preparation). Comparisons of implicit and explicit self-esteem among Chinese, Japanese, and North American university students.

Yamaguchi, S., Lin, C., & Aoki, S. (2005). [*Relationship between expressed self-esteem and interpersonal impressions*]. Unpublished data. University of Tokyo.

Yamaguchi, S., & Murakami, F. (2000, October). *Nihonjin no kouteitekina jikokan: The Implicit Association Test ni yoru kentou* [Positive self-regard among Japanese: An examination by the Implicit Association Test]. Paper presented at the 48th conference of the Japanese Group Dynamics Association, Tokyo.

22 Understanding human potential, creativity and achievement: Indigenous, cultural and psychological perspectives

Uichol Kim and Young-Shin Park

Psychology developed in the late 19th century attempting to emulate the success of the natural sciences. Wundt is considered as the founding father of modern psychology (Boring, 1921/1950). He was instrumental in establishing the experimental method in psychology. However, he recognized the limitation of experimental methods and emphasized the importance of *Völkerpsychologie* ("cultural psychology"; Danziger, 1983). He observed that thinking is heavily conditioned by language and customs and regarded *Völkerpsychologie* to be a "more important branch of psychological science which was destined to eclipse experimental psychology" (Danziger, 1983, p. 307). In the latter part of his life he devoted himself to examining sociocultural influences in psychological processes by writing a ten-volume work on *Völkerpsychologie* (Wundt, 1916).

When psychology became institutionalized in North America, psychologists adopted a top-down approach in search of abstract, universal laws of human behavior, emulating natural sciences. Behaviorism emerged as the dominant scientific paradigm and provided the paradigmic direction, method, and substance (Koch & Leary, 1985). The subject matter of psychology became tailored to fit into the narrow definition of science espousing positivism and operationalism (Koch & Leary, 1985). With the entrenchment of behaviorism, influences from the cultural sciences tradition became eliminated (Danziger, 1983).

Although psychology flourished as a discipline and became very successful in terms of number of students, faculty members, research projects, funding and professional organizations (Koch & Leary, 1985), it experienced a crisis of confidence in the 1970s (Cronbach, 1975; Kim, 1999; Koch & Leary, 1985). Elms (1975) noted that, "whether they are experiencing an identity crisis, a paradigmatic crisis, or a crisis in confidence, most seem agreed that a crisis is at hand" (p. 967). The crisis emerged from the inappropriate emulation of the natural sciences and the elimination of subjective aspects of human functioning (i.e., consciousness, agency, and meaning).

Although concepts of agency and consciousness were central in theories developed by Wilhelm Wundt and William James, subsequent theorists have expunged them. The concept of agency refers to the belief that people have control over their actions and they possess "the power to originate actions for given purposes" (Bandura, 1997, p. 2). Bandura (1999) points out that "it is ironic that a science of human functioning should strip people of the very capabilities that make them unique in their power to shape their environment and their own destiny" (p. 21). As such, "psychology has undergone wrenching paradigm shifts" and "in these transformations, the theorists and their followers think, argue and act agentically, but their theories about how other people function grant them little, if any, agentic capabilities" (p. 21).

In human sciences, we are both the subject and the object of investigation. Although the objective third-person point of view is necessary, it is not sufficient. We need to supplement it with the first-person analysis (i.e., agency, meaning and intention; Bandura, 1997) and the second-person analysis (e.g., discourse analysis; Harré & Gillet, 1994). Physical or physiological forces may influence human behavior, but they do not determine it. Human behavior is shaped by the goals that people set for themselves, the skills that they develop and the outcomes that shape their subsequent actions (Kim & Park, 2005). People are agents of their action and motivated to control their lives: "The striving for control over life circumstances permeates almost everything people do throughout the life course because it provides innumerable personal and social benefits" and "unless people believe that they can produce desired effects by their actions, they have little incentive to act" (Bandura, 1997, p. 1).

Creativity is composed of visible and inferred aspects. In science, we organize our data into analytical, theoretical, and epistemological frameworks and publish them in scientific journals. Publications in scientific reports reinforce the perception that the process of research and discovery is objective, rational, and transparent. Holten (1988) points out that the phenomenological and agentic aspects of science (e.g., motives, presuppositions, intuition, insight, methodological judgments, interpretive decisions, and conceptual leaps) are inseparable from objectivity and through subjectivity seminal works in science have been achieved. Albert Einstein noted that "science as an existing, finished [corpus of knowledge] is the most objective, most unpersonal [thing] human beings know, [but] science as something coming into being, as aim, is just as subjective and psychologically conditioned as any other of man's efforts" (cited in Holten, 1988, pp. 6–7).

The inferred aspects can become an integral and explicit part of science in the transactional model of science (see Figure 22.1). Figure 22.1 is an integration of the triadic reciprocal causation and dual causal linkage model proposed by Bandura (1997). Human agency, intention and goal are central components, linking environmental factors on the one hand with human action on the other. Human beings are actors, who not only react and interact with the environment, but also manage and change their environment to meet

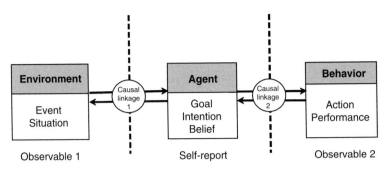

Figure 22.1 Transactional model of causality (adapted from Kim, 1999).

their needs. It is important to examine how an individual perceives or interprets a particular event or situation (Causal linkage 1) and how it influences their goal, intention and beliefs. Since human beings are conscious of the inner state, this intermediate state is assessed through self-report. The second step involves assessing how the event or situation affects, motivates and directs individuals' behavior (Causal linkage 2).

Bandura (1997) identifies self-efficacy as an important agentic factor that links environment and behavior. He defines self-efficacy as "beliefs in one's capabilities to organize and execute the courses of action required to produce given attainments" (p. 3). An outcome is probabilistic rather than determined since a given performance may not always result in the same outcome. In addition, people develop relational, social and collective efficacy to manage the environment in concert with others (Bandura, 1997; Kim & Park, 2005). Behaviors have multiple determinants and culture plays an important role in influencing the goals that people pursue.

Bandura (1997) has found that successful performance or attainment can increase self-efficacy, which can in turn motivate the individual to seek a more challenging goal. An opposite pattern of results has been found for failure experiences. Successful mastery experiences could also lead to *transformative* changes, which can affect other aspects of a person's life. For example, in a series of studies of over 400 snake phobics, who were tormented for 20 to 30 years, Bandura (2004) was able to treat their phobia in a matter of few hours by increasing their self-efficacy through modeling. He found that the mastery of snake phobia transformed their lives and improved areas that were unrelated to snake phobia (e.g., reducing their social timidity, becoming more expressive and increasing their desires to overcome other fears). Nine large-scale meta-analyses were conducted to examine the causal linkage between efficacy beliefs and individual functioning across diverse milieus that used multiple methods, analytic strategies and experiments, and these confirmed the predictive generality of the social cognitive theory (Bandura, 2004).

Bandura (1997) identified four types of control: primary, secondary, proxy and collective control. *Primary control* and *collective control* represent direct control over the environment. If a single person exerts direct control over the environment, then it is an example of primary control. If people work together in concert to manage the environment, then it is an example of collective control (e.g., democracy). *Secondary control* and *proxy control* are examples of indirect control over the environment. If a person obtains assistance from another person in managing the environment, it is an example of proxy control. If a person adjusts to a given environment and regulates him/herself to adapt to the environment, it is an example of secondary control. The effectiveness of each type of control depends on the individual, group and culture.

Bandura (2002, 2004) applied his theory to various settings to help people to take control over their lives. His social cognitive theory has been used to teach diabetic children to manage their health, employees to reduce cholesterol levels, patients with coronary artery disease to implement lifestyle changes, patients with arthritis to manage their pain, and employees, students and athletes to become higher achievers. It has also been used to develop television dramas to foster society-wide changes in health promotion and AIDS prevention in Tanzania, India and Mexico and to reduce the fertility rate and elevate the rights of women in China.

Culture

Culture is not a variable, quasi-independent variable, category, dimension, or a mere sum of individual characteristics. Culture is an emergent property of individuals interacting with and managing their environment. Culture represents the collective utilization of natural and human resources to achieve desired outcomes (Kim, 2000). Differences in cultures can exist if we set different collective goals, utilize different methods and resources to realize the goal and attach different meaning and values to them.

Although human beings have not changed biologically over the past 7000 years, cultural changes have been rather dramatic. Biology cannot explain cultural developments, which are recorded outside of our body and any given individual. Cultural transformations during the last seven millennia have changed the way that we understand and manage our world. Modern nations did not evolve in a logical, sequential, or evolutionary manner. Modern nations arose through clashes of ideas, individuals and cultures (Kim, 2003). We were able to integrate these ideas into new forms. Cultures and nations undergo changes through dialectical transformations. We do not live in a world of certainty, purely determined by physical or biological forces, but we live in a world of possibilities influenced by our generative and creative capabilities (Bandura, 1997).

Our physiology provides us with the basis, but culture helps us to use our physiology to achieve desired outcomes. To use an analogy, computers consist of hardware and software. Our physiology is like the hardware of a computer and culture is like the software (Hofstede, 1991). A computer operates differently depending on the type of software that is downloaded on to it. The socialization experiences of children affect their attitudes, values and behavior and they will differ from other children who grew up in another cultural environment (Kim, Triandis, Choi, Kagitcibasi, & Yoon, 1994). When children are born, although they have the potential to learn any language, they usually learn one language. As adults, their native language feels natural and other languages sound alien. Language and culture provide people with ways to organize their thoughts, communicate with others and manage the world.

People possess self-reflectiveness, agency and creativity that computers do not possess (Bandura, 1999). Computers have to be programmed to run and they operate based on that program. Human beings have the capability not only to change their values, beliefs and skills but also to change themselves, others and their culture. Without culture, human beings would be like other animals, reduced to basic instincts. Without culture, we would not be able to think, feel, or behave the way we do. Culture allows us to know who we are, define what is meaningful, communicate with others and manage our environment. It is *through* culture that we think, feel, behave and manage with our reality (Shweder, 1991). Just as we use our eyes to see the world, we use our culture to understand our world. Because we think *through* our culture, it is difficult to recognize our own culture (Shweder, 1991). For a person born and raised in a particular culture, his/her own culture feels supremely natural.

Western liberal democracy

In the West, the liberal tradition focuses on a rational individual's rights to freely choose, define and search for self-fulfillment (Kim, 1995). The content of self-fulfillment depends on the goals that individuals freely choose. The nature of the goal can vary from one individual to another and can range from hedonistic self-fulfillment to altruism. This freedom of choice is collectively guaranteed by individual human rights.

From a societal point of view, an individual's status or role is not ascribed or predetermined but attained through educational, occupational and economic achievements. Individuals interact with others using mutually accepted principles (e.g., equality, equity, non-interference and detachability), or through mutually established rules, contracts and laws. Individuals with similar goals are brought together into a group and they remain in the group as long as it satisfies their needs. Laws and regulations are institutionalized to protect individual rights and articulate their duties. Everyone is able to assert these rights through the legal system. The state is governed by elected officials, whose role is to protect individual rights and the viability of public institutions. Liberal education provides the necessary training for children to discover and cultivate their rationality. Only those individuals who are considered rational are allowed to participate in political decision-making.

For example, children, the mentally insane and criminals are not given the basic right to vote.

East Asian perspective

Rather than focusing on individual rights and rationality, the East Asian worldview focuses on relationships and emotions that bind individuals together. The Chinese, Japanese and Korean word for human being is *ingan* (人間). Literally translated, it means "human between." The human essence is defined in terms of what happens between individuals and not solely within an individual. Relational emotions that link individuals together, not the private emotions, are emphasized. Relationship, not the individual, is the basic unit of analysis and maintaining harmony is an important goal. Although Western science and technology have been adopted, traditional values and beliefs that emphasize human-relatedness coexist with, and have not been replaced by, individualistic Western values.

East Asian philosophy acknowledges the existence of conflict between opposing forces, such as *yin* (陰) and *yang* (陽). Unlike the West, East Asian philosophy focuses on the balance or harmony between opposing forces. The focus is not on the dichotomous contrast between black and white, right and wrong, but in the shades of gray that occupy the two extreme poles. In East Asia, extremes should be avoided and the middle path should be taken. The East Asian value of self-cultivation, relatedness and harmony has been used to transform past-oriented Confucian societies into future-oriented economic powerhouses.

Educational achievements in East Asia

The 20th century has often been called the Pacific Era to characterize the phenomenal achievements in economics, education and nation-building. At the turn of the century, East Asian societies were far behind in science and technology, lacking in educational, economic and political infrastructure and experiencing national turmoil. Despite limited natural resources, East Asian governments and companies were able to design appropriate educational, political and economic systems to kinetically transform latent human resources into powerful nations. Currently, Japan has the second largest economy in the world. South Korea and Taiwan have one of the fastest growing economies in the past 30 years. China is emerging as a major international player with a rapidly expanding economy.

In 1960, South Korea (abbreviated as Korea) had all the problems of a resource-poor, low-income and under-developed nation (Kim & Park, 2005). The vast majority of people were dependent on agricultural products produced on scarce farmland. The literacy rate and educational level were among the lowest in the world. Korea was one of the poorest countries, with the per capita gross national product (GNP) at a meager $82. Since 1965,

Korea has undergone a phenomenal transformation in the economic, educational, social and political spheres. The Korean economy has been dramatically transformed, growing at an average annual rate of 8%. The per capita GNP increased from $82 in 1960 to $1640 in 1981. By 1997, the per capita GNP reached $10,000.

The phenomenal economic growth in Korea has been spurred by educational transformations. Currently, the literacy and high-school enrollment rate is 99 and 80% of students enroll in a college or university (Park & Kim, 2004). The economic miracle in Korea is closely tied to the educational aspiration and investment made by adolescents and parents. By 1983, Korea had the highest percentage of adolescents wishing to obtain a university degree and the number of parents who wanted their children to at least graduate from university in the world (Park & Kim, 2004).

In international comparisons of academic achievement of middle-school students (National Center for Educational Statistics, 2000, abbreviated as TIMSS; Organisation for Economic Co-operation and Development, 2003, abbreviated as PISA), East Asian students are the top achievers in mathematics, sciences and reading literacy. In the 39-nation study of Grade 8 students, students from Singapore are the top performers, followed by students from Korea, Taiwan, Hong Kong and Japan (TIMSS). In sciences, Taiwanese students are the top performers, followed by students from Singapore, Hungary, Korea and Japan. In the 31-nation study of Grade 9 students (PISA), Japanese students are at the top in mathematics, Korean students are at the top in sciences and they are near the top in reading literacy (Korea is ranked 6th and Japan 8th). The US students are ranked 19th in mathematics and 18th in sciences (TIMSS) and 15th in reading literacy, 19th in mathematical literacy and 14th in scientific literacy (PISA).

These results baffle many psychologists since the results are inconsistent with existing psychological theories. Traditional psychological and educational theories that emphasize biology (i.e., innate ability, IQ), individualistic values (e.g., intrinsic motivation, ability attribution and self-esteem) and structural features (e.g., high educational spending, small class size and individualized instruction) cannot explain the relatively poor performance of American students and the high performance of East Asian students.

First, at the turn of the 20th century, Asians were regarded as a "kind of inferior species, who could be used for unskilled labor and menial jobs, but could never be accepted as equals into the white community" (Vernon, 1982, p. 2). When the number of Asian immigrants began to increase, the US Congress passed the National Origins Act in 1924 barring immigrations from Asia (Kim, 1992). These laws were passed due to fears that this "genetically inferior" Asian race would pollute the genetic pool of the USA and lead to nation degeneracy (Chorover, 1980).

Recently, Lynn and Vanhanen (2002) proclaimed the same eugenic ideal, but with a different set of results. In their study of 60 nations, they found that East Asians had the highest IQs: 106 for Koreans, 105 for Japanese, 104 for

Taiwanese and 103 for Singaporeans. The Europeans and Americans had lower scores: 98 for the USA, 100 for the United Kingdom and 102 for Germany. They conclude that the IQ scores accurately reflect the racial superiority of the Mongolian race. East Asians have now become a superior race due to their genes, although they were considered as genetically inferior only 80 years ago.

Second, although the US government spends more money per student than the East Asian governments and Americans schools have smaller classes with individualized instruction, American students perform far below their East Asian counterparts. Despite significantly greater investments made by the US government, American students lag far behind East Asian students.

Third, developmental theories developed by Freud, Piaget, behaviorists and humanists largely ignore the role played by parents. Although attachment theory examines the role of parents, separation and individuation are viewed as necessary for secure attachment and healthy human development. In East Asia, parents play a central role in child development by defining the goals of socialization, teaching them the necessary cognitive, linguistic, relational and social skills and providing them with a supportive family environment. Parents play an important role throughout one's lifetime and maintenance of strong familial relationships is the key to education and economic success and maintaining a high quality of life (Kim & Park, 2005).

Fourth, concepts such as guilt have a very different connotation and utility in East Asia (Kim & Park, 2005). In Western psychoanalytic and psychological theories, guilt is presumed to be based on irrational beliefs, unrealistic fear, or forbidden wishes. Extensive use of guilt is believed to cause later developmental problems in adolescence. In East Asia, it is considered appropriate that children feel guilty or indebted toward their parents for all the devotion, indulgence, sacrifice and love that they receive from them. Children feel indebted since they cannot return the love and care that they received from parents. Guilt in East Asia is viewed as an important interpersonal emotion that promotes filial piety, achievement motivation and relational closeness.

The phenomenal educational attainment in East Asian societies has been systematically documented (Kim & Park, 2003, 2005; Stevenson, Azuma, & Hakuta, 1986; Stevenson & Lee, 1990). The main factor that is responsible for the high performance is the socialization practices that promote and maintain a strong relational and emotional bond between parents and children. It is the role of the parents to provide a positive family environment for their children and pressure children to succeed (Azuma, 1986; Ho, 1986; Kim & Park, 2003, 2005). Children learn to discipline themselves and develop their academic skills with the help of their parents. This type of socialization promotes the development of proxy control. A second major factor is the emphasis on self-regulation, especially the belief of persistent effort. The third major factor is the compatibility of values between the family and school environment that promotes collective efficacy.

Interdependence and proxy control

Relationship, not the individual, is the basic unit in East Asia. The parent–child relationship provides the basis for the development of the self. Parental devotion, sacrifice and support are important features of the traditional socialization practice that still remain in modern East Asia (Azuma, 1986; Ho, 1986; Kim & Park, 2005). In East Asia, a mother remains close to the child to make the child feel secure, to make the boundary between herself and the child minimal and to meet all of the needs of the child. Children's strong dependency needs, both emotional and physical, are satisfied by their mother's indulgent devotion, even if that means a tremendous sacrifice on her own part.

A mother's job is to use her close relationship with her children to encourage them to discipline themselves and to succeed in school. She becomes a mediator between the home environment and the school environment by socializing appropriate values and norms. As children grow up, they are expected to extend and transfer their interdependent identification and loyalty from their mothers to their teachers.

In East Asia, the relationship between teachers and their students is seen as an extension of the mother–child relationship. A typical climate in schools affirms maternalism, pressures the students to strive for personal excellence and encourages them to cooperate in a group. Children are motivated to please the teacher and their attention is focused on the teacher. Even in a class size that is as large as 40–60, East Asian students are more attentive, less disruptive and more devoted to doing their schoolwork than students in the West (Kim & Park, 2005).

Self-regulation

The second important value is the emphasis on self-regulation, especially the emphasis on persistent effort. Consistent with Confucian philosophy, individual striving is viewed as a necessary component of the self-cultivation process. Excellence in performance provides evidence that a child has developed a moral character through perseverance and persistence. It is a visible demonstration that a child has deeper abilities to be a virtuous person. Holloway, Kasgiwagi, and Azuma (1986) point out that "the emphasis on individual effort includes a sense of responsibility to the group to which one belongs" (p. 272). In East Asia, individuals are pressured to contribute to the group through hard work and success is collectively defined and shared. While natural talent and ability are emphasized in the West, in East Asia effort and self-cultivation are highly valued.

Lebra (1976) has found, in a free-association task, that over 70% of Japanese respondents (both young and old, men and women) attribute success to diligence, effort and endurance and only 1% attribute it to ability. Other researchers (Holloway et al., 1986; Kim & Park, 2003; Park & Kim,

2004; Stevenson et al., 1986, 1990) similarly found that East Asian students, parents and teachers attribute poor performance in school to a lack of effort rather than ability. Euro American students, parents and teachers are most likely to attribute failure to a lack of ability (Holloway et al., 1986; Stevenson et al., 1986, 1990).

Collective control

In East Asia, there is a greater congruence of values emphasized in the family, school and society than there is in the West. In the West, individualistic values are often in conflict with a relatively hierarchical classroom structure, curriculum and the teacher–student relationship (White & LeVine, 1986). In addition, students, parents, teachers and administrators often hold different views about the meaning of success and the factors that lead to success (White & LeVine, 1986). In the West, development of one's talent, whether it is in sports, music, or the arts, is emphasized and academic achievement may not be considered as the primary goal. The diversity of viewpoints is considered to be the strength in individualistic societies, but it is can lead to conflicts among the students, parents and teachers when it comes to academic achievement.

In East Asia, students, parents and teachers unanimously agree that academic achievement is the primary goal for children and adolescents to attain and they work together towards this goal. There is greater agreement among all parties about the goals of education and the method of achieving these goals. This collective agreement among family, school and society promotes collective efficacy and is a key factor in motivating students to attain a high level of achievement (Kim & Park, 2005).

Organizational culture

In East Asia, researchers note that industrialization, urbanization and capitalism have not significantly altered the underlying cultural value system that emphasizes human-relatedness (Kim & Park, 2005). The phenomenal economic progress of East Asian countries has been achieved due to the maintenance of human-relatedness. Capitalism itself became modified to fit underlying East Asian cultural values that emphasize human-relatedness (Kim, 1988, 1994; Misumi, 1985; Yu & Yang, 1994).

With modernization, the focus has changed from status quo, conservatism and harmony with nature to change, progress and control of the environment (Kim, 2001a). Traditionally, learning has been linked to Confucian classics and literature, but currently it is defined by the acquisition of scientific and technological knowledge. The primary role of the parents is to educate their children in a highly competitive world. Although women did not traditionally receive a formal education, currently both men and women are educated to succeed in life and to raise their children.

Contrary to the Western emphasis on individual rights, competition and contractual relationship between employees and employers, organizations in East Asia are managed as an extension of the family (Kim, 1998; Misumi, 1985; Yu & Yang, 1994). In these societies, companies and governments encourage paternalism, cooperation and contribution to the group. Employers in a company look after their employees in the same way that parents look after their children and the employees are expected to be loyal, committed and hard-working.

In a national survey of personnel managers from mining and manufacturing firms in Korea, the vast majority (over 80%) of managers strongly endorsed the ideas of paternalism and collectivism (Kim, 1994). These companies provide occupational and welfare services to their employees to foster paternalism, in-group solidarity and collectivism, which are found to increase production, efficiency, solidarity, loyalty, job satisfaction and social control (Kim, 1994).

In comparative studies of US and Japanese managers, the nature and role of a group are viewed very differently (Sullivan, Suzuki, & Kondo, 1986). The authors found that American managers gave rewards based on individual performance and they provided greater rewards to individuals when an employee worked alone. In the minds of American managers, the successful person working alone can expect the greatest amount of reward. The Japanese managers, in contrast, distributed rewards equally and gave greater rewards to individuals who worked in a group and who had been influenced by the group. Japanese managers see groups as *productivity enhancers* (i.e., as a facilitating factor; Sullivan et al., 1986). Consistent with this belief, Japanese managers rewarded individuals who worked with their group members in a highly interdependent manner and who were highly influenced by the group's attitudes and advice. Similarly, Gabrenya, Wang, and Latané (1985) found that for meaningful, skill-related tasks, the US students who worked in a group tended to loaf (called "social loafing"), while Chinese students tended to work harder in a group (called "social striving").

Justice and organizational effectiveness

In decision-making and negotiation theories developed in the West, a tit-for-tat strategy is considered to be the most effective (Axelrod & Hamilton, 1981). In other words, if your partner cooperates, then you cooperate with the partner. If your partner does not cooperate, then you do not cooperate (i.e., *lex talionis*, "an eye for an eye, a tooth for a tooth, and a life for a life"). Systematic researches suggest that this is the most effective strategy in inducing cooperation and positive outcome in the West and this model has been widely used in psychological, economic, social and political sciences (Axelrod & Hamilton, 1981).

In East Asia, the seniority norm is prevalent. In the seniority norm, reward is not based on individual performance, but on how long a person has been with the group. In a typical university in Japan, Korea or Taiwan, senior professors are paid much more than junior professors (Kim, 1995). They have the largest offices and have access to the greatest resources, even though the junior professors may be much more productive than the senior professors. Moreover, the junior professors are expected to serve the senior professors and handle much of the administrative burden. It creates a temporary imbalance with the senior professors receiving much more benefit than the junior professors. Equity is achieved when the junior professors become senior professors, since they will receive all the benefits that are linked to their status and they will have junior professors serving them (see Figure 22.2). In the long-term relational perspective, justice and equity are maintained. Yuki and Yamaguchi (1996) called this phenomenon the long-term equity within a group.

In the relational perspective, individuals are motivated to maintain the group. Since senior professors are obtaining benefits beyond their contribution, they are motivated to remain in the group and to maintain the group. The junior professors will only receive the greater benefits as along as they remain in the group (i.e., when they become senior professors). As a result, they are motivated to maintain the group. The seniority norm enhances group solidarity, commitment and loyalty and it has been widely adopted in East Asia (Kim, 1998; Yuki & Yamaguchi, 1996). However, since the reward is not directly linked to performance, it could also lead to incompetence, corruption and nepotism (Kim, 1998, 2001b).

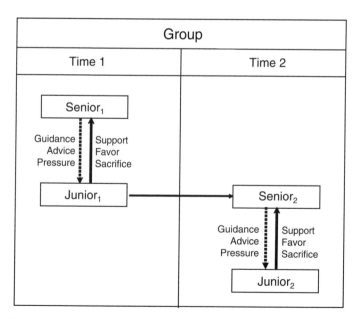

Figure 22.2 Relational model of equity (adapted from Kim, 1998).

In addition to the seniority norm, East Asians interact with others differently depending on the relationship. When *Person A* has contributed 70% to the overall outcome and *Person B* has contributed 30%, then the equitable distribution would be to give $70 to *Person A* and $30 to *Person B*. In the West, this type of distribution is considered fair and just (Kim, Park, & Suzuki, 1990; Leung & Bond, 1984). In East Asia, if *Person A* is not related to *Person B* (i.e., is an out-group member), then the reward is distributed equitably 70:30. If, however, the partner is an in-group member, then the high performer will divide the reward equally (i.e., 50:50; Kim et al., 1990; Leung & Bond, 1984). In other words, the high performer will sacrifice his/her reward and give it to the in-group member (see Figure 22.3). The sacrificial behavior of the high performer can promote a sense of gratitude, loyalty and harmony. Although there is a temporary imbalance, the high performer expects future benefits from the friend or from the in-group (Yamagishi, Jin, & Miller, 1998). This type of distribution is based on the indigenous parent–child model, where it is the role of parents to sacrifice for their children and of children to feel indebted to the parents (Park & Kim, 2004).

In families, East Asian parents willingly make personal sacrifices for their children since their own parents took care of them unconditionally when they were young (Park & Kim, 2004). Children are expected to return their sense of gratitude to the parents, but not the favor. They are expected to raise their own children with the same degree of sacrifice, devotion and love as their parents did. This flow of sacrifice, devotion and love is what binds family members together through generations and keeps them strong. It is the flow of emotions from one generation to another that is valued in East Asia, not the tit-for-tat exchange.

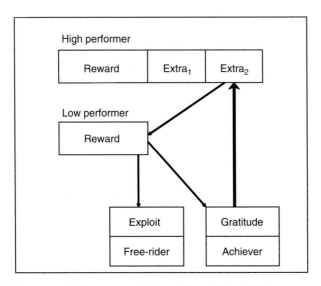

Figure 22.3 Harmony within a group (adapted from Kim, 1998).

This long-term relational perspective among in-group members, rather than the short-term tit-for-tat strategy, is accepted as being just, fair and effective in East Asia since it promotes group solidarity, loyalty and harmony. The long-term relational perspective is a cultural norm and it has been widely adopted and implemented in East-Asian schools, organizations and companies. This principle is behind the Sunshine Policy that president Kim Dae-jung has been pursuing with North Korea (Kim, 2001b). It is, however, not without its problems.

There are two possible outcomes for organizations adopting the long-term relational perspective. The low-performing employee will receive the same benefits as the high-performing employee. In the ideal situation, the low-performing employee should feel a sense of shame, indebtedness and gratitude and work harder to contribute to the group. This will create synergy and organizational dynamism and it is responsible for the high level of productivity in East Asia. If, however, the low-performing employee simply accepts the reward without the intention or motivation to contribute to the group (known as free-riding), then it will lead to organizational ineffectiveness and discontent (Yamagishi et al., 1998).

The high-performing employees expect to be rewarded in the long term. If they are not rewarded, then they will leave the organization (Kim, 1998; Yamagishi et al., 1998). Thus, if the long-term contingency is not rectified, the high-performing employees will leave the company and the fate of the company is left to low-performing free-riders who do not contribute to the company. As a result, the company will face financial and moral bankruptcy. This is the basis of the Asian economic crisis that has plagued East Asia (Kim, 2001b).

The long-term relational perspective has contributed to the phenomenal educational and economic progress in East Asia. It has, however, also contributed to incompetence, nepotism and corruption. Strong leaders, such as Park Chung-hee, Lee Kwan Yew and Mohamad Mahathir, used the long-term relational perspective to justify their policies. However, in order for the long-term relational perspective to be effective in companies, organizations and society, the system must be trusted by the people. Institutions in East Asia are not trusted since they lack transparency, integrity and accountability (Helgesen & Kim, 2002; Kim, 2001b). Although East Asian countries have developed economically, they are ranked low in transparency: Japan was ranked 24th, Korea 47th, Taiwan 35th and China 71st in 2004 (Transparency International, 2005).

The problem can be resolved when the system becomes transparent and everyone knows who the high and low performers are (Kim, 1998). The low performer will be compelled to work harder or leave the group since he or she will experience a sense of shame. The high performer will be rewarded equitably in the long run. Transparency is also necessary to ensure that every member of the group will behave with integrity. Finally, individuals need to be held accountable for their behavior. Without transparency, integrity and accountability, some individuals and groups will not be motivated to work hard and contribute to the group, and corruption and conflicts could emerge.

Discussion

Human behavior is influenced by physical and physiological factors but it is are not determined by them. Human behavior is mediated by cognitive and emotional factors of agency, meaning, intentions, and goals. We must be cautious of external impositions that may distort our understanding. First, psychologists imposed the natural sciences model on to the study of human beings. Although psychologists were able to achieve a modest degree of methodological sophistication, psychological knowledge became distorted.

The second imposition is the assumption of the universality of psychological theories. With very little development, testing and data, psychological theories are assumed to be universal. This assumption is particularly problematic since most theories are developed in the USA and tested mainly on university students in a laboratory setting. Theories that were tested on less than 1% of the total population have been assumed to be universal. We do not know very much about people of other cultures and erroneous conclusions have been made since psychologists assumed that their theories were universal.

Third, experts or professionals have imposed their views on the lay public. Psychologists have been premature in developing theories, concepts and methods without understanding the phenomenon itself. General psychology has largely failed to describe psychological phenomena from the inside, from the experiencing person. Instead, psychologists have dissected the world into cognitions, motivations, emotions and behavior, whereas in real life these elements are components of experience and not the unit of experience. General psychology can be best described as the *psychology of psychologists*. It represents the way psychologist understand people and not necessarily the way people understand themselves and the world.

Psychology needs to examine human potential, creativity and imagination. Psychology is a discipline that can link humanities (which focus on human experience and creativity) with social sciences (which focus on analysis and verification). However, psychologists focused our attention on scientific analysis and ignored the creative side of human potential. Psychology has the potential to become a basic science that can provide the basis to understand ourselves and how we manage our environment.

References

Axelrod, R., & Hamilton, W. D. (1981). The evolution of cooperation. *Science, 211,* 1390–1396.

Azuma, H. (1986). Why study child development in Japan? In H. Stevenson, H. Azuma, & K. Hakuta (Eds.), *Child development and education in Japan* (pp. 3–12). New York: W. H. Freeman.

Bandura, A. (1997). *Self-efficacy: The exercise of control*. New York: Freeman.

Bandura, A. (1999). Social cognitive theory: An agentic perspective. *Asian Journal of Social Psychology*, *2*, 21–42.

Bandura, A. (2002). Environmental sustainability by sociocognitive deceleration of population growth. In P. Schmuck & W. Schultz (Eds.), *The psychology of sustainable development* (pp. 209–238). Dordrecht, The Netherlands: Kluwer.

Bandura, A. (2004). Swimming against the mainstream: The early years from chilly tributary to transformative mainstream. *Behavior Research and Therapy*, *42*, 613–630.

Boring, E. G. (1950). *A history of experimental psychology*. Englewood Cliffs, NJ: Prentice Hall. (Original work published 1921)

Chorover, S. L. (1980). *From genesis to genocide: The meaning of human nature and the power of behavior control*. Cambridge, MA: MIT Press.

Cronbach, L. J. (1975). The two disciplines of scientific psychology. *American Psychologist*, *30*, 671–684.

Danziger, K. (1983). Origins and basic principles of Wundt's Volkerpsychologie. *British Journal of Social Psychology*, *22*, 303–313.

Elms, A. C. (1975). The crisis in confidence in social psychology. *American Psychologist*, *30*, 967–976.

Gabrenya, W. K., Jr., Wang, Y. E., & Latané, B. (1985). Social loafing on an optimizing task: Cross-cultural differences among Chinese and Americans. *Journal of Cross-Cultural Psychology*, *16*(2), 223–242.

Harré, R., & Gillet, G. (1994). *The discursive mind*. Thousand Oaks, CA: Sage.

Helgesen, G., & Kim, U. (2002). *Good government: Nordic and East Asian perspectives*. Copenhagen, Denmark: Danish Institute of International Affairs.

Ho, D. Y. F. (1986). Chinese patterns of socialization: A critical review. In M. H. Bond (Ed.), *The psychology of the Chinese people*. Oxford, UK: Oxford University Press.

Hofstede, G. (1991). *Cultures and organizations: Software of the mind*. New York: McGraw-Hill.

Holloway, S., Kasgiwagi, K., & Azuma, H. (1986). Causal attributions by Japanese and American mothers and children about performance in mathematics. *International Journal of Psychology*, *21*, 269–286.

Holten, G. (1988). *Thematic origins of scientific thought: From Kepler to Einstein* (Rev. ed.). Cambridge, MA: Harvard University Press.

Kim, H. C. (Ed.). (1992). *Asian Americans and the Supreme Court: A documentary history*. New York: Greenwood.

Kim, K., Park, H. J., & Suzuki, N. (1990). Reward allocations in the United States, Japan and Korea: A comparison of individualistic and collectivistic cultures. *Academy of Management Journal*, *33*, 188–198.

Kim, U. (1995). Psychology, science and culture: Cross-cultural analysis of national psychologies in developing countries. *International Journal of Psychology*, *30*, 663–679.

Kim, U. (1998). Understanding Korean corporate culture: Analysis of transformative human resource management. *Strategic Human Resource Development Review*, *2*, 68–101.

Kim, U. (1999). After the "crisis" in social psychology: Development of the transactional model of science. *Asian Journal of Social Psychology*, *2*, 1–19.

Kim, U. (2000). Indigenous, cultural and cross-cultural psychology: Theoretical, philosophical and epistemological analysis. *Asian Journal of Social Psychology, 3,* 265–287.

Kim, U. (2001a). Culture, science and indigenous psychologies: An integrated analysis. In D. Matsumoto (Ed.), *Handbook of culture and psychology* (pp. 51–76). Oxford, UK: Oxford University Press.

Kim, U. (2001b). Analysis of democracy and human rights in cultural context: Psychological and comparative perspectives. In H. S. Aasen, U. Kim, & G. Helgesen (Eds.), *Democracy, human rights, and peace in Korea: Psychological, political, and cultural perspectives* (pp. 53–94). Seoul, Korea: Kyoyook Kwahasa.

Kim, U. (2003). Science, religion, philosophy and culture: Psychological analysis of Western, Islamic and East Asian worldviews. In U. Kim, H. S. Aasen, & S. Ebadi (Eds.), *Democracy, human rights and Islam in modern Iran: Psychological, social, cultural perspectives* (pp. 443–496). Bergen, Norway: Fagbokforlaget.

Kim, U., & Park, Y. S. (2003). An indigenous analysis of success attribution: Comparison of Korean students and adults. In K. S. Yang, K. K. Hwang, P. Pedersen, & I. Daibo (Eds.), *Progress in Asian social psychology: Conceptual and empirical contributions* (pp. 171–195). New York: Praeger.

Kim, U., & Park, Y. S. (2005). Integrated analysis of indigenous psychologies. *Asian Journal of Social Psychology, 8*(1), 75–95.

Kim, U., Triandis, H. C., Choi, S. C., Kagitcibasi, C., & Yoon, G. (Eds.). (1994). *Individualism and collectivism: Theory, method and application.* Thousand Oaks, CA: Sage.

Kim, U. M. (1994). Significance of paternalism and communalism in the occupational welfare system of Korean firms: A national survey. In U. Kim, H. C. Triandis, C. Kagitcibasi, S. C. Choi, & G. Yoon (Eds.), *Individualism and collectivism: Theory, method and application.* Thousand Oaks, CA: Sage.

Koch, S., & Leary, D. E. (1985). *A century of psychology as science.* New York: McGraw-Hill.

Lebra, T. S. (1976). *Japanese patterns of behavior.* Honolulu, HI: East-West Center.

Leung, K., & Bond, M. H. (1984). The impact of cultural collectivism on reward allocation. *Journal of Personality and Social Psychology, 47,* 793–804.

Lynn, R., & Vanhanen, T. (2002). *IQ and the wealth of nations.* Westport, CT: Praeger.

Misumi, J. (1985). *The behavioral science of leadership.* Ann Arbor, MI: The University of Michigan.

National Center for Educational Statistics [TIMSS] (2000). *Mathematics and science in eighth grade: Findings from the Third International Mathematics and Science Study.* Washington, DC: US Department of Education.

Organisation for Economic Co-operation and Development [PISA] (2003). *Education at a glance: OECD indicators.* Paris: OECD

Park, Y. S., & Kim, U. (2004). *Adolescent culture and parent–child relationship in Korea: Indigenous psychological analysis* [in Korean]. Seoul, Korea: Kyoyook Kwahaksa.

Shweder, R. A. (1991). *Thinking through cultures: Expeditions in cultural psychology.* Cambridge, MA: Harvard University Press.

Stevenson, H., Azuma, H., & Hakuta, K. (Eds.). (1986). *Child development and education in Japan.* New York: W. H. Freeman.

Stevenson, H., & Lee, S. Y. (1990). Context of achievement: A study of American, Chinese and Japanese children. *Monographs of the Society for Research in Child Development, 55*(1–2, Serial number 221).

Sullivan, J. J., Suzuki, T., & Kondo, Y. (1986). Managerial perceptions of performance: A comparison of Japanese and American work groups. *Journal of Cross-Cultural Psychology, 17*, 379–398.

Transparency International (2005). *Corruption perception index*. (Available at: www.transparency.org/policy_and_research/surveys_indices/cpi)

Vernon, P. E. (1982). *The abilities and achievements of Orientals in North America*. New York: Academic Press.

White, M. I., & LeVine, R. A. (1986). What is an *li ko* (good child)? In H. Stevenson, H. Azuma, & K. Hakuta (Eds.), *Child development and education in Japan* (pp. 55–62). New York: W. H. Freeman.

Wundt, W. (1916). *Elements of folk psychology: Outlines of a psychological history of the development of mankind*. [E. L. Schaub, Trans.]. London: George Allen & Unwin.

Yamagishi, T., Jin, N., & Miller, A. S. (1998). In-group favoritism and culture of collectivism. *Asian Journal of Social Psychology, 1*, 315–328.

Yu, A. B., & Yang, K. S. (1994). The nature of achievement motivation in collectivistic societies. In U. Kim, H. C. Triandis, C. Kagitcibasi, S. C. Choi, & G. Yoon. (Eds.), *Individualism and collectivism: Theory, method and applications* (pp. 239–250). Thousand Oaks, CA: Sage.

Yuki, M., & Yamaguchi, S. (1996). Long-term equity within a group: An application of the seniority norm in Japan. In H. Grad, A. Blanco, & J. Georgas (Eds.), *Key issues in cross-cultural psychology* (pp. 288–297). Lisse, The Netherlands: Swets & Zeitlinger.

Section IV

Organizational, applied and international psychology

23 Investigating five leadership themes: Roles, decisions, character, relationships, and journeys

Leon Mann

The subject of leadership can be approached in many different ways. How we approach leadership – who and what we choose to study, the activities and events that we analyze, and the conceptual frameworks that we use to understand leadership – determines what we see and, therefore, conclude about the main issues: Who is a leader? How important are leaders? What difference do they make? What drives and motivates them? What makes a capable leader? What is the essence of effective leadership? How do we nurture leadership?

Yukl (1998) in a review of leadership theory and research observed that "most of the research on leadership during the past half century has been conducted in the United States, Canada and Western Europe." Similarly, House and Aditya (1997) noted that "almost all of the prevailing theories of leadership and about 98 percent of the empirical evidence at hand, are distinctly American in character: individualistic rather than collectivistic, stressing follower responsibilities rather than rights . . ." (p. 409). But there is a long tradition of writing about political, military, and spiritual leadership in many Asian countries and it is important to note the recent emergence of a strong research interest in leadership in China and other Asian countries, especially in regard to the moral dimension of leadership. Rost (1991), who conducted a historical review of the literature on leadership, concluded that "leadership . . . has come to mean many things to all people" (p. 7) and that "scholars and practitioners of leadership are no more sure of what leadership is in 1990 than they were in 1930" (p. 17). While the diversity of views about leadership may indicate a field without direction, a more positive reading is that there are many valid ways to define, approach, and understand leadership and this testifies to both the complexity and the richness of the field.

Five approaches to leadership

The conceptual framework that I use to study leadership draws upon five recurring themes in leadership writing and research. The five themes are:

(1) leadership as a set of roles, activities, and behaviors; (2) leadership and crucial decisions; (3) leaders and their personal characteristics and attributes; (4) leadership as a set of vital social relationships; and (5) leadership as a journey. Some themes are broader in scope than others, and while the five themes touch on different aspects of leadership they, of course, overlap. I do not claim this is an exhaustive list of themes. It could be argued, for example, that one of the most important approaches to leadership is missing, namely, leadership as the exercise of authority, power, and influence. Thus, Rost (1991) writes that *"Influence* is probably the word most often used in the leadership definitions of the 1980s" (p. 79).

Some themes are dominant in Western studies of leadership. For example, the study of leader characteristics and attributes is prominent in Western research, perhaps because of the tendency to focus on the individual to explain social phenomena and the emphasis on assessment and selection of people for leadership training and development. Other themes have received less attention – for example, the factors underpinning the nature and dynamics of leader–follower relationships, the theme of leadership career and of leadership as a personal and shared journey, and the study of leadership as the exercise of strategic decision making. I will return later to the theme of leadership as a journey and discuss why it is a powerful entry point to the study of leadership.

Looking at leaders

The five approaches to leadership will be illustrated in reference to team leaders. The five approaches are just as applicable to the analysis of leadership at the top of organizations and institutions, but the focus is on team leadership because I am able to draw on my own research to illustrate and compare the five themes. There are many kinds of teams – for example, sales and marketing teams, hospital emergency teams, product-development teams, search and rescue teams – and accordingly many kinds of team leadership roles and tasks (Cohen & Bailey, 1997). My specific interest is in Research and Development (R&D) teams (Mann, 2005). R&D teams include university research teams investigating the structure of brain cells, pharmaceutical development teams, and automobile product-development teams. These teams are made up of scientists, technologists, engineers, and sometimes psychologists and other professionals who work on a new idea, concept, or product. The leader's role in R&D teams is to manage, coordinate, and motivate the team to produce creative and innovative work. The leadership task in R&D teams corresponds to what Robert Kelley (1998) calls "small-l leadership," as practiced among peers. "Small-l" leaders manage their teams by working closely together with colleagues, gaining their trust and respect, rather than by resorting to the exercise of power and authority. In contrast, "large-L leadership," which is more strategic and direction setting, is found at the top of organizations in the form of senior executive teams, policy-making groups, company boards, and so on.

In brief, the leadership task varies across levels in the organization and is related to the nature and purpose of the team. This, in turn, is relevant to an analysis of the most useful approaches to the study of team leadership. The themes that we follow provide different meanings and insights into leadership. The perspective taken makes a difference to what is studied – for example, the individual leader, or the relationship between leader and followers, or the nature of the task on which leaders are engaged. The themes also influence an understanding of the importance of leaders, the nature of leadership, and the lessons learned. For example, if leadership is essentially all about the leader's personal attributes, presumably there is less interest in looking at what they actually do when interacting with peers and followers.

Application of the five themes in the study of team leaders

Over the past decade I have studied leadership of R&D project teams in Australian organizations, investigating the importance of the team leader for team performance and innovativeness, comparing new and experienced leaders. The Australian Research Council (ARC) provided support for a project titled "Effective R&D Project Leaders," a longitudinal study of 29 new leaders and 29 experienced leaders, together with their teams. The ARC study involved leaders from four research organizations, which differed in the type of R&D performed. BHP Research carried out research on steel and aluminum products. ICI conducted research on paints and explosives. CSIRO, a publicly-funded organization, conducted research in areas such as forests, materials, water, information technology, plants, entomology, environment, and nutrition. DSTO, also a publicly funded organization, conducted research on defense and surveillance systems, airplane and ship structures. When I began studying team leaders there was no plan to examine leadership from five different themes or perspectives. But looking back, it is apparent that the five themes influenced the way that I approached the study. In the remainder of this chapter I draw on data and findings from the ARC study to illustrate the five themes and their relevance to team leadership.

Leaders and activities/behaviors (roles)

The tradition of defining leadership and classifying leader and manager roles according to the tasks and activities performed stems from Henry Mintzberg (1973), R. E. Quinn (1988), and Gary Yukl (1998). This approach is about what leaders actually do. Senior leaders devise plans, make strategy, allocate resources, monitor organizational performance, handle disputes, and so on.

What do team leaders do? Bain and Mann (1997) identified four leader roles as important for R&D teams. They are: (1) knowledge builder (provides scientific knowledge and expertise to the team); (2) stakeholder liaison (coordinates the team's tasks with outside stakeholders who provide authority and resources to the team); (3) standards upholder (establishes standards and priorities); and (4) team builder (engages in activities to build relationships within the team).

The knowledge-builder role is at the core of the team's task – bringing together the ideas, experience, and creativity of the team to discover new things, find solutions, design new products, and develop new knowledge. The leader does this by leading from the front, through expert knowledge and expertise, by encouraging new approaches and methods to unlock puzzles and problems, by encouraging team members to search widely for information and new ideas. In a world in which information and knowledge are the keys to innovation and competitive advantage, leaders who are outstanding knowledge builders are a precious asset for their organization.

The team-builder role describes the task of creating a climate where team members have cordial relationships, trust each other, feel valued for their contributions, have some autonomy in how they perform their work and, importantly, feel free to express their ideas and opinions.

The stakeholder-liaison role involves acting as the team's representative, ambassador, spokesman, and advocate for resources to the wider organization and to the outside world. The term "boundary spanning" describes the leader's liaison function in meeting with and briefing managers, customers, funding agencies, etc., about the team's work and its progress.

The standards-upholder role is a more routine leadership role, which involves the leader in monitoring the team's work and ensuring that it complies with proper scientific, safety, environmental, and ethical standards set down by the organization and the industry.

The significance of the first three leadership roles – knowledge builder, team builder, and stakeholder liaison – is very evident from the study of team performance in the ARC study. All 58 leaders were rated by their teams on the Project Leader Questionnaire (Bain & Mann, 1997), which measures leadership role performance. Leaders who performed well as knowledge builders, team builders, and stakeholder liaisons (as rated by members of their team) were in charge of teams whose project work was evaluated highly by customers and by team members themselves. Thus, the leader's standing as a knowledge builder, team builder, and stakeholder liaison, was positively correlated with ratings of team performance, .35, .36, and .42 (using team-member ratings) and .24, .43, and .30 (using customer ratings) (see Table 23.1). And when the role profiles of leaders of the 16 best-rated teams are compared with leaders of the 16 worst-rated teams, the superiority of the leaders of the best teams on the knowledge-builder, team-builder, and stakeholder-liaison roles is readily apparent (see Figure 23.1).

My doctoral student, Pauline Lee (2005) focused on the leader's role as a knowledge builder and knowledge sharer in her study of the performance of 34 product-development teams at Holden Engineering in Australia. Consistent with findings from the ARC study, she found that leaders who were highly rated as knowledge builders were in charge of the best performing teams ($r = .60$).

Table 23.1 Correlations between team leader role performance and project performance

Leader role performance (team-rated)	Project performance as rated by	
	Team (n = 52–54)	Customer (n = 25–27)
Knowledge builder	.35**	.24
Stakeholder liaison	.42**	.30
Standards upholder	.05	−.12
Team builder	.36**	.43*

*p < .05; **p < .01.

Leader performed

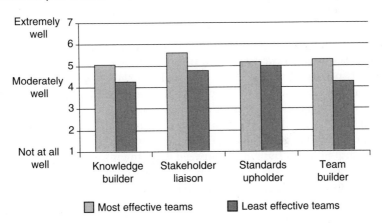

Figure 23.1 Most and least effective teams. Ratings of the leader's role performance.

The ARC study findings show the significance of the leader's ability to perform a variety of roles that contribute to the team's performance. While some team leaders are good in all roles, many excel in only one role and lead with that strength. Their colleagues will cover for shortcomings as long as the leader is at least competent in the other roles. But team leaders weak in all roles are considered "passengers," and lose the respect of their colleagues – and when that happens their team is in trouble, as we found in some teams in the ARC study.

Leadership and decision making

Leading any organization or project involves making strategic and consequential decisions, but, surprisingly, the links between leadership and decision making are under-explored in the research literature. There are, however, models linking leadership and decision making, such as Vroom and Yetton's (1973) normative decision model, Heller and Yukl's (1969) participative leadership model, Janis and Mann's (1977) conflict theory of decision making, and Janis's (1972) analysis of the vulnerability of policy-making groups to groupthink, a pattern of flawed thinking and decision making, due to leadership failure and conformity pressures in "knowledge" teams.

Leaders of project teams often face difficult decisions, for example, recognizing that the use of an incorrect procedure has compromised months of research activity, or deciding to drop a veteran team member who is not performing. Perhaps the most important decision that team leaders face is whether to fight to protect a cherished project that is running into major difficulties and is consuming large amounts of time and resources. We found many examples in the ARC study of leaders who faced difficult decisions, and how they handled them had major consequences for both their team and the organization.

An example of a leader whose flawed decision making had negative repercussions was "Walt," the leader of the "Pygmalion" project, which worked on a new process to remove impurities from compound substances. Walt was a new, inexperienced leader who was frustrated by what he considered unreasonable demands from the project customer. Walt, without consulting his manager and colleagues, decided to abandon the project about 6 months after it had begun. His precipitous decision meant that his team was left without a project to work on and the manager was left to deal with a political dispute and bitter recrimination between departments in the organization.

A contrasting example was "Terry," the new leader of the "Geodiscovery" project, whose bold decision making had benefits for his team. Three years into the project and 6 months after Terry became leader, there was a crisis in the "Geodiscovery" project. The complex working prototype at the heart of the project had failed a series of critical tests. Terry, who was not an expert in the field, had relied extensively on the advice of his senior team members, two of whom insisted that the problem could be fixed with more time and resources. Terry's own inquiries led to a different conclusion – that the prototype was inherently flawed and therefore would continue to fail. Despite strong opposition, Terry, with the support of his manager, asserted his leadership authority and discarded the prototype for a simpler approach. The "Geodiscovery" team then made rapid progress and produced a simpler, successful prototype that was well accepted by the organization.

We did not set out to study the decision-making performance of leaders in the ARC study. But tracing the project journey of many of the 58 teams provided rich case examples of leaders making tough decisions in difficult situations, some of which saved their projects.

Leaders and their personal characteristics and attributes

A focus on the personal attributes and characteristics of leaders has been a dominant theme in Western models of leadership (see Drath, 2001). Ralph Stogdill (1948) was an early proponent of this approach, which emphasizes "personal factors associated with leadership," and focuses on the physical characteristics and personality traits, such as self-confidence, high energy, assertiveness, persistence, and stress tolerance, of successful leaders. Little attention in Western research has been given to the moral dimension of leadership, although there are exceptions (Greenleaf, 1996). A welcome development is the emphasis by Chinese researchers on the moral dimension of leadership and its significance for the way that subordinates evaluate their leaders (Hui & Tan, 1999).

The leader-as-attributes approach is vulnerable to the fundamental attribution bias, a tendency to overestimate personal (internal) factors in making judgments and accordingly to make heroes out of successful leaders and give them too much credit for the successful performance of their organization. A more up-to-date and sophisticated version of the leadership-as-attributes theme is the current interest in the "emotional intelligence" of leaders (Goleman, 1998), with its emphasis on self-awareness, social awareness, empathy, and self-management.

Two important leader attributes are self-awareness and openness to learning. I will illustrate these attributes from the ARC study of R&D leaders.

Self-awareness: Good calibration

A high degree of self-awareness and self-management are among the characteristics of emotionally intelligent leaders (Goleman, 1998). Snyder (1979) observed that self-awareness and self-monitoring are twin aspects of being alert to one's strengths and weaknesses and also alert to social cues and the impact one has on others. Some so-called leaders are oblivious to the consequences of their behavior and how they are regarded by others.

One test of self-awareness is whether there is close agreement between how the leader thinks he is performing and how his followers think he is performing. We have data on 47 team leaders in the ARC study and how they rated themselves on transformational leadership and how their team colleagues rated them (see Table 23.2). We found that approximately half of the team leaders (53%) were well-calibrated, i.e., how they saw themselves was matched by how their team members saw them. But 30% had an *inflated* view of their leadership style not shared by their team members. And, interestingly, 17% of team leaders had a *deflated* view of themselves, i.e., they had a lower opinion of their leadership ability than their own team members.

The over-estimators or self-inflated leaders are an interesting group because they are out of touch with the reality of how they were regarded by their teams; in some cases strikingly so. For example, two quite inexperienced

Table 23.2 Self–other agreement. Leaders and their team members' ratings of transformational leadership

Self–other agreement	Transformational leadership (7-point scale)	Transformational leadership (7-point scale)	Project team performance (5-point scale)
	Leader-rated	Team-member rated	Customer-rated
Over-estimators (*n* = 14)	5.89	4.20	3.50
In agreement (*n* = 25)	5.31	5.23	4.17
Under-estimators (*n* = 8)	4.13	5.61	4.50

leaders regarded themselves as outstanding transformational leaders while their team members regarded them as disappointing failures. An extreme gap or discrepancy between self and other assessment is always a sign of trouble.

Evidence from the ARC study shows that customers of teams in which the leader had an inflated self-view tended to have a low opinion of the team and its work. As Table 23.2 shows, teams with leaders who are well-calibrated (i.e., evaluate themselves similarly to how they are evaluated by others) have, in the opinion of customers, better performing teams (4.17) than teams led by leaders who have an inflated view of their leadership style (3.50). Interestingly, the humble leaders who do not think all that highly of themselves have, in the opinion of customers, very good teams. This is an intriguing finding and merits further attention. Most of the humble leaders were highly experienced leaders and it is likely that they set much higher standards when they assess or evaluate themselves.

Leader learning

Another important attribute of excellent team leaders is their openness to learning. Every 4 months we asked each leader: "How much have you learned over the past 4 months from the work you do?" We found that leaders who reported they learned "a great deal" were among the very best leaders, while those who reported "not much" were among the worst. The best leaders are never satisfied with what they know and strive continually to learn new things. Both new and experienced leaders continue to learn how to manage people, teams and projects, how to deal with customers and other stakeholders, how their organization works, and they learn new scientific and technical knowledge that helps advance successful completion of the project. Hirst, Mann, Bain, Pirola-Merlo, and Richver (2004) found, as expected, that new leaders tend to report that they have learned more than experienced leaders. New leaders who reported that they learned a great deal headed projects highly regarded by their customers (*r* = .59). Consistent with that finding, Hirst et al. (2004) found that for the new leaders the amount of self-reported learning had a significant impact on their subsequent facilitative leadership style and team performance 8 and 12 months later.

Why are leaders who say that they learn a great deal associated with the best-performing teams? I suggest that such leaders have a strong "learning orientation" (Coad & Berry, 1998). They are open to new ideas; they enthuse colleagues with their curiosity; they find new insights in events frequently overlooked or ignored by others; they learn from experience, including overcoming obstacles; and probably because they are also good teachers, sharing the things that they have learned. The areas where the leader's self-reported learning appears to make most difference to team performance are learning about team management, learning how to deal with external stakeholders, and learning about their organization.

Transformational leadership style

The concept of transformational leadership (Bass, 1990) sits somewhat awkwardly in the five-themes framework as it belongs to both the leader-attributes perspective and the concept of leadership as a relationship. The transformational style of leadership – based on a close, personalized relationship with followers – inspires team members with the importance of their work and motivates them to strive for outstanding results and performance. Mann and Gillespie (2005) found that transformational leaders are more trusted, are more respected in the knowledge-building and team-building roles, and are also more self-aware – that is, more in touch with how others see them.

The transformational leadership style makes a difference in both direct and indirect ways. We found in the ARC study that transformational leaders help buffer the team from the adverse effects of seemingly insurmountable obstacles (Pirola-Merlo, Hartel, Mann, & Hirst, 2002). They also foster a team climate that encourages innovative team performance (Mann & Gillespie, 2005). An interesting finding is that the positive effects of transformational leadership on innovative team performance were especially evident in teams led by new leaders, and, consistent with Keller (1992), the correlation between transformational leadership and project performance was stronger in fundamental research teams ($r = .68$) than in product-development teams ($r = .40$). This demonstrates how the nature of the project or task has a bearing on the most effective leadership style for that task. It takes an inspiring transformational leader to help the team meet the challenge of a complex, fundamental research project.

Leadership as relationships

Leadership is essentially a relationship between the leader and his/her followers. While the leader–follower dyad dominates the "relationship" theme, there is now greater attention paid to "relational leadership"

(Drath, 2001), in which the focus is widened to the concept of shared leadership in teams, groups, and organizations. Other perspectives include Robert Greenleaf (1996) whose concept of servant as leader helped challenge the traditional view of leadership as controlling and influencing followers and raised the idea of leaders who want to serve people.

The Western emphasis on social influence in leadership (Rost, 1991) has led to studies of the different types of power that leaders use to influence followers and others. Yukl (1998) writes: "The effectiveness of a manager [leader] depends on several types of power *relationships* [italics added] including the downward power of the leader over subordinates, the upward power of subordinates over the leader, the upward power of the leader over superiors, and the lateral power of the leader over other people in the organization" (p. 197).

Some Western models of the leader–follower relationship point to an exchange arrangement involving obligations, favors, and commitments. Leader–member exchange theory (LMX theory; Graen & Uhl-Bien, 1995) describes how different exchange relationships emerge between leaders and particular subordinates. (Note the term "subordinate.") The basic premise is that leaders usually establish a special exchange relationship with a small number of trusted subordinates (the "in-group") who function as assistants, lieutenants, or advisors. The exchange relationship established with the remaining subordinates (the "out-group") is substantially different. This is a highly instrumental view of leadership based on the premise that the leader provides selected followers with tangible rewards, more pay, a larger office, better promotion opportunities, and favors in exchange for the follower's greater commitment, loyalty, and support. The relevance of LMX theory to leader–follower relationships in Asian societies is now an active research topic.

A matter of trust

The follower's trust in the leader is central to an understanding of the leader–follower relationship. Gillespie and Mann examined in the ARC study the importance of trust in the leader for team climate and team performance (Gillespie, 2004; Gillespie & Mann, 2005). They reported that trust in the leader is based on two components: first, a belief in the competence and reliability of the leader, and, second, recognition that the leader is willing to share vital information and keep personal confidences. Most team leaders in the ARC study were trusted, but not all. Lack of trust was mainly due to doubts about the leader's competence and reliability rather than concerns about disclosure of personal confidential information.

The competence–reliability aspect of trust is a fundamental aspect of the leader–follower relationship. Leaders who are incompetent and unreliable are not trusted because they compromise the reputation of the team and seriously jeopardize its performance. Thus, the most trusted leaders were rated significantly more highly by team members on all four leadership roles – knowledge builder, team builder, stakeholder liaison, and standards upholder – and on transformational leadership.

Gillespie and Mann (2005) investigated the dynamic relationship between trust in the leader, positive team climate, and good team performance. For example, does increased trust in the leader over time (say, 8 months) have a subsequent positive effect on team climate and team performance? Analyzing data from the ARC study, Gillespie and Mann found that an increase in leader trustworthiness indeed had a subsequent impact on team climate ($r = .42$) and on team performance ($r = .38$) (see Figure 23.2). Gillespie and Mann also found that an increase in team performance over time was followed months later by an increase in trust in the leader ($r = .28$). Thus the relationship between trust in the leader and team performance is reciprocal and dynamic.

Other relationships

The leader–follower relationship is not the only one of interest for an understanding of leadership. Other relationships include the relationship between leaders and their teachers and mentors, between leaders and other leaders in the organization, and between leaders and their parents, families, and friends. Again, the dominant Western model depicts leadership as mainly how leaders motivate and influence followers and implies that the only significant relationship is between leader and follower (see Rost, 1991). Accordingly, Drath's

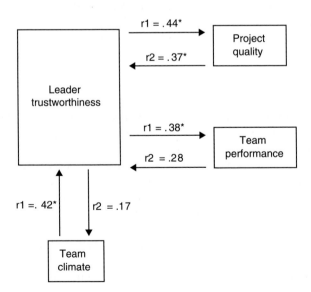

Figure 23.2 Bidirectional effects of changes in leader trustworthiness on team climate, project quality and team performance (Gillespie & Mann, 2005). * $p < .05$.

(2001) concept of relational leadership and his call for greater attention to shared leadership in groups, teams, and organizations is important.

Leadership as a journey

Finally, we come to the theme of leadership as a journey. This theme has two related aspects – leadership as personal growth and development, and leadership as guiding a shared project to a valuable goal and conclusion.

The concept of the personal leadership journey is a way of describing the careers and development of leaders who have been influential through their ideas, decisions and actions. The perspective is essentially psychological and developmental as it traces the early development and formative experiences of future leaders as a key to their ideas and commitment to a cause or ideology.

Bennis and Thomas (2002) refer to "leadership crucibles," formative experiences that shape the leaders' values, their concept of what constitutes leadership, and their readiness to take on the challenge of leadership. Writers taking this perspective refer to childhood experiences and identity formation in adolescence and early adulthood as a key to leadership mission and values. Examples include Eric Erikson (1969) writing about Mahatma Gandhi and Howard Gardner (1995) writing about Martin Luther King. Gandhi's experience with personal discrimination as a young Indian lawyer in South Africa was crucial in forming his decision to become a leader and advocate for his people in India. Che Guevara's (1952) *Motorcycle Diaries*, a record of his eight-month trip through South America in 1952 when he was 24 years old, describes the impact of observing abject poverty and discrimination on his decision to quit medicine and become a revolutionary.

While research at the Center for Creative Leadership (McCauley & Van Velsor, 2004) examines the effect of hardships and other experiences on leader development, there have not been, to my knowledge, systematic longitudinal studies of leaders tracing their development and how they learn, change, and grow over time, or, for that matter, lose their way and decline.

The concept of leadership as a shared journey refers to the idea of the leader at the head of a challenging project with a worthwhile goal or destination. This meaning evokes the idea of the leader as the head of a lengthy and difficult mission to discover something, change something, or make a difference to other people's lives.

Intrepid explorers and influential political leaders are among the most compelling examples of leadership as taking charge of a difficult, path-breaking project. A striking example was the race in 1911 between a British team led by Robert Falcon Scott and a Norwegian team led by Roald Amundsen to be the first to reach the South Pole. Amundsen's precise and strategic planning led to success and the safe return of his team, while Scott's flawed leadership contributed to the demise of his team who perished on the return journey from the South Pole. The story of Scott and Amundsen is compelling because it contrasts the stark difference between successful and failed leaders and how the leader's preparation and aptitude for a hazardous journey can spell the difference between survival and death.

In China, the concept of leader and journey is evoked by the epic Long March, in which Mao Zedong led 100,000 of his followers to a secure base in Shaanxi, a journey of over 8000 kilometers that began in 1934 and lasted for almost a year. Mao was known as the Great Helmsman, evoking another metaphor of the leader on a journey. Other political and historical leaders who led their people on long journeys include Moses and the Hebrews in the Sinai desert, Mahatma Gandhi and his followers in 1930 on the 300 mile Salt March in defiance of the British government's salt tax, and Martin Luther King and the Civil Rights marches in the USA in the 1960s. The stories of these journeys led by political and spiritual leaders have taken on a larger than life, mythical quality.

On a modest scale, the ARC study of R&D team leaders touches on both meanings of the theme of leadership as a journey.

Leadership development

The ARC study design included a comparison between 29 new leaders at the beginning of their career and 29 seasoned, experienced leaders. The idea was to examine the magnitude of difference in leadership capabilities and performance produced by experience. Unexpectedly, we found *on average* only small differences between new leaders and experienced leaders in capabilities, style and performance, but there was a striking finding. Most of the approximately 20% of teams in the ARC study that struggled and performed poorly were led by new, relatively inexperienced leaders (Mann, 2005).

Shared journey

The ARC study used a longitudinal design to track teams and their leaders over one year with follow-up interviews 18 months later. Some of the teams had been together for almost 10 years and had major projects that in many cases took years to complete. R&D projects are like a journey of many stages with milestones to be met and obstacles to be overcome. Throughout the different phases of a project there are changes in the kind of work done – from more routine to more creative – and also in the team's progress and achievements. The key point is that sustained leadership is necessary to steer the project and its team through its lengthy and difficult journey. This is illustrated in the next section.

The project journey

We asked leaders to reconstruct progress made and the obstacles encountered by their team during the year of the ARC study. An example is Dr Lazor ("Laz") Strezov, leader of Project M, a team at BHP Research, which worked for eight years on a revolutionary technology for casting super-thin steel strips from molten steel. Figure 23.3 shows Laz's reconstruction of progress and obstacles in Project M's journey during 1997. At the beginning of 1997, progress to objectives was rated at 10%, then flattened at 35% in May–June as disappointing results emerged from the first trials of the thin strip process in a commercial plant. A change of project objectives to simplify the thin-strip casting process was decided at the end of June. The changes seem to have worked, as progress increased rapidly from a low of 10% in July to reach 85% by the end of 1997. Corresponding to fluctuations in progress there were obstacles, which were significant in the first half of the year and peaked at "very significant" in mid-year.

Most leaders reported encountering obstacles during the project journey (Pirola-Merlo et al., 2002). As Table 23.3 shows, 50% of teams experienced

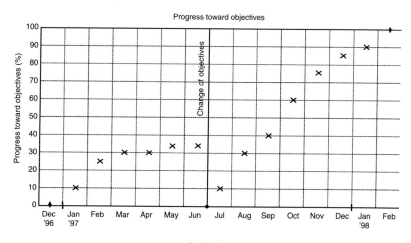

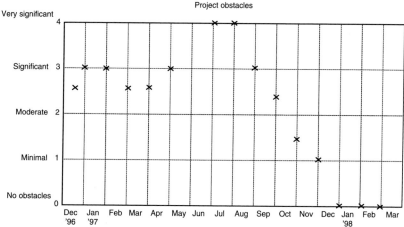

Figure 23.3 Reconstruction of progress toward objectives and obstacles encountered over 16 months in a project (Laz Strezov, leader of Project M, BHP).

Table 23.3 Obstacles reported by team leaders over 15 months

Obstacle	Proportion of teams affected (%)
Technical problems	50
Availability of suitable staff	44
Funding/resource shortages	44
Relationships between team members and relationships with stakeholders	33
Conceptual issues	22
Organizational restructure	14
Time/workload pressures	8

$n = 34$ leaders. *Source*: Pirola-Merlo, Hartel, Mann, and Hirst (2002).

technical problems (as in the case of Project M), 44% had funding and resource shortages, 44% lack of suitable staff, and 33% reported difficult and strained relationships between team members and with stakeholders. Some teams had to deal with multiple, persistent obstacles. When a team encounters obstacles it often produces a sharp deterioration in team climate. Team members become demoralized, blame one another, communication breaks down, and team performance begins to suffer. However, Pirola-Merlo et al. (2002) found that many teams overcome obstacles, maintain positive team morale, and complete their projects successfully. The key is how the team leader responds to the obstacles. Team leaders who are transformational and facilitative in their leadership style – they work hard to reinforce important goals, inspire team members to believe that worthwhile goals can still be attained, and involve team members in finding solutions to problems – are able to maintain a positive team climate and, in turn, achieve good outcomes. Thus, transformational and facilitative leaders protect their teams and counteract the otherwise debilitating effects of setbacks and obstacles during the project journey. An example in the ARC study is Laz Strezov of BHP Research.

Which are the most compelling approaches?

In sum, the five themes offer a framework for studying different aspects of leaders and leadership. They are useful and complementary and together help build a more complete picture of the task of leaders and the nature of leadership. It is interesting that although not planned, the five themes together seem to cover many of the relevant issues that managers raise about the performance of team leaders and their importance for innovative project work. But three questions remain as we determine whether the five themes are useful for the study of leadership.

Do these themes correspond to how people think of leadership?

When I invite people in Western audiences to indicate which theme most closely fits their concept of leadership, most choose the leader's characteristics and attributes. I expect that in group-oriented cultures, such as China and Japan, the themes of leadership as a relationship and leadership as a journey would be chosen in keeping with traditional writings on the lives of popular historical figures and military heroes and on the central role of relationships in family, work, and community.

The journey theme is compelling because it evokes two powerful ideas. First, the impact on the leader of family, teachers, and community, character-forming experiences, and life-altering events that shape the leader's values and interests. Second, the nature and significance of the project on which the leader is engaged with his or her team of followers. Genuine leaders are trying to create something valuable or to change an unsatisfactory situation. What is this project? And what makes it so valuable that people are prepared to commit years of effort and sacrifice? When that question is asked the importance of studying leaders engaged with others in challenging, difficult work and what enables them to succeed when others fail becomes obvious. And there are clear implications for the research approach and methodologies that should be taken, for example, an emphasis on studying emergent, appointed or elected leaders in genuine leadership settings, and a low priority on studies of so-called leaders assigned to that role in contrived laboratory situations.

Can we simplify the five approaches? Are they all distinct?

It can be argued that some themes belong with other approaches. For example, decision making could be part of the theme of leadership roles or part of the theme of a leadership journey, inasmuch as influential leaders make crucial decisions throughout their careers (see Lipshitz & Mann, 2004). It can also be argued that leadership as a journey underpins all themes. Thus, leadership as a personal journey encompasses the theme of individual differences in leader attributes, values, self-awareness, and learning – and changes in these characteristics over time. Similarly, leadership as a shared journey encompasses themes of leadership roles, decision making, and social relationships, especially trust, to complete a valuable project. Consistent with this idea, Bain, Mann, Atkins, and Dunning (2005) found that the leader's performance as knowledge builder, team builder, and particularly stakeholder liaison, was most significant for team performance at the late, concluding phases of a project. The importance of different leadership roles at different stages of a project is indicated by these findings.

Is each theme understood the same way across cultures?

Some themes may be interpreted differently across cultures. For example, the leader attributes and relationships themes have different meanings across cultures. Hui and Tan (1999) point out that moral character has been a major criterion for Chinese leadership since historic times and that an emphasis on the leader's "moral integrity" is a feature of how leaders are evaluated in all Chinese communities.

In the GLOBE project (House et al., 1999), the major study of leadership worldwide, the central question is the extent to which specific leader attributes and leadership behaviors are seen to contribute to effective leadership – and whether these attributes and behaviors are universally endorsed across cultures. This is an implicit leadership theory, as it concerns the beliefs and assumptions that people have about the characteristics that distinguish effective and ineffective leaders and moral and immoral leaders. The GLOBE study, based on samples of middle managers from 60 different countries who were asked to endorse what they believed were the facilitators of effective leadership, found that most leadership attribute dimensions apply across cultures, but some dimensions, for example, self-protective (self-centered, loner, evasive) and autonomous (independent, individualistic), vary by culture.

Conclusion and recommendations

The study of leadership is informed by five themes that examine leadership in a range of roles, activities and behaviors, crucial decisions, personal characteristics and values, types of relationships, and formative events and shared experiences in working with others on challenging projects. The different perspectives were illustrated by drawing on an empirical study of 58 research and development teams and their leaders in Australian organizations. Each perspective contributes to the analysis of leadership factors in the performance of R&D teams engaged in innovative work.

I conclude with four brief suggestions for future work. First, the importance of attending to the leadership level when examining the nature of leadership. While drawing freely on the leadership literature across the board, the analysis in this chapter is limited to the level of team leaders at the first or second supervisory level in organizations. It is important to check whether the five themes are as relevant to leadership at more senior levels. The theme of leadership as decision making would, I suggest, be more important at the senior level. Second, following the example of Drath (2001) and others, it is important to attend to the wider network of key relationships that support effective leaders. Third, it is important to attend to the longitudinal aspect of leadership development and performance as expressed in the theme of the leadership journey. This is crucial for understanding readiness to take on and relinquish leadership, the interest in leading diverse projects and tasks, and how leaders mature and change. The theme of leadership as a journey also underpins the analysis of changing roles, personal attributes, and crucial decisions over time. The implication for learning about leaders from observing how they have performed throughout their career is obvious. Finally, it is important to attend to cultural differences and similarities in the meaning of leadership, whether in regard to preferred leader characteristics, the nature of the leader–follower relationship, or the kinds of leaders who are respected for their service in their respective societies.

Acknowledgments

To Andrew Pirola-Merlo, Giles Hirst, Paul Bain, Marinella Padula and Nicole Gillespie, and to the Australian Research Council for its support for the "Effective R&D Project Leaders" study. A version of this chapter was presented as the Cunningham Lecture at the Annual meeting of the Academy of the Social Sciences in Australia, November 2003.

References

Bain, P. G., & Mann, L. (1997). *The Project Leadership questionnaire: Validation and preliminary norms*. Working Paper Series. Melbourne Business School, University of Melbourne.

Bain, P. G., Mann, L., Atkins, L., & Dunning, J. (2005). R&D project leaders: Roles and responsibilities. In L. Mann, *Leadership, management, and innovation in R&D project teams* (pp. 49–70). Westport, CT: Praeger.

Bass, B. M. (1990). *Handbook of leadership: A survey of theory and research*. New York: Free Press.

Bennis, W., & Thomas, R. (2002). *Geeks and geezers: How era, values, and defining moments shape leaders*. Boston, MA: Harvard Business School Press.

Coad, A. F., & Berry, A. J. (1998). Transformational leadership and learning orientation. *Leadership & Organization Development Journal, 19*(30), 164–172.

Cohen, S. G., & Bailey, D. E. (1997). What makes teams work: Group effectiveness research from the shop floor to the executive suite. *Journal of Management, 23*, 239–290.

Drath, W. H. (2001). *The deep blue sea: Rethinking the source of leadership*. San Francisco: Jossey-Bass.

Erikson, E. (1969). *Gandhi's truth: On the origins of militant non violence*. New York: Norton.

Gardner, H. (1995). *Leading minds: An anatomy of leadership*. New York: Basic Books.

Gillespie, N. (2004). *Leadership and trust: The nature and determinants of interpersonal trust in knowledge-based teams*. Unpublished doctoral dissertation, University of Melbourne.

Gillespie, N., & Mann, L. (2005). How trustworthy is your leader? In L. Mann, *Leadership, management, and innovation in R&D project teams* (pp. 93–121). Westport, CT: Praeger.

Goleman, D. (1998). *Working with emotional intelligence*. New York: Bantam.

Graen, G. B., & Uhl-Bien, M. (1995). Relationship-based approaches to leadership: Development of leader–member exchange (LMX) theory of leadership over 25 years: Applying a multi-level multi-domain perspective. *Leadership Quarterly*, 6(2), 219–247.

Greenleaf, R. K. (1996). *On becoming a servant leader*. San Francisco: Jossey-Bass.

Guevara, C. (1952). *Motorcycle diaries: A journey around South America*. Melbourne, Australia & New York: Ocean Press.

Heller, F., & Yukl, G. (1969). Participation, managerial decision making, and situational variables. *Organizational Behavior and Human Performance*, 4, 227–241.

Hirst, G., Mann, L., Bain, P., Pirola-Merlo, A., & Richver, A. (2004). Learning to lead: The development and testing of a model of leadership learning. *Leadership Quarterly*, 15, 311–327.

House, R. J., & Aditya, R. N. (1997). The social science study of leadership: Quo vadis? *Journal of Management*, 23(3), 409–474.

House, R. J., Hanges, P. J., Ruiz-Quintanilla, A., Dorfman, P. W., Javidan, M., Dickson, M. et al. (1999). Cultural influences on leadership and organizations: Project GLOBE. In W. H. Mobley (Ed.), *Advances in global leadership* (Vol. 1, pp. 171–233). Stamford, CT: JAI Press.

Hui, C. H., & Tan, G. C. (1999). The moral component of effective leadership: The Chinese case. In W. H. Mobley (Ed.), *Advances in global leadership* (Vol. 1, pp. 249–266). Stamford, CT: JAI Press.

Janis, I. L. (1972). *Victims of groupthink*. Boston, MA: Houghton Mifflin.

Janis, I. L., & Mann, L. (1977). *Decision making: A psychological analysis of conflict, choice, and commitment*. New York: Free Press.

Keller, R. T. (1992). Transformational leadership and the performance of research and development project groups. *Journal of Management*, 18(3), 489–501.

Kelley, R. E. (1998). *Star performer*. New York: Times Books.

Lee, P. (2005). *Knowledge sharing and team performance: The role of leadership and trust*. Unpublished doctoral thesis, University of Melbourne.

Lipshitz, R., & Mann, L. (2004) *Decision making and leadership: Mapping the domain*. Unpublished manuscript, Melbourne Business School, University of Melbourne.

Mann, L. (2005). *Leadership, management, and innovation in R&D project teams*. Westport, CT: Praeger.

Mann, L., & Gillespie, N. (2005). Transformational leaders of project teams. In L. Mann, *Leadership, management, and innovation in R&D project teams* (pp. 71–91). Westport, CT: Praeger.

McCauley, C. D., & Van Velsor, E. (Eds.). (2004). *The Center for Creative Leadership handbook of leadership development* (2nd ed.). San Francisco: Jossey-Bass.

Mintzberg, H. (1973). *The nature of managerial work*. New York: Harper & Row.

Pirola-Merlo, A., Hartel, C., Mann, L., & Hirst, G. (2002). How leaders influence the impact of affective events on team climate and performance in R&D teams. *Leadership Quarterly*, 13(5), 561–581.

Quinn, R. E. (1988). *Beyond rational management: Mastering the paradoxes and competing demands of high performance*. San Francisco: Jossey-Bass.

Rost, J. C. (1991). *Leadership for the twenty first century*. New York: Praeger.

Snyder, M. (1979). *Public appearances/private realities: The psychology of self-monitoring*. New York: Freeman.

Stogdill, R. M. (1948). Personal factors associated with leadership: A survey of the literature. *Journal of Psychology, 25*, 35–71.

Vroom, V. H., & Yetton, P. W. (1973). *Leadership and decision making.* Pittsburgh, PA: University of Pittsburgh Press.

Yukl, G. (1998). *Leadership in organizations* (3rd ed.). Englewood Cliffs, NJ: Prentice Hall.

24 Leadership competency and implicit assessment modeling

Zhong-Ming Wang

New challenges and approaches

During the 1980s and 1990s human resource management (HRM) and leadership competency assessment have rapidly become the focus for implementing talent strategy and developing Chinese approaches to industrial and organizational psychology (Wang, 1996, 2003). From research and application activities, several emerging strategies for leadership competency assessment and development are proposed, which are closely related to the recent challenges posed by globalization and organizational reform (e.g., Campbell & Deirdre, 2001; Gatewood & Field, 2001; Leung, Smith, Wang, & Sun, 1996; Riggio, Murphy, & Pirozzolo, 2002; Verburg, Drenth, Koopman, van Muijen, & Wang, 1999; Wang, 1993, 1999). The practice and focus of leadership examination and assessment systems development has made significant changes in the past 25 years in China. Many Chinese organizations have made efforts to develop recruitment programs with more accurate predictors and long-term person–job fit requirements. Some of them try to link leadership assessment with systematic succession planning, particularly among international joint ventures, township companies and private firms as well as government offices (e.g., Feng, 1998; Wang, 2003). These changes have called for new frameworks and methodologies for leadership competency assessment and human resource development (Anderson & Herriot, 1997; Wang & Mobley, 1999; Wilhelm & Engle, 2005).

Some developments in personnel assessment in China

In the mid-1980s, we already had quite a few organizations that were trying to build up a comprehensive and scientific assessment system for senior civil servant selection and promotion (Wang, 1996, 1999). A number of studies adopted new methods such as assessment centers and situational simulation tests to evaluate verbal ability, written communication ability, interpersonal ability, delegating ability, organizing ability, analytic ability, management creativity, and policy implementation ability, as well as job evaluation and job ranking for compensation design (Zhang, 1988). More recently, the focus of studies on personnel assessment and selection has moved from applicant-characteristics analysis to competence-performance analysis and a group approach to evaluation, e.g., role–set assessment methods and multi-level measurement practices, in many industrial sectors and governmental departments (Smith & Wang, 1996; Wang, 2001) on the basis of leadership competency modeling. In a recent project of the national assessment systems development, a leadership competence model with six key components was formulated to include four culture-general functional competencies (planning, organizing, leading, controlling) and two culture-specific competencies (relationship and teamwork competence). In addition, a national executive assessment system was designed to have modules of moral (integrity, value and commitment), motivation (achievement, organizational, relationship motives), personality (conscientiousness, emotional adaptation, group compatibility), managerial skills (strategic decisions, organizing and coordinating, motivating and directing, process monitoring), and managerial performance (behavioral performance, task performance, business performance). All these developments demonstrate the nationwide emphasis on leadership competency assessment in HR and industrial organizational psychology.

Also, more efforts have been devoted to developing the national leadership examination and testing systems such as Personnel Examination and Assessment Center by the Test Center of the Ministry of Personnel as well as the National Leadership Examination and Assessment Center by the Central Government in China in collaboration with experts and researchers from the key universities. More systematic requirements for civil servants' public selection and assessment are constructed and implemented nationwide by the National Public Selection and Assessment Center. More executive development programs and overseas study tour programs have been conducted to enhance leadership competence among executives and managers. Attention has been paid to the principles and methodology in the assessment and selection of both leaders and employees (Li & Shi, 2000; Wang, 1997a).

New challenges and coping strategies for leadership assessment

With the recent developments of leadership competency assessment, several challenges need to be addressed in strategic leadership development and strategic HRM methodology:

1   *Alternative competency models.* Given the shift of focus in leadership assessment to the cross-cultural and executive level of positions, alternative competency models need to be constructed to capture and redefine the taxonomy and models of leadership competency under different cultural settings.
2   *Special assessment strategies.* With higher levels of leadership competence, special assessment strategies need to be developed for identifying

and selecting highly competent executives, senior civil servants, and global entrepreneurs.

3   *Global leadership packages.* Using those special assessment strategies, global leadership packages need to be designed in order to develop cross-cultural leadership teams in joint ventures and cross-regional ventures, both at home and overseas.

4   *Integrated criterion systems.* To develop a comprehensive leadership assessment system, integrated criterion systems need to be formulated to assess the dynamic development of leadership competence to achieve job- and career-span total validity.

To cope with these challenges, several types of competency-modeling approach are considered to be useful, e.g., tacit knowledge and successful intelligence with a global dimension (Sternberg, 1997; Wang, 1997a) and strategic job modeling (Shippmann et al., 2000; Wang, 2003). There is also an increasing demand for more culture-specific approaches and theoretical models with a trend towards the development of Chinese culture-based and work-oriented constructs (Wang, 1996). In discussing the indigenous or emic approaches to Chinese personality structure, McCrae, Paul, and Michelle (1996) noticed two major efforts: Fanny M. Cheung and her colleagues' new Chinese Personality Assessment Inventory (CPAI) intended to measure both normal personality traits and psychopathology from a distinctively Chinese perspective (Cheung, Leung, Fan, Song, Zhang, & Zhang, 1996); and K. S. Yang's new survey of indigenous Chinese personality adjectives (Yang, 1993). In a recent study on the personality structure and its relationship with performance, Tao (1999) formulated and tested a culture-based hierarchical model of personality. This hierarchical model defines personality at four hierarchical levels: operational level, interpersonal level, societal level and regulational level. Empirical research showed that the operational level of competency was more closely related to task and individual performance whereas the other higher levels of leadership competence were significantly correlated with organizational performance. Further efforts are made to identify these cultural and contextual boundaries and formulate more culture-based concepts of leadership competence.

New approaches to leadership competency assessment

Validity has been a methodological focus in recent assessment studies (Murphy, 2003). Several new approaches have been developed to enhance the validity of leadership assessment. The following are the specific approaches:

1   *Talent strategy approach.* Leadership competency assessment is used as an effective approach to implementing talent strategy, regional development strategy and global business strategy. Talent requirements and developmental plans are incorporated into the leadership

competency modeling procedure and personnel assessment and promotion package.

2 *Person–job–organization fit approach*. Leadership competency assessment is adopted for retaining, utilizing, and developing core personnel for better person–job–organization fit, usually by long-term career programs and motivational packages. This approach emphasizes long-term fit through phase-based competence modeling and assessment indicators (Wang, 1997a).

3 *Strategic leadership approach*. Leadership competency assessment is conducted to integrate strategic leadership with decision competency and entrepreneurial competency modeling. This approach mainly targets the executive level of leadership teams and entrepreneurs (McCauley, Ruderman, Ohlott, & Morrow, 1994; Wang 1997b).

4 *Innovative methodology approach*. With the rapid development of leadership competency assessment research and practice in China, we have more opportunities to conduct empirical research in order to advance the innovative methodology for strategy- and e-based assessment and leadership selection (Aguinis, Nenle, & Beaty, 2001; Wang, 2002, 2003).

Key issues on leadership competency modeling

How can we develop leadership competency models under different cultural, business and administrative settings? Several studies have been carried out to examine the Chinese characteristics of leadership (Lin, Chen, & Wang, 1987; Peterson, 1988; Wang, 2001, 2003; Wang & Chen, 2002). Among these, Lin and his group (1987) conducted a comparative study using a modified Japanese scale of leadership to investigate the leadership styles of Chinese managers. An additional dimension of leadership character was identified in addition to the conventional two dimensions of performance and maintenance. Apparently, Chinese employees regard personal morals and character as elements of leadership competency more than other nationalities do. More recently, Wang (2001, 2003) and Wang and Chen (2002) conducted empirical studies on managerial competency models for Chinese CEOs and senior civil servants with an emphasis on performance-related competency elements. Selecting more skillful entrepreneurs and executives has become one of the main tasks for strategic development in various types of company. There are four criteria for selecting those candidates: (1) ideological and political qualifications; (2) responsibility and management abilities; (3) decision-making skills; and (4) business knowledge. However, what would be the competency structure within the Chinese context? What are the key issues in leadership competency structure? What are the main organizational constraints in utilizing managerial competencies in China? In a joint research project, 221 Chinese top managers from 180 enterprises participated in the survey of managerial competencies (Wang & Kakabadse, 2006). The results revealed six reliable managerial competency factors: (1) change uncertainty; (2) people performance; (3) communication feedback; (4) independence; (5) work motivation; and (6) leadership skills.

In general, recent empirical research showed that a hierarchical model more effectively demonstrated functional competence, while a dimensional model could capture higher-level administrative competence, and a growth model better illustrated entrepreneurial competence. However, how those higher-order leadership competencies could be effectively assessed and comprehensively captured was always an important question for research (McClelland, 1973; Wang, 2003). Several issues need to be addressed before we can systematically understand leadership competence assessment and development processes in different cultural and socioeconomic settings.

Cultural representation for leadership assessment

One of the key issues is how cultural representations such as *Guanxi* (relationship) can be built into the leadership assessment. Although *Guanxi* and the relationship dimension are widely recognized as the key elements of Chinese culture and business practice (e.g., Bond, 1996; Li & Tsui, 2000; Liang, 2000), the implications of *Guanxi* in leadership competency modeling is not yet clearly understood. In particular, further efforts need to be made to develop leadership models using emic–etic approaches. For example, Graen and Uhl-Bien (1995) studied *Guanxi* and professional leadership with the leader–member exchange (LMX) model while Wang and Schneider (2001) formulated a model for cross-cultural leadership teams through cross-cultural perspectives.

In a recent review of Chinese management studies, Tsui, Farh, and Xin (2000) suggested that *Guanxi* is more pervasive and important in lateral than in vertical dyads, indicating that relationship-based constructs are possibly more connected with same-level networks than across other aspects of work behavior or competence. In another study involving more than 250 employees, Liang (2000) demonstrated a multidimensional structure of relationship (or *Guanxi*) orientation: task accomplishment, harmony maintenance, social support, and information channel. Among these, task accomplishment is demonstrated as a habitual tendency to solve problems through various kinds of relationship and social networks; harmony maintenance shows conflict avoidance in interpersonal interactions; social support represents a relationship behavior in obtaining sentimental or task-support from other people, whereas information channel means impression management behavior through various types of information channels. The four dimensions of relationship orientation are interdependent with harmony seeking as a core of the constructs.

Methodological issues for measurement errors and variance

Once we have a culture-based leadership competency model, we still need to improve the methodology of how to effectively assess and comprehensively capture those culturally specific leadership competencies and eliminate measurement errors and variance. Validity generalization has been the key issue (Murphy, 2003). Several methodological considerations from previous studies are worth noting:

1 *Situational judgment testing and single dimension error.* In previous research, situational judgment testing was recommended as a useful method for assessing tacit knowledge or executive leadership competence. However, situational judgment testing usually produced more general, overlapping or unidimensional leadership competence. We need to adopt a new methodology to represent information from different dimensions of assessment.

2 *Developmental variance.* Leadership competency has the nature of career-path development for those managers who enter the organizations with high potential. We need to develop a new methodology to capture the incremental and developmental variance along with the increases in managers' experience within the organizations.

3 *Situational specificity and cross-dimensional variance.* Another key issue in assessing leadership competency and capturing the situational features is how to estimate the specialties of leadership contexts and organizational settings. Further studies need to be carried out to further understand the situational specificity of particular management systems and leadership models. Although various kinds of instruments or methods have been developed to measure leadership competence on specific dimensions of the models, we will need a methodology to measure cross-dimensional variance on the competence models.

4 *Growth validity and integrated criteria.* I use the term "growth validity" to describe the incremental validity evidence and predictive power from a sequential selection process. So, with a phase-based predictor set design, we may formulate an incremental growth validity indicator. Another approach to enhancing incremental validity is to integrate various kinds of criteria (e.g., Schmitt & Chan 1998). A crucial task here is to build up a performance model or criterion model using various levels of indicators and constructs. A useful framework is the person–job–organization-fit model (e.g., Kristof-Brown, 2000; Schneider, Goldstein, & Smith, 1995; Wang, 2001). As Wang (2001) indicated, criteria at levels of person, job and organization need to be selected to build up a model of integrated criteria.

Three strategies for implicit assessment modeling

So far, we have discussed three key issues in leadership competency assessment, e.g., cultural representation, cross-dimensional interaction and developmental variance. Although we mostly used statistical techniques with separate analyses to provide partial solutions in the past, the results were not satisfactory. We may need to link leadership competency models with an implicit assessment modeling approach to provide total validity. The total validity is an integrated validity of assessment with hierarchical, interactive and adaptive predictors. The hierarchical predictors refer to performance across levels of organizations. Often we need to formulate a model to configure competencies across levels in order to effectively predict the potential career development across levels of organizations. The interactive predictors represent the team and project-based groups whereas the adaptive predictors are design to capture competencies along with the development of one's career in the organization. Many recent studies focused upon managerial ability and leadership competencies (e.g., Feng, 1998; Wakabayashi & Chen, 1999; Wei & Zhang, 1999; Wang, 2001). With an emphasis on cross-cultural managerial value orientation and competency-performance framework, Wang and Schneider (2001) conducted a three-year longitudinal study on multicultural leadership team development and found that four key competencies were crucial for working in multicultural leadership teams in joint ventures: (1) cultural competence; (2) achievement competence; (3) decision competence; and (4) team competence. In order to capture the hierarchical, interactive and adaptive variance, three strategies of implicit assessment modeling are formulated in order to achieve total validity.

Culture-specific hierarchical modeling strategy

The hierarchical culture-specific strategy for implicit assessment modeling is to search for higher-order culture-specific constructs. Here are two recent studies that used the hierarchical implicit assessment strategy. The first study was about functional modeling for officials from state-owned enterprises. In this study, a field interview was conducted among 348 managers to collect critical incidents, and a leadership competence model was built for six categories of function and position: administrative, technical, finance, sales, production, and HR functions. Then a system of competency assessment was developed, which included a cognitive ability test, a set of critical behavioral indicators, a situational judgment test, and an in-basket test. Altogether, more than 24,000 Chinese middle managers participated in the second stage of this study. An implicit assessment approach was adopted in the sense that cross-regional cultural differences were analyzed and region-specific competence models were built with higher-order factors.

Cultural elements such as group, relationship, *Guanxi*, and collectivism were widely examined in the leadership and HR management research. It was recognized that culture would be a higher-order factor and be constructed as an element or a dimension of leadership competency. Wang and Chen (2002) used a strategic and hierarchical analysis technique and conducted leadership critical incident analysis to formulate a Linear Structural Relations (LISREL) model of managerial competency structure. In this study, the hierarchical culture-specific implicit assessment modeling was conducted to represent cultural variance in the Chinese context. The basic idea was to link work activity, competencies and work context with strategic objectives in the organizations. With a sample of 568 managers, a structural multidimensional model of managerial competency was formulated. It was shown that there was an implicit managerial competency model behind the assessment and personnel decisions. Specifically, the relationship-based constructs appeared to be the higher-order factors underlying the first-order factorial structure. This result indicated that within the Chinese setting, relationship-based higher-order constructs seem to dominate the competency modeling process and may affect the general mental model of assessment. These constructs include integrity, extraversion, relationship motive, and relationship coordination, which formulated into second-order constructs. The validation evidence indicated that the higher-order factors such as coordination and relationship competencies had higher predictive validity for leadership performance, especially organizational performance (r = .38–.46). The hierarchical models demonstrated higher incremental validity to cognitive ability tests than that of multifactor models (+ 22%). In this way, this higher-order competency model demonstrates the hierarchical implicit modeling approach.

Interactive cross-dimensional modeling strategy

The second strategy is interactive cross-dimensional modeling to represent the interactive variance of leadership assessment. The usual way of modeling is to hypothesize that dimensions are relatively independent and treat them as single dimensions. However, in the complex leadership competency assessment situation, cross-dimensional variance may contribute significantly to the validity. An example is the assessment project using the executive leadership competency model (Wang, 2002, 2003) for assessment and selection of executive and senior governmental officials. The difficulty of competency modeling for high-level executive positions was the complexity and multidimensionality of their responsibilities and key skills. In order to solve this problem, a position–role-set critical incident analysis was conducted to evaluate the cross-functional responsibilities among the set of positions. Both criticality and sustainability of competency components were then evaluated among two different samples: 424 candidates for governmental positions in Guangzhou city and 684 administrative directors for governmental departments in three other provinces. A three-dimensional leadership competency model of accountability value, decision making and innovative learning was constructed with interactive assessment modeling. The within-dimensional measures and cross-dimensional indicators were respectively used to code the correspondent competency elements and then correlated with indicators of performance. The preliminary results showed that cross-dimensional competency information was more predictive than the within-dimensional competency information for administrative performance.

Adaptive growth modeling strategy

The third strategy is adaptive assessment modeling, i.e., emphasizing the developmental and phase-dependent nature of leadership competency. In our study, we used a growth model to characterize the main developmental features of leadership competence. Schneider, Goldstein, and Smith (1995) proposed an ASA model to represent key features of this growth process: attraction, selection, and attrition. Wang (1999, 2001) modified the model with the Chinese research findings and proposed a three-phase attraction, selection, and development (ASD) growth model. Instead of attraction, selection and attrition, the ASD model adopts a scheme of attraction, selection and development to reflect the "development" nature of the later career stages of most managers in Chinese entrepreneurial firms. This model was tested in a recent study conducted by Wang's group (2003) among 628 entrepreneurs and their team members from six provinces on leadership competency modeling and assessment, and the results demonstrated its validity and generalizability in capturing the adaptability of competence among both managerial personnel and senior governmental officials at the three phases of development. For instance, at the attraction phase, value accountability was more crucial in predicting the performance of the first stage of jobs, thus emphasizing work values and adaptation to the leadership situation, while at the selection phase, strategic decision competence was more predictive for leadership performance. Moreover, in our study, the progressive innovation competence was found to be the best predictor for performance at the stage of development. A crucial method for a valid adaptive assessment is to develop "growth phase incidents," i.e., from situations of personal entrepreneurship, team entrepreneurship and corporate entrepreneurship in order to achieve dynamic person–job–organization fit. Our research showed that for high adaptive implicit assessment, it was important to formulate a phase-based competency-performance model. We call it the synthetic implicit assessment model, and it is composed of the three implicit modeling approaches (hierarchical, interactive and adaptive implicit assessment modeling).

Conclusion

Models of leadership competency

On the basis of recent research and developments on leadership assessment and selection, three models for leadership competencies under the Chinese cultural, business and administrative setting are summarized:

1 Hierarchical model, demonstrating functional competence;
2 Dimensional model, characterizing administrative competence; and
3 Growth model, representing entrepreneurial competence.

We argue that the conventional assessment methodology may be suitable for measuring the hierarchical model of functional leadership competence but not effective in capturing higher-level more complicated leadership competence. We need a new approach to assess the higher-order models of leadership competence such as the dimensional model for administrative leadership competence and the growth model for entrepreneurial competence.

Implicit assessment modeling strategies

Our recent research indicated that even for hierarchical models of leadership competence, we will still need to use the "culture-specific representation hierarchical strategy" in order to build up models for particular cultural settings. We call it an implicit assessment modeling strategy. When we are assessing dimensional model of administrative competence, a cross-dimensional interactive strategy should be used to construct the implicit assessment model. Furthermore, for measuring the entrepreneurial competence, a more strategic assessment model will be needed to capture the growth model. From recent empirical research in China, we have adopted the ASD adaptive strategy and generated evidence for incremental growth validity.

Total validity for leadership competency assessment

In general, the new approach for total validity has proved to be effective in conducting leadership competence implicit assessment modeling: developing culture-specific structures; focusing upon performance-based leadership compatibility and team effectiveness; and emphasizing entrepreneurial competence and organizational performance. The implicit assessment modeling strategies underlying effective personnel assessment and selection can be conducted to integrate those assessment approaches with strategic objectives. In order to achieve total validity, those three strategies need to be integrated in the same way that culture-specific higher-order constructs are collected in relation to cross-dimensional modeling strategy and adaptive growth assessment strategy. This implicit managerial modeling process has proved to be crucial in building up total validity. Further research is needed to integrate the leadership competency models with implicit assessment strategies so as to establish more comprehensive leadership competency assessment models.

Acknowledgment

This chapter was supported by NSF China grants (No. 39870247, No. 70071050) and by the Key Research Center grant of Zhejiang University, China.

References

Aguinis, H., Nenle, C. A., & Beaty, J. C. C., Jr. (2001). Virtual reality technology: A new tool for personnel selection, a chapter from the special issues. *International Journal of Selection and Assessment, 9*(1/2), 70–83.

Anderson, N., & Herriot, P. (1997). *International handbook of selection and assessment.* Chichester, UK: Wiley.

Bond, M. H. (1996). Chinese values. In M. H. Bond (Ed.), *Handbook of Chinese psychology* (pp. 208–226). Hong Kong: Oxford University Press.

Campbell, J. P., & Deirdre, J. K. (2001). *Exploring the limits in personnel selection and classification.* London: LEA.

Cheung, F. M., Leung, K., Fan, R., Song, W. Z., Zhang, J. X., & Zhang, J. P. (1996). Development of the Chinese Personality Assessment Inventory (CPAI). *Journal of Cross-Cultural Psychology, 27,* 181–199.

Feng, C. J. (1998). Exploration of leadership ability structure and assessment indicators [in Chinese]. *Local Government Administration, 7,* 5–7.

Gatewood, R. D., & Field, H. S. (2001). *Human resource selection* (5th ed.). New York: Harcourt College Publishers.

Graen, G. B., & Uhl-Bien, M. (1995). Development of leader–member exchange (LMX) theory of leadership over 25 years: Applying a multi-level multi-domain perspective. *Leadership Quarterly, 6*(2), 219–247.

Kristof-Brown, A. L. (2000). Perceived applicant fit: Distinguishing between recruiters' perceptions of person–job and person–organization fit. *Personnel Psychology, 53*(3), 643–670.

Leung, K., Smith, P. B., Wang, Z. M., & Sun, H. F. (1996). Job satisfaction in joint venture hotels in China: An organizational justice analysis. *Journal of International Business Studies, 27*(5), 947–962.

Li, C. P., & Shi, K. (2000). Issues in developing employee quality assessment system [in Chinese]. *China Human Resource Development, 3,* 33–35.

Li, J. T., & Tsui, A. S. (2000). Management and organizations in the Chinese context: An overview. In J. T. Li, A. S. Tsui, & E. Weldon (Eds.), *Management and organizations in the Chinese context.* Hong Kong: Saint Martin's Press.

Liang, J. (2000). *The structural analysis of Guanxi orientation behavior and validation in organizational context* [in Chinese]. Unpublished MA thesis in I/O psychology. Zhejiang University, Hangzhou.

Lin, W. Q., Chen L., & Wang D. (1987). The construction of the CPM scale for leadership behavior appraisal [in Chinese]. *Acta Psychologica Sinica, 19*(2), 199–207.

McCauley, C. D., Ruderman, M. N., Ohlott, P. J., & Morrow, J. E. (1994). Assessing the developmental components of managerial jobs. *Journal of Applied Psychology*, *79*(4), 544–560.

McClelland, D. C. (1973). Testing for competence rather than for "intelligence." *American Psychologist*, *28*(1), 1–14.

McCrae, R. R., Paul, T. C., & Michelle, S. M. Y. (1996). Universal aspects of Chinese personality structure. In M. H. Bond (Ed.), *Handbook of Chinese psychology*. Hong Kong: Oxford University Press.

Murphy, K. R. (2003). *Validity generalization: A critical review*. London: LEA.

Peterson, M. (1988). PM theory in Japan and China: What's in it for the United States? *Organizational Dynamics*, *16*(4), 22–38.

Riggio, R. E., Murphy, S. E., & Pirozzolo F. J. (2002). *Multiple intelligences and leadership*. London: LEA.

Schmitt, N., & Chan, D. (1998). *Personnel selection: A theoretical approach*. London: Sage.

Schneider, B., Goldstein, H. W., & Smith, D. B. (1995). The ASA framework: An update. *Personnel Psychology*, *48*(4), 747–773.

Shippmann, J. S., Ash, R. A., Carr, L., Hesketh, B., Pearlman, K., Battista, M. et al. (2000). The practice of competency modeling. *Personnel Psychology*, *53*(3), 703–736.

Smith, P. B., & Wang, Z. M. (1996). Chinese leadership and organizational structures. In M. H. Bond (Ed.), *Handbook of Chinese psychology* (pp. 322–337). Hong Kong: Oxford University Press

Sternberg, R. J. (1997). Tacit knowledge and job success. In N. Anderson & P. Herriot (Eds.), *International handbook of selection and assessment*. New York: Wiley.

Tao, Q. (1999). *The relationship between personality indicators and performance in organizational settings* [in Chinese]. Unpublished MA thesis in I/O psychology. Zhejiang University, Hangzhou.

Tsui, A. S., Farh, J.-L., & Xin, K. R. (2000). Guanxi in the Chinese context. In J. T. Li, A. S. Tsui, & E. Weldon (Eds.), *Management and organizations in the Chinese context*. Hong Kong: Saint Martin's Press.

Verburg, R. M., Drenth, P. J. D., Koopman, P. L., van Muijen, J. J., & Wang, Z.-M. (1999). Managing human resources across cultures: A comparative analysis of practice in industrial enterprises in China and The Netherlands. *The International Journal of Human Resources Management*, *10*(3), 391–410.

Wakabayashi, M., & Chen, Z. G. (1999). The practices of managerial skills for Asian managers: Comparisons based on managers in Japanese, Chinese and Taiwanese corporations. *Forum of International Development Studies*, *12*. Nagoya University.

Wang, Z. M. (1993). Psychology in China: A review dedicated to Li Chen. *Annual Review of Psychology*, *44*, 87–116.

Wang, Z. M. (1996). Culture, economic reform and the role of industrial and organizational psychology in China. In M. D. Dunnette & L. M. Hough (Eds.), *Handbook of industrial and organizational psychology* (2nd ed.). Palo Alto, CA: Consulting Psychologists Press.

Wang, Z. M. (1997a). Integrated personnel selection, appraisal and decisions: A Chinese approach. In N. Anderson & P. Herriot (Eds.), *International handbook of selection and assessment*. New York: Wiley.

Wang, Z. M. (1997b). Effective team management and cooperative decisions in Chinese organizations. In C. Cooper (Ed.), *Trends in organizational behaviour*. New York: Wiley.

Wang, Z. M. (1999). Developing joint-venture leadership teams. In W. H. Mobley,

M. J. Gessner, & V. Arnold (Eds.), *Advances in global leadership* (Vol. 1). New York: JAI Press.

Wang, Z. M. (2001). *Managerial psychology* [in Chinese]. Beijing, China: People's Educational Press.

Wang, Z. M. (2002). HRM strategies in managing virtual organizations in China: A case analysis of banking e-commerce projects. In R. L. Heneman, & D. B. Greenberger (Eds.), *Human resource management in virtual organizations*. Greenwich, CT: Information Age Publishing.

Wang, Z. M. (2003). Managerial competency modeling and the development of organizational psychology: A Chinese approach. *International Journal of Psychology, 38*(5), 323–334.

Wang, Z. M., & Chen, M. K. (2002). Managerial competency modeling: A structural equations analysis [in Chinese]. *Psychological Science, 6*, 420–428.

Wang, Z. M., & Kakabadse, A. (2006). Top management competencies in Chinese industrial organizations: A cross-cultural and structural analysis, Monograph. *Journal of Management Development*, in press.

Wang, Z. M., & Mobley, W. H. (1999). Strategic human resource management for twenty-first-century China. In P. M. Wright, L. D. Dyer, J. W. Boudreau, & G. T. Milkovich (Eds.), *Research in Personnel and Human Resources Management* (Suppl. 4, pp. 353–366). Stamford, CT: JAI Press.

Wang, Z. M., & Schneider, B. (2001). Final report of multi-cultural joint venture leadership teams in China. *Executive Brief No. 9 (February)*. Minneapolis, MN: PDI Global Research Consortia.

Wei, J. X., & Zhang, X. S. (1999). Evaluation of managerial competency [in Chinese]. *China Telent, 2*, 11–13.

Wilhelm, O., & Engle, R. W. (2005). *Handbook of understanding and measuring intelligence*. London: Sage.

Yang, K. S. (1993). *Indigenous psychological research in Chinese societies* [in Chinese]. Taipei, China: Taiwan University Psychology Department and Gui Guan Press.

Zhang, H. C. (1988). Psychological measurement in China. *International Journal of Psychology, 23*, 101–117.

25 Control processes in the formation of task units

Daniel Gopher

What is a task?

"Task" is one of the most fundamental and frequently used terms in the study of human behavior. Psychology is the science of people performing tasks. Every report of experimental work includes a mandatory section of "task" description. The key component of my own work, in applied cognition and human factor engineering, is the attempt to understand what the tasks are that people are involved with when performing daily missions, and how these tasks are mapped to the constructs and data bases provided by cognitive psychology. Yet, the operational definition of the term "task" is fuzzy, and its status as a theoretical construct in human performance models is not clear. This state of ambiguity is clearly reflected in the fact that while there are some general standards on what type of details should be included in the description of a task in experimental reports, these standards are open to interpretation and personal taste. A review of the experimental literature reveals a wide variety in the specific characteristics of tasks that are reported, the detail in which they are reported, and the degree in which these details are considered in the interpretation of results.

Every task can be described along many dimensions and with many specific features. Figure 25.1 illustrates some of the common dimensions and descriptive features, including: stimulus type; presentation mode; transformation and computation requirements; response type; performance instructions; and reward structure. These are all separate elements, which can be combined in numerous ways that include all or part of them, to create a variety of tasks, and serve different goals. A task is thus a specific combination of these elements in the service of goal-directed behavior.

Webster's unabridged dictionary (McKechnie, 1959) proposes three definitions for the term "task":

1   A piece of work assigned to or demanded of a person.
2   Any undertaking or a piece of work.
3   An undertaking involving labor or difficulty.

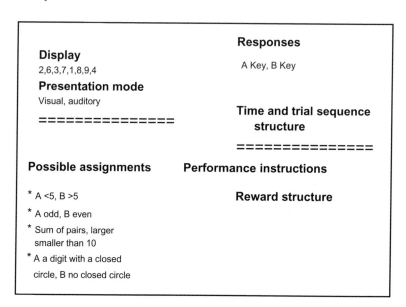

Figure 25.1 The many components that make a task.

Note the emphasis on the "undertaking" or the "coping" with a demand. Tasks are the elementary units of goal-directed behavior. They encompass the structural and dynamic constraints on performance in the service of intentions or instructions. Tasks are a joint product of top-down constraints and the properties of the environment. Information-processing modes, response types, memory representations and performance competency are all defined, bounded and developed within their respective task shells. The term "task shell" denotes the integrated joint product of all structural and dynamic properties that compose a task. Task shells have an independent status, which is akin to the Gestalt fundamental idea of the whole being more than the sum of its composing parts (Kellman, 2000; Koffka, 1935). Similarly, it is argued that task shells have a marked influence on the work of their elements: stimuli, responses, representations, transformations, etc.

Shells are important for the understanding of interaction, facilitation and interference effects on performance, within and between tasks.

Shells also delineate the boundaries of an acquired skill, the value of practice, and the cost of transfer. The formation of a task shell is the building block of the conduct of purposive behavior. Nonetheless cognitive psychology has overlooked the importance of incorporating the construct of a task shell in its models, and studying its formation and influence on behavior.

Control processes in the formation of task units

An investigation of the nature of task shells, and the process by which they are formulated and maintained, is well within the contemporary focus in cognitive psychology, on the study and modeling of the work and influence of control and executive processes on human behavior (Gopher & Koriat, 1999; Monsell & Driver, 2000). Control processes are the class of processes that initiate, coordinate, synchronize, and regulate the conduct of goal-directed behavior. They are also those that bind together all task elements to establish a coherent task shell, in the service of intentions.

Contemporary research in cognitive psychology appears to be undergoing a shift of interest. Whereas the classical information-processing approach has focused on questions concerning elementary components of tasks, basic architecture, and the flow of information in the human processing system, there is now a growing interest in questions pertaining to the regulatory processes underlying supervisory control functions (e.g., Allport, Styles, & Hsieh, 1994; Baddeley & Hitch, 1994; Bjork, 1999; Carlson, Khoo, Yaure, & Schneider, 1990; Carlson, Wenger & Sullivan, 1993; Gopher, 1993, 1996; Gopher, Armony, & Greenshpan, 2000; Gopher, & Koriat, 1999; Kramer, Larish, & Strayer, 1995; Kramer, Larish, Weber, & Bardell, 1999; Meyer & Kieras, 1997; Meiran, 1996; Norman & Shallice, 1986; Rogers & Monsell, 1995; Rubinstein, Meyer, & Evans, 2001; Shallice, 1994; Yee, Hunt, & Pelegrino, 1991).

Experimental psychology and cognitive neuroscience have made significant steps towards understanding how the brain processes information in specific domains such as sensory modalities, motor control, memory, spatial cognition and language. However, only recently there has been a significant move to consider how the flow of purposive behavior is integrated, controlled, coordinated, and synchronized. Experimental research, using diversified research paradigms such as concurrent task performance, task switching and speeded responses, has demonstrated the influence and importance of control and strategic processes on task performance (Gopher et al., 2000; Kramer, et al., 1999; Mayr & Keele, 2000; Meiran, 2000; Meyer & Kieras, 1997; Sohn & Carlson, 2003; Yeung & Monsell, 2003). Developmental studies demonstrate the importance of acquiring control at a young age (Johnson & Munkata, in press). Studies of old adults and clinical populations show the severe performance degradation resulting from impaired control. These studies are corroborated by neurophysiological and brain-imaging studies, which locate major control functions in the frontal and prefrontal areas, but also suggest a model of distributed control activity across multiple brain areas (Kanwisher & Duncan, 2003; Monsell & Driver, 2000). In the context of the present chapter, it is somewhat surprising that a concept of "task shell" has not emerged as a topic of investigation, despite the fact that it is crucial in the control-processes domain, and one of the major and important products of control. I will return to consider this neglect in the final section of this chapter.

The following sections describe three examples from research conducted in our laboratory, which demonstrate the formation of a task shell, its main features, and its influence on performance for three different tasks. All examples are based on laboratory studies that simulate complex daily life tasks. They speak for the importance of studying the task-shell construct and point to research questions that need to be addressed in future research. The three tasks are:

1   Typing with a two-hand chord keyboard (the importance of representation format).
2   Flying with a single-eye, helmet-mounted display (influencing basic execution modes).
3   Training under variable priorities and emphasis changes (the significance of global task setting).

Typing with a two-hand chord keyboard: The importance of representation format

The first example examines the process of acquiring typing skills on a two-hand chord keyboard. Typing and data entry using a standard computer keyboard is one of the most prevalent tasks in our technological age. Yet, touch typing, which is the most efficient mode of data entry, is a skill exercised by only a small percentage of the users. Most users are one- or two-finger typists with continuing visual guidance. The difficulty of acquiring touch-typing skills is associated with the design features of the QWERTY keyboard, in which the blind location of multiple letter keys and numerous finger trajectories has to be learned. In a sequence of studies we investigated the prospects of an alternative keyboard, which differs in its design principles and operation rules (Gopher & Raij, 1988). The new system comprises two separate panels, both with five keys (one for each finger) and two additional colored keys used to change character groups (Figure 25.2). Letters and characters are entered by typing a specific chord for each letter (a chord is a combination of 1–5 fingers pressed together). For five fingers there are 31 possible chord combinations, 26 of which are sufficient to represent the Latin alphabet. Moving the thumb to a different color key creates a new chord combination family. Thus, each of the two keyboards is able to represent the full character set of the standard QWERTY keyboard. With two keyboards, performers can divide the work between the hands as they wish, increase their typing speed, or type two independent texts simultaneously. The new design raises many interesting theoretical and applied issues related to the acquisition of competence and the best application of the system. In the context of the present chapter we focus on one study, which examined the best mapping rule for the assignment of letter chords across the two hands (Gopher, Karis, & Koenig, 1985). The question can be stated as follows: if on the right-hand panel the letter A is entered by using a chord

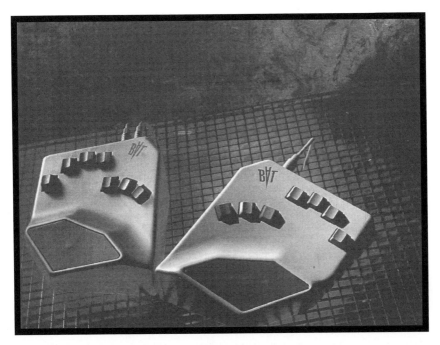

Figure 25.2 A photograph of the two-hand chord keyboard.

combination of the thumb and index finger, and the chord for the letter B combines the thumb, middle and ring fingers (see Figure 25.3), what will be the corresponding chords for these letters on the left-hand panel? The efficiency of three mapping principles was compared in a training study. Two principles were hand symmetry (same finger chords are used to enter the same letter on both panels) and spatial congruency (same key locations on both panels). Note that each of the two principles creates a conflict in terms of the other. With hand symmetry the same fingers are used but key positions on the two panels are mirror images of one another. Under spatial congruence the key positions are the same, but different finger combinations are used to enter the same letter. A third design combines the two principles. When the panels are tilted upright vertically such that the two palms face each other, letter chords on the two panels use both the same fingers and key positions (Figure 25.3).

Figure 25.4 depicts the learning curves of three groups of subjects, who were presented with pairs of English letters and asked to enter them as fast as possible, using both hands. Figure 25.4 presents the average typing speeds of seven 90-minute training sessions. Because subjects were unable to be completely parallel, letter pairs were usually entered such that the left hand letter was leading, while the right hand followed and completed the pair. As the figure shows, letter entry times for the three groups were about equal during

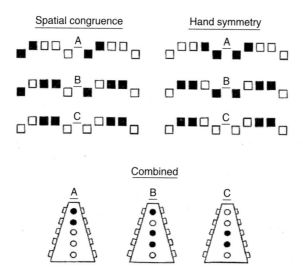

Figure 25.3 Coding principles for associating letters with chord entries (from Gopher, Karis, & Koenig, 1985).

the first session and all groups improved with training. However, with the progress of training, an increasing difference between mapping rules was observed. The combined vertical principle was superior, followed by spatial congruency, with hand symmetry having lowest performance. The differences were equally evident for right- and left-hand performances. Subsequent experiments indicated that the performance superiority of the combined vertical group resulted from its mapping rule, rather than the different posture of the hands (Gopher et al., 1985). The increased influence of the representation rule with the progress of training is an important support for the idea of a gradual development of a global task shell, which binds together the elements of a task and influences its performance. If the main role of the mapping principles was only that of a memory aid, for better memorization of the association between letters and their entry chords, we would expect a different pattern of results. The largest difference between groups should have appeared early in training, and all groups should have converged to similar performance levels with the progress of training, when direct connection between letters and corresponding motor chords has been established, thus eliminating the need for a memory aid. The results show the exact opposite pattern. Representation principles became more important late rather than early in the acquisition of competence (see also Gopher, 1984, for similar results). Furthermore, it should be noted that mapping rules created a difference only in the way in which chords were assigned to letters on the left-hand panel. On the right-hand panel, chord combinations for letter entries were the same under all three mapping principles (Figure 25.3). Yet, the differences in performance created by the representation rules were equally potent on

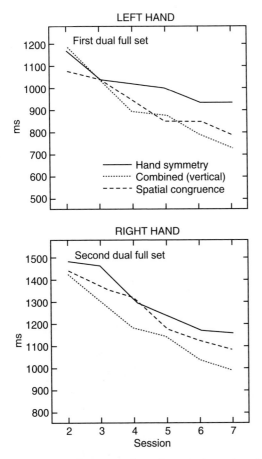

Figure 25.4 Response times for entering pairs of letters with a two-hand chord keyboard (from Gopher, Karis, & Koenig, 1985).

both hands. This outcome is a strong demonstration of the influence of task-shell properties on the processing and performance of the task-composing elements. The representation principles created a difference in entering the same finger chords, and these differences increased with training. The representation format has become a dominant organizing and differentiating property of the acquired typing competency.

Flying with a single-eye, helmet-mounted display (HMD): Influencing basic execution modes

The second example of the effects of a task shell on performance comes from an experimental study investigating the training of subjects to fly with a single-eye, helmet-mounted display (Seagull & Gopher, 1997). Monocular helmet-mounted night-vision systems have been incorporated in modern helicopters to improve pilots' ability to fly at night. These systems are based on a thermal sensor (FLIR) installed on the nose of the helicopter, which is sensitive to the heat emission of objects in the forward flight path. Thermal energy is converted to the optical range and presented on a small single-eye display located on the pilot's helmet (Figure 25.5). The horizontal visual angle of the sensor is limited (20–40 degrees depending on model). To enable full scanning of the outside visual field the sensor is installed on a servomotor, which is driven by the pilot's head movements. Scanning of the outside environment is thus exclusively dependent on head movements, rather than the normal close coupling of eyes and head motion. While moving the head is the most adaptive behavior to assure adequate coverage of the outside visual field, pilots make deliberate efforts to limit their head movements to reduce the risk of disorientation. Visual orientation based on the HMD is very difficult due to the combined effect of several factors: the single sensor monocular field of view; absence of peripheral visual flow; lack of visual reference; the large displacement between the sensor position and the pilot eye points of regard; all coupled with the rapid movement of the helicopter through the landscape and the influence of wind direction change. Additional voluntary head movements further complicate the situation because they create another source of image movement on the display. Head movements are required and are adaptive, as well as disruptive and dangerous. Our study

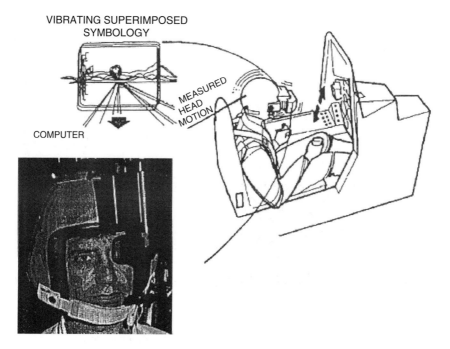

Figure 25.5 A single-eye, helmet-mounted display (HMD).

was aimed at training subjects to move their heads with HMDs to improve performance, without losing orientation.

Participants piloted a simulated H-19 helicopter through a computer-generated, simulated narrow canyon, using either a single-eye HMD or normal binocular vision, through the window field of view, which was projected onto a large screen (Figure 25.6). Each training trial lasted 3 minutes (if the subject did not crash earlier). Subjects could control the pitch, yaw and roll of the helicopter, but moved at a fixed speed of 15 ms^{-1}. Five groups of Technion students, with no prior flight experience, were given a total of 120, 3-minute training trials in five sessions, preceded and followed by pre- and post-training test flights, comprising equal numbers of 4-minute binocular and pure HMD flight trials. One group was trained only under normal binocular, out of the window viewing conditions. A second group was trained only with HMD. Groups three and four were trained with HMD, but in addition were given a secondary task of capturing targets. Subjects were required to move their heads and capture with a square reticule, displayed at the center of their HMD, a diamond target, which appeared every 10–12 seconds, at random locations in the canyon, along their flight path. When captured the target changed its color and disappeared. In group four, the reticule recentered itself automatically, while in group three subjects had to actively reset it. Group 5 was trained with HMD, but was given a demanding secondary task, which appeared at the center of the eye field but did not require any head movement (thus was irrelevant to head-movement training).

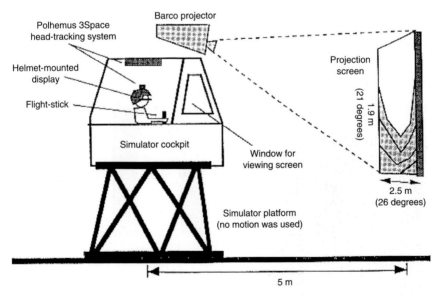

Figure 25.6 The flight simulator used for simulation of an H-19 helicopter in a low-level flight through a canyon (from Seagull & Gopher, 1997).

Because the task was very difficult, and subjects had no prior experience in flight situations, crashing before the end of a trial was very common. A good performance measure was, therefore, average flight duration in test trials before a crash occurred (maximum 240 seconds). Figure 25.7 presents this data for the five experimental groups in binocular and HMD flight trials. As can be seen, in the post-training test flights, all groups had about equal levels of performance under normal binocular viewing conditions. Flight-time scores were somewhat higher for the group that was trained under the binocular condition throughout, but this difference failed to reach statistical significance. In contrast, the two groups that were trained with HMD and a secondary task that forced them to move their head, showed significantly better flight performance with HMD, which equaled their performance under normal viewing conditions. Hence, the training approach was successful, although subjects were not aware of this. They were not informed that the main purpose of introducing the secondary task was to train them to fly with an HMD. The most interesting results for the purpose of the present chapter come from the analysis of head movements, comparing the data from the pre- and post-training test flights. These data are presented in Figure 25.8. The barographs depict the changes in the average amount of head movement from the pre- to the post-training test flights. The zero line represents the pre-training levels, positive values indicate an increase and negative values a decrease of head movements in post-training flights as compared to pre-training. As can be seen there is a distinct difference between the two groups that were trained with HMD and a secondary task that required head movements and the other three groups in which such movements were not

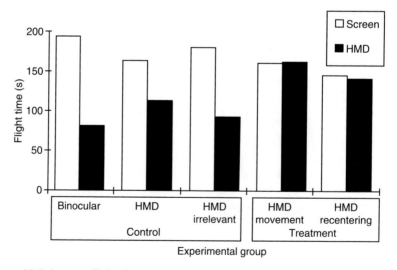

Figure 25.7 Average flight times under normal and helmet-mounted viewing conditions during the post-training test trials (from Seagull & Gopher, 1997).

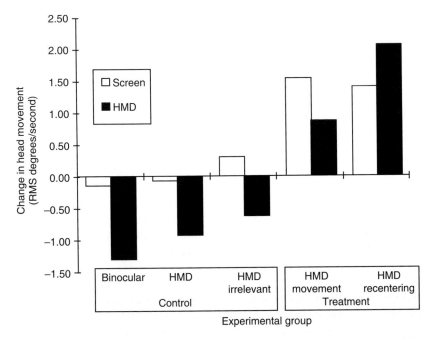

Figure 25.8 The changes in head movements from before training to after training;
RMS = root mean square (from Seagull & Gopher, 1997).

required. For these latter groups there is no difference in the number of head movements in the normal viewing conditions as a result of training, while there is a considerable reduction in head movements from pre- to post-training during HMD flights. Subjects indeed learned the harmful consequences of head motion and reacted by limiting their head movements. Note also that their flight performance was much worse in HMD flights (Figure 25.7). The effect was most pronounced in the binocular-only group. In contrast, the two groups that were trained with the secondary task increased their number of head movements substantially. Moreover, they show a similar increase in their head movements under the normal binocular viewing condition. This increase did not affect their flight performance under normal viewing conditions, which was not different from the levels of the other three groups. It appears that in the two secondary-task groups training had established a new task shell, which changed the fundamental relationship between eye and head movements in scanning the visual field. Thereby it changed one of the earliest acquired, frequently used, unconsciously coordinated and executed processing modes. A new task shell was developed, which adapted behavior to the new constraints and operational requirements of the task and the environment. It influenced the delicate balance between its composing elements; balance that has been long automated to the point, figuratively speaking, of being almost hard wired. Interestingly, this change occurred without influencing the overall success in task performance. The present example of flying with a single-eye HMD attests not only to the power of the emerging task shell, but also to its important adaptive role in coping with changes in the environment and in task requirements.

Training under variable priorities and emphasis changes: The influence of manipulating the global task set

The third example of the influence of a task shell on the performance of its composing elements comes from a sequence of studies investigating the effect of a training protocol, in which subjects were required to change their attention-allocation policies and emphasis on elements, while performing complex and attention-demanding tasks. One study investigated performance of demanding dual tasks (Gopher, 1993). Another study investigated the acquisition of competence in a difficult, multi-element computer game (Gopher, Weil, & Siegel, 1989). A third study examined the transfer of training from a computer game to actual flight (Gopher, Weil, & Bareket, 1994). I briefly review here the logic and the results of the dissertation work of Michael Brickner, which is summarized in Gopher (1993). Subjects were trained under dual-task conditions to perform concurrently pursuit-tracking and letter-typing tasks. Figure 25.9 depicts the experimental display of the two tasks. A continuous two-dimensional tracking task required subjects to follow the X symbol, controlled by a right-hand joystick, and the movements of a target square generated by the computer forcing function. The joystick

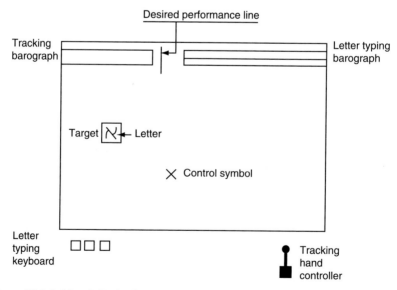

Figure 25.9 Subjects' display in concurrent performance of tracking and letter typing with priority manipulations (from Gopher, 1993).

control dynamic was a mix of acceleration and velocity control. A second, letter-typing task was performed by entering three finger-chord combinations, using the keys of a left-hand panel. The task was a Hebrew analogue of the chord keyboard system, described in the first example above. A Hebrew letter was displayed inside the tracking target square. It had to be responded to by entering its corresponding finger chord as fast as possible. A correct entry led to the immediate presentation of a new letter. In addition to the tracking and typing tasks, subjects were also presented with feedback indicators at the upper part of the computer screen. Indicators comprised a short vertical desired performance line, and two moving barographs, one for each task. The desired performance line indicated the required performance level on each task, and the moving barographs depicted the momentary difference between actual and desired performances. Positioning the desired performance to the left or right of the center point of the display indicated a reciprocal change in the task priorities. More effort and higher priority had to be allocated to a task when the line moved away from the base of its performance barograph, because higher performance level was now required to reach the desired performance line. Similarly, lower efforts and priority were demanded when the line moved closer to the barograph base of a task. Priority levels were determined relative to baseline performance distributions of each of the tasks, and manipulated in a commensurate manner, such that when the priority of one task was increased the priority of the other task decreased and vice versa. Five levels of priorities were employed: 0.75, 0.65, 0.50, 0.35, 0.25 (Gopher, Brickner, & Navon, 1982).

Variable priority training was administered during two sessions, comprising 50, 3-minute trials, 35 of which fell under the relevant training condition, namely, priority levels were changed in each 3-minute trial. Training performance of the variable priority group (VP) was compared with two other groups: One group – no priority (NP) – was given the two tasks, without the feedback indicators, and instructed to perform both of them to the best of its ability, assigning equal importance to two tasks. A second group – equal priority (EP) – was given the augmented feedback display, but practiced only under equal-priority conditions (desired performance line located at the center). This group was added to control for the possible influence of the augmented feedback display. Of the 35 priority change trials of the VP group, seven were performed under equal priorities, which was the only priority condition practiced by the other two groups. Figure 25.10 shows the performance results for tracking and letter typing, in the equal-priority trials of the three experimental groups. As can be seen, while all groups have about equal performance levels at the beginning of training and all groups improve with the progress of training, the VP group progresses much faster, and demonstrates substantially better performance on both tasks at the end of training. The other two groups display lower performance, and the differences between them were not significant statistically. In a third additional transfer session of the experiment, the augmented feedback display was removed for

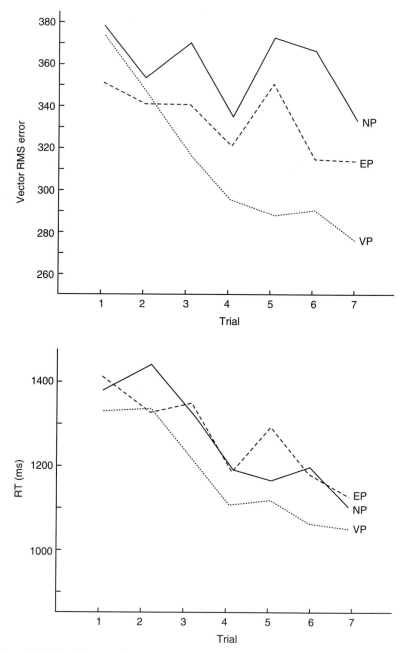

Figure 25.10 Average tracking errors (upper panel) and letter-typing response time (lower panel) in seven equal-priority trials (from Gopher, 1993).

all groups. Subjects were instructed to put equal emphasis on both tasks while reciprocal manipulations of task difficulty were introduced. Subjects were not informed about these difficulty changes. Difficulty manipulations were analogous to the change in the relative demands of tasks through the manipulation of desired performance level. This time however, subjects were uninformed and were not given an online feedback on their performance. Subjects trained under variable priorities were again significantly better than the other two groups in their dual-task performance, and their ability to adjust performance to changes in task difficulty.

From the perspective of the influence of a formulated task shell on the performance of elements, the results of both training and transfer are revealing. Instructed variation in the relative priority of the two concurrently performed tasks required subjects to develop a task frame that allowed flexible allocation of efforts between the tracking and typing, and adoption of differential attention policies. As the results show, this general framework (task shell) led to an improved dual-task performance of both tracking and typing at the end of training. These outcomes are especially striking because the superiority was revealed in the performance of equal-priority trials. Recall that for the VP group the equal-priority condition was practiced in only 20% of the trials. Hence, the NP and EP groups had five times more replications of this condition. Practice in the NP and EP groups was also more uniform and consistent, as they practiced only one variant of task priority as compared to five in the VP group. Consistency and number of trials have been shown to be the strongest determinants of performance improvement with practice (Newell & Rosenbloom, 1981; Schneider, 1985). Yet, the training protocol based on emphasis change overpowered both of them. Furthermore, the superiority of the group trained with this protocol was generalized to the transfer condition, when subtle changes in the properties of the concurrently performed tasks changed their demands and required detection and reallocation of performance efforts. It seems that the general task shell, which was created in response to the requirement for flexible allocation of effort among demanding concurrent tasks, was better suited to coping with the dynamic of change in the balance of demands between the two difficult tasks. These demands may be influenced by many local transients of each of the performed tasks, external conditions, or the performer's state of mind. A task shell formulated to adapt flexibly to changes may better coordinate the management of efforts with such transients. It is another clear demonstration of the role of the task shell in coordinating and controlling the work of the elementary units. Subsequent studies have shown the advantage of emphasis-change training in acquiring competence in performing a complex computer game that involved demanding visual scanning, and dealing with multiple elements and multiple procedures, under severe time pressure (Gopher et al., 1989). The emphasis-change protocol was applied in the creation of a task shell, by leading subjects to experience game variants, in each of which one element was made figure and emphasized, while all others were de-emphasized and became ground. An application of this approach has also shown a strong positive transfer from emphasis-change training on the computer game to the actual flight performance of cadets in the Israeli air force flight-training school (Gopher et al., 1994).

Concluding remarks and further thoughts

Three demonstrations were presented for the strong and enduring influence of task shells on real-life, complex task performances. In two cases (chord keyboards and HMDs) indirect emerging consequences of external task features (chord acquisition format, viewing conditions) were those that were dominant in the creation of task shells. In the example of training under variable priorities and emphasis change, the creation of a task shell was led by top-down, direct intentional efforts/voluntary priority shifts during training. Performers may not be cognizant of the emergence of a task shell, its properties, constraints and far-reaching influences on short- and long-term performances. Nonetheless, it represents performers' goal-directed adaptive strategy, given task constraints and reward structure.

The three experimental studies showed that task shells are integrative global constructs that do not occur immediately. They gradually develop with experience and training and are most clearly revealed when performers achieve competence in task performance. As such, the study of task shells is closely linked to the study of training and skill acquisition. Task shells evolve around leading dimensions: dominant task features (e.g., mapping principles); environmental constraints (e.g., viewing conditions); control strategies (e.g., flexibility in shifting efforts). Once established the global properties of the shell bind together its composing elements and influence their work in ways that cannot be predicted from a separate study of the elements. In the domain of skilled performance, the concept of a "task shell" has the same theoretical status as the "good figure" in Gestalt models of perception (Gibson, 1979; Kellman, 2000).

Scattered evidence in support of the task-shell notion can be found in many experimental works, in particular in detailed accounts of the development of expertise, and in reports on structural differences in task representations between novices and experts. One striking example is the study of Chase and Ericsson (1981), which showed how their subject, who had a well-organized knowledge base of running times, became a world champion in memorizing long sequences of auditorily presented digits. He converted subgroups of digits into running times, developed and organized encoding, storage and retrieval systems, based on his knowledge. Another example comes from the performance analysis of master chess players and in particular masters of multi-board games. These players are unable to show their power unless they play against opponents who have reached at least a medium level of expertise, a level at which their game has an organization and plan, and is not chaotic as in the case of beginners (Chase & Simon, 1973; De

Groot & Gobet, 1996). When confronting a well-organized player multi-board masters can read the board rapidly and plan their moves in the allotted time. Examining the performance of music virtuosos or champion tennis players provides many examples of the influence of global task shells on the performance of elements (see Sudnow, 1981, for an interesting observational study of piano playing). A compelling example of the power of a well-developed task shell may be the case of face recognition. Extensive scientific work has been conducted to investigate the special perceptual sensitivity of humans to the presentation of a human-face figure. The literature is rich with behavioral, physiological and neuroimaging studies of face recognition arguing for a unique status of human faces as perceptual objects (Bruce, 1988; Bruce & Young, 1998). A consideration of the face-recognition literature from the vantage point of a well-developed, ecologically functional task shell, may give the study of this topic a fresh perspective. For example, can different types of face-recognition sensitivity be revealed or developed as a result of different frameworks and constraints on experience?

Relevant information on the nature and processes involved in the development of task shells can also be extracted from contemporary research under the aforementioned task-switching paradigm. This popular paradigm is employed to investigate the processes and costs involved in switching performance from one task to another (e.g., Allport et al., 1994; Gopher et al., 2000; Rogers & Monsell, 1995). By inference it can be used to identify the distinctive features that single out one task unit from another and signify the properties of its task shell.

While there is ample incidental evidence across a wide range of problem areas and research paradigms to support the viability of the task-shell notion, it should be recognized that it is not a systematic study of the shell nature, fundamental properties, mechanisms and processes that govern the development and operation of shells. Major topics in such a study should include: the course of development of task shells and the differences between alternative modes of guided experience; the nature of organizing principles and the determinants of the emerging dominance of shell dimensions; the neuronal substrates of task shells, uncovering the associated brain processes, structures and mechanisms, associated with the formation of task shells and accompanying their operation.

Afterthoughts

The chapter began with a general undisputed observation that psychology is the science of people performing tasks. It was further stated that the task construct is, on the one hand, fundamental to the study of behavior and, on the other hand, fuzzy and ill defined. The claim was also made that the formation of a task shell represents a combined, adaptive product of intentions, environmental constraints, internal constraints, and reward structure in the service of goal-directed behavior. It is therefore somewhat puzzling that this construct has not been a subject of direct research. This is even more puzzling in the contemporary Zeitgeist when control processes and executive control have become mainstream in cognitive research. The formation and maintenance of a task shell are clearly the most important of control functions. The reasons for this neglect can only be speculated. One possibility is technical, due to the duration and effort required in following the formation and stabilization of a task shell. It should be noted that the performed tasks in each of the three reviewed experimental examples required considerable training and multiple sessions before the influence of task shells emerged clearly. Even then, the revealed differences were far from reaching their final power. The vast majority of the laboratory studies reported in the experimental literature are of relatively short duration, and such studies are thus concluded before a stable task shell can be expected to be established. In contrast, well-formulated task shells govern behavior in the majority of daily-performed tasks. An interesting speculation is that this difference may, in part, explain the difficulties of generalizing from laboratory studies to performance in operational settings. While short-duration laboratory studies may present valid information on the work of the elements, this information may have substantially changed when a coherent task shell is established. Another possibility is that the study of control processes is still at the stage of attempting to identify, understand and model the elementary processes of control. It has not yet reached the point of investigating their integrative products, such as a task shell. I hope that the present chapter has highlighted the importance of studying task shells, raised questions and pointed to directions that may lead to productive research.

References

Allport, A., Styles, E., & Hsieh, S. (1994). Shifting intentional set: Exploring the dynamic control of tasks. In C. Umilta & M. Moskovitch (Eds.), *Attention and performance, XV: Conscious and nonconscious information processing* (pp. 421–452). Cambridge, MA: MIT Press.

Baddeley, A., & Hitch, G. J. (1994). Developments in the concept of working memory. *Neuropsychology, 8*, 485–493.

Bjork, R. A. (1999). Assessing our own competence: Heuristic and illusions. In D. Gopher & A. Koriat (Eds.), *Attention and performance XVII. Cognitive regulation of performance: Interaction of theory and application* (pp. 435–460). Cambridge, MA: MIT Press.

Bruce, V. (1988). *Recognizing faces*. Hillsdale, NJ: Lawrence Erlbaum Associates, Inc.

Bruce, V., & Young, A. (1998). *In the eyes of the beholder: The science of face recognition*. London: Oxford University Press.

Carlson, R. A., Khoo, B. H., Yaure, R. G., & Schneider, W. (1990). Acquisition of a problem-solving skill: Levels of organization and use of working memory. *Journal of Experimental Psychology: General, 119*, 193–214.

Carlson, R. A., Wenger, J. L., & Sullivan, M. A. (1993). Coordinating information from perception and working memory. *Journal of Experimental Psychology: Human Perception and Performance, 19*, 531–548.

Chase, W. G., & Ericsson, A. E. (1981). Skilled memory. In J. A. Anderson (Ed.), *Cognitive skills and their acquisition.* Hillsdale, NJ: Lawrence Erlbaum Associates, Inc.

Chase, W. G., & Simon, A. (1973). *The mind's eye in chess.* In W. G. Chase (Ed.), *Visual information processing.* New York: Academic Press.

De Groot, A., & Gobet, F. (1996). *Perception and memory in chess.* Assen, Germany: Van Gorcun.

Gibson, J. J. (1979). *The ecological approach to visual perception.* Boston, MA: Houghton Mifflin.

Gopher, D. (1984). On the contribution of vision-based imagery to the acquisition and operation of a transcription skill. In W. Prinz, A. Sanders, & H. Heuer (Eds.), *Cognition and motor processes* (pp. 195–208). New York: Springer-Verlag.

Gopher, D. (1993). The skill of attention control: Acquisition and execution of attention strategies. In D. E. Meyer & S. Kornblum (Eds.), *Attention and performance XIV: Synergies in experimental psychology, artificial intelligence, and cognitive neuroscience – a silver jubilee* (pp. 299–322). Cambridge, MA: MIT Press.

Gopher, D. (1996). Attention control: Explorations of the work of an executive controller. *Cognitive Brain Research, 5*, 23–38.

Gopher, D., Armony L., & Greenshpan, Y. (2000). Switching tasks and attention policies. *Journal of Experimental Psychology: General, 109*, 306–339.

Gopher, D., Brickner, M., & Navon, D. (1982). Different difficulty manipulations interact differently with task emphasis: Evidence for multiple resources. *Journal of Experimental Psychology: Human Perception and Performance, 8*, 146–157.

Gopher, D., Karis D., & Koenig, W. (1985). The representation of movement schema in long term memory: Lessons from the acquisition of a transcription skill. *Acta Psychologica, 60*, 105–134.

Gopher, D., & Koriat A. (Eds.). (1999). *Attention and performance XVII: Cognitive regulation of performance: Theory and application.* Cambridge, MA: MIT Press.

Gopher, D., & Raij, D. (1988). Typing with a two hand chord keyboard – will the QWERTY become obsolete? *IEEE Transactions in System Man and Cybernetics, 18*, 601–609.

Gopher, D., Weil, M., & Bareket, T. (1994). Transfer of skill from a computer game trainer to flight. *Human Factors, 36*, 1–19.

Gopher, D., Weil, M., & Siegel, D. (1989). Practice under changing priorities: An approach to training of complex skills. *Acta Psychologica, 71*, 147–179.

Johnson, M. H., & Munkata, Y. (Eds.). (in press). Processes of change in brain and cognitive behavior. *Attention and performance XXI.* London: Oxford University Press.

Kanwisher, N., & Duncan, J. (Eds.). (2003). Functional neuroimaging of visual cognition. *Attention and performance XX.* London: Oxford University Press.

Kellman, P. J. (2000). An update on Gestalt psychology. In B. Landau, J. Sabini, J. Jonides, & E. Newport (Eds.), *Perception cognition and language: Essays in honor of Henry and Lila Gleitman.* Cambridge, MA: MIT Press.

Koffka, K. (1935). *Principles of Gestalt psychology.* New York: Harcourt Brace.

Kramer, A. F., Larish, J. L., & Strayer, D. L. (1995). Training for attentional control in dual task setting: A comparison of young and old adults. *Journal of Experimental Psychology: Applied, 1*, 50–76.

Kramer, A. F., Larish, J. L., Weber, T. A., & Bardell, L. (1999). Training for executive control: Task coordination strategies and aging. In D. Gopher & A. Koriat (Eds.), *Attention and performance XVII. Cognitive regulation of performance: Interaction of theory and application* (pp. 617–652). Cambridge, MA: MIT Press.

Mayr, U., & Keele, R. (2000). Changing internal constraints on action: The role of backward inhibition. *Journal of Experimental Psychology: General, 12,* 4–26.

McKechnie, J. I. (Ed.). (1959). *Webster's new twentieth century dictionary* (2nd ed.). New York: Simon & Schuster.

Meiran, N. (1996). The reconfiguration of processing mode prior to task performance. *Journal of Experimental Psychology: Learning, Memory and Cognition, 22,* 1423–1442.

Meiran, N. (2000). Modeling cognitive control in task switching. *Psychological Research, 63,* 234–249.

Meyer, D. E., & Kieras, E. D. (1997). A computational theory of executive cognitive processes and multiple task performance: Part 1, Basic mechanisms. *Psychological Review, 104,* 3–75.

Monsell, S., & Driver, J. (2000). Control of cognitive processes. *Attention and performance XVIII.* Cambridge, MA: MIT Press.

Newell, A., & Rosenbloom, P. S. (1981). Mechanisms of skill acquisition and the law of practice. In J. A. Anderson (Ed.), *Cognitive skills and their acquisition.* Hillsdale, NJ: Lawrence Erlbaum Associates, Inc.

Norman, D. A., & Shallice, T. (1986). Attention to action: Willed and automatic control of behavior. In R. J. Davidson, G. E. Schwartz, & D. Shapiro (Eds.), *Consciousness and self regulation* (Vol. 4). New York: Plenum Press.

Rogers, R. D., & Monsell, S. (1995). Costs of a predictable switch between simple cognitive tasks. *Journal of Experimental Psychology: General, 124,* 207–231.

Rubinstein, J., Meyer, D. E., & Evans J. E. (2001). Executive control of cognitive processes in task switching. *Journal of Experimental Psychology: Human Perception and Performance, 27,* 763–797.

Schneider, W. (1985). Training high performance skills: Fallacies and guidelines. *Human Factors, 27,* 285–301.

Seagull, F. J., & Gopher D. (1997). Training head movement in visual scanning: An embedded approach to the development of piloting skills with helmet mounted displays. *Journal of Experimental Psychology: Applied, 3,* 463–480.

Shallice, T. (1994). Multiple levels of control processes. In C. Umilta & M. Moskovitch (Eds.), *Attention and performance, XV: Conscious and nonconscious information processing.* Cambridge, MA: MIT Press.

Sohn, M.-H., & Carlson, R. A. (2003). Implicit temporal tuning of working memory strategy during cognitive skill acquisition. *American Journal of Psychology, 116,* 239–256.

Sudnow, D. (1981). *Ways of the hand.* New York: Harper & Row.

Yee, P. L., Hunt, E., & Pelegrino, J. W. (1991). Coordinating cognitive information: Task effects and individual differences in integrating information from several sources. *Cognitive Psychology, 23,* 615–680.

Yeung, N., & Monsell, S. (2003) Switching between tasks of unequal familiarity. *Journal of Experimental Psychology: Human Perception and Performance, 29,* 455–469.

26 States of mind: Political systems as implicit theories of psychology

Diane F. Halpern

Political belief systems are, at their heart, psychological theories. They are implicit theories of motivation, personality, mental health, human development, education, and social interaction – topics that are the very lifeblood of psychology. We cannot separate the way in which people think and act from the society in which they live; we cannot view human thought and behavior without seeing them through the lens of the viewer's own culture. If social scientists want to understand the underlying beliefs of any political system, we need to look at the way that the society responds to questions like: What is normal? How can workers be motivated? When will people help others? How can violence be reduced? Why do we go to war? How should we raise children? Why do we love or hate? When do we cooperate or compete?

These are among the many questions that are found in psychology textbooks, but they are also the stated and unstated assumptions behind political theories and public policies – the way that societies answer these everyday fundamental questions and enact laws that reflect their answers about motivation, human development, where to draw the line between normal and abnormal, the reasons for war, and so on is a combination of the psychological and political. There are some universal principles and standards for answering these questions, but there are also variations that depend on the time, place, and tradition.

The main thesis of this chapter is that political beliefs – the reasoning behind the structures, actions, and laws of a political system – follow from individual and shared psychological theories. In any society, the psychological and political are closely intertwined. This thesis is theoretical in nature and not one that can be tested with strong research designs (e.g., random assignment) because it rests on the cumulative effects of historical events on different cultures. I present here some examples that support my main thesis, with the recognition that it is a difficult thesis to falsify because the explanation is post hoc and there is a virtually endless list of possible alternative explanations.

References have been made to the theoretical links and conceptual overlap between theories of psychology and theories of political science numerous times over the last century. For the purposes of this chapter, political science is the study of the behavior, process, and structures of governing groups, their use of power, and the rules or more formally, laws, they formulate to regulate human behavior. Psychology includes the study of individual and group behavior (and thoughts and emotions). Almost 100 years ago, a neurologist named Adolf Meyer proposed a formal linking of psychology and political science with the concept of "civic medicine," a conceptual model of health with the goal of reorganizing communities, schools, and politics in ways that would create an atmosphere that would be conducive to mental hygiene – an older term for good mental health (Shore, 2001). Because thoughts and emotions underlie behavior, it is easy to see how these concepts blur, making it difficult to draw clear demarcations between psychology and political science or any of the other social sciences.

How people create their world views

Although people the world over are similar in basic ways, there are some group-level differences in addition to within-group differences in how people in different cultures understand the underlying reasons for human behavior. The differences tend to be those of extent or degree, such that some groups attend more to interpersonal relationships and show greater concern for community; others are more concerned with personal achievement and individual advancement. This basic dichotomy is used repeatedly in cross-cultural research. As a way of understanding across-culture differences in how people explain, or make sense of, or frame information about the world, Lipmann (1925, p. 25) referred to the way people make meaning as the "mystery off there" the "swarming confusion of problems that populate public life" (p. 358). People explain events according to their cognitive frames or structures or points of view (Kinder, 2003).

Cognitive psychologists conceptualize the way that people store knowledge about the world as a set of interlinking nodes that form a knowledge map or network of concepts that is analogous to the neural network or the physiological hardware that "runs" the thinking programs in the mind. For each person, knowledge is organized within the cognitive maps such that meaning is embedded in the web of concepts and the ways in which concepts are related to each other. Each individual's concept maps are built in a society of shared meaning and to the extent that every person in a society shares the same conceptual meaning as represented in their maps, a political system that depends on society's members "seeing things the same way" will be firmly entrenched.

An example should help with this abstract idea. If there is a shared understanding in a society that children assume adult responsibilities at a specific age, then other indicators of becoming adult at that age will be reflected in the laws, which might include the age at which someone could be given a death penalty or held to other adult standards such as the legal age for drinking alcohol or serving in the military. Because cognitive maps are built from experiences (and some predispositions to link certain concepts in a limited number of ways), concepts maps depend, at least in part, on geographical ones because people who live in the same places and share similar experiences will develop similar understandings about the nature of the world. Thus, how we understand has a meaningful link to where we are raised, making the metaphor of cognitive maps even more appropriate to understanding how we understand.

Whenever someone is presented with new information, it is fitted into an appropriate place in an individual's existing concept map, and opinions about the new information are determined in ways that are consistent with its position among the existing items in the map. So, if you meet a new person who is from Germany or the United States, your pre-existing beliefs and attitudes about people from that country get shifted in part to the new person, most often without any conscious awareness. Many people are distressed by the idea that they are not consciously aware of the forces that influence the way that they think about political issues. In fact, there are considerable data to support the conclusion that we are often unaware of the influences on the way we make decisions, or on what we recall in a particular context because we do not know what served as the recall cues, or whether we will evaluate an ambiguous situation as favorable or unfavorable. For example, the concept of implicit memory (Roediger, 1990) is based on the notion that people have knowledge that they cannot describe in words and that they do not know that they have, and that knowledge is used in cognitive processes such as making decisions. No one can know how their implicit or tacit memories are affecting the way that they think and act. Unconscious and preconscious processes influence all of us; it is generally accepted that no one can provide an accurate description of all of the cognitive processes that influence her or his own thoughts and feelings, so the fact that there are such processes that influence political beliefs is "nothing special" when considered from the domain of cognitive psychology. This idea is often upsetting to social scientists from sister disciplines, such as economics, who assume that humans will reason rationally. The way a fact or concept is evaluated depends on prior knowledge that may be shared, in part, with the broader community with little or no conscious awareness, including a larger set of beliefs about the world.

What follows are several examples that show ways in which implicit or tacit theories of psychology underlie political beliefs.

Example 1. A natural experiment: The rapid and unanticipated change in the Russian political system

The messages that anyone takes away from cross-cultural and cross-national research and theorizing about two disciplines – psychology and political science – that rarely "talk" depend on the vantage point from which the listener attends to these topics. What follows is a brief overview of some earlier work that I did with a Russian colleague, Alexander Voiskounsky, in which we compared North American and post-Soviet/Russian psychology and their relationships to their respective political systems (Halpern & Voiskounsky, 1997). We took advantage of a unique natural experiment – the rapid change in the Russian political system created a unique opportunity to study the way in which topics of psychological inquiry are framed and develop as they relate to the prevailing political thought. Prior to 1991 and for many years following the "capitalist revolution," as some have called the rapid change from Soviet-style communism to Russian-style capitalism, there had been very little exchange of information between psychologists in the West and in the former Soviet Union. The seminal work of the great Russian physiologist, Ivan Pavlov, and developmental/learning psychologist Lev Vygotsky, were well known in the West, but fewer than a handful of other Soviet psychologists had been influential in the development of Western psychological thought.

It was only when I worked in other countries, including semesters in Russia, Turkey, and Canada, a summer session in Mexico, a Fulbright in Italy and briefer stays elsewhere, that I could see how myopic psychology in the United States really is. Few psychologists in the United States can name any, or more than a few, living psychologists in their field from other countries in the world. Similarly, knowledge of Western developments in psychology had also been extremely limited in the republics of the former Soviet Union. Political events permitted a unique opportunity to see how two major world powers defined contemporary psychological issues under different political systems and the way in which they collected and interpreted data that bear on these issues.

In what seemed like an almost overnight about-face, the Soviet Union, which was built on communist principles, became capitalist Russia. The great experiment in Soviet political systems of the 20th century was over and the change was profound. There are countless personal vignettes told by Russian citizens and frequent visitors about a moment or incident when the magnitude of the change from communism to capitalism "hit home." For me, it occurred during a visit to the prestigious Academy of Sciences Institute for Psychology in Moscow. During an earlier visit in 1990, when the Soviet Union was still a communist country, I sat stiffly at a long formal table with serious officials under the watchful eyes of large portraits of Lenin and Gorbachov (who was the Soviet leader at that time). I presented my research in a formal auditorium before a stern group of scientists. On a return visit in 1994, in the new capitalist Russia, I sat at the same long formal table with the same officials, but this time only two bright rectangles of wallpaper marked the places where the portraits of Lenin and Gorbachov had been hanging. This may seem like an insignificant indicator of the magnitude of the change, but the two blank rectangles spoke as loudly as the men whose portraits had previously occupied that space. The psychologists who met at this formal table in the Institute of Psychology were no longer under the watchful gaze of communism.

Evidence for the strong influence of political system, and with it place, historical period, and social system, on the way that psychology has been defined and investigated can be seen in the way that different fields of psychology developed in the United States and the former Soviet Union. The free market economy in the United States created an emphasis on the importance of individual work. In a free market, each individual's standard of living depends on how well, how long, and how hard the individual works. Americans view their work as more than a source of income; for many, work is so central to their lives that it is also a key component to their identity. At the same time, the nature of modern work has become increasingly complex and cognitive in nature. Given these emphases, it is not surprising that one of the dominant research topics in the psychology of aging in the United States is to find ways to slow or reverse intellectual decline, so that older adults can continue to work at quality jobs as they age.

The emphasis in the United States on individual work has many possible origins that contrast this perspective to more collectivist orientation in many other societies. One theory for the prevalence of individualism in the United States, which is a dominant theme in cross-cultural psychological research, is grounded in unique aspects of United States history. What is it about the history of the United States that could account for such a strong emphasis on the individual? The character traits of independence, risk-taking, and self-reliance are associated with the American frontier experiences that were part of the everyday life of the immigrants that make up the United States. Collins (2004) suggested that the frontier effect is not just history because its effects can be seen today in the language we use and the way attitudes vary across the United States. According to Collins, it is not a coincidence that exploration of outer space is called the last frontier, signifying a continuation of the spirit of exploration and adventure; California and other western states lead the country in political reforms, and voters in the United States repeatedly insist on their right to own handguns, even semiautomatic weapons. The United States is one of the few countries that still has the death penalty, perhaps because in the frontier it was necessary to take the law into one's own hands and the death penalty is consonant with that position. Emphasis on individualism grew, in part, from the frontier experience in the United States, an experience that was not duplicated in other countries. Individualism, in turn, created different types of expectations across a wide range of contexts with consequences for policies that can be recognized as stemming from an individualistic orientation. Research into the cognitive aspects of aging is consistent with this orientation, in part because it would help to achieve the goal of keeping older adults independent into old age.

By contrast, the Soviet government and post-Soviet governments in the years immediately following the collapse of the Soviet Union, overtly and covertly discouraged research into the psychology of aging, especially in those psychological topics that pertained to an age-related intellectual decline. Kol'tsova, Meshalkina, and Olegnik (1997), contemporary Russian psychologists, have offered this explanation:

With few exceptions, the heads of the Communist Party were very old men, commonly called the somewhat pejorative term "gerontocrats" – a Russian slang for old bureaucrats. The system required many long years of devoted service before an individual could rise to a high-level government post, so it was only in old age that most officials could attain the highest offices. One explanation for the absence of funding and research into cognitive aging was that these elderly bureaucrats did not want to fund research that might show a cognitive decline in old age.

(p. 281)

There were other reasons, as well, for the paucity of psychological research on aging in the former Soviet Union. Under the communist system, every aged individual was guaranteed a retirement in exchange for a lifetime of work. These old people were no longer the producers in society, so the limited research money available to psychologists would not be wisely spent if the subjects and beneficiaries of the research were the nonproductive elderly. Thus, the political views of work and growing older, and the psychological views of work and aging have parallel influences on each other. It is not possible to determine which is causal or primary, but there are parallel influences within countries and cultures that influence both.

Example 2. Systems of thought

A somewhat radical approach to the proposal that psychological theories are the basis for political theories and actions is the idea that people from widely different geographical regions of the world have fundamentally different systems of thought that cannot be explained solely by different learning histories or life experiences. The idea is that different ways of thinking and differences in what people value or prefer are caused by differences in their cognitive "tools," the underlying thought mechanisms that people use to understand the world. This radical view is advanced by a respected cognitive psychologist from the United States, Richard Nisbett (2003). Specifically, Nisbett claims that Asians and Westerners "think differently," with central Europeans somewhere between the two on most measures. Of course he acknowledges that Asians are a diverse group, but the major population group is Chinese, so he uses the Chinese as an example. The implications of this idea are that social attitudes and values – essential components of psychological theories and of political theories and systems – are not solely taught, but are fundamentally different in different parts of the world.

For the Chinese, the largest Asian group, the chief moral system was Confucianism, which is an elaboration of the obligation between an emperor and his subjects. According to Nisbett (2003), this tradition fosters a sense of collective agency, which is a common theme, possibly the dominant theme, in Asian psychology (Sugiman, 1997). In understanding "collective agency," it is important to keep in mind the fact that "95 percent of the Chinese population belongs to the same Han ethnic group" (Nisbett, 2003, p. 31), so the considerable homogeneity means that huge numbers of people would never have contacted anyone with different beliefs or practices. As a means of developing his premise, Nisbett uses an example from the ancient Chinese who had to manage a complex irrigation system that required people to share water resources. At the same time, they were ruled by powerful government officials, which created conditions in which getting along was paramount in their world of social constraints. Thus a combination of ethnic homogeneity, the need for cooperative behavior for survival (sharing water resources), and strong sanctions against disharmony all created a strong emphasis on maintaining harmony as the highest good. Harmony is a major theme in Asian life that does not appear at anywhere near the same frequency in other cultures.

Of course, history is complex, and I am simplifying it to make my main points because simplification and selection are necessary when looking for meaningful patterns among a vast array of possibilities. A brief chapter cannot capture the complexity of this topic without simplification, so I have focused on only a few examples. To complete this analysis, I return to the emphasis on the individual that was inherent in the United States frontier experience, including the need to take justice into one's own hands, which meant that there was a need for individuals to be in control of their destiny. By contrast, Asian history did not engender the universal and deep-seated feeling that control is as important for Asian identity (in part because of Confucian heritage and its hierarchical relationships, the almost complete ethnic homogeneity, which made individualism less likely, and the compelling multiple needs for conformity). Taken together, it would be expected that Asians, in general, would be more accepting of a government that takes more control over individuals. Thus, an underlying sense of collectivism became the underlying assumption as the natural form of government in Asian countries because it was fundamental and deeply rooted in Asian thought through history. Similarly, individualism became the psychological basis for capitalistic societies because of their historical experiences.

Example 3. Social domination orientation

History has traditionally been taught as a timeline of wars, or in other words, a timeline of which country dominated other ones. Warfare has occurred throughout time, but it is not constant in any society, and by studying its intermittent starts and stops and those countries that are more militaristic than others, there should be long-view lessons about war as social domination. One of the strongest points made by evolutionary psychologists is that war is predominantly a male activity (Messquida & Wiener, 1999). Although it is clear that women always defended themselves and others in times of war, it was rare for women to wage war as the aggressors, and one of the best predictors of war-like behavior is the proportion of males in the young adult age range in a society. Surprisingly this conclusion seems to hold up even when young adult males are not the ones making the decision to go to war. Many have argued that evolutionary psychology has done a poor job of informing politics (Edwards, 2003), but the sex difference in aggression and in the tendency to seek political power is incontrovertible. Sex differences in overt political behaviors are mirrored in sociopolitical attitudes (Sidanius & Kurzban, 2003), with women having more favorable attitudes towards *reducing* differences in hierarchy relationships and men having more favorable attitudes towards *increasing* differences in hierarchy relationships. Men also have more xenophobia, more punitive attitudes in general, and more predatory attitudes than women. Thus, if this hypothesis has predictive validity, large differences in sex ratios in any society should be discernible in its international relations and internal policies, with more overall aggression in societies with higher proportions of young adult males than comparable societies with lower proportions in this male age range.

Studies of social domination usually show that racism and sexism tend to go together in that attitudes towards racial groups other than one's own correlate with attitudes towards women, so that if one is negative, the other also tends to be negative. Strong patriarchal societies place strong value on having sons, and in some places in the world there is an excess of boys that can only be achieved by selective abortion, infanticide, malnutrition of girls, exporting girls, and so on. There are modern societies formed from traditional warrior societies where racism justifies war against other groups and sexism permits the high proportion of boys needed to wage wars. The social dominance orientation that underlies a political system of patriarchy is resistant to change because there are multiple cognitive structures, strong values, and other psychological underpinnings that support its existence despite rational evidence and legal sanctions. Market economy explanations would predict that an oversupply of either sex, say males for example, should lead to an over-valuation of females because they are in short supply, which would be followed, after some "lag time" with a greater supply of females. Eventually the sex ratios would equalize. Unfortunately, old value systems are often stronger than rational arguments and there are still many places, perhaps most places, where sons are more highly prized than daughters. Those societies where sex ratios are extreme can be expected to be more aggressive, more xenophobic, more hierarchical in their government structure, and to display other overt manifestations of social domination.

Example 4. In- and out-group processes in the United States and post-Soviet Russia

Processes that perpetuate prejudice are complex (Plous, 2004) but, because of the limitations of this chapter (length and general audience), I will use only some examples of the interplay between psychology and political beliefs as they pertain to prejudice. Consider, for example, the tendency to categorize people on the basis of some characteristic (e.g., race, income) and then perceive members of the other group as relatively homogeneous, inferior to one's own, and a threat to the limited resources that our own group so rightfully deserves (e.g., employment, land, housing, etc.). To some extent, the preference for members of one's own group seems to be universal. Despite this sorry conclusion, prejudice is rooted in very different circumstances in different parts of the world. Consider, for example, the countries that comprise the former Soviet Union and the United States. In the former Soviet Union, prejudice exists among ethnic groups, especially when ethnic groups are vying for land they believe is historically theirs, creating a type of in-group/out-group dichotomy that appears arbitrary to those who do not know the regional history.

Ethnic Russians living in Estonia face legally sanctioned discrimination based on whether they can trace their ancestry to Estonian soil before or after World War II. The rationale for these laws, which establish different criteria for citizenship for ethnic Russians in Estonia, is based on the involuntary take-over of Estonia by the Soviet authorities 60 years ago, and it is the children and grandchildren of these unwelcome "guests" who are now finding themselves as noncitizens in the only country they have ever known. The bloodless secession from the Soviet Union has created a new class of "stateless" people who lost their jobs and their status when Estonia first became a new independent republic. From the perspective of a native Estonian, these laws are just; but from a distance, it is not hard to see how an ethnic Russian who grew up in Estonia and never lived anywhere else might see these laws as overt discrimination.

American-style prejudice is based on some salient group characteristic, which is most likely to be race, sex, or age. Discrimination against minority groups was overt and bloody early in the 20th century, especially prejudice against African Americans. (I am not including the earlier periods of slavery and the Civil War in the 19th century.) Modern prejudice and discrimination are now less overt. The term "modern racism" is often used as a label for the subtler forms of racism that are practiced in American society. Modern racism can be found in biases in deciding who should get a home mortgage and other credit decisions and in hiring where criteria tend to be subjective. Laws that provide an advantage for African Americans for entry into elite colleges or government contracts are interpreted as affirmative action or reverse discrimination depending on one's underlying psychology.

Although there are differences among countries with different political systems, there are also similar across-society processes in social domination. In the former Soviet Union, Jews were (and still are) perceived as a distinct ethnic group, even if they come from different regions of this vast country and have different customs from each other. They have been the scapegoat for all of Russia's ills for many centuries and have endured countless pogroms and bloody acts of violence (including the active participation of some Soviet republics in the extermination of Jews during World War II). As modern Russia re-embraces religion, religious intolerance has grown also and seems likely to continue to increase. Thus, although there are distinctive features of prejudice that can be attributed to time and place, there are also commonalities that transcend sociopolitical norms.

The role of place in a shrinking world

The basic premise in this chapter is that psychological theories and political theories and the laws that follow from them are inextricably entwined. It is useful to think of the way that people understand the world and the emotions that they attach to events as the basis for political beliefs and political systems. The understanding and emotions come from the long periods of experiences that create the histories of countries. But, new technologies are changing how we think about world geography. Places that once sounded so foreign to me are now close, and I can communicate as easily with colleagues and friends in Beijing or Moscow as I can with those in my Los Angeles neighborhood.

New technologies have created new opportunities to create a common world history. As president of the American Psychological Association in 2004, one of my projects was to post translated versions of quality materials about the psychology of prejudice on a website that would be available to members of the general population who want to understand how psychologists study and understand this topic. (see http://www.understandingprejudice.org/apa). The kind of world history we create is up to us. We can communicate across all national boundaries and share a common history; today's young adults talk of being President of Europe – not of one country in Europe. Why not president of other continents? How will psychology affect the in- and out-group processes, the shared histories, the common understandings? How will we help create the political?

Conclusion

Psychological theories about human motivation, violence, human development, and almost every aspect of behavior and the thoughts and emotions that underlie behavior serve as the basis for political thoughts and actions. It is our beliefs about how people are and should and can be that lead us to decide if we should have the death penalty, offer an olive branch or go to war, spend money on cognitive aging research, decide whom to hate or when to cooperate, and so on. Although only a few examples were presented in this chapter, there is an almost endless possibility of examples that make the linkages between psychological and political theories clear. As technologies continue to make national boundaries less meaningful, the distinctions between the psychological and political will continue to blur. Psychologists will need to be more active in shaping future political systems in directions that are beneficial for the citizens of the world.

References

Collins, M. (2004). The American perspective. *Contemporary Review*, *284*, 71–76.

Edwards, J. (2003, May). Evolutionary psychology and politics. *Economy and Society*, *32*, 280–298.

Halpern, D. F., & Voiskounsky, A. E. (1997). *States of mind: American and post-Soviet perspectives on contemporary issues in psychology*. New York: Oxford University Press.

Kinder, D. R. (2003). Communication and politics in the age of information. In D. O. Sears, L. Huddy, & R. Jervis (Eds.), *Oxford handbook of political psychology* (pp. 357–393). New York: Oxford University Press.

Kol'tsova, V. A., Meshalkina, N. B., & Olegnik, Y. N. (1997). A life-span approach to the study of psychogerontology in Russia. In D. F. Halpern & A. E. Voiskounsky (Eds.), *States of mind: American and post-Soviet perspectives on contemporary issues in psychology*. New York: Oxford University Press.

Lipmann, W. (1925). *The phantom public*. New York: Harcourt.

Messquida, C. G., & Wiener, N. I. (1999). Male age composition and severity of conflicts. *Politics and the life sciences*, *18*, 181–189.

Nisbett, R. E. (2003). *The geography of thought*. New York: Free Press.

Plous, S. (2004). Understanding prejudice. (Available at: http://www.understandingprejudice.org Accessed 10 July 2004)

Roediger, H. L. (1990). Implicit memory: Retention without remembering. *American Psychologist*, *45*, 1043–1056.

Shore, M. F. (2001). How psychiatrists and political scientists have grown up since 1938. *Psychiatry*, *64*, 192–196.

Sidanius, J., & Kurzban, R. (2003). Evolutionary approaches to political psychology. In D. O. Sears, L. Huddy, & R. Jervis (Eds.), *Oxford handbook of political psychology* (pp. 146–181). New York: Oxford University Press.

Sugiman, T. (1997). A new theoretical perspective of group dynamics. In K. Leung, U. Kim, S. Yamaguchi, & Y. Kashima (Eds.), *Progress in Asian social psychology* (Vol. 1, pp. 37–53). New York: Wiley.

27 Russian psychology at the crossroads

Vladimir A. Barabanschikov

Many psychologists outside Russia either consider Russian psychology as a kind of *terra incognita*, or do not discriminate between current studies and former Soviet psychology. Foreign colleagues often ask the following questions:

1 What is going on in Russian psychology today?
2 Has it changed since the decomposition of the USSR?
3 What is the attitude of modern Russian psychologists to Marxism and to the classical works by Soviet psychologists (L. S. Vygotsky, A. N. Leontiev, S. L. Rubinstein, V. V. Davydov, etc.)?
4 What is the Russian way of psychology?

One may easily note that the questions reflect not only an interest in Russian psychology, which has been somewhat opposed to Western psychology for rather a long time, but also interest in the development of science against a background of radical changes in the state, and its economic system and political order.

Soviet psychology is presented here first. As the topic is inexhaustible, I only focus on the most important issues: the philosophical basis of Soviet psychology; the conceptual structure; the methods of research; and applied work. The second part of the chapter is about what has become of Russian psychology since 1991, the year of the collapse of the USSR, outlining the changes that have occurred in Russian psychology over the past 10–12 years. The conclusion sums up the achievements of these years and consider the prospects for the future.

Speaking about both Soviet and Russian psychology, the chapter does not go into details of specific schools or theories but rather the whole of the knowledge about the human mind and behavior accumulated at different stages of development of the country. Such wholes are formed on the basis of common language, shared cultural traditions, common economic, political and social style of life, and develop as relatively independent formations. However, they also incorporate international components reflecting the tendencies of the world's science and practice.

Soviet psychology

Russian psychology as a scientific discipline emerged in the second part of the 19th century and, from its very beginning, was an integral part of the European psychology movement. Before the Revolution of 1917, Russian psychology was a polymorphous body comprising both subjective and objective studies of the human internal world. It was based on a peculiar blend of philosophical materialism and idealism, and it combined the experimental method with speculations often rooted in religion. The idea of *reflexes* (I. M. Sechenov, V. M. Bekhterev, & I. P. Pavlov) coexisted with the idea of *the soul* (N. A. Berdyaev, N. O. Lossky, & E. N. Trubetskoy) in the same sociocultural space.

The rise of Soviet psychology in the 1920s was a response to radical changes in the sociopolitical and economic system of Russia. Marxism became the only philosophical basis of both ideology and science, which signaled the materialist worldview, the use of the dialectic method, the emphasis on the role of labor in human development, and the belief in the priority of society over individual. The solidification of the philosophical background in combination with the strict ideological and state regulation played an important role in the making of the specific way of the Soviet or, as it was called in the earlier days, Marxist psychology.

The cultural- (or socio-) historical theory proposed by L. S. Vygotsky and further developed by A. R. Luria, A. N. Leontiev, A. V. Zaporozhets, P. Ya. Galperin, D. B. Elkonin, and others, was the first unique contribution to Soviet psychology. The nucleus of the theory was shaped by the concept of *social determination and historical development of the human mind*, stemming directly from the works of K. Marx and F. Engels. According to Vygotsky, one cannot expect to discover what human nature is inside an organism, specifically in the brain. It is outside every given individual, and it is determined by a continuously changing system of social relations into which the individual is incorporated. That is why Vygotsky connected the future developments of psychology not with the studies of the invariable structure of consciousness and its external expression (either in movement or secretion), but with the studies of social life generating conscience.

In Vygotsky's opinion, the major difference between the behaviors of humans and animals is the mediation of human behavior with a tool, that is, something that humans place between themselves and nature in order to reach their goals. Using tools, a human modifies the external reality as well as him- or herself. Any mediator may be a tool, including a sign. A tool is always an element of culture, a carrier of sociohistorical experience. Once being born, a human individual emerges into the supra-individual, historically developing world of culture; his/her psychological development is realized as a process of mastering this world. Cultural products, including human relations that originally exist in their external form, become internalized, or incorporated, into the individual mind thus providing a means of voluntary control of individual's own behavior, as well as the behavior of other individuals.

The use of tools dramatically modifies the structure of psychological phenomena. Unlike the natural psychological functions, predetermined with the natural possibilities of an organism, the higher psychological functions, that is complex forms of perception, voluntary memory, discourse thinking, etc., are mediated with a sign. Such being the case, they become realizable and voluntary (Vygotsky, 1996).

The problems of mastering culture as studied by Vygotsky (e.g., the studies of mechanisms of means created by society not only to modify the reality, but also for the sake of the development of cognitive abilities) are very important today. This is specifically true in connection with the advance of modern information technologies and with the role of modern tools in changing everyday environments.

The cultural-historical theory formulated a most important principle typical of all the subsequent Soviet psychology. The principle is: in order to disclose the internal world of a human, one should go into the wider context of life. The principle contradicts the principles of a classical psychological experiment, according to which the researcher is studying the process in isolation from other psychological phenomena, but psychological processes are studied from the subject's relations with the world. From this time on, Soviet psychology studied psychological phenomena in different contexts of human existence.

In the 1930s the role of the state in the regulation of science grew dramatically. The directions considered ideologically alien were suppressed (in fact, some were eradicated). To avoid the ideological pressures, many psychologists shifted to those areas of psychological knowledge oriented towards the solution of practical tasks: pedology, psychoanalysis, and psychotechnics. *Activity* became the central scientific problem, which was also deeply rooted in the philosophy of Marxism. Rubinstein (1946) and Leontiev (1972) tackled this problem most extensively.

Considering "activity" (its German equivalent, *tätigkeit*, is a better word for the concept), one usually means the goal-directed modification of the world by a person, in the course of which the person's self also changes. This may involve work (both physical and/or mental), play, or learning. The nature of any activity is social. It may be characterized according to the motivation, and may be implemented through several actions, each being subordinate to a specific goal. Actions in their turn develop as systems of operations related to the conditions in which the activity takes place.

Within the framework of the theory described, mind is considered as an internal component of activity that provides for orientation of the individual in the environment and regulation of his/her activity. Psychological processes are not only expressed, but also are formed and develop in the activity.

These ideas imply at least three things. First, activity is *the main determinant* of mental processes. What and how a person perceives, memorizes or experiences is determined by what is being done and how it is done. For example, thresholds of different sensory modalities may become higher or lower, depending on the requirements and organization of a given activity (Ananiev, 1960). Involuntary memorizing may become more efficient than voluntary memorizing, if the goal of the subject's activity includes the material to be memorized (Smirnov, 1965; Zinchenko, 1961). Now that the information-processing approach to cognition has been pushed almost to its limits, the psychological content of human activity becomes specifically important.

Second, in the context of the activity paradigm, any psychological process may be interpreted in terms of *internal activities*. This is exactly what is meant when we speak about perceptual, mnemic or intellectual activities. It is assumed that the internal activity stems genetically from the external activity, and has the same structure. It is formed in the course of learning, going through several specific stages of development. Studies by Zaporozhets (1960), Galperin (1998), and many others, provided evidence that the object-oriented practical action is internalized by the subject; the action acquires a shape of compact internal process. Vygotsky's ideas on internalization of a sign are transformed here into the internalization of activity (action).

Third, the activity paradigm casts powerful light on *the regulatory function* of mind that maintains the activity in agreement with its objectives, means and conditions. Research was aimed at the so-called subjective components of activity: motive, goal, plan of activity, scheme of situation, etc., united in a multi-level dynamic system. Analysis of the components and their interrelations made it possible to raise the problems of the genesis of the system of practical activity (Shadrikov, 1978), of relations between the conscious and non-realized components of cognitive activity (Brushlinsky, 1979), and of cognitive representation of psychological components of activity (Lomov, 1984), etc.

One should note here that the analysis of psychological phenomena as a rule was restricted to individual activity. However, interaction of one individual with the world is never self-sufficient. It is always a component, or participation, in human *joint activities*. Even the finest psychophysical experiment cannot totally eliminate the influence of the experimenter and get rid of the thousands of invisible threads connecting the experimenter with the subject. To understand any individual activity as a whole, one should describe its function as a part of a certain joint activity and the individual's function in the group. Joint activity is always distributed among the group members and is characterized by common goals, plans, joint decision making, and estimation of results. Its internal content is described in terms of interpersonal relations and the process of interaction/communication.

In the mid-1970s, B. F. Lomov and his coworkers launched studies of psychological phenomena in the context of *joint activity and communication (or interaction)*. The Russian word *obschenie* means a specific form of human interaction with others, in the course of which not only the exchange of information takes place, but also the exchange of actions and states. The result of this process is the establishment and/or implementation of specific new relations between people. So, in English translation it may mean communication, or interaction, or both at once, and the present chapter further uses either of these two words, or both, depending on what is more appropriate.

Studies of perception, memory, thinking and representations, conducted within the framework of this new paradigm, show that interaction appears to be another foundation and most important determinant of psychological processes and personality. The effect of interaction may be pinpointed by way of organization, selection, estimation and correction of information received by subjects, by some peculiarities of composition of subjective scales, by selection of reference points and transformation of images, by widening the background for generalization and abstraction in concept formation, etc.

Research made it possible to specify communication/interaction as a phenomenon. Now it may be defined as an open system making possible distribution (and redistribution) of functions among the participants, their cooperation (or opposition) in solving a common problem, exchange of roles, etc. Cycles and stages of interactions were also described (Lomov, 1984).

In reality, interaction and activity are tightly interwoven. However, they are independent in their essence. One can hardly think of interaction as a sequence of actions that the participants exercise in turns. Rather it is a kind of common action, or cooperation. In comparison with the structure of individual activity, the process of interaction/communication is peculiar in that it may be characterized by the availability of a common information resource, interrelation of the motives, goals, and programs of the participants, the conjugation of their actions, the differentiation of their positions and functions in the group, etc. The purpose of these studies was to reveal a unique stratum of human existence signaling a specific set of qualities, functions and regularities of the human mind.

In spite of the importance of sociocultural determinants of the structure of activities and interaction/communication, there was still another category that became the central concept of Soviet science. The category of *reflection* was considered to be connected with the nature of mind. Mental phenomena were considered as a variety of forms of subjective reflection of the objective reality. From this viewpoint, not only cognitive processes, which were the primary interest of the scholars, but also emotions, feelings and will were considered. This was a major point of overlap of the scientific views of the majority of Soviet psychologists.

The category of psychological reflection and mental image as its product are closely connected with Marxist gnosiology. This implies two important things. First, it means that the mind is included within the overall interrelations of the phenomena of the material world. Owing to the ability to reflect, the mind is a relatively independent whole playing an active role in biological and social life according to biological and social laws. This is the way that the ontological plane of analysis of mental phenomena was introduced, thus providing the background for a search of the regularities of their internal movement.

Second, the specific circumstances of human life are considered to be the source of the content of psychological phenomena. For a person, reflecting the reality opens up the possibility of orientation, of expression of integrity and of regulation of his/her own behavior. So far as reflection and mental images of reality do not exist by themselves, but pertain to a subject, a realistic being, their content appears to be always biased, not mirror-like. Within the framework of this approach a number of special concepts were formulated to reveal peculiarities of mind and behavior. Examples are "the operative image" by Oshanin (1999), "the image of the world" by Leontiev (1977) and "the anticipative reflection" by Anokhin (1978). Search for regularities of generation, formation and functioning of subjective images of reality in the process of human activity was considered to be the primary objective of Soviet psychology.

The basic categories of Soviet psychological science were developed within a relatively short time. These concepts provided vast possibilities for studies of different aspects of human mind and behavior. They were the cornerstones of many schools and directions in Soviet psychology, though the structure of categories and their understanding varied. Moreover, the system of categories was open and allowed for incorporation of new categories, as, for example, "relation" and "personality," the elaboration of which started in the 1980s.

Soviet psychology may be also characterized by the peculiarity of its *methodology*. As early as in the 1930s, the basic dialectical ideas, such as diversity, unity, contradiction, qualitative leap, etc., were introduced into scientific thinking. The attention of Soviet psychologists was focused on the diversity of qualities of psychological phenomena (e.g., natural and higher psychological functions) and the peculiarities of their determination. They identified the levels of organization of mind and behavior (activities); they conducted efficient research in the genesis of psychological functions. One may say that the Soviet psychologists elaborated the foundation and worked in the general paradigm of *dialectical psychology*. However, it was never termed that way: sometimes it was defined as *Marxist psychology*, reflecting the philosophical source. The version of the systems approach proposed by B. F. Lomov in the 1970s was also based on the principles of dialectics.

The empirical methods and procedures were a direct extension of the concepts that were worked out. In particular, together with the traditional laboratory experiment, a so-called "forming experiment" based on Vygotsky's theory was widespread. This kind of experiment was designed to study the process of formation of psychological functions with ascribed qualities. Examples of such studies were given by Leontiev's work on formation of pitch hearing and the cycle of work by Galperin and coworkers dedicated to the formation of mental actions. In the studies of interaction, the "peer interaction design" proposed by Bekhterev was widely implemented. The method was based on comparison of peculiarities of psychological processes in the conditions of joint and individual problem solving. As a rule, these procedures were combined with other methods, more typical of Western psychology.

The domain of *applied psychology* was relatively narrow, though continuously expanding. It was the weakest link in Soviet psychology. Not only was the volume of research relatively small, but also the methodology of the work was poor. In spite of this, one should acknowledge the achievements of Soviet psychology in solving problems of education (Davydov, 1972; Elkonin, 1976; Talyzina, 1975), of health care (Luria, 1963; Zeigarnik, 1976) as well as in the design and putting into use of new technologies (Lomov, 1966; Oshanin, 1999; Zinchenko & Munipov, 1983). There may be different attitudes to Soviet psychology. One may accept or reject its conceptual structure and methodology. But one cannot simply ignore its unique design, and efficiency in raising and solving a number of basic and applied problems. Soviet psychology covered a long and difficult path, it was easily recognizable, and it was highly esteemed in the world's psychological community.

Russian psychology today

The year of 1991 was a turning point: Russia stepped onto the road of non-socialist development. The ideology, that is the main values of the society, changed. The regulatory role of the State was considerably curtailed. The economy became liberal. The industrial production was dramatically reduced, the well-being of the overwhelming majority of people abruptly declined. In particular, financial support of science was reduced several times. Judging by the economic, political and social features, the situation was reminiscent of that in the 1920s, exactly when Soviet psychology emerged. But, under the new historical conditions, Russian psychological science began to move in a different, to a certain extent an opposite, direction.

Removal of ideological barriers and reinstatement of the values common to all mankind has led to the criticism of Marxism and *widening of the foundation of psychological science*. Some philosophical ideas, earlier rejected as alien, became incorporated in psychological thinking. These are phenomenology by E. Husserl and M. Heidegger, existentialism by S. Kirkegaard and J.-P. Sartre, and hermeneutics (P. Ricoeur). Many researchers were trying to elaborate the ideas of Kant and Russian religious philosophers V. S. Soloviev, N. A. Berdyaev, S. N. Trubetskoy, S. L. Frank, and others. Citation of Marxist works became a rare event, and the conceptual structure of the areas of knowledge that have been quite recently called dialectical and historical materialism seemed to be almost forgotten. It does not mean, of course, that it was commonly accepted that phenomenology or instrumentalism were better than the realism of the dialectical theory of cognition (Lektorsky, 2001). However, one may ascertain the advent of philosophical pluralism supporting co-existence of different schools and currents of thinking. Consequently, the soil became fertile enough for the growth of psychology in any direction.

The attitude towards Marxism represents a complicated problem of the Russian philosophy. Here one may discriminate between the two aspects: Marxism as a philosophy and Marxism as a kind of "state religion" that was dominant in the USSR. The latter is rejected without further consideration, whereas the Marxist philosophy is thoroughly analyzed. Marxist conceptions of the active nature of human cognition, studies of converted forms of consciousness, and a number of ideas in philosophical anthropology directly related to psychology deserve thoughtful consideration. On the contrary, Marxist ideas of violence or human domination over the world, over the natural and social circumstances of life, generate many doubts. Some aspects of Marxism seem to be restricted to the framework of the industrial society.

One may also acknowledge the growing interest in the Eastern traditional cultures, which consider the attitude of man towards the world from the opposite side. They do not emphasize the man, or person, but rather the world, nature, and space. Consequently, the logic of human action is different. For example, the Chinese principle of *u vei* (which may be interpreted as "non-interference," or "evasive adaptability") suggests agreement of action with natural rhythms, including the cosmic ones.

Finally, the removal of ideological restrictions has given rise to mysticism, irrationalism and clerical teachings. Books on chiromancy, astrology, and parapsychology overwhelm the shelves of the bookstores.

Erosion of the philosophical basis has affected the content of activities of many psychologists. The researchers became disinterested in studies of the background of their science. The interest, however, began to recover at the beginning of the new millennium. The problem of the conceptual structure and methodology of psychology attracts ever-growing attention. The rapidly developing studies in the history of psychology bring back the once forgotten names: G. I. Chelpanov, G. G. Shpet, A. F. Lazursky, and many others.

The development of new world views is accompanied with *criticism of certain tenets of Soviet psychology*. The criticism is focused on the concept of reflection that was earlier considered as generic in relation to mind, on the interpretative status of the category of activity and on the overestimation of the dominant role of society in relation to personality and consciousness. However, neither a radical modification of the conceptual basis has occurred nor have the results of studies conducted in the Soviet time been reconsidered. But a widening and *smooth reconstruction of the conceptual backgrounds of psychology* are in fact taking place. Psychology is now considered as mainly a humanitarian branch of knowledge, the problem of personality becomes the principal one and the epistemological plane of studies becomes subordinate to the ontological plane. The concepts of "interaction/communication" (that is *obschenie*), "relation," "experience," and "internal world" are playing a growing constructive role in the studies. Attempts are made to reinstate the metaphysical concept of "the soul." The earlier developed fields, such as psychology of cognitive processes, psychophysics and psychophysiology are becoming subordinate and the researchers are quickly trying to modify their programs. Particular emphasis is laid on the studies of cognitive styles, intelligence, understanding and other phenomena bearing a strong person-aligned component of cognitive processes. However, the spirit of positive science has not totally evaporated; these studies are still being conducted.

Three of the most vivid features of modern psychological studies in Russia can be further characterized.

First of all, there is the rise and rapid growth of the so-called *subject-centered approach* in the analysis of human mind and behavior (Abulkhanova, 1973; Ananiev, 1968; Brushlinsky, 2003; Rubinstein, 1973). In line with this approach, all psychological phenomena and forms of activity are considered in their specific relation to their subject. An individual as a subject is capable of managing his/her own resources and, as a result of this, of constructing relations with the world. Activity, self-determination, self-regulation, self-development and self-perfection are the main characteristics of the life of the subject. They are the objectives of most intensified current studies. A number of existential problems awaiting solution are connected with these studies: the problem of the purpose of life, of the attitude to the highest values, the problem of self-realization, etc. It is important that the concept of subject may be related not only to a person, but also to any social body.

In the 1990s Russian psychologists rediscovered an unfinished manuscript by S. L. Rubinstein, "Man and the World." It is an outline of a radically new Soviet philosophical and psychological conception of man. Rubinstein rejects some ideas of orthodox Marxism, particularly the materialistic principle "existence determines consciousness." He introduces new ideas of the infinite personality, of persons' continuous breakthrough beyond their own limits, of freedom and responsibility, and emphasizes the significance of ethical and esthetical attitudes of man towards the world (Rubinstein, 1973). This was a major theoretical step toward the humanistic psychology that would bring closer the positions of Soviet and Western psychologists.

Another important feature of modern Russian studies is their attachment to the principle of *development*, the basic principle of the work of many Soviet psychologists. Emergence or formation of different psychological phenomena, or types of activities, peculiarities of stages and levels of psychological development of a subject still remain the focus of attention. The area of studies in psychogenesis is growing rapidly to incorporate new topics, such as early and late ontogenesis, human highest professional and creative achievements (acme), psychological make-up of people of different historical epochs and even paleogenesis of psychological functions. In these studies, psychological development is interpreted as a polymorphous process leading not only to generation of something new, but also to transformation and/or decomposition of inefficient forms of psychological organization and behavior.

Finally, a tendency towards the *holistic* cognition of the phenomena studied should be mentioned. The researchers have become more and more interested in the interaction of phenomena that are different in their nature, in the multiple of forms of these phenomena, in their structure and levels of organization. What is the logic of mutual transformations and mutual incorporation of psychological realities? How and on what principles can the heterogeneous psychological knowledge be consolidated? For example, within the framework of the activities approach, perception is described as a process of construction of an objectified image of reality. Within the framework of the cognitive approach it would be described as information reception, processing and use. The ecological approach requires the description of perception as a function of proximal stimulation. Each approach seeks for the integrity of the description of its objective. However, what is the psychological essence of perception as a whole? How may one make (using the concepts) a three-dimensional picture of the perceptual process?

Finding solutions to these and similar problems requires a more profound implementation of the ideas of the systems approach, in particular, the ideas of the multi-systemic nature of existence of the person and of systemic determination of mind and behavior (Barabanschikov & Nosulenko, 2004; Lomov, 1984). According to these views, at any given time one finds oneself at a certain point where many different systems cross. In each system the person has unique qualities and features. Thus, a multiplicity of bases generates a multiplicity of qualities and their determinants.

The need for the systems approach as a methodological principle arises from the peculiarities of the current cognitive situation in science. The emergence of new branches, the widening of the conceptual and methodological approaches of psychology, not only fails to bring about a new qualitative leap, but also reduces its organization. The subject matter of psychological studies is being split into rapidly growing numbers of parts and particles, thus generating insurmountable difficulties when comparison of results is needed. The extreme expression of this discontinuity is the opposition of the scientific and the humanitarian paradigms of studies. It is possible that this inability of modern psychology to incorporate the different bases of psychological phenomena into a single conceptual system reflects the deep roots of methodological crises.

These tendencies develop in the conditions of a continuously *expanding informational field* of psychological science. Any professional publication is now accessible in Russia. Modern information technologies are used extensively.

Unlike the Soviet period, Russian psychology is now widely open to the world of science and practice. It is greatly influenced by ideas and techniques of Western humanistic psychology. The studies of academic psychologists are to a certain extent influenced by cognitive sciences. There is a great interest in Western psychometric studies and testing. Some traditions of psychoanalysis are being reinstated. Finally, regardless of continuously growing doubts about the scientific value of their methods, transpersonal psychology and neuro-linguistic programming (NLP) are literally flourishing in Russia.

The frequency of citation in Russia of works of Russian and foreign psychologists in 2003 (relative citation index; Allakhverdov, 2004) may illustrate the current situation in Russian psychology.

As can be seen in Figure 27.1, the highest citation index cluster comprises the founders of Soviet psychology (Vygotsky, Rubinstein, Leontiev, Ananiev). Two clusters in the middle represent classics of world psychology (Freud, Jung, Maslow, Rogers, Lewin) and outstanding Soviet psychologists (Lomov, Brushlinsky, Myasischev, Luria, and others). Finally, the cluster with low citation index includes outstanding representatives of Western cognitive psychology and behaviorism (Miller, Bruner, Neisser, Skinner, and others). One may conclude that the modern Russian psychology, in particular its part engaged in basic research, is based on the fundamental ideas of Soviet psychology, and is trying to develop them whenever possible. The focus of attention, however, has shifted toward the problems of personality and the relations of a person with the world. Russian psychologists manifest growing interest in the ideas and methods of humanistic psychology and psychoanalysis, whereas the experimental psychology connected with cognitive and behavioral approaches is peripheral. It is also indicative that there are no universal leaders in modern Russian psychology, though the traditions and schools are preserved and have become open to cooperation as never before.

There are changes in the research priorities and in *the structure of methods of psychological studies*. Not so much the general methodology, as the specific means and technologies of obtaining new knowledge become the matter of particular interest. The question of how to study, to assess, and to modify the development of psychological processes, human states, and qualities of a

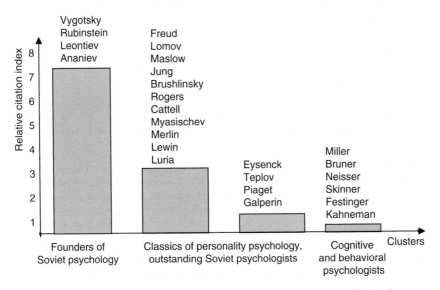

Figure 27.1 Citation of works by Soviet and Western psychologists in Russian psychological literature in 2003.

person, becomes the main one. There are rapid developments in special methodologies (particularly in practical activities). Tests, training and psychotherapeutic techniques are developed and widely used. Observation as a major method has been reinstated. The same refers to the so-called natural experiment (A. F. Lazursky). One may also note a tendency to use ideographic methods. The ideal research is often conceived of as that conducted within the situation of realistic activity and interaction in a natural environment. Some ideas are discussed concerning reconstruction and design of social and life scenarios.

In comparison with this picture, the role played by laboratory experimentation, which was the background of the most outstanding achievements of the Russian psychology in the past, has reduced dramatically. The same is true of the almost forgotten models and simulations. This tendency is sometimes referred to as "the positivism-induced tiredness." But the causes may be entirely different. During the past decade the status of psychology has radically changed. Society now perceives psychology as a *useful* branch of knowledge that helps to solve not only the problems of social life (education, health care, economy, politics, etc.) but also the problems of individuals. The number of psychologists has grown several times. There are about 70 higher education facilities in Moscow alone, which train professional psychologists, compared with about one dozen in the USSR. Being previously a narrow profession, psychology has now become almost a mass occupation. That is why the misbalance of basic and applied studies that existed before has shifted its focus towards applied work and practice. Russian psychology is no longer mainly an academic discipline. More than that, it now attaches specific attention to practice: psychotherapy, psychoanalysis, etc. These are the roots of the specific interest in the individual, the tendency to study personality as a whole, and, consequently, of the use of non-experimental means.

The problem of personality today is a specific motive force in Russian psychology. This problem is not only being elaborated very thoroughly, but it is shaping modern research strategies, thus bringing up other areas of psychological research and practical activities.

Direction towards applied work seems to provide the most outstanding difference between modern Russian psychology and Soviet psychology. It is not so much the search for new knowledge as for new ways of applying it that is important for modern psychologists. The main breakthrough is connected with education, health care, economics and business, politics and social activities. Whereas the work of psychologists in the first two areas is based on old Russian traditions and the substantial conceptual contribution by Vygotsky, Davydov, Luria, Zeigarnik, and others, the other work is based mainly on Western ideas and methods. The area of social problems is growing, thus providing a zone of proximal development for Russian psychology.

In spite of the fact that the necessity of integration of theoretical and applied knowledge is clearly acknowledged, the prospects of integration remain unclear. An aphoristic formula "practice is the criterion of truth" often cannot be applied to the realities of psychological work. The paradox is that the methods of applied work of different competing schools may be equally efficient. It is not the psychological technology, but the person who applies the technology that plays the leading role.

Conclusion

There were two metaphors describing Russian psychology at different stages of its history. One was: "All ruins, as those of Troy" (by N. N. Lange), while the other one was: "The construction site" (by B. M. Teplov), where a new unprecedented building is being erected, or even a whole new town. The current state of Russian psychology may be paradoxically described by both metaphors simultaneously. The crisis connected with the dismantling of totalitarian world views and fall of the economy is combined with the high interest of the society in psychological phenomena and the development of new areas and directions of psychological activity. Psychology is acquiring the status of a practical discipline, and the psychological culture of society is rapidly growing.

Russian psychology at this stage is developing extensively, implementing the potential accumulated by Soviet psychology. The difficulties may be described as external and limited. They have no effect on the deep mechanisms of knowledge generation as may be illustrated by the fact of emergence of new areas of theory and practice. In this situation, one may consider positive the fact that the main conceptions of Soviet psychology, especially those by Vygotsky and Rubinstein, remain not only deeply rooted in the science, but also widely open to other schools and directions.

Russian psychology today has no specific direction of movement; one may say that it is at the crossroads. The current stage of its development may be characterized as the stage of adaptation to the new social and economic structure of the country. Participating in this process by solving the problems of modern society, it is becoming an indispensable part of the new life and a factor in its development. Consequently, the design of its new dress will depend on how Russian psychology adapts itself to the new social, economic and political conditions of life. Whether it is going to be a beautiful dress, or an invisible one, we shall see in the near future.

Finally, some general conclusions. There is no doubt that the radical restructuring of the country has affected the forms and directions of development of psychological science. However, this influence is indirect, mediated, and the effects are ambiguous. There is evolution of science. Science cannot be constructed according to architectural design, as if it were a house. Science is a living organism in which, for example, categories play the role of genes responsible for the interpretative potential, and methods play the role of channels of reception of new knowledge. The state creates the general atmosphere (possibilities and limitations) in which science exists and formulates the most significant problems. Peculiarities of problem solving shape the peculiar ways of any national science.

References

Abulkhanova, K. A. (1973). *On the subject of psychological activity*. Moscow: Nauka. (in Russian)

Allakhverdov, V. M. (2004). *Afterword to the Congress//Psychology*, #2 [3rd Congress of the Russian Psychological Society, May 2003], pp. 62–68. (in Russian)

Ananiev, B. G. (1960). *Psychology of sensory cognition*. Moscow: Academy of Pedagogical Sciences. (in Russian)

Ananiev, B. G. (1968). *Man as an objective of cognition*. Leningrad: Leningrad State University. (in Russian)

Anokhin, P. K. (1978). *Philosophical aspects of the functional system theory*. Moscow: Nauka. (in Russian)

Barabanschikov, V. A., & Nosulenko, V. N. (2004). *Systems, perception, interaction*. Moscow: Institute of Psychology RAS. (in Russian)

Brushlinsky, A. V. (1979). *Thinking and prognosing*. Moscow: Mysl. (in Russian)

Brushlinsky, A. V. (2003). *Subject-centered psychology*. St Petersburg: Aleteia. (in Russian)

Davydov, V. V. (1972). *Types of generalization in education*. Moscow: Pedegogika. (in Russian)

Elkonin, D. B. (1976). *Psychology of learning: Younger schoolchildren*. Moscow: Prosveschenie. (in Russian)

Galperin, P. Ya. (1998). *Psychology as an objective science*. Moscow-Voronezh: APSN. (in Russian)

Lektorsky, V. A. (2001). *Epistemology: Classic and non-classic*. Moscow: URSS. (in Russian)

Leontiev, A. N. (1972). *Problems of development of mind*. Moscow: Moscow State University. (in Russian)

Leontiev, A. N. (1977). *Activity, consciousness, personality*. Moscow: Politizdat. (in Russian)

Lomov, B. F. (1966). *Man and technology*. Moscow: Sovetskoe Radio. (in Russian)

Lomov, B. F. (1984). *Methodological and theoretical problems of psychology*. Moscow: Nauka. (in Russian)

Luria, A. R. (1963). *Development of higher cortical functions*. Moscow: Moscow State University. (in Russian)

Oshanin, D. A. (1999). *Objectified action and operative basis*. Moscow-Voronezh: APSN. (in Russian)

Rubinstein, S. L. (1946). *Fundamentals of general psychology*. Moscow: Uchpedgiz. (in Russian)

Rubinstein, S. L. (1973). *Problems of general psychology*. Moscow: Nauka. (in Russian)

Shadrikov, V. D. (1978). *Genesis of the system of professional activities*. Moscow: Nauka. (in Russian)

Smirnov, A. R. (1965). *Problems of psychology of memory*. Moscow: Prosveschenie. (in Russian)

Talyzina, N. F. (1975). *Managing the process of knowledge*. Moscow: MSU. (in Russian)

Vygotsky, L. S. (1996). *Developmental psychology as a cultural phenomenon.* Moscow-Voronezh: APSN. (in Russian)

Zaporozhets, A. V. (1960). *Development of voluntary movements.* Moscow: Academy of Pedagogical Sciences. (in Russian)

Zeigarnik, B.V. (1976). *Pathopsychology.* Moscow, MSU. (in Russian)

Zinchenko, P. I. (1961). *Involuntary memorizing.* Moscow: Prosveschenie. (in Russian)

Zinchenko, V. P., & Munipov, V. M. (1983). *Fundamentals of ergonomics.* Moscow: Mashinostroenie. (in Russian)

28 Towards a history of applied psychology in the 20th century

Helio Carpintero

The history of applied psychology may be considered hitherto as a "neglected" area. It is true that it seems that things are beginning to change in that respect; recent works are taking the field into account (Ash, 2002; Benjamin & Baker, 2004). Nevertheless, more work needs to be done than that which has been carried out so far.

It has been a truism to consider applied psychology as a mere translation or a simple transfer of principles and concepts from theory to concrete issues. In fact, the pressure of society and its new demands went much further than that. They required new concepts and techniques, and a theoretical widening of the previous intellectual frame. Both developments run in parallel. What is needed, then, is a broad overview in which the emerging questions are presented in connection with the main lines of the dominant theory, while stressing the novelties added to it.

An early definition of the field was provided by William Stern in his pioneer work on "applied psychology" (*Angewandte Psychologie*): "the science of psychological facts that are relevant for their practical utility" (Stern, 1903; see Dorsch, 1963). Here is stressed its condition of a science; no reference is made to any "scientific" use whatever of some previously acquired concepts. Nevertheless, the utility value and the social implications of knowledge are here brought into consideration as a differential trait.

The variety of possible applications is unlimited, in principle. Human behavior has an endless variety of forms, origins and development courses, each of them with specific characteristics of their own. Intervention needs always to be adapted to the peculiarities of each field. On some occasions a mere transfer of well-established principles could be made to new phenomena and problems not previously worked out. At other times, the creation of new mental instruments that could fit well with the new types of data was required. For instance, the creation of such widely acknowledged concepts as IQ, mental age, role playing, and many others, was required by the new methodologies employed in dealing with those various topics.

It is true that, in its early days, psychology was conceived as a descriptive and explanatory theory of mental life, far from everyday life questions. As Wundt put it, it was the "whole content of consciousness in its immediate being" that was at stake, and this was a wholly theoretical question. He also rejected the differentialistic approach introduced by J. McKeen Cattell, and qualified his ideas as *"ganz amerikanisch,"* obviously implying a devaluation of the adequate theoretical level (Boring, 1950, p. 533). A similar position was also adopted by E. B. Titchener, who, in the USA, rejected individual psychology as being interested only in the study of the mind, but not of minds (Boring, 1950, p. 413). As he wrote, "to the strictly methodical man of science, technology should appear scrappy and provisional" (Titchener, 1972, p. 68), far from the soundness of true conceptual thought. Nevertheless, mankind's daily needs could not wait indefinitely; the pressure of the street finally pressured laboratories by asking them for help.

The background to the new practical attitude was basically determined by the psychology of individual differences. This was one of the various consequences of Darwin's views. As one of its own pillars, Darwinism assumed the existence of continuous changes in individuals. This variability introduced a differential adaptability among individuals and paved the way for the appearance of new types of adaptation. The situation was found not only among non-human species, but also in many fields directly related to human beings.

Galton stressed the importance for mankind of such a treasure of variations. "The living world does not consist of a repetition of similar elements, but of an endless variety of them" (Galton, 1883, p. 3). Diversity among individuals multiplies their possibilities for adaptation. As Quetelet had shown, the assessment of values related to individuals required the support of statistics, in order to determine their normal magnitude and, above all, the dimensions of what he called "the average man" (*"l'homme moyen"*) (Quetelet, 1835, Vol. II, p. 250). As a consequence, any project devised to deal with individuals had to rely on concrete measures, which could only be obtained through contact with the individuals themselves. The well-known story of A. Bertillon, the French founder of the scientific police, shows how many difficulties he had to overcome in order to have his innovative methods accepted. After some initial doubts on the value of photographic records taken from delinquent people, he was able to manage a difficult case, identifying an individual, and then solving the problem. The case was a sort of "experimentum crucis" that proved the soundness of his methods.

Mental phenomena, similar to body variations in size and shape, also show different values in different subjects. They can be placed along a continuum, which includes a larger or shorter range of normal degrees, and has at its ends the categories of abnormality and exceptionality. Comparisons among people brought about the need for solving inequalities and disadvantages. Some voices began to rise in favor of a psychological intervention that could correct the situation. As a result, the new science began to focus on day-to-day questions. For instance, the French psychotechnician J. Fontègne, criticizing education, noted the interest of workers in a change in psychological habits; as he wrote, "It is a commonplace to repeat that our teaching, on the whole or very nearly, needs to be changed . . . Workers accuse it of being too abstract, not taking real life into consideration . . . In 1866, at the International Association of Workers gathering in Geneva, socialists asked for . . . a living knowledge that would substitute a dead one, and for a progressive transformation that would change the play instinct into an instinct of work" (Fontègne, 1923, p. 1). Social urges would then require a change of the so-called instincts, in order to tackle the new demands.

Moreover, psychologists also became more and more interested not only in gaining theoretical knowledge, but also in seeing how their "findings may also contribute their quota to the sum-total of human happiness" (Hall, Baird, & Geissler, 1917, p. 6); as they also noted, "applied psychology can no longer be relegated to a distinctly inferior plane" (Hall, Baird, & Geissler, 1917, p. 6). In fact, Hall proved to be a far-sighted person, and some of his thoughts seemed prophetic in a certain way: "The world needs a new psychology greater in all its dimensions more than it needs anything else. All the great problems of our age are becoming more and more psychological, the better we understand them . . ." (Hall, 1923, p. 437). Accepting such views in various degrees, and not always in a univocal sense, little by little the new community of professionals accepted being involved in practical affairs, and in trying to solve them.

The initial points

There is not an initial year in which applied psychology might have been born. The variety of directions from which psychologists began to be solicited seems to have had different origins in time.

In the field of clinical psychology, the year 1896 has a singular value. In that year, US psychologist Lightner Witmer examined and treated a school student with reading difficulties, and, convinced of the importance of this type of intervention, at the annual American Psychological Association convention in Boston (McReynolds, 1996, p. 238), he urged his colleagues to tackle social problems and published a paper titled "Practical work in psychology" (Witmer, 1896), insisting on the topic. Also the same year, an Italian psychiatrist, Giulio Cessare Ferrari, wrote a paper very similar in its sense: "Mental tests for examining the insane" (*I 'testi mentali' per l'esame degli alienati*"; Guicciardi & Ferrari, 1896). Moreover, the previous year, the well-known German psychiatrist Emil Kraepelin (Kraepelin, 1895) had published a pioneer paper on "Psychological research in psychiatry" (*Der psychologische Versuch in der Psychiatrie*), stressing the benefits that could be obtained in psychiatry from the application of the new psychological experimental procedures. This surge of interest in applied psychology in so many places and different settings at the same time could be thought of as a case of a "multiple discovery," in R. K. Merton's sense (Merton, 1973).

Research in educational psychology seemed well consolidated in the early years of the 20th century. Let us take 1905 as a symbolic year for the new field. Two seminal works were produced that year: the appearance of the Binet–Simon Metric Scale for Intelligence, in *L'Année Psychologique*, the famous Binet journal (Binet & Simon, 1905), and the book *Child Psychology and Experimental Pedagogy*, by E. Claparède, in Geneva (Claparède, 1905). The following year, 1906, an Institute for Pedagogy and Experimental Psychology was created in Leipzig (Germany); two years before, E. L. Thorndike (1903) had written his first handbook on the subject. The institutionalization of the field had clearly begun.

Finally, industrial and applied social psychology could perhaps select 1910 as its starting point. Around that year, many important contributions began to spring forth: Mosso's studies on work fatigue (1903); Taylor's views on labor productivity and scientific management (1911); Münsterberg's seminal book *Psychology and Industrial Efficiency* (1913); Marbe's *Foundations of Forensic Psychology* (*Grundzüge der forensischen Psychologie*) (1913), among others.

As Whipple noted in his classic work on tests, "now tests have become objects of attention for many workers whose primary interest is in education, social service, medicine, industrial management and many other fields in which applied psychology promises valuable returns" (Whipple, 1914, p. v). Interest in useful instruments rapidly spread among specialists of various social and human fields of study.

Clearly, these are mere approximations made for didactic purposes to some initial points of the past. It can be seen how all these various applications had diverse beginnings. The reason is that in each case, the occasion of the initiation of the intervention was provided by some specific demand requiring an urgent solution.

The new paradigm

Theoretical psychology was born under the pressure of scientific queries, while applied research developed under personal demands presented to psychologists. Well known is the case of Witmer, who founded a psychological clinic in the University of Pennsylvania as a response to the demand of one of his students, a teacher with a schoolboy with profound language problems (McReynolds, 1996; Routh, 1996). Similarly, Münsterberg and Marbe were required by some friends involved in court processes, to help them with their expertise in analyzing some witnesses' declarations that were vital for the final outcome. Moreover, many teachers and educators demanded an instrument for evaluating and discriminating among students, those capable of a normal rhythm of learning and those that were not – a demand that stimulated Binet to carry out his classic research.

It may be affirmed that applied psychology, in its various directions, was built according to a model that largely differed from the basic research.

Applied interventions, produced under social demand, were based on problem data and the characteristics of each case. As a consequence, the action devised was usually adjusted to the specific situation, and largely independent from the constraints of any precise theoretical school. Little by little, these interventions came to cover all the main areas of human behavior, especially those in which people had to deal with specific dimensions of the human operator and his mental and behavioral peculiarities.

As a result, new instruments were devised to measure and analyze human performance in different settings (tests, simulators, sociograms, role-playing situations, etc.) and, above all, new concepts were defined that could be adapted to the new characteristics of the problem. Mental age, IQ, signal detectability, decision making, psychological complex, and many other concepts, were born in practical research and then transferred to the larger field of psychological theory.

As is well known, Kuhn maintained that each scientific paradigm is displayed as a "disciplinary matrix" that includes not only "symbolic generalizations," but also shared values, instrumental technologies and some concrete models in which solving procedures had obtained relevant results (Kuhn, 1970/1978, p. 271). Looking for all these factors in the various branches of applied psychology, it is clear that they seem to be idiosyncratic for each specialty, and are very different from those that can be found in the various consolidated theoretical schools. Another decisive trait may serve to characterize applied psychology since its early days: applied psychologists have always focused on human behavior, while experimental theorists have largely dealt with models and problems of animal behavior, at least in the first half of the 20th century, until the advent of cognitivism.

All these peculiarities testify to the originality of the psychological intervention model, which cannot be conceived as a mere transfer of ideas but as the emergence of a scientific field of its own.

This theoretical originality can also be confirmed when looking at the conceptual framework in which many applied contributions were constructed by their authors. It is well known that Münsterberg, although a close collaborator of William James at Harvard, was not at all a pragmatist, but a follower of J. G. Fichte's philosophical ideas, rooted in the Kantian discoveries, and stressing the primacy of the "practical reason," and the need for each individual to become "the man you are" (Marias, 1967, p. 309). Stern, for his part, another of the pioneers of the field, maintained a personalistic conception of psychology; he viewed it as a knowledge of the "person," that is, "a living totality, individual, unique, tending to goals ... open to the surrounding world, and having feelings" (Stern, 1938/1957, p. 69). They all stressed the relevance of the control principle: knowledge had to empower man to modify and influence the processes under study, enabling society to get rid of limitations and abnormalities.

World War I and the early institutionalization of psychological intervention

Cattell's quotation has been frequently repeated: In the war days, "the army testing put psychology on the map of the United States" (see Samelson, 1979, p. 154). Among the facts that proved him to be right, one should perhaps mention the million people tested in the USA with the Army Alpha and Army Beta instruments during the war time; the pilot testing carried out in Italy by Gemelli, or in France, by Camus and Neper; the testing of lorry drivers for the German army; or the creation of the Health of Munitions Workers Committee (1915), in the United Kingdom, which would soon turn into the National Institute for Industrial Psychology (1921). Many other institutions were born in the same period: the Institute for Work in Moscow (1920), the Institute for Professional Guidance in Barcelona (Spain) (1918), the Laboratory for Industrial Psychotechnology, at Charlottenburg (Germany) (1918), the Psychological Laboratory at the University of Sacro Cuore (Milano, Italy) (1921), the Laboratory for Experimental Psychology, at the School for Higher Studies (*Ecole des Hautes Etudes*) (Paris, France, 1921), among others.

The multiplication of centers and groups immediately brought the need for coordination and collaborative work. In 1919, politicians had finally created the League of Nations in Geneva, to bring together all the nations to a forum in which problems would be discussed, avoiding a new war confrontation. Following that model, the psychologists, largely due to the efforts of the Swiss Claparède, gave birth to an association, the International Society for Psychotechnology (*Société Internationale de Psychotechnique*), to enhance communication among professionals. Its first gathering took place in Geneva, in 1920. The new society would serve the scientific and technical development of the applied field. In its new form, as the International Association of Applied Psychology (IAAP), it has continued to work on the same goals to the present day.

The evolution of the field

The proceedings of the first 13 congresses of the IAAP (1920–1958) may help us to detect some changes produced in the field throughout those years (Gundlach, 1998). We have examined the question in more depth elsewhere (Carpintero & Herrero, 2002), but we will give some hints of it here.

The first conference took place in Geneva, in September 1920, thanks to the efforts of Claparède. He had founded there, in 1912, with the collaboration of P. Bovet, the Jean Jacques Rousseau Institute for Educational Sciences, which was soon integrated into the University of Geneva. This institution hosted the meeting, which was also largely supported by the League for Mental Hygiene of Paris, the leaders of which – the French researchers H. Piéron and J. M. Lahy – were also deeply involved in the new project.

Sixty people from several European countries gathered there. There were no contributions forthcoming from three countries – the USA, the UK or Germany – in which there were many groups working in this field. In the following years, things changed considerably and, when the 13th Congress gathered in Rome, in 1958, about 700 persons attended it, coming from all the continents, except Australia.

Interesting information may be obtained from the comparison of the main topics dealt with by the participants at those meetings. Terms appearing in the title of the presented papers have been examined, and after counting them, they were ranked for the following two periods: 1920–1934 (Congresses 1–8), and 1949–1958 (Congresses 9–13). The division took as its limit World War II, which clearly produced a serious break in the normal development of these meetings.

For some terms, their rank order is similar in both periods: such is the case of "Test" (2nd/2nd), "Vocation" (3rd/3rd), "Guidance" (4th/5th), and "Work" (5th/8th); very different are the results obtained for: "Psychotechnics" (1st/0; no ranking), and for "Psychology" (0/1st rank), and also for "Intelligence" (9th/0), and "Personality" (0/7th) (Carpintero & Herrero, 2002).

It seems that, first of all, "Psychotechnology," conceived at the beginning as a special branch of knowledge, was finally absorbed by "Psychology," the larger field that included intervention in its own tasks. Moreover, "Tests" maintained its relevant position, being the basic instruments at the disposal of psychologists. School and Industrial specialties maintained their pre-eminence, and, at the same time, topics related to clinical psychology and personality clearly rose in the second period. Finally, it could also be said that, while in the first period an emphasis on intelligence (IQ) can be detected, researchers became more and more interested in personality and individuality in the second one.

These changes may serve to qualify the turning point experienced by psychological interventions in the 1940s and 1950s. During that period well-devised actions became fully integrated into the body of psychological knowledge, then largely influenced by more holistic views on the human subject. In the long run, old divisions between theory and applications were effaced and both lines converged into one broader and more inclusive body of knowledge, which has been continuously growing since the middle of the century. A symbol of such convergence can be considered to be the appearance of the well known "Boulder model" that would become so influential in the clinical field. The model of the "researcher–practician" was elaborated by an APA conference of experts on the training of clinicians, held in 1949 at the University of Colorado in Boulder (USA) (Raimy, 1950). There an integration of theory and intervention was proposed as the best model to be applied in the training of psychologists. The scheme also inspired many other lines of development among professionals in the following decades. Such integration of the two main aspects of the psychologist's activity has guided most of the curriculum building that has taken place everywhere since then.

Political interference

Applied psychology, dealing with human behavior in historical societies, could not escape criticisms and interference by political movements, which have proclaimed certain human values and also tried to control individuals as psychology does.

On many occasions politicians have interfered in psychologists' work. A landmark of such an attitude is the famous decree against pedology ordered by the Central Committee of the Communist Party in the USSR, in 1936, in which all practices with IQ tests and intelligence measurement were abolished. Political reasons seem to have dictated this singular decision.

The study of intelligence and inborn abilities has been repeatedly affected by political upheavals. Well-known criticisms by Gould (1981), Eysenck and Kamin (1981), Herrnstein and Murray (1994), among others, have brought their arguments to the attention of general readers, showing the multiplicity of dimensions immersed in the apparently neutral practice of intelligence testing.

It may be assumed, as a general thesis, that "a free psychology may, in fact, be symptomatic of a free society" (Gilgen, 1982, p. 37). Its practitioners, and its clients, are clearly distributed in a similar way as the renta per capita: some years ago, while there were more than 400 psychologists per million inhabitants in the USA and Canada, this figure only reached 81 per million in Eastern Europe, and 7 per million in the former USSR and in Asia, and probably less in Africa (Rosenzweig, 1982).

The last quarter of the 20th century was filled with enormous changes in the world: the reshaping of all of the former USSR empire, the tremendous modernization of China, the development and growth of the European Union, the "conflict among religions," the movements in the Islamic world, just to mention the biggest ones. It has been a time for gigantic advances in genetics and biological power. The assessment of the impact of all these changes on our science is an urgent task to be completed.

In our days, applied psychologists are facing new demands in a changing world. They have been called to offer help and advice to people suffering from AIDS, from the effects of terrorist attacks, from technological changes that are deeply affecting the world of work. The phenomenon of globalization, the new dimensions of the information society, and genome engineering, for instance, demand from psychologists new ways of dealing with the mental and behavioral problems that are springing up in contemporary societies (Wilpert, 1999).

The coming time will probably make the old words of Hall, quoted above, increasingly true: "All the great problems of our age are becoming more and more psychological, the better we understand them . . ." (Hall, 1923, p. 437). It is the new deal for psychologists, be they theoreticians or practitioners. In the 21st century, psychology will continue to be a scientific instrument in favor of the health and growth of human persons.

References

Ash, M. G. (2002). La psicología como ciencia y profesión desde 1850: La perspectiva de un historiador [Psychology as a science and a profession since 1850: The point of view of a historian]. *Revista de Historia de la Psicologia, 23*(3–4), 249–264.

Benjamin, L. T., Jr., & Baker, D. B. (2004). *From séance to science. A history of the profession of psychology in America.* Belmont, CA: Wadsworth-Thomson.

Binet, A., & Simon, T. (1905). Méthodes nouvelles pour le diagnostic du niveau intellectuel des anormaux [New methods for the assessment of the intellectual level of abnormal people]. *L'Année Psychologique, XI*, 191–244.

Boring, E. G. (1950). *A history of experimental psychology* (2nd ed.). New York: Appleton.

Carpintero, H., & Herrero, F. (2002). Early applied psychology: The early days of the IAAP. *European Psychologist, 7*(1), 39–52.

Claparède, E. (1905). *Psychologie de l'enfant et pédagogie expérimentale* [Child psychology and experimental pedagogy]. Geneva: Kündig.

Dorsch, F. (1963). *Geschichte und Probleme der angewandten Psychologie.* Bern, Switzerland: Hans Huber.

Eysenck, H. J., & Kamin, L. (1981). *The intelligence controversy.* New York: Wiley.

Fontègne, J. (1923). *Manualisme et éducation.* Paris: L. Eyrolles.

Galton, F. (1883). *Inquiries into human faculty and its development.* London: Macmillan.

Gilgen, A. R. (1982). *American psychology since World War II. A profile of the discipline.* Westport, CT: Greenwood Press.

Gould, S. (1981). *The mismeasure of man.* New York: Norton.

Guicciardi, G., & Ferrari, G. C. (1896). I "testi mentali" per l'esame degli alienati [Mental tests for the assessment of the insane]. *Rivista Sperimentale di Freniatria e Medicina Legale delle Alienazioni Mentali, XXII*, 297–314.

Gundlach, H. (Ed.). (1998). Applied psychology. In *The first-thirteenth congress proceedings of the International Association of Applied Psychology* (13 vols.). London & New York: Routledge.

Hall, G. S. (1923). *Life and confessions of a psychologist.* New York: Appleton.

Hall, G. S., Baird, J. W., & Geissler, L. R. (1917). Foreword. *Journal of Applied Psychology, 1*(1), 5–7.

Herrnstein, R., & Murray, C. (1994). *The bell curve. Intelligence and class structure in American life.* New York: The Free Press.

Kraepelin, E. (1895). Der psychologische Versuch in der Psychiatrie [Psychological research in psychiatry]. *Psychologische Arbeiten, I*, 1–91.

Kuhn, T. S. (1978). Reflections on my critics. In I. Lakatos & A. Musgrave (Eds.), *Criticism and the growth of knowledge* (reprint, pp. 231–278). Cambridge, UK: Cambridge University Press. (Originally published in 1970)

Marbe, K. (1913). *Grundzüge der forensischen Psychologie* [Foundations of forensic psychology]. Munich: Beck.

Marias, J. (1967). *History of philosophy.* New York: Dover.

McReynolds, P. (1996). Lightner Witmer: A centennial tribute. *American Psychology, 51*(3), 237–240.

Merton, R. K. (1973). *The sociology of science: Theoretical and empirical investigations* (pp. 343–370). Chicago: University of Chicago Press.

Mosso, A. (1903). *Fatigue*. New York: Putnam.

Münsterberg, H. (1913). *Psychology and industrial efficiency*. Boston, MA: Houghton Mifflin.

Quetelet, A. (1835). *Sur l'homme et le developpement de ses facultés, ou essai de physique sociale* (2 vols.). Paris: Bachelier.

Raimy, V. C. (Ed.). (1950). *Training in clinical psychology*. New York: Prentice Hall.

Rosenzweig, M. (1982). Trends in development and status of psychology: An international perspective. *International Journal of Psychology, 26*, 514–530.

Routh, D. K. (1996). Lightner Witmer and the first 100 years of clinical psychology. *American Psychologist, 51*(3), 244–247.

Samelson, F. (1979). Putting psychology on the map: Ideology and intelligence testing. In A. R. Buss (Ed.), *Psychology in social context*. New York: Irvington.

Stern, W. (1903). Angewandte psychologie [Applied psychology]. *Beiträge zur Psychologie der Aussage, I,* 4–45.

Stern, W. (1957). *Psicología general desde el punto de vista personalístico* [General psychology from the personalistic standpoint]. Buenos Aires, Argentina: Paidos. (Originally published 1938)

Taylor, F. W. (1911). *The principles of scientific management*. New York: Harper & Brothers.

Thorndike, E. L. (1903). *Educational psychology*. New York: Lemcke & Buechner.

Titchener, E. B. (1972). *Systematic psychology: Prolegomena*. Ithaca, NY: Cornell University Press.

Whipple, G. M. (1914). *Manual of mental and physical tests. Part I: Simpler processes*. Baltimore, MD: Warwick & York.

Wilpert, B. (1999). The changing nature of work and of work & organizational psychology. In *La Psicología al Fin de Siglo* [Psychology at the end of the century]. XVII Interamerican Congress of Psychology (pp. 409–422). Caracas, Venezuela: Interamerican Psychological Society (SIP).

Witmer, L. (1896). Practical work in psychology. *Pediatrics, 2*, 462–471.

Author index

Aberle, D.F. 232
Abulkanova, K.A. 425
Ackerman, N.W. 131
Adams, M.M. 191
Ader, R. 160
Aditya, R.N. 351
Adler, P.S. 13
Aguinis, H. 374
Agurto, S. 185
Aikawa, A. 327
Ait-Ouarasse, O. 285, 287
Ajzen, I. 168, 170
Alexander, F. 131, 132
Alexander, F.G. 129
Allakhverdov, V.M. 427
Allik, J. 286, 289, 291
Allport, A. 387, 401
Allport, G.W. 105
Altman, I. 234, 235
Alvarez-Borda, B. 162
Ames, D.R. 263, 265, 273
Ananiev, B.G. 420
Anderson, C.W. 13
Anderson, J.R. 46
Anderson, K.L. 187
Anderson, N. 371
Angleitner, A. 105
Annis, R.C. 231, 232, 236
Anokhin, P.K.
Anthony, J.L. 148
Aoki, S. 323
Armony, L. 387, 401
Armstrong, C. 167, 170
Ash, M.G. 433
Ash, R.A. 373
Ashmann, S. 13
Ashton, M.C. 100
Asimov, I. 37
Atkins, L. 366

Axelrod, R. 341
Azuma, H. 252, 307, 308, 310, 316, 338, 339, 340

Bachman, J.G. 321
Bacon, M. 236, 239
Baddeley, A. 387
Baddeley, A.D. 84
Bahuchet, S. 231, 232, 236
Bailey, D.E. 352
Bailey, J.A. 182, 184, 190
Bain, P.G. 353, 354, 358, 366
Baird, J.W. 435
Baker, D.B. 441
Baker, J.A. 126
Balls-Organista, P. 235
Banahan, B.F. 126
Banaji, M.R. 325, 326
Bandura, A. 168, 169, 332, 333, 334, 335
Barabanschikov, V.A. 426
Baral, R.L. 326
Barbaranelli, C. 106, 107
Bardell, L. 387
Bareket, T. 396, 400
Baron, R.M. 285
Barry, H. 236, 239
Barth, F. 305
Bartlett, L. 11
Basgall, J.A. 113
Bass, B.M. 231, 359
Battista, M. 373
Baumeister, R.F. 170, 319, 320, 326
Beaty, J.C.C. Jr. 374
Becker, G. 13
Becker, M.H. 170

Bell, P.A. 269, 270, 274
Belsky, J. 252
Benedict, R. 249, 252, 255, 308
Benet-Martinez, V. 263, 274, 276
Benjamin, L.T. Jr. 433
Bennett, A.B. Jr. 106
Bennett, J.A. 232, 233
Bennett, L. 131
Bennis, W. 362
Ben-Zur, H. 143
Bergen, R.K.
Berger, R.E. 321
Berkowitz, L. 319
Berkowitz, W. 236, 239
Bermudez, J. 106
Bermudez-Rattoni, F. 162
Bernstein, B. 41
Berry, A.J. 359
Berry, J.W. 92, 102, 105, 229, 230, 231, 232, 233, 234, 235, 236, 237, 238, 239, 279, 284
Best, S.R. 142
Bethea, L. 190
Biaggio, M.K. 129
Bill, V.L. 7, 9
Binet, A. 435
Binger, C.A.L. 131
Bingham, G.E. 248, 250
Bjork, R.A. 387
Blackwell, B. 126
Blascovich, J. 326
Bloom, B. 47
Blow, F.C. 128
Bochner, S. 285
Bock, P.K. 286
Boettger, R. 261

Bonanno, G. 141
Bond, M. 106
Bond, M.H. 93, 343, 375
Bond, R. 236, 285, 291
Bongaerts, T. 56
Boring, E.G. 331, 434
Bornstein, M.H. 247,
    248, 250, 251, 252, 253,
    254
Bortner, R.W. 126, 132,
    134
Boyd, R. 233
Bradley, R.H. 248
Brand, R.J. 125
Brandon, A.D. 130, 131,
    134
Bransford, J.D. 4, 5
Brett, P. 57
Breugelmans, S.M. 281
Brickner, M. 397
Brislin, R.W. 91
Brody, J.E. 125
Bronfenbrenner, U. 232,
    245, 252
Brouwers, S.A. 281, 292
Brown, A.L. 4, 45
Brown, B. 234, 235
Brown, J. 250
Brown, J.D. 57
Brown, J.S. 45
Browne, A. 182, 188
Bruce, F.C. 191
Bruce, V. 401
Bruner, J. 10
Brushlinsky, A.V. 420,
    425
Bryk, A.S. 13, 291
Buck, M.J. 250
Burger, J.M. 262
Byrne, C.M. 142, 153
Byrne, D.G. 128

Cabrera, N.J. 248
Cai, T.S. 105
Camara Bastos, M.H. 37
Campbell, D.T. 279
Campbell, J.D. 319, 320,
    326
Campbell, J.P. 371
Campbell, K. 82
Canchica, A. 37
Caplan, D. 56
Cappa, S.F. 51
Caprara, G.V. 106, 107

Caragata, L. 51
Carlson, R.A. 387
Carpintero, H. 438, 439
Carr, L. 373
Carter, K. 319
Caruso, M. 37, 39
Case, R. 86
Cashmore, R. 252
Cattell, R.B. 127
Caudill, W.A. 326
Cavalli-Sforza, L.L. 231,
    232, 236
Cavanagh, P. 41
Ceci, S.J. 72
Cha, J-H. 212
Chan, D. 376
Chang, A. 264, 269, 270
Chang, M-H. 52
Chase, W.G. 400
Chee, M.W.L. 56
Chen, C. 320
Chen, D. 325
Chen, J. 160, 162
Chen, L. 374
Chen, M.C. 106
Chen, M.K. 374, 378
Chen, Z. 106
Chen, Z.G. 377
Cheung, F.M. 92, 94, 95,
    99, 373
Cheung, S.F. 92
Chi, M.T.H. 45
Child, I. 236, 239
Child, I.L. 255
Chiu, C. 263, 274, 276
Chiu, C.C. 265, 266, 274
Chiu, C.Y. 266, 272, 273
Chiu, L-H. 211, 212
Choi, I. 209, 211, 212,
    263, 267
Choi, S.C. 335
Chong, D. 264, 269, 270
Chorover, S.L. 337
Chua, H. 222
Chun, K. 235
Church, A. 106
Cialdini, R.B. 322
Claparède, E. 436
Coad, A.F. 359
Cocking, R.R. 4
Cohen, A. 128
Cohen, A.K. 232
Cohen, J. 293
Cohen, L. 51

Cohen, N. 160
Cohen, S.G. 352
Cohn, A.E. 131
Coker, A.L. 190
Cole, M. 11, 247
Coleman, J.S. 13
Collins, A. 11, 45
Collins, M. 409
Collins, W.A. 247
Comrey, A.L. 106, 107
Condorcet, J.-A.-N. 26
Confucius. 322
Conner, M. 167, 170
Coopersmith, S. 319
Cope, J. 62
Costa, P. 91
Costa, P.T. 105, 106, 143,
    290
Costello, E.J. 143
Cote, L.R. 250
Cotton, S. 252
Cousins, S.D. 210
Cowan, C.P. 248
Cowan, P.A. 248
Crane, R.J. 129, 130
Crane, R.S. 130, 134
Crisp, R. 269, 270, 274
Cromer, A. 209
Cronbach, L.J. 331
Cronin, V. 57
Cross, S.E. 210
Cui, H. 106, 107, 108,
    110, 111, 112, 114, 115
Curtis, N. 129

Dahlberg, L.L. 184, 185,
    190
Dai, X.Y. 105
Dalal, R. 267
Daniels, G. 131
Danziger, K. 331
Darlington, C.D. 72
Darwin, C. 126, 129
Das, J.P. 74, 76, 77, 80, 81,
    82, 83, 84, 87
Dasen, P.R. 229, 230,
    232, 234, 235, 236, 279,
    284
Dash, U.N. 74
Davis, A. 232
Davis, K.E. 264
Davydov, V.V. 423
De Groot, A. 401
de la Torre, J. 133

DeCourcey, W. 248
Deffenbacher, J.L. 130, 131, 134
Dehaene, S. 51
Deirdre, J.K. 371
Dekel, R. 143
Delaney, M. 57
Demetrikopoulos, M.K. 162
Demm, P.M. 134
Dempster, F.M. 86
Denckla, M.B. 83
Denious, J.E. 184, 191, 192
Dennis, J. 248
Denny, J.P. 232, 233
Desai, S. 184
DeSilva, H. 126
Di Blas, L. 107
Diamond, J.B. 15
Diaz, E. 142, 153
Dickson, M. 38, 39, 42, 367
Diener, E. 326, 327
Diener, M. 326, 327
DiMaggio, P.J. 12
Ding, X-S. 52
Dinnel, D.L. 319
Doi, T. 307
Donahue, E.M. 105
Donald, M. 80
Donovan, S. 5
Dorfman, P.W. 367
Dorsch, F. 433
Drath, W.H. 357, 360, 362, 367
Drenth, P.J.D. 371
Driver, J. 387
Dubanoski, J. 91, 93, 102
Duncan, J. 387
Dunn, A.J. 159
Dunn, J. 250
Dunning, J. 366
Dupoux, E. 51
Durkheim, E. 261, 262

Edelman, S. 164
Edgecomb, J.L. 128
Edleson, J.L. 182
Edwards, J. 412
Elias, M.F. 128
Eliot, R.S. 125
Elkonin, D.B. 423
Ellis, R. 51

Ellsberg, M.C.L. 182, 183, 185, 189
Elms, A.C. 331
Elson, B. 262, 268, 272, 274, 275
Engel, G. 131
Engeström, Y. 11
Engle, R.W. 371
Enriquez, V. 231
Ericsson, A.E. 400
Erikson, E. 362
Erikson, E.H. 252
Esteban, L. 26
Evans, J.E. 387
Exton, M.S. 160
Eysenck, H.J. 85, 143, 440
Eysenck, M.W. 143

Fairbank, D.W. 143
Fairbank, J.A. 143
Fan, R. 93, 373
Fang, L. 106
Fang, Y. 162
Farh, J.-L. 375
Farnham, S.D. 325
Farrell, D. 57
Feldman, D.A. 232, 233
Feng, C.J. 371, 377
Feng, Z-K. 55
Fernald, A. 211
Fernandez Heres, R. 37
Ferrari, G.C. 435
Field, H.S. 371
Figueredo, A.J. 185
Fincham, F.D. 248, 263
Finkelhor, D. 185
Fiske, A.P. 210
Fitzgerald, L. 182
Flynn, J.R. 73
Flyr, M.L. 248
Folkman, S. 140, 156
Fontègne, J. 435
Forde, D. 233
Forsyth, D.R. 321
Forzi, M. 107
Foucault, M. 36, 39, 46
Frede, S. 160
Freire, P. 30
French, T.M. 129
French, V. 248
Freud, S. 126, 127, 129, 133

Friedman, M. 125, 126, 131, 132
Friedman, M.J. 142, 153
Frith, C. 74
Fuchs, R. 169, 170
Fuller, L.269
Fung, Y. 209
Furnham, A. 285

Gabrenya, W.K. Jr. 341
Gaertner, L. 320
Gale, J. 56
Galperin, C. 250
Galperin, P.Ya. 420
Galton, F. 434
Gamoran, A. 13
Gan, Y.G. 94, 95
Garcia-Moreno, C. 185
Gardner, H. 362
Gatewood, R.D. 371
Gazmararian, J.A. 191
Geary, D.C. 106
Geertz, C. 246
Geffner, R. 190
Geissler, L.R. 435
Georgas, J. 237, 290, 291
Georgiou, G. 85, 86
Gergen, K.J. 230
Gergen, M.M. 230
Ghoshal, S. 13
Gibson, J.J. 400
Gierse, C. 160
Gilbert, D.T. 264, 265
Gilbert, T.F. 43
Gilgen, A.R. 440
Gillespie, N. 359, 360, 361
Gillet, G. 332
Gilman, S. 128
Ginzburg, K. 143
Gjerde, P. 307, 308, 312
Glaser, R. 36
Glass, D.C. 126, 132, 134
Gleser, G.C. 155
Goady, J. 57
Gobet, F. 401
Goldberg, J. 86
Goldberg, L. 94
Goldberg, L.R. 105
Goldman, P. 9
Goldstein, H. 291
Goldstein, H.W. 376, 379
Goleman, D. 357
Gollwitzer, P.M. 169
Gönçü, A. 245

Gong, Y. 106
Goodman, L.A. 182, 183, 184
Goodman-Turkanis, C.G. 11
Goodnow, J.J. 250, 252
Goodrum, S. 187
Gopher, D. 387, 388, 389, 390, 391, 392, 393, 394, 395, 396, 397, 398, 399, 400
Gordon, R. 143
Gorsuch, R.L. 126, 127, 128
Gottemoeller, M. 182, 183, 189
Gould, S. 71, 440
Grace, M.C. 155
Graen, G.B. 360, 375
Gramsci, A. 225
Grassi, F. 51
Green, B.L. 140, 142, 155
Green, M. 262, 266, 268
Greene, A.F. 128
Greene, A.G. 128
Greenfield, P.M. 295
Greenholtz, J. 320
Greenleaf, R.K. 357, 360
Greeno, J.G. 11
Greenshpan, Y. 387, 401
Greenwald, A.G. 324, 325, 326
Greer, S. 159
Grych, J.H. 248
Guevara, C. 362
Guicciardi, G. 435
Gundlach, H. 438
Guo, H.F. 162
Guo, Y. 160
Guthrie, G.M. 106
Guyton, A.C.133

Hahn, R. 106, 107
Hakuta, K. 51, 338, 340
Hall, E.T. 210
Hall, G.S. 435, 440
Hall, J.H. 248
Hall, M.W. 5, 6, 7
Hallahan, M. 212, 267
Halpern, D.F. 408
Halverson, R. 15
Hamada, W.C. 91, 93, 102
Hambling, J. 131

Hamburger, W. 131
Hamilton, D.L. 262, 266
Hamilton, V.L. 263, 264, 274
Hamilton, W.D. 341
Han, J. 162
Hanges, P.J. 367
Harkness, S. 246, 305
Harré, R. 332
Harris, D. 37
Harris, R. 131
Harrison, E.E. 128
Hartel, C. 364, 365
Hassard, J. 37, 38
Hausmann, R.G. 45
Haynes, O.M. 250
Heatherton, T.F. 170
Hecht, S.A. 148
Heider, F. 261, 275
Heine, S.J. 319, 320, 322, 327
Heise, L. 182, 183, 185, 187, 189
Helgesen, G. 344
Heller, F. 356
Herrero, F. 438, 439
Herriot, P. 371
Herrnstein, R. 440
Herskovits, M.J. 279
Hertzman, M. 216
Herzog, T. 212, 267
Hesketh, B. 373
Heslet, L. 190
Hetherington, E.M. 247
Hetts, J.J. 324
Hewstone, M. 267
Hiland, D.N. 128
Hirsch, J. 51
Hirst, G. 358, 364, 365
Hitch, G.J. 387
Ho, D.Y.F. 338
Hoefnagel-Hohle, M. 56
Hofferth, S. 248
Hofstede, G. 284, 290, 334
Hogg, J.A. 130, 131, 134
Holden, G. 190
Holden, G.W. 250
Holloway, S. 339, 340
Holten, G. 332
Holtgraves, T. 321
Hong, Y. 263, 274, 276
Hong, Y.Y. 265, 266, 272, 273, 274

Horowitz, E. 62
Horowitz, M. 62
Hotaling, G.T. 188
Hou, Y. 162
Houlihan, M. 82
House, R.J. 351, 367
Hsieh, S. 387, 401
Hsu, F.L.K. 210
Hu, X-Y. 54
Huang, J. 161
Huckin, T. 57
Hui, C.H. 225, 357, 367
Hulme, C. 84
Hunt, E. 387
Husband, A.J. 160
Hutchins, E. 11

Illich, I. 28
Inoue, N. 327

Jacobs, G.A. 129, 130
Jaffe, P.G. 190
Jahoda, G. 232
James, W. 320, 327
Janis, I.L. 356
Jansen, H. 185
Jared, D. 83
Jarman, R.F. 77
Jasinski, J.L. 182
Jasook, K. 211
Jaspars, J.M. 263
Javidan, M. 367
Jenkins, C.D. 125
Jeong, H. 45
Ji, L. 212, 214, 216
Jin, N. 343, 344
John, O.P. 105
Johnson, C.H. 191
Johnson, E.H. 129, 130
Johnson, K. 185, 186, 187, 189, 190, 192, 193
Johnson, M.H. 387
Johnston, J. 9
Jones, E.E. 263, 264
Jones, S. 169
Jouriles, E. 190
Junid, F.B. 261, 267

Kaczmarek, L. 162
Kaczmarek, M. 146, 155
Kaestle, C.F. 39
Kagitcibasi, C. 335
Kakabadse, A. 374
Kalis, B. 131

Kamin, L. 440
Kanagawa, C. 210
Kaniasty, K. 142, 153
Kanwisher, N. 387
Kaplan, B. 91
Kar, B.C. 81
Karasawa, M. 316, 324
Karis, D. 388, 390, 391
Karp, S.A. 216
Kasgiwagi, K. 339, 340
Katigbak, M.S. 106
Kaur, J. 264, 269, 270
Kawai, H. 301, 315
Keane, T.M. 141
Keele, R. 387
Keita, G.P. 182
Keller, F. 47
Keller, R.T. 359
Keller, S.E. 162
Kelley, H.H. 261, 263, 271
Kelley, R.E. 352
Kellman, P.J. 386, 400
Kenny, D.A. 285
Kentle, R.L. 105
Kernis, M.H. 320
Khazan, I. 248
Khoo, B.H. 387
Kidman, A. 164
Kieras, E.D. 387
Kiesler, S.B. 326
Kim, B.J. 213
Kim, H. 210
Kim, H.C. 337
Kim, K. 333, 336, 338, 343
Kim, K.H.S. 51
Kim, U. 231, 331, 334, 335, 337, 339, 340, 341, 342, 343, 344
Kim-Prieto, C. 267
Kinder, D.R. 406
King, M. 190
King, M.G. 160
Kirby, J.R. 77, 82
Kishor, S. 185, 186, 187, 189, 190, 192, 193
Kitayama, S. 210, 284, 313, 319, 322, 324, 327
Klaric, J.S. 143
Kluckhorn, C. 308, 314
Knight, N. 225
Knight, R. 252

Knowles, E. 212
Kobayashi, C. 324
Koch, S. 331
Koenig, W. 388, 390, 391
Koffka, K. 386
Kohn, M.L. 225
Kol'tsova, V.A. 409
Kondo, Y. 341
Koo, J. 263
Koopman, P.L. 371
Kop, P.F.M. 281
Koriat, A. 387
Korol, M. 155
Kosakai, T. 313, 314
Koss, M.P. 182, 183, 184, 185, 187
Koss, P.G. 190
Kraepelin, E. 435
Kramer, A.F. 387
Krasner, S.S. 130
Kristel, O. 262, 266, 268
Kristof-Brown, A.L. 376
Kroeber, A. 233
Kroeber, A.L. 308, 314
Krohne, H.W. 140
Krueger, J.I. 319, 320, 326
Krug, E.G. 184, 185, 190
Kruger, A. 235
Kuhn, T.S. 437
Kunda, Z. 262
Kurland, D.M. 86
Kurt, J. 183
Kurzban, R. 412
Kwon, S. 13

Lamb, M.E. 248
Larish, J.L. 387
Latané, B. 341
Lauterbach, D. 139, 142, 154
Laux, L. 140
Lave, J. 11
Lawrence, A. 84
Lazarus, R.S. 141, 156
Leary, D.E. 331
Lebra, T.S. 321, 339
Lee, F. 211, 212, 263, 267
Lee, K. 100
Lee, K.-M. 51
Lee, P. 354
Lee, S.-Y. 320, 340
Lehman, D.R. 319, 320, 322, 327

Leidy, M.S. 248
Lektorsky, V.A. 423
Leonard, A.C. 155
Leong, F.T.L. 91, 94
Leontiev, A.N. 419, 422
Lerner, J. 262, 266, 268
Lerner, J.S. 261
Leung, F. 164
Leung, K. 93, 94, 95, 99, 283, 295, 343, 371, 373
Leventhal, H.169
Levin, D.T. 218
Levine, J.M. 11
LeVine, R.A. 249, 250, 255, 340
Levinson, D.J. 146
Lewis, H.B. 216
Li, C.P. 372
Li, J. 162
Li, J.T. 375
Li, M. 112
Li, S. 106
Li, X. 52, 159
Liang, J. 375
Liao, W.C. 126
Lichter, E. 182, 184, 190
Lickel, B. 262, 266
Liederman, P.H. 248
Lim, C.S.M. 266, 272
Lim, H.K. 273, 275
Lin, C. 323
Lin, W. 160, 161, 162, 163, 164
Lin, W.Q. 374
Lin, X. 164
Lin, Y. 51
Lipmann, W. 406
Lippke, S. 172, 173, 174
Lipsey, T.L. 142
Lipshitz, R. 366
Liu, Y. 160, 164
Lloyd, G.E.R. 209
Lomax, A. 236, 239
Lomov, B.F. 420, 421, 422, 423, 426
London, P. 130, 132, 134
Lonigan, C.L. 148
Lonner, W.J. 91
Lopez, C. 36, 37
Lozano, R. 184, 185, 190
Luria, A.R. 77, 81, 253, 423
Lushene, R.D. 126, 127, 128

Luszczynska, A. 170, 175, 177
Lynn, R. 337

Maccoby, E.E. 105
Maccoby, E.E. 247, 251
Machover, K. 216
Madsen, G. 160
Mahoney, M.R. 188
Malcuit, G. 250
Malinowski, B. 308
Malone, P.S. 264, 265
Mann, L. 352, 353, 354, 356, 358, 359, 360, 361, 363, 364, 365, 366
Marbe, K. 436
March, J.G. 13
Marias, J. 437
Marin, A.J. 187
Marin, G. 235
Markus, H.R. 210, 284, 313, 319, 322, 327
Marrou, H.I. 26
Marsella, A.J. 91, 93, 102
Martin, J.A. 251
Mashima, M. 312, 316
Maslach, C. 106
Masuda, T. 211, 217, 218, 221, 222
Mathews, K.A. 126, 132, 134
May, J. 269, 270, 274
May, R. 126
Mayr, U. 387
McCartney, K. 251
McCauley, C.D. 362, 374
McClelland, D.C. 375
McConnell, M. 248
McCrae, R. 91
McCrae, R.R. 105, 106, 143, 286, 288, 289, 291, 373
McCusker, C. 225
McFarlane, A.C. 142, 155
McFarlin, D.B. 326
McGillicuddy-De Lisi, A.S. 250
McGrath, J.E. 140
McHale, J. 248
McKay, B. 233
McKechnie, J.I. 385
McKeown, R.E. 190
McLaughlin, M.W. 13

McRae, K. 83
McReynolds, P. 435, 436
Mead, M. 255, 308
Meier, B. 160
Meiran, N. 387
Meissner, P.B. 216
Menon, T. 263, 265, 266, 272, 273, 274
Mercy, J.A. 184, 185, 190
Merton, R.K. 435
Meshalkina, N.B. 409
Messquida, C.G. 411
Meyer, D.E. 387
Meyer, J. 12
Michaels, S. 7
Micheaux, D. 9
Michelle, S.M.Y. 373
Middleton, D. 11
Middleton, R. 238
Miller, A.S. 343, 344
Miller, J.G. 230, 265, 294
Miller, R.S. 322
Mintzberg, H. 353
Mishra, R.C. 231, 232, 236
Mishra, R.K. 84
Mistry, J. 245
Misumi, J. 340, 341
Mitchell, T. 321
Miyamoto, Y. 221
Mo, M. 52
Mobley, W.H. 371
Mok, M. 84
Monsell, S. 387, 401
Moran, E. 233
Morelli, G.A. 249
Morikawa, H. 211
Morris, K.L. 248
Morris, M.W. 212, 263, 265, 266, 267, 272, 273, 274, 276
Morris, P.A. 245, 252
Morrow, J.E. 374
Morse, H. 91, 93, 102
Mosen, M. 160
Moses, J.A. 131
Moses, L. 131
Mosier, C. 245
Mosso, A. 436
Muir, C. 84
Munipov, V.M. 423
Munkata, Y. 387
Munro, D.J. 209, 210
Munroe, R.H. 229

Munroe, R.L. 229
Münsterberg, H. 436
Murakami, F. 322, 324
Murdock, G.P. 232, 238
Murphy, K.R. 373, 375
Murphy, S.E. 371
Murray, C. 440
Muthén, B.O. 288

Naglieri, J.A. 76, 77, 80, 81, 82
Nahapiet, J. 13
Nakamura, H. 209, 225
Nakazato, H. 106
Nam, K.D. 212
Narodowski, M. 36, 37
Needham, J. 225
Nenle, C.A. 374
Neria, Y. 143
Newell, A. 399
Newman, S.E. 45
Newmann, F.M. 13
Nickerson, J. 131
Nimkoff, J. 238
Nisbett, R.E. 73, 209, 210, 211, 212, 213, 214, 216, 217, 218, 222, 262, 263, 264, 268, 269, 271, 274, 275, 276, 300, 410, 411
Nobeji, M. 327
Nomoto, T. 312, 316
Norenzayan, A. 209, 212, 213, 223, 263
Norman, D.A. 387
Norman, P. 167, 170
Norman, W.T. 105
Norris, F.H. 142, 146, 153
Nosek, B.A. 325
Nosulenko, V.N. 426
Nsamenang, B. 236

O'Connor, M.C. 13
Odbert, H.S. 105
O'Dekirk, J.M. 143
Ofiesh, G.D. 46
Oguchi, T. 322
Ohlott, P.J. 374
Okagaki, L. 248, 250
Okun, M.A. 322
Olegnik, Y.N. 409
O'Malley, P.M. 320
Ong, P. 264, 269, 270
Oniszczenko.W. 146, 147
Orantes, A. 35, 37

Ormsby, C.E. 162
Orr, J. 13
Osaka, E. 312
Oshanin, D.A. 422, 423
Ostendorf, F. 105
Overing, J. 306
Ozaki, Y. 322
Ozer, E.J. 142

Painter, K. 250
Palincsar, A.S. 45
Paller, K.A. 86
Pandey, J. 232, 234
Park, H. 267
Park, H.J. 333, 336, 338, 343
Park, Y.S. 337, 339, 340, 343
Parke, R.D. 248
Parrila, R. 85, 86
Parrila, R.K. 81
Pascual, L. 250
Paul, T.C. 373
Pearlman, K. 373
Pease-Alvarez, L. 51
Pedhazur, E.J. 150, 156
Pedhazur-Schmelkin, L. 150, 156
Peeters, G. 323
Pelegrino, J.W. 387
Pelham, B.W. 324
Pellegrino, J. 5
Pelto, P. 236
Pena, R. 185
Peng, K. 209, 212, 214, 216, 263, 267, 320
Perani, D. 51
Perilla, J.L. 146
Peters, R.S. 261
Peterson, M. 374
Pettigrew, T.F. 267, 273, 275
Pfeiffer, J. 131
Piaget, J. 44
Piedmont, R.L. 105, 106, 107
Pike, K.L. 92, 102
Piker, S. 286
Pirola-Merlo, A. 358, 364, 365
Pirozzolo, F.J. 371
Planken, B. 56
Plomin, R. 247
Plous, S. 412

Plunkett, J. 131
Polifroini, M. 262, 272, 274, 275
Pomerleau, A. 250
Poortinga, Y.H. 229, 230, 232, 234, 281, 284, 288, 289, 290, 291, 295
Posner, M.I. 82
Powell, W.W. 12
Ptacek, J. 188, 191
Putnam, R.D. 225
Pynoos, R.S. 146

Qian, M. 106
Quetelet, A. 434
Quinn, R.E. 353
Quiroz, P.A. 13

Radomska, A. 147
Raij, D. 388
Raimy, V.C. 439
Ramasamy, M. 264, 269, 270
Ramirez-Amaya, V. 162
Ramos, L. 182
Rappoport, R. 233
Rapport, N. 306
Ratner, H. 235
Raudenbush, S.W. 291
Reheiser, E.C. 130, 131, 132
Reiser, M. 131
Relkin, N.R. 51
Renner, B. 168, 170, 177
Renzetti, C.M. 182
Resnick, L.B. 5, 6, 7, 9, 11
Reyes, J.A.S. 106
Ribes, E. 29, 32
Rice, A.P. 128
Richardson, K. 73
Richerson, P. 233
Richver, A. 358
Riggio, R.E. 371
Ripley, M. 131
Robbins, M.A. 128
Robinson, A. 126
Rodger, A. 41
Rodriguez, N. 146
Roediger, H.L. 407
Roese, N.J. 271
Rogers, R.D. 387, 401
Rogers, R.W. 170
Rogoff, B. 11, 245

Roland, J. 47
Roldan, E. 37, 40, 46
Rolland, J.P. 106
Rosenberg, M. 320
Rosenbloom, P.S. 399
Rosenfeld, A. 248
Rosenfeld, I. 134
Rosenman, R.H. 125, 126, 131, 132, 134
Rosenzweig, M. 440
Roskies, E. 128
Ross, L. 262, 263, 275
Rost, J.C. 351, 352, 360, 361
Rothman, A.J. 167, 170
Rotman, T. 248
Routh, D.K. 436
Rowan, B. 12
Rowlinson, M. 37, 38
Rozin, P. 263
Rubinstein, J. 387
Rubinstein, S.L. 419, 425
Ruch, W. 106
Rudel, R.G. 83
Ruderman, M.N. 374
Rudman, L.A. 326
Rueda, M.R. 82
Ruiz-Quintanilla, A. 367
Ruscio, A.M. 141
Ruscio, J. 141
Russell, D.E.H. 185
Russell, S.F. 129, 130
Russo, N.F. 182, 183, 184, 187, 191, 192
Ryle, G. 28

Sabatier, C. 250
Sakuma, M. 324
Salmon, D. 38
Saltzman, L.E. 184, 191
Samayoa, H.H. 37
Samelson, F. 438
Sameroff, A.J. 251
Sanchez, M. 51
Sanchez-Burks, J. 211, 263
Sanders, J. 274
Saraswathi, T.S. 232, 234
Saul, L.J. 131
Scarr, S. 251
Schils, E. 56
Schleifer, J. 162

Schlenker, B.R. 322
Schmader, T. 262, 266
Schmitt, N. 376
Schneider, B. 13, 375, 377, 379
Schneider, W. 387, 399
Schnieder, R.A. 131
Schofield, T.J. 248
Scholz, U. 172, 175, 176, 177
Schon, D. 5
Schooler, C. 225, 326
Schumacher, E.F. 46
Schüz, B. 172, 177
Schwartz, M.S. 185
Schwartz, S.H. 286
Schwarzer, R. 167, 168, 169, 170, 172, 173, 174, 175, 176, 177
Scott, A. 262, 272, 274, 275
Seagull, F.J. 392, 393, 394, 395
Secada, W.G. 13
Sedikides, C. 320
Segall, M.H. 229, 230, 232, 234, 279, 284
Seidenberg, D. 83
Seitz, A. 9
Sénéchal, C. 231, 232, 236
Shadrikov, V.D. 420
Shallice, T. 387
Shane, B. 183
Shao, F. 160, 162, 163
Sharkin, B.S. 134
Sheffield, C.J. 183
Shi, K. 372
Shibata, T. 327
Shih, H. 210
Shiomura, K. 325
Shippmann, J.S. 373
Shiraishi, D. 106
Shocken, D.D. 128
Shore, M.F. 406
Shweder, R.A. 105, 230, 231, 335
Sidanius, J. 412
Siegel, D. 396, 399
Sigel, I.E. 250
Siler, S. 45
Simon, A. 400
Simon, H.A. 13
Simon, T. 436
Simons, D.J. 218

Singelis, T. 284
Singer, R. 169
Singh, R. 262, 264, 266, 269, 270, 272, 273, 274, 275
Sinha, D. 231, 232, 236, 294
Siu, I. 84
Skinner, B.F. 45
Skitka, L. 261
Slavin, R.E. 45
Smirnov, A.R. 420
Smith, D.B. 376, 379
Smith, E.E. 213
Smith, M.C. 126
Smith, P. 236
Smith, P.B. 285, 291, 371, 372
Smith, P.H. 190
Sniehotta, F.F. 172, 175, 176, 177
Snow, C. 56
Snyder, C.R. 113
Snyder, M. 357
Sobolewski, A. 146
Sohn, M.-H. 387
Sokolow, M. 131
Solomon, E.P. 130
Solomon, Z. 143
Song, W. 106
Song, W.Z. 93, 94, 95, 373
Soon, C.S. 56
Spevack, M. 128
Spielberger, C.D. 126, 127, 128, 129, 130, 131, 132, 134
Spillane, J.P. 15
Sriram, N. 56
Srull, T.K. 321
Stark, R.S. 130, 131, 134
Steffe, L.P. 56
Steinberg, A. 146
Steinberg, L. 247
Stelmack, R. 82
Stern, W. 433, 437
Sternberg, R.J. 373
Stevens, M.J. 202
Stevenson, H. 338, 340
Stevenson, H.H. 320
Steward, J. 233
Stogdill, R.M. 357
Story, D.A. 130, 131, 134
Straus, R. 125
Strauss, M.A. 186

Strelau, J. 139, 140, 141, 143, 146, 147
Stumpf, H. 106
Styles, E. 387, 401
Suchman, L. 13
Sudermann, M. 190
Sudnow, D. 401
Sue, S. 92
Sugarman, D.B. 188
Sugiman, T. 410
Suh, E.M. 105
Sullivan, J.J. 341
Sullivan, M.A. 230, 231, 387
Sun, H. 164
Sun, H.F. 94, 95, 371
Super, C.M. 246, 305
Supplee, K. 129
Surkis, A. 128
Sutton, F.X. 232
Sutton, S. 168
Sutton, S.R. 167, 170
Suzuki, N. 343
Suzuki, T. 341
Swartz, L. 249, 252
Sydeman, S.J. 130, 131, 132
Syme, S.L. 125

Takano, Y. 312
Talbert, J.E. 13
Talyzina, N.F. 423
Tamis-LeMonda, C.S. 248, 250
Tan, E.W.L. 56
Tan, G.C. 357, 367
Tan, S.P. 273, 275
Tang, C. 160
Tao, Q. 373
Tay, A.Y.L. 269, 270, 274
Taylor, F.W. 436
Teasley, S.D. 11
Tedeschi, J.T. 321
Teles, L. 45
Tetlock, P.E. 261, 262, 264, 266, 268, 269, 270, 272, 273, 274, 275
Thibaut, J.W. 263
Thiel, T. 56
Thoennes, P. 185
Thomas, R. 362
Thomson, N. 84
Thorndike, E.L. 23, 436
Thorndike, R.M. 91

Tian, J. 162
Titchener, E.B. 434
Tjaden, P. 185
Toguchi, Y. 320
Tomasello, M. 235
Tomlinson, M. 249, 252
Tomo, R. 312, 316
Torgesen, J. 84
Triandis, H.C. 105, 210, 225, 239, 335
Troadec, B. 232
Tronick, E.Z. 249
Trull, T.J. 106
Tsui, A.S. 375
Tucher, W.I. 131
Tulkin, S.R. 248
Tyack, D. 12
Tyler, L. 73

Uchida, Y. 324
Uhl-Bien, M. 360, 375
Umberson, D. 187

van de Koppel, J.M.H. 231, 232, 236
Van de Vijver, F. 93, 237
Van de Vijver, F.J.R. 281, 283, 285, 287, 288, 289, 290, 291, 292, 295
van der Valk, J.M. 131
Van Hemert, D.A. 281, 289, 290, 291
van Muijen, J.J. 371
Van Velsor, E. 362
Vanhanen, T. 337
Varnum, M.E.W. 225
Vary, M.G. 155
Vasquez, O. 11
Vaughan, E. 36, 40, 47
Vayda, A.P. 233
Verburg, R.M. 371
Vernon, P.E. 337
Visser, P. 262, 272, 274, 275
Vohs, K.D. 319, 320, 326
Voiskounsky, A.E. 408
Vrana, S. 142, 154
Vroom, V.H. 356
Vygotsky, L. 11, 251
Vygotsky, L.S. 74, 419

Wachs, T.D. 247
Wada, S. 92
Wahlsten, D. 82

Wakabayashi, M. 377
Wallston, K. 167, 170
Wang, B. 160, 162
Wang, C.-M. 56
Wang, D. 106, 107, 108, 110, 111, 112, 113, 114, 115, 374
Wang, J. 164
Wang, Q. 52
Wang, W. 160, 162, 163
Wang, X. 162
Wang, X.-D. 62
Wang, X.-P. 61
Wang, Y.E. 341
Wang, Z.M. 371, 372, 373, 374, 375, 376, 377, 378, 379
Ward, C. 94, 285
Washburne, C. 47
Washinton, W. 162
Waterman, A.S. 319
Watkins, D. 288
Watson, P.J. 142, 153
Watts, C. 185
Weber, M. 12
Weber, T.A. 387
Wedding, D. 202
Wei, J.X. 377
Wei, X. 160
Weil, M. 396, 399, 400
Weinstein, N.D. 167, 170
Weiss, D.S. 142
Welles-Nyström, B. 250
Wenger, E. 6, 11
Wenger, J.L. 387
Werner, C. 234, 235
Whetstone, M.R. 322
Whipple, G.M. 436
White, J.W. 185
White, M.I. 340
Whitehead, W.E. 126
Whiting, J.W. 252, 255
Whiting, J.W.M. 232, 255
Wiener, N.I. 411
Wilhelm, O. 371
Williams, L.M. 182
Williams, T. 13
Wilpert,, B. 440
Winkvist, A. 185
Winter, O. 131
Witkin, H.A. 216, 235, 236
Witmer, L. 435
Wolf, S. 131

Wolff, H. 131
Woodruff, W.J. 190
Worden, T.J. 128, 129
Wraith, R. 143
Wu, G. 106
Wundt, W. 331
Wurm, M. 125

Xie, Y. 160
Xin, K.R. 375

Yagi, Y. 327
Yamagishi, T. 343, 344
Yamaguchi, S. 322, 323, 324, 325, 342
Yamauchi, T. 45
Yang, J. 105, 160, 162
Yang, K. 106, 107
Yang, K.S. 93, 340, 341, 373
Yao, S.Q. 105
Yaure, R.G. 387
Yee, P.L. 387
Yeh, C. 316
Yetton, P.W. 356
Yeung, N. 387
Yik, M.S. 93
Yllo, K. 185
Yoon, G. 335
Young, A. 401
Younger, B. 184
Yu, A.B. 340, 341
Yuan, N.P. 182, 184, 190
Yuki, M. 342
Yukl, G. 351, 353, 356, 360

Zangari, J.M. 131
Zaporozhets, A.V. 420
Zawadzki, B. 139, 143, 146, 147, 155
Zeidner, M. 143
Zeigarnik, B.V. 423
Zhang, H.C. 371
Zhang, J. 164
Zhang, J.P. 93, 373
Zhang, J.X. 92, 93, 94, 95, 373
Zhang, S. 106
Zhang, X.-C. 52, 61
Zhang, X.S. 377
Zhang, Z. 212
Zhang, Z.-Y. 55
Zhao, S. 211, 263

Zheng, L. 162
Zhou, F. 107, 112
Zhu, R. 106

Ziegelmann, J.P. 172, 173, 174
Zinchenko, P.I. 420

Zinchenko, V.P. 423
Zuo, Y. 106
Zwi, A.B. 184, 185, 190

Subject index

Absolutism 230
Academic rigor 19–20
Accomplice 274–275
Accomplishment 19
Accountability 15
Accountability demands 261, 269–270
Accountable Talk 20
Acculturation 240
Actions 270–272
Activity 419–420
Adaptive growth modeling 379
Affordances 219–222, 225–226
Agency 265, 274–275, 332
Aggression 129–131
AHA! syndrome 129
Alcohol abuse 188
Amae 307
American Psychological Association
   (APA) 200
Amygdala 162
Analytic perception 209, 263, 300
Anger 129–131, 133, 134
Anthropology 11, 233–234
Anxiety 126–131, 133
Applied psychology 423, 433–442
Apprenticeship
   cognitive 45
   learning 21
Arousal 79
ASD model 379
Assessment 59–60
Attention 79, 214–223, 224–225
Attributions 270–272

Behavioral intervention, immunity
   163–164
Beliefs 10
Bell, Andrew 36, 38
Big Five Model 105, 111, 288

Big Seven Model 107, 108–109, 111
Blood pressure 129–131
Boulder conference 201–202, 439
Bounded rationality 13–14
British Psychological Society 203
Buddhism 301–303

Cancer, behavioral intervention 163–164
Cardiac rehabilitation 175–177
Cardiovascular disease 125–132
Categorization 212–214, 225
Causal analysis 264
Causal attribution 212, 263
Change blindness 218–219
Child development 245–246, 252,
   253–255
China
   personality 106–107, 108–109,
      111–118
   professional psychology 203–204
   second-language learning 51–70
Chinese Personality Assessment
      Inventory 93–102
Chinese Personality Scale 107, 110–111
Chord keyboard 388–391
Civic medicine 406
Clinical psychology 435
Cognitive apprenticeship 45
Cognitive Assessment System 80–81
Cognitive maps 406–407
Cognized environment 233
Collective control 333–334, 340
Collective punishment 268, 275
Collectivism 236–237, 284, 314, 411
Communication 420–421, 424
Concept maps 407
Conditioning, immunity 160–162
Consciousness 332
Continuum models 170–171

Control
  collective 333–334, 340
  proxy 334, 339
  types 333–334
Covariation detection 215
Creativity 332
Cross-cultural psychology
  approaches 92–93
  conceptual biases 281–283
  ecocultural approach 229–243
  growth 295
  history 279
  long-term viability 294–295
  multilevel models 291–294
  personality 91–103, 105–106
  SWOT analysis 279–298
Cross-national study 312–313
Cultural adaptation 233–235
Cultural psychology 230, 231, 294–295,
    305–318
Cultural transmission 239–240
Cultural universals 232
Culture 334–335
  accountability demands 269–270
  agency 265
  attention 214–223, 224–225
  cognition 211–214, 223–225, 300–301,
    425–426
  concept 229–230
  fluid 305–318
  gender-based violence 188–190
  group 310–312
  historical antecedents 255–256
  interpretation 246–247
  legal actions 270
  moral actions 270
  motivated actions 268–273
  motivated reasoning 262–263
  organizational 340–345
  parenting 247–252
  perception 209, 214–223, 225,
    262–263
  personal 305, 308–310
  personality 112–114, 286, 288–291
  self-descriptions 210
  situation/individual-centered theories
    211, 267–268
  social constructivism 230
  socialization 210–211, 335
  theory and methodology 253–255
  thoughts 268–273
Culture-comparative approach 231

Decision making 355–356

Dependency 339
Depression 133, 134
Derived etic 92, 105, 106, 231
Development
  child development 245–246, 252,
    253–255
  in Russian psychology 425
Developmental science 253–256
Dialectical psychology 422
Disaster 142–153
Disengagement 170
Dispositional attributions 265–266
Dose–response effect 142, 153
Drug abuse 188
Dyslexia 83, 84

Ecological adaptation 233–235
Ecological demands 236
Education
  East Asia 336–340
  learners 29–32
  Mutual Teaching Method 36–47
  schooled 24, 25–29, 32–34, 72–73
Educational psychology 23–24, 25,
    436
Effort 18–19, 339–340
Electro-acupuncture 161
Emic approach 92–93, 106, 231
Encoding 85
Enculturation 239, 249
Equity 342
Error of commission 91
Error of omission 91
Etic approach 92–93, 106
European Federation of Psychology
    Associations (EFPA) 202–203
Evaluations 19
Event-related potentials 82
Event script 314–317
Expectations 19
Expertise 10, 400–401
External partners 15–16

Face recognition 401
Factor analysis 71
Field dependence 216–217
Five Factor Model 105, 111, 288
Fluid culture 305–318
Flying 391–396
Flynn effect 73
Foreign Language Classroom Anxiety
    Scale 62
"Forming experiment" 422
Frame switching 263

Fundamental attribution error 262, 268, 275

Gender-based violence 182–185, 188–192, 193
General intelligence 71–77, 87
Globalization 294, 308
GLOBE project 367
Goal setting and pursuit 167–170
Group culture 310–312
Guanxi 375
Guilt 338

Health action process approach 171–172, 177–178
Health behavior change 167–179
  continuum models 170–171
  health action process approach 171–172, 177–178
  models 170–172
  motivation 167–169
  physical activity 172–177
  self-regulation 169–170
  stage models 171
Heart disease 125–132
Helmet-mounted display 391–396
Hierarchical modeling 377–378
Holistic perception 209, 262–263, 300, 425–426
Hostility 129–131
Human capital 10, 13
Hypertension 129–131
Hypothalamus 162

Immunocompetence 159–166
Implementation intentions 169
Implicational analysis 264
Implicit assessment modeling 377–379, 380
Implicit theories 407
Imposed etic 92, 105–106, 230
Impression management 321
In-groups 412–414
Indigenous psychology 231, 294–295
Individual-centered 211, 267–268
Individualism 236–237, 284, 411
Industrial psychology 436
Information technology 57, 58, 68
Initiative 169, 326–327
Institutional theory 12
Instruction 45
Insular cortex 162

Intelligence
  Flynn effect 73
  general 71–77, 87
  politics 440
  rules 81
  social-cultural history 73
  socializing 20
  speed of processing 82, 83–87
  tests 72
  tools 82
Interaction 420–421, 424
Interactive cross-dimensional modeling 378–379
Interdependency 339
Internalized dialogue 261
International Association of Applied Psychology 438
Internet 45, 46
Intimate partner violence 184–188, 191–192
Intuitive pragmatic politicians 261, 267–269, 273
Intuitive principled theologians 262, 272–273
Intuitive prudent prosecutors 261, 269–270, 274
Intuitive scientists 263
IQ
  East Asians 337–338
  harmful idea 73
  schooling 72–73
  validity of concept 71, 72

Japanese
  mind and body 299–304
  organizations 341, 342
  self-esteem 319–330
Joint activities 420

Knowledge
  distribution 14–15
  telling 3, 4–5

Lancaster, Joseph 36, 38–39
Leadership 351–370
  activities 353–355
  adaptive growth modeling 379
  approaches 351–353
  ASD model 379
  attributes 357–359, 367
  behaviors 353–355, 367
  competency assessment 371–383
  cultural representation 375
  decision making 355–356

development 363
distributing 14–15
diversity of views 351
GLOBE project 367
hierarchical modeling 377–378
implicit assessment modeling
    377–379, 380
interactive cross-dimensional
    modeling 378–379
journey 362–365, 366
knowledge builder 353, 354
large-L 352
leader–member exchange theory 360
learning 358–359
personal characteristics 357–359
relationships 359–362
roles 353–355
self-awareness 357–358
small-l 352
stakeholder liaison 353, 354
standards upholder 353, 354
team builder 354
team leadership 352–355, 356,
    357–359, 360–361, 363–365
transformational style 359
trust 360–361
Learners 29–32
Learning 33
apprenticeship 21
assessment 59–60
communities 5–8, 59
leadership 358–359
opportunities 15
organizations 14–16
self-management 20–21
LearningWalks 9
Legal actions 270
Liberal democracy 335–336
Long-term equity within a group 342

Map routines 14
Marxism 418, 424
Marxist psychology 418, 422
Mastery learning 10
Mediation 285–286
Memory span 84
Mental chronometry 82
Mental images 421–422
Meta-norm violators 262
Methodology 313–314, 422–423,
    427–428
Mind and body 299–304
Moderation 285–286
Modesty 321–322

Moral actions 270
Moral cleansing response 262
Moral outrage 262, 266
Motivated actions 264–273
Motivated reasoning 262–263
Motivation 10, 167–169
Multilevel models 291–294
Multimedia technology 57, 58
Mutual Teaching Method 36–47

Naming speed 83–87
Narrative autobiography 314
Natural disaster 142–153

Organizations
culture 340–345
design 3, 9–14
learning 14–16
resources 12–13
theory 13–14
Orthopedic rehabilitation 172–174
Out-groups 412–414
Outcome expectancies 168–169

P300 82
Pan Deng English Learning Program
    55–68
Parenting 245–260, 338, 339, 343
PASS theory 76, 77–81
Perceived self-efficacy 168–169
Peripheral electric stimulation 161
Person-centered 211, 267–268
Personal culture 305, 308–310
Personality
Big Five Model 105, 111, 288
Big Seven Model 107, 108–109, 111
Chinese 106–107, 108–109, 111–118
Chinese Personality Assessment
    Inventory 93–102
Chinese Personality Scale 107,
    110–111
cross-cultural issues 91–103, 105–106
culture 112–114, 286, 288–291
Physical activity promotion 172–177
Physical assault 185–188
Planning 79, 169
Pleasant feelings 326–327
Politicians, intuitive 261, 267–268, 273
Politics 306–308, 405–415, 440
Posttraumatic stress disorder 141,
    148–155
Pragmatic politicians 261, 267–268, 273
Pregnancy, unwanted 191–192
Prejudice 412–414

Principled theologians 262, 272–273
Principles of Learning 6–8, 16, 18–21
Process variables 237–240
Processes 232
Professional psychology 199–206
Prosecutors, intuitive 261, 269–270, 274
Protocols 3, 8–9
Proxy control 334, 339
Prudent prosecutors 261, 269–270, 274
Psychobehavioral intervention 163–164
Psychoimmunology 159–166
Psychological differences studies
    283–284
Psychological practice 199
Psychological vital signs 132–134
Psychology of psychologists 345
Psychotherapy 303–304
PTSD-Factorial Version 146

Racism 412, 413
Rape 185–188
Rapid automatized naming 83
Rationality 263
Raven's Progressive Matrix 61
Reactive inhibition 85, 86
Reflection 421–422
Relapse management 170
Relativism 230–231
Research and Development team leaders
    352–355, 356, 357–359, 360–361,
    363–365
Respondeat superior 266
Risk perception 167–169
Role differentiation 238
Russia
    political system 407–410
    prejudice 412–414
    psychology 408–410, 417–431

Sanctioning enquiries 264
Satisficing 13
Schooled education 24, 25–29, 32–34,
    72–73
Scientists, intuitive 263
Second-language learning 51–70
Self-awareness 357–358
Self-Description Questionnaire 63
Self-descriptions 210
Self-efficacy 168–169, 333
Self-enhancement 320
Self-esteem 319–330
    definition 319–320
    enhanced initiative 326–327
    explicit 325–326

implicit 324–326
"lower" 320–321
moderate 322, 323–324
modesty 321–322
pleasant feelings 326–327
Self-management 20–21
Self-regulation
    effort 339–340
    goal pursuit 169–170
Seniority norm 341–342
Separation assault 188
Settlement patterns 238
Severity bias 262, 275
Sex differences 411–412
Sexism 412
Simultaneous processing 79
Situated learning 11
Situation-centered 211, 267–268
Situation-matching set 263
Social capital 13, 14–15
Social cognitive theory 333–334
Social constructivism 230
Social desirability 291
Social domination orientation
    411–412
Social explanations 264
Social-functionalism 264–268
Social stratification 238
Socialization 210–211, 239, 257, 335,
    338
Sociocognitive theory 11
Sociocultural theory 11
Sociopolitical events 306–308
Soviet psychology 408–410, 417,
    418–423
Speed of processing 82, 83–87
Spiral learning 10
Stage models 171
Standard operating procedures (SOPs)
    13, 14
State–Trait Anger Expression Inventory
    130–131
State–Trait Anxiety Inventory 127–128
Stress
    heart disease 125
    immunity 162–163
    temperament 139–141, 153–155
Subject-centered approach 425
Substance abuse 188
Successive processing 79, 84
SWOT analysis 279–298
Sympathetic nervous system 163
Systems approach 426
Systems of thought 410–411

Tacit theories 407
Task
　basic execution modes 391–396
　control processes 387–388
　definition 385–386
　global task set 396–400
　representation format 388–391
　shell 386, 387–388, 400–402
　switching 387, 401
Team leadership 352–355, 356, 357–359,
　360–361, 363–365
Technology 46, 57, 58, 68, 414
Telling 3, 4–5
Temperament 139–158
　disaster 142–143
　PTSD symptoms 148–150, 153
　stress 139–141, 153–155
Theologians, intuitive 262, 272–273
Thought
　cultural differences 268–273
　systems 410–411
Tools
　behavior 418–419
　intelligence 82
　learning communities 5–8

Training 3, 5–8
Trait anxiety 127
Transactional model 332–333
Transformational leadership 359
Trauma characteristics 147, 148,
　150–153, 154–155
Trust 360–361
Two-hand chord keyboard 388–391
Type-A behavior 125–126, 131–132
Typing task 388–391

Ultimate attribution error 267, 268, 273,
　275
Universalism 230, 231
Universalist psychology 231

Variable priority training 396–400
Vicarious responsibility 262, 266
Violence against women 181–197
Vygotsky 418–419

War
　sex differences 411–412
　WWII 306, 438
Western liberal democracy 335–336